February 26–28, 2014
Monterey, California, USA

**Association for
Computing Machinery**

Advancing Computing as a Science & Profession

FPGA'14

Proceedings of the 2014 ACM/SIGDA International Symposium on
Field Programmable Gate Arrays

Sponsored by:
ACM SIGDA

Supported by:
Altera, Microsemi, Microsoft Research, Xilinx, Atomic Rules, Algo-Logic, and BEEcube

With logistical support from:
The Trimberger Family Foundation

**Association for
Computing Machinery**

Advancing Computing as a Science & Profession

The Association for Computing Machinery
2 Penn Plaza, Suite 701
New York, New York 10121-0701

Notice to Past Authors of ACM-Published Articles
ACM intends to create a complete electronic archive of all articles and/or other material previously published by ACM. If you have written a work that has been previously published by ACM in any journal or conference proceedings prior to 1978, or any SIG Newsletter at any time, and you do NOT want this work to appear in the ACM Digital Library, please inform permissions@acm.org, stating the title of the work, the author(s), and where and when published.

ISBN: 978-1-4503-2671-1 (Digital)

ISBN: 978-1-4503-3098-5 (Print)

Additional copies may be ordered prepaid from:

ACM Order Department
PO Box 30777
New York, NY 10087-0777, USA

Phone: 1-800-342-6626 (USA and Canada)
+1-212-626-0500 (Global)
Fax: +1-212-944-1318
E-mail: acmhelp@acm.org
Hours of Operation: 8:30 am – 4:30 pm ET

Printed in the USA

Foreword

It is our great pleasure to welcome you to the *2014 ACM International Symposium on FPGAs (FPGA 2014)*. This year's symposium continues the tradition of being a premier forum for the presentation of FPGA-related research across a wide variety of topics: new FPGA architectures and circuit designs, Computer-Aided Design (CAD) and high level synthesis algorithms and flows, applications well-suited to FPGAs, and design studies. In addition to facilitating the sharing of research results through the paper and poster presentations, FPGA provides an excellent opportunity for researchers from around the world to mingle and discuss research results and ideas.

This year we received 110 submissions from 19 different countries. The program committee accepted 20 full (ten page) papers (acceptance rate 18%) and 10 short (four page) papers (overall acceptance rate 27%). Full papers each have a twenty minute oral presentation, while short papers will have a five minute oral presentation, followed by a poster presentation at which attendees can further discuss the work with the authors. Finally we will have four poster sessions in which a total of 45 additional research projects will be displayed on posters, and at which you may ask detailed questions of the authors.

This year the symposium begins with a workshop related to the emerging role of FPGAs in the datacenter. The symposium also includes an evening panel on the topic of low power FPGAs – bring your questions for our panel of experts, and enjoy a lively discussion on whether FPGAs will make inroads into markets dominated by power, form factor and cost constraints.

Putting together *FPGA 2014* was a team effort. We first thank the authors, workshop and panel presenters and organizers for providing the content of the program. We are grateful to the program committee who worked very hard to review the papers and provide detailed feedback to authors. We are in debt to all the members of the program committee who took on additional responsibility as finance, publicity, webmaster, tutorial, panel and session chairs, and to Lisa Tolles of Sheridan Communications for assembling the proceedings. Last but certainly not least, we greatly appreciate the support of our sponsor, ACM SIGDA, and our corporate supporters Algo-Logic, Altera, Atomic Rules, BeeCube, Microsemi, Microsoft and Xilinx. We also thank the Trimberger Family Foundation for additional logistical support.

Welcome to FPGA 2014!

Vaughn Betz　　　　　　　　　**George A. Constantinides**
FPGA 2014 General Chair　　　　*FPGA 2014 Program Chair*
University of Toronto　　　　　　*Imperial College London*

Table of Contents

Session 5: Processors and Systems
Session Chair: Miriam Leeser *(Northeastern University, USA)*

Session 6: Applications 2
Session Chair: Lesley Shannon *(Simon Fraser University, Canada)*

Session 7: Tools and Models 1
Session Chair: Deming Chen *(University of Illinois at Urbana-Champaign, USA)*

Session 8: Tools and Models 2
Session Chair: Kyle Rupnow *(Nanyang Technological University, Singapore)*

Poster Session 1

Poster Session 2

Poster Session 3

Poster Session 4

FPGA 2014 Symposium Organization

General Chair: Vaughn Betz *(University of Toronto, Canada)*

Program Chair: George A. Constantinides *(Imperial College London, UK)*

Finance Chair: Brad Hutchings *(Brigham Young University, USA)*

Publicity Chair: Jason Anderson *(University of Toronto, Canada)*

Workshop Chair: Derek Chiou *(University of Texas, Austin, USA)*

Program Committee:

Jason Anderson *(University of Toronto, Canada)*
Kia Bazargan *(University of Minnesota, USA)*
Vaughn Betz *(University of Toronto, Canada)*
Mike Butts *(Synopsys, USA)*
Deming Chen *(University of Illinois at Urbana-Champaign, USA)*
Peter Cheung *(Imperial College, UK)*
Ray Cheung *(City University of Hong Kong, Hong Kong)*
Derek Chiou *(University of Texas, Austin, USA)*
Paul Chow *(University of Toronto, Canada)*
Jason Cong *(University of California at Los Angeles, USA)*
George Constantinides *(Imperial College London, UK)*
Haohuan Fu *(Tsinghua University, China)*
Jonathan Greene *(Actel, USA)*
Scott Hauck *(University of Washington, USA)*
Mike Hutton *(Altera, USA)*
James Hoe *(Carnegie-Mellon University, USA)*
Brad Hutchings *(Brigham Young University, USA)*
Ryan Kastner *(University of California Santa Barbara, USA)*
Martin Langhammer *(Altera, UK)*
Miriam Leeser *(Northeastern University, USA)*
Guy Lemieux *(University of British Columbia, Canada)*
Philip Leong *(University of Sydney, Australia)*
David Lewis *(Altera, Canada)*
Mingjie Lin *(University of Central Florida)*
John Lockwood *(Algo-Logic Systems, USA)*
Wayne Luk *(Imperial College London, UK)*
Patrick Lysaght *(Xilinx, USA)*
Stephen Neuendorffer *(Xilinx, USA)*
Jonathan Rose *(University of Toronto, Canada)*
Kyle Rupnow *(Nanyang Technological University, Singapore)*
David Rutledge *(Lattice Semiconductor, USA)*
Graham Schelle *(Xilinx)*
Herman Schmit *(Altera, USA)*
Lesley Shannon *(Simon Fraser University, Canada)*

Program Committee (continued):

Juergen Teich *(University of Erlangen, Germany)*
Russell Tessier *(University of Massachusetts at Amherst, USA)*
Steve Trimberger *(Xilinx, USA)*
Frank Vahid *(University of California Riverside, USA)*
John Wawrzynek *(UC Berkeley, USA)*
Yu Wang *(Tsinghua University, China)*
Steve Wilton *(University of British Columbia, Canada)*
Michael Wirthlin *(Brigham Young University, USA)*

Additional Reviewers

Ameer Abdelhadi
Samuel Bayliss
Tobias Becker
Srinivas Boppu
Stuart Byma
Andrew Canis
Thomas Chau
Jeff Chromczak
Donald Donglong Chen
Ying Chen
Yu-Ting Chen
Yushu Chen
S. Alexander Chin
Jongsok Choi
Young-kyu Choi
Veronica Cojocaru
James Davis
Ashutosh Dhar
Carl Ebeling
Wenyi Feng
Blair Fort
David Galloway
Lin Gan
Farnaz Gharibian
Vadim Gutnik
Ce Guo
Connie Kangni Guo
Conghui He
Hui Huang
Muhuan Huang

Safeen Huda
Dana How
Alexandre Isoard
Faramaz Khosravi
Jin Hee Kim
Dirk Koch
Choden Konigsmark
Maysam Lavasani
Austin Lesea
Josh Levine
Will Xiangyu Li
Ruolong Lian
Chen-Hsuan Lin
Benben Liu
Jianxiong Liu
Charles Lo
Jason Luu
Zihong Lv
Xiaoyu Ma
Chris Madill
Valavan Manohararajah
Fernando Martin del Campo
Bailey Miller
Bill Biao Min
Vincent Mirian
Mohammad Reza Mohammadnia
Xinyu Niu
Gabriel Noaje

Hossein Omidian
Bogdan Pasca
Anand Ramachandran
Alex Rodionov
Sascha Roloff
Naman Saraf
Moritz Schmid
Bernhard Schmidt
Aaron Severance
Gokhan Sayilar
Edward Stott
Shao Lin (Tom) Tang
Jason Thong
Tim Todman
Zahid Ullah
Tim Vanderhoek
Jasmina Vasiljevic
Jihe Wang
Tengpeng Wei
Ruediger Wilenberg
Justin Wong
Bingjun Xiao
Edward Yang
Gavin Xiaoxu Yao
Yi Yuan
Xi Yue
Daniel Ziener
Wenlai Zhao
Hongbin Zheng

FPGA 2014 Sponsor & Supporters

Sponsor:

Supporters:

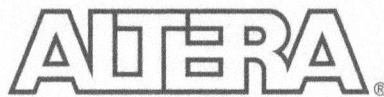

Also with the support of:

With additional logistics from:

Trimberger Family
Foundation

Fast and Effective Placement and Routing Directed High-Level Synthesis for FPGAs

Hongbin Zheng [1]   Swathi T. Gurumani [1]   Kyle Rupnow [3,1]   Deming Chen [2,1]

[1] Advanced Digital Sciences Center, {hongbin.zheng, swathi.g}@adsc.com.sg

[2] University of Illinois at Urbana-Champaign, dchen@illinois.edu

[3] Nanyang Technological University, k.rupnow@ntu.edu.sg

ABSTRACT

Achievable frequency (f_{max}) is a widely used input constraint for designs targeting Field-Programmable Gate Arrays (FPGA), because of its impact on design latency and throughput. f_{max} is limited by critical path delay, which is highly influenced by lower-level details of the circuit implementation such as technology mapping, placement and routing. However, for high-level synthesis (HLS) design flows, it is challenging to evaluate the real critical delay at the behavioral level. Current HLS flows typically use module pre-characterization for delay estimates. However, we will demonstrate that such delay estimates are not sufficient to obtain high f_{max} and also minimize total execution latency.

In this paper, we introduce a new HLS flow that integrates with Altera's Quartus synthesis and fast placement and routing (PAR) tool to obtain realistic post-PAR delay estimates. This integration enables an iterative flow that improves the performance of the design with both behavioral-level and circuit-level optimizations using realistic delay information. We demonstrate our HLS flow produces up to 24% (on average 20%) improvement in f_{max} and upto 22% (on average 20%) improvement in execution latency. Furthermore, results demonstrate that our flow is able to achieve from 65% to 91% of the theoretical f_{max} on Stratix IV devices (550MHz).

Categories and Subject Descriptors

B.5.2 [**Hardware**]: Design Aids—*optimization*

Keywords

High-Level Synthesis, Layout driven, Scheduling

1. INTRODUCTION

The size and complexity of FPGAs are continually growing to meet the demands for applications of yet more complexity. However, design at the register-transfer level (RTL)

FPGA'14, February 26–28, 2014, Monterey, CA, USA.
Copyright 2014 ACM 978-1-4503-2671-1/14/02 ...$15.00.
http://dx.doi.org/10.1145/2554688.2554775.

is a challenging, time-consuming process. In contrast, recent advancements in high-level synthesis (HLS) tools, which generate RTL from high-level language descriptions, have provided shorter design cycles. There are numerous academic [1–6] and commercial [7–10] examples of HLS tools.

Despite the rise in popularity of HLS tools, it remains challenging for users to specify and obtain a desired target frequency. HLS tools accept user constraints such as target f_{max}; using desired clock cycle latency and microbenchmarking based pre-characterized component latencies [7], HLS tools estimate datapath latency and allocate operations to control cycles. However, actual datapath delay is often significantly different from estimated delay. Individual components can be pre-characterized using a design flow, but in a full design, further optimizations in logic synthesis, technology mapping, register packing, placement and routing will not be modeled. In actual designs, different implementations of the same operation may have different delay due to variations in optimizations or interconnect delay which can be up to 70% of circuit delay [11], and inaccurate estimates lead to sub-optimal designs.

Currently, HLS tools depend primarily on logic synthesis tools to identify and optimize the design's critical path instead of regenerating RTL to improve implementation quality. Logic synthesis tools attempt to fix timing closure using retiming and/or resynthesis [12]. Although logic synthesis tools optimize some paths that do not meet f_{max} constraints, they are limited to a restrictive set of transformations that maintain the exact behavior of the RTL. Such limitations force users to undergo design iterations to improve performance – challenging in RTL, but even more challenging with HLS because the mapping between design description and implementation details is obfuscated by HLS transformations. Meanwhile, relatively minor (automatic) behavioral level transformations can change the number of control cycles, computation scheduling, and operation pipelining, which can significantly impact lower-level implementations.

Behavioral level transformations to improve f_{max} and execution latency require accurate estimates of physical implementation details. Lack of details leads to significant under- or over-estimation of computation delays. Under-estimated delays produce RTL that cannot meet the f_{max} constraint, while over-estimation leads to longer latency in cycles that can overwhelm performance advantages of high f_{max}. Although pre-characterization is accurate for single operations in isolation, technology mapping, placement and routing (PAR) information is critical for accurate estimates in even small designs. Accurate delay information is available after logic synthesis, and PAR; thus, in this work we iteratively enhance the RTL and back-annotate post-RTL-implementation delays to improve RTL generation, specifically to improve both f_{max} and application execution latency. Achieving maximal f_{max} does not guarantee minimal execution latency; thus, we must also minimize the number of clock cycles while maintaining f_{max}.

In this work, we develop a new HLS tool that integrates with Altera Quartus' synthesis and fast PAR tool [13], and is able to iteratively improve the generated RTL quality. [1] Integrated with Quartus, we ensure that we leverage state-of-the-art logic synthesis and PAR optimization and generate RTL implementations for **real-world** FPGA devices. We will demonstrate that this technique improves f_{max} by 24% and execution latency by 22%, which corresponds to between 65% and 91% of the theoretical f_{max} of the Stratix IV device we use. This work is designed to reduce user design iteration and improve ability to achieve user objectives. However, it is also important that the synthesis process remains feasible – therefore, we use Quartus' fast-PAR, and furthermore demonstrate that our benchmarks typically converge in few iterations with fast overall runtime.

This work contributes to HLS targeting FPGAs by:

1. An iterative, fast PAR directed HLS flow that optimizes using behavioral-level and back-annotated post PAR physical-level information to reduce the latency of the hardware by up to 22% and increases the f_{max} by up to 24%, compared to a non-iterative flow.

2. A demonstration of the importance of flattening for logic optimization and place and route; PAR reduces latency by 28% and 12% over the non-flattened and non-PAR flows, respectively.

3. A demonstration that our accurate delay estimation model converges quickly: our fast-PAR based iterative synthesis converges within 3 iterations for all tested benchmarks.

2. MOTIVATION

Our proposed method improves RTL generation through iterative refinement of delay estimates, which influences optimization and allocation decisions during binding and scheduling within HLS. Such a method is not the only method to improve f_{max} through behavioral-level transformations; however, although other methods improve f_{max}, there is still significant optimization opportunity.

We develop a new HLS framework based on LLVM to create a baseline for our iterative fast PAR HLS flow. Our HLS framework includes word-level logic synthesis based on ABC [15], SDC-based scheduling [16], functional unit binding, and multi-cycle chaining. Related work has demonstrated the importance of multi-cycle constraints generation for both performance and resource consumption [5]. However, their multi-cycle generation focuses on relaxing the timing requirements, it is not suitable for an iterative flow. We discuss our multi-cycle constraints in section 3.3.4.

By setting the number of iterations to 1, our HLS framework can be used as a non-iterative flow. Therefore, in order

---

[1] We believe we could also use Vivado [14] given an interface to extract timing information.

to establish the performance of our framework in comparison to current state-of-the-art HLS, we compare our flow in non-iterative mode to the VAST HLS framework [5]. We use the CHStone [17] suite of benchmarks and dataflow benchmarks from [18]. In both VAST HLS and our HLS framework, we target a Stratix IV FPGA (EP4SGX70), speed-grade 2 with a target f_{max} of 500MHz. In our flow, all of the dataflow benchmarks are able to achieve the maximum f_{max} (480MHz) of 36×36 MULT blocks without iteration, and thus we concentrate only on the CHStone benchmarks for the rest of this paper.

Fig. 1a shows the achieved f_{max}, together with the theoretical maximum f_{max} of the Stratix IV 36×36 MULT and Dual-port RAM components. Although our new flow increases f_{max} for all of the benchmarks, there is still a significant gap between the achieved and theoretical f_{max}: inaccurate component-based delay estimates limit scheduling and binding quality and produce RTL that cannot achieve a high f_{max}. We will demonstrate that iterative refinement of delay estimates can further narrow this gap.

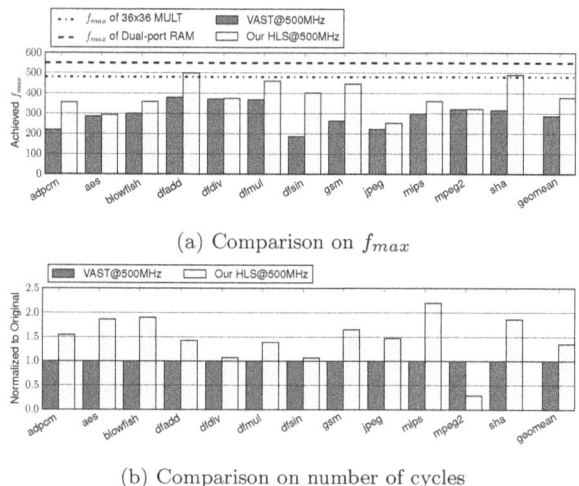

(a) Comparison on f_{max}

(b) Comparison on number of cycles

Figure 1: Performance comparison

Furthermore, Fig. 1b demonstrates that this f_{max} improvement comes at the cost of increased latency in clock cycles. In most cases, this clock cycle increase overwhelms f_{max} improvement – on average, our flow improves f_{max} but slightly degrades execution latency by 2%. We will demonstrate that the iterative refinement solves this issue to produce designs with both improved f_{max} and overall improved latency.

Based on this initial analysis, we demonstrate that although our non-iterative HLS flow is competitive with the current state-of-the-art in HLS, there is still significant opportunity to improve f_{max} and execution latency. Inaccurate delay estimates limit both f_{max} and latency in clock cycles. In the next section, we will present our iterative flow that integrates with Quartus for accurate delay estimation.

3. ITERATIVE PAR-DIRECTED HLS FLOW

Our LLVM-based HLS framework begins with a control-dataflow graph (CDFG), and performs analysis and optimization both at the LLVM-IR level and our own FPGA-specific intermediate representation. In this work, we con-

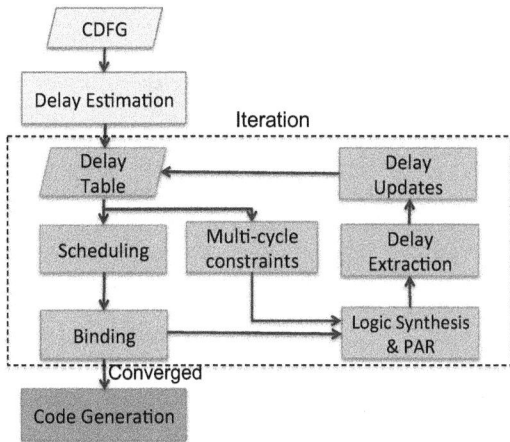

Figure 2: PAR-directed HLS Flow

centrate on iterative refinement of the delay estimates at the CDFG-level; our flow starts from pre-characterized component delays, and iteratively refines these delays with back-annotated post-synthesis and PAR information. During each iteration, our HLS optimizes design performance considering both the user's f_{max} constraints and the annotated delay estimates. As high level goals, this tool is intended to reduce design iteration, and simplify the process of achieving a user-defined f_{max}, while maintaining reasonable total synthesis time. The first goals are achieved simply through improving the tool's ability to achieve frequency and latency targets without user interaction. For the final goal, to maintain reasonable synthesis time, we examine several of Quartus' synthesis options including Quartus' fast-PAR tool which has the potential to reduce iteration runtime by up to 10× [19, p. 2-35]. Furthermore, our accurate estimation allows fast convergence; as we will demonstrate, all benchmarks converge in just 3 iterations.

We divide our flow into three stages: Initialization, Iteration, and Finalization: Initialization performs an initial synthesis based on pre-characterized delay estimates, then Iteration repeats a cycle of back annotation and regeneration of optimized RTL; Finalization performs a final RTL code generation and full Quartus synthesis. An overview of our flow is shown in Fig. 2. During Iteration, there are two different options for how to update the delay information as well as optional iterative constraints generation. We describe these stages in the following sections.

3.1 Component Pre-characterization

As a one-time task for each target platform, we perform component pre-characterization [7] for 188 micro-benchmarks of elementary operations, MUXs and storage elements. Each micro-benchmark is synthesized in Quartus for the target platform, and we measure resource use, critical delay and power consumption using LegUp's file format and measurement infrastructure [1].

3.2 Initialization Stage

Initialization begins with a simplified baseline synthesis similar to a non-iterative HLS flow. Firstly, we refine the CDFG to build a modified CDFG which contains only non-computation operations, and chains of computational operations are replaced by data dependence edges (data edges).

Then we estimate the delay of the data edges in the modified CDFG by accumulating the delay of individual computational operations in the original chains using the pre-characterized, platform-specific component delays as in [7].

Based on these delay estimates, we build a delay table and the corresponding inputs to the SDC scheduler. Using the estimates, the scheduler assigns operations to clock cycles, preserving the f_{max} (clock period) constraint and CDFG dependency constraints. If delay estimates perfectly match post-synthesis and PAR delays, this schedule would inherently meet the f_{max} constraint.[2] Differences between the achieved f_{max} and the constraint are due to inaccurate delay estimates. Furthermore, the number of control steps generated by the scheduler corresponds to the latency in clock cycles; excess clock cycle latency is also directly related to inaccuracy in delay estimates.

Following scheduling, we perform binding of the scheduled CDFG to functional units/registers and generate the RTL description. Currently, we bind all computational operations to pure combinational functional units (i.e. functional units without pipeline register). Hence, the functional units are shared only if their sharing does not introduce multiplexers. Optionally, we also generate simple multi-cycle constraints in order to further improve delay estimation quality in designs with multi-cycle data propagation paths. Using this initial RTL, we perform an initial Quartus logic synthesis, and fast-PAR to generate timing information and then continue to the Iterate stage.

3.3 Iteration Stage

After Initialization, Iteration will repeatedly extract the Quartus timing information, back-annotate to update the CDFG, repeat HLS scheduling and binding, generate constraints, and finally repeat synthesis in Quartus. Currently, the number of iterations of this stage is a user-provided constraint, but this could easily be converted to a technique with automatic convergence. However, it is important to note that an automatic convergence technique should examine both frequency and latency in clock cycles: examining only frequency may erroneously exit early while latency in clock cycles is still being optimized through behavioral-level retiming. Furthermore, it is important to allow (sometimes negative) variation in performance without early-exit conditions: we frequently observe temporary reductions in achievable frequency while optimizing latency in clock cycles.

We will now present details for the steps in our iteration stage: RTL synthesis, timing extraction, back annotation, and constraints generation.

3.3.1 RTL Synthesis

We integrate with Altera Quartus tool to perform logic synthesis and PAR on the generated RTL. Though this is a generic step in HLS flows, we explore three different synthesis options to study the impact of synthesis quality on delay estimation and compare them in section 4.1.

Non-flattened (NO FLAT) – By applying Altera's "keep" synthesis attribute, we force functional units to be instantiated as sub-modules, disable flattening and logic optimization across blocks. Although disabling optimization obviously degrades design quality within the iterations, this option tests the importance of logic optimization for the accu-

---

[2] Assuming, of course, that each individual computation has delay less than the clock period constraint

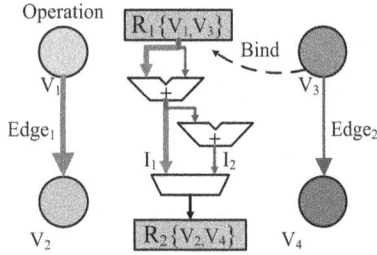

Figure 3: An example of path ambiguities

racy of Quartus' timing estimates. The **NO FLAT** flow is similar to the block-level floorplanning-based delay estimation approach widely used in ASIC HLS flows and macro-based FPGA synthesis [20–22].

No PAR Flow (NO PAR) – This flow runs logic synthesis with flattening and logic optimizations, but does not perform PAR. Using the "post map" option in Altera Time-Quest, we perform timing analysis on the mapped, optimized but pre-PAR circuit. This option tests the importance of placement and routing information for accurate timing estimates relative to optimization alone.

Fast PAR Flow (FAST PAR) – In this flow, we run logic synthesis (also with hierarchy flattening and logic optimization) followed by fast placement and routing of the design using the "early timing estimation" option to perform a quick PAR, and timing analysis.

3.3.2 Timing Extraction

As stated in section 3.2, every data edge in our CDFG corresponds to a chain of computational operations; there may be many gate-level paths in the post-synthesis implementation that correspond to a single data edge in the CDFG. However, among the set of gate-level paths, only the critical paths, i.e. the gate-level paths with the largest delay, have an impact on the data edge delay and HLS scheduling.

To find the set of gate-level paths that affect the delay of data edges in our CDFG, we take advantage of a property of HLS: each node in our CDFG is allocated a register to store the input and/or output operands. Thus, the set of paths that affect the critical path are the set of paths from the source register to the sink register, a set of paths easily extracted from post-synthesis timing reports. However, the binding step in HLS may reuse the same register for multiple different operations – thus, gate-level paths between the same pair of registers may affect different critical paths in the CDFG, which creates some ambiguity in how to back annotate the extracted values to the CDFG.

For example, in Fig. 3, there are two data edges whose source and sink registers are identical, but they use different combinational paths. If we simply use the critical path delay between R1 and R2 to annotate both data edges, we over-estimate delay of $Edge_1$ by including a functional unit only used in $Edge_2$. Correspondingly, this over-estimate may result in an inefficient CDFG schedule and produce hardware with lower frequency, higher latency in clock cycles or both.

For this reason, we further filter the paths based on the MUX input ports used in binding. Paths that use the same source and sink registers but different MUX ports will thus correctly use different sets of combinational paths, and we can correctly annotate the relevant information to the CDFG.

We generate "path filter" for each data edge in the CDFG, so that Quartus correctly reports the corresponding critical gate-level path delay for the date edge according to the filter. A path filter is described by the source and sink register of the path, and the MUX input for the path. However, we have to apply the *keep* synthesis attribute to the MUX inputs, otherwise we cannot exactly match the MUX input with the filter in the post-synthesis implementation. These *keep* attributes prevent logic synthesis from optimizing away the nodes with this attribute, and have a negative impact on the quality of the extracted delays. Hence, we use register based path filtering whenever possible, and only use the MUX input based path filtering when necessary. Given a register and the MUX that connects to the register, the algorithm to generate path filters for all data edges with the given sink register while minimizing keep attribute application is shown in Algorithm 1.

Algorithm 1: Path Filter Generation

Input: Register R, the MUX *mux* connected to R
Output: Path filters for data edges taking R as sink
1   Allocate set All_Regs and Intersected_Regs;

2   **foreach** $i \in$ *inputs of mux* **do**
3   Srcs $\leftarrow$ All registers connect to R through i;
4   **foreach** $R_{src} \in Srcs$ **do**
5   **if** $R_{src} \in All\_Regs$ **then**
6   Insert R_{src} into Intersected_Regs;
7   **else**
8   Insert R_{src} into All_Regs;

9   **foreach** $i \in$ *inputs of mux* **do**
10   $O_d \leftarrow$ the annotated operation of i;
11   $E \leftarrow$ Data Edges taking O_d as sink;
12   **foreach** $Edge\ (O_s, O_d) \in E$ **do**
13     $R_{src} \leftarrow$ result register of O_s;
14   **if** $R_{src} \in Intersected\_Regs$ **then**
15   Generate MUX based filter for edge (O_s, O_d);
16   Apply keep attribute to i;
17   **else**
18   Generate Reg based filter for edge (O_s, O_d);

From line 2 to line 8 the algorithm builds the set of *Intersected_Regs*, with an auxilliary set of *All_Regs*. *All_Regs* contains all registers that connect to register R through any input of the MUX (e.g., the MUX that drives R2 in Fig. 3). For each source register we test whether it is already in the *All_Regs* set (line 5). If the source register is already in *All_Regs* it indicates that we inserted this register into the set earlier when we visited other MUX input. This means the source register connects to R through more than one MUX input (e.g., register R1 in Fig. 3), and we insert the source register into *Intersected_Regs* (line 6). Otherwise, we insert the register to *All_Regs* to indicate that this register connects to R through some MUX input.

After we build the *Intersected_Regs* set, we generate the path filters for all paths connected to R. We visit all operations that will write to R; if the source register is in *Intersected_Regs*, there are multiple paths from this source register to R (as in Fig. 3). Therefore, we generate a path filter that includes the MUX input information and apply the "keep" attribute to the MUX input so that the filter will exactly match during timing extraction. If, instead, the source is not in *Intersected_Regs*, the path between source and sink is unambiguous and we use a register based filter to match the gate-level paths and data edge delay.

Time Complexity – We now analyze the time complexity of applying the algorithm to all registers of the design. Line 2 to line 8 are equivalent to visiting all registers that connect to R. This requires a depth-first search on the RTL combinational cone rooted on R. With proper caching, this step scales linearly with the number of RTL nodes in the design. In Lines 9 to 18, we visit all data edges whose sink operation is bound to register R, hence the upper bound of the number of edges visited for this part is N_E, the number of date edges in the CDFG. The time complexity of applying the algorithm to a design with N RTL nodes, N_R registers and N_E data edges is $O(N + N_R \times N_E)$. [3]

3.3.3 *Back Annotation*

After we have extracted the relevant timing information from the post-synthesis timing reports, we now back-annotate this information to the CDFG to refine timing estimates for the following HLS RTL generation. As stated in section 3.2, SDC will generate a CDFG schedule that preserves timing and dependence constraints as provided by the timing estimates and CDFG dependence edges. Any improvement in the accuracy of the timing estimates will be reflected in improved frequency, latency in clock cycles or both.

However, due to the non-deterministic nature of CAD tools, there may be some random variation in delays extracted from Quartus' timing reports. If we were to completely replace all original timing estimates with post-synthesis values, this random variation may be sufficient to prevent the iterative flow from converging. Based on an examination of the delay distribution of all critical data edges in the design, we find that Quartus produces delays in a normal distribution with a standard deviation of 0.5 clock period. However, this stability does not guarantee that individual paths are also stable between tool iterations; thus, in the back annotation process we ensure some memory of prior delay values in order to minimize quality of results variation due to large changes in path delay.

For the back annotation *update function*, we explore two options that will be compared in detail in section 4.2.

Moving Average (MAVG) – This update function is a simple filter that averages the current extracted timing value with the timing value of the previous iteration. Specifically, $est_{n+1} = (est_n + delay_n)/2$, where $delay_n$ is the extracted timing value from Quartus; est_n is the timing estimate of iteration n calculated by the same equation recursively, starting from pre-characterization based delay estimation (est_0). This two-point moving average moderates the timing estimates from changing too quickly, but will also quickly forget poor estimates from either initial or intermediate updates because the importance of any individual sample decreases exponentially with growing iterations. The moving average should work well if there are benchmarks that require significant changes in the estimates, but moderation of effects of any randomness in the estimates.

Average (AVG) – This update function simply performs the average of the delay estimates of all iterations up to the

current point. Whereas the moving average has exponentially decreasing importance of older datapoints, this update function linearly decreases importance. A full average more strongly moderates estimates from changing too quickly, but may suffer from a single poor estimate that skews the average. The average function should work well to more strongly moderate random variation in delay estimates as long as no individual estimate is particularly poor.

3.3.4 *Constraint Generation*

In order to improve the synthesis quality as well as the quality of the back-annoted delay, we can also generate multi-cycle constraints for multi-cycle operations. Related studies also consider multi-cycle constraints [5], but their multi-cycle constraints may over-relax the timing requirement of gate-level paths in hardware. Over-relaxed timing requirements may lead to sub-optimal implementations of gate-level paths; over-estimated delays from sub-optimal gate-level paths may generate low-performance hardware. Instead, we implement a more appropriate technique: for each data edge, we round the estimated delay up to the next integer number of cycles and generate an appropriate constraint. Although our approach is a coarser-grained approach to multi-cycle constraint generation, it gives Quartus sufficient optimization opportunity and allows the iterative process to properly track variation in delay estimates of long paths. The simple multi-cycle constraints are generated based on the estimated critical delay from the CDFG; given an estimated delay est_n, we generate the multi-cycle constraint $\lceil est_n - 0.5 \times T_{clk} \rceil$ cycles. The value 0.5 tightens constraints by a half cycle on average in order to encourage optimization. This simple constraint allows Quartus to optimize delay of multi-cycle operations.

In section 4.2, we will compare iterative flows with and without constraint generation. However, in the experiments we found that the multi-cycle constraints increase the synthesis time due to the low efficiency of passing multi-cycle constraints to Quartus through Tcl scripts. [4] To overcome this, we heuristically filter the constraints based on the slack ratio calculated by $1 - est_n/Cycles$, where $Cycles$ is the number of cycles **available** for the combinational path, and est_n is its estimated delay. We only generate the multi-cycle constraints if the slack ratio is smaller than a user defined threshold. This allows our flow to generate multi-cycle constraints to tweak the critical paths while avoiding the overhead of passing multi-cycle constraints for all paths.

3.4 Finalization Stage

After the user-specified number of iterations, the finalization stage performs RTL generation and a final full place and route of the design.

4. EXPERIMENTAL RESULTS

For our experiments, we pair together our HLS platform and QuartusII 13.0 synthesis and fast PAR tool targeting a Stratix IV device (EP4SGX70), speedgrade 2. We compare multiple options in Quartus synthesis, timing estimate

---

[3] Please note that the nodes in the combinational cone are at word-level, not bit-level.

[4] We observed that the multi-cycle constraints file is read and evaluated 7 times by Quartus during the synthesis process, and each constraint may require one second to process in larger benchmarks. After initial reading and processing, Quartus also spends considerable time annotating these constraints to its timing netlist.

update functions and constraints generation as described in section 3. For each tested HLS flow, we use the CHStone [17] set of benchmarks. Since we already compared our non-iterative baseline HLS tool to a state-of-the-art published work [5] in Section 2 and demonstrated comparable performance, we compare several versions of our iterative HLS flow to each other in this section. The RTL of each synthesis run in each flow, as well as intermediate RTL in the iterative flows are verified with post-fitting timing simulation, as well as to obtain detailed latency in clock cycles. We report the f_{max} and also calculate the latency of the hardware by multiplying the number of cycles and the minimal achievable clock period, i.e. the reciprocal of f_{max}. In these experiments, we set the number of iterations to 10; as we will see, in practice, all benchmarks converge in 3 iterations.

4.1 Quartus Synthesis Options

First, we compare the three options for Quartus synthesis: NO-FLAT, NO-PAR, and FAST-PAR. For all benchmarks, the first iteration is based on component pre-characterization and hence it is identical regardless of the Quartus synthesis option. Thus, we normalize benchmark performance to the first iteration. We repeat the experiment with three user f_{max} constraints: 400MHz, 450MHz and 500MHz.

Table 1 shows the geometric mean of cycles, clock period (**CP**, the reciprocal of f_{max}) and execution latency for each of the three synthesis options, normalized to performance of the first (non-iterative) solution. Initially, we can see that all three methods for iteratively refining the delay estimates are successful in reducing the clock period, i.e. improving the achievable f_{max} – any technique that refines the timing estimates based on (even partial) synthesis information will assist the SDC scheduler in assigning operations to control cycles and correctly determining the necessary total cycles. However, in the NO-FLAT and NO-PAR synthesis flows, this f_{max} improvement comes at a significant cost to the latency in clock cycles as well as the total execution latency. NO-FLAT synthesis increases the number of clock cycles by 22%, with execution latency increased by 13% on average. Similarly, the NO-PAR synthesis flow improves f_{max} through increasing the latency in clock cycles.

Examining execution latency in more detail, Fig. 4 shows the per-benchmark execution latency of the final solution of the NO-FLAT, NO-PAR and FAST-PAR synthesis options, normalized to the non-iterative flow for each user f_{max} constraint. First, the NO-FLAT synthesis significantly degrades performance of the final design. As expected, disabled logic optimization leads to increased execution latency of 8% to 17% on average and up to 58%. Furthermore, disabled logic optimization significantly increases the area consumption of the circuit as there can be no cross-module sharing or optimization; thus, the jpeg benchmark cannot create a feasible design due to increased resource use in the NO-FLAT option. Comparing to the NO-PAR synthesis, with lower user f_{max} constraints, the NO-PAR synthesis has close to the same final execution latency as FAST-PAR, yet the execution latency remains on average worse than FAST-PAR. As the target f_{max} increases, the execution latency difference also grows – at 450MHz, the latency of FAST-PAR is on average 10% faster than NO-PAR. This emphasizes that logic synthesis and optimization alone are not sufficient to generate accurate timing estimates, especially in higher frequencies where the routing delay impact is emphasized.

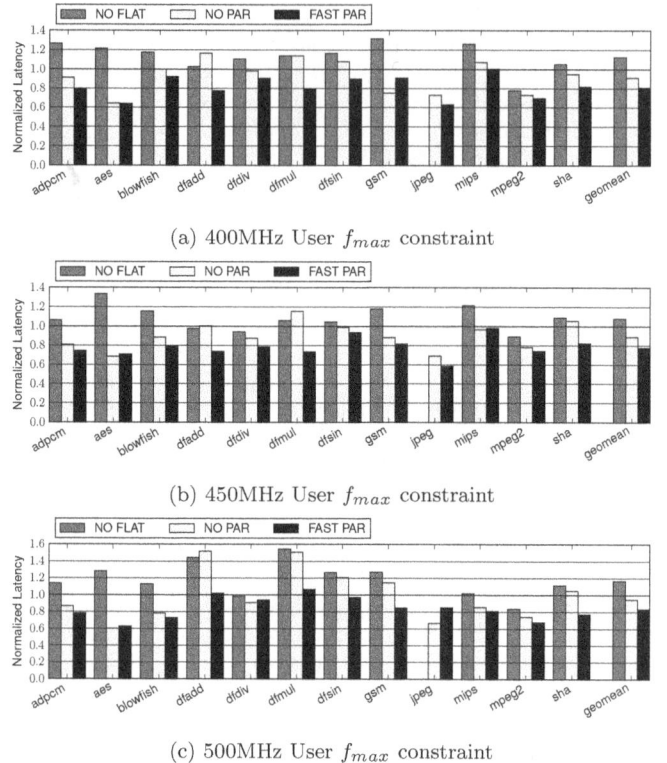

(a) 400MHz User f_{max} constraint

(b) 450MHz User f_{max} constraint

(c) 500MHz User f_{max} constraint

Figure 4: Comparison of Quartus Synthesis Options

Based on this information, we select FAST-PAR synthesis as the superior synthesis technique for the Iteration stage. Given this decision, we will now investigate the impact of timing estimate update functions and the use of multi-cycle timing constraints for the iterative flow using FAST-PAR.

4.2 FAST-PAR Updates & Constraints

Using FAST-PAR synthesis, we now investigate the impact of the two update functions, each with or without constraints. We denote the average update function AVG and average with multi-cycle constraints as AVG+C. Similarly, we denote the moving average function options as MAVG and MAVG+C. As in the previous section, we synthesize each benchmark from the CHStone set for iterations with each of 400MHz, 450MHz, and 500MHz f_{max} constraints.

Table 2 shows the geometric mean cycles, clock period and execution latency for each of AVG, AVG+C, MAVG, and MAVG+C for each of the user constraints. In all cases, all four update function combinations provide overall improvement in both f_{max} and total execution latency. Both the AVG and MAVG functions produce similar quality results on average, at the end of 3rd iteration. When we let our flow continue to run for 10 iterations, we observed that AVG flow improves execution latency by 2% than the MAVG flow. However, this small improvement is at the cost of 3x additional runtime. Fig. 5 compares the convergence property of AVG and MAVG for the AES benchmark as a histogram of the magnitude of estimation updates of 10 iterations. The tighter distribution of estimation updates in the AVG function lets the flow to further refine the design to get the additional improvement.

6

Table 1: Performance Metrics Normalized to non-Iterative Flow (The smaller the better)

	400MHz			450MHz			500MHz		
	CP	cycles	latency	CP	cycles	latency	CP	cycles	latency
No Flat	0.92	1.22	1.13	0.89	1.22	1.08	0.93	1.25	1.17
No PAR	0.83	1.10	0.91	0.81	1.10	0.89	0.86	1.10	0.95
Fast PAR	0.83	0.97	0.81	0.81	0.96	0.78	0.87	0.95	0.83

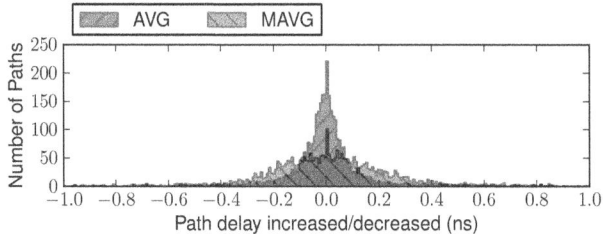

Figure 5: Convergence Comparison on AES (450MHz)

Table 2: Geometric Means of Performance Metrics (Normalized to Non-iterative, the smaller the better)

		AVG	AVG+C	MAVG	MAVG+C
400	CP	0.84	0.83	0.84	0.84
	cycles	1.00	0.97	0.99	0.95
	latency	0.84	0.81	0.83	0.80
450	CP	0.81	0.81	0.80	0.81
	cycles	0.98	0.96	0.99	0.97
	latency	0.80	0.78	0.79	0.78
500	CP	0.88	0.87	0.86	0.89
	cycles	0.99	0.95	0.98	0.95
	latency	0.87	0.83	0.84	0.84

(a) 400MHz User f_{max} constraint

(b) 450MHz User f_{max} constraint

(c) 500MHz User f_{max} constraint

Figure 6: Update Function, Constraints in Iterative FAST-PAR

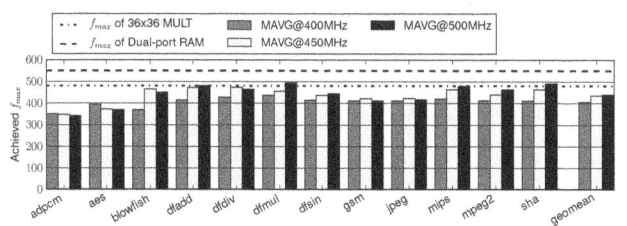

Figure 7: Achieved f_{max}

When we add multi-cycle constraints generation to each of the update functions, we see a further average improvement in output quality for both AVG and MAVG functions. Multi-cycle constraints enable Quartus to specifically optimize and reduce the delay of multi-cycle operations, which produces a tighter distribution of delays more amenable to meeting the user f_{max} constraint. Following the description in section 3.3.4, we only generate multi-cycle constraint for paths whose slack ratio, i.e. $(1 - est_n/Cycles)$, is smaller than 0.3, where $Cycles$ is the number of available cycles and est_n is its estimated delay.

Fig. 6 shows the per-benchmark normalized latency of each of the four update function combinations for 400MHz, 450MHz and 500MHz. Examining the results in detail, we find several distinct cases of applications: improving latency in clocks, f_{max}, both, and degrading latency in clocks in order to meet f_{max}. Fig. 7 also shows the final achieved frequency using MAVG of each of the application for each user constraint; we see that on average we achieve over 400MHz and we commonly reach physical limitations of the device such as the f_{max} of the 36×36 MULT.

4.2.1 Reduce Clock Cyles, f_{max} unchanged

In ADPCM, GSM, and SHA, execution latency improvement is mainly due to reductions in the number of clock cycles. Fig. 8 shows SHA as an example. We plot cycles,

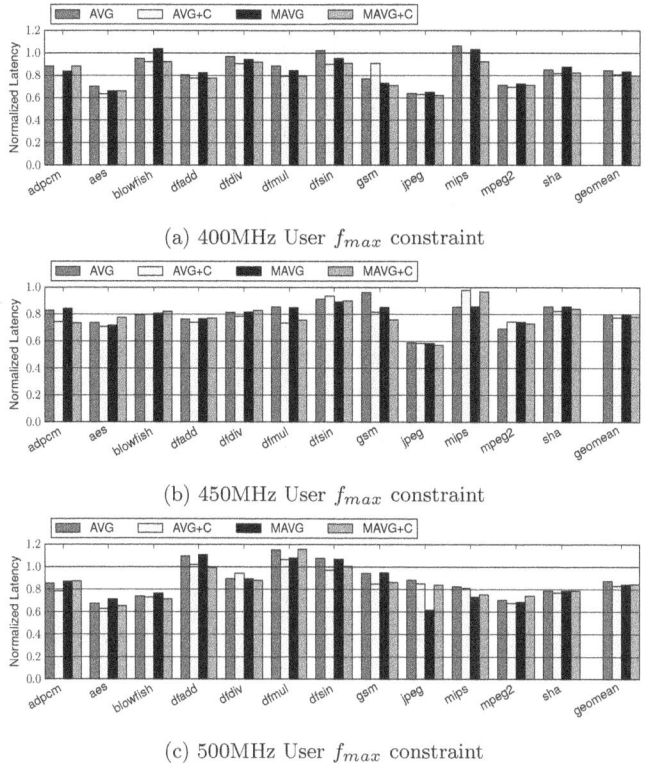

f_{max} and execution latency per iteration normalized to the first iteration for each of the 10 iterations. In the first few iterations, both f_{max} and cycles reduce significantly, and later iterations recover the goal f_{max}. However, we can see that the primary performance impact is due to a 20% reduction in cycles in the second iteration that is stable throughout the remaining iterations. SHA is a bit-level operation intensive benchmark, and Quartus is able to perform significant optimizations on these bit level paths.

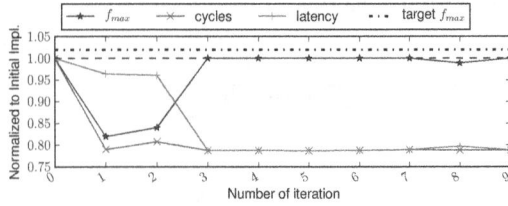

Figure 8: SHA 500MHz: less cycles, equal f_{max}

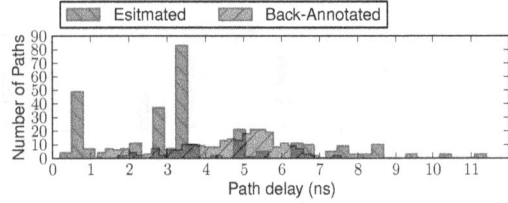

Figure 9: Delay Distribution: SHA 500MHz

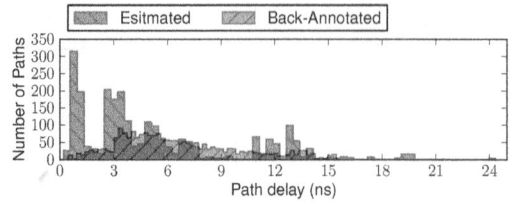

Figure 11: Delay Distribution: JPEG 450MHz

tion, our flow is performing a tradeoff between the latency in cycles and the achievable f_{max}. Through iterative refinement of timing violations and reduction in clock cycle latency, we converge on a series of equivalent solutions ~30% better than the initial iteration.

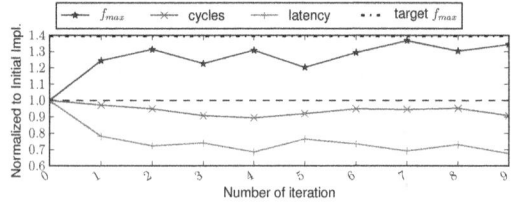

Figure 12: BLOWFISH 500MHz: improve f_{max}, cycles

We can verify this behavior by examining the distribution of estimated path latencies from the first and last iterations as in Fig. 9. The initial estimates include many long paths such as 7ns to 12ns paths, but the final delay demonstrates that many of these paths are much shorter, which allows the SDC scheduler to optimize the control and generate RTL with lower latency in clock cycles.

4.2.2 Improved f_{max}, unchanged cycles

In other benchmarks such as JPEG, MIPS and MPEG2, execution latency improvement is primarily due to increased f_{max}. For example, JPEG increases f_{max} by over 60% as shown in Fig. 10. In the first iteration, there is a large negative slack on a critical path due to an inaccurate overestimate. By the second iteration, we have significantly improved the f_{max} without affecting the latency in cycles. Observing the variation in delay distributions in Fig. 11, we observe a significant number of paths with estimated delay of less than 3ns but actual delays are longer than 3ns. After optimization of back-annotated delays, the design's critical path is through the MUX on the 64-bit data port of a RAM, which cannot be optimized through iteration in our current framework. We do not consider optimizing such paths in order to create multi-cycle MUXs and leave this further optimization for future work.

4.2.4 Improve f_{max} by increasing cycles

Finally, in certain cases, our flow increases the number of cycles in order to meet a target f_{max} similar to the other frequency improvement techniques presented in section 2. Particularly in the floating point benchmarks, DFMUL, DFADD, DFDIV and DFSIN, we need to increase the latency in clock cycles in order to meet f_{max} through a finer-grained division of operations into clock cycles. In most cases, our improvement to f_{max} offsets the cycles increment to achieve an overall execution latency improvement. However, there are certain cases such as MIPS at 400MHz, DFADD at 500MHz and DFMUL at 500MHz that produce designs with increased execution latency without multi-cycle constraints. In these particular cases, the AVG+C update model with multi-cycle constraints for **all** data edges allows Quartus to properly optimize the multi-cycle paths and produce an overall execution latency improvement. For example, Fig. 13 demonstrates the delay distribution of DFMUL with and without multi-cycle constraints applied. We can see that with multi-cycle constraints, the delay paths are generally reduced as well as more strongly clustered into groups of similar paths. Many long paths are reduced to single or two-cycle paths, yielding an overall reduction in clocks by ~ 10% at the same f_{max}, and thus an improvement in execution latency. In our benchmark set, we found no individual benchmark that could not be improved through either AVG or AVG+C with multi-cycle constraints for all data edges.

4.3 Resource Consumption

We present the resource consumption for the different flows in Table 3. Although the NO FLAT flow significantly increases resource use due to disabled logic optimizations, there is little difference in resource usage between iterative and non-iterative flows or between different options of the iterative flows.

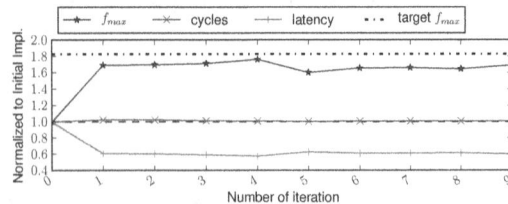

Figure 10: JPEG 450MHz: increase f_{max}, less cycles

4.2.3 Improve both f_{max} and cycles

In addition, our flow is able to simultaneously optimize both cycles and f_{max} in benchmarks such as AES and BLOWFISH. Considering BLOWFISH, we see that in each itera-

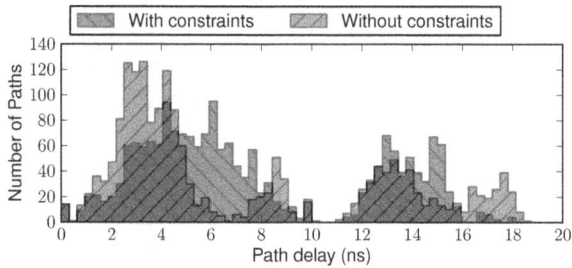

Figure 13: Delay Distribution of DFMUL (f_{max} : 500MHz)

Table 3: Average Resource Consumption (450MHz)

		ALM	REG	DSP	Membits
Non-Iterative		5989	5122	55	69167
NO PAR		6160	5259	55	69167
NO FLAT		14164	4574	51	36532
Fast PAR	AVG	6107	5263	55	69167
	AVG+C	6159	5271	55	69167

4.4 Runtime Comparison

We show runtime of different flows in Table 4, including the run-time of the initial non-iterative (pre-characterization based) flow. The flows with fast-PAR, but without multi-cycle constraints generation have average runtime of ∼12 minutes: 3-4× slower than the NO-PAR flow. With the addition of filtered multi-cycle constraints, there is a minimal overhead over the no-constraints FAST-PAR flows. There was no significant difference between AVG and MAVG and hence only the AVG results are reported. Using only FAST-PAR without constraints, our flow remains feasible compared to a single, non-iterative flow.

5. RELATED WORK

The problem of achieving timing closure is a classical problem in digital design. However, most prior work in the FPGA domain has concentrated on logic synthesis optimizations in order to improve timing closure when implementing RTL [23]. Similarly, most prior work in behavioral level optimization for timing closure concentrates on transformations such as memory partitioning [24], pipelining [25], retiming [12], and multi-cycle chaining [26]. Although these efforts all aid in achieving timing closure, they neglect the impact of physical implementation details on the achievable frequency; interconnect delay alone can contribute up to 70% of circuit delay [11]. However, integrating physical design information into the high level synthesis process is a comparatively under-studied area.

Initial efforts to integrate physical information into a synthesis process provided layout feedback to the binding process to improve f_{max} on an analytical model of a Xilinx XC4000 [27]; thus, although they attempt to model physical information, it is based on an analytical model rather than true feedback from the placement and routing process. Similarly, Cong et. al [28] presented placement-driven scheduling and binding for multi-cycle communications in a island-style architecture that bears some similarity to FPGA architectures. However, this work concentrates on optimizing inter-island communication as each island in the ar-

chitecture contains a computational element, register file and finite state machine. Another approach uses placement of block-level macros, and custom relational placement followed by heuristically determined critical wires to guide scheduling and binding refinements [20]. Although this approach is intended for FPGA architectures, it ignores detailed placement and routing information, and the macro-based technique does not allow optimization either within the macros or across block boundaries. Following the concept of integrating physical information, several commercial HLS tools [8,9] have integrated logic synthesis feedback for delay estimation, but they currently do not consider interconnect delays; as demonstrated in section 4.1, place and route information is an important component of accurate delay estimations.

In the ASIC domain, the concept of integrating physical information in high level synthesis is more widely employed, but the differences in design flows make the specific techniques inapplicable to FPGA design flows. Optimizations such as technology mapping [29] and packing [30] for FPGA architectures can significantly impact the number of logic levels and thus the combinational path delays. Nevertheless, these techniques have conceptual similarity to a place-and-route directed high level synthesis FPGA flow. Several ASIC HLS flows have integrated floorplanning to estimate wire delays to iteratively improve scheduling and binding operations [21,22]. In order to avoid full logic synthesis in each iteration, Zhenyu et. al [31] presented an incremental floorplanning technique; however, this technique only considers inter-block interconnect delay, not logic optimization within the blocks. In contrast, in the FPGA domain, rather than floorplanning block-level placements, we must perform full logic optimization, place and route in order to determine accurate timing estimates. Altera Quartus does offer an incremental synthesis option, but it does not optimize within blocks marked for incremental synthesis, preventing iterative enhancements of design-wide logic optimization. Other ASIC HLS flows similarly use interconnect wire delay information to optimize functional unit binding [32,33] as well as operation scheduling [34].

6. CONCLUSION

We have presented a placement and routing directed HLS flow for FPGAs that iteratively optimizes the design considering both behavioral-level and physical-level information by back-annotating post placement and routing delay information. We used the flow to reduce the latency of the hardware by up to 22% and increase the f_{max} by upto 24%, compared to a non-iterative flow. In addition, we demonstrated the importance of a full (fast) PAR compared to both synthesis without flattening and logic optimization, and synthesis with logic optimization but without place and route, achieving 28% and 12% improvement, respectively over the other synthesis options. Our flow achieved from 65% to 91% of the theoretical f_{max} on the Stratix IV device.

7. ACKNOWLEDGMENT

This work was supported by A*STAR under the HSSP grant.

8. REFERENCES
[1] A. Canis, J. Choi, M. Aldham, V. Zhang, A. Kammoona, J.H. Anderson, S. Brown, and

Table 4: Flow Runtime for 3 Iterations (Minutes)

	adpcm	aes	blowfish	dfadd	dfdiv	dfmul	dfsin	gsm	jpeg	mips	mpeg2	sha	geomean
Non-Iterative	.12	.08	.14	.02	.02	.01	.09	.09	.70	.02	.10	.02	.06 (1×)
NO PAR	7	4	6	2	3	2	8	4	13	2	2	2	4 (65×)
FAST PAR	29	11	15	8	19	6	32	14	37	6	5	7	12 (219×)
FAST PAR+C[†]	33	10	17	9	22	12	57	17	48	5	6	8	15 (266×)

[†] +C = Generate multi-cycle constraints to guide the PAR process

T. Czajkowski. Legup: high-level synthesis for fpga-based processor/accelerator systems. In *FPGA*, pages 33–36, 2011.

[2] D. Chen, J. Cong, Y. Fan, G. Han, W. Jiang, and Z. Zhang. xpilot: A platform-based behavioral synthesis system. *SRC TechCon*, 5, 2005.

[3] S. Gupta, N. Dutt, R. Gupta, and A. Nicolau. Spark: a high-level synthesis framework for applying parallelizing compiler transformations. In *ICVD*, pages 461–466, 2003.

[4] Alexandros Papakonstantinou, Karthik Gururaj, John A. Stratton, Deming Chen, Jason Cong, and Wen mei W. Hwu. Fcuda: Enabling efficient compilation of cuda kernels onto fpgas. In *SASP*, pages 35–42, 2009.

[5] Hongbin Zheng, Swathi Gurumani, Liwei Yang, Deming Chen, and Kyle Rupnow. High-level synthesis with behavioral level multi-cycle path analysis. In *FPL*, 2013.

[6] K. Rupnow, Yun Liang, Yinan Li, Dongbo Min, Minh Do, and Deming Chen. High level synthesis of stereo matching: Productivity, performance, and software constraints. In *FPL*, pages 1–8, 2011.

[7] Z. Zhang, Y. Fan, W. Jiang, G. Han, C. Yang, and J. Cong. Autopilot: A platform-based esl synthesis system. *High-Level Synthesis: From Algorithm to Digital Circuit*, pages 99–112, 2008.

[8] Synopsys, Inc. *Synphony High-Level Synthesis Solution*, 2012. http://www.synopsys.com/.

[9] Cadence, Inc. *C-to-Silicon Compiler*, 2012. http://www.cadence.com/.

[10] CALYPTO. *Catapult C Synthesis*, 2012. http://www.calypto.com/catapult_c_synthesis.php.

[11] Valavan Manohararajah, Gordon R. Chiu, Deshanand P. Singh, and Stephen D. Brown. Predicting interconnect delay for physical synthesis in a fpga cad flow. *IEEE TVLSI*, 15(8):895–903, August 2007.

[12] R.K. Ranjan, V. Singhal, F. Somenzi, and R.K. Brayton. On the optimization power of retiming and resynthesis transformations. In *ICCAD*, pages 402–407, 1998.

[13] Altera Inc. *Quartus II Software*. http://www.altera.com/products/software/.

[14] Xilinx Inc. *Vivado High-Level Synthesis*. http://www.xilinx.com/products/design-tools/vivado/integration/esl-design/hls/index.htm.

[15] Berkeley Logic Synthesis and Verification Group. *ABC: A System for Sequential Synthesis and Verification*, release 70930 edition. http://www.eecs.berkeley.edu/~alanmi/abc/.

[16] J. Cong and Z. Zhang. An efficient and versatile scheduling algorithm based on sdc formulation. In *DAC*, pages 433–438, 2006.

[17] Y. Hara, H. Tomiyama, S. Honda, H. Takada, and K. Ishii. Chstone: A benchmark program suite for practical c-based high-level synthesis. In *ISCAS*, pages 1192–1195, 2008.

[18] M.B. Srivastava and M. Potkonjak. Optimum and heuristic transformation techniques for simultaneous optimization of latency and throughput. *IEEE TVLSI*, 3(1):2–19, 1995.

[19] Altera Inc. *Quartus II Handbook*, 2013. http://www.altera.com/literature/manual/TclScriptRefMnl.pdf.

[20] R. Huang and R. Vemuri. Forward-looking macro generation and relational placement during high level synthesis to fpgas. In *PDPS*, pages 139–, 2004.

[21] D.W. Knapp. Fasolt: a program for feedback-driven data-path optimization. *IEEE TCAD*, 11(6):677–695, 1992.

[22] P. Prabhakaran and P. Banerjee. Simultaneous scheduling, binding and floorplanning in high-level synthesis. In *VLSI Design. Proceedings., Eleventh International Conference on*, pages 428–434, 1998.

[23] Deshanand P. Singh and Stephen D. Brown. An area-efficient timing closure technique for fpgas using shannon's expansion. *Integration, the VLSI Journal*, 40(2):167 – 173, 2007.

[24] Yuxin Wang, Peng Li, Peng Zhang, Chen Zhang, and J. Cong. Memory partitioning for multidimensional arrays in high-level synthesis. In *DAC*, pages 1–8, 2013.

[25] Yu-Chin Hsu and Yuan-Long Jeang. Pipeline scheduling techniques in high-level synthesis. In *ASIC Conference and Exhibit, 1993. Proceedings., Sixth Annual IEEE International*, pages 396–403, 1993.

[26] Jinhwan Jeon, Daehong Kim, Dongwan Shin, and Kiyoung Choi. High-level synthesis under multi-cycle interconnect delay. In *ASP-DAC*, pages 662–667, 2001.

[27] Min Xu and Fadi J. Kurdahi. Layout-driven rtl binding techniques for high-level synthesis using accurate estimators. *ACM TODAES*, 2(4):312–343, October 1997.

[28] J. Cong, Yiping Fan, G. Han, Xun Yang, and Zhiru Zhang. Architecture and synthesis for on-chip multicycle communication. *IEEE TCAD*, 23(4):550–564, 2004.

[29] Alan Mishchenko, Satrajit Chatterjee, and Robert Brayton. Improvements to technology mapping for lut-based fpgas. In *FPGA*, pages 41–49, 2006.

[30] Taneem Ahmed, Paul D. Kundarewich, and Jason H. Anderson. Packing techniques for virtex-5 fpgas. *ACM TRETS*, 2(3):18:1–18:24, 2009.

[31] Zhenyu Gu, Jia Wang, R.P. Dick, and Hai Zhou. Unified incremental physical-level and high-level synthesis. *IEEE TCAD*, 26(9):1576–1588, 2007.

[32] Yung-Ming Fang and D. F. Wong. Simultaneous functional-unit binding and floorplanning. In *ICCAD*, pages 317–321, 1994.

[33] G. Lucas, S. Cromar, and Deming Chen. Fastyield: Variation-aware, layout-driven simultaneous binding and module selection for performance yield optimization. In *ASP-DAC*, pages 61–66, 2009.

[34] Michael C. McFarland and Thaddeus J. Kowalski. Incorporating bottom-up design into hardware synthesis. *IEEE TCAD*, 9(9):938–950, 1990.

Optimizing Effective Interconnect Capacitance for FPGA Power Reduction

Safeen Huda, Jason Anderson
Dept. of ECE, University of Toronto
Toronto, ON, Canada

Hirotaka Tamura
Fujitsu Laboratories Limited
Kawasaki, Japan

ABSTRACT

We propose a technique to reduce the effective parasitic capacitance of interconnect routing conductors in a bid to simultaneously reduce power consumption and improve delay. The parasitic capacitance reduction is achieved by ensuring routing conductors adjacent to those used by timing critical or high activity nets are left floating - disconnected from either V_{DD} or GND. In doing so, the effective coupling capacitance between the conductors is reduced, because the original coupling capacitance between the conductors is placed *in series* with other capacitances in the circuit (series combinations of capacitors correspond to lower effective capacitance). To ensure unused conductors can be allowed to float requires the use of tri-state routing buffers, and to that end, we also propose low-cost tri-state buffer circuitry. We also introduce CAD techniques to maximize the likelihood that unused routing conductors are made to be adjacent to those used by nets with high activity or low slack, improving both power and speed. Results show that interconnect dynamic power reductions of up to ~15.5% are expected to be achieved with a critical path degradation of ~1%, and a total area overhead of ~2.1%.

1. INTRODUCTION

Process scaling has served as the linchpin of the unprecedented growth the semiconductor industry has seen over the past 50 years. Through process scaling, the performance, energy efficiency, and density of a digital system can all be increased, and these trends combine to offer significant increases in the total computational power of chips with each passing process node. However, as the industry continues to venture into deep submicron territory, several challenges have emerged which are beginning to degrade the expected returns from process scaling. One of the most significant bottlenecks has been the poor scalability of interconnect power; for example, [1] and [2] show that interconnect is becoming an ever more dominant factor in the performance and power dissipation of a digital system. As such, the optimization of interconnect is becoming an ever more critical aspect of digital system design.

While interconnect optimization has been explored extensively in the ASIC domain [3, 4], there is little published literature on the optimization of interconnect in FPGAs. This is because in ASICs, the width and spacing of wires can be arbitrarily chosen and as such they can be optimized to meet a target delay and/or power consumption on a net-by-net basis. In contrast, FPGAs have fixed, prefabricated interconnect structures whose geometry (width and spacing to other interconnect) cannot be altered to optimize the power and/or performance of a specific net.

In this work, we propose a technique to reduce the total parasitic capacitance of FPGA interconnect structures. We first note that the majority of the capacitance in the interconnect lies in the coupling capacitance, C_C, between adjacent routing conductors, and moreover, the coupling capacitance is expected to become an increasingly dominant component of interconnect capacitance, based on ITRS projections [5]. We then note that if a routing conductor is left in a floating state, the adjacent routing conductors will see reduced capacitive loading. This is because (as we will demonstrate) the effective capacitance seen by an adjacent conductor is that of the series combination of the coupling capacitance between the two conductors, and the total capacitance to ground of the conductor left in a floating state. Since the series combination of two capacitors results in an equivalent capacitance which is *less* than the capacitance of either of the two original capacitors, it follows that the total capacitance seen between a conductor and an adjacent floating conductor is less than in the case where the adjacent conductor is tied to a rail (V_{DD} or GND).

To implement this desired capacitance reduction technique, we propose a novel lightweight buffer topology which allows for tri-state operation, while requiring minimal area overhead. We further propose CAD techniques to ensure that nets which would benefit the most from reduced parasitic capacitance (i.e. timing critical nets or nets with high activity factor) have unused adjacent routing conductors, thus allowing our optimization to be applied. Results show that interconnect dynamic power reductions of up to ~15.5% can be achieved as C_C approaches a value three times as large as C_P (the plate capacitance – the capacitance between a wire and adjacent metal layers/substrate). The power savings are achieved at a critical path degradation of ~1% (on average), and a total area overhead of ~2.1%.

The remainder of this paper is organized as follows: Section 2 reviews FPGA interconnect hardware, describes interconnect scaling trends, and general approaches to the physical optimization of interconnect. The proposed effective parasitic capacitance reduction technique and necessary circuits are presented in Section 3 and Section 4, respectively. The interconnect architecture model and CAD tool modifications needed to maximize the available gains of our proposed technique are described in Sections 5 and 6, respectively. The experimental study is described in Section 7. Finally, Section 8 concludes the paper.

FPGA'14, February 26–28, 2014, Monterey, CA, USA.
Copyright 2014 ACM 978-1-4503-2671-1/14/02 ...$15.00.
http://dx.doi.org/10.1145/2554688.2554788.

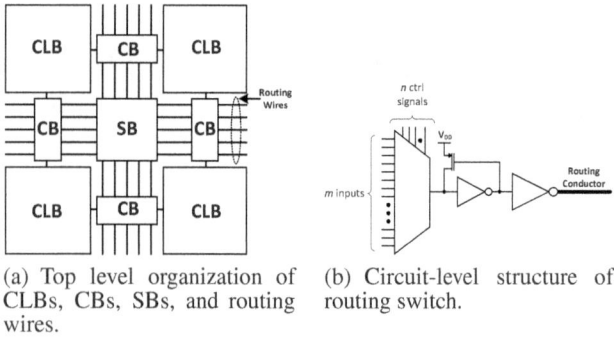

(a) Top level organization of CLBs, CBs, SBs, and routing wires.

(b) Circuit-level structure of routing switch.

Figure 1: Conventional FPGA circuit structures.

2. BACKGROUND

2.1 FPGA Routing Circuitry

Electrical connectivity between logic blocks (CLBs) in an FPGA is facilitated by the *programmable routing network*. The routing network is comprised of fixed-length routing wires, Connection Boxes (CBs) which connect CLBs to routing wires, and Switch Boxes (SBs) which are used to stitch together routing wires to form paths. A simple organization of routing wires is shown in Fig. 1(a). The switch boxes and connection boxes are simple pass-transistor based multiplexors, with an output driver circuit to buffer and re-condition the output signal. Routing switch circuitry is shown in Fig. 1(b). The pull-up PMOS on the multiplexer output is present because the mux is typically implemented using NMOS transistors (which are poor at passing logic "1").

2.2 Interconnect Power and Capacitance Scaling Trends

Due to the large capacitances of the routing wires in a modern FPGA, the power dissipated in the routing network is a dominant component of the total power dissipated, as much as 62% [6]. As such, any effort to reduce the power consumption in the routing network will potentially allow for an appreciable reduction in overall power. The significant power consumption in the routing network is attributed to the large capacitance of routing conductors. We estimate that the total load capacitance of a length-4 wire in a commercial FPGA fabricated in a 65nm CMOS process is near 200fF as follows: Based on the tile area data in [7], we estimated a single tile length in each dimension as $170\mu m$ for an FPGA in 65nm CMOS, which implies a wire capacitance of 170fF for a length-4 wire, assuming a wire capacitance per length of $0.25fF/\mu m$. We anticipate that the additional parasitic capacitance of a length-4 wire (resulting from the diffusion capacitance of the many multiplexors connected to a length-4 wire) will push the total load capacitance close to 200fF. Fig. 2 shows the two primary sources of capacitance in a routing conductor: C_P, the plate capacitance, which is the capacitance between a routing conductor and conductors in adjacent layers and/or the substrate, and C_C, the capacitance between a routing conductor and adjacent routing conductors within the same metal layer. Due to the evolution of the parameters related to wire geometries through process scaling, minimum width wires in intermediate metal layers have considerably greater height than width, as depicted in the figure. This leads to a growing disparity in the capacitances of C_C and C_P. Using ITRS projections [5] and simple models for wire capacitance, it can be estimated that C_C will scale to be approximately twice as large as C_P, although prior work using more sophisticated capacitance models has estimated that C_C is approximately 85% of the total interconnect capacitance

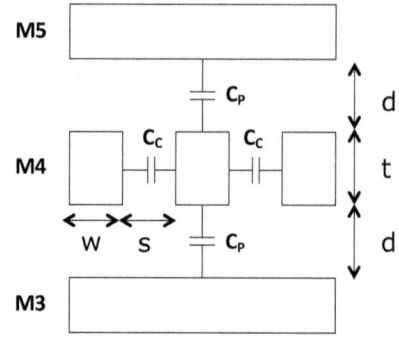

Figure 2: Interconnect capacitance components.

[8] - implying that $C_C/C_P \approx 5.7$ - in a 90nm process. Moreover, in FPGAs specifically, it is believed that C_C can be up to three times larger than C_P, depending on wire width and spacing [9]. Thus, it is widely believed that C_C is the dominant component of the total capacitance of interconnect, and as such, any technique to reduce C_C will lead to favourable reductions in total wire capacitance.

2.3 Wire Planning in ASICs and FPGAs

Due to the increasing sensitivity of key system-level metrics (such as speed and power) on interconnect parameters, much work has been done on interconnect optimization in the ASIC domain [10],[11]. Broadly speaking, the interconnect optimization problem serves to optimize a chip's speed and/or power consumption through judicious selection of wire width and spacing, under constraints of total wiring area. For example, a timing critical net would be routed with an intermediate wire width (to reduce interconnect resistance and thus reduce interconnect delay) and increased wire spacing to reduce wire capacitance (and thus further reduce delay). On the other hand, a high activity signal would be routed with both minimum width and maximum spacing to ensure minimum routing conductor capacitance, thus minimizing dynamic power consumption.

Previous work has investigated the optimization of interconnect in FPGAs [12], however it only considered the optimization of wire spacing and width of the prefabricated routing network. These optimizations provided some control over the wire width and spacing of conductors used by a particular net. For example, if a net were timing critical, the router would endeavor to route the net using the portion of the interconnect network which had favorable wire width/spacing. However, depending on placement and wiring congestion, such low-capacitance conductors may not be readily accessible, and moreover, the prior work considered only timing optimization, not power.

3. PROPOSED PARASITIC CAPACITANCE REDUCTION TECHNIQUE

The proposed parasitic capacitance reduction technique is inspired by the observation that two capacitors connected in series results in a total capacitance that is smaller than either of the two capacitors. More specifically, if two capacitors, C_1 and C_2 are connected in series, the total resulting capacitance is:

$$C_{eq} = \frac{C_1 \cdot C_2}{C_1 + C_2} \quad (1)$$

We are therefore inspired to reduce the effective parasitic interconnect capacitance of a routing conductor by making use of this property. We again note that the coupling capacitance between adjacent routing conductors is becoming increasingly dominant, and

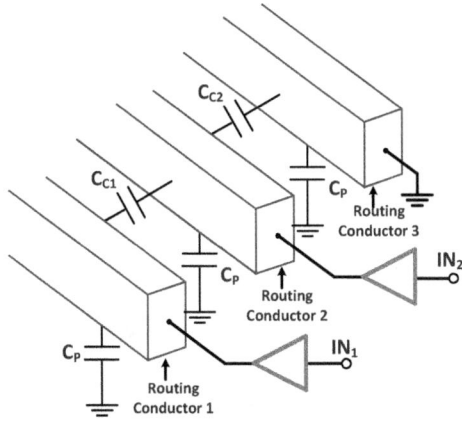

(a) Interconnect drivers and their respective loads.

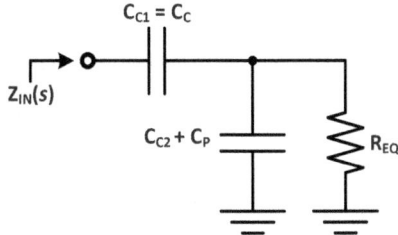

(b) Equivalent circuit representing routing conductors 2 and 3, from the perspective of routing conductor 1.

Figure 3: Effective impedance of coupled routing conductors.

so it would be advantageous if we could reduce the coupling capacitance by combining this capacitance with a second capacitance in series. We devised an approach whereby this can be achieved under certain circumstances.

Fig. 3(a) shows three routing conductors, with their respective driver circuits. Routing conductor 1 is coupled with routing conductor 2 through coupling capacitor C_{C1} and similarly, routing conductor 2 is coupled with routing conductor 3 through C_{C2}. From the perspective of routing conductor 1, routing conductor 2 and coupling capacitors C_{C1} and C_{C2} together form the equivalent, approximated circuit shown in Fig. 3(b). In the figure, R_{eq} is the effective output resistance of the driver driving routing conductor 2, and it is assumed (pessimistically, as will later become apparent) that the effective driver resistance for the buffer driving routing conductor 3 is near 0 (the conductor is grounded). The input impedance of this circuit has the following s-domain transfer function:

$$Z_{in}(s) = \frac{R_{eq}(2 \cdot C_C + C_P)s + 1}{C_C s [R_{eq}(C_c + C_p)s + 1]} \quad (2)$$

where it is assumed that $C_{C1} = C_{C2} = C_C$. We now note that if $R_{eq} \gg T_{PW\_AVG}/2\pi(C_C + C_P)$, where T_{PW_AVG} represents the average signal pulse width, $Z_{in}(s) \approx (2 \cdot C_C + C_P)/(C_C(C_C + C_P))$. This implies that if the driver impedance can be set to be very large, the effective impedance seen from routing conductor 1 looking towards routing conductor 2 is that of capacitor C_{C1} in *series* with the parallel combination of capacitors C_{C2} and C_P, which means that the effective parasitic loading on routing conductor 1 can therefore be *reduced*. Note however, that setting the driver resistance to be large enough such that such reductions in effective parasitic capacitance are achievable is not a practical solution, as this will make the buffer excessively slow (since the buffer delay is, to first order,

equal to the buffer resistance multiplied by the total output loading). Note however that a buffer with a reasonably small effective output resistance can be made to have a much larger output resistance if that buffer can be put into a tri-state mode. Putting a buffer into tri-state mode requires disconnecting all paths to either V_{DD} or GND, which ensures that there are no low impedance paths to either rail.

Therefore, we have shown that the parasitic capacitance arising from the coupling between two adjacent conductors can be reduced when the driver of the neighbouring conductor is put into tri-state mode. In this work, we assume that a routing conductor can in general be put into a tri-state mode, only if it is unused. As such, parasitic capacitance reduction can be observed only when an active routing conductor is adjacent to one or more unused routing conductors. The remaining sections will detail the circuitry to enable tri-state mode capable buffers, and CAD tool support to encourage routing conductors to remain unused if they are adjacent to a used routing conductor.

Returning now to routing conductor 3 in Fig. 3(a), the analysis above assumed the conductor was grounded. The reason this is a pessimistic assumption as far as capacitance reduction is concerned is as follows: if instead conductor 3 were tri-stated, as may be the case in a real FPGA, the consequence would be that capacitor C_{C2} would be in *series* with the plate capacitance of conductor 3 (C_P). This would mean that the capacitance of the capacitor labeled $C_{C2} + C_P$ in Fig. 3(b) would in fact be $C_P + C_{C2}[C_P/(C_{C2} + C_P)]$ which is less than $C_{C2} + C_P$. This would provide a further reduction in coupling capacitance between conductor 1 and conductor 2 (for the case of conductor 2 being tri-stated).

4. TRI-STATE BUFFERS

A conventional tri-stateable buffer is shown in Fig. 4. In this buffer, a header transistor is added to cut off all paths from V_{DD} to the input and output stages of the buffer. As can be seen in Fig. 4, when signal TS is high, transistor M5 is shut off, thus disconnecting the output from V_{DD}. Given that an unused routing switch will have its input held at V_{DD}, this leads to the gate of M6 being pulled to GND, which ensures that the output is also disconnected from GND; thus, the output is completely disconnected from either rail when an unused switch is put into tri-state mode. Note that transistor M3 cannot be disconnected from V_{DD}, as this ensures that the input of the buffer can be held at V_{DD}. This approach to designing tri-stateable buffers however is costly because of the transistor stacking in the pull-up paths. To maintain the same buffer delay

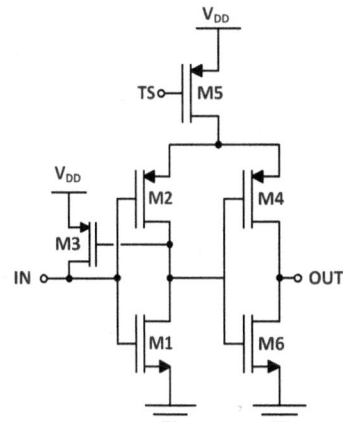

Figure 4: Conventional tri-state buffer.

13

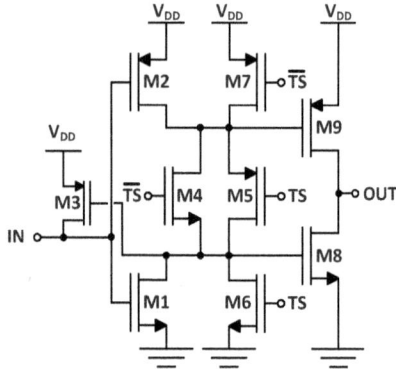

Figure 5: Alternative conventional tri-state buffer.

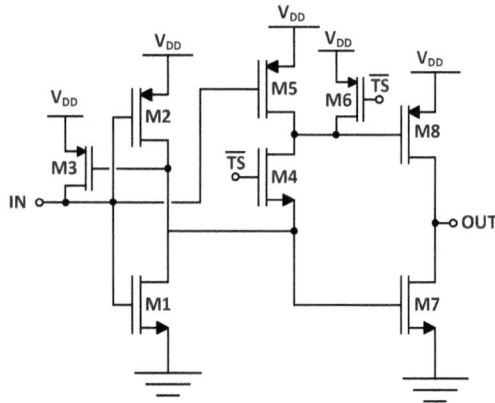

Figure 6: Proposed tri-state buffer.

as that of a conventional buffer, the transistor widths need to be at least doubled. In reality, the transistor width must be increased by a factor greater than two to compensate for speed degradation due to the body effect. Therefore, the traditional approach to designing tri-stateable buffers results in high area cost, since it not only requires an increased number of transistors, but it also necessitates a significant increase in the widths of the PMOS transistors in the input and output stages of the buffer.

An alternative conventional tri-stateable buffer topology is shown in Fig. 5 - this topology consists of a split inverter (formed by transistors M1 and M2), separated by a transmission gate (transistors M4 and M5) which together form the input stage, and a conventional output stage consisting of transistors M8 and M9. Note that in this topology, there is no transistor stacking in the output stage. As such, this topology does not require increased transistor sizing of the transistors in the output stage (which dominate the area of the buffer), thus allowing for a more area efficient design. The buffer works as follows: when TS is low, the transmission gate consisting of transistors M4 and M5 is on which effectively shorts the gate of M9 to the gate of M8. Thus, in this mode M1 and M2 are connected to form a single inverter which directly drives the output stage. When TS is high however, M4 and M5 are both off, which leads to the connection between the gates of M8 and M9 being severed; M6 and M7 are both turned on pulling the gates of M8 and M9 to GND and V_{DD}, respectively. Thus, in this mode both M8 and M9 are off, leaving the output tri-stated. This topology therefore uses a clever arrangement of transistors in the input stage of the buffer to ensure that tri-state mode is achieved without transistor stacking in the output stage, which results in area savings compared to the design in Fig. 4.

In this work, we propose to further optimize the buffer topology shown in Fig. 5 for use in FPGAs. Referring to Fig. 5, we can note some potential optimizations. We first observe that in FPGAs, an unused routing buffer will always have its input set to V_{DD}; this means that in tri-state mode, M1 is always guaranteed to be on, which makes transistor M6 unnecessary. Furthermore, because the input is guaranteed to be set to V_{DD}, the drain of M2 can safely be connected directly to the gate of M8; thus M1 and M2 would form a conventional inverter driving the gate of M8. This is advantageous because previously the path to V_{DD} from the gate of M8 was through two stacked PMOS transistors: M2 and M5. By eliminating this stack of transistors, we are able to reduce the sizes of the PMOS transistors in the input stage, which results in appreciable area reduction since the area of PMOS transistors dominates the total area of the input stage. Finally, transistor M5 can be repositioned to have its source connected to V_{DD} and its drain connected to the gate of M9 - again this eliminates any stacking in the pull-up path from the gate of M9 to V_{DD}, and also marginally reduces the parasitic capacitance connected to the gate of M8 (we have eliminated the diffusion capacitance arising from the drain of M5 at this node). Our optimized tri-stateable buffer topology is shown in Fig. 6, and together with the set of optimizations we discussed above, aims to offer a very area efficient tri-stateable buffer topology.

A detailed description of our proposed buffer is as follows: When the buffer is used (i.e. it is not tri-stated), since TS is low, transistor M6 is off, while M4 is on. During a rising transition at the input, M1 turns on, and the gates of M8 and M7 are both pulled to ground, which turns M8 on, M7 off, and allows the output to be pulled to V_{DD}. During a falling transition at the input, M2 and M5 both turn on, which results in M8 turning off, M7 turning on, thus causing the output to be pulled to GND. Observe that M5 pulls the gate of M8 to rail V_{DD} when the input is low.

When operating in tri-state mode, TS is high and therefore, M6 is on, M4 is off, which keeps the gate of M8 pulled to V_{DD} (thus keeping it turned off). Since an unused buffer has its input tied to V_{DD} (the input stage of the buffer acts as a latch when the input is at V_{DD}, since M3 forms a feedback loop allowing the input to hold its state at V_{DD}), M1 turns on, thus pulling the gate of M7 to GND and turning it off.

There is one issue regarding the tri-state buffer of Fig. 6 that warrants additional discussion, which is regarding the feasibility of "floating" unused conductors. This practice is acceptable in the FPGA context because such unused conductors feed downstream switches and pins via input NMOS-based multiplexors (see Fig. 1(b)). Naturally, the select inputs of such downstream multiplexors would not be configured to pass a signal from an incoming unused conductor. Note that the ability to tri-state wires is unique to the inherent interconnect architecture of FPGAs; tri-stating signals in general CMOS logic is not acceptable, owing to the potential for significant short-circuit current if a CMOS gate's input floats to a voltage mid-way between the two rails.

4.1 Buffer Comparison

To assess the merits of the proposed tri-state buffer over the two conventional topologies, we sized the buffers to allow for a target delay of approximately 185 ps - representing a $\sim$10% delay overhead over a conventional buffer (not tri-stateable). Comparisons of the area overhead (in minimum transistor widths) and tri-state leakage power reduction (relative to a conventional, non-tri-stateable buffer) are shown in Table 1.

The comparison shows that the conventional tri-state buffer topology (Fig. 4) offers superior leakage power reductions when oper-

Buffer Topology	Area Overhead [Min W. Xtors]	Tri-state Mode Leakage Reduction [%]
Conventional (Fig. 4)	99	45
Alternative Conventional (Fig. 5)	6.5	11
Proposed (Fig. 6)	3	25.4

Table 1: Comparison of area and tri-state leakage of buffer topologies.

ating in a tri-state mode. This is expected since the conventional topology employs transistor stacking, which results in reduced V_{SG} of the PMOS transistors, thus resulting in reduced leakage. The alternative conventional tri-state buffer (Fig. 5) offers dramatic reductions in area overhead, owing to the fact that there are no stacked transistors in the output stage of the buffer (recall that the transistors in the output stage of the buffer are the dominant component of the total buffer area). Thus, the area overhead is reduced from 99 minimum width transistors to ~6.5 minimum width transistors. However, the lack of transistor stacking results in poor tri-state mode leakage power, as we only observed an 11% reduction in leakage power compared to a conventional buffer which is not tri-stateable. The proposed buffer offers further reductions in area overhead compared to the alternative conventional tri-state buffer, as the area overhead is reduced from ~6.5 minimum width transistors to 3 minimum width transistors. The proposed buffer topology also shows decreased tri-state mode leakage power compared to the alternative conventional design. This is because the proposed topology is able to employ narrower transistors in the input stage, which results in reduced leakage current. However, the proposed buffer is still unable to match the low leakage power of the conventional tri-state buffer; again, this is because the proposed topology does not employ stacking, and as such, cannot offer the same levels of leakage reduction. Thus, the combined low cost/low power of the proposed topology makes it an attractive option to implement tri-state buffers in an FPGA. Note however, our proposed capacitance reduction technique does not rely on any specific topology, indeed a conventional tri-state buffer topology may be employed, albeit at a much larger area penalty.

5. INTERCONNECT MODELLING

In this work, we assume that the layout of the the routing conductors forming the interconnect network matches that of the standard VPR-style staggered interconnect model; Fig. 7 depicts the assumed organization of the routing conductors comprising a routing channel.

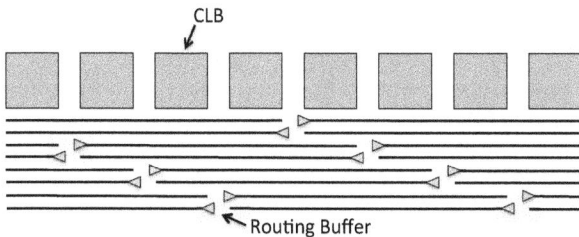

Figure 7: Assumed layout of routing conductors within a channel.

Note in this assumed organization of routing conductors, adjacent conductors do not necessarily have complete overlap with one another. Rather, because the start points of interconnect are staggered, some adjacent conductors will only partially overlap with one another. Fig. 8 shows a detailed view of the coupling capaci-

tances between adjacent conductors. Note that because of the staggered nature of the routing layout considered in this work, all tracks (except for those at the boundaries of a channel) will have exactly three neighbours. In the figure, track (i, j) is coupled with routing tracks $(i-1, j)$, $(i-1, j+1)$, and $(i+1, j)$. Thus track (i, j) has three neighbours which for this paper we number as follows: track $(i-1, j)$ is neighbour 1, track $(i-1, j+1)$ is neighbour 2, and track $(i+1, j)$ is neighbour 3. We note that tracks (i, j) and $(i+1, j)$ completely overlap with one another, and model the coupling between these two tracks with a capacitor with capacitance C_C. As previously mentioned, some tracks do not overlap completely with adjacent tracks, and this is the case with tracks $(i-1, j)$ and $(i-1, j+1)$, which have a 75% and 25% overlap with track (i, j), respectively. As such, we model the coupling between tracks $(i-1, j)$ and (i, j) and between tracks $(i-1, j+1)$ and (i, j) with capacitances of $0.75C_C$ and $0.25C_C$, respectively. Note that this example showed the various overlaps with neighbouring tracks when i is an odd number. When i is an even number, track (i, j) will have complete overlap with track $(i-1, j)$, 25% overlap with track $(i+1, j-1)$ and 75% overlap with track $(i+1, j)$.

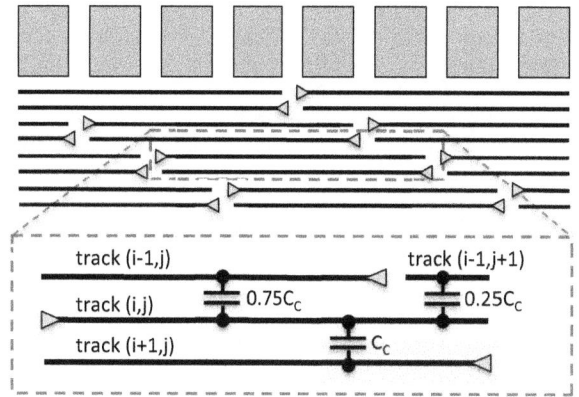

Figure 8: Detailed view of routing conductor layout.

6. TOOL SUPPORT

One of the premises of the proposed capacitance reduction technique is that power and/or timing critical switches will have adjacent tracks which are *unused* and thus can be put into tri-state mode. Therefore, special effort must be made during the physical implementation of a circuit to ensure that such situations arise so as to optimize both power and timing. In order to ensure that power and timing critical nets have unused adjacent tracks, we have made modifications to a conventional FPGA router. The router is modified to encourage power and timing critical signals to be routed with unused adjacent tracks.

The modifications to the router in this work bears some similarity to a previously proposed crosstalk-aware router for FPGAs [13], in that signals are routed such that they have unused adjacent tracks (if they have high activity or are timing critical). However, the difference between this work and prior work is that here we proposed to leave adjacent conductors unused to reduce the effective capacitance of used routing conductors, thereby reducing power and improving speed. This is in contrast to previous work, where adjacent conductors were left unused (and were grounded, not tri-stated as is the case in our work) to reduce coupling between active routing conductors, thereby mitigating the delay penalty due to crosstalk.

The VPR router incorporates the PathFinder algorithm [14]. PathFinder routes individual driver/load connections one at a time. A cost function is used to find a low-cost path through the routing fabric from a driver to a load. The cost function incorporates metrics of timing performance and *routability* (i.e. the ability to legally route all of the connections in the circuit) in order to yield a routed circuit with a favorable quality of results. The cost function implemented in VPR is:

$$\begin{aligned} Cost_n &= (1 - Crit_i) \cdot cong\_cost_n \\ &+ Crit_i \cdot delay\_cost_n \end{aligned} \quad (3)$$

where n is the routing resource (e.g. wire segment) being considered for addition to a partially-completed route, i is the driver/load connection being routed, $Crit_i$ is the timing criticality of the connection (equal to 1 for connections on the critical path, and decreasing to 0 as the slack of the connection increases), $cong\_cost_n$ is the congestion cost of routing resource n which gives an indication of the *demand* for the routing resource among nets, while $delay\_cost_n$ is the delay of routing resource n.

The rationale for cost function (3) is that when connection i is being routed to a routing resource n, if the connection has high criticality (i.e. $Crit_i$ is close to 1), then the cost of using the routing resource is principally given by the delay of that resource (equal to $delay\_cost_n$). For such timing-critical connections, the principal concern should be to route the connections using the fastest routing resources, with less focus on the demand for such resources by other nets. On the other hand, if the criticality of the connection being routed is low (i.e. $Crit_i$ is close to 0), then the $cong\_cost_n$ is the dominant part of the cost of using a resource. As such, connections with sufficient timing slack are encouraged to use resources with less demand, potentially pursuing more circuitous routes to reduce demand on overcongested nodes.

Turning now to our modification of the VPR router, for a routing segment, n, we use the following cost function:

$$\begin{aligned} Cost_n &= (1 - Crit_i) \cdot [cong\_cost_n \\ &+ PF \cdot (\alpha_i \cdot cap\_cost_n \\ &+ power\_cost\_infringe_n)] \\ &+ Crit_i \cdot delay\_cost_n \end{aligned} \quad (4)$$

where α_i is the activity factor for connection i being routed (normalized to a [0:1] range), PF is a scalar tuning parameter (determined empirically), and cap_cost_n is the effective capacitance of node n (taking into account current occupancies of adjacent conductors). The term $power\_cost\_infringe_n$ is equal to:

$$\sum_{m=1}^{3} neighbour\_cost(m) \cdot max\_activity(n,m) \quad (5)$$

where $neighbour\_cost(m)$ models the difference in coupling capacitance seen by neighbour m (recall our definitions for neighbour numbers from Section 5) if node n is not in a floating state, and $max\_activity(n,m)$ is the maximum activity factor corresponding to the nets using the mth neighbouring conductor of node n. Recall that during routing, multiple nets may be using a single routing conductor (it is only towards the end of routing when congestion is resolved that a conductor is used by at most one net), and as such we pessimistically assume the worst case activity factor among all nets using a neighbouring conductor in our cost function. Thus $power\_cost\_infringe_n$ models the worst case increase in power if node n is not kept in a floating state.

The motivation for the modification to the cost function is as follows: while routing a circuit, we wish to route connections which have high switching activity and/or criticality such that their neighbouring tracks are unoccupied. Occupied adjacent tracks cannot be put into a floating state, and therefore, such a scenario would lead to a lost opportunity for capacitance reduction. In general, when routing connection i, we need to consider two cases: 1) connection i has sufficient timing margin, or 2) connection i is timing critical. For the former case, we strive to optimize the routing for two different situations. First, we attempt to guide nets with high activity factor to use tracks with unoccupied neighbours; the term $(1 - Crit_i)\alpha_i \cdot PF \cdot cap\_cost_n$ attempts to optimize for this goal. The term cap_cost_n models the capacitance of a track given the occupancies of adjacent tracks (i.e. unoccupied adjacent tracks will lead to a lower capacitance). As such if the current net has high activity factor (α_i), the router will attempt to find routing solutions where adjacent tracks are unused for this net. The second goal is to avoid using tracks adjacent to high activity nets. This is to ensure that the capacitance of the tracks seen by such nets in minimized. This optimization goal is dealt with by the term $(1 - Crit_i) \cdot PF \cdot power\_cost\_infringe_n$. The term $power\_cost\_infringe_n$ models the impact to power resulting from use of the current track.

On the other hand, if the connection being routed has high criticality, then as always, we seek to optimize the timing of this net. While the cost function has no specific changes to optimize the timing of critical nets, in our cost function the $delay\_cost_n$ term models the effect of used/unused adjacent tracks (i.e. tracks with unused adjacent tracks will see a lower value for $delay\_cost_n$). As such, the router will naturally seek out paths where tracks have unused adjacent tracks in a bid to optimize the timing for that net.

7. EXPERIMENTAL STUDY

In order to assess the merits of the proposed capacitance reduction technique, we used our modified version of VPR to place and route the set of benchmark circuits packaged with VPR 6.0 [15] as well as circuits from the MCNC benchmark suite. We performed post-routing analysis to estimate the power reductions achievable using our proposed technique versus a baseline architecture. Our baseline architecture contains unidirectional wire segments (direct-drive) which span 4 CLB tiles, uses the Wilton switch block [16], and has logic blocks with ten 6-LUTs/FFs per CLB. All benchmark circuits were initially routed on the baseline architecture to determine the minimum number of tracks per channel needed to route each circuit successfully (W_{min}). For each circuit, we then computed $W = 1.3 \times W_{min}$ to reflect a medium-stress routing scenario. The computed W value for each circuit was used for all experimental runs of the circuit. We use the ACE switching activity estimator tool [17] to compute switching activity for each signal in each benchmark circuit; these are required by our modified CAD flow (see (4)) to optimize routing for power reduction. We used SPICE simulations with a commercial 65nm process to determine the added delay of our proposed tri-stateable buffer over a conventional buffer, to assess the capacitance reductions achievable for the various values of C_C/C_P considered in this study, and to study leakage power under various modes of operation.

7.1 CAD Tool Optimization

We first begin by analyzing the impact of our cost function modifications on power reduction/critical path delay, and optimize the scalar term (PF) in (4) accordingly. Fig. 9 shows the variation in both interconnect power reduction and critical path delay as PF is varied from 0 to 50, assuming that $C_C/C_P = 1.5$. The results show interesting trends: First, as PF is varied from 0 to 10, we see a steady increase in the achieved power reductions. This is intuitively expected because as PF is increased, the router is encour-

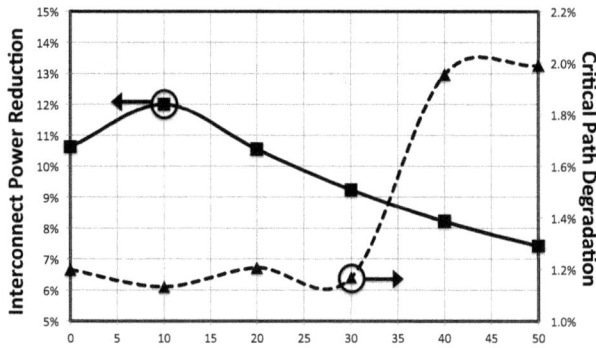

Figure 9: Interconnect dynamic power and critical path vs _PF_.

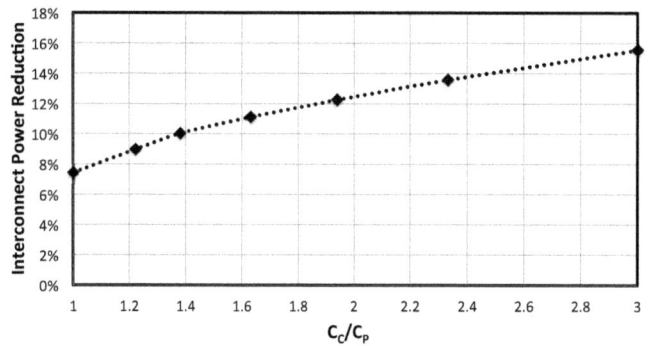

Figure 10: Interconnect dynamic power ratio vs C_C/C_P.

aged to spend more effort in creating situations where high activity nets have unused adjacent conductors. Thus, as _PF_ is increased, more high activity nets will have unused adjacent conductors, thus allowing for increased power reduction. However, as _PF_ is further increased from 10 to 50, we see a decrease in the achieved power reductions. This is because larger values of _PF_ causes the router to place too much emphasis in creating situations where conductors adjacent to high activity nets are unused; in doing so, the router ends up increasing the average wirelength used to route each net, thus increasing dynamic power consumption. Thus a _PF_ value of 10 serves as an reasonable balance between creating situations where the proposed technique can be used to decrease capacitance for high activity nets, while the average wirelength used by the router does not degrade the overall achieved power reductions.

The plot also shows the variation in critical path degradation as a function of _PF_. Due to the increased pull-down resistance of the first stage of our proposed tri-stateable buffer, our buffer suffers from a $\sim$10% delay increase compared to a conventional buffer. However, we are able to reduce the overall buffer delay penalty by using our proposed capacitance reduction technique. Thus, careful attention must be paid to the range of _PF_ values which leads to minimized increases in critical path. The trend in Fig. 9 shows that the degradation to critical path remains constant over the range $0 \leq PF \leq 30$, indicating the router is able to route the critical path with a sufficient number of unused neighbouring conductors such that the overall degradation in critical path is restricted to $\sim$1% within this range. However, as _PF_ is further increased from 30 to 50 we see a distinct degradation in critical path; this is attributed to the fact that increasing _PF_ in these ranges results in increased wirelength for the critical path, thus resulting in increased critical path delay. Since a _PF_ value of 10 results in the best power reduction and the minimal critical path degradation, we assume a _PF_ value of 10 for the remainder of this paper.

7.2 Power Reduction Results

In lieu of a specific value for C_C/C_P which would vary with process node, and would depend on the specific layout of an FPGA tile, we assess the available power reductions and performance improvement as the ratio C_C/C_P is varied from 1-3. Fig. 10 shows the interconnect dynamic power reduction as a function of the ratio C_C/C_P. Note that previously it was shown that interconnect dynamic power accounts for 62% [6] of the total power consumption in a 90nm FPGA. Though, given that interconnect power does not scale as favourably as other contributors to total dynamic power (such as the power dissipated in individual logic elements), it is likely that interconnect dynamic power accounts for an even greater portion of the total dynamic power in 32nm and beyond.

As expected, the power reductions afforded by the proposed technique increase as the ratio C_C/C_P increases. Given that ITRS data shows the ratio C_C/C_P increasing with every passing technology node, it follows that the proposed technique offers excellent scalability – it is expected to allow for improved quality of results with each passing technology node. The interconnect power reductions exceed 15% as C_C/C_P approaches a value of 3 (i.e. C_C accounts for 75% of the total capacitance). Finally, Table 2 shows a circuit-by-circuit breakdown of power reductions, critical path degradations, and area overheads for the circuits considered in this work. Two sets of results are given for each circuit, one for $C_C/C_P = 1$ and a one for $C_C/C_P = 2$, since we believe that C_C/C_P for interconnect of an FPGA fabricated in the latest process technology would have a value between these two bounds.

7.3 Area

The proposed tri-stateable buffer uses three additional transistors: _M4_, _M5_, and _M6_. These transistors were sized such that the proposed buffer had a worst-case delay overhead of $\sim$10%. The resulting area overhead of the additional transistors is thus 3 minimum-width transistors (_M4_, _M5_ and _M6_ were all minimum width) in addition to an SRAM cell needed for the mode configuration of each routing buffer. This results in an increase in routing area of 5.1%, and an overall area overhead of 2.1%.

7.4 Leakage Power Reduction

Note that while the main thrust of this work is in the use of tristate buffers to reduce coupling capacitance and thus save dynamic power, one additional benefit worth noting is that tri-state buffers may be used to reduce leakage power for unused blocks; this was alluded to in Section 4.1, where we noted that simulation results showed that standby leakage power of the proposed buffer was $\sim$25% less than a conventional buffer. In our experiments, we counted the number of used and unused buffers in each design, and determined the overall reductions in leakage power of the routing buffers on a circuit-by-circuit basis; results show that routing static power can be reduced by $\sim$14.5%.

8. CONCLUSION

In this work, we presented a novel technique to reduce the capacitance of nets in FPGAs. We have shown that keeping unused routing conductors tied to a rail (V_{DD} or GND) is suboptimal and imposes an unnecessary increased coupling capacitance to used routing conductors. Thus, we showed how unused routing conductors may be exploited, since when they are left floating, they result in decreased capacitance to adjacent routing conductors. We then presented a low-cost tri-stateable buffer to allow for our proposed capacitance reduction technique with minimal area overhead. We

Circuit	$C_C/C_P = 1$			$C_C/C_P = 2$			Total Area Overhead %
	Routing Dynamic Power Reduction %	Critical Path Incr. %	Routing Static Power Reduction %	Routing Dynamic Power Reduction %	Critical Path Incr. %	Routing Static Power Reduction %	
alu4	8.1	1.6	14.9	12.0	0.9	14.9	1.8
apex2	7.9	0.9	14.1	11.9	1.4	14.1	2.1
apex4	7.5	-1.0	12.7	11.4	0.6	12.6	2.1
bigkey	9.7	1.1	13.7	14.3	1.6	13.8	1.8
clma	7.6	0.9	14.8	12.9	1.3	14.8	2.7
des	10.8	1.0	15.7	16.2	1.4	15.6	1.8
diffeq	8.0	0.5	14.6	12.5	0.7	14.8	2.1
dsip	9.4	0.9	15.6	14.2	2.3	15.7	2.1
elliptic	7.4	0.8	14.0	11.7	1.3	14.0	2.7
ex1010	6.7	1.1	13.6	11.1	1.7	13.6	2.4
ex5p	7.6	0.4	14.4	11.4	2.0	14.2	2.1
frisc	7.3	0.8	13.2	11.7	1.1	13.1	2.7
misex3	8.1	0.7	13.5	11.9	2.1	13.7	2.7
pdc	6.5	2.2	12.6	10.7	1.6	12.5	2.4
s298	7.9	0.2	14.4	13.0	0.2	14.3	1.8
s38417	7.1	1.1	13.4	11.6	1.6	13.4	2.4
s38584.1	6.7	0.8	13.0	11.0	1.1	13.1	2.4
seq	7.4	0.9	13.2	11.6	1.3	13.2	2.1
spla	6.1	5.0	12.9	10.1	1.8	12.9	2.4
tseng	10.5	-0.6	14.2	15.2	1.0	14.3	2.4
LU8PEEng	6.0	0.5	12.7	10.6	0.7	12.7	2.7
LU32PEEng	8.0	1.0	14.3	12.0	1.5	14.3	2.4
blob_merge	6.2	0.4	13.2	10.4	0.6	13.2	2.4
boundtop	8.5	0.7	13.5	13.3	0.9	13.6	2.1
ch_intrinsics	14.2	0.7	15.5	19.2	1.0	15.6	1.8
diffeq1	11.6	0.8	16.7	16.4	0.6	16.7	2.1
diffeq2	13.1	1.8	18.0	17.6	0.6	18.0	1.8
mcml	8.0	0.8	14.9	13.3	1.0	14.9	2.1
mkDelayWorker32B	7.7	2.7	18.1	13.2	1.0	18.1	2.1
mkPktMerge	10.0	0.7	21.0	16.5	0.9	21.0	1.5
mkSMAdapter4B	7.8	0.7	15.3	12.4	1.1	15.2	2.1
or1200	7.6	0.2	16.3	12.4	0.3	16.3	2.1
raygentop	8.1	0.6	13.8	12.9	0.8	13.9	2.1
sha	6.8	0.5	13.1	11.0	0.7	13.3	1.8
stereovision0	7.1	0.7	13.8	12.0	1.0	13.8	1.8
stereovision1	6.4	1.3	14.3	11.0	1.9	14.3	2.4
stereovision2	8.7	1.0	14.1	12.9	1.3	14.1	2.7
stereovision3	14.6	0.3	15.4	19.2	0.4	15.8	1.8
geomean	**8.2**	**0.9**	**14.5**	**12.8**	**1.1**	**14.5**	**2.1**

Table 2: Detailed power reductions, critical path increases and area overheads for each circuit.

further present CAD techniques to optimize the routing of a design to maximize capacitance reductions with our proposed technique. Results have shown interconnect dynamic power reductions of up to ~15.5% when the ratio between coupling capacitance and plate capacitance of a wire, C_C/C_P, reaches a value of 3. These savings come with a critical path degradation of ~1%, on average, and a total area overhead of ~2.1%.

9. REFERENCES

[1] N. Magen, A. Kolodny, U. Weiser, and N. Shamir, "Interconnect-power dissipation in a microprocessor," in *SLIP '04*, 2004, pp. 7–13.

[2] R. Krishnamurthy, S. Mathew, M. Anders, S. Hsu, H. Kaul, and S. Borkar, "High-performance and low-voltage challenges for sub-45nm microprocessor circuits," in *ASICON 2005*, vol. 1, 2005, pp. 283–286.

[3] M. L. Mui, K. Banerjee, and A. Mehrotra, "A global interconnect optimization scheme for nanometer scale VLSI with implications for latency, bandwidth, and power dissipation," *IEEE T-ED*, vol. 51, no. 2, pp. 195–203, 2004.

[4] X.-C. Li, J.-F. Mao, H.-F. Huang, and Y. Liu, "Global interconnect width and spacing optimization for latency, bandwidth and power dissipation," *IEEE T-ED*, vol. 52, no. 10, pp. 2272–2279, 2005.

[5] ITRS, "ITRS 2011 Report." [Online]. Available: http://www.itrs.net/Links/2011ITRS/Home2011.htm

[6] T. Tuan, A. Rahman, S. Das, S. Trimberger, and S. Kao, "A 90-nm low-power FPGA for battery-powered applications," *IEEE TCAD*, vol. 26, no. 2, pp. 296–300, 2007.

[7] H. Wong, V. Betz, and J. Rose, "Comparing FPGA vs. custom CMOS and the impact on processor microarchitecture," in *ACM FPGA*, 2011, pp. 5–14.

[8] D. Sinha and H. Zhou, "Statistical timing analysis with coupling," *IEEE TCAD*, vol. 25, no. 12, pp. 2965–2975, 2006.

[9] Altera, personal communication.

[10] J.-A. He and H. Kobayashi, "Simultaneous wire sizing and wire spacing in post-layout performance optimization," in *ASP-DAC*, 1998, pp. 373–378.

[11] K. Moiseev, S. Wimer, and A. Kolodny, "Timing optimization of interconnect by simultaneous net-ordering, wire sizing and spacing," in *IEEE ISCAS*, 2006, pp. 21–24.

[12] V. Betz and J. Rose, "Circuit design, transistor sizing and wire layout of FPGA interconnect," in *IEEE CICC*, 1999, pp. 171–174.

[13] S. J. E. Wilton, "A crosstalk-aware timing-driven router for FPGAs," in *ACM FPGA*, 2001, pp. 21–28.

[14] L. McMurchie and C. Ebeling, "PathFinder: A negotiation-based performance-driven router for FPGAs," in *ACM FPGA*, 1995, pp. 111–117.

[15] J. Rose, J. Luu, C. W. Yu, O. Densmore, J. Goeders, A. Somerville, K. B. Kent, P. Jamieson, and J. Anderson, "The VTR project," in *ACM FPGA*, 2012, pp. 77–86.

[16] S. J. Wilton, "Architecture and algorithms for field-programmable gate arrays with embedded memory," Ph.D. dissertation, 1997.

[17] J. Lamoureux and S. Wilton, "Activity estimation for field-programmable gate arrays," in *IEEE FPL*, 2006, pp. 1–8.

Towards Interconnect-Adaptive Packing for FPGAs

Jason Luu, Jonathan Rose, and Jason Anderson

Dept. Electrical and Computer Engineering, University of Toronto
Toronto, Ontario, Canada
vpr@eecg.utoronto.ca

ABSTRACT

In order to investigate new FPGA logic blocks, FPGA architects have traditionally needed to customize CAD tools to make use of the new features and characteristics of those blocks. The software development effort necessary to create such CAD tools can be a time-consuming process that can significantly limit the number and variety of architectures explored. Thus, architects want flexible CAD tools that can, with few or no software modifications, explore a diverse space. Existing flexible CAD tools suffer from impractically long runtimes and/or fail to efficiently make use of the important new features of the logic blocks being investigated. This work is a step towards addressing these concerns by enhancing the packing stage of the open-source VTR CAD flow [17] to efficiently deal with common interconnect structures that are used to create many kinds of useful novel blocks. These structures include crossbars, carry chains, dedicated signals, and others. To accomplish this, we employ three techniques in this work: *speculative packing*, *pre-packing*, and *interconnect-aware pin counting*. We show that these techniques, along with three minor modifications, result in improvements to runtime and quality of results across a spectrum of architectures, while simultaneously expanding the scope of architectures that can be explored. Compared with VTR 1.0 [17], we show an average 12-fold speedup in packing for fracturable LUT architectures with 20% lower minimum channel width and 6% lower critical path delay. We obtain a 6 to 7-fold speedup for architectures with non-fracturable LUTs and architectures with depopulated crossbars. In addition, we demonstrate packing support for logic blocks with carry chains.

Categories and Subject Descriptors

B.5.2 [**Design Aids**]: Automatic Synthesis, Optimization

Keywords

FPGA; Algorithms; Packing; Clustering; Architecture

1. INTRODUCTION

The architecture of an FPGA logic block has a significant impact on the overall performance, area, and power consumption of circuits implemented on the device. Over the years, market demands and technological innovations have driven the evolution of FPGA logic blocks from simple groups of LUTs and flip-flops [2] to more complex blocks such as memories with configurable aspect ratios [21] [1], multipliers with selectable size and quantity [1], and general-purpose logic blocks with different modes of operation. As the economics of technology scaling continues to drive more applications towards programmable devices, we expect new ideas to arise in the architecture of FPGA logic blocks to meet the demands of a changing market.

As FPGA architects seek to explore increasingly sophisticated logic blocks, the difficulty of conducting experiments to evaluate their quality has correspondingly increased. One reason for this difficulty is that many CAD tools employed in these experiments have restrictive architectural assumptions that require significant changes before any evaluation work can be done. The release of VTR 1.0 [17], an open source FPGA architecture exploration CAD flow, was a recent effort by Rose et al. towards addressing this problem by greatly expanding the scope of FPGA architectures that can be targetted without software changes. However, this flexibility created new challenges in the packing stage of the FPGA CAD flow. Packing assigns a technology-mapped user netlist to the various physical logic blocks of a target FPGA architecture. To support a greater variety of logic blocks, pack time in VTR 1.0 increased to the point where it rivals placement time on the VTR heterogeneous architectures. For more complex architectures, pack time in VTR can regularly exceed place-and-route time [14]. Our work seeks to address this runtime issue while simultaneously expanding the scope of architectures that can be explored. We first describe precisely why the VTR packer is slow before describing our approach to this problem.

VTR provides the architect great freedom when specifying logic block architectures including the ability to specify any arbitrary interconnect structure within a logic block. Support for arbitrary interconnect enables the natural expression of a wide range of architectural constructs. These include carry chains, crossbars, optionally registered inputs/outputs, and control signals, which can be expressed by simply stating how various components are connected together. However, this level of customization creates a computationally challenging packing problem. The packing algorithm must determine if the internal connectivity within a logic block can successfully route the sections of the netlist that are assigned into that logic block. The packing algorithm in VTR [9], as with other prior attempts on supporting arbitrary interconnect [18] [20], employs heavy use of detailed routing to check for routability. This results in a packer that is often unnecessarily slow.

Our goal is to develop a packing tool and algorithm that runs quickly for architectures with simple interconnect, spends medium computational effort on architectures with moderately complex interconnect, and only uses heavy computational effort on architectures with very complex interconnect. Our approach is to automatically use a faster, simpler algorithm when interconnect structures that are easier to deal with are encountered. For example, if an architecture contains full crossbars, then computationally intensive routing checks within the logic block are not necessary because routing is guaranteed as long as the number of pins to be connected is below a certain threshold. Similarly, if an architecture has an inflexible carry chain, then we know that the blocks that form that chain must be kept together in a strict order.

In this work, we enhance the packing stage of VTR [17]. We enable the packer in VTR to adapt computational effort based on architect-specified interconnect through three techniques: First, *speculative packing* attempts to save runtime by optimistically skipping detailed legality checks at intermediate steps and then checking all legality rules after a logic block is full. Second, *pre-packing* groups together netlist blocks that should stay together as one unit during packing. This helps the packer deal with interconnect structures with limited or no flexibility, such as carry chains and registered input/output pins. Third, *interconnect-aware pin counting* reduces the more complex routing problem to a simple counting problem, which is inferred from the architecture.

2. PRIOR WORK

Much of the prior work in packing focused on simple logic blocks that consist only of LUTs and flip-flops interconnected by full crossbar interconnect [12] [19] [3] [8] [7] [4].

There have been several attempts to make packers that have more general types of interconnect within the logic block. Ni [15] proposed a tool that targets the same simple style logic block described above but with arbitrary logic elements instead of just pairs of LUTs and flip-flops. Wang [20] and Lemieux [6] proposed different ways to target logic blocks with depopulated crossbars. Cong proposed a tool, RASP, where a variety of different interconnect in a logic block is permitted but the user is then responsible for creating custom heuristics to map to that logic block [5]. Paladino [16] proposed a packer that focuses on modelling control signals and carry chains within a logic block. All these methods provide point solutions to specific constructs, but do not give a general, comprehensive strategy towards automatically handling arbitrary interconnect structures.

A few related works have attempted to model arbitrary interconnect in logic blocks. Sharma [18] proposed a placement algorithm that can explore FPGAs with arbitrary general interconnect. That work could be extended to target arbitrary interconnect within a logic block. Sharma's approach is to regularly sample the underlying interconnect during annealing-based placement by employing detailed routing repeatedly. However, this approach results in extremely long

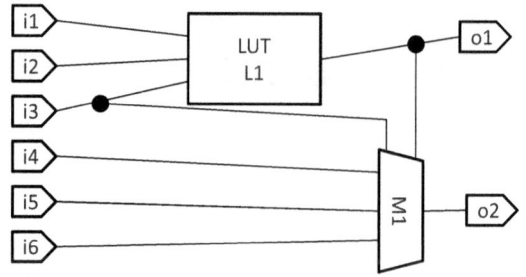

Figure 1: Example of a netlist with a LUT, a mux, and some I/O pads.

runtime. Similar to Sharma's work but in the context of FPGA packing, Luu [9] proposed a greedy packer, called AAPack, that employed detailed routing to check the legality of all intermediate (partial) packing solutions. Although Luu benefited from a much smaller routing problem, namely working at the logic block level, Luu's tool still ran two orders of magnitude slower than T-VPack [12] on the simple FPGA architectures. AAPack 6.0 is the current packer used in VTR 1.0.

3. PROBLEM DEFINITION

The inputs to packing are a technology-mapped logical netlist and a description of the physical logic blocks of a target architecture [9]. The output of packing is a netlist of physical logic blocks that implement the input user netlist. This netlist of logic blocks is then placed and routed in the subsequent stages of the FPGA CAD flow.

A technology-mapped netlist is a flattened view of a user circuit. It consists of blocks, called *atoms*, that are connected together by *nets*. Examples of atoms include LUTs, flip-flops, memory slices, and I/Os. Atoms are classified based on what kind of functionality they represent. We call this the atom's *logic model*. During packing, each atom will be mapped to a unique physical unit, called a *primitive*, within one of the logic blocks. Fig. 1 shows an example of a netlist. This netlist consists of one atom of logic model *LUT*, one atom of logic model *mux*, six atoms of logic model *input pad*, and two atoms of logic model *output pad*.

The target architecture defines the different types of logic blocks available. A logic block definition includes the primitives that exist in the block, a hierarchical description of how those primitives are organized, and the routing structures within the logic block. Each type of logic block can appear in the FPGA in different quantities. For example, there may be one configurable multiplier block for every four soft logic blocks.

The primitives within a logic block are organized in a hierarchy. At the top of the hierarchy is the logic block itself. Below the logic block, the architect can specify any arbitrary tree hierarchy of *subclusters* and primitives. A subcluster is a node in the logic block hierarchy that can contain other subclusters or primitives.

The interconnect within a logic block provides connectivity between subclusters, primitives, and logic block input/output pins. In this expanded definition of the packing problem, the architect is allowed to specify any arbitrary interconnect network within a logic block. This extension enables a far more powerful expression of different architec-

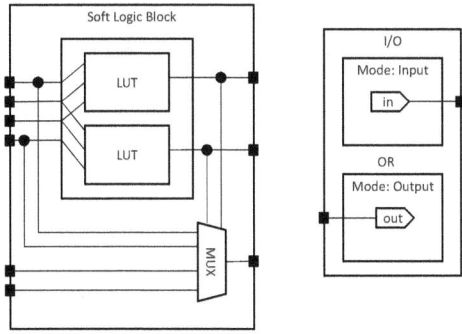

Figure 2: Example of an architecture with I/Os and soft logic blocks.

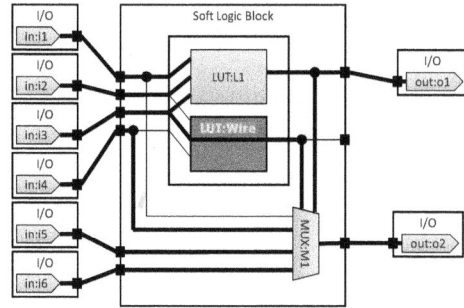

Figure 3: Example of a packing solution mapping a netlist to a set of logic blocks

tures but does create a potentially more difficult packing problem.

Structures in modern logic blocks can have different *modes*, which are mutually exclusive states of the logic; for example, a fracturable LUT can either be in its large, unfractured state, or be two smaller, "fractured" LUTs that share some inputs. We represent modes in the architecture definition in much the same way as how hierarchy is expressed. Each mode is represented as a subcluster where the subcluster can only be used if none of its siblings (in the logic block hierarchy) are used.

Fig. 2 shows an example of an architecture with soft logic blocks and I/O logic blocks. The soft logic block consists of a subcluster of two 3-input LUT primitives and a single 4-to-1 mux primitive. Unlike the routing muxes within the FPGA that implement nets, this mux primitive is used to implement actual logic in the user netlist. The data lines of the mux are driven by the input pins of the logic block. The two 3-LUTs drive the select lines of the mux primitive. The LUT primitives have special properties. They can operate as interconnect wires in addition to logic. The two 3-LUTs are driven by four logic block inputs so they share two input pins. Unlike LUT and mux primitives, input and output pads are implemented in their own dedicated logic blocks. An I/O logic block has two modes of operation. It can implement one input pad or one output pad.

3.1 Packing Problem

The packing problem is defined as the assignment of netlist atoms to primitives, while optimizing for multiple objectives, under the constraint that the final mapping is *legal*. Ultimately, we want the packer to produce a netlist that gives good area and delay results after placement and routing. To acheive this practically, we set the objectives of packing to minimize the number of logic blocks, minimize the number of connections that must route across multiple logic blocks, and group together connected atoms where those connections are timing critical. A legal solution is a packing solution that can be physically realized. We determine legality by checking for various conditions. The main conditions are as follows: 1) All atoms are assigned to unique primitives and each of those primitives can implement the atom assigned to it, 2) All nets within a logic block can be routed, and 3) Modes within a logic block are mutually exclusive.

3.2 Example of Packing

Fig. 3 gives an example packing of the input circuit shown in Fig. 1 into an FPGA with the logic block types shown in Fig. 2. The lightly shaded primitives, such as LUT:L1 and MUX:M1, name the atoms that they implement. The dark LUT shows a LUT that is used to implement a wire. The thick edges show the physical interconnect edges that implement nets. The I/O logic blocks are set to either inpad or outpad mode, depending on what I/O atom got assigned to them.

4. INTERCONNECT-AWARE PACKING

This section describes the modifications that we made to an existing packing tool (AAPack) [9] to enable the packer to adapt to the underlying interconnect of the target logic blocks. We begin with an overview of the original packing algorithm. We then describe the various modifications that we made.

The packing algorithm starts by selecting an empty logic block in the FPGA to be packed. The algorithm then fills the logic block by attempting to assign candidate atoms to unused primitives. Candidate atoms are chosen using an attraction function, where atoms with a higher score are considered before atoms with a lower score. Once the logic block is full, the algorithm "closes" that block and opens up a new, empty, logic block to be filled. Packing terminates when all atoms in the netlist have been mapped into logic blocks.

The attraction function is a weighted sum of two terms [17]. The first term scores the timing criticality of a candidate while the second term scores the connectivity of a candidate with the logic block that is currently being filled. The algorithm first only considers unpacked atoms that share one or more nets with the packed atoms inside the currently active logic block. This keeps the algorithm scalable and prevents unrelated logic from being packed together. If no such atoms remain, then the algorithm selects atoms from unrelated logic.

Up to this point, the algorithm description is about the same as many other greedy FPGA packers [12] [3] [4]. The part that distinguishes this packer, the part that enables architecture adaptiveness, is in the stage where the algorithm determines which primitive, if any, a candidate netlist atom should map to within a logic block. We call this stage intra-logic block placement and routing.

Intra-logic block placement finds a suitable primitive within the logic block to assign the candidate atom then assigns modes within the logic block based on that placement. This stage is also responsible for checking most of the legality constraints. These checks include whether or not the primitive can implement the atom, if modes assigned are legal, and if basic routability (in the form of pin counting) passes. If placement is successful, then the original packing algorithm [9] would invoke intra-logic block routing to attempt detailed routing, using the PathFinder algorithm [13], to ensure routability. If detailed routing fails, then the placement and routing process repeats itself until a successful primitive is found or until there are no more unused primitives to try.

Among all the legality checks, detailed routing consumes, by far, the most time. The main focus of our techniques is to avoid this computationally intensive check when the interconnect in the architecture is simple enough for us to skip it.

4.1 Speculative Packing

Speculative packing is a technique to avoid unnecessary invocations of detailed routing. This technique first attempts to optimistically pack a logic block by not invoking detailed routing until the logic block is filled. We call the optimistically filled logic block the *speculated solution*. If detailed routing of the speculated solution succeeds, then the solution is accepted. Otherwise, the packer rejects the speculated solution and reverts back to the conservative method of [9] that invokes detailed routing for every partial packing.

The runtime impact from speculative packing depends heavily on how often the final route of a speculated solution succeeds. In the best case, the final route always succeeds resulting in speedup. In the worst case, the final route never succeeds which results in wasted speculation time. Thus, if a logic block contains simple interconnect from which the packer can form routable speculated solutions, then speculative packing enables the packer to expend less computational effort routing. If a logic block contains more complex interconnect, then the computational effort expended by the packer depends on how often the packer assembles a routable speculated solution.

4.2 Interconnect-Aware Pin Counting

Pin counting is a technique that approximates the routability problem with a simpler counting problem. Pin counting checks if a particular assignment of atoms to a logic block/subcluster uses more pins than supplied by the logic block/subcluster. If pins are overused, then that assignment is proven unroutable. If pins are not overused, then in the pin counting approach, we optimistically assume that the assignment is routable. Pin counting is one of the many checks performed in intra-logic block placement. This implies that during speculative packing, when detailed routing is skipped, pin counting becomes the only check for routability. Therefore, more accurate pin counting reduces computational effort by increasing the chance that speculated solutions will route.

Interconnect-aware pin counting is our more precise version of pin counting. In addition to analyzing pins, this technique also analyzes the underlying physical interconnect with the intention of capturing clues about how those pins are related. We begin by describing what information this

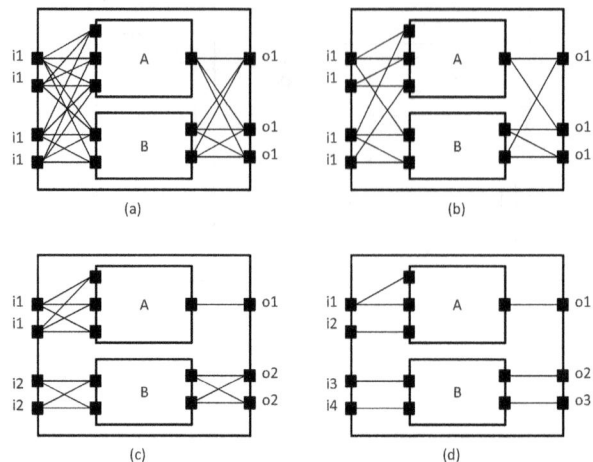

Figure 4: Examples on how pins are grouped into pin classes

technique extracts from the interconnect, and then we describe how packing uses that information.

Prior to the packing stage, we analyze the architecture of each logic block, and group the pins of each block and subcluster into separate *pin classes* based on the interconnect structures. Intuitively, pin classes are an attempt to approximate arbitrary interconnect with a set of non-overlapping full crossbars. Input pins of the same class drive the same crossbar, output pins of the same class are driven by the same crossbar. Pins are grouped into pin classes using the following process: First, all pins are set to have their own, individual, pin class. Then, pin classes are merged together based on connectivity while subject to constraints. Pin classes are constrained by subcluster/logic block and by type. Pins in the same pin class must be on the periphery of the same subcluster/logic block. Furthermore, pins of the same pin class must be either all input pins or all output pins. Subject to these constraints, if two pins of a subcluster/logic block belong to different pin classes but can connect (through the interconnect) to a common primitive pin within that subcluster/logic block, then those pin classes are merged together. When two pin classes merge, all pins contained in either of the original pin classes are grouped into one new pin class. In the event that the primitive has logically equivalent pins (for example, an AND gate has logically equivalent input pins), then those primitive pins are considered as one pin for the purposes of determining pin classes. At any point during the construction of pin classes, if a pin gets assigned to two different pin classes, then all pins in both pin classes are merged into a single pin class. The process ends when no more pin classes can be merged together.

Fig. 4 illustrates different examples of pin classes on a subcluster with two primitives, four input pins, and three output pins. The labels on the subcluster pins show which pin class each pin belongs to. Fig. 4 (a) has a large, well populated crossbar at the inputs and outputs. The subcluster input pins all belong to the same pin class *i1* and the subcluster output pins all belong to another pin class *o1*. Fig. 4 (b) has a sparser crossbar than (a). Our technique optimistically approximates these cases as the same, thus (b) has the

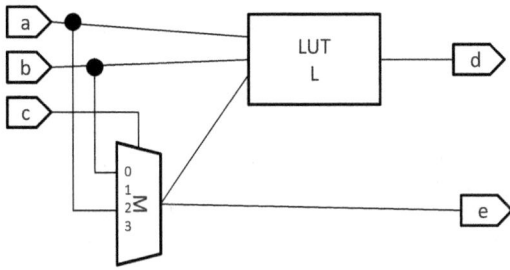

Figure 5: Example netlist to illustrate pin counting.

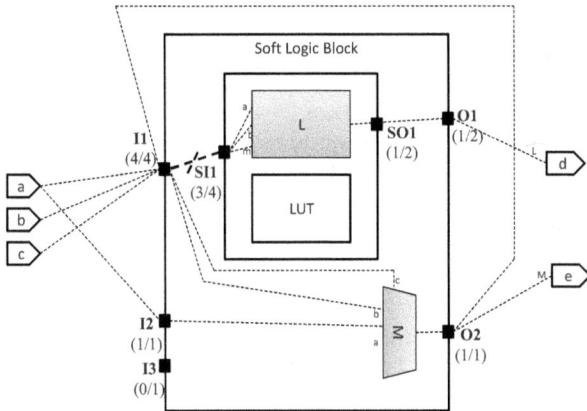

Figure 6: Example intermediate solution to illustrate pin counting.

same pin classes as (a). Fig. 4 (c) has disconnected smaller crossbars. This is reflected in the two pin classes for the inputs and two pin classes for the outputs. Finally, Fig. 4 (d) has no interconnect flexibility so all subcluster pins belong to separate pin classes.

During packing, every time a candidate atom is placed inside a logic block, pin counting updates the utilization of the pin classes of used subclusters within the logic block then updates the pin classes of the logic block itself. If, after the update, there exists a pin class that uses more pins than is supplied by that pin class, then pin counting declares the intermediate solution unroutable. Without loss of generality, we describe the update procedure for just the logic block. A net adds a count of one to a pin class of input pins if and only if the net drives a primitive input pin through that pin class and the driver of that net cannot reach the primitive input pin solely from within the logic block. A net adds a count of one to a pin class of output pins if and only if the primitive output pin of that net drives that pin class and there exists one primitive input pin driven by the net that cannot be reached solely from within the logic block.

To illustrate the nuances of pin counting, we revisit the logic block described in Fig. 2. We show the effect of packing the netlist in Fig. 5 to that logic block. This netlist consists of a LUT L and a logical mux M. Fig. 6 shows an intermediate packing solution that placed the LUT L in the top LUT position and the mux M in the mux location. We start by describing the pin classes in the logic block, then we describe the utilization of each pin class.

The logic block input pin classes are I1, I2, and I3. The logic block output pin classes are O1 and O2. The dual-LUT subcluster input pin class is SI1 and the subcluster output pin class is SO1. There is some subtlety in determining pin class I1. All four top input pins of the logic block belong to the same pin class. A LUT has logically equivalent inputs so the top three input pins are grouped together and the second, third, and fourth input pins are grouped together. Moreover, since the second and third input pins are common to both groups, all four pins are merged into the same pin class. The capacity of each pin class is determined by the number of pins it grouped. We label this value in the figure as the denominator of the fraction displayed beside each pin class. For pin class I1, the capacity is 4.

The utilization of each pin class is determined by the nets connected to the primitives within the logic block. This value is displayed as the numerator in the fraction beside each pin class in the figure. Observe the following subtlety: Net a requires two logic block input pins because of the lack of internal flexibility in the logic block. This behaviour is captured by the separation into pin classes I1 and I2. This is in contrast to net b which only needs to consume one pin because of internal fanout within the logic block. This connectivity is captured in pin class I1. Net M from the logical mux must traverse outside the logic block to reach the LUT input. This is represented as consuming one count of pin class O2 and one count of pin class I1. Net c illustrates how interconnect-aware pin counting is optimistic. Without the ability to detect that it is necessary to route through the dual-LUT subcluster to reach the mux select line, we see that our pin counting technique optimistically uses 3 of 4 pins in SI1, when in fact all 4 must be used in a detailed route. These examples illustrate which properties interconnect-aware pin can capture and which it cannot capture.

To summarize, we list the properties and limitations of interconnect-aware pin classes as follows:

- Acts as an optimistic filter. Cases that fail interconnect-aware pin counting will fail to route while cases that pass may or may not successfully route.

- Sparse interconnect is approximated as fully flexible.

- Does not account for situations where a net routes through a subcluster without connecting to any primitive within the subcluster.

- Internal feedback/feedfoward connections within a logic block/subcluster are discovered before packing and accounted for during pin counting.

- Only returns pass/fail. Does not give hints to guide future candidate selection.

4.3 Pre-Packing

Logic blocks sometimes contain inflexible routing structures. These structures can cause complications in a greedy packer because different stages of the packer become necessarily coupled. We illustrate this coupling using carry chains as an example. A carry chain is an important structure that enables the fast computation of wide logical adders by chaining together smaller physical adders using fast, inflexible carry links. In the packing stage of the VTR CAD flow, a logical adder is represented by multiple smaller adder

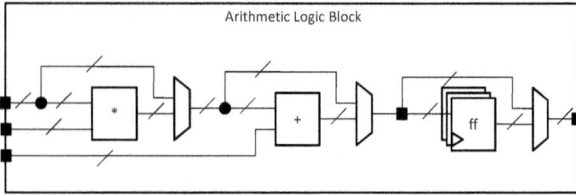

Figure 7: A bus-based arithmetic logic block

atoms that link together to form the logical adder. The packer must map the adder atoms to physical adder primitives in such a way that the physical chain can implement those logical links. An incorrect grouping or placement of the atoms during packing can result in failed (internal-to-the-block) routing because carry connections may become impossible to route. This example shows how inflexibility in interconnect can cause strong coupling among the candidate selection and placement stages in packing. This coupling is not unique to carry chains. We observe this coupling effect in multiple other logic block constructs including primitives with registered inputs/outputs, datapath arithmetic blocks with compound operations such as multply-add, and others.

We employ a pre-packing technique to capture coupling from restrictive interconnect in a generic and simple way. The architect is asked to identify (in the architecture file) groups of primitives joined together using inflexible interconnect. These groups and their links are called *pack patterns*. Before packing, groups of netlist atoms that match a pack pattern are grouped together into what is called a *molecule*. We call this stage the *pre-packing* stage. During packing, molecules are treated as though they are an atom and can only map to primitives that form the same pack pattern as the molecule.

Fig. 7 shows an example of the concept of pack patterns and molecules. This arithmetic logic block can perform both basic multiplication and addition, as well as combined operations such as multiply-add and registered arithmetic. If the architect intends for combined operations to be kept together during packing, then the architect should indicate that intent by specifying four pack patterns as follows: 1) Multiply-add, 2) Registered multiply, 3) Registered add, and 4) Registered multiply-add.

4.4 Other Modifications

Unlike the previous modifications which enable the packer to adapt to the detailed interconnect of a logic block, the enhancements described in this section are general improvements to the packer. We discuss three important improvements: First, more accurate timing analysis during packing that uses delay values from the architecture description file. Second, best-fit intra-logic block placement. Third, special case handling for high fanout nets.

Accurate Timing Analysis

The original AAPack tool computes timing criticality based on a delay graph that is a function of only the netlist. We modified the delay graph to also include architectural information. The delay model of an atom is taken from the delay model of the smallest physical primitive in the architecture that can implement that atom. In addition, we model interconnect delay between atoms with a single constant based on inter-logic block wire delays.

Best-Fit Placement

We modified the intra-logic block placement function to employ best-fit placement instead of first-fit placement. The intra-logic block placer in [9] employs a first-fit algorithm to determine where to place a candidate atom within a logic block. This can lead to quality of results being heavily dependant on how a logic block is described in the architecture file because the placer will not examine any other primitives after it encounters one unused primitive that can implement the candidate atom.

Our best-fit placement iterates through all valid primitives and returns the primitive with the least cost that can implement the candidate atom. The base cost of a primitive is equal to the number of pins of that primitive. This encourages the placer to select smaller primitives before bigger primitives. When a primitive is used, the cost of each unused primitive is reduced by 0.1^a where a is the depth of the used primitive to the closest ancestor of that unused primitive and the value 0.1 is an empirically derived parameter. This encourages the placer to consider primitives in used sections of the logic block hierarchy before unused sections.

High Fanout Nets Handling

The original AAPack tool, along with many prior academic packers, have scalability problems with circuits that contain high fanout nets. In the original AAPack, all atoms connected to a high fanout net are considered during packing. Since a high fanout net reaches many atoms, that pool of weakly connected atoms is considered several times over the course of packing. This ultimately results in a runtime cost that is quadratic with the number of terminals for a high fanout net.

We modified the attraction function to initially ignore high fanout nets when packing to a logic block. When these candidate atoms are exhausted, then the algorithm prioritizes selecting candidate atoms connected by high fanout nets that are connected to the currently active cluster before considering completely unrelated logic. A net is considered to be high fanout when it exceeds 64 terminals.

5. RESULTS

In this section, we measure the impact of the new algorithms introduced in the previous section on the quality of results and runtime of the packer. We also illustrate how the new, complete packer adapts to architectures with increasing levels of interconnect complexity. We label the prior version of AAPack, released in the VTR 1.0 suite, as AAPack 6.0, and this new version released in VTR 7.0 as AAPack 7.0.

5.1 Experimental Setup

We use the VTR 7.0 CAD flow [11] in these experiments as shown in Fig. 8. This flow takes as input a benchmark Verilog circuit and an FPGA architecture description file. The flow maps the circuit to the architecture described in that file then outputs statistics about that final mapping. We use Odin II for elaboration, ABC for logic synthesis, one of AAPack 6.0 or AAPack 7.0 for packing, and VPR 7.0 for placement and routing. VPR is left at default values [10] except the placement option inner_num is set to 10.0[1].

---

[1]This placement algorithm option aligns VPR 7 placement with prior versions of VPR.

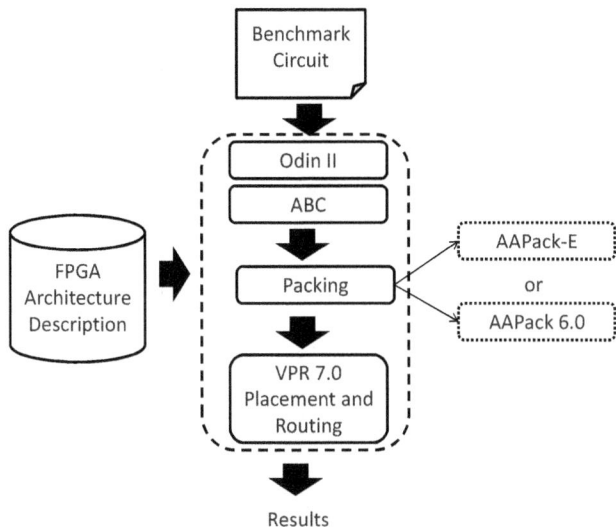

Figure 8: The experimental CAD flow

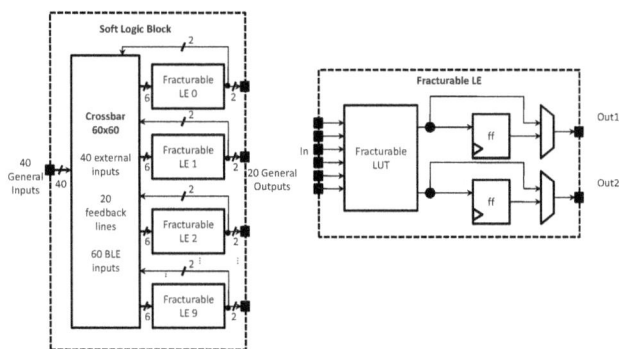

Figure 9: The baseline soft logic block architecture.

We use the VTR 7.0 benchmarks for our experiments. The VTR 7.0 benchmarks are a standard set of Verilog circuits that come from a variety of different applications including computer vision, medical, math, soft processors, etc. These circuits contain heterogeneous elements, such as memories and multipliers, which differentiate them from older FPGA benchmarks. These benchmarks range from a few hundred 6-LUTs in size to just over a hundred thousand 6-LUTs. Most contain memories and/or multipliers of varying quantities and sizes. For example, the circuit `stereovision2` contains 564 logical multipliers and the circuit `mcml` contains 30 logical multipliers and 10 memory blocks totalling 5 Mb. These benchmarks are very similar to the VTR 1.0 benchmarks [17], but have some minor Verilog changes.

The baseline FPGA architecture used in these experiments is a 40nm CMOS heterogeneous architecture released in VTR 7.0 called `k6_frac_N10_mem32K_40nm.xml`. Fig. 9 shows the soft logic blocks of this architecture which is loosely modelled from an Altera Stratix IV FPGA [1]. A soft logic block has 40 inputs, 20 outputs, and 10 fracturable 6-LUTs. A fully populated internal crossbar connects all logic block inputs to fracturable LUT inputs and provides feedback connections within the logic block. Each fracturable 6-LUTs can optionally operate as two five LUTs with some shared inputs. The 5-LUTs are set to share all 5 inputs. This shar-

Table 1: Results of VTR CAD flow using AAPack 7.0 across 19 benchmarks.

Circuit	Min W	Crit Delay (ns)	Pack Time (s)	Num Ex Nets	Num CLBs
bgm	114	25.71	198.2	21.1K	2930
blob_merge	72	10.47	17.45	3069	543
boundtop	58	6.51	6.56	2200	233
ch_intrinsics	48	3.89	0.77	430	37
diffeq1	50	21.50	0.72	717	36
diffeq2	52	17.04	0.52	468	27
LU8PEEng	108	111.81	84.89	16.3K	2104
LU32PEEng	168	115.39	429.25	54.2K	7128
mcml	94	81.73	681.78	52.4K	6615
mkDelayWorker32B	80	7.40	19.99	5224	447
mkPktMerge	48	4.57	0.64	972	15
mkSMAdapter4B	54	5.85	5.26	1597	165
or1200	72	13.29	8.3	2499	257
raygentop	70	5.04	7.54	1964	173
sha	50	13.77	10.58	1304	209
stereovision0	58	4.23	33.54	7936	905
stereovision1	102	5.65	38.63	11.1K	889
stereovision2	154	19.68	82.37	34.5K	2395
stereovision3	34	2.72	0.17	122	13

ing more closely resembles a Virtex 6 fracturable LUT [21] than a Stratix IV fracturable LUT. It was chosen because this reduces the size of the internal crossbar to more closely match the number of switch points in a Stratix IV depopulated internal crossbar. All LUTs have optionally registered outputs. This architecture contains fracturable multipliers, where each multiplier can operate as one large 36x36 multiplier or two fracturable 18x18 multipliers. A fracturable 18x18 multiplier can operate as one 18x18 multipier or two 9x9 multipliers. Finally, this architecture contains configurable memories. Each memory has 32Kb and can operate in aspect ratios ranging from 32Kx1 to 512x64. The area and delay values of this architecture are mostly chosen to match a Stratix IV FPGA [1].

The machine used in this experiment has two Intel Xeon 5160 processors running at 3 GHz. Each processor has two cores with 4 MB of L2 cache. Each machine has a total of 8 GB of shared memory. Although this machine is capable of parallelism, we chose to run our experiments single-threaded.

5.2 AAPack 7.0 vs AAPack 6.0

In this experiment, we compare AAPack 7.0 with the original AAPack 6.0 in the context of the full CAD flow. The architecture used is the baseline architecture previously described.

Table 1 shows the absolute values of running the VTR flow using AAPack 7.0. The leftmost column lists the circuit used. After that, from left to right, the columns are as follows: 1) The minimum channel width (min W) needed to route the circuit; 2) The critical path delay in nanoseconds when the circuit is routed at 1.3 times minimum W for the current flow (this follows historical precedant to route the circuit under reasonable stress); 3) The time needed to pack the circuit in seconds; 4) The number of external nets (nets that are routed between logic blocks); and 5) The number of soft logic blocks used in each benchmark. This table serves as the baseline values from which the later relative comparisons are made.

Table 2: Relative comparison of AAPack 7.0 over AAPack 6.0.

Circuit	Min W	Crit Delay	Pack Time	Num Ex Nets	Num CLBs
bgm	0.71	0.83	0.45	0.89	1.00
blob_merge	0.78	1.00	0.16	0.82	1.00
boundtop	0.78	0.85	0.03	0.86	0.95
ch_intrinsics	0.89	1.01	0.04	0.92	0.93
diffeq1	1.00	0.96	0.10	0.94	0.92
diffeq2	1.08	0.93	0.07	0.91	1.00
LU8PEEng	0.77	0.95	0.18	0.98	1.02
LU32PEEng	0.72	0.97	0.18	0.98	1.02
mcml	0.48	0.97	0.08	0.89	0.97
mkDelayWorker32B	0.80	0.92	0.07	0.91	1.01
mkPktMerge	1.00	1.06	0.14	0.99	1.00
mkSMAdapter4B	0.77	0.89	0.02	0.91	0.97
or1200	0.86	0.98	0.06	0.87	0.97
raygentop	0.92	1.00	0.11	0.90	1.01
sha	0.74	1.00	0.04	0.71	0.99
stereovision0	0.66	0.78	0.06	0.92	1.09
stereovision1	0.82	0.92	0.06	0.92	1.09
stereovision2	0.71	0.92	0.08	0.94	1.06
stereovision3	1.00	0.90	0.05	0.89	1.00
geomean	0.80	0.94	0.08	0.90	1.00
stdev	0.17	0.07	0.12	0.05	0.04

Table 3: Relative place-and-route runtime comparison of circuits packed by AAPack 7.0 over circuits packed by AAPack 6.0.

Circuit	Place Time	Fixed Route Time
bgm	0.90	0.68
blob_merge	0.89	0.74
boundtop	0.88	0.65
ch_intrinsics	0.87	0.83
diffeq1	0.93	0.91
diffeq2	0.92	0.92
LU8PEEng	0.89	0.78
LU32PEEng	0.96	0.93
mcml	0.96	0.59
mkDelayWorker32B	0.89	0.87
mkPktMerge	1.01	0.95
mkSMAdapter4B	0.90	0.72
or1200	0.90	0.78
raygentop	0.94	0.85
sha	0.77	0.80
stereovision0	0.92	0.82
stereovision1	0.95	1.04
stereovision2	1.01	0.76
stereovision3	1.09	1.25
geomean	0.92	0.82
stdev	0.04	0.13

Table 2 measures how well AAPack 7.0 performs relative to AAPack 6.0. Each value is presented as a ratio of AAPack 7.0 over AAPack 6.0. The columns are the same as columns 1-5 of Table 1. For packer runtime, AAPack 7.0 is 12-fold faster than AAPack 6.0. This illustrates the effectiveness of our techniques. The interconnect of this architecture is simple enough that the combination of interconnect-aware pin counting and LUT/FF molecules is sufficient for speculated solutions to always route. This enables AAPack 7.0 to successfully skip many of the intermediate detailed routing checks that AAPack 6.0 invokes resulting in a speed up. Profiling the packer revealed that detailed routing checks dropped from over 90% of pack time in AAPack 6.0 to approximately 10% in AAPack 7.0 which further confirms this causative link. In terms of quality of results, AAPack 7.0 absorbs nets better resulting in a 10% reduction in the number of external nets which leads to the 20% reduction in minimum channel width. Critical path delay is reduced by 6%. These quality of results improvements show that pre-packing, best-cost placement, and more accurate timing analysis are effective techniques towards reducing inter-logic block routing stress and enabling better delay optimizations. We conclude that AAPack 7.0 produces packed circuits that are better than AAPack 6.0 and can do so at much lower runtime.

Table 3 measures the effect of packing quality on placement and routing runtime. The leftmost column lists the circuit used. The middle column lists the relative time needed to place the circuit. The rightmost column lists the relative time needed to route the circuit at a fixed route of 1.3 times minimum W. Each value is presented as a ratio of AAPack 7.0 over AAPack 6.0. The results show that placement time is reduced by 8% and fixed route time by 18% on average. The speedup from using AAPack 7.0 in placement and fixed channel width routing is a result of the reduction in the number of external nets. Fewer external nets reduces the time needed for the placer to update costs and reduces the load on the router. We conclude that the higher quality

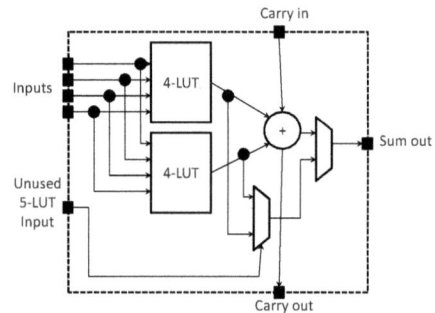

Figure 10: Interaction between 5-LUT and carry chain adder

packing from AAPack 7.0 reduces the runtime of placement and routing.

5.3 Architecture Adaptiveness

In this experiment, we measure how well AAPack 7.0 adapts to architectures with varying levels of interconnect complexity. We make two main comparisons. The first compares how AAPack 7.0 performs on different architectures with respect to a baseline architecture. The second compares how AAPack 7.0 performs on these same architectures against AAPack 6.0.

We run the VTR benchmarks using the same VTR flow as earlier on five different architectures with varying types of interconnect. All these architectures are variations of the k6_frac_N10_mem32K_40nm.xml baseline. The first architecture has simpler soft logic blocks by replacing the fracturable 6-LUTs with non-fracturable 6-LUTs. The second architecture adds carry chains to the baseline. Fig. 10 shows how the adder is integrated with the fracturable LUT. When the fracturable 6-LUT is operating in dual 5-LUT mode, each 5-LUT further fractures into two 4-LUTs that drive one hardened adder bit. Dedicated carry links join all 20 hard adders together and also establishes connections to the

Table 4: Comparison of how AAPack 7.0 performs on different architectures vs the baseline architecture.

Architecture	Pack Time	Num Ext Nets	Num CLBs
Non-fracturable	0.41	1.02	1.33
Carry Chain	1.50	1.20	1.14
Xbar 0.5	1.73	1.02	1.01
Xbar 0.25	1.46	1.09	1.01
Xbar 0.1	14.21	1.09	1.07

Table 5: Comparison of AAPack 7.0 vs AAPack 6.0 across different architectures.

Architecture	Pack Time	Num Ext Nets	Num CLBs
Non-fracturable	0.15	0.97	1.00
Xbar 0.5	0.15	0.90	1.00
Xbar 0.25	0.13	0.88	1.00
Xbar 0.1	0.41	0.87	0.79

soft logic block carry input and carry output pins. The next three architectures replace the complete internal crossbar of the baseline with a depopulated crossbar. A depopulated crossbar is a crossbar where some of the switch points are removed thus reducing area at the cost of less connectivity. A crossbar that uses 25% of all possible switch points is 25% populated. The third, fourth, and fifth architectures have crossbars populated at 50%, 25%, and 10% respectively.

Table 4 shows the results of AAPack 7.0 on different architectures normalized to the results from the baseline architecture. The leftmost column lists the architecture being investigated. Moving rightwards, the next columns are pack time, number of external nets, and number of soft logic blocks. The values shown are the geometric mean across all 19 benchmarks normalized to the baseline. These results show the general trend that AAPack 7.0 runtime is faster for architectures with simpler interconnect and slower for architectures with more complex interconnect. AAPack 7.0 runs more than twice as fast for a simple, non-fracturable LUT architecture. AAPack 7.0 runs slower for architectures with a carry chain or a depopulated internal crossbar. At the extreme, a very sparse 10% populated crossbar runs 14-fold slower than the same architecture with a full crossbar because interconnect-aware pin counting no longer accurately captures the complexities of sparsity. This experiment also demonstrates other findings. First, it shows a proof-of-concept that pre-packing enables the packer to target carry chain architectures. Second, this experiment shows that quality of results for architectures with depopulated internal crossbars can remain fairly high. For example, at 50% population, the packer produces 1% more soft logic blocks and 2% more external nets on average.

The next experiment examines how AAPack 7.0 performs compared to AAPack 6.0 for the same set of architectures. We exclude the carry chain architecture in this comparison because AAPack 6.0 is not capable of packing to architectures with carry chains. Table 5 shows the results of this experiment. The columns are the same as for Table 4. The values shown are the geometric mean across all 19 benchmarks of the AAPack 7.0 runs normalized to the AAPack 6.0 runs. For classic, non-fracturable LUT, architectures, pack time is 6.7-fold faster with 3% fewer external nets. AAPack 7.0 is 6-fold faster for soft logic blocks that contain crossbars at 50% and 25% population. We notice a large 10% to 12% reduction in external nets which indicates that AAPack 7.0 packs to soft logic blocks with depopulated crossbars better than AAPack 6.0. Lastly, we notice that for the very low 10%-populated crossbar, AAPack 6.0 no longer packs efficiently requiring 27% more CLBs than AAPack 7.0. However, AAPack 7.0 only runs 2.4-fold faster than AAPack 6.0 for this architecture because the sparsity of the crossbar causes AAPack 7.0 to invoke detailed rout-

ing for many of the partially packed solutions. These results show that AAPack 7.0 performs better than AAPack 6.0 across all architectures and AAPack 7.0 better adapts to architectures with complex interconnect than AAPack 6.0.

6. CONCLUSIONS AND FUTURE WORK

We have presented key enhancements in AAPack 7.0 that enables the tool to adapt to the underlying interconnect of an FPGA architecture. These enhancements speed up a state-of-the-art flexible packer by 12-fold, while simultaneously lowering minimum channel width by 20% and lowering critical path delay by 6% on a modern style FPGA. We demonstrate that these enhancements provide more robust packing across a diverse range of architectures, including architectures with carry chains and architectures with depopulated crossbars. This work is a key step towards a flexible packing tool that can adapt its computational effort based on the difficulty of the underlying interconnect architecture.

In the future, we intend to use AAPack 7.0 to investigate new logic block architectures. We identify the interplay between fracturable LUTs, carry chain architecture, and depopulated crossbars as an interesting direction to explore.

7. REFERENCES

[1] Altera Corporation. Stratix IV Device Family Overview. http://www.altera.com/literature/hb/stratix-iv/stx4_siv51001.pdf, November 2009.

[2] V. Betz, J. Rose, and A. Marquardt. *Architecture and CAD for Deep-Submicron FPGAs*. Kluwer Academic Publishers, Norwell, Massachusetts, 1999.

[3] E. Bozorgzadeh, S. Memik, and M. Sarrafzadeh. RPack: Routability-driven Packing for Cluster-Based FPGAs. In *ASP-DAC '01: Proceedings of the 2001 Asia and South Pacific Design Automation Conf.*, pages 629–634, New York, NY, USA, 2001. ACM.

[4] D. Chen, K. Vorwerk, and A. Kennings. Improving Timing-Driven FPGA Packing with Physical Information. *Int'l Conf. on Field Programmable Logic and Applications*, pages 117–123, 2007.

[5] J. Cong, J. Peck, and Y. Ding. RASP: A general logic synthesis system for SRAM-based FPGAs. In *Proceedings of the 1996 ACM fourth international symposium on Field-programmable gate arrays*, pages 137–143. ACM, 1996.

[6] G. Lemieux and D. Lewis. *Design of Interconnection Networks for Programmable Logic*. Kluwer Academic Publishers, Norwell, Massachusetts, 2004.

[7] J. Lin, D. Chen, and J. Cong. Optimal Simultaneous Mapping and Clustering for FPGA Delay Optimization. In *ACM/IEEE Design Automation Conf.*, pages 472–477, 2006.

[8] A. Ling, J. Zhu, and S. Brown. Scalable Synthesis and Clustering Techniques Using Decision Diagrams. *IEEE Trans. on CAD*, 27(3):423, 2008.

[9] J. Luu, J. Anderson, and J. Rose. Architecture Description and Packing for Logic Blocks with Hierarchy, Modes and Complex Interconnect. In *Proceedings of the 19th ACM/SIGDA international symposium on Field programmable gate arrays*, FPGA '11, pages 227–236, New York, NY, USA, 2011. ACM.

[10] J. Luu, J. Goeders, T. Liu, A. Marquardt, I. Kuon, J. Anderson, J. Rose, and V. Betz. VPR User's Manual (Version 7.0). http://code.google.com/p/vtr-verilog-to-routing/downloads/list, 2013.

[11] J. Luu, J. Goeders, M. Wainberg, A. Somerville, T. Yu, K. Nasartschuk, M. Nasr, S. Wang, T. Liu, N. Ahmed, K. B. Kent, J. Anderson, J. Rose, and V. Betz. Verilog-to-Routing 7.0. https://code.google.com/p/vtr-verilog-to-routing/, 2013.

[12] A. Marquardt, V. Betz, and J. Rose. Using Cluster-Based Logic Blocks and Timing-Driven Packing to Improve FPGA Speed and Density. *ACM Int'l Symp. on FPGAs*, pages 37–46, 1999.

[13] L. McMurchie and C. Ebeling. PathFinder: A Negotiation-Based Performance-Driven Router for FPGAs. In *ACM Int'l Symp. on FPGAs*, pages 111–117, 1995.

[14] K. E. Murray, S. Whitty, S. Liu, J. Luu, and V. Betz. Titan: Eabling Large and Complex Benchmarks in Academic CAD. 2013.

[15] G. Ni, J. Tong, and J. Lai. A New FPGA Packing Algorithm Based on the Modeling Method for Logic Block. In *IEEE Int'l Conf. on ASICs*, volume 2, pages 877–880, Oct. 2005.

[16] D. Paladino. Academic Clustering and Placement Tools for Modern Field-Programmable Gate Array Architectures. Master's thesis, University of Toronto, Toronto, Ontario, Canada, 2008.

[17] J. Rose, J. Luu, C. W. Yu, O. Densmore, J. Goeders, A. Somerville, K. B. Kent, P. Jamieson, and J. Anderson. The VTR Project: Architecture and CAD for FPGAs from Verilog to Routing. In *ACM Int'l Symp. on FPGAs*, pages 77–86, 2012.

[18] A. Sharma, S. Hauck, and C. Ebeling. Architecture-adaptive routability-driven placement for FPGAs. In *Field Programmable Logic and Applications, 2005. International Conference on*, pages 427–432. IEEE, 2005.

[19] A. Singh, G. Parthasarathy, and M. Marek-Sadowksa. Efficient Circult Clustering for Area and Power Reduction in FPGAs. *ACM Trans. on Design Automation of Electronic Systems*, 7(4):643–663, Nov 2002.

[20] K. Wang, M. Yang, L. Wang, X. Zhou, and J. Tong. A Novel Packing Algorithm for Sparse Crossbar FPGA Architectures. In *Int'l Conf. on Solid-State and Integrated-Circuit Technology*, pages 2345–2348, 2008.

[21] Xilinx Inc. Xilinx Virtex-6 Family Overview. http://www.xilinx.com/support/documentation/data_sheets/ds150.pdf, 2009.

Rent's Rule Based FPGA Packing for Routability Optimization

Wenyi Feng, Jonathan Greene, Kristofer Vorwerk, Val Pevzner, Arun Kundu
Microsemi Corporation, 3870 N 1st Street, San Jose, CA 95134
{wenyi.feng, jonathan.greene, kris.vorwerk, val.pevzner, arun.kundu}@microsemi.com

ABSTRACT
Packing is a critical step in the CAD flow for cluster-based FPGA architectures, and has a significant impact on the quality of the final placement and routing results. One basic quality metric is routability. Traditionally, minimizing cut (the number of external signals) has been used as the main criterion in packing for routability optimization. This paper shows that minimizing cut is a sub-optimal criterion, and argues to use the Rent characteristic as the new criterion for FPGA packing. We further propose using a recursive bipartitioning-based k-way partitioner to optimize the Rent characteristic during packing. We developed a new packer, PPack2, based on this approach. Compared to T-VPack, PPack2 achieves 35.4%, 35.6%, and 11.2% reduction in wire length, minimal channel width, and critical path delay, respectively. These improvements show that PPack2 outperforms all previous leading packing tools (including iRAC, HDPack, and the original PPack) by a wide margin.

Categories and Subject Descriptors

B.7.2 [**Integrated Circuits**]: Design Aids – Placements and Routing.

Keywords

Rent's rule; FPGA packing; clustering; routability optimization; recursive bipartitioning; k-way partitioning

1. INTRODUCTION

Modern FPGA architectures [1][2][3][4] use cluster-based logic blocks. Cluster-based architectures are preferred over a flat architecture due to their potential to achieve significant area and speed improvement. The FPGA CAD flow for such architectures typically employs a packing step before placement. This step groups logic resources into clusters and significantly reduces the problem size for the time-consuming placement and routing step. As such, it has a huge impact on the quality of final results. One basic metric (out of many quality metrics) is routability.

Routability optimization has been considered a difficult problem at the packing stage since there were no accurate means available to estimate routability at this stage. It is closely related to placement wire length minimization. Previous FPGA packing algorithms used cut minimization as the main criterion. Such a criterion aims to minimize the number of inter-cluster signals

during packing, and has been shown to correlate to the final placement wire length (hence, routability) to a degree. This paper contradicts this commonly used criterion. Our contributions include:

- We show that cut minimization is a sub-optimal criterion, and propose using the Rent characteristic as the new goal for routability optimization in packing. The Rent characteristic of the packing solution (i.e., cluster-level netlist) is directly correlated to the placement wire length and serves as a better criterion for routability optimization.

- We propose to use recursive bipartitioning-based k-way partitioning to optimize the Rent characteristic.

- We experimentally verify that our approach achieves superior quality compared to leading methods.

2. PREVIOUS WORK
2.1 Architecture Model

Our architecture model is similar to what is used in VPR[5]. A configurable logic block (CLB) has N basic logic elements (BLEs), with each BLE being a K-input LUT and a FF. However, unlike VPR, we assume no bandwidth constraint for the input interconnect block (IIB) [12]. We use such a model for both its practicality and its friendliness for partitioning-based packing approaches, as discussed in [11]. Recent work [12][13] showed that the IIB can be made area-efficient without any input constraint. Furthermore, most IIBs used in major commercial architectures [1][3][4] do not have input bandwidth constraints (with the only exception being [2]). However, our approach is not limited to such an architecture and can be modified to work with architectures with input constraints.

2.2 Previous FPGA Packing Approaches

A packing tool takes a netlist of LUTs and FFs and groups them into clusters. During clustering, the packing tool needs to obey a set of constraints while at the same time optimizing certain objectives. The common constraints are input bandwidth and FF related control constraints. In this paper we ignore the FF constraints for ease of discussion.

The majority of the previous packing approaches are seed-based [5][6][8][17] with T-VPack[5] being the default packer in VPR. These approaches are fast but likely to become stuck in local minima. The leading approaches for routability optimization are iRAC[17] and HDPack[8].

Another class of packing approaches is based on k-way partitioning [16][11]. Such an approach first calls a k-way partitioner to partition the netlist into an initial set of clusters, then uses a legalization step to fix the clusters. Both of them use hMetis to do direct k-way partitioning. In [16], the legalization process needs to fix oversized clusters as well as input constraints. In PPack[11], the approach is applied to architectures without input constraints and made timing driven.

For routability optimization, all previous approaches use cut minimization as the primary goal. In [5], T-VPack's improved routability over VPack is attributed to its capability to reduce cut size. In both iRAC[17] and PPack[11], the reduction in cut size is shown to be superior to T-VPack and used as an explanation for their superior improvement in routability.

2.3 Rent's Rule

Rent's rule [15] is an empirical relationship between the size of a group of logic cells and the number of its external connections:

$$T = T_0 N^p \qquad (1)$$

T is the average number of terminals required by a group containing an average of N cells, T_0 is the average number of terminals per cell, and p is a constant between 0 and 1 called the *Rent exponent*. Typical values of p range from 0.4 to 0.8. In general, netlists with a higher Rent exponent (assuming the same T_0) will be more difficult to place and route [10], resulting in longer average placement wire length and more wiring requirement.

For real designs, the relationship between T and N usually cannot be ideally modelled by equation (1) using only two parameters. We use the following general representation [9] instead:

$$T = f(N) \qquad (2)$$

and call the curve corresponding to the above function the Rent characteristic curve, or just the *Rent characteristic*. For two curves $T1$ and $T2$, if $T1 \geq T2$ for all values of N, then $T1$ will have higher interconnect complexity, just as a higher Rent exponent would indicate in the simple case.

Extracting the Rent characteristic curve and/or Rent's rule of a netlist is commonly done using recursive bipartitioning [15][18].

Input: A netlist of N basic cells
Output: Rent characteristic and/or Rent's rule

1. Recursively bipartition the netlist. At each recursive level i, calculate the average number of cells N_i per partition and the average number of external nets T_i over all partitions. Partitioning stops when each partition is just one basic cell. The curve of (T_i, N_i) is the Rent characteristic of the netlist.
2. Do a linear regression of the curve (T_i, N_i) using log-log scale. The slope of the curve is Rent exponent p and the intercept at $\log(N_i)=0$ is $\log(T_0)$.

Fig. 1. Extracting Rent characteristic and/or Rent's rule

One implementation detail in the extraction is the treatment of multi-terminal nets during recursive bipartitioning. If a multi-terminal net S is cut in a bipartitioning step, then we need to reconstruct the partial net of S in each partition (if S still has more than one terminal in the partition) instead of ignoring it. This allows subsequent partitionings to take this net into proper consideration, which helps in minimizing the Rent exponent.

The extraction approach above depends heavily on the bipartitioning technique. In practice, the latest high quality partitioning tools like hMetis[14] and MLpart[7] have been used.

The extraction routine generates a partitioning tree (Fig.2). This tree reveals a natural circuit structure and hierarchy of the original netlist found through recursive bipartitioning in the form of a binary tree of disjoint sub-circuits.

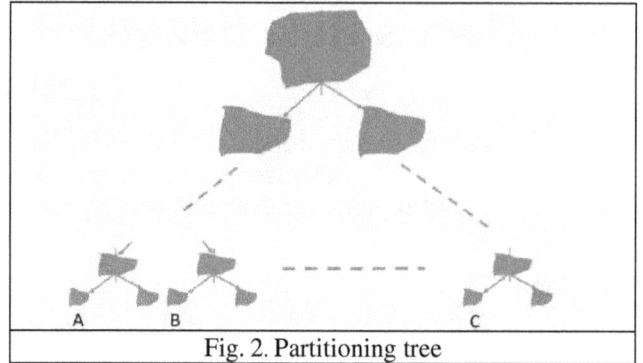

Fig. 2. Partitioning tree

3. OUR APPROACH

3.1 The Principle

An FPGA packer takes in a netlist of BLEs and generates a set of clusters, each cluster being a group of BLEs. As a result, the original BLE-level netlist becomes a cluster-level netlist. How can we optimize the Rent characteristic of the cluster-level netlist in packing? What is the relationship between the BLE-level netlist and cluster-level netlist with regard to the Rent characteristic? The following example illustrates the principle.

Suppose we need to pack a netlist of 2^n BLEs into a set of clusters, and cluster size is 8. We apply recursive bipartitioning on the BLE level netlist to build the partitioning tree as we would in the extraction of its Rent characteristic. We assume that the bipartitioner is ideal in achieving a perfect balance between two sub-partitions in every step. The partitioning tree at the bottom level is level 0 with each partition being a BLE. The tree at level 3 would have 2^{n-3} partitions and we use them as the packing solution of 2^{n-3} clusters. The cluster-level netlist would then have the exact same Rent characteristic as the original BLE-level netlist from the top level down to level 3.

So the principle is: *use recursive bipartitioning to do packing; and the packing solution achieves an optimal Rent characteristic by retaining the natural hierarchy of the BLE-level netlist.* Neither seed-based approaches nor direct k-way partitioning-based approaches have any view of a natural hierarchy during packing, hence they cannot optimize the Rent characteristic as effectively as our approach.

The ideal case discussed above is not practical: we assume both netlist and cluster size being a power of two, and an ideal bipartitioner. Next we discuss the practical implementation based on the above principle.

3.2 Recursive Bipartitioning-Based Packing: PPack2

PPack2 has the same basic steps as the original PPack[11], but with two main differences:

- Using a bipartitioning-based k-way partitioner instead of a direct k-way partitioner.
- Considering the hierarchy when rebalancing.

A recursive bipartitioning-based k-way partitioner works as follows. For a graph targeting k partitions, the graph is first bipartitioned into two equal or close-to-equal parts. If k is even, then the graph is partitioned equally, with each subgraph targeting $k/2$ partitions; otherwise, the graph is partitioned with the first part targeting $(k-1)/2$ partitions and the second part $(k+1)/2$ partitions (note: this requires the bipartitioner to be capable of generating uneven partitions). Then each sub-graph is partitioned recursively until k partitions are produced. The recursive bisection-based k-way partitioner in the hMetis package partitions like this.

The partitioning tree would be the same (down to the level when the number of partitions is k) as that for extracting Rent characteristic on the BLE-level netlist when k is a power of two. For other cases, there will be some small differences. As a result, the Rent characteristic of the cluster-level netlist will be slightly different from that of the BLE-level netlist.

The rebalancing step is needed if there are any partitions exceeding the capacity N. Surplus BLEs are moved from oversized partitions to undersized partitions. To minimize the disturbance to the hierarchy, we evaluate each BLE move considering both the cut/SOED (sum of external degrees) change and the impact on the hierarchy (measured by the distance in the tree between the source and the target partition). A larger distance means a greater disturbance to the hierarchy and is less favored. For example, in Fig. 2, if we need to move a surplus BLE out of partition A, and partition B and C are two possible target partitions with spare capacity, then moving to B is favored over moving to C (assuming the cut/SOED change is the same between the two moves).

4. EXPERIMENTAL RESULTS

For comparison, we used VPR4.3 and MCNC-20 benchmark designs. We established a baseline by first running T-VPack + VPR. Then we ran PPack2 + VPR. We also reproduced PPack results[11].

The baseline CLB has $K=4$, $N=8$, and $I=32$, i.e., 8 LUT4s without an input bandwidth constraint. Length-1 segments are used in the routing. For placement, the grid size is set to the smallest square grid for each design. Low-stress routing is set to be 20% over the minimal channel width reported by the baseline T-VPack flow. Wire-lengths and critical path delays are from VPR's report after low-stress routing. All reported numbers are geometric average of 20 designs. The machine used to run the experiments is a 3.2GHz 64-bit Linux machine.

4.1 Clustering Results

Table 1 compares the usual clustering statistics from three different packing tools, T-VPack, PPack and PPack2. The columns are: the total number of external nets (i.e., the cut size), the average number of external inputs and outputs per cluster, and the Rent exponent of the cluster-level netlist. (The number of clusters produced is the same for all three tools, all being the minimal possible, and not listed.)

Table 1. Summary of Clustering Results ($N=8$, $I=32$)

Packer	Ext Nets	AveIn	AveOut	Rent Exp
T-VPack	1381.4	13.7	4.3	0.63
Ratio	100%	100%	100%	100%
PPack	974.6	14.3	3.0	0.52
Ratio	71%	104%	70%	84%
PPack2	1348.3	11.7	4.2	0.48
Ratio	98%	85%	98%	77%

In terms of external nets, PPack solutions are the best (71%), significantly smaller than the other two. In terms of average

number of terminals per cluster (i.e., T_0 in Rent's rule), which is the sum of average inputs and outputs per cluster, PPack2 is the smallest at 15.9, followed by PPack at 17.3, then T-VPack at 18.0. In terms of Rent exponent, PPack2 is the smallest at 0.48 and T-VPack is the biggest at 0.63.

Rent's rule has two parameters, T_0 and p. The comparisons show that PPack2 has the smallest values in both, indicating the lowest interconnect complexity for the cluster-level netlists, followed by PPack, then T-VPack. The results also show that optimizing the Rent characteristic and Rent's rule is not the same as minimizing cut (PPack2 achieves the best Rent characteristic while PPack achieves the smallest cut) .

Fig.3 shows Rent characteristic curves for design clma for both the BLE-level netlist and three cluster-level netlists. It is a log-log chart with the X axis being the size of partition in terms of BLEs and the Y axis being the average number of external connections for all partitions at a size. The curve of the BLE-level netlist starts from $x=0$ (corresponding to 1 BLE). The curves for the three cluster-level netlists start from $x=3$ (corresponding to $N=8$). We can see that the curve of PPack2 closely matches that of the BLE-level netlist, as expected with our approach, and is the best of three packers. The curve of PPack is in turn better than that of T-VPack. For most other designs, their curves are similar to the curves of this design.

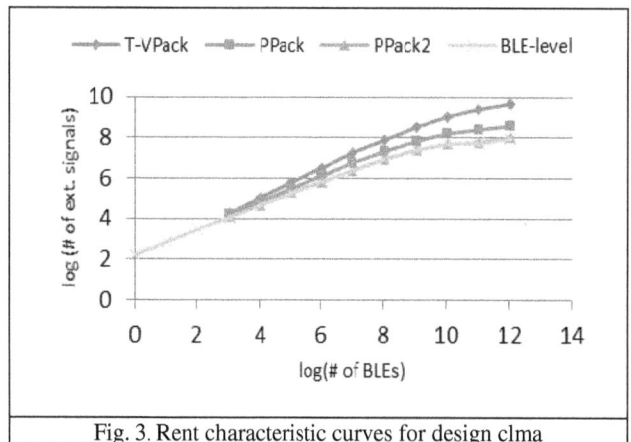

Fig. 3. Rent characteristic curves for design clma

4.2 Placement and Routing Results

Table 2 summarizes the results for all previous leading packers and PPack2.

Table 2. Summary of VPR Results ($N=8$, length-1 routing)

Packer	Clusters	Wire Length	Minimal Channel Width	Critical Path Delay
T-VPack(I=18)	100.0%	100.0%	100.0%	100.0%
iRAC	107.8%	78.0%	74.1%	N/A
HDpack	101.4%	76.8%	75.5%	93.9%
[16]	100.0%	N/A	81.3%	97.4%
T-VPack(I=32)	100.0%	100.0%	100.0%	100.0%
PPack	100.0%	77.4%	77.4%	98.1%
PPack2	100.0%	64.6%	64.4%	88.8%

The first part of the table presents results for the architecture with input bandwidth constraint (I=18), normalized to T-VPack(I=18) (more on how these numbers are obtained can be found in [11]). The second part of the table shows results for the architecture with no such constraint, normalized to T-VPack(I=32). PPack2 is the best in terms of improvement in both routability and delay, and outperforms all previous packers by a wide margin. Combining these results and the clustering results in Table 1, we clearly show that it is the Rent's rule and characteristic, not the cut size, of a clustering solution that determines the quality of placement and routing.

4.3 Runtime

Table 3 compares the runtime for all three packers. PPack2 runtime is similar to PPack and about 10x T-VPack runtime. However, both placer and router run faster in PPack2. We believe that the placer runtime saving is from the smaller number of nets incident on each cluster (i.e., value T_0), which results in lower computation needed to evaluate a move during annealing; while the router runtime saving is from the lower wire length. The absolute runtime increase (although at 10x relative) in the packer is in fact small since the total runtime is dominated by the placer and router. As a result, the PPack2 flow achieves a net saving of 14% in total runtime.

Table 3. Summary of Runtime (seconds)

Packer	Packer	Placer	Router	Total
T-VPack	0.13	15.45	2.89	18.74
Ratio	100%	100%	100%	100%
PPack	1.38	14.04	2.21	17.88
Ratio	1021%	91%	77%	95%
PPack2	1.44	12.70	1.91	16.19
Ratio	1065%	82%	66%	86%

5. DISCUSSIONS

Rent's rule and recursive bipartitioning were also used in previous packers, but in different ways from this paper. In iRAC[17], local Rent's rule of a cluster is compared to Rent's rule of the CLB, and used to guide depopulation of clusters. In HDPack[8], recursive bipartitioning is used to obtain a rough placement of the primitive netlist; the placement info is then incorporated in the cost function during packing. This paper is the first to relate recursive bipartitioning to the optimization of the Rent characteristic of the cluster-level netlist.

Though we used architectures without input bandwidth constraints in the experiments, the same principle can also be applied to architectures with such constraints. One simple approach is to fix any illegal cluster (i.e., exceeding input limit) by splitting after packing without considering the limit. Such a fix has a minimal impact on the hierarchy and the benefit of the approach is expected to be retained. However, it will increase the cluster count somewhat. For example, if we limit the input bandwidth of the baseline CLB (N=8, K=4) to be 18 ($2N$+2), 6 out of 20 designs will not require any increase since the maximum input does not exceed 18, and the rest of the designs will require some increase in the cluster count (up to 15%). This indicates that I=18 is too tight for some natural clusters for the CLB. Naturally, the need for splitting clusters can be reduced if the input bandwidth is relaxed. For example, if we allowed 24 inputs for the CLB, then none of the 20 designs would require any fixing.

6. CONCLUSION

This paper proposed using the Rent characteristic as the optimization goal for FPGA packing. We showed that this goal can be achieved with recursive bipartitioning-based k-way partitioning. We developed PPack2 and showed that it outperforms all previous packing tools by a wide margin in all aspects.

7. REFERENCES

[1] Microsemi SoC products group (formerly Actel). http://www.actel.com.

[2] Altera Corp. http://www.altera.com.

[3] Lattice Semiconductor Corp. http://www.latticesemi.com.

[4] Xilinx Corp. http://www.xilinx.com.

[5] V.Betz, J.Rose and A.Marquardt. Architecture and CAD for Deep-submicron FPGAs. Kluwer Academic Publishers, February, 1999.

[6] E.Bozogzadeh, S.Ogrenci-Memik, and M.Sarrafzadeh, RPack: routability-driven packing for cluster-based FPGAs, Proceedings, *ASPDAC*2001, pp. 629–634.

[7] A.E.Caldwell, A.B.Khang, and I.L.Markov, Improved algorithms for hypergraph partitioning, *ASPAC2000*, pp. 343-348.

[8] D.Chen, K.Vorwerk, and A.Kennings, Improving timing-driven FPGA packing with physical information, *FPL*2007, pp. 117-123.

[9] J.Dambre, et al., A comparison of various terminal-gate relationships for interconnect prediction in VLSI circuits, *IEEE Trans. on VLSI*, vol. 11 pp. 24-34, 2003.

[10] W.E. Donath, Placement and average interconnection lengths of computer logic. *IEEE Trans. on Circuits and Systems*, vol. CAS-26, pp. 272-277, April, 1979.

[11] W.Feng, K-way partitioning based packing for FPGA logic blocks without input bandwidth constraint, *FPT2012*, pp. 8-15.

[12] W.Feng and S.Kaptanoglu, Designing efficient input interconnect blocks for LUT clusters using counting and entropy, *FPGA*2007, pp. 23-32.

[13] J.Greene, et al., A 65nm flash based FPGA fabric optimized for low cost and power, *FPGA*2011, pp. 87-96.

[14] G.Karypis and V.Kumar, Multilevel k-way hypergraph partitioning, *DAC1999*, pp. 343-348.

[15] B.S.Landman and R.L.Russo, On a pin versus block relationship for partitions of logic graphs. *IEEE Trans.On Computers.* vol. C-20, pp. 1469-1479, 1971.

[16] Z.Marrakchi, H.Mrabet and H.Mehrez, Hierarchical FPGA clustering based on multilevel partitioning approach to improve routability and reduce power dissipation, *ReConfig*2005, pp. 25-29.

[17] A.Singh and M.Marek-Sadowska, Efficient circuit clustering for area and power reduction in FPGAs, *FPGA*2002, pp. 59-66.

[18] X.Yang, E.Bozorgzadeh and M.Sarrafzadeh, Wire length estimation based on rent exponents of partitioning and placement, *SLIP2001*, pp. 25-31.

Modular Multi-ported SRAM-based Memories

Ameer M. S. Abdelhadi and Guy G. F. Lemieux
Department of Electrical and Computer Engineering
University of British Columbia
Vancouver, B.C., V6T 1Z4, Canada
{ameer,lemieux}@ece.ubc.ca

ABSTRACT

Multi-ported RAMs are essential for high-performance parallel computation systems. VLIW and vector processors, CGRAs, DSPs, CMPs and other processing systems often rely upon multi-ported memories for parallel access, hence higher performance. Although memories with a large number of read and write ports are important, their high implementation cost means they are used sparingly in designs. As a result, FPGA vendors only provide dual-ported block RAMs to handle the majority of usage patterns. In this paper, a novel and modular approach is proposed to construct multi-ported memories out of basic dual-ported RAM blocks. Like other multi-ported RAM designs, each write port uses a different RAM bank and each read port uses bank replication. The main contribution of this work is an optimization that merges the previous live-value-table (LVT) and XOR approaches into a common design that uses a generalized, simpler structure we call an invalidation-based live-value-table (I-LVT). Like a regular LVT, the I-LVT determines the correct bank to read from, but it differs in how updates to the table are made; the LVT approach requires multiple write ports, often leading to an area-intensive register-based implementation, while the XOR approach uses wider memories to accommodate the XOR-ed data and suffers from lower clock speeds. Two specific I-LVT implementations are proposed and evaluated, binary and one-hot coding. The I-LVT approach is especially suitable for larger multi-ported RAMs because the table is implemented only in SRAM cells. The I-LVT method gives higher performance while occupying less block RAMs than earlier approaches: for several configurations, the suggested method reduces the block RAM usage by over 44% and improves clock speed by over 76%. To assist others, we are releasing our fully parameterized Verilog implementation as an open source hardware library. The library has been extensively tested using ModelSim and Altera's Quartus tools.[1]

Categories and Subject Descriptors

B.3.2 [**MEMORY STRUCTURES**]: Design Styles – *Cache memories, Shared memory*; C.1.2 [**PROCESSOR ARCHITECTURES**]: Multiple Data Stream Architectures (Multiprocessors) – *Interconnection architectures, Parallel processors (e.g. common bus, multiport memory, crossbar switch)*

Keywords

Embedded memory; block RAM; multi-ported memory; shared memory; cache memory; register-file; parallel memory access

FPGA'14, February 26–28 2014, Monterey, CA, USA
Copyright 2014 ACM 978-1-4503-2671-1/14/02...$15.00.
http://dx.doi.org/10.1145/2554688.2554773

1. INTRODUCTION

Multi-ported memories are the cornerstone of all high-performance CPU designs. They are often used in the register files, but also in other shared-memory structures such as caches and coherence tags. Hence, high-bandwidth memories with multiple parallel reading and writing ports are required. In particular, multi-ported RAMs are often used by wide superscalar processors [1], VLIW processors [1][2], multi-core processors [3][4], vector processors, coarse-grain reconfigurable arrays (CGRAs), and digital signal processors (DSPs). For example, the second generation of the Itanium processor architecture employs a 20-port register file constructed from SRAM bit cells with 12 read ports and 8 write ports [3]. The key requirement for all of these designs is fast, single-cycle access from multiple requesters. These multiple requesters require concurrent access for performance reasons.

One way of synthesizing a multi-ported RAM is to build it from registers and logic. However, this is only feasible for very small memories. Another way is to alter the basic SRAM bit cell to provide extra access ports, but area growth is quadratic with the number of ports, so this requires a custom design for each unique set of parameters (number of ports, width and depth of RAM). Since FPGAs must fix their RAM block designs for generic designs, it is too costly to provide highly specialized RAMs with a large number of ports. A multi-ported RAM can also be emulated through banking or multi-pumping. Banking uses hashing and arbitration to provide access, but it leads to unpredictable (multi-cycle) access latencies under collisions; this complicates system design and compromises performance. Multi-pumping provides a few extra ports, but it is limited by the amount of overclocking. Hence, a method of composing arbitrary, multi-ported RAMs from simpler RAM blocks is required.

In this paper, a modular and parametric multi-ported RAM is constructed out of basic dual-ported RAM blocks while keeping minimal area and performance overhead. The suggested method significantly reduces SRAM use and improves performance compared to previous attempts. To verify correctness, the proposed architecture is fully implemented in Verilog, simulated using Altera's ModelSim, and compiled using Quartus II. A large variety of different memory architectures and parameters, *e.g.* bypassing, memory depth, data width, number of reading or writing ports are simulated in batch, each with over million random memory access cycles. Stratix V, Altera's high-end performance-oriented FPGA, is used to implement and compare the proposed architecture with previous approaches. Major contributions of this paper are:

- A novel I-lVT architecture to produce modular multi-ported SRAM-based memories. It is built out of dual-ported SRAM blocks only, without any register-based memories. To the authors' best knowledge, compared to other multi-ported approaches, the I-LVT consumes the fewest possible SRAM cells. It also provides improved overall performance.

---

[1] http://www.ece.ubc.ca/~lemieux/downloads/

- A fully parameterized Verilog implementation of the suggested methods, together with previous approaches. A flow manager to simulate and synthesize various designs with various parameters in batch using Altera's ModelSim and Quartus II is also provided. The Verilog modules and the flow manager are available online [5].

Notation and abbreviations used for the rest of the paper are listed in Table 1. The rest of this paper is organized as follows. In section 2, conventional RAM multi-porting techniques in embedded systems are reviewed. Previous attempts to provide multi-ported memories are reviewed in section 3. The proposed invalidation-based live-value-table method is described in detail and compared to previous methods in section 4. The experimental framework, including simulation and synthesis and results, are discussed in section 5, and conclusions are drawn in section 6.

Table 1. List of notations and abbreviations

n_W	Write ports number	WAddr	Write address
n_R	Read ports number	RAddr	Read address
w	Data width	WData	Write data
d	Memory depth	RData	Read data
n_{M20K}	Number of M20K blocks	RBankSel	Read bank selector
n_{BypReg}	Number of bypass registers	LVT	Live-value-table
f_{fb}, f_{out}	LVT feedback/out functions	I-LVT	Invalidation LVT

2. RAM MULTI-PORTING TECHNIQUES IN EMBEDDED SYSTEMS

This section provides a review of current methods of creating multi-ported RAMs in embedded systems. Creating multi-ported access to register-based and SRAM-based memories is described in subsection 2.1. Multi-pumping is described in subsection 2.2. Replicating a memory bank to increase the number of read and write ports is described in subsections 2.3 and 2.4, respectively.

2.1 Register-based RAM

Multi-ported RAM arrays can be constructed using basic flip-flop cells and logic. As depicted in Figure 1, each writing port uses a decoder to steer the relevant written data into the addressed row. Each read port uses a mux to choose the relevant register output. This method is not practical for large memories due to area inflation, fan-out increase, performance degradation, and a decline in routability.

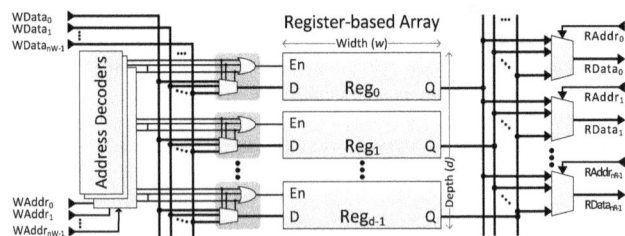

Figure 1. Register-based multi-ported RAM.

2.2 RAM Multi-pumping

A time-multiplexing approach can be applied to a single dual-ported SRAM block to reuse access ports and share them among several clients, each during a different time slot. As depicted in Figure 2, addresses and data from several clients are latched then given round-robin access to a dual-ported RAM. The RAM must operate at a higher frequency than the rest of the circuit. If the maximum RAM frequency is similar to the pipe frequency, or a large number of access ports are required, then multi-pumping

cannot be used. A number of designs utilize multi-pumping to gain additional access ports while keeping area overhead minimal [6][7]. The 2.3GHz Wire-Speed POWER processor uses double-pumping to double the writing ports [8].

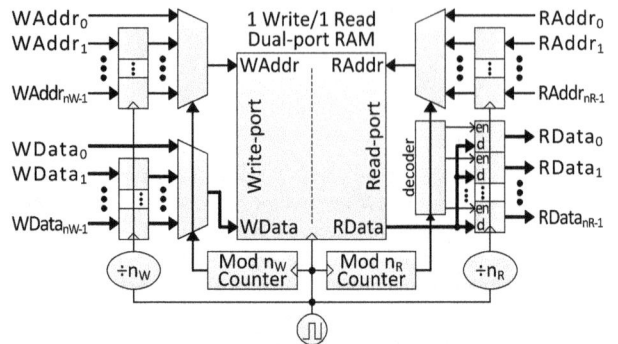

Figure 2. Multi-pumping: RAM is clocked faster than the pipeline in the periphery, allowing multiple accesses during one pipeline cycle.

2.3 Multi-read RAM: Bank Replication

To provide more reading ports, the whole memory bank can be replicated while keeping common write address and data as shown in Figure 3. Any data will be written to all bank replicas at the same address, hence reading from any bank is equivalent. This method incurs high SRAM area and consumes more power. However, the replication approach has two strong advantages over other multi-porting approaches. The first is the simplicity and modularity of bank replication. The second is that read access time is unaffected as the number of ports increases; only write delays increase due to fan-out, but this can be hidden via pipelining and bypassing. The bank replication technique is commonly used in state-of-the-art processing architectures to increase parallelism. The 2.3GHz Wire-Speed POWER processor replicates a 2-read SRAM bank to achieve 4 read ports [8]. Each of the two integer clusters of the Alpha 21264 microprocessor has a replicated 80-entry register file, thus doubling the number of read ports to support two concurrent integer execution units. Similarly, the 72-entry floating-point register file is duplicated, supporting two concurrent floating-point units [9].

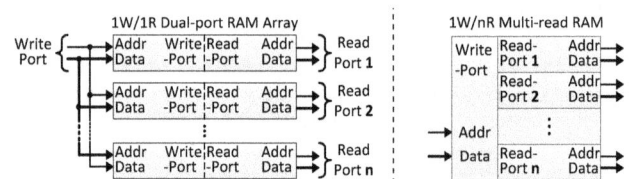

Figure 3. (left) Replicated dual-ported banks with a common write port. (right) Symbol used in this paper equivalent to a multi-read RAM block.

2.4 Multi-write RAM: Emulation via multi-banking

Multi-ported memories are very expensive in terms of area, delay, and power for a large number of ports. The overhead of multi-porting can be reduced by multi-banking if one relaxes the guaranteed access delay constraint. As depicted in Figure 4, the total RAM capacity can be divided into several banks, each with few ports (e.g. dual-port). A fixed hashing scheme is used to match each access to a single bank; often, the address MSBs are used. Arbitration logic steers access from multiple ports to each bank. Since two ports can request access to data in the same bank at the same time, a conflict resolving circuit determines which port grants access to a specific bank. The other port will miss the arbitration and is required to request access again. Not only does the multi-banking approach provide unpredictable access latency due to the arbitration miss, but it also degrades delay due to the additional access circuitry. Several approaches have been proposed to improve multi-banking [10][1][11][12]. State-of-the-art memory controllers and processor caches are based on multi-banking due to area and power efficiency. For example, the Pentium 5 has a data cache with 8 interleaved banks and two access ports [13].

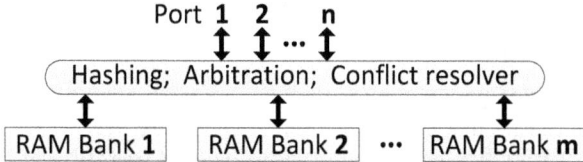

Figure 4. Multi-banking: RAM capacity is divided into several banks. Ports access a RAM bank with a fixed hashing scheme.

3. MODULAR MULTI-PORTED SRAM-BASED MEMORIES: PREVIOUS WORK

In this section a review of two previous modular designs of multi-ported SRAM-based memories are provided. The first approach is based on multi-banking with a live-value-table (LVT) [14] and is described in subsection 3.1. The second approach retrieves the latest written data by utilizing logical XOR properties [15] and is described in subsection 3.2.

3.1 LVT-based Multi-ported RAM

For each RAM address, the LVT stores the ID of the bank replica that holds the latest data. As depicted in Figure 5 (left), an LVT-based multi-ported RAM uses a different bank replica for each writing port, while each bank has several reading ports. All banks are accessed by all read addresses in parallel; the LVT helps to steer the read data out of the correct bank since it holds the ID of last accessed (written) bank for each address.

Actually, the LVT itself is a multi-ported RAM with the same memory depth and number of writing ports as the implemented multi-ported memory. However, since the LVT stores only bank IDs, the data (line) width of the LVT table is only $[log_2]$ of the number of banks, which is equal to the number of writing ports. Furthermore, the LVT doesn't have write data, instead it writes a fixed bank ID for each port as described in Figure 5 (right).

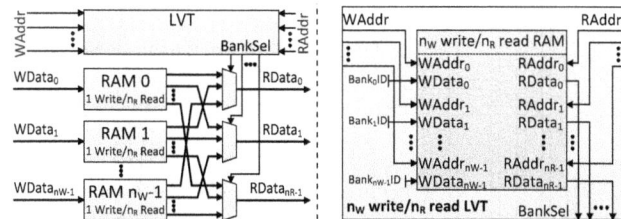

Figure 5. (left) LVT-based multi-ported RAM. (right) An LVT implemented using multi-ported RAM.

Since an LVT is a narrow, multi-port memory, it is implemented as a registered-based, multi-ported RAM. As explained in subsection 2.1, register-based RAM is not suitable for building

large memories. While the LVT width is only $\log_2$ of the number of writing ports, the depth of the LVT is still similar to the depth of the original RAM. *This is the main cause of the area overhead.* In this paper, to reduce this area overhead, two methods of constructing SRAM-based LVTs are described. The methodology of constructing SRAM-based LVTs is also generalized. To the authors' best knowledge this is the first attempt to build an LVT out of SRAM blocks only.

Assuming that bank IDs are binary encoded, the total number of registers required to implement the LVT is

$$d \cdot \lceil \log_2 n_W \rceil. \tag{1}$$

For deep memories, the large number of registers and huge read multiplexers make register-based LVTs impractical. For example, on a Stratix V GX A5 device (185k ALMs), Quartus II failed to synthesize a 16k-deep memory with two write ports.

A register-based LVT with SRAM banks requires n_W multi-read banks for each write port. Each multi-read bank supports n_R reading ports, allowing the LVT to select the required data block. The total number of SRAM cells is

$$d \cdot w \cdot n_W \cdot n_R. \tag{2}$$

Using Altera's Stratix V M20K block RAMs, the total number of required M20K blocks is

$$n_{M20K}(d,w) \cdot n_W \cdot n_R. \tag{3}$$

Where $n_{M20K}(d,w)$ is the number of M20K Blocks required to construct a RAM with a specific depth and data width. This value, described by equation (4), is derived from Figure 6, which shows how Altera's M20K blocks can be configured into several RAM depth and data width configurations [16]. The total amount of utilized SRAM bits can be either 16Kbits, or 20Kbits. Assuming that the RAM packing process minimizes the number of blocks cascaded in depth to avoid additional address decoding, each 16K lines will be packed into single bit-wide blocks, and the remainder will be packed into the minimal required configuration as follows

$$n_{M20K}(d,w) = \left\lfloor \frac{d}{16k} \right\rfloor \cdot w + \begin{cases} d\%16k > 8k & w \\ 8k \geq d\%16k > 4k & \lceil w/2 \rceil \\ 4k \geq d\%16k > 2k & \lceil w/5 \rceil \\ 2k \geq d\%16k > 1k & \lceil w/10 \rceil \\ 1k \geq d\%16k > \frac{1}{2}k & \lceil w/20 \rceil \\ \frac{1}{2}k \geq d\%16k & \lceil w/40 \rceil \end{cases} \tag{4}$$

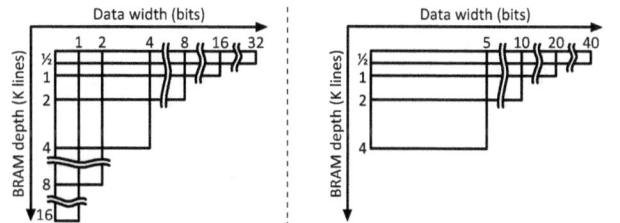

Figure 6. Altera's M20K BRAM configurations (left) 16Kbit (right) 20Kbit.

3.2 XOR-based Multi-ported RAM

While the LVT-based multi-port RAM just shown implements its LVT as a register-based multi-ported RAM, the XOR-based multi-ported RAM is implemented using SRAM blocks [15]. This makes it more efficient for deep memories. However, as will be shown, it is inefficient for wide memories.

The XOR-based method utilizes the special properties of the XOR function to retain the latest written data for each write port. XOR is commutative $a \oplus b = b \oplus a$, associative $(a \oplus b) \oplus c = a \oplus (b \oplus c)$, zero is the identity $a \oplus 0 = a$, and the inverse of each element is itself $a \oplus a = 0$.

As illustrated in Figure 7, each write port has a bank with multi-read and a single write. Part of the read ports are used as a feedback to generate new data and rewrite a specific bank, while the other read ports generate the data outputs. To perform a write, the new data is XOR'ed together with all the old data from the other banks; the result is rewritten to the corresponding bank. Hence if an address A is written through write port i with data $WData_i$, $Bank_i$ will be rewritten with

$$Bank_i[A] \leftarrow Bank_0[A] \oplus Bank_1[A] \oplus ...$$
$$\oplus WData_i \oplus ... \oplus Bank_{n_W-1}[A]. \quad (5)$$

A read is performed by XOR'ing all the data for the corresponding read address from all the banks, hence,

$$RData_i[A] \leftarrow Bank_0[A] \oplus Bank_1[A] ... \oplus Bank_{n_W-1}[A]. \quad (6)$$

Substituting $Bank_i[A]$ from (5) into (6) and applying commutative and associative properties of the XOR shows that each bank appears twice in the XOR equation, hence will be cancelled since XORing similar elements is 0. The only remaining item will be $WData_i$, the required data.

The XOR-based multi-ported RAM requires n_W multi-read banks for each write port. Each multi-read bank supports $n_W - 1$ read ports to feedback the other ports via XORs, and n_R read ports. Each feedback read port is of width d, to match the write data, so these feedback memories can be quite large. The number of required SRAM cells is

$$d \cdot w \cdot n_W \cdot (n_R + n_W - 1). \quad (7)$$

Using Altera's Stratix V M20K block RAMs, the total number of required M20K blocks is

$$n_{M20K}(d, w) \cdot n_W \cdot (n_R + n_W - 1). \quad (8)$$

Since FPGA block RAM is synchronous, data feedbacks are read with a one-cycle read delay. Hence, the written data, their addresses and write-enables must be retimed to match the feedback data. This requires the following number of registers

$$n_W \cdot (w + \lceil \log_2 d \rceil + n_W). \quad (9)$$

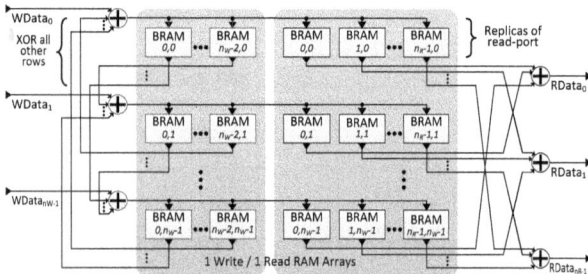

Figure 7. XOR-based multi-ported RAM.

4. INVALIDATION TABLE

As described in the previous section, the XOR-based multi-ported memories requires $n_W \cdot (n_R + n_W - 1)$ manipulated copies of the RAM content, while the LVT approach requires another register-

based multi-ported memory with the same number of read and write ports for bank IDs.

This work proposes to implement LVTs using SRAM blocks only, which has a major advantage over register-based LVTs and a lower SRAM area compared to the XOR-based approach. Instead of requiring multiple write ports to each multi-read bank in regular LVT method, we suggest a design with a single write port each like the XOR method. This makes it feasible to implement the LVT using standard dual-ported RAMs. However, writing an ID to one bank requires also invalidating the IDs in the other banks, which produces the need for the multiple write ports. Instead, we suggest writing an ID to only one specific bank and invalidating all the other IDs with a single write by using an invalidation table. Since the *invalidation table* has the same functional behavior as an LVT, we call it an invalidation-based LVT, or I-LVT.

The I-LVT doesn't require multiple writes to indicate the last-written bank. Instead, as described in Figure 8, the I-LVT reads all other bank IDs as feedback, embeds the new bank ID into the other values through a feedback function f_{fb}, then rewrites the specific bank. To extract back the latest written bank ID, all banks are read and data is processed with the output function f_{out} to regenerate the required ID. Selection of these two functions, f_{fb} and f_{out}, is what distinguishes different I-LVT implementations.

The I-LTV requires n_W multi-read banks, each with n_R read ports for output extraction. Furthermore, an additional $n_W - 1$ read ports are required in each bank for feedback rewriting. The data width of these read ports varies depending on the feedback method and the bank ID encoding. In this paper, two bank ID encoding methods are presented, binary and one-hot. The binary method employs exclusive-OR functions to embed the bank IDs, while the second uses mutual-exclusive conditions to invalidate table entries and generate one-hot-coded bank selectors. The two methods are described in subsections 4.1 and 4.2, respectively.

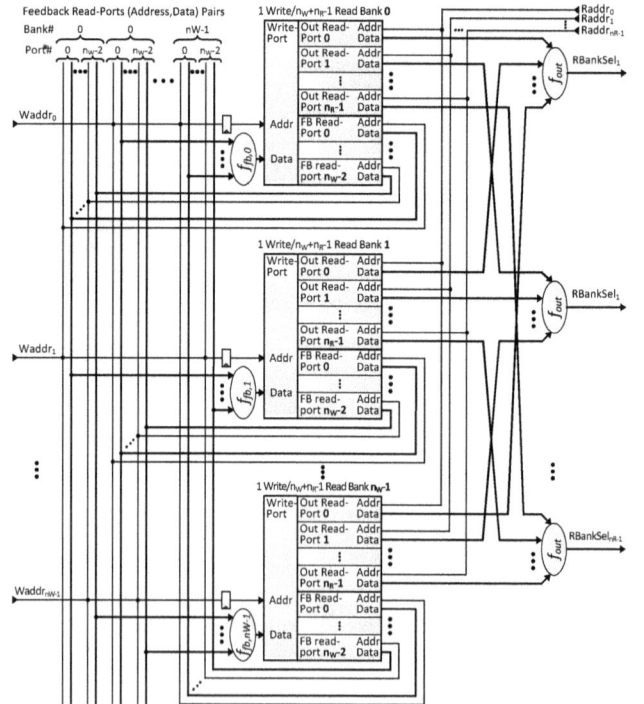

Figure 8. Generalized approach for building the I-LVT.

4.1 Bank ID Embedding: Binary-coded selectors

This approach attempts to reduce the SRAM cell count in the I-LVT by employing binary-coded bank IDs. The special properties of the exclusive-OR function are utilized to embed the latest written bank ID, hence invalidating all other IDs. The current written bank ID is XOR'ed with the content of all the other banks from the same write address as described in the following feedback function,

$$f_{fb,k} = k \oplus_{\substack{0 \leq i < n_W \\ i \neq k}} Bank_i[WAddr_k], \qquad (10)$$

where k is the ID of the currently written bank.

Similar to the XOR-based method described in subsection 3.2, the last written bank ID is extracted by XOR'ing the content of all the banks from the same read address as described in the following output extraction function

$$f_{out,k} = \oplus_{0 \leq i < n_W} Bank_i[RAddr_k]. \qquad (11)$$

Without loss of generality, if address A in bank k is written with the feedback function from Equation (10), then

$$Bank_k[A] = k \oplus_{0 \leq i < n_W; \, i \neq k} Bank_i[A]. \qquad (12)$$

If one of the read ports, say read port r, is trying to read from the same address, namely $RAddr_r = A$, then the read bank selector will be generated using the same output extraction function from (11), hence

$$RBankSel_r = \oplus_{0 \leq i < n_W} Bank_i[A]. \qquad (13)$$

Due to XOR operation associativity, $RBankSel_r$ from (13) can be expressed as

$$RBankSel_r = Bank_k[A] \oplus_{0 \leq i < n_W; \, i \neq k} Bank_i[A], \qquad (14)$$

Substituting $Bank_k[A]$ from (12) into (14) provides

$$RBankSel_r =$$
$$k \oplus_{0 \leq i < n_W; \, i \neq k} Bank_i[A] \oplus_{0 \leq i < n_W; \, i \neq k} Bank_i[A]. \qquad (15)$$

The last two series in (15) can be reduced revealing that $RBankSel_r = k$, the ID of the latest writing bank into address A, as required.

Figure 9 provides an example of 2W/2R binary-coded I-LVT. (As will become apparent in the next section, when there are only 2 write ports, the binary-coded and one-hot-coded I-LVTs are identical.) Figure 10 shows a 3W/2R binary-coded I-LVT.

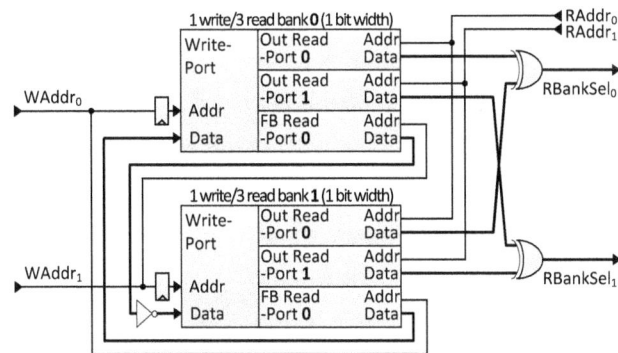

Figure 9. A 2W/2R SRAM-based I-LVT; identical for binary-coded or one-hot-coded bank selectors.

The required data width of the I-LVT SRAM blocks is $\lceil \log_2 n_W \rceil$. Also, n_W multi-read banks are required each with n_R output ports for ID extraction and $n_W - 1$ feedback ports for ID rewriting. Hence, the number of required SRAM cells is

$$d \cdot \lceil \log_2 n_W \rceil \cdot n_W \cdot (n_W + n_R - 1). \qquad (16)$$

Respectively, the number of required M20k block RAMs is

$$n_{M20K}(d, \lceil \log_2 n_W \rceil) \cdot n_W \cdot (n_W + n_R - 1). \qquad (17)$$

Similarly, the number of registers required for retiming is

$$n_W \cdot (\lceil \log_2 d \rceil + 1). \qquad (18)$$

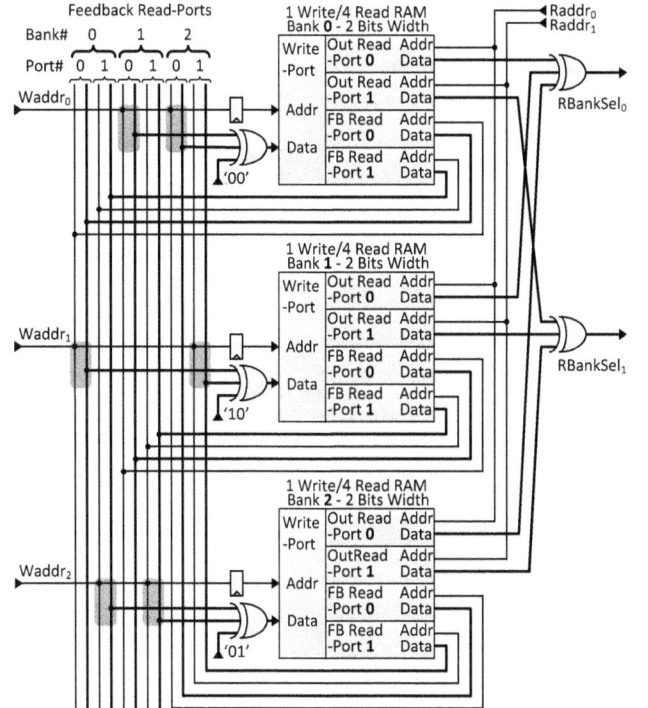

Figure 10. A 3W/2R SRAM-based I-LVT with binary-coded selectors.

4.2 Mutual-exclusive Conditions: One-hot-coded Selectors

The previous binary-coded I-LVT incurs a long path delay through the feedback and output extraction functions, which causes a performance reduction in structures with more ports. Employing a one-hot thermometer ID encoding reduces the feedback paths to just a few inverters, from the n_W-wide XOR used earlier.

Mutual-exclusive conditions are used to rewrite the RAM contents. A specific bank is written data that contradicts all the other banks, hence only this specific bank will be valid and all the others are invalid. By checking the appropriate mutual-exclusive condition for each bank, only the latest written bank will hold the valid data.

Equations (19), (20), and (21) describe mutual-exclusive feedback functions for n_W values 1, 2, and 3, respectively. The angle brackets in theses equations are used for bit selection and concatenation, while the square brackets in other equations are used for RAM addressing. As can be seen from these equations, writing to one bank will invalidate all the other banks at the same address since one mutual negated bit is shared between each two lines. For example, writing to bank 2 when $n_W = 3$ (Equation (20)) will write $Bank_1\langle 0\rangle \leftarrow \overline{Bank_0\langle 0\rangle}$ which will invalidate bank 0, and $Bank_1\langle 1\rangle \leftarrow Bank_2\langle 1\rangle$ which will invalidate bank 2.

$$n_W = 2: \begin{cases} f_{fb,0}: Bank_0\langle 0\rangle \leftarrow Bank_1\langle 0\rangle \\ f_{fb,1}: Bank_1\langle 0\rangle \leftarrow \overline{Bank_0\langle 0\rangle} \end{cases} \quad (19)$$

$$n_W = 3: \begin{cases} f_{fb,0}: Bank_0\langle 1:0\rangle \leftarrow \langle Bank_2\langle 0\rangle, Bank_1\langle 0\rangle\rangle \\ f_{fb,1}: Bank_1\langle 1:0\rangle \leftarrow \langle Bank_2\langle 1\rangle, \overline{Bank_0\langle 0\rangle}\rangle \\ f_{fb,2}: Bank_2\langle 1:0\rangle \leftarrow \langle \overline{Bank_1\langle 1\rangle}, \overline{Bank_0\langle 1\rangle}\rangle \end{cases} \quad (20)$$

$$n_W = 4: \begin{cases} f_{fb,0}: Bank_0\langle 2:0\rangle \leftarrow \langle Bank_3\langle 0\rangle, Bank_2\langle 0\rangle, Bank_1\langle 0\rangle\rangle \\ f_{fb,1}: Bank_1\langle 2:0\rangle \leftarrow \langle Bank_3\langle 1\rangle, Bank_2\langle 1\rangle, \overline{Bank_0\langle 0\rangle}\rangle \\ f_{fb,2}: Bank_2\langle 2:0\rangle \leftarrow \langle Bank_3\langle 2\rangle, \overline{Bank_1\langle 1\rangle}, \overline{Bank_0\langle 1\rangle}\rangle \\ f_{fb,3}: Bank_3\langle 2:0\rangle \leftarrow \langle \overline{Bank_2\langle 2\rangle}, \overline{Bank_1\langle 2\rangle}, \overline{Bank_0\langle 2\rangle}\rangle \end{cases} \quad (21)$$

Equation (22) generalizes the feedback function to $f_{fb,k}\langle i\rangle\big|_{0 \le i < n_W - 1}$:

$$Bank_k[WAddr_k]\langle i\rangle \leftarrow \begin{cases} i < k & \overline{Bank_i[WAddr_k]\langle k-1\rangle} \\ else & Bank_{i+1}[WAddr_k]\langle k\rangle \end{cases}. \quad (22)$$

This equation shows that each bank is using bits from all other banks to write its own content. To prove that each two banks are mutually exclusive, one bit of these banks should be mutually negated. Suppose $0 \le k_0 \le n_W - 1$ a bank ID, and $0 \le i_0 \le n_W - 1$ a bit index. From Equation (22) if $i_0 \ge k_0$ then another bank ID k_1 and bit index i_1 exist such that $Bank_{k_0}\langle i_0\rangle \leftarrow Bank_{k_1}\langle i_1\rangle$, $k_1 = i_0 + 1$, and $i_1 = k_0$. Hence, $i_1 < k_1$ and from (22) $Bank_{k_1}\langle i_1\rangle \leftarrow \overline{Bank_{k_0}\langle i_0\rangle}$ as required. The proof in case of $i_0 < k_0$ is identical.

The output extraction function checks for each one-hot output selector if the read data from a specific bank matches the mutual-exclusive case. Hence, only one case will match due to exclusivity. The output extraction function consists of an $n_W - 1$ bit wide comparator for each one-hot selector.

An example of a 2W/2R one-hot-coded I-LVT is shown in Figure 9, while a 3W/2R one-hot I-LVT is depicted in Figure 11.

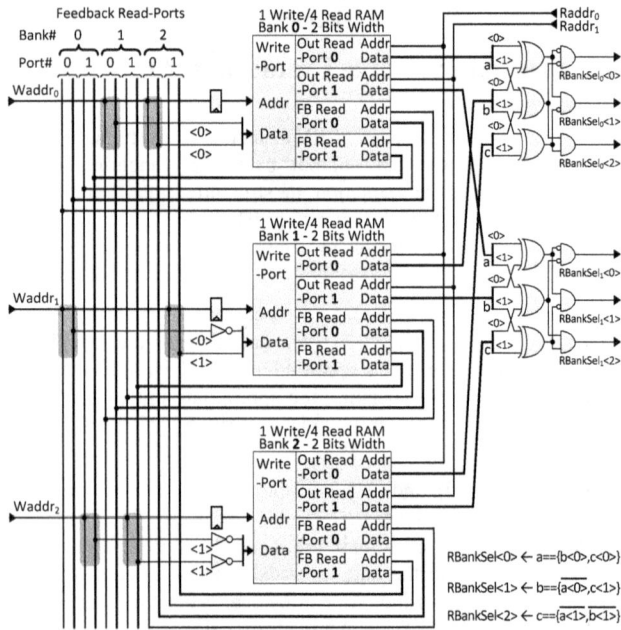

Figure 11. A 3W/2R SRAM-based I-LVT with one-hot-coded selectors.

The one-hot-coded I-LVT requires $n_W - 1$ SRAM bits to save the mutually exclusive cases. However, the feedback read ports requires only one bit, since only one bit is used by the feedback function from each bank. n_W multi-read banks are required each with n_R output ports for one-hot selectors extraction and $n_W - 1$ feedback ports for mutually exclusive cases rewriting. Hence, the number of required SRAM cells is

$$d \cdot (n_W - 1) \cdot n_W \cdot n_R + d \cdot n_W \cdot (n_W - 1). \quad (23)$$

Respectively, the number of required M20k block RAMs is

$$n_{M20K}(d, n_W - 1) \cdot n_W \cdot n_R + B_{M20K}(d, 1) \cdot n_W \cdot (n_W - 1). \quad (24)$$

Similarly, the number of registers required for retiming is equal to the binary-coded case and is described by (18).

4.3 Data Dependencies and Bypassing

The new I-LVT structure and the previous XOR-based multi-ported RAMs incur some data dependencies due to feedback functions and the latency of reading the I-LVT to decide about the last written bank. Data dependencies can be handled by employing bypassing, also known as forwarding.

Figure 12 illustrated two types of bypassing based on write data and address pipelining. Bypassing is necessary because Altera dual-port block RAMs cannot internally forward new data when one port reads and the other port writes the same address on the same clock edge, constituting a read-during-write (RDW) hazard. Both bypassing techniques are functionally equivalent, allowing reading of the data that is being written on the same clock edge, similar to single register functionality. However, the fully-pipelined two-stages bypassing shown in Figure 12 (right) can overcome additional cycle latency. This capability is required if a block RAM has pipelined inputs (*e.g.*, cascaded from another block RAM) that need to be bypassed.

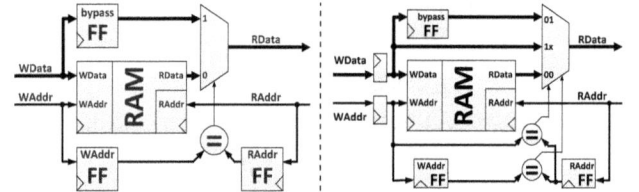

Figure 12. RAM bypassing (left) single-stage (right) 2-stages fully pipelined.

The single-stage and the two-stage bypass circuitry for a w bits data width and d lines depth block RAM requires w registers for data bypassing, two $\lceil \log_2 d \rceil$ wide address registers and one enable register, for a total of

$$n_{BypReg}(d, w) = w + 2\lceil \log_2 d \rceil + 1. \quad (25)$$

The most severe data dependency that I-LVT design suffers from is write-after-write (WAW), namely, writing to the same address that has been written before in the previous cycle. This dependency occurs because of the feedback reading and writing latency. A single-stage bypassing for the feedback banks should solve this dependency.

Two types of reading hazards are introduced by the proposed I-LVT design, read-after-write (RAW) and read-during-write (RDW). RAW occurs when the same data that have been written in the previous clock edge are read in the current clock edge. RDW occurs when the same data are written and read on the same clock edge.

Due to the latency of the I-LVT, reading from the same address on the next clock edge after writing (RAW) will provide the old data. To read the new data instead, the output banks of the I-LVT should be bypassed by a single-stage bypass to overcome the I-LVT latency.

The deepest bypassing stage is reading new data on the same writing clock edge (RDW), which is similar to single register stage latency. This can be achieved by 2-stage bypassing on the output extract ports of the I-LVT or the XOR-based design to allow reading on the same clock edge. The data banks, which are working in parallel with the I-LVT should also be bypassed by a single-stage bypass to provide new data. Table 2 summarizes the required bypassing for data banks, feedback banks and output banks for each type of bypassing of the XOR-based, binary-coded and one-hot-coded I-LVT designs.

Since XOR-based multi-ported RAM requires bypassing for all the $n_W \cdot (n_W + n_R - 1)$ banks to read new data when RAW or RDW, the additional registers required for the bypassing are

$$n_W \cdot (n_W + n_R - 1) \cdot n_{BypReg}(d, w). \qquad (26)$$

RAW for binary-coded method requires bypassing the I-LVT only. Since the I-LVT is built out of $n_W \cdot (n_W + n_R - 1)$ blocks, each with $\lceil \log_2 n_W \rceil$ bits width data, the following amount of additional registers is required

$$n_W \cdot (n_W + n_R - 1) \cdot n_{BypReg}(d, \lceil \log_2 n_W \rceil). \qquad (27)$$

RAW for one-hot-coded method requires bypassing the whole I-LVT, $n_W \cdot (n_W - 1)$ feedback banks with 1 bit width and $n_W \cdot n_R$ output banks with $n_W - 1$ bits width, hence a total registers of

$$n_W \cdot (n_W - 1) \cdot n_{BypReg}(d, 1) + n_W \cdot n_R \cdot n_{BypReg}(d, n_W - 1). \qquad (28)$$

RDW for both binary and one-hot-coded methods require bypassing the $n_W \cdot n_R$ data banks in addition to the I-LVT, hence the following amount of registers is added to the previous count in (27) and (28)

$$n_W \cdot n_R \cdot n_{BypReg}(d, w). \qquad (29)$$

Table 2. Bypassing for XOR-based and binary/one-hot-coded I-LVT multi-ported memories

	XOR-based		I-LVT based		
	Feedback banks	Output banks	Data banks	Feedback banks	Output banks
Allow WAW	1-stage	None	None	1-stage	None
New data RAW	1-stage	1-stage	None	1-stage	1-stage
New data RDW	1-stage	2-stage	1-stage	1-stage	2-stage

4.4 Initializing Multi-ported RAM Content

Due to the special structure of the proposed I-LVT-based multi-ported memories and the previously proposed XOR-based method, RAM data may have replicas in several banks. Hence, initializing the multi-ported RAM with a specific content requires special handling.

For the XOR-based multi-ported RAM, the first multi-read bank should be initialized to the required initial content; all the other multi-read banks should be initialized to zero.

The binary/one-hot-coded I-LVT-based multi-ported RAM requires initializing all the I-LVT banks with zeros. The binary-coded I-LVT will generate a selector to the first data bank (indexed zero), since XOR'ing all the initial values (zeros) will

generate zero. Similarly, the one-hot-coded I-LVT will be initialized to the first mutually exclusive case, hence the first bank will be selected. Only the first data bank should hold the initial data; the remaining banks can be left uninitialized. The initial values for each bank in the binary/one-hot-coded I-LVT-based and XOR-based designs are shown in Figure 13.

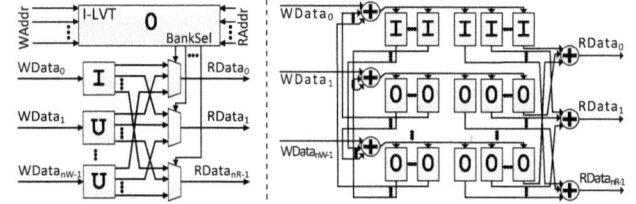

Figure 13. Initial value for each bank (left) I-LVT-based (right) XOR-based. Initial values are 0: zeros, I: initial content, and U: uninitialized.

4.5 Comparison and Discussion

In this section, we compare the previous LVT and XOR approaches to the new I-LVT approaches for building multi-port memories. Using the equations provided, we will illustrate why the I-LVT approach is superior in terms of number of BRAMs required, and number of registers required. Also, between the two I-LVT methods proposed, we will inspect the number of BRAMs and registers used by each bypassing method.

Table 3 summarizes SRAM resource usage for each of the three multi-ported RAM approaches: the XOR-based and the binary/one-hot-coded I-LVT. Both the general SRAM cell count and the number of Altera's M20K blocks are described. Comparing the SRAM cell counts, the XOR-based approach consumes fewer SRAM cells than the one-hot I-LVT if

$$w < n_R + 1. \qquad (30)$$

This inequality is unlikely to be satisfied, since even if the data width is only one byte, the number of reading ports n_R would need to be larger than 8, which is very rare. Hence, for most of the common cases, the one-hot-coded I-LVT approach will consume fewer SRAM cells.

Comparing the XOR-based approach to the binary-coded approach, the XOR-based approach consumes fewer SRAM cells only if

$$w < \left. \frac{\lceil \log_2(n_W) \rceil \cdot (n_W + n_R - 1)}{(n_W - 1)} \right|_{n_W > 1}. \qquad (31)$$

Both (30) and (31) show that the XOR-based approach will consume less SRAM cells only for a very narrow data widths which are uncommonly used. Hence, the I-LVT approach will be the choice for most applications. Comparing the two I-LVT approaches, Table 3 shows that the one-hot-coded I-LVT consumes fewer SRAM cells than the binary-coded I-LVT if

$$1 < n_W \le 3 \ OR \ n_R < \left. \frac{(n_W - 1) \cdot (\lceil \log_2(n_W) \rceil - 1)}{(n_W - 1) - \lceil \log_2(n_W) \rceil} \right|_{n_W > 3}. \qquad (32)$$

Table 4 summarizes register usage for all multi-ported RAM architectures and bypassing. Only the register-based LVT architecture is directly proportional to memory depth. As a consequence, it consumes much more registers than other architectures, making register-based LVTs impractical for deep memories.

Table 3. Summary of SRAM-based memory usage

	SRAM bits	M20K blocks[1]
Register-based LVT	$d \cdot w \cdot n_W \cdot n_R$	$n_{M20K}(d,w) \cdot n_W \cdot n_R$
XOR-based	$d \cdot w \cdot n_W \cdot n_R + d \cdot w \cdot n_W \cdot (n_W - 1)$	$n_{M20K}(d,w) \cdot n_W \cdot n_R + n_{M20K}(d,w) \cdot n_W \cdot (n_W - 1)$
Binary-coded I-LVT	$d \cdot w \cdot n_W \cdot n_R + d \cdot \lceil \log_2 n_W \rceil \cdot n_W \cdot (n_W - 1) + d \cdot \lceil \log_2 n_W \rceil \cdot n_W \cdot n_R$	$n_{M20K}(d,w) \cdot n_W \cdot n_R + n_{M20K}(d,\lceil \log_2 n_W \rceil) \cdot n_W \cdot (n_W - 1) + n_{M20K}(d,\lceil \log_2 n_W \rceil) \cdot n_W \cdot n_R$
One-hot-coded I-LVT	$d \cdot w \cdot n_W \cdot n_R + d \cdot n_W \cdot (n_W - 1) + d \cdot (n_W - 1) \cdot n_W \cdot n_R$	$n_{M20K}(d,w) \cdot n_W \cdot n_R + n_{M20K}(d,1) \cdot n_W \cdot (n_W - 1) + n_{M20K}(d, n_W - 1) \cdot n_W \cdot n_R$

Table 4. Summary of register usage

	No bypass	Additional registers for single-stage[2]	Additional registers for two-stage
Register-based LVT	$d \cdot \lceil \log_2 n_W \rceil$	None	None
XOR-based	$n_W \cdot (w + \lceil \log_2 d \rceil + 1)$	$n_W \cdot (n_W - 1) \cdot n_{BypReg}(d,w) + n_W \cdot n_R \cdot n_{BypReg}(d,w)$	None
Binary-coded I-LVT	$n_W \cdot (\lceil \log_2 d \rceil + 1)$	$n_W \cdot (n_W - 1) \cdot n_{BypReg}(d,\lceil \log_2 n_W \rceil) + n_W \cdot n_R \cdot n_{BypReg}(d,\lceil \log_2 n_W \rceil)$	$n_W \cdot n_R \cdot n_{BypReg}(d,w)$
One-hot-coded I-LVT	Same as Binary-coded	$n_W \cdot (n_W - 1) \cdot n_{BypReg}(d,1) + n_W \cdot n_R \cdot n_{BypReg}(d,n_W - 1)$	Same as Binary-coded

[1] $B_{M20K}(d,w)$ is the number of Altera's M20K blocks required to construct a RAM with d lines depth and w bits width and is described in (4).

[2] $Reg_{bypass}(d,w)$ is the number of additional registers required to bypass a RAM with d lines depth and w bits width and is described in (25).

With a single-stage bypassing, the XOR-based design consumes fewer registers than the binary-coded if

$$w < \lceil log_2(n_W) \rceil. \tag{33}$$

Equation (33) is unlikely to be satisfied. Even if the data width is just one byte ($w = 8$), the number of write ports n_W would need to be larger than 256, which is impractical.

On the other hand, with a single-stage bypass, the XOR-based design consumes fewer registers than the one-hot-coded I-LVT design if

$$w < \left.\frac{1+n_R}{1+\frac{n_R}{n_W-1}}\right|_{n_W>1}. \tag{34}$$

In a typical compute-oriented designs, $n_R = 2 \cdot n_W$. Assuming that $n_R = 2 \cdot (n_W - 1)$ requires that $3 \cdot w - 1 < n_R$; even for a one byte data width, this requires $23 < n_R$ to satisfy (34), which is impractical. Therefore, for a single-stage bypass, the I-LVT based designs will consume fewer registers than the XOR-based design.

Considering two-stage bypassing, I-LVT based designs will consume $n_W \cdot n_R \cdot Reg_{bypass}(d,w)$ more registers, as described in (29). In this case, XOR-based design consumes fewer registers than the binary-coded I-LVT design only if

$$w < \lceil log_2(n_W) \rceil \cdot \left(1 + \frac{n_R}{n_W-1}\right). \tag{35}$$

On the other hand, XOR-based design consumes fewer registers than the one-hot-coded I-LVT design only if

$$w < n_R + 1. \tag{36}$$

Similar to (30), which is equal to (36), this is unlikely to be satisfied in practical designs. Hence, in the case of two-stage bypassing, the I-LVT-based design will consume fewer bypassing registers than the XOR-based method.

In the next section, we will show these analytical results are in agreement with experimental results.

5. EXPERIMENTAL RESULTS

In order to verify and simulate the suggested approach and compare to previous attempts, fully parameterized Verilog modules have been developed. Both the previous XOR-based multi-ported RAM method, and the proposed I-LVT method have been implemented. To simulate and synthesize these designs with various parameters in batch using Altera's ModelSim and Quartus II, a run-in-batch flow manager has also been developed. The Verilog modules and the flow manager are available online [5].

To verify correctness, the proposed architecture is simulated using Altera's ModelSim. A large variety of different memory architectures and parameters are swept, *e.g.* bypassing, memory depth, data width, number of reading or writing ports, and simulated in batch, each with over million random memory access cycles.

All different multi-ported design modules were implemented using Altera's Quartus II on Altera's Stratix V 5SGXMA5N1F45C1 device. This is a high-performance device with 185k ALMs, 370k ALUTs, 2304 M20K blocks and 1064 I/O pins.

We performed a general sweep and tested all combinations of configurations of the following parameters:

- Writing ports (n_W): 2, 3 and 4 writing ports.

- Reading ports (n_R): 3, 4, 5 and 6 reading ports.

- Memory depth (d): 16 and 32 K-lines.

- Data width (w): 8, 16, and 32 bits.

- Bypassing: No bypassing, single-stage and two-stages.

Following this, we analyzed the full set of results. In this paper, we omit many of the in-between settings because they behaved as one might expect to see via interpolation of the endpoints.

Figure 14 plots the maximum frequency derived from Altera's Quartus II STA at 0.9V and temperature of 0 °C. The results show a higher Fmax for binary/one-hot coded I-LVT compared to XOR-based approach for all design cases. With 3 or more writing ports, the one-hot-coded I-LVT supports a higher frequency compared to all other design styles. Compared to the XOR-based approach, the one-hot-coded I-LVT improves Fmax by 38% on average for all tested design configurations, while the maximum Fmax improvement is 76%.

Figure 15 (top) plots the number of Altera's M20K blocks used to implement each multi-ported RAM configuration. The proposed binary/one-hot-coded I-LVT consumes the least BRAM blocks in all cases. The average reduction of the best of binary/one-hot-coded I-LVT compared to XOR-based approach is 19% for all tested design configurations, while it can reach 44% for specific configurations. The difference of consumed Altera's M20Ks between binary-coded I-LVT and one-hot-coded I-LVT is less than 6%. Both I-LVT methods make a significant improvement in BRAM consumption, but binary-coded I-LVT consumes the least BRAMs for more than 3 writing ports. To clarify the difference in

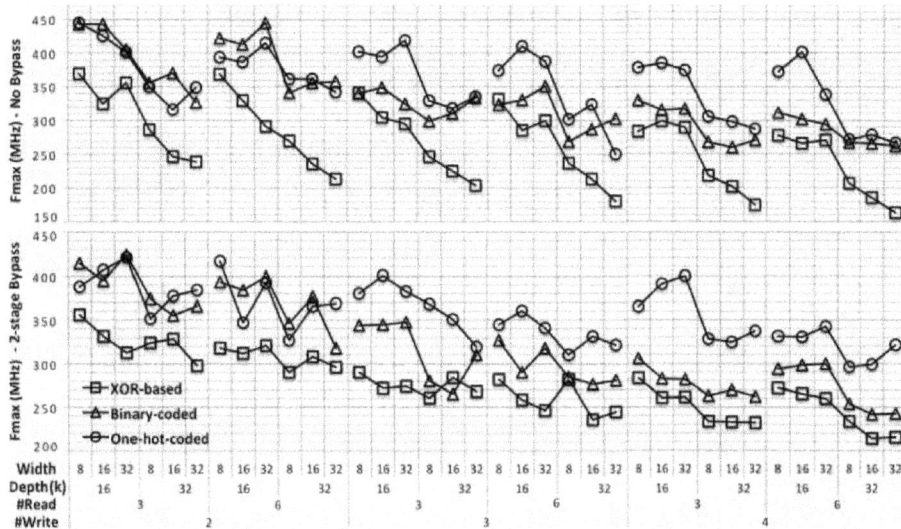

Figure 14. Fmax (MHz) T=0C (top) No bypass (bottom) Two-stage bypass.

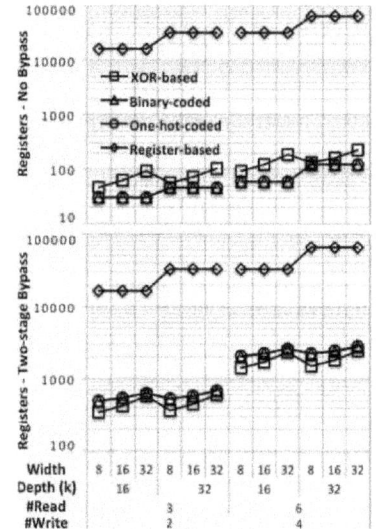

Figure 16. Registers (top) no-bypass (bottom) two-stage bypass.

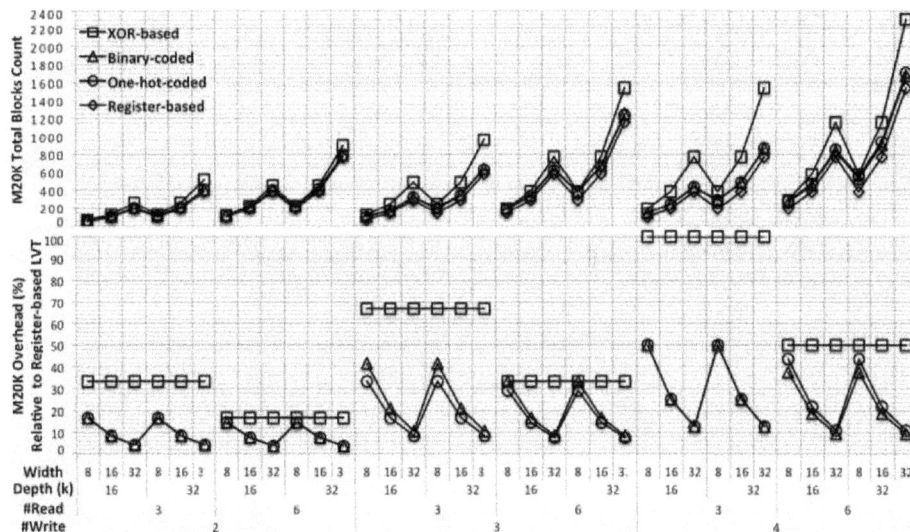

Figure 15. M20K blocks (top) total count (bottom) overhead percentage relative to register-based LVT.

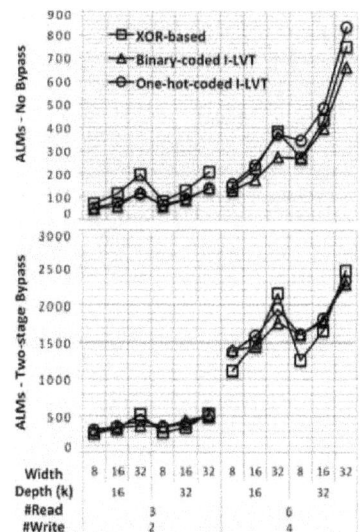

Figure 17. ALMs (top) no-bypass (bottom) two-stage bypass.

BRAM consumption, Figure 15 (bottom) shows the percentage of BRAM overhead above the register-based LVT, which uses the fewest possible BRAMS overall. The XOR-based design consumes more BRAMs in all cases, up to 100% more than the register-based LVT. On the other hand, I-LVT-based methods consume only 12.5% more BRAMs in the case of 32-bit wide memories.

The number of registers required for various designs and bypassing styles is shown in Figure 16. The I-LVT-based methods consume fewer registers compared to the XOR-based method for no bypassing or single-stage bypass cases. For two-stage bypassing, the I-LVT based methods must bypass the data banks, hence the register consumption goes higher than the XOR-based method. However, the register consumption of the register-based LVT method is the highest overall and can be three orders of magnitude higher since it is directly proportional to memory depth. Furthermore, some register-based LVT configurations failed to synthesize on our Stratix V with 185k ALMs.

Figure 17 shows the number of ALMs consumed by each design with different bypassing methods. Single-stage bypassing consumes more ALMs than the non-bypassed version due to address comparators and data muxes. On the other hand, two-stage bypassing requires an additional address comparator and a wider mux; hence it consumes more ALMs than a single-stage bypass. In all bypass modes, as memory data width goes higher, the XOR-based method consumes more ALM's than the I-LVT methods due to wider XOR gates.

Since the register-based LVT approach is not feasible with the provided deep memory test-cases, the register-based LVT trends are derived analytically from Table 3 and 4 and not from experimental results. Hence, the register-based LVT trend was added as a reference baseline to Figure 15 and 16 only.

6. CONCLUSIONS AND FURTHER DIRECTIONS

In this paper, we have proposed the use of an invalidation-based live-value-table, or I-LVT, to build modular SRAM-based multi-ported memories. The I-LVT generalizes and replaces two prior techniques, the LVT and XOR-based approaches. A general I-LVT is described, along with two specific implementations: binary-coded and one-hot-coded. Both methods are purely SRAM based. A detailed analysis and comparison of resource consumption of the suggested methods and previous methods is provided. The original LVT approach can use an infeasible number of registers. Unlike the LVT, the I-LVT register usage is not directly proportional to memory depth; hence it requires magnitudes fewer registers. Furthermore, the proposed I-LVT method can reduce BRAM consumption up to 44% and improve Fmax by up to 76% compared to the previous XOR-based approach. The one-hot-coded I-LVT method exhibits the highest Fmax, while keeping BRAM consumption within 6% of the minimal required BRAM count. Meanwhile, the binary-coded I-LVT uses fewer BRAMs than the one-hot coded when there are more than 3 write ports.

A fully parameterized and generic Verilog implementation of the suggested methods is provided as open source hardware [5]. As future work, the suggested multi-ported memories can be tested with various other FPGA vendors' tools and devices. Furthermore, these methods can also be tested for ASIC implementation using dual-ported RAMs as building blocks, and compared against memory compiler results. Also, to improve Fmax, time-borrowing techniques can be utilized. The goal would be to recover the frequency drop due to the multi-ported RAM additional logic, feedback and bank selection logic. One possible approach uses shifted clocks to provide more reading and writing time [17]. However, adapting this method to multi-ported memories is not trivial due to internal timing paths across the I-LVT.

7. ACKNOWLEDGMENTS

The authors would like to thank Altera for donations of hardware and software, as well as NSERC for funding.

8. REFERENCES

[1] J.H. Tseng and K. Asanovic, "Banked multiported register files for high-frequency superscalar microprocessors," *Int'l Symp. on Computer Architecture (ISCA)*, May 2003, pp. 62–71.

[2] J.A. Fisher, "Very Long Instruction Word architectures and the ELI-512," *Int'l Sym. on Comp. Arch. (ISCA)*, 11(3), June 1983.

[3] E.S. Fetzer and J.T Orton, "A fully-bypassed 6-issue integer datapath and register file on an Itanium microprocessor," *IEEE Int'l Solid-State Circuits Conf.*, vol. 1, Feb. 2002, pp. 420–478.

[4] H. Bajwa and X. Chen, "Low-Power High-Performance and Dynamically Configured Multi-Port Cache Memory Architecture," *Int'l Conf. on Elec. Eng.*, Apr. 2007, pp. 1–6.

[5] http://www.ece.ubc.ca/~lemieux/downloads/

[6] B.A. Chappell, T.I Chappell, M.K. Ebcioglu, and S.E. Schuster, "Virtual multi-port RAM employing multiple accesses during single machine cycle," *U.S. Patent 5 542 067*, Jul. 30, 1996.

[7] H. Yokota, "Multiport memory system," *US Patent 4 930 066*, May 29, 1990.

[8] Ditlow *et al.*, "A 4R2W register file for a 2.3GHz wire-speed POWER™ processor with double-pumped write operation," *IEEE Int'l Solid-State Circuits Conf.*, Feb. 2011, pp. 256–258.

[9] R.E. Kessler, "The Alpha 21264 microprocessor," *IEEE Micro*, vol. 19, no. 2, pp. 24–36, Mar./Apr. 1999.

[10] H.J. Mattausch, "Hierarchical N-port memory architecture based on 1-port memory cells," *European Solid-State Circuits Conference (ESSCIRC '97)*, Sept. 1997, pp. 348–351.

[11] J. Weixing, S. Feng, Q. Baojun Qiao, and S. Hong, "Multi-port Memory Design Methodology Based on Block Read and Write," *IEEE Int'l Conference on Control and Automation)*, May 2007.

[12] Z. Wang Zuo, "An Intelligent Multi-Port Memory," *Journal of Computers*, vol. 5, no. 3, pp. 471–478, Mar 2010.

[13] D. Alpert and D. Avnon, "Architecture of the Pentium microprocessor," *IEEE Micro*, 13(3), pp. 11–21, June 1993.

[14] C.E. LaForest and J.G. Steffan, "Efficient Multi-ported Memories for FPGAs," *ACM/SIGDA Int'l Symp. on Field-Programmable Gate Arrays (FPGA '10)*, Feb. 2010.

[15] C.E. LaForest, M.G. Liu, E.R. Rapati, and J.G. Steffan, "Multi-ported memories for FPGAs via XOR," *ACM Int'l Symp. on Field-Programmable. Gate Arrays (FPGA '12)*, Feb. 2012, pp. 209–218.

[16] Altera Corporation, *Stratix V Device Handbook*, June 2011.

[17] A. Brant, A. Abdelhadi, A. Severance, G. Lemieux, "Pipeline Frequency Boosting: Hiding Dual-Ported Block RAM Latency using Intentional Clock Skew," *IEEE International Conference on Field-Programmable Technology (FPT)*, December 2012.

Revisiting And-Inverter Cones

Grace Zgheib[†]   Liqun Yang[‡]   Zhihong Huang[‡]   David Novo[†]

Hadi Parandeh-Afshar[†]   Haigang Yang[‡]   Paolo Ienne[†]

[†]Ecole Polytechnique Fédérale de Lausanne (EPFL)
School of Computer and Communication Sciences, 1015 Lausanne, Switzerland
{grace.zgheib, david.novobruna, hadi.parandehafshar, paolo.ienne}@epfl.ch

[‡]Chinese Academy of Sciences
Institute of Electronics, Beijing, China
yangliqun10@mail.ucas.ac.cn, {huangzhihong, yanghg}@mail.ie.ac.cn

ABSTRACT

And-Invert Cones (AICs) *have been suggested as an alternative to the ubiquitous* Look-Up Tables (LUTs) *used in commercial FPGAs. The original article suggesting the new architecture made some untested assumptions on the circuitry needed to implement AIC architectures and did not develop completely the toolset necessary to assess comprehensively the idea. In this paper, we pick up the architecture that some of us proposed in the original AIC paper and try to implement it as thoroughly as we can afford. We build all components for the logic cluster at transistor level in a 40 nm technology as well as a LUT-based architecture inspired by Altera's Stratix IV. We first determine that the characteristics of our LUT-based architecture are reasonably similar to those of the commercial counterpart. Then, we compare the AIC architecture to the baseline on a number of benchmarks, and we find a few difficulties that had been overlooked before. We thus explore other design possibilities around the original design point and show their detailed impact. Finally, we discuss how the very structure of current logic clusters seems not perfectly appropriate for getting the best out of AICs and conclude that, even though they are not confirmed as an immediate blessing today, AICs still offer rich research opportunities.*

Categories and Subject Descriptors

B.6.1 [**Logic Design**]: Design Styles—*Logic arrays, Combinatorial Logic*; B.7.1 [**Integrated Circuits**]: Types and Design Styles—*Gate arrays*

Keywords

FPGA Logic Block, And-Inverter Cones, Transistor Design

1. INTRODUCTION

Field-Programmable Gate Arrays (FPGAs) are an important class of semiconductors with a tangible and growing market share. The key of their future growth is in the capability of the vendors to improve their effectiveness (e.g., the ability to run user designs at higher speeds) and their efficiency (e.g., run the same user design at a considerable lower silicon real-estate cost). Vendors and researchers alike actively work on the architecture of FPGAs, and seldom two generations of devices by the same vendors have shared the very same architecture. Yet, some important architectural elements have now been constant for many years, and among them the use, at least in all widely available commercial devices, of *Look-Up Tables (LUTs)* as the basic logic element.

A couple of years ago, some researchers argued that the costly versatility of LUTs goes wasted in most cases when the logic synthesis process uses representations other than the classic algebraic one [4]. Inspired by some modern synthesizers representing circuits as networks of AND-invert operations [8], Parandeh-Afshar et al. suggested replacing LUTs with a new logic element in the form of a binary tree of AND gates with conditional inversion. This new logic element is called *And-Inverter Cone (AIC)* [10] and its configuration bits would decide the function of a specific AIC by selecting whether the output of each AND gate is inverted or not. The authors argued that the similarity of the logic element to the representation used for synthesis would guarantee an efficient mapping and somehow compensate for the lack of versatility of AICs compared to LUTs.

The original paper on AICs claimed that hybrid FPGAs made of a blend of AICs and LUTs could reduce delay up to approximately 30% and area by some 15%. These results were obtained on a set of relatively small benchmarks, all of them combinational. Perhaps more importantly, the modeling of the new logic cluster was somewhat rough and no real global routing results were presented, the overall routing contribution being estimated through statistical parameters extrapolated from LUT-only experiments. Some aspects of the architecture have been refined in successive papers without really addressing the fundamental modeling questions [12, 11]. We think that a more comprehensive analysis of AICs is worth it, before they can be considered as serious alternative to LUTs.

This paper attempts a more thorough analysis of AIC architectures close to the suggested original design [10]. To this end, in Section 2 we develop at the transistor-level precise models of both a LUT logic cluster (primarily to benchmark our design ability and to establish a fair reference) and an AIC logic cluster. We compare the resulting designs with the original expectations of the authors and notice a few divergences, leading to some exploration of the design space. Section 3 explains how we use the data collected in the previous section. We run a tangibly larger set of benchmarks, not limited to combinational ones and including some large designs. Since results are not necessarily what we would expect, we use them to drive some changes in the architecture, and analyze which aspects of AICs remain promising and which ones somewhat disappointing; all this is covered in Section 4. Finally, we draw our conclusion on the perspectives for AICs in Section 5.

2. LUT- AND AIC-BASED CLUSTERS

In this section we build the components that will make up our architectures: we start by presenting our design methodology and we then use it to produce the building blocks for the LUT-based reference logic cluster. We then pause in Section 2.3 to compare our results with common models used in the literature, and the results are a mixed blessing; we discuss why we think that the differences do not compromise our final results. In the following subsections, we attack the components of the AIC-based logic cluster and in Section 2.7 we discuss how our findings relate to the original AIC paper [10]. We conclude this part by exploring the design space, at transistor-level, of critical components.

2.1 Full-Custom Design Methodology

Although the original AIC paper contained some analysis of the critical path [10], no comprehensive design experiments at the transistor level have been performed. This is one of the main contributions of this paper.

All the components needed for our designs and described in the upcoming sections have been implemented in a commercial 40 nm CMOS technology. The circuits have been developed full-custom at the transistor level in the Cadence Design Platform Virtuoso. Speed characterization has been performed by simulating the circuits with Cadence simulation tool Spectre using the transistor models provided by the foundry. We report timing data in the typical corner (typical process, room temperature, nominal voltage). Unless specified differently in the following sections, transistor sizes are optimized for speed. Approximately, this means that we usually increase the size of critical transistors until we observe only marginal gains in speed. Although not strongly formalized, we apply this strategy consistently on all our functional blocks. We mainly use normal V_t transistors and low V_t transistors. The sizing of all transistors is performed manually.

Of course, the effort needed prevented us from layouting the circuits we developed. The use of front-end data has two impacts: on the measurements of timing and of area. Concerning timing, we used a number of other designs for another FPGA architecture we have designed (with complete layout and back-annotation): our experience suggests that, on average, paths degrade by a factor of $1.6\times$ after layout, and thus we have corrected our front-end data by applying the same factor. Concerning area, for consistence

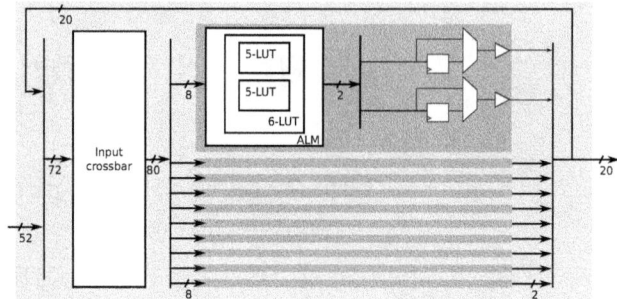

Figure 1: Reference LUT-based logic cluster. It is composed of ten fracturable 6-LUTs and all outputs can be registered; an input crossbar creates some local routing network.

with the numbers reported by VPR, we have applied the same classic methodology [2]. Specifically, we measure area using *minimum-width transistor areas* (or T_{mw}) as the unit, assume as usual that the die size is determined by the active area, and estimate the area (in minimum-width transistor areas) occupied in the actual layout by each transistor T as

$$\text{Area}(T) = 0.5 + \frac{\text{Drive Strength}(T)}{2 \times \text{Drive Strength}(T_{Minimum-Width})}. \tag{1}$$

As explained in Section 3.2, we use our measured values to build appropriate architecture files for VPR. It should be noted, though, that we restricted ourselves to the design of all of the logic clusters that we use and describe in detail in the next sections; on the other hand, we rely on existing architectural descriptions, provided with the *Verilog-to-Routing (VTR)* toolflow [13], for what concerns the characterization of the global routing. Indeed, these descriptions, widely used in the research community, exist and target commercial technology nodes similar to ours.

2.2 Reference LUT-Based Logic Cluster

For our reference LUT-based cluster we chose to loosely mimic the Altera Stratix-IV architecture. The logic cluster of this architecture, shown in Figure 1, was implemented drawing inspiration from the details provided in the Altera datasheets [1] and other descriptions in the literature. Each cluster, or *Logic Array Block (LAB)*, is composed of ten *Adaptive Logic Modules (ALMs)* having eight inputs each. The ALM is the basic logic block of the Stratix-IV architecture and can be configured as either one 6-input LUT, or *6-LUT*, or two 5-LUTs with some input sharing. The output(s) of the LUT(s) are used either as combinational outputs or sequential outputs, using two registers.

In addition to the LUTs and registers, the ALM architecture of the Stratix-IV includes two dedicated full adders and a carry chain used to implement arithmetic functions. These adders and carry chain, along with all related multiplexers, were not included in the implemented reference cluster to provide a more accurate area to delay comparison between the AIC-based and the LUT-based architectures, since carry chains are not used in our experiments.

Each LUT-based logic cluster has 52 inputs from the global interconnect and 20 outputs from the LUTs. The input crossbar receives the 52 external inputs and the 20 outputs from the LUTs, and has 80 outputs to feed the ten ALMs. It is implemented as a half-populated crossbar with

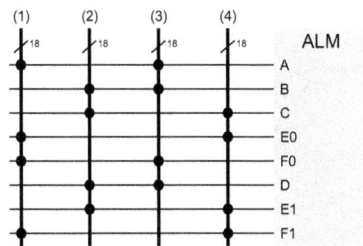

Figure 2: Topology of the LAB input crossbar. The half-populated crossbar has 72 inputs and 80 outputs, connecting the LAB input to the ALM inputs using a specific pattern.

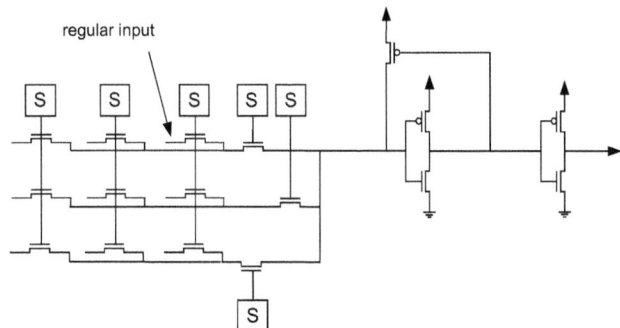

Figure 3: Two-level multiplexer [6]. All our crossbars are implemented with this type of two-level structure (without any fast inputs). Their topology differs only in the size of the $h \times v$ first-level array. The LUT-based logic cluster crossbar has a 6×6 structure.

the topology shown in Figure 2 [9]. It may be noted here that the crossbar in the original AICs paper was fully populated [10].

The eighty 36-input multiplexers of the crossbar are implemented as a two-level structure, similar to the ones used in Stratix-II [6], as indicated in Figure 3. Using the optimization criteria mentioned in Section 2.1, the transistors of the first and second layers result in transistors around 600 nm wide. The transistors in the multiplexers of the LUTs are usually somewhat larger than 600 nm except the last level which are significantly larger. These transistor sizes are not fundamentally different from those which could be obtained from recently published automated transistor sizing techniques [3].

2.3 How Good Is Our Reference?

The natural question at this point is whether our model of LUT-based cluster has any resemblance, quantitatively, to the commercial architecture that inspired it. We will report all numbers on the LUT-based cluster in Section 2.7, but anticipate some key figures in Table 1. We took as a reference numbers extracted from the standard VTR architecture files [13] which are mainly based on simulation data and approximations. Firstly, we notice that some critical values match remarkably well, such as the 6-LUT delay or the total cluster area. Besides these, there are a number of parameters which are different but within what appear to us reasonable margins (for instance, if one considers the sum of setup time and clock to output of the flip-flops the difference is around 50% which is significant but, we believe, not

		Our	[13]
6-LUT		298 ps	261 ps
FF	T_setup	192 ps	66 ps
	T_clock_to_Q	96 ps	124 ps
Mux	comb. inputs	224 ps	25 ps
	seq. inputs	163 ps	45 ps
Input crossbar		192 ps	95 ps
Cluster area		53,600 T_{mw}	53,894 T_{mw}

Table 1: Reference LUT-based cluster vs. Stratix-IV. We compare here some key parameters of our reference design with some available model of Stratix-IV [13].

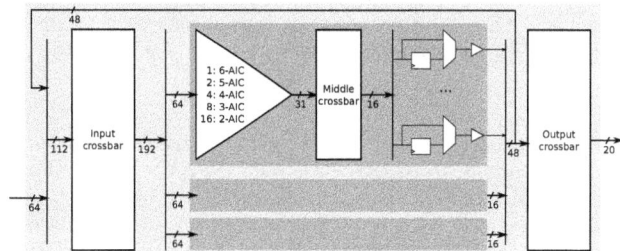

Figure 4: AIC-based cluster with three 6-AICs. The cluster architecture is unmodified from the original AIC paper [10].

truly worrying). Finally, there are some parameters which are unjustifiably different: the output multiplexer delays are very much slower in our design. We believe that our model contains a buffer to drive the highly loaded cluster outputs whereas the competing model does not: 25 ps are certainly sufficient only for a simple multiplexer in a 40 nm node. We believe that such differences do not jeopardize the quality of the results of Section 4, though. Firstly, the key computational element is reasonably well matched in our model, and thus does not suggest any suspicious low-quality implementation of LUTs that would bias the results in favor of AICs. Secondly, all worst discrepancies correspond to components which either exist practically identical in the AIC cluster or which are redesigned for it following the very same methodology and circuit structure. In other words, if we are making a mistake, the error is independent of the cluster type and is systematic across the simulated architectures: it should thus bring only a minimal bias to our conclusions.

2.4 AIC-Based Cluster

The AIC-based logic cluster proposed in Parandeh-Afshar et al. [10] has three 6-level AICs (or *6-AIC*) with 64 inputs and 31 outputs. Figure 4 shows a block diagram of the AIC-based logic cluster. A small crossbar, referred to as the *middle crossbar*, is placed at the end of each 6-AIC to select only 16 out of the 31 outputs. These 16 outputs can either be used as combinational outputs or sequential outputs using dedicated registers, exactly as in the LUT-based cluster. In order to maintain the same number of outputs per cluster as in the reference architecture, an additional crossbar, referred to as *output crossbar*, selects 20 cluster outputs out of the total 3×16 signals, registered or non-registered, coming from the middle crossbar or the registers.

The cluster has 64 inputs—the original paper assumed that the reference Stratix-III logic cluster also has 64

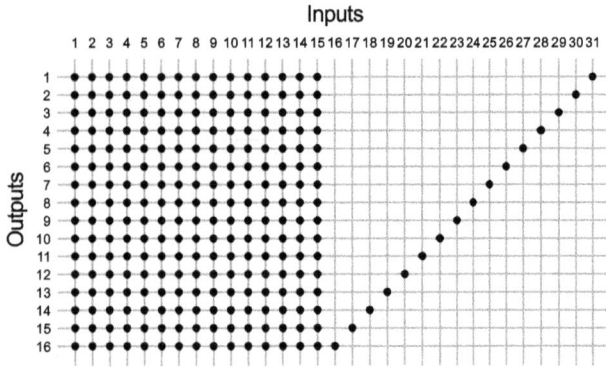

Figure 5: AIC-based logic cluster middle crossbar. The connectivity of the middle crossbar is that of a full-capacity minimal crossbar, but the implementation is as in Figure 3.

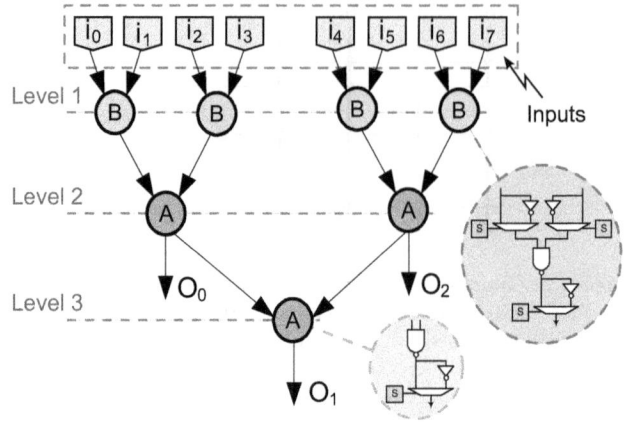

Figure 6: AIC logic element. The enhanced AIC architecture with programmable inversion at the inputs of the first level nodes, reproduced from the paper which introduced the improvement [12].

inputs—coming from global routing and 48 feedback connections coming from the AICs selected outputs. A third crossbar, the *input crossbar*, connects the 64 cluster inputs and the 48 feedbacks—112 in total—to the 192 AICs inputs. (A small detail is that, due to the symmetry of the AND gates at the input of the 6-AIC, only 111 inputs are implemented, but this has hardly any impact on area and delay.)

2.5 Topology of the Crossbars

The three crossbars of the AIC-based logic cluster are also all implemented as two-level multiplexers (see Figure 3). The basic implementation of the input crossbar is fully-populated with a 14×8 first level array. Our transistor-size optimization results in very similar transistors as the input crossbar of the LUT-based cluster: transistors are also about 600 nm wide. We considered two additional input crossbars: a 75%-populated sparse crossbar and a half-populated crossbar built with the same transistors sizes. The 75% and 50% crossbars are referred to using the *75p* and *50p* notations, respectively, in the experimental results. Note that Parandeh-Afshar et al. used a 75%-populated crossbar [10].

The middle and output crossbars have the connectivity of full-capacity minimal crossbars. Full-capacity minimal crossbars, or simply *minimal crossbars*, have fewer switches than full crossbars but maintain the full-capacity property. This property guarantees that any set of inputs that does not exceed the number of outputs can be connected to all outputs; however, the order of the outputs cannot be fully controlled [5]. Figure 5 shows the connectivity of the middle crossbar, with 31 inputs and 16 outputs. It is implemented with multiplexers with $in - out + 1 = 31 - 16 + 1 = 16$ inputs, in a 4×4 array of large transistors: 1 μm in width. The output crossbar has 48 inputs and 20 outputs. It is implemented with 29-input two-level multiplexers whose input array is 6×5; the transistors are also 600 nm wide as in the input crossbar.

2.6 AIC Logic Element

The And-Inverter Cone was introduced as a full binary tree of AND gates with programmable output inversion [10]. Then an enhanced AIC architecture was proposed as a shadow logic, placed behind LUTs [12]. Irrespective of its architectural placement, this enhanced design adds to the initial AIC architecture programmable inversions at the inputs of the first level nodes, as shown in Figure 6. Naturally, allowing the inputs to be inverted internally uses more compact AICs with less depth and helps reducing the number of clusters used per circuit. We designed the logic element using the enhanced AIC architecture. The optional inversion is implemented literally with an inverter and a multiplexer. Transistor sizes vary between 240 nm and 1 μm in width.

2.7 The Good, the Bad and the Ugly

Table 2 summarizes the two clusters designed and the break out in the different elements. There is some good, as expected: the AICs are not very significantly slower than the LUTs and yet are much smaller. They contribute for a quite small fraction to the cluster size (less than 10%), suggesting that even if they were not sufficiently well utilized, more could be added, allowing more logic to be packed within the same cluster, or that their structure could be made more complex at a very limited cost.

There is some bad, or at least surprise, in that the delay of the crossbars is only moderately variable with their size, which is a significant penalty in the case of the middle crossbar. Essentially, this reflects the fact that the topology of the crossbars is the same and, to a good extent, optimizing transistor sizes only helps compensating the different parasitic capacitances.

But, finally, there is something really ugly: the input crossbar, which was anticipated by the original authors to be the dominant component of the cluster area-wise, is in fact humongous; not only it takes 80% of the cluster, but it is itself almost twice the size of the complete LUT cluster itself. Of course, this is also due to the fact that the crossbar is full, but this is not the whole story: even with a 75% populated crossbar (80% of the area, approximately) or half-populated (60% of the area), we are far from having two clusters of similar size as we originally expected, and the AIC-based cluster remains at best 60% larger than the LUT-based cluster.

2.8 Exploring Transistor Sizing

From Table 2, the area of the AIC-based cluster is about $2.3\times$ that of the LUT-based cluster. This area difference

		AICs		LUTs	
		Area (T$_{mw}$)	Delay (ps)	Area (T$_{mw}$)	Delay (ps)
Crossbars	Input crossbar	102,393.6 (80.85%)	203.2	12,330 (22.4%)	192
	Middle crossbar	7,310.4 (5.77%)	118.4	-	-
	Output crossbar	3,849 (3.04%)	166.4	-	-
Logic	5-LUT	-	-	24,550	302.08
	6-LUT	-	-	(44.6%)	298.4
	Adder	-	-	1,440 (2.6%)	-
	6-AIC	9,870.21 (7.79%) [3 AICs]	449.6	-	-
	5-AIC		388.8	-	-
	4-AIC		318.4	-	-
	3-AIC		252.8	-	-
	2-AIC		184	-	-
FF Mux Buff	Tclk2Q	3,223.2 (2.55%)	171.2 17.6 80	16,720 (30.4%)	96 193 (avg)
	Total	126,646.41		55,040	

Table 2: Delay and area comparison between the AIC and LUT Clusters.

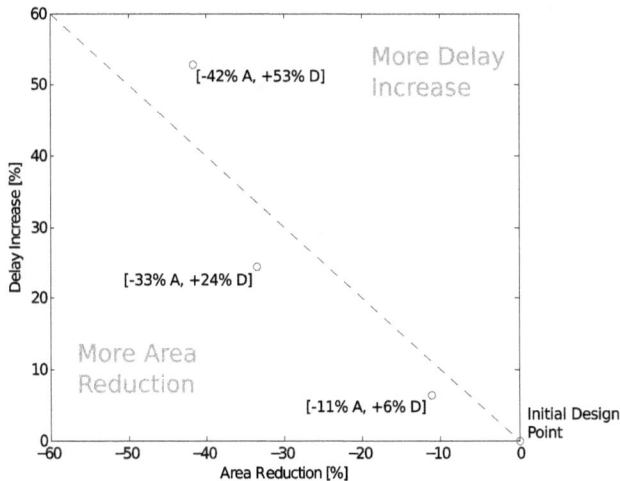

Figure 7: Transistor sizing delay vs. area trade-off. Different transistor sizes in the AIC cluster's input crossbar result in sensibly different and potentially interesting Pareto solutions.

is mainly due to the AIC input crossbar—accounting for more than 80% of the cluster area; thus, we decided to go back to the transistor-level circuits and see if other design points would make sense by trading off delay for area. Figure 7 shows three other optimization points with their relative area and delay values. Clearly, there exists other design points of potential interest: the second smallest (68,140 T$_{mw}$, 252.8 ps) saves a significant area (33% area reduction) for an additional delay (24% delay increase, roughly 50 ps) which is fairly small compared to the total combinatorial cluster delay (of the order of the nanosecond). Accordingly, we decided to use also this design point in our experiments and will be referring to it throughout this paper as *68k*.

3. EXPERIMENTAL SETUP

Now that we have all circuit elements we need, we can proceed to assemble them and compare the two architectures on benchmarks. In this section we explain how we run the experiments of Section 4. In particular, we explain first how we performed technology mapping and then we explain the various choices we have made to create architecture description files for VPR, in order to perform packing, placement, and routing.

3.1 AIC Technology Mapper

We use the AIC technology mapper described in Parandeh-Afshar et al. [10] and include a final area recovery pass [12]. The mapping includes basically three phases. Initially, the input AIG circuit description is forward traversed—from inputs to outputs—generating for each AIG node all the possible cuts, both for an AIC and a LUT mapping. Then, the circuit is backward traversed selecting for the visible nodes the cuts that are optimal for delay, and amongst those, the one leading to a smaller area. Note that after having chosen a cut for a node, this cut will cover all the AIG nodes between its inputs and output. The inputs become visible nodes and the process is repeated until the whole circuit is covered. However, this covering has prioritized delay over area in all the paths of the circuit, including the non critical ones. Accordingly, we implement a final area recovery phase to choose area optimal cuts for the paths that are not critical. The area optimal cuts still need to satisfy the constraint that the relaxed path cannot include more logic levels than the critical path obtained in the previous phase.

3.2 VPR Architecture Files

After technology mapping, the *AAPack* [7] tool of VPR is used to pack the mapped logic blocks into clusters of the predefined FPGA architectures. Thus, each FPGA architecture was modeled using the XML format. The basic logic blocks are defined along with their respective configuration modes

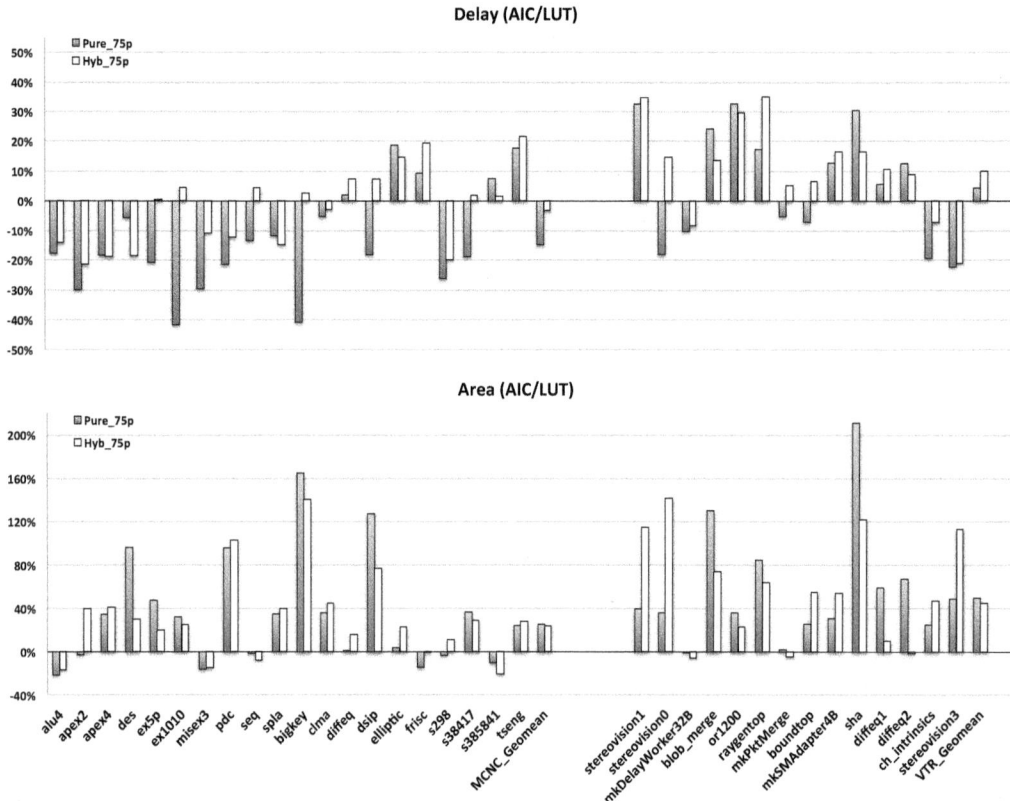

Figure 8: Speedup and area reduction of reference architectures. Reproducing the results of both reference architectures [10] shows that the pure AIC architecture has a more direct effect on the speedup of the MCNC benchmarks than the hybrid architecture, with respect to the LUT architecture. This speed up comes at the expense of around 25% area increase. However, the performance of both these architectures deteriorates on the VTR benchmarks.

and delay metrics. All logic delays and local routing delays were taken from the transistor level implementation, as reported in Table 2. Starting with the LUT-based architecture, used as reference, the Stratix-IV cluster is designed in which LUTs are configured as two 5-LUTs or one 6-LUT and the crossbar is half populated as described in Section 2.2.

The basic AIC architecture is modeled as described in Section 2.4, where three 6-AICs are used as basic logic blocks. The fracturable nature of the AIC is explicitly defined in the XML file by allowing multiple configurations of the same cone. The hybrid architecture file is created by combining the two cluster definitions of the LUT and AIC architectures, respectively into one XML file. The LUT clusters are placed at every third column of the FPGA grid. The different areas of the LUT and AIC clusters are accounted for by specifying the relative size of the AIC cluster with respect to the LUT, and the length of the global routing is adapted accordingly.

For the first comparison between AICs and LUTs [10], the MCNC benchmark set [14] was used to run experiments. More precisely, and due to some tool flow limitations, the benchmarks of the original paper were limited to the biggest 10 combinatorial circuits of the MCNC set. However, in this work, we were able to overcome these limitations and test the performance of the AICs on sequential circuits. Furthermore, we also run our experiments on the more recent set of benchmarks provided with the VTR tool flow. These

VTR benchmarks are bigger and use multipliers and memory blocks. For this purpose, we updated our architecture files to include the multipliers and RAM blocks that we took from the sample architectures of VTR. Some of the biggest benchmarks take too long to pack and were omitted from the experiments.

To compute the area of each packed and routed circuit, we are relying on the VPR built-in estimation of the routing area, while the logic area is computed by counting the number of blocks, for each block type, and multiplying it by its respective area.

All architectural files can be downloaded here:

http://lap.epfl.ch/downloads/fpga14

4. EXPLORING ARCHITECTURES

We finally report our results through VPR over all benchmarks. We start by running experiments for the basic AIC architecture as proposed by the original authors and we repeat some of the design explorations they originally suggested. Then, analyzing our use of the resources, we explore a few neighboring design points which do not change radically the structure of the AIC cluster but try to minimize the problems of the straightforward architecture. We conclude this section with some analysis of what we think works well with AICs and what needs further research or dramatic improvement.

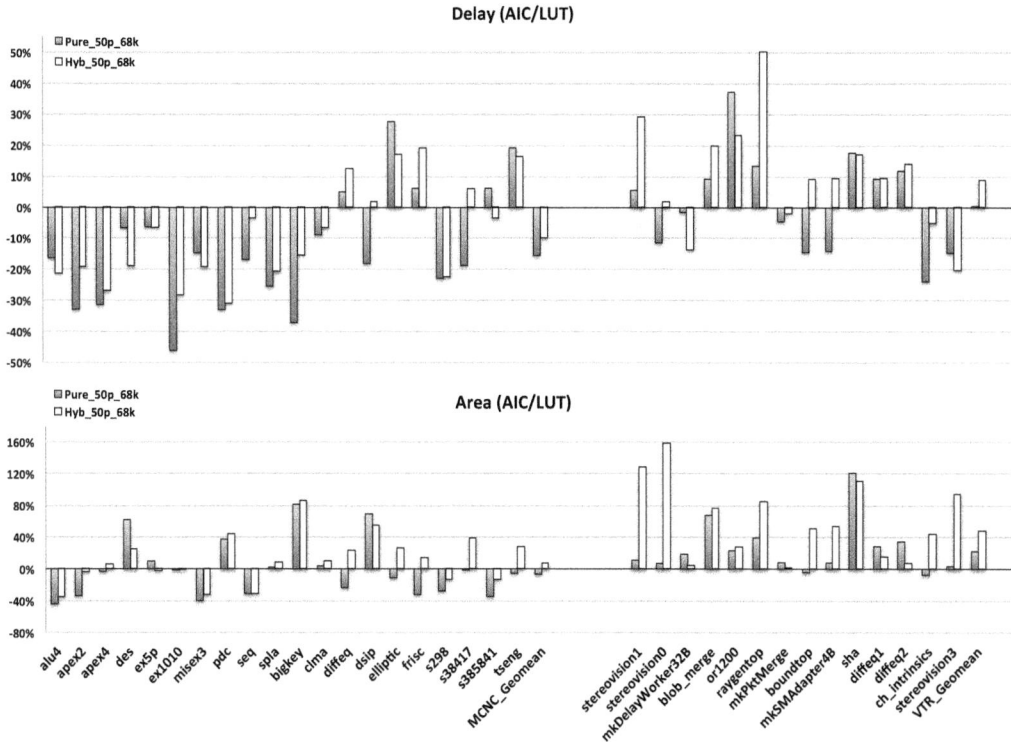

Figure 9: Effects of the input crossbar's architectural modifications on delay and area. Decreasing the population of the input crossbar to 50% and choosing an optimization point that reduces the area of the crossbar, improves the performance of both pure AIC and hybrid architecture. The best speedup and area results are achieved using the pure AIC architecture when considering only the MCNC benchmarks.

4.1 Plain-Vanilla AIC Architecture

In the first experiment, the benchmarks are mapped, packed, placed and routed onto three different architectures: (1) the reference architecture, which is made of LUT-based logic clusters such as the one depicted in Figure 1; (2) the pure AIC architecture as originally described, which is made of AIC-based logic clusters such as the one depicted in Figure 4; and (3) the hybrid LUT-AIC architecture, which combines LUT and AIC logic clusters in a ratio of 1 to 3, respectively. Throughout the experimental setup and results sections, we will use *pure* to identify AIC-only architectures and *hybrid* (or *hyb* for short) to refer to mixed LUT-AIC architectures.

Figure 8 shows in the top graph the relative delay of the pure and hybrid architectures with respect to the reference LUT architecture. The results are separated per benchmark suite. The MCNC benchmarks, the combinatorial subset which was used in the original AIC paper as well as the sequential subset, show consistent speedups when executed on AICs, especially in the pure architecture. The results show an average speedup of 15% for the pure architecture and a 3% for the hybrid one. However, the subset of VTR benchmarks, which are bigger and make use of memories and DSP blocks, performs generally worse in the AIC architectures than in the reference LUT architecture. In particular, the pure and hybrid architectures achieve a 4% and 10% slow down, respectively.

Moreover, Figure 8 shows in the bottom graph the relative areas (logic and routing areas) corresponding to the same

architectures and benchmarks with respect to the LUT reference architecture. The pure AIC architecture requires on average 25% and 50% more area for the MCNC and VPR benchmarks, respectively. The hybrid architecture requires slightly less area but the overhead is still quite significant. Some benchmarks are particularly big in AICs increasing the area by more than a factor of 3.

In summary, the original AIC architectures only show interesting speedups for a limited set of benchmarks. The main reasons are the rather big crossbars, which increase logic cluster area beyond the reference logic cluster, and the inclusion of bigger size and synchronous benchmarks. In the following, we explore a few AIC architectural variations to try and unleash the AICs' theoretical potential.

4.2 Playing with the Input Crossbar Sparsity

Realizing from Table 2 that the input crossbar contributes to about 80% of the total cluster area, we considered changing the input crossbar in two ways: (1) by reducing its population and making it more sparse, and (2) by changing its optimization so that we gain in area even if it comes at the expense of delay.

Depopulating the input crossbar by reducing the number of used switches, we first explored a 75% sparse crossbar and then a 50% sparse crossbar. Having less switches constrains the packer, making it harder to cluster logic blocks. However, the experiments revealed that such a constraint is still acceptable and promises good results. Moving from a full crossbar to a 50% sparse crossbar reduces the overall cluster

51

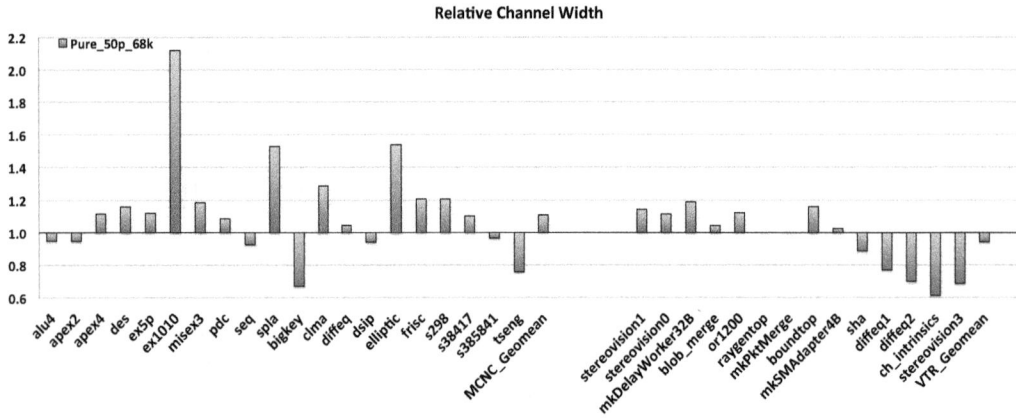

Figure 10: Relative channel width of the pure AIC architecture with an optimized half-populated crossbar, with respect to the reference LUT architecture.

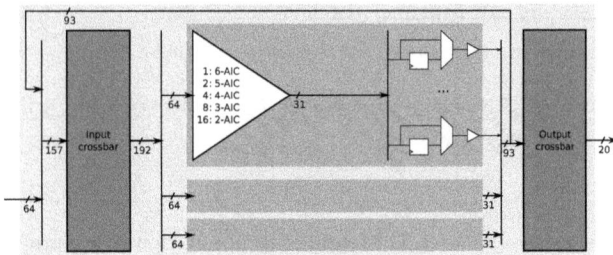

Figure 11: AIC-based cluster without middle crossbar.

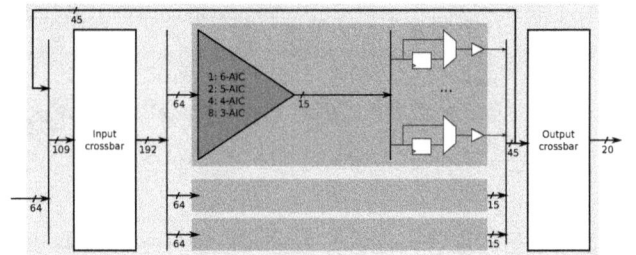

Figure 12: AIC-based cluster without middle crossbar and without outputs for 2-AICs.

area by about 10%. In order to further reduce the cluster area, we explore different optimizations of the input crossbar as mentioned in Section 2.8. From Figure 7, we choose the 68k optimization point where the crossbar size decreases by 33% at the expense of a delay increase of 24% (referred to as 68k).

The results of Figure 9 confirm our intuition since the experiments performed using a 50% sparse input crossbar with the chosen design point reveal to be the most promising: the delay decreases by 16% for the pure AIC architecture and 10% for the hybrid architecture with respect to the reference LUT architecture. For the pure AIC architecture, not only the delay is reduced but also the overall area is reduced by around 7% for the MCNC benchmarks. This particular architecture appears to be the most rewarding in terms of delay and area, especially for the MCNC set.

To gain a sense of the stress the AIC architectures might add on global routing, Figure 10 shows the relative channel width of the pure AIC architecture with 50% sparse crossbar (and 68k optimization point) over the reference LUT architecture. The demand for routing channels depends on the benchmark used, and although on average the channel widths used for AICs and LUTs are comparable, some oddities in the results can be highlighted. For instance, the MCNC benchmarks, which are known to be small, tend to require more channels on AICs than the VTR benchmarks which are rather large and complex. We believe that the nature of the benchmarks directly impact the efficiency with which it can map and pack on AIC clusters.

4.3 Removing the Middle Crossbar

Table 2 suggests that the middle crossbar adds to the delay of the logic path around 166 ps in order to reduce the number of AIC outputs. In this experiment, we remove the middle crossbar trying to gain more in delay at the expense of almost doubling the number of flip-flops and output multiplexers, as shown in Figure 11. However, the experimental results of Figure 13 show that removing the middle crossbar (with a 75% sparse input crossbar designed using the 68k optimization point that trades delay for area) does almost as well as if the middle crossbar were kept and the input crossbar sparsity were reduced to 50%, on average (the results of Section 4.2). Nevertheless, removing the middle crossbar has a bigger impact on the area. It is true that the number of flip-flops and multiplexers doubled; but that is not the main source of area overhead. The feedback connections to the input crossbar as well as the direct connections to the output crossbar doubles, which has a direct impact on the area of the crossbars, the area of the cluster and by that the overall circuit area.

4.4 Limiting the AIC Element Outputs

Limiting the AIC outputs is one possible remedy to the extra area overhead observed after removing the middle crossbar. In this experiment we remove the outputs that exist at the second level of the AICs, which results in a reduction from 31 to 15 in the number of AIC outputs. Figure 12 depicts the corresponding logic cluster architecture. Note that the input and output crossbars are slightly smaller than the

52

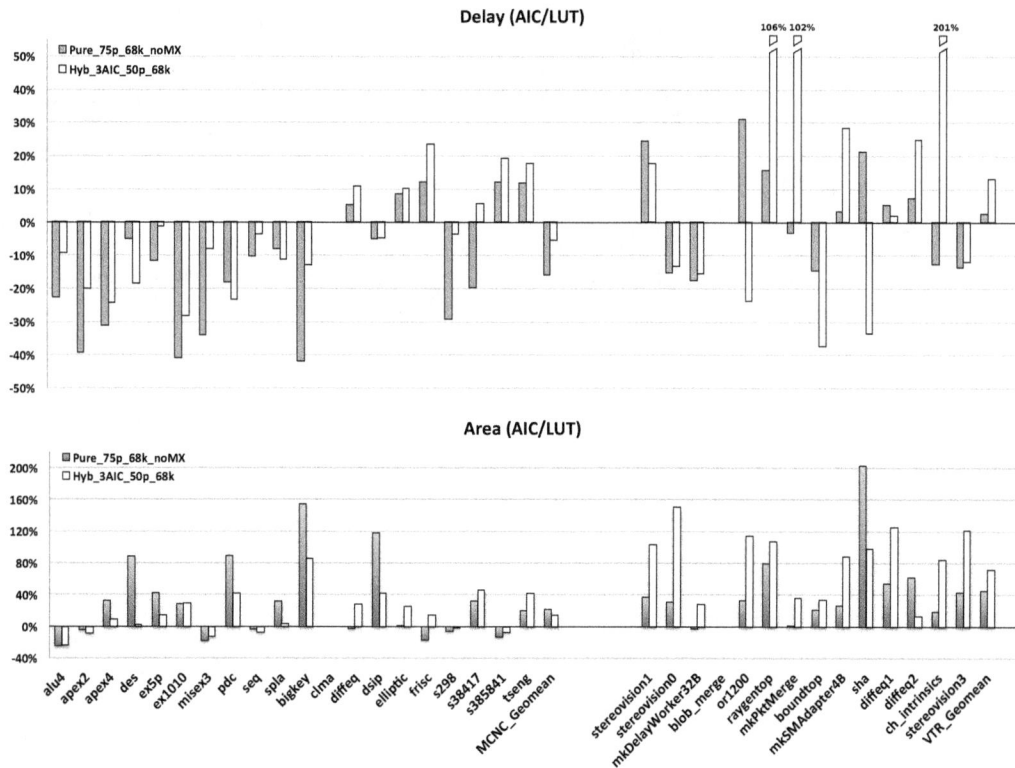

Figure 13: Minimal effects resulting from removing the middle crossbar. To compensate for the middle crossbar either bigger input/output crossbars are used (*Pure_75p_68k_noMX*, Figure 11) or the AIC's second-level outputs are not used (*Hyb_3AIC_50p_68k*, Figure 12).

ones used in the original AIC architecture of Figure 4. Such an architectural change required some modifications in the mapper in order to prevent the use of 2-AICs and restrict the AIC outputs to levels 3 to 6.

Figure 13 shows the relative delay and area of this new architecture (*Hyb_3AIC_50p_68k* in the figure) with respect to the reference LUT architecture. In general, removing the 2-AIC outputs seems detrimental for both area and speed. Often, the logic that would ideally map onto a 2-AIC is now forced to go onto a LUT. This results in some substantial impact on the global routing due to the forced change of clusters. LUT and AIC clusters are located in different columns, thus switching between LUTs and AICs over a small subfunction compromises the locality of the design and introduces major routing overhead.

4.5 What Is Promising and What Is Not

We have seen that despite the theoretical potential of AICs, realizing a logic cluster architecture that enables competitive implementations is far from trivial. We believe that the original work on AICs underestimated the effects of the crossbars, especially in area. We have shown that the circuit area/delay numbers are heavily influenced by the different AIC cluster architectures but also by the area/delay trade-offs played at the component level, as illustrated in Figure 7.

In order to provide further insights on why the AIC performance varies so much depending on the benchmark, Figure 14 details the critical path of four selected benchmarks when running on five different architectures. The *bigkey*

benchmark shows delay advantages in all its AIC executions being an example of a small benchmark with a very short critical path that can fit in about 3 logic blocks. At the opposite end of the spectrum, the *sha* benchmark includes a long critical delay path and shows an increase in delay in all its AIC executions. The reference LUT execution manages to reduce significantly the global routing delay by using very short hops. We suspect that the area increase of the AIC implementations reduces the locality and forces longer global wires, also in the critical path. The *tseng* benchmark is another example that systematically performs poorly in AIC architectures, suffering from the same problem of *sha* despite a much shorter critical path. Finally, the *boundtop* benchmark shows speedups for the pure AIC architecture while it slows down in the hybrid one. For this benchmark the penalty of moving from LUT to AIC clusters and vice versa—each type of cluster is placed in different columns, not always contiguous—overcomes the benefits in logic delay.

Further analysis reveals that the AIC packing is extremely focused on achieving the maximum density, thus apparently resulting in poor locality and seldom using any local feedback within the same cluster. Thus, the AICs are mainly using global routing, leading to a longer critical path.

5. CONCLUSIONS

We have revisited the idea of replacing LUTs in FPGAs with AICs, tried to build at transistor level the complete logic necessary and have adapted VPR to place and route

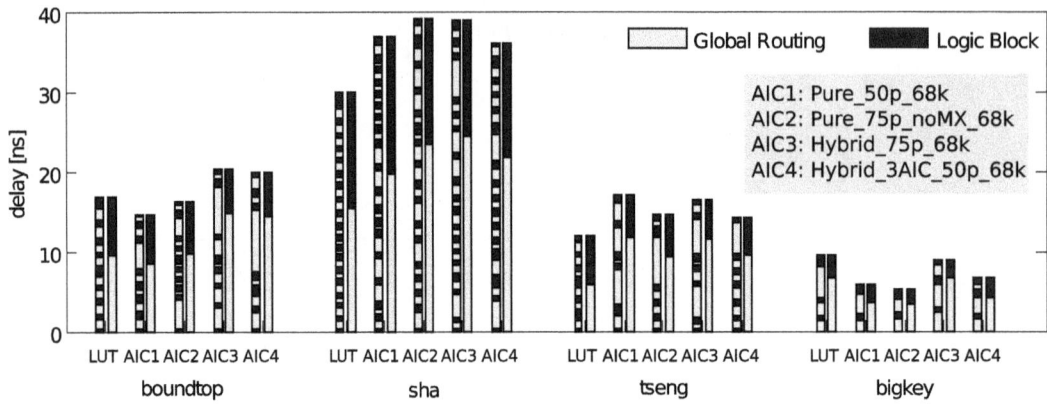

Figure 14: Detailed critical path. Distribution between logical delay and global routing delay of four selected benchmarks when running on five different architectures. Each pair of bars shows the same path twice: on the left with the succession of logic and routing delays as they occur on the path and on the right accumulating the two components.

benchmarks. The results are a mixed blessing: some aspects of the AIC-based architecture are significantly worse than expected, most notably the size of the input crossbar and of the cluster. Although this cannot but impact the overall results, it is surprising that even with very fat logic clusters we could find some design points which improve delay reasonably while not deteriorating the overall silicon real-estate cost. Although average results are never truly excellent, results on individual benchmarks display a remarkable heterogeneity, with several benchmarks achieving delay improvements of around 30-40% at almost no area cost. We conclude that AICs still promise some potentially significant improvements, although achieving them does not appear as immediate as we hoped at first. Looking at the resulting implementations, we foresee opportunities to better utilize AICs by tailoring the logic synthesis and technology mapper to AICs, and using a packer that can trade off wire length for a lower packing density [9].

6. REFERENCES

[1] Altera Corporation. *Stratix IV Device Handbook, vols. 1 and 2.* http://www.altera.com/literature/.

[2] V. Betz, J. Rose, and A. Marquardt. *Architecture and CAD for deep-submicron FPGAs.* Kluwer Academic, Boston, Mass., 1999.

[3] C. Chiasson and V. Betz. COFFE: Fully-Automated Transistor Sizing for FPGAs. In *Proceedings of the IEEE International Conference on Field-Programmable Technology*, 2013.

[4] G. De Micheli. *Synthesis and Optimization of Digital Circuits.* McGraw-Hill, New York, 1994.

[5] G. Lemieux, P. Leventis, and D. Lewis. Generating highly-routable sparse crossbars for PLDs. In *Proceedings of the 8th ACM/SIGDA International Symposium on Field-Programmable Gate Arrays*, pages 155–164, 2000.

[6] D. Lewis et al. The Stratix II logic and routing architecture. In *Proceedings of the 13th ACM/SIGDA International Symposium on Field Programmable Gate Arrays*, pages 14–20, Monterey, Calif., Feb. 2005.

[7] J. Luu, J. H. Anderson, and J. Rose. Architecture description and packing for logic blocks with hierarchy, modes and complex interconnect. In

Proceedings of the 19th ACM/SIGDA International Symposium on Field Programmable Gate Arrays, pages 227–36, Monterey, Calif., Feb. 2011.

[8] A. Mishchenko, S. Chatterjee, and R. Brayton. DAG-aware AIG rewriting: A fresh look at combinational logic synthesis. In *Proceedings of the 43rd Design Automation Conference*, pages 532–36, San Francisco, Calif., July 2006.

[9] K. E. Murray, S. Whitty, S. Liu, J. Luu, and V. Betz. Titan: Enabling large and complex benchmarks in academic CAD. In *Proceedings of the 23rd International Conference on Field-Programmable Logic and Applications*, Porto, Portugal, Sept. 2013.

[10] H. Parandeh-Afshar, H. Benbihi, D. Novo, and P. Ienne. Rethinking FPGAs: Elude the flexibility excess of LUTs with And-Inverter Cones. In *Proceedings of the 20th ACM/SIGDA International Symposium on Field Programmable Gate Arrays*, pages 119–28, Monterey, Calif., Feb. 2012.

[11] H. Parandeh-Afshar, G. Zgheib, D. Novo, M. Purnaprajna, and P. Ienne. Shadow AICs: Reaping the benefits of And-Inverter Cones with minimal architectural impact. In *Proceedings of the 21st ACM/SIGDA International Symposium on Field Programmable Gate Arrays*, page 279, Monterey, Calif., Feb. 2013. Poster.

[12] H. Parandeh-Afshar, G. Zgheib, D. Novo, M. Purnaprajna, and P. Ienne. Shadow And-Inverter Cones. In *Proceedings of the 23rd International Conference on Field-Programmable Logic and Applications*, Porto, Portugal, Sept. 2013.

[13] J. Rose, J. Luu, C. W. Yu, O. Densmore, J. Goeders, A. Somerville, K. B. Kent, P. Jamieson, and J. Anderson. The VTR Project: Architecture and CAD for FPGAs from Verilog to Routing. In *Proceedings of the 20th ACM/SIGDA International Symposium on Field-Programmable Gate Arrays*. ACM, 2012.

[14] S. Yang. Logic synthesis and optimization benchmarks user guide, version 3.0. Technical report, Microelectronics Center of North Carolina, Research Triangle Park, N.C., Jan. 1991.

Scalable Multi-Access Flash Store for Big Data Analytics

Sang-Woo Jun*, Ming Liu*, Kermin Elliott Fleming†, Arvind*
Department of Electrical Engineering and Computer Science
Massachusetts Institute of Technology
Cambridge, MA 02139
{wjun, ml, arvind}@csail.mit.edu*
{kermin.fleming}@intel.com†

ABSTRACT

For many "Big Data" applications, the limiting factor in performance is often the transportation of large amount of data from hard disks to where it can be processed, i.e. DRAM. In this paper we examine an architecture for a scalable distributed flash store which aims to overcome this limitation in two ways. First, the architecture provides a high-performance, high-capacity, scalable random-access storage. It achieves high-throughput by sharing large numbers of flash chips across a low-latency, chip-to-chip backplane network managed by the flash controllers. The additional latency for remote data access via this network is negligible as compared to flash access time. Second, it permits some computation near the data via a FPGA-based programmable flash controller. The controller is located in the datapath between the storage and the host, and provides hardware acceleration for applications without any additional latency. We have constructed a small-scale prototype whose network bandwidth scales directly with the number of nodes, and where average latency for user software to access flash store is less than 70µs, including 3.5µs of network overhead.

Categories and Subject Descriptors

H.3.4 [**Information Storage and Retrieval**]: Systems and Software—*Distributed systems*

Keywords

Storage system, Big Data, FPGA networks, SSD, Flash

1. INTRODUCTION

We have entered the "Big Data" age. The evolution of computer networks and the increasing scale of electronic integration into our daily lives has lead to an explosion of data to be analyzed. Thanks to the steady pace of Moore's Law, our computing abilities on these data have been growing as well. However, effective computation requires a very low-latency random access into the data. As a result, it is highly desirable for the entire working set of the problem to fit in main memory to achieve good performance.

However, modern Big Data application datasets are often too large to be cached in the main memory of any host at a reasonable cost. Instead, they are spread among multiple machines in a cluster interconnected with some network fabric, and often also stored in a cheaper, higher density secondary storage such as hard disks. This means data often has to be accessed from a secondary storage device over a network, each of which has significantly higher access latency than local main memory. The primary performance bottleneck is the seek time of magnetic disks, which has to be amortized by large sequential data access. As a result, the storage device characteristics in large part dictated the design of the rest of the system.

With the recent advancement of low latency and high bandwidth flash devices as alternatives to disks, the performance bottleneck has shifted from the storage device to the network latency and software overhead. As a result, modern high performance storage systems need to optimize all aspects of the system, including the storage, network and software stack. Current attempts to increase the performance of storage systems include use of hardware implementation of the network stack and better I/O fabric. However, even state-of-the-art networked storage systems still suffer hundreds of microseconds of latency. This large gap between the performance of main memory and storage often limits our capacity to process large amounts of data.

Another facet of high performance storage systems under active investigation is providing a computation fabric on the storage itself, effectively transporting computation capabilities to where the storage is, instead of moving large amounts of data to be processed. However, the processing power that can be put on a storage device within the power budget is often limited, and its benefits are sometimes limited when heavy computation is required. For applications that require heavy computation, it is effective to use hardware acceleration to assist data processing. Due to the high development and production cost of dedicated ASIC accelerator chips, reconfigurable hardware fabrics such as FPGAs are popular choices for implementing power-efficient application-specific accelerators.

In this work, we propose a novel high-performance storage architecture, which we call BlueDBM (Blue Database Machine). The high-level goal of BlueDBM is to provide a high-performance storage system that accelerates the processing of very large datasets. The BlueDBM design aims to achieve the following goals:

- **Low Latency, High Bandwidth**: To increase the performance of response-time sensitive applications, the network should add negligible latency to the overall system while maintaining high bandwidth.

- **Scalability**: Because Big Data problems are constantly increasing in size, the architecture should be scalable to higher capacity and node count.

- **Low-Latency Hardware Acceleration**: In order to reduce data transport and alleviate computationally bound problems, the platform should provide very low-latency hardware acceleration.

- **Application Compatibility**: As a general storage solution for Big Data, existing applications should run on top of our new storage hardware without any modification.

- **Multi-accessibility**: In order to accommodate distributed data processing applications, the system should be capable of handling multiple simultaneous requests from many different users.

The BlueDBM architecture distributes high performance flash storage among computational nodes to provide a scalable, high-performance and cost-effective distributed storage. In order to achieve this, BlueDBM introduces a low-latency and high-speed network directly between the flash controllers. The direct connection between controllers not only reduces access latency by removing the network software stack, but also allows the flash controllers to mask the network latency within flash access latency. As we will demonstrate, controller-to-controller latencies in such a network can be insignificant compared to flash access latencies, giving us the potential to expose enormous storage capacity and bandwidth with performance characteristics similar to a locally attached PCIe flash drive.

To further improve the effectiveness of the storage system, BlueDBM includes a FPGA-based reconfigurable fabric for implementing hardware accelerators near storage. Because the reconfigurable fabric is located in the datapath of the storage controller through which data has to travel anyways, no latency overhead is introduced from using the accelerators.

The key contribution of this paper is a novel storage architecture for Big Data applications, which include a low-latency communication link directly between flash controllers and a platform for accelerator implementation on the flash controller itself. We demonstrate the characteristics of such an architecture on a 4-node prototype system. We are also engaged in building a much larger system based on the architecture.

To test these ideas, we have constructed a small 4-node prototype of our system using commercially available FPGAs [10] coupled to a custom flash array, networked using high speed inter-FPGA serial links. The prototype has an average latency to client applications of about $70\mu s$, which is an order of magnitude lower than existing distributed flash systems such as CORFU [13], and rivals the latency of a local SSD. Our shared 4-node prototype provides 4x the bandwidth of a single flash card with marginal impact on access latency. We also implemented a word counting application with hardware accelerator support from our storage platform, showing 4x performance increase over a pure software implementation. We are currently building a newer system employing the same ideas but with more modern hardware, which will deliver an order of magnitude performance increase over the prototype system.

The rest of the paper is organized as follows. Section 2 provides background on storage deployment and FPGA based acceleration in Big Data. Sections 3 to 5 describes the system in detail, and Section 6 discusses the prototype we have built to demonstrate the performance of the system. Section 7 provides the experimental results obtained from the prototype and its evaluation. Section 8 concludes the paper.

2. RELATED WORK

Storage systems that require high capacity are usually constructed in two ways: (i) building a Storage Area Network (SAN) or (ii) using a distribute file system. In a SAN, large amounts of storage are placed in a storage node such as a RAID server, and these storage devices are connected together using a dedicated network (i.e. SAN), providing the abstraction of locally attached disk to the application servers. However, the physical storage network is usually ethernet based running on protocols such as iSCSI or FCoE, which adds milliseconds of software and network latency. An alternative organization is to distribute the storage among the application hosts and use the general purpose network along with a distributed file system (e.g., NFS [7], Lustre [6], GFS [18]) to provide a file-level sharing abstraction. This is popular with distributed data processing platforms such as MapReduce [3]. While a distributed file system is cheap and scalable, the software overhead of concurrency control and the high-latency congestion-prone general purpose network degrades performance. Nevertheless, traditionally, these network, software and protocol latencies are tolerable because they are insignificant compared to the seek latency of magnetic disks.

This is changing with recent developments in high-performance flash devices. Large flash storage offer two benefits over magnetic disks, namely superior random read performance and low power consumption, while still providing very high density. Such advantages make them alternatives to magnetic disks. Flash chips offer access latency in the order of tens of microseconds, which is several orders of magnitude shorter than the 10 to 20 millisecond disk seek time. By organizing multiple chips in parallel, very high throughput can be obtained. As a result, the storage device is no longer a bottleneck in high capacity storage systems. Instead, other parts of the system such as network latency and software stack overhead now have a prominent impact on performance. It has been shown that in a disk-based distributed storage system, non-storage components are responsible for less than 5% of the total latency, while in a flash-based system, this number rises to almost 60% [14].

Flash has its own drawbacks as well. Its characteristics include limited program erase cycles, coarse-grain block level erases, and low write throughput. As a result of these characteristics, hardware (e.g., controllers, interfaces) and software (e.g., file systems, firmware) traditionally designed for hard disks are often suboptimal for flash. Much research has gone into developing techniques such as intelligent address translation in the Flash Translation Layer (FTL) to control area under use [12] [24] [26]. Our storage architecture is similarly motivated by and designed for these flash characteristics.

Recent efforts such as CORFU [13] attempts to build distributed file systems tailored for flash storage characteristics, but still suffers millisecond-level latency. Other attempts such as QuickSAN [14] have studied directly connecting flash storage to the network in order to bypass some of the software latency. This brings down the latency of the system to hundreds of microseconds. We hope to further improve performance by removing protocol and software overhead.

In data centers, several research efforts have suggested providing side-channels for communication between nodes within the data center to alleviate and bypass network congestion. [19] attempts to resolve congestion using software architectural approaches. Halperin et al.[20] examine adding wireless links to data-centers as an auxiliary communication mechanism.

Moving computation to data in order to circumvent the I/O limitations has been proposed in the past. Computation in main memory (e.g. Computational RAM [16]) has been studied, but it failed to see much light due to the fast advancement of I/O interfaces. However, in light of power consumption walls and Big Data, moving computation to high capacity secondary storage is becoming an attractive option. Samsung has already demonstrated the advantages of having a small ARM processor on the storage device itself [22] for in store computation. They have shown power and performance benefits of offloading I/O tasks from host CPU to the storage device. However, benefits are only seen if the offloaded task have low computing complexity and high data selectivity because of the weak ARM processor.

FPGAs have been gaining popularity as application specific accelerators for Big Data due to its low power consumption, flexibility and low cost. FPGA accelerators are currently being used in database management systems [4], in providing web services [15], as well as in other domains such as machine learning [23] and bioinformatics [27].

3. SYSTEM ARCHITECTURE

The distributed flash store system that we propose is composed of a set of identical storage nodes. Each node is a flash storage device coupled with a host PC via a high-speed PCIe link. The storage device consists of flash chips organized into busses, controlled by a flash controller implemented on reconfigurable FPGA fabric. The storage devices are networked via a dedicated storage network implemented on multi-gigabit low latency serial links using SERialize/DESerializer (SERDES) functionality provided within the FPGA fabric. The host servers are networked using generic Ethernet communications. The construction of the system is shown in Figure 1.

To use BlueDBM, the host PCs run high level applications (e.g. databases) which generate read/write commands to the file system. The file system forwards the requests to the locally attached FPGA, which fulfills the requests by accessing either the local or remote flash boards. Data is

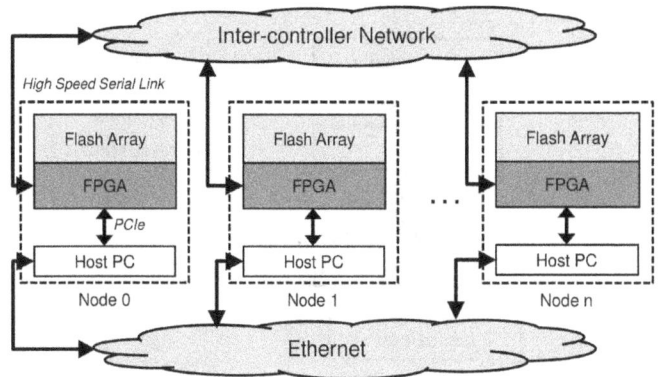

Figure 1: BlueDBM top level system diagram consisting of multiple storage nodes connected using high speed serial links forming an inter-controller network

globally visible and accessible from all host PCs, and the address space is shared and unified among all nodes. Alternatively, the application may issue commands to instruct a hardware accelerator on the FPGA to process the data directly from the flash controllers.

This organization fulfills our goal of (i) low latency/high bandwidth by using parallel flash chips, PCIe and high-speed transceivers coupled with a thin networking protocol; (ii) scalability through homogeneous nodes and a network protocol that maintains low latency over multiple hops and is topologically flexible; (iii) low-latency hardware acceleration by providing a hook to software to invoke accelerator operations on data without passing through host; (iv) application compatibility by providing a generic file system and exposing the abstraction of a single unified address space to the applications; and (v) multi-accessibility by providing multiple entry points to storage via many host PCs.

The hardware and software stacks of the system are presented in Figure 2. Hardware running on the FPGA has 5 key components: (i) client interface, (ii) address mapper, (iii) flash controller, (iv) inter-FPGA router and (v) accelerator. The client interface handles the communication of data and commands with the host over PCIe. Together with the driver and file system software on the host, they provide a shared unified address space abstraction to the user application. The address mapper maps areas in the logical address space to each node in the network. The flash controller includes a simple flash translation layer to access the raw NAND chips on the flash board. The router component implements a thin protocol for communication over the high speed inter-FPGA SERDES links. Finally, accelerators may be placed before and after the router for local or unified access to data. The flash controller and related components are explain in detail below. The inter-FPGA network and accelerators are explained separately in the next sections.

3.1 File System, Client Interface and Address Mapper

The client interface module on the FPGA works in concert with the driver and file system software on the host server to handle I/O requests and responses over PCIe. We implemented a generic file system using FUSE [1]. FUSE intercepts file system command made to its mount point and

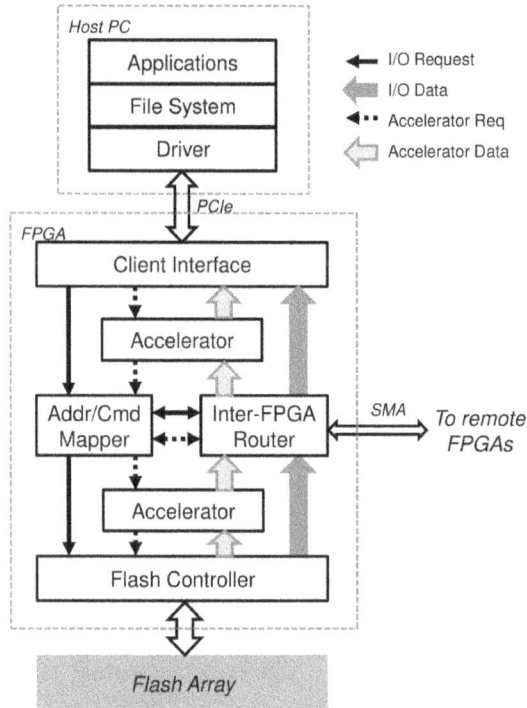

Figure 2: Hardware and software stack of a single node

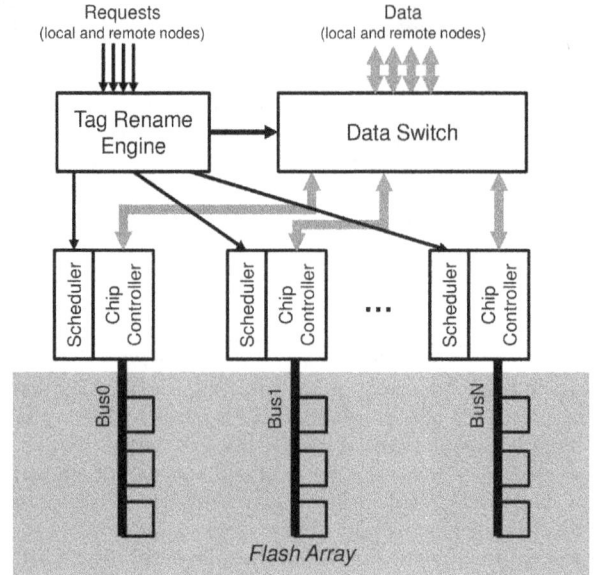

Figure 3: Flash controller featuring a scheduler and chip controller per bus, virtualized using a tagging mechanism

allows us to convert file system commands into load/store operations to our flash device. Currently the entire combined storage of all nodes in the system is translated to a single flat address space.

For each I/O request, the address mapper module determines which storage node the data resides in. All storage nodes in the system need to agree on the same mapping scheme, which is currently defined programmatically. Due to the low latency serial communication fabric, there is little difference in performance between fetching from a local node or fetching from a remote node. Therefore, the current mapping scheme focuses on utilizing as much device parallelism as possible, by striping the address space such that adjacent page addresses are mapped to different storage nodes.

3.2 Flash Controller

We use a flash array for fast random access storage. These arrays are populated with NAND chips organized into several buses with chips on each bus sharing control and data paths. The flash board exposes raw chip interfaces to the FPGA via GPIOs and the flash controller accesses the chips. The architecture of the flash controller is shown in Figure 3. We use an independent chip controller and scheduler per bus to communicate with the raw flash chips. Not only can buses be accessed in parallel, data operations on different flash chips on the same bus may be overlapped to hide latency. We designed the flash controller to take advantage of these properties. In addition, we use a tag renaming table and a data switch to manage sharing among multiple hosts in a distributed setting.

The system includes a simple implementation of the Flash Translation Layer (FTL). The current FTL focuses only on providing maximum read performance through parallel ac-

cess to as many flash chips as possible. We achieve this by simply permutating a portion of the logical address bits such that spatially local requests have a high probability of being mapped to different bus controllers, buses and chips thereby improving overall system throughput.

3.3 Controller Virtualization and Communication

Because multiple clients can access all storage in the system through a very thin layer of controllers, there needs to be an efficient way to match the commands against the data flowing in and out of the flash chips. For example, data being read from the flash device needs to be routed back to where the read command originated. A possible solution is to implement a distributed agreement protocol between each node, but this is complex and requires additional data transfer across the network. Instead, we use a two-layer tagging scheme to keep track of this information.

In the first layer, each command that is issued from a client interface is given a 8-bit tag value. A list of unoccupied tags are kept in a free tag queue. We dequeue when a new request is issued, and enqueue back when a request retires. On the command issuer side, this tag is correlated with information such as the request page address in a tag mapping table structure. When the request needs to be processed at a remote node, the tag is sent to the target node with the rest of the request information. However, because each node keeps a separate list of free tags, there can be tag collisions at the remote node. This is solved using a second layer of tagging scheme, which translates the original tag to the target node's unique local tag. The first layer tag is stored in another tag map table with information such as the request source and the original tag value. After the request has been handled, the data is sent back to the request origin node tagged with the original tag value it was requested with, so it can be reused for future operations.

4. INTER-CONTROLLER NETWORK

Conventional computer networking infrastructures, like Ethernet and TCP, are designed to provide general purpose functionality and operate at large scales over long distances. As a result, they come at a cost of significant time and processing overhead. But this cost was often overlooked in the past when constructing SANs, because the latency of magnetic disks dominated over the network infrastructure . However, in the case of flash-based deployment, such networking overhead becomes a serious issue. Furthermore, conventional method of networking storage devices requires the storage traffic to share the host-side network infrastructure. This results in reduced effective bandwidth, because the link between the host and its storage has to be shared for local and remote data. Finally, because the network and storage management are composed separately, the combined latency adds up to hundreds of microseconds of latency.

BlueDBM solves these issues by having a dedicated storage data network directly connecting the flash controllers to each other. For this purpose, we constructed a simple packet-switched storage network protocol over a high-speed serial link provided by the FPGA package. The protocol was implemented completely inside the FPGA, and provides sub-microsecond latency communication between controllers. Because the flash controller manages the storage device as well as the network, all data transport of words within a page could be pipelined, effectively hiding the network latency of accessing a page. The protocol includes a flooding peer discovery functionality, allowing hot-plugging of nodes into any topology required by the application.

4.1 Routing Layer

Figure 4 depicts the architecture of the router. The routing mechanism for our storage network is a packet-switched protocol that resembles a simplified version of the Internet Protocol. Each node maintains a routing table of all nodes in the network, where each row contains information including which physical link a packet should take to get to that node and how many network hops away it is. This table is populated on-line via a flooding discovery protocol. This allows hotplugging nodes into the network while the system is live, and also to automatically maintain the shortest path between all pairs of nodes.

The networking infrastructure is constructed such that the flash controller or accelerators can declare in code their own virtual communications links of various widths, and the router will organize and schedule packets in order to multiplex all of the virtual lanes onto a single physical link. This not only allows the writing of simple, easy to understand code for the network infrastructure, but also provides a clean and efficient abstraction of the network for the accelerator platform. An accelerator can declare, at compile time, multiple virtual links according to its requirements, reducing the burden of network management in accelerator development.

4.2 Physical Layer

In our current implementation we make use of the high-speed serial transceivers provided in the FPGA silicon as the physical link. The transceivers provide not only high bandwidth and low latency, they also provide relatively reliable data transport over up to two meters, which is sufficient in data center racks.

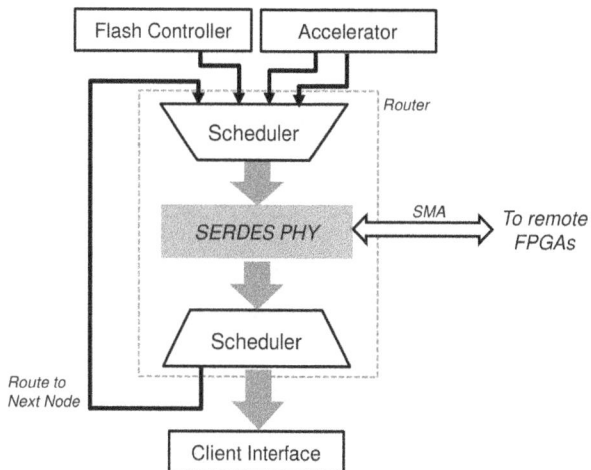

Figure 4: Inter-node network router.

Please note that the choice of physical communication fabric in our system is flexible. While in this particular system, we do not choose general-purpose media such as ethernet or Infiniband [5] as a physical transport for performance reasons, we could have easily chosen other such high-speed communications fabrics given that it is supported by the FPGA or hardware. Heterogeneous controller networks can also be constructed. For example, ethernet could be used across racks in a data center, while high speed inter-FPGA serial links can be used within a rack.

5. CONTROLLER AS A PROGRAMMABLE ACCELERATOR

In order to enable extremely low latency acceleration, our system provides a platform for implementing accelerators along the datapath of the storage device (Figure 5, right). One advantage is that operations on the data can be completed faster with dedicated hardware. In addition, because the combined throughput of the BlueDBM cluster can easily surpass the bandwidth of any single hostside link (i.e. PCIe), accelerators that filter or compress data can be used to process more data than the hostside link fabric allows. This setup is more advantageous compared to using the accelerator as a separate appliance (Figure 5, left), where data must be transported from storage to the accelerator via the host, and then transported back after computation.

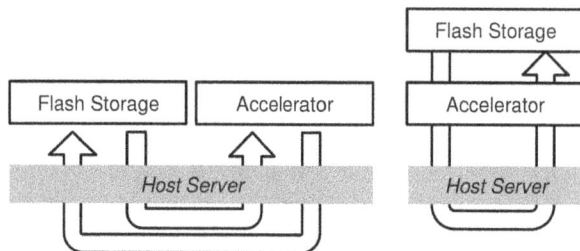

Figure 5: Flow of data when using an accelerator as a separate appliance (left) versus an accelerator in the data path of the storage device (right)

5.1 Two-Part Implementation of Accelerators

In BlueDBM, accelerators can be implemented both before and after the inter-FPGA router (Figure 2). The *local* accelerator, which is located between the flash storage and the router, is used to implement functions that only require parts of the data. For example, compressing pages before writing them to flash. The *global* accelerator located between the router and the client interface implements higher-level functionalities that require a global view of data. Examples includes table join operations in a database accelerator, or the word counting example that will be described shortly. Both accelerators can work in concert, for example to implement compression and decompression algorithms, to reduce the amount of data transported over the inter-FPGA link.

5.2 Example Accelerators

To demonstrate the accelerator architecture, we have implemented a simple word counting accelerator on the Blue-DBM platform. The accelerator exposes an interface to specify the word being counted, in the form a FUSE virtual file. Once the word is registered, the accelerator accesses its virtual access points to storage and network to count the number of the registered word in all storage devices in the network. The resulting output can also be accessed via a FUSE virtual file. An example invocation of the accelerator looks like the following:

```
echo "would" > fuse/input ; cat fuse/output
```

We have already implemented other effective application specific FPGA-based hardware accelerators serving as separate appliances to a host machine. These include application specific compression [21], database query accelerators and network link compression algorithms. Most of these can be ported to the BlueDBM platform with minor modifications, and we are in the process of doing this. We expect both compute and data bound applications to see notable performance improvements with these accelerators.

6. PROTOTYPE SYSTEM

Our prototype flash system, a photo of which is shown in Figure 6(a), is based around the Xilinx ML605 board and our custom built flash board. The ML605 board and the flash board is coupled using the FPGA Mezzanine Card (FMC) connector, as seen in Figure 6(b), and plugged into a PCIe slot on the host server. The implementation overhead was greatly reduced by building on top of an abstraction layer [25], which mapped physical physical device details into logical services. We have also used similar abstractions of the serial network [17] for early functionality, but eventually implemented a routing protocol in favor of dynamic reconfiguration of the network.

Each flash board hosts 16GB of flash storage arranged in four parallel buses comprised of 8 512MB Micron SLC flash chips. An on-board Xilinx CPLD is used to decode command signals for all buses. Our custom flash board uses slightly older, less dense flash chips with asynchronous interfaces. These older chips with asynchronous signalling lowers the throughput of each flash bus to a maximum of around 25MB/s, even though our controllers can handle chips with much larger bandwidths.

We network the processing nodes of our system by way of the Virtex-6 GTX high speed transceivers. Each transceiver

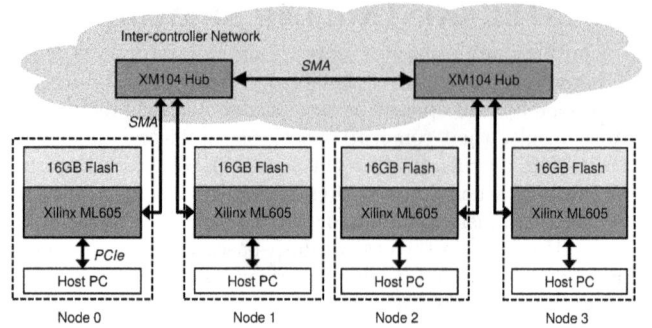

Figure 7: Prototype physical implementation with 4 storage nodes and 2 hubs

is capable of transporting up to 5Gbps. Unfortunately, our flash cards utilize the same mezzanine connector as most of the ML605's serial transceivers. As a result, each node can only connect to one other node via the only remaining SMA port on the ml605 board. Therefore, the prototype uses a tree topology shown in Figure 7, and connects the processing nodes using extra ML605s which act as hubs. These ML605s do not have attached flash cards, enabling us to use most of its transceivers for inter-FPGA communication using the Xilinx XM104 connectivity card.

Hosts in our system run the Ubuntu distribution of Linux. We use the file system FUSE[1] to interface with our storage system though eventually we plan to implement a true file system.

7. RESULTS

Using our prototype system, we first characterize the inter-controller network. Then we examine the raw latency and throughput of the entire storage system. Finally, we measure the performance of simple applications running on the system, taking advantage of multi-accessibility and accelerators.

7.1 FPGA Resource Usage

The approximate area breakdown of each node in our flash system is shown in Table 1. Our design, which is largely unoptimized for either timing or area, is dominated by its use of large buffers. This area corresponds to approximately 35% of the resources of the medium sized Virtex-6 chip. The rest of the area is free to be used for accelerator implementation.

Most structures in our system are constant in size regardless of the number of processing nodes in the system. Notable exceptions to this scaling include the routing table and packet header size. However, even with a thousand-node system, we can easily fit the routing table within a few BRAMs on the FPGA given that each entry is merely 128 bits. Packet headers will require 10 bits to identify the source/destination node in a thousand-node system, which means a corresponding increase in FIFO sizes. However, this area increase remains insignificant compared to the rest of the design on the FPGA. Thus we are able to scale to thousands of nodes without significant impact on area.

7.2 Network Performance

Figure 8 summarizes the typical throughput and latency characteristics of our inter-FPGA network architecture. We

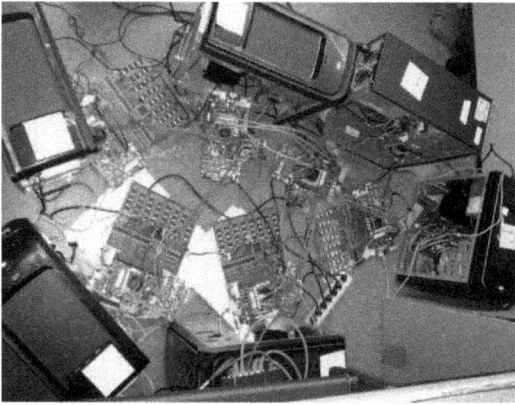

(a) Four-node prototype system

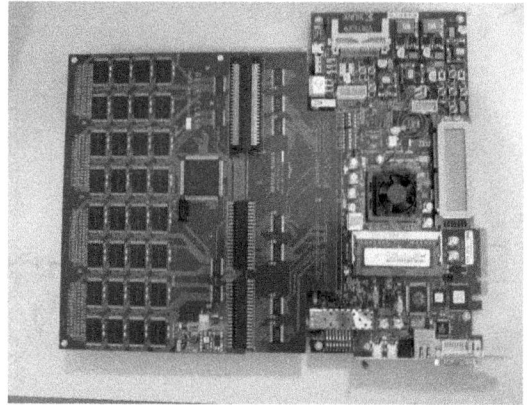

(b) ML605 and attached flash card

Figure 6: Prototype system

	LUTS	Registers	BRAM
Client Interface	17387	17312	51
Flash Controller	10972	8542	151
Networking	24725	27530	16
Total	53084 (35%)	53384 (17%)	218 (52%)

Table 1: Synthesis metrics for controller components at 100MHz.

achieve approximately 450MB/s or 70% of the theoretical link bandwidth with average packet latency of around $0.5\mu s$ per hop. Latency scales linearly with the number of hops traversed because we maintain flow-control on a per-hop basis, as opposed maintaining flow-control on the end-to-end traversal. Considering that the typical latency of a flash read is several tens of microseconds, requests in our network can, in theory, traverse dozens of nodes before the network latency becomes a significant portion of the storage read latency, potentially enabling the addressing of multiple terabytes worth of data across many nodes.

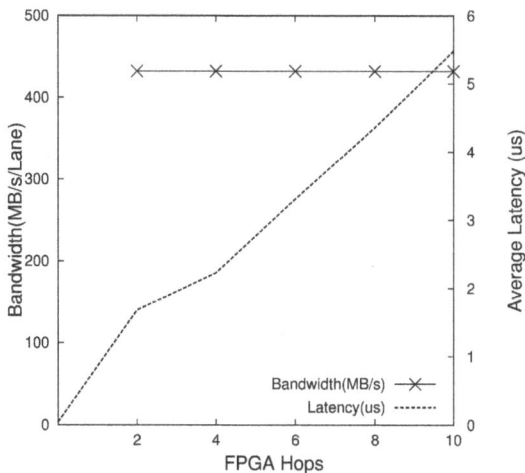

Figure 8: Throughput and latency of our inter-FPGA network using a 5Gbps SERDES connection on the Virtex-6 ML605.

In our current system, each compute node only supports a single lane connection due to physical constraints discussed previously. However, the maximum bandwidth per chip in the latest generation of FPGAs tops 10GB/s per chip for moderately sized FPGAs [11]. Based on this, we believe that BlueDBM can scale to hundreds of processing nodes while delivering average-case performance similar to a good commodity SSD array and best-case performance rivalling or surpassing local PCIe SSDs such as FusionIO [2]. Indeed, we are currently building a much bigger machine that will demonstrate the BlueDBM architecture at a much larger scale.

7.3 Raw Latency

Figure 9(a) shows the average read latency of our storage system from the perspective of the host user application. It is the average time from when a request is made for a single 2048-byte page to when the entire page is received by the application. Latency is measured by making repeated blocking requests one at a time, to random pages, which may reside on different nodes, buses and blocks.

The total read latency can be broken down into flash chip latency, controller latency and software latency. Chip latency is the access time of a single flash chip and is a characteristic of the NAND flash device. Our SLC chips average around $27\mu s$. The controller latency is incurred in moving the data from a flash chip to the appropriate client interface, and includes the inter-FPGA network latency. The software latency accounts for the time to transfer the page across the PCIe bus and through the driver and FUSE file system.

From Figure 9(a), we observe that flash chip latency remains constant with more nodes as expected. Because by construction, the underlying storage network is abstracted away, the driver and file system layers are thin and simple. Their latencies total $4\mu s$ and also remains constant with increasing number of nodes. The network latency is minimal compared to flash latency as shown previously. Moreover, the tight coupling between the inter-FPGA network and the flash controller means that the network does not have to wait for the entire page to be read from the controller before sending it. Network latency can be hid by pipelining individual words streamed out of the controller across the network. As a result, the end-to end latency of fetching a page from

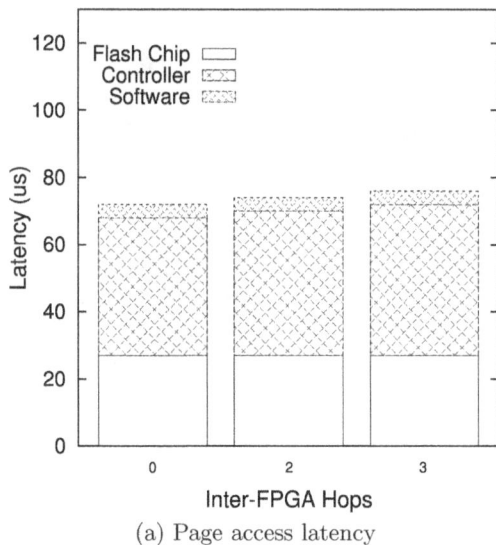

(a) Page access latency

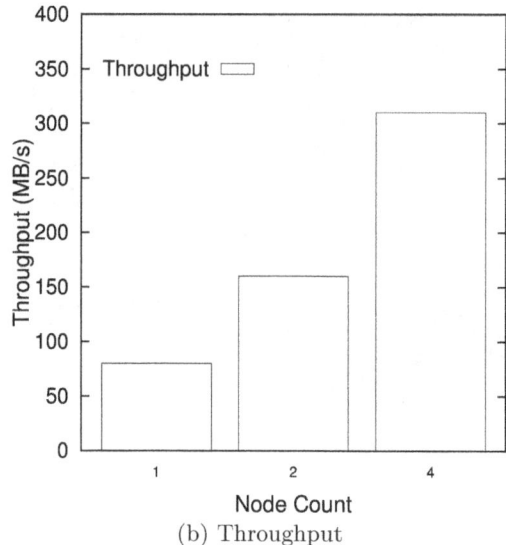

(b) Throughput

Figure 9: Raw latency and throughput measurements of our 4-node prototype

remote storage is much less than the sum of storage and network latencies accounted for separately. In our prototype, end-to-end page read latency increase is a marginal $2\mu s$ per additional network hop. We expect this trend to continue for larger networks. The total latency of our system is an order of magnitude lower than existing networking solutions such as Ethernet or fibre channel.

7.4 Raw Throughput

Figure 9(b) shows the sequential read throughput of the system with increasing number of distributed nodes. Throughput was measured by running a benchmark on a single host that requests a continuous stream of pages from the total address space in order. Each request is serviced by either a local or a remote node depending on the mapping of the requested address.

The throughput of our system achieves linear scaling with the addition of more storage nodes. A single node provides 80 MB/s of bandwidth. A 2-node system doubles the bandwidth to 160 MB/s, while a 4-node system further scales up to 310 MB/s, or 3.8x the speed of a single node. The reason the performance is not a full 4x is because our prototype implementation of the PCIe driver is hitting its maximum throughput. Future iterations of the system will remove this limitation. It is conceivable that by adding more storage nodes, we can achieve throughput and capacity comparable to commercial SAN or PCIe flash products such FusionIO or PureStorage Flash Array [8], but at a much lower dollars per gigabyte.

It should be noted that the throughput of a single node of the prototype system is limited by the low throughput of the custom flash boards. With modern flash chips (200 MB/s per chip) organized into more buses, we would be able to achieve the same linear scaling at much higher bandwidth, until we saturate the bandwidth of PCIe or the inter-FPGA links. We are currently designing a new flash board to build a faster and larger system for real-world big data applications.

7.5 Multi-Access Performance Scaling

Effective multi-access capability of a storage system is crucial in a distributed processing environment such as MapReduce. We demonstrate this ability by running computationally heavy workloads on multiple consumer nodes and measuring the achieved performance of the system.

Figure 10 shows the performance scaling of the system in a multi-access setting. Throughput is shown normalized against a single-access scenario in a four-node system. It can be seen that the total bandwidth delivered by the system linearly increases with the number of consumers. This is because the total available bandwidth of the system exceeds the amount a single server node could process. This shows that our system is an effective way to share device storage and bandwidth among multiple hosts, where each host may not always require the maximum bandwidth from the storage device, because for example, it is doing computation on the data or waiting for external input.

However, if all nodes are constantly requesting maximum throughput, we will not see linear scaling. In such a case, the total throughput of the system will saturate at the maximum internal bandwidth, after which node throughput will decrease. It is worthy to note that this is a baseline experiment to demonstrate the raw performance of the system, without advanced hot block management features such as DRAM caching or deduplication. After such advanced features are implemented, we expect to show better performance even on bandwidth intensive workloads.

7.6 Application-Specific Acceleration

Figure 11 shows the performance results of the word counting application, implemented with (i) an in-datapath hardware accelerator, (ii) an off-datapath hardware accelerator treated as a separate appliance, and (iii) software only. All experiments were run on the two-node configuration, where the maximum bandwidth is 140MB/s. It can be seen that while the accelerator on the datapath makes almost maximum use of the device bandwidth at 128MB/s, the software implementation of the application is not nearly as fast

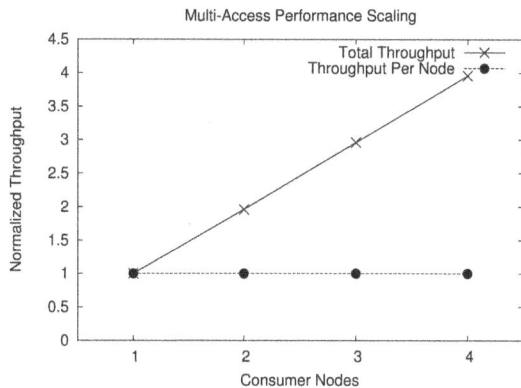

Figure 10: Performance scaling in multi-access scenario

(31MB/s), because it is bound by the CPU. Even the hardware accelerator, implemented as a separate appliance suffers significant throughput loss because of the overhead involved in streaming the fetched data into the accelerator.

Because out host server provides only one PCIe slot, we could not implement the off-datapath accelerator as a physically separate appliance. Instead, the accelerator shares the FPGA fabric and PCIe link of the flash controller. In order to utilize the accelerator, data read from flash storage is transferred back to the FPGA, this time to the accelerator implementation instead of the flash controller. However, even though the flash controller and accelerator share some of the same resources, because they share no control structure inside the FPGA and the direction of heavy data transfer on PCIe is different, we do not think the performance characteristics of this configuration is very different from a physically separate implementation.

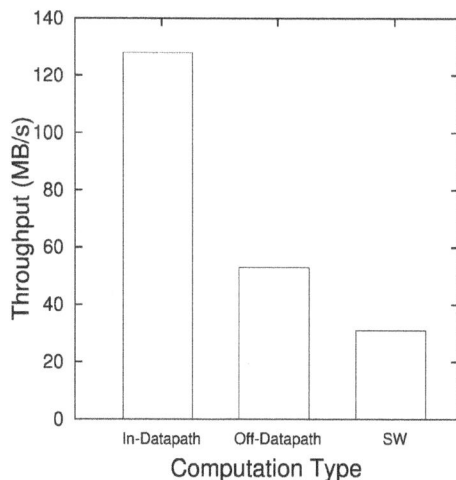

Figure 11: Word counting accelerator performance scaling

8. CONCLUSION AND FUTURE WORK

"Big Data" processing requires high-performance storage architectures. In this paper, we have examined an architecture for a scalable distributed flash store, wherein each node possesses a moderate amount of storage resources and

reconfigurable fabric for accelerator implementation, and is connected to other nodes by way of a low-latency and high-bandwidth controller-to-controller network. We have demonstrated that by having the inter-FPGA network connecting the controllers directly, each node is able to access remote storage with negligible performance degradation. Not only does the controller-to-controller network provide pooling of storage capacity, but it also allows combining the throughput of all nodes on the network, resulting in linear throughput scaling with more nodes. We also demonstrated that offloading computation into the storage controller as an accelerator provides performance benefits against implementing acceleration as a separate appliance.

We are in the process of building a 20-node BlueDBM rack-level system using more modern, faster and higher capacity flash boards with newer Xilinx VC707 FPGA boards [11]. The new flash board is planned to deliver more than 1GB/s of throughput per storage node, and the server-side PCIe bandwidth will perform at more than 3GB/s. The new system will be used to explore real Big Data problems at the storage hardware level. Some planned improvements and experimentations include:

Improved FTL: Our current system is designed for read-intensive applications. We have thus far assumed that writes occur infrequently. Our next step is to optimize writes to flash memory by designing wear leveling, garbage collection, write amplification reduction algorithms specifically for a controller networked flash storage system.

DRAM Caching: We can cache reads and writes to the SSD in DRAM on the FPGA board. This can reduce writes to the flash and improve performance. We may use a cache coherence protocol to synchronize the cache of individual nodes. Additionally, because of our low latency inter-FPGA network, we could create a shared global DRAM cache from DRAM of all the nodes and dynamically partition them according to the workload characteristics.

Database Acceleration: Existing applications can already take advantage of BlueDBM's distributed flash store, but we aim to further accelerate database management systems such as Postgres or SciDB [9] by offloading database operations to the FPGA. Specifically, filtering, aggregation and compression tasks could be done directly at the storage level.

We believe our system holds great promise both for high-speed rack-level storage networking and for large-scale application acceleration in Big Data.

9. ACKNOWLEDGEMENTS

This work was funded in part by Quanta (#6922986) and Samsung (#6925093). We also thank Xilinx for their generous donation of hardware.

10. REFERENCES

[1] FUSE: Filesystem in Userspace. http://fuse.sourceforge.net/. Accessed: Sept. 2013.

[2] FusionIO. http://www.fusionio.com. Accessed: Sept. 2013.

[3] Hadoop Distributed File System. http://hadoop.apache.org/docs/stable/hdfs_user_guide.html. Accessed: Sept. 2013.

[4] IBM Netezza.
http://www-01.ibm.com/software/data/netezza/.
Accessed: Sept. 2013.

[5] Infiniband. http://www.infinibandta.org/.
Accessed: Sept. 2013.

[6] Lustre.
http://wiki.lustre.org/index.php/Main_Page.
Accessed: Sept. 2013.

[7] NFS Specifications.
http://tools.ietf.org/html/rfc1094. Accessed:
Sept. 2013.

[8] PureStorage FlashArray.
http://www.purestorage.com/flash-array/.
Accessed: Sept. 2013.

[9] SciDB. http://scidb.org/. Accessed: Sept. 2013.

[10] Virtex-6 FPGA ML605 Evaluation Kit. http://www.
xilinx.com/products/devkits/EK-V6-ML605-G.htm.
Accessed: Sept. 2013.

[11] Virtex-7 Datasheet.
http://www.xilinx.com/support/documentation/
data_sheets/ds180_7Series_Overview.pdf.
Accessed: Sept. 2013.

[12] M. Balakrishnan, A. Kadav, V. Prabhakaran, and
D. Malkhi. Differential raid: rethinking raid for ssd
reliability. In *Proceedings of the 5th European
conference on Computer systems*, EuroSys '10, pages
15–26, New York, NY, USA, 2010. ACM.

[13] M. Balakrishnan, D. Malkhi, V. Prabhakaran,
T. Wobber, M. Wei, and J. D. Davis. Corfu: a shared
log design for flash clusters. In *Proceedings of the 9th
USENIX conference on Networked Systems Design
and Implementation*, NSDI'12, pages 1–1, Berkeley,
CA, USA, 2012. USENIX Association.

[14] A. M. Caulfield and S. Swanson. Quicksan: a storage
area network for fast, distributed, solid state disks. In
*Proceedings of the 40th Annual International
Symposium on Computer Architecture*, ISCA '13,
pages 464–474, New York, NY, USA, 2013. ACM.

[15] S. R. Chalamalasetti, K. Lim, M. Wright,
A. AuYoung, P. Ranganathan, and M. Margala. An
fpga memcached appliance. In *Proceedings of the
ACM/SIGDA international symposium on Field
programmable gate arrays*, FPGA '13, pages 245–254,
New York, NY, USA, 2013. ACM.

[16] D. Elliott, M. Stumm, W. M. Snelgrove, C. Cojocaru,
and R. McKenzie. Computational ram: Implementing
processors in memory. *IEEE Des. Test*, 16(1):32–41,
Jan. 1999.

[17] K. E. Fleming, M. Adler, M. Pellauer, A. Parashar,
Arvind, and J. Emer. Leveraging Latency-Insensitivity
to Ease Multiple FPGA Design. In *20th Annual
ACM/SIGDA International Symposium on
Field-Programmable Gate Arrays (FPGA 2012)*,
February 2012.

[18] S. Ghemawat, H. Gobioff, and S.-T. Leung. The google
file system. In *Proceedings of the nineteenth ACM
symposium on Operating systems principles*, SOSP
'03, pages 29–43, New York, NY, USA, 2003. ACM.

[19] A. Greenberg, J. R. Hamilton, N. Jain, S. Kandula,
C. Kim, P. Lahiri, D. A. Maltz, P. Patel, and
S. Sengupta. Vl2: a scalable and flexible data center
network. *Commun. ACM*, 54(3):95–104, Mar. 2011.

[20] D. Halperin, S. Kandula, J. Padhye, P. Bahl, and
D. Wetherall. Augmenting data center networks with
multi-gigabit wireless links. *SIGCOMM Comput.
Commun. Rev.*, 41(4):38–49, Aug. 2011.

[21] S. W. Jun, K. Fleming, M. Adler, and J. Emer. Zip-io:
Architecture for application-specific compression of big
data. In *Field-Programmable Technology (FPT), 2012
International Conference on*, pages 343–351, 2012.

[22] Y. Kang, Y. suk Kee, E. Miller, and C. Park. Enabling
cost-effective data processing with smart ssd. In *Mass
Storage Systems and Technologies (MSST), 2013
IEEE 29th Symposium on*, 2013.

[23] K. Nagarajan, B. Holland, A. George, K. Slatton, and
H. Lam. Accelerating machine-learning algorithms on
fpgas using pattern-based decomposition. *Journal of
Signal Processing Systems*, 62(1):43–63, 2011.

[24] S. Nath and A. Kansal. Flashdb: dynamic self-tuning
database for nand flash. In *Proceedings of the 6th
international conference on Information processing in
sensor networks*, IPSN '07, pages 410–419, New York,
NY, USA, 2007. ACM.

[25] A. Parashar, M. Adler, K. Fleming, M. Pellauer, and
J. Emer. LEAP: A Virtual Platform Architecture for
FPGAs. In *CARL '10: The 1st Workshop on the
Intersections of Computer Architecture and
Reconfigurable Logic*, 2010.

[26] D. Tsirogiannis, S. Harizopoulos, M. A. Shah, J. L.
Wiener, and G. Graefe. Query processing techniques
for solid state drives. In *Proceedings of the 2009 ACM
SIGMOD International Conference on Management of
data*, SIGMOD '09, pages 59–72, New York, NY,
USA, 2009. ACM.

[27] F. Xia, Y. Dou, G. Lei, and Y. Tan. Fpga accelerator
for protein secondary structure prediction based on
the gor algorithm. *BMC Bioinformatics*, 12(Suppl
1):S5, 2011.

Dynamic Voltage & Frequency Scaling with Online Slack Measurement

Joshua M. Levine, Edward Stott and Peter Y. K. Cheung
Department of Electrical and Electronic Engineering, Imperial College London, London, UK
{josh.levine05,ed.stott,p.cheung}@imperial.ac.uk

ABSTRACT

Timing margins in FPGAs are already significant and as process scaling continues they will have to grow to guarantee operation under increased variation. Margins enforce worst-case operation even in typical conditions and result in devices operating more slowly and consuming more energy than necessary. This paper presents a method of dynamic voltage and frequency scaling that uses online slack measurement to determine timing headroom in a circuit while it is operating and scale the voltage and/or frequency in response. Doing so can significantly reduce power consumption or increase throughput with a minimal overhead. The method is demonstrated on a number of benchmark circuits under a range of operating conditions, constraints and optimisation targets.

Categories and Subject Descriptors

B.8.1 [**Hardware**]: PERFORMANCE AND RELIABIL-ITY—*Reliability, Testing, and Fault-Tolerance*

Keywords

dynamic voltage and frequency scaling; FPGA; self-test; timing measurement

1. INTRODUCTION

Dynamic voltage and frequency scaling (DVFS) promises to alleviate some of the operating margins required to guarantee safe operation of circuits under effects such as process and environmental variation. In this paper we use online timing slack measurement to directly quantify the performance of circuits while they are operating. By feeding this information back through a controller we tune voltage and clock frequency in a closed loop and optimise power efficiency or throughput. Our technique offers an excellent trade-off between the degree of optimisation and implementation overhead, in terms of area and performance.

FPGA'14, February 26–28, 2014, Monterey, CA, USA.
Copyright 2014 ACM 978-1-4503-2671-1/14/02 ...$15.00.
http://dx.doi.org/10.1145/2554688.2554784.

As process scaling continues, operating margins are expected to grow in order to compensate for increasing variation and unreliability. FPGAs are particularly affected by large margins as their function is not known during device manufacturing and may change during its lifetime. In normal use these margins result in large timing model safety guardbands, which in turn require the device to be operated more conservatively than would otherwise be required in all but the worst-case operating conditions.

The novel contributions of this work include:

- A low overhead, yet accurate, DVFS system for performance and lifetime enhancement.
- A calibration and guardbanding technique to ensure optimised and safe operation.
- Controllers for maximising throughput or efficiency and for meeting dynamic constraints, including power.

2. BACKGROUND

2.1 Operating Margin

Operating margins exist to ensure that a circuit continues to work across a range of conditions that impact on performance. They exist as parameters built into datasheets, timing models and system specifications and they are inherently pessimistic, resulting in worst-case operation even in typical conditions. The dominant margins in a VLSI system are detailed below:

Load: A system must be able to meet throughput and latency requirements under the heaviest computational workload. If it runs under these assumptions with a varying workload then there will be idle clock cycles and wasted energy. This has been the main motivation for implementing DVFS to date.

Variation: Static timing analysis (STA) guarantees operation over all (or nearly all) possible timing variations. The average device performs better than the STA model but will not be able to exploit this. Statistical static timing analysis is less conservative than STA for intra-die variation but it is still a "one-size-fits-all" policy.

Degradation: Phenomena such as NBTI can cause circuits to slow down over time. Normally, a timing margin ensures correct operation over the whole device lifetime. This is wasteful when a device is new and it cannot accommodate the non-deterministic nature of many degradation mechanisms.

Temperature: Circuit performance varies with temperature — typically it deteriorates as temperature rises. Here too, margins must be applied to assume the worst case.

Noise: Several stochastic effects influence circuit timing on a cycle-to-cycle basis, including thermal noise, crosstalk, power supply ripple and clock jitter. Timing margins must consider the possibility that these effects are compounded.

Data: The data arrival time at a particular register depends on the logic function that is implemented and the transitions that occur on all the fan-in nodes. Usually, only the slowest combination is considered: the critical path. However, the critical path may not be exercised frequently and the average delay may be significantly faster. Indeed, some physical paths may be impossible to exercise due to dependencies between their inputs.

The margins listed here have differing statistical properties and the gains to be made by reducing them depends on the application. For example, a mission critical system with a single FPGA must meet guaranteed specifications, so increasing the average throughput over many varying devices is not much use —the slowest must still meet the specifications. However, a data centre with many FPGAs that share a workload could make power savings and performance gains since it is the average efficiency and throughput of the devices that will determine the performance of the whole cluster.

Many of the margining factors in VLSI are becoming more severe and STA models are becoming increasingly conservative in comparison to the actual performance of the majority of devices for the majority of their operating life[11]. As silicon features become smaller, they become more difficult to manufacture consistently, they are more susceptible to external influences and they become increasingly unstable over time. All of this erodes the benefits brought by process scaling.

FPGAs are particularly sensitive to margins because their ultimate application is unknown during manufacture and test and may change after it is deployed. The resources in the device may be used in any configuration and any combination of them may ultimately fall on a critical path.

2.2 Dynamic Voltage & Frequency Scaling

Dynamic voltage and frequency scaling is used to reduce the size of the operating margins and achieve better than worst case operation. Real-time information on operating parameters (e.g. workload or temperature) is used to control the device's voltage and/or frequency in an attempt to conserve power (DVS) or increase throughput (DFS). To date, the main categories of DVFS systems are as follows:

Static timing analysis (STA): The most common implementation of DVFS today is based on STA. STA is executed for a number of different voltage nodes and a table is constructed to record the maximum operating frequency at each. As the load changes, the table is consulted to find an operating frequency that meets the throughput requirement and the voltage is set accordingly. The timing analysis at each node respects all the other operating margins as normal. Intel SpeedStep is an example of this[1].

Characterised: There are a number of offline techniques for measuring circuit timing, for example Transition Probability[8]. This can be used to build a DVFS table that

Table 1: A summary of DVFS methods and the operating margins that they can reduce

Method	Load	Var.	Deg.	Temp.	Noise	Data
STA	✓					
Char.	✓	✓	✓			
TRC	✓	✓	✓	✓		
OSM[1]	✓	✓	✓	✓		
Razor	✓	✓	✓	✓	✓	✓
Asynch.	✓	✓	✓	✓	✓	✓

[1]This work

is optimised for a particular device, eliminating the process variation margin. If the characterisation is re-run at intervals during deployment the degradation margin can also be reduced, but only if the application can tolerate the necessary downtime.

Tunable replica circuit (TRC): This technique takes an online timing measurement by testing the performance of a stand-alone, on-die circuit[2, 9]. The speed of this circuit, often based around a ring oscillator, indicates the speed of the application circuit and can track changes due to temperature and degradation. It is also sensitive to inter-die variation. Since timing measurements are indirect, margins must still be included to allow for discrepancies between the behaviour of the sensor and the circuit. For example, degradation in the application circuit is data-dependent and the TRC may not exhibit the same degree of ageing.

Online slack measurement (OSM): This method uses direct timing measurement of the application circuit to respond to variation, temperature, and degradation. It is more accurate than the TRC since timing changes in the application circuit are measured directly. This measurement technique and associated tool flow was proposed in recent work by the authors [6, 7]. In this work, we apply the technique to DVFS and address the calibration and guardbanding considerations that govern the reliability of the system.

Razor: Like OSM, Razor[3] is based on shadow registers inserted into the design. Here, the shadow registers are used to detect timing errors rather than measure timing slack. Multiplexers and stall circuitry are used to correct timing errors in a single clock cycle. By tolerating timing errors, Razor can reduce margins for stochastic timing variations such as noise and data. Whilst it is an attractive concept, it has not yet found commercial application due to the challenges of metastability, area overhead and timing constraints of the error correction logic.

Feedback for Razor-based DVFS comes from the error rate and each error must be corrected, incurring some timing and throughput overhead. Razor was proposed for CPU applications where stalls and queuing are already accommodated — the timing and area overheads would be more severe in general-purpose logic. Since Razor must stall the processor to correct errors that occur, it is less suitable for the tightly-coupled, deterministic applications frequently implemented on FPGAs.

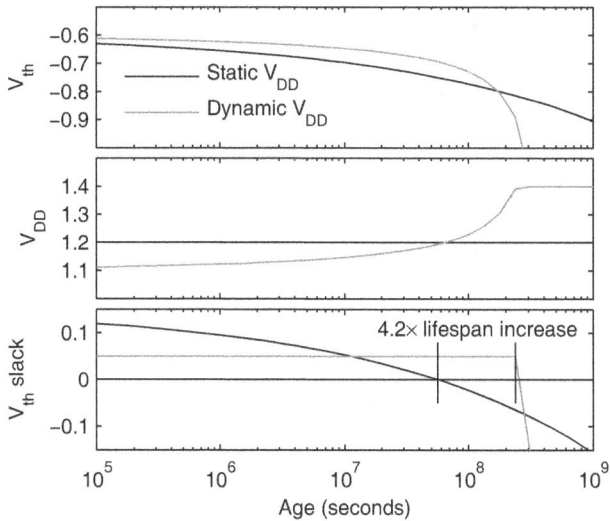

Figure 1: DVS can be used to extend lifespan by scaling V_{DD} to match changes in V_{th}

Table 2: Glossary of terms

f_{sta}	Maximum frequency defined by timing model at V_{nom}
f_{sig}	Maximum frequency defined by output checker
f_{set}	Requested operating frequency
f_{clk}	Operating frequency
f_{cal}	Calibration frequency
V_{DD}	Operating voltage
V_{nom}	Nominal/STA operating voltage
V_{min}	Minimum voltage for data integrity
V_{set}	Requested operating voltage
ΔV_{DD}	Voltage scaling step size
V_{th}	Transistor threshold voltage
P	Operating power
P_{set}	Requested operating power
$d_i(t_\phi)$	Discrepancy rate of RUM i at phase offset t_ϕ
$t_{\mathrm{sR},i}$	Data arrival slack at RUM i
$t_{\mathrm{sS},i}$	Data arrival slack at shadow register i
t_{sC}	Data arrival slack of circuit critical path
$t_{\mathrm{RS},i}$	Shadow register delay offset for RUM i
$t_{\mathrm{aR},i}$	Data arrival delay at RUM i
$t_{\mathrm{aS},i}$	Data arrival delay at shadow register i
Δt_{cal}	Clock period step size of calibration sweep
Δt_{clk}	Clock period step size for frequency scaling
t_{G}	Data arrival slack guardband
t_{H}	Data arrival slack hysteresis
t_{M}	Slack measurement latency
t_{L}	Voltage and frequency control latency
t_ϕ	Phase offset (lead) of shadow clock, in units of time
$\Delta t_\phi(f)$	Phase step size for frequency f

Asynchronous: The advantages of unclocked logic have been recognised for some time. Execution proceeds at exactly the speed of the logic delay and there are no clocking margins. However, asynchronous logic has also failed to find widespread use — this is due to the large area overhead of the handshaking logic and incompatibility with existing design flows.

2.3 Life extension through DVS

An interesting application of DVS is to increase the lifespan of a device. This is illustrated in the simulation results of NBTI degradation in Fig. 1, based upon degradation models from [10]. The simulation assumes that there must be a certain headroom of supply voltage V_{DD} over threshold voltage V_{th} for the circuit to meet timing requirements. Normally, a static V_{DD} would include a guardband to allow for a decrease in V_{th} (PMOS is affected by NBTI — V_{th} is negative) over the lifespan of the product. Once this guardband is eroded, the device fails.

With DVS the guardband is not necessary — instead, V_{DD} is gradually increased to follow the change in V_{th} via timing slack measurements. This means that V_{DD} is lower when the device is new, which reduces the rate of degradation. V_{DD} can also be scaled a certain amount above the normal supply voltage V_{nom}, allowing operation to continue even when the degraded V_{th} would normally mean timing failure. In this simulation a 4.2× increase in lifespan is forecast based on the point where V_{th} headroom is exhausted.

3. METHOD

3.1 Slack Measurement

In this work the DVFS controller makes voltage and frequency scaling decisions based on information about the circuit's timing performance. We use online timing slack measurement [6] to directly quantify the timing headroom available in the critical paths of the circuit whilst they are operating. To do this, shadow registers are added to the design in the configuration illustrated in Fig. 2. A shadow reg-

ister S is attached to a sink register K if, according to STA, it lies at the end of one or more critical paths. S latches the same input, D, as K, but at a variable phase offset t_ϕ. By sweeping t_ϕ and counting mismatches between the outputs of K and S we build a discrepancy profile $d(t_\phi)$ for K that indicates the amount of timing slack. Registers K which are attached to shadow registers are known as registers-under-monitor (RUMs). All RUMs in a single clock domain share a common shadow clock, which is used to set t_ϕ.

Shadow registers are added to the circuit using an automated tool flow[7]. The flow first compiles the unmodified circuit, then executes a timing analysis to identify all the registers where the data arrival delay is near-critical. The placement and routing of the circuit are back-annotated so that its timing characteristics are mostly unaffected by the addition of shadow registers. RUMs are chosen by a metric called critical delay margin (CDM), whereby a register is shadowed if its timing model data arrival delay $t_{\mathrm{aR,STA}} > (1-\mathrm{CDM})t_{\mathrm{aC,STA}}$, where $t_{\mathrm{aC,STA}}$ is the timing model critical path delay of the whole circuit. The value of CDM is set to ensure that any path which may be critical under intra-die variation is monitored.

Following RUM selection, shadow registers are added to the circuit netlist, which is recompiled with the earlier back-annotation to generate the final bitstream. The placement of the shadow registers is unconstrained as we want to give priority to the constraints of the application circuit. This technique is succesful thanks to the general over-provision of routing resources in FPGA architectures — the shadow registers are accommodated with very little change to re-

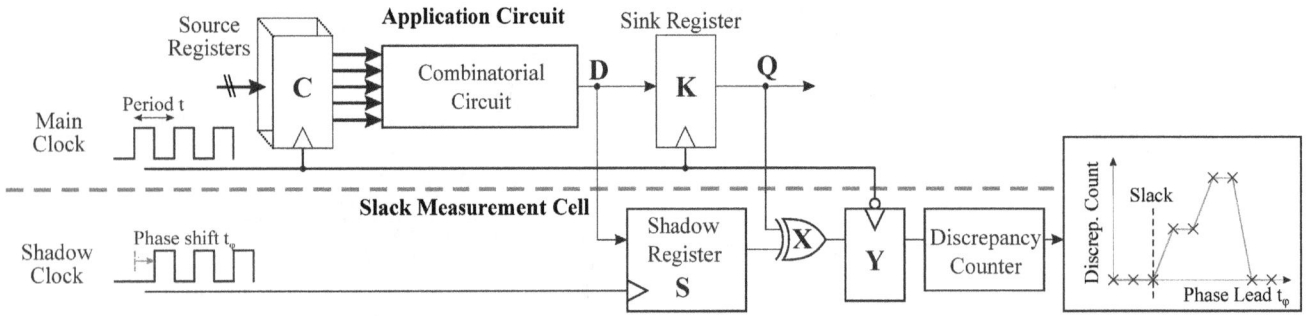

Figure 2: Block diagram of online timing slack measurement circuit

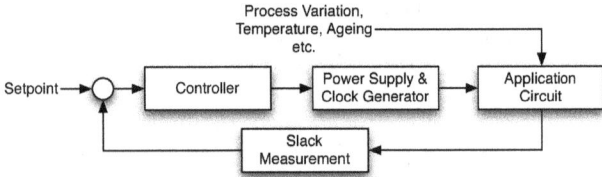

Figure 3: Block diagram of DVFS controller

Table 3: The system can be controlled in one of three modes, depending on which parameter is constrained

Mode	Constraint	Goal	Scaling
DVS	Throughput	Min. power	Voltage
DFS	Voltage	Max. throughput	Frequency
DVFS	Power	Max. throughput	Frequency and voltage

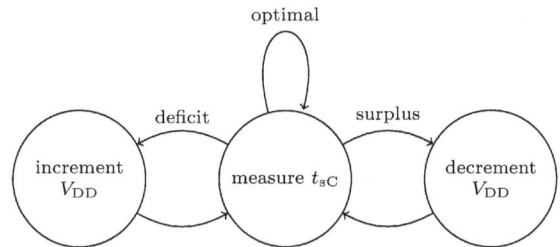

Figure 4: State diagram for dynamic voltage scaling with static throughput constraint

ported timing. However, shadow registers are not necessarily located near their associated RUM and data arrival times may be significantly different between them. To compensate for this, an offline calibration process is used to measure each shadow register delay offset. The offsets are stored in a table and used to correct the online timing slack measurements. A full discussion of calibration and its effect on measurement accuracy in the context of DVFS is given in Section 3.3.

For online slack measurement, discrepancy counts $d_i(t_\phi)$ are gathered for each RUM index i and each increment of shadow clock phase t_ϕ. From this, the shadow register timing slack, $t_{sS,i}$, is defined as the greatest t_ϕ for which $d_i(t_\phi) = 0$, where t_ϕ is the absolute phase in units of time. Then, RUM timing slack $t_{sR,i}$ is derived as $t_{sR,i} = t_{sS,i} - t_{RS,i}$, where $t_{RS,i}$ is the calibration offset for RUM index i. Finally, an aggregate circuit timing slack t_{sC} is defined according to the smallest $t_{sR,i}$, viz. $t_{sC} = \min_i(t_{sR,i})$

Online timing slack measurement is well suited to FPGAs in particular because the shadow registers can be added freely to any part of the circuit without significantly affecting its normal operation. It also makes use of their highly flexible clock generation resources, extensive clock distribution and over-provision of routing. Applying the same technique to ASICs would be possible, but the relative design and area overheads of doing so would be greater.

3.2 Control Algorithm

The general form of our DVFS system is shown in Fig. 3. It is a closed-loop controller, where the state of the plant is compared to a setpoint and adjustments are made to the plant inputs as necessary. Here the plant is the application circuit, timing slack and power are the system states which are measured and frequency and voltage are the inputs that are changed. The controller can work in one of three modes, depending on whether an external constraint is given for throughput, voltage or power. The modes are listed in Table 3 with their optimisation objectives and control action.

We have designed three forms of controller for different applications — they are statically constrained, dynamically constrained and power constrained. The design of each is discussed in the following sections.

3.2.1 Statically constrained

A simple use of DVFS is to optimise operation of a design under static constraints. Either frequency or voltage are fixed, typically according to system or device specifications. If frequency is fixed then voltage is reduced until timing slack reaches a minimum safe guardband and the device consumes minimum power for the required throughput. If voltage is fixed then frequency is adjusted and maximum throughput is achieved. This type of operation increases efficiency or throughput by removing most of the timing margin. Frequency and voltage are adjusted to track any changes to circuit timing from sources such as temperature variation and degradation.

The controller for our statically-constrained system is a simple stepping algorithm, shown in Fig. 4 for voltage scaling mode. Overall timing slack, t_{sC}, is measured on a continual basis. If a slack deficit is detected, voltage is increased (or clock frequency is decreased) by a fixed step. If there is a slack surplus, voltage is decreased (or clock frequency is

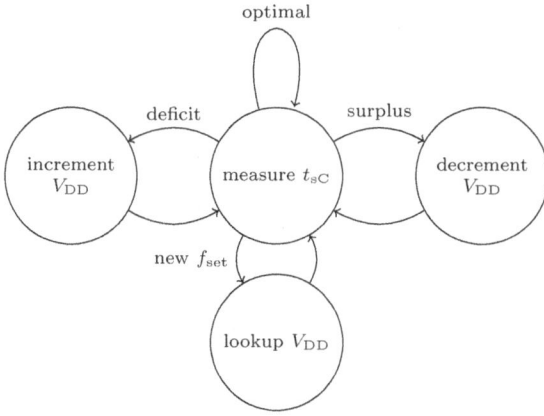

Figure 5: State diagram for dynamic voltage scaling with dynamic throughput constraint

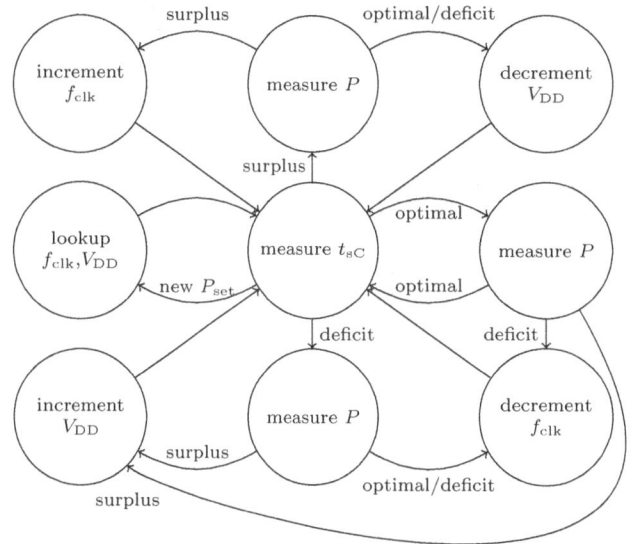

Figure 6: State diagram for dynamic voltage and frequency scaling with dynamic power constraint

increased). The definitions of slack surplus and deficit are discussed in Section 3.3.

3.2.2 Dynamically constrained

The most common use for traditional, STA-based DVFS is for systems with a number of voltage–throughput operating points. As the computational workload varies, frequency and voltage are scaled in tandem to reduce power consumption. In our implementation, voltage or frequency is set according to a system constraint while the other parameter is scaled to optimise timing slack.

Dynamic frequency and voltage constraints may change on a frequent basis — too fast for a stepping controller to track effectively. Also, it would be unsafe to set one parameter according to the constraint and let the other adapt. For example, if the voltage setting was reduced, clock frequency would have to be reduced first to an appropriate level. To address this, our controller uses a table to make coarse frequency and voltage changes and then makes fine adjustments based on timing slack measurements. The table is generated from an offline test over the anticipated operating corners with a suitable guardband added to allow for potential inaccuracies such as degradation. The table can be updated during run-time with data from timing slack measurement.

The controller for a dynamic throughput DVS system is shown in Fig. 5. It measures and responds to t_{sC} in the same way as the static throughput controller. Additionally, it consults a lookup table whenever the throughput constraint f_{set} is changed to jump to a safe, near-optimal voltage. Following a table look-up, frequency and voltage jumps are executed in a specific order: frequency first when the frequency decreases and voltage first when the frequency increases.

3.2.3 Power constrained

Another useful application of DVFS is to make a system meet an exact power constraint. This can be achieved to an extent with a model or table that estimates power from voltage but inaccuracy arises due to the dependence of power on data. We have developed a closed-loop controller that adjusts both frequency and voltage freely to meet a power constraint, illustrated in Fig. 6.

Like the other dynamically-constrained modes, it makes continuous measurements of t_{sC} while also responding to

constraint changes with a table look-up. Here, the power constraint P_{set} is used to index a frequency and voltage pair, which result in approximately the requested power consumption and a guaranteed safe timing slack. The response to t_{sC} is more complex in this mode as there is a further input variable to consider: measured power consumption. Plus, with frequency and voltage left unconstrained there is an extra degree of freedom to control. Adjustments are made to eliminate any surplus or deficit in one input variable without tending the other towards deficit. For example, if t_{sC} is optimal and P is in deficit then f_{clk} will be reduced, as this will reduce power consumption without cutting timing slack.

3.3 Calibration & Guardbanding

3.3.1 Shadow path offset

Timing slack measurements are made at the shadow registers so any data delay offset between the shadow registers and the RUMs must be calibrated for. This is done with a one-time offline calibration process, defined in algorithm 1.

The calibration algorithm determines the shadow path offset $t_{RS,i}$ for each RUM i by comparing timing slack measurements with a frequency sweep analysis. First, a timing slack measurement is made at a safe operating frequency f_{cal} and, since the system is not yet calibrated, this establishes the data arrival delay at the shadow registers $t_{aS,i}$. The calibration process must then traverse the maximum operating frequency of the circuit and so it uses a measurement f_{sig}, the highest frequency that produces the correct output sequence from a defined set of inputs, determined by a signature generator. f_{sig} is used only to define the limits of the calibration sweep and its accuracy does not contribute to the final calibration accuracy.

Starting at $0.95f_{sig}$, the clock frequency is stepped upwards such that the period decreases by $-\Delta t_{cal}$ at each interval. Shadow register discrepancy counts $d_i(t_\phi)$ are recorded at each frequency and at all phase offsets (t_ϕ) between 0 and $1/f_{clk}$. Any frequency where the RUM is safely clocked will

Algorithm 1 Shadow register delay offset calibration

for all $i \in \{\text{RUMs}\}$ **do**
    $f_{\text{clk}} \leftarrow f_{\text{cal}}$
    measure $t_{\text{sS},i}$
    $t_{\text{aS},i} \leftarrow 1/f_{\text{cal}} - t_{\text{sS},i}$
    measure f_{sig}
    $f_{\text{clk}} \leftarrow 0.95 f_{\text{sig}}$
    done $\leftarrow$ FALSE
    repeat
        set PLL frequency f
        measure $d_i(t_\phi)$ for $0 \le t_\phi < 1/f_{\text{clk}}$
        if $0 \in d_i$ **then**
            $t_{\text{aR},i} \leftarrow 1/f$
        else
            done $\leftarrow$ TRUE
        end if
        $f_{\text{clk}} \leftarrow \frac{1}{1/f - \Delta t_{\text{cal}}}$
    until done
    $t_{\text{RS},i} \leftarrow t_{\text{aR},i} - t_{\text{aS},i}$
end for

produce $d_i(t_\phi) = 0$ for one or more steps of t_ϕ. Hence, the RUM arrival delay $t_{\text{aR},i}$ is set to the reciprocal of the highest frequency before $d_i(t_\phi) > 0$ for all t_ϕ. This is similar to the error detection technique of Razor, except that we sweep t_ϕ instead of using a static phase offset — this avoids the need for onerous timing constraints. Finally, the shadow path calibration offset $t_{\text{RS},i}$ is calculated from the difference of $t_{\text{aR},i}$ and $t_{\text{aS},i}$.

For the greatest accuracy, calibration is carried out post-configuration on every device. We have not attempted to optimise calibration for execution time but we estimate the overall burden in a manufacturing environment to be comparable to other automated test and commissioning processes.

3.3.2 Measurement resolution

It is important to establish the resolution of timing slack measurements to ensure that the circuit remains timing-safe. For example, if slack were reported as 50ps with a resolution of ± 100ps then the circuit would not be safe from errors. The main limit to the resolution of slack measurement arises from the phase step resolution $\Delta t_\phi(f_{\text{clk}})$. This quantity is determined by the implementation of the FPGA clock generation hardware and is a function of the clock frequency. The accuracy of the shadow path offset calibration must also be considered — this is dependent on $\Delta t_\phi(f_{\text{cal}})$. We have designed the calibration and measurement algorithms to give conservative results. This means the actual slack will always be greater than or equal to the measured slack. The analysis which ensures this is given in Table 4, where the resolution intervals are given for all the intermediate quantities that determine a slack measurement.

Note that conservative measurement is achieved by taking different readings of $t_{\text{sS},i}$ for calibration and for measurement. In measurement, we round down and set $t_{\text{sS},i}$ to be the lowest t_ϕ for which $d_i(t_\phi) = 0$. This way, $t_{\text{sS},i}$ is less than or equal to the true slack. $t_{\text{RS},i}$, the calibration offset is subtracted to find $t_{\text{sR},i}$ so to preserve this property $t_{\text{RS},i}$ should be greater than or equal to the true offset. This means that during calibration $t_{\text{sS},i}$ is set to the lowest t_ϕ for which $d_i(t_\phi) > 0$. The end result is that reading of $t_{\text{sR},i}$ may

Table 4: Resolution intervals for slack measurement quantities

Qty.	Derivation	Interval
Calibration		
$t_{\text{sS},i}$	From $d_i(t_\phi)$	$[-\Delta t_\phi(f_{\text{cal}}), +0]$
$t_{\text{aS},i}$	$1/f_{\text{cal}} - t_{\text{sS},i}$	$[-0, +\Delta t_\phi(f_{\text{cal}})]$
$t_{\text{aR},i}$	f_{clk} sweep	$[-\Delta t_{\text{cal}}, +0]$
$t_{\text{RS},i}$	$t_{\text{aR},i} - t_{\text{aS},i}$	$[-(\Delta t_{\text{cal}} + \Delta t_\phi(f_{\text{cal}})), +0]$
Measurement		
$t_{\text{sS},i}$	From $d_i(t_\phi)$	$[-0, +\Delta t_\phi(f_{\text{clk}})]$
$t_{\text{sR},i}$	$t_{\text{sS},i} - t_{\text{RS},i}$	$[-0, +(\Delta t_\phi(f_{\text{clk}}) + \Delta t_{\text{cal}} + \Delta t_\phi(f_{\text{cal}}))]$

be up to $\Delta t_\phi(f) + \Delta t_{\text{cal}} + \Delta t_\phi(f_{\text{cal}})$ less than the true value, but never greater.

3.3.3 Calibration stability

The calibration offset $t_{\text{RS},i}$ is subject to variation due to temperature and degradation. However, the magnitude of $t_{\text{RS},i}$ is typically small compared to $t_{\text{aR},i}$, the data delay it is used to measure. Therefore, considering the measurement resolution that is currently achievable, a one-time calibration is sufficiently accurate for use over the lifetime of the FPGA configuration. In the case that resolution is increased such that calibration stability does affect accuracy, corner measurements, guardbanding and recalibration could be employed. The small magnitude of $t_{\text{RS},i}$ means that any guardbands would reduce performance by a smaller margin than if they were applied to the circuit as a whole.

One calibration stability factor that cannot be ignored is voltage. Voltage has a very strong affect on delay and the change in $t_{\text{RS},i}$ between V_{nom} and V_{min} is sufficient enough to affect accuracy. If DVS is used, we measure $t_{\text{RS},i}$ at a number of voltage nodes and interpolate between them during operation depending on V_{DD} at that time.

3.3.4 Guardbanding

In the absence of any fault tolerance or correction it is important that the system does not scale frequency or voltage to the point where timing errors are introduced. In section 3.3.2 we analysed the measurement resolution and showed that the actual slack is greater than or equal to the measured slack. However, thresholds for voltage and frequency scaling must still include a guardband to allow for timing fluctuations that vary faster than we can measure them. The guardband must be set so that if it is violated, the condition is detected and corrected (by adjusting frequency or voltage) before the remaining timing slack is eroded and failure occurs.

We consider two sources of timing fluctuation for guardbanding purposes. Stochastic effects are uncorrelated and include power supply ripple, clock jitter and noise. Drift effects are longer term and include external temperature and degradation.

The guardband calculation is:

$$t_{\text{G}} = \sum_m a_m \quad + \quad \sum_n b_n (t_{\text{M}} + t_{\text{L}})$$

Here, t_G is the guardband, t_M is the measurement latency and t_L is the control latency. a_m are the stochastic timing fluctuations, expressed as peak-to-peak variation in critical path delay, and b_n are the timing drifts, expressed as a maximum change in critical path delay per unit time. b_n are multiplied by the sum of the measurement and control latencies to obtain the maximum change in delay that could occur during the period the system needs to measure and respond to a guardband violation. All the timing fluctuation terms are summed to calculate the guardband. If any fluctuation parameter is dependent on frequency or voltage then we take its maximum value over the operating range. During operation, the controller takes action if overall timing slack falls below the guardband slack. Hence, a slack deficit occurs when $t_{sC} < t_G$.

An important factor in guardbanding is the allowance for data variation. Since timing slack measurement relies on normal operating inputs to stimulate paths, we cannot guarantee that the most critical paths are always exercised. There are two ways to allow for this in the guardband calculation. First, the measurement latency t_M can be set to a period during which critical path excitement can be reasonably expected. Secondly, an extra stochastic fluctuation factor a_m can be estimated that represents that maximum difference between the slack measured and the true slack of the critical path. We find this to be satisfactory for applications with moderately high data entropy. Where this is not the case potential solutions include lightweight test vector insertion and statistical analysis of the data arrival profiles — this is an area of ongoing research.

3.3.5 Hysteresis

While the guardband defines when the circuit is running with too little slack, we also need to decide when the slack is great enough to safely increase clock frequency or reduce voltage. A hysteresis band is needed so that an adjustment does not immediately cause a guardband violation. The hysteresis band is set thus:

$$t_H = \max(\Delta t_{clk}, \Delta V_{DD} \frac{dt_{sC}}{dV})$$

Here, t_H is the hysteresis, Δt_{clk} is the period increment for frequency scaling, ΔV_{DD} is the voltage increment for voltage scaling and $\frac{dt_{sC}}{dV}$ is the maximum sensitivity of slack to voltage. In operation, there is a slack surplus when $t_{sC} > t_G + t_H$.

An additional hysteresis parameter is needed in power-constrained DVFS mode. Power hysteresis, P_H, is chosen such that when a system is using optimal power ($P = P_{set}$), a single step of voltage or frequency made to optimise timing slack will not lead to a power surplus ($P < P_{set} - P_H$). Hence, P_H depends on Δt_{clk} and ΔV_{DD}, plus characterised sensitivities of power to period and power to voltage:

$$P_H = \max(\Delta t_{clk} \frac{dP}{dt_{clk}}, \Delta V_{DD} \frac{dP}{dV})$$

3.4 Experimental Hardware

Experiments are carried out with a thermally-controlled FPGA with an adjustable core voltage and power measurement. The FPGA model used is an Altera Cyclone IV EP4CE22F17C6, a 60nm device with 22,000 LEs. Temperature is regulated by applying a PID-controlled thermoelectric element to the FPGA package. This arrangement is capable of spanning the FPGA's rated temperature range

Figure 7: Experimental hardware, showing FPGA board in the centre with water-cooled thermoelectric element. FPGA core power is provided by the programmable PSU to the right.

of 0°C to 85°C (273-358K) with high accuracy. The FPGA core is powered directly from a programmable bench power supply (PSU) and this is set to vary the voltage between 0.9V and 1.2V. 0.9V is the minimum voltage at which all of the FPGA hardware is functional — below this level failure of the reset, configuration and PLL circuitry prevents operation. 1.2V is the nominal core voltage of the device and we have chosen not to exceed this so as to avoid excessive degradation. Accurate power measurements are made by the power supply.

Only the core supply of the FPGA is varied, this powers soft logic, DSPs and BRAM, leaving clock generation and I/O unaffected. While these experiments have used external power supply equipment, the hardware required to implement DVFS is already available on some commercial FPGA boards. The latest high-performance designs from both Xilinx and Altera include sophisticated power supply controllers which allow the FPGA to alter supply voltages and measure power. Alternatively, with the inclusion of few additional components (an ADC, current-sense resistor and digital-potentiometer) the required control and measurement can be provided to the FPGA.

Clock generation is already provided by on board PLLs. For the purposes of these experiments the PLL is reconfigured each time a new frequency is required, this incurs a stall as the voltage controlled oscillator locks on the new frequency. It is possible to preselect the new frequency on a different PLL and use one of the architecture's clock multiplexers to seamlessly switch between these in a single cycle. Finally, the necessary slack measurement and control circuitry can be automatically added to arbitrary designs with minimal overhead.

4. RESULTS

4.1 Benchmarks and Overhead

We tested DVFS on a range of benchmark operations. The mathematical operators are single or double precision floating point units, generated by FloPoCo[4], the filter is a 16 bit IIR with 12 taps generated by Spiral[5] and the DCT is 8 bit, 8 point. They are listed in Table 5 with their resource usages and timing model operating frequencies. Table 6 shows the resource and timing overhead of implementing timing slack measurement. The number of RUMs varies with the size of the benchmark and the distribution of timing slacks — circuits with many near-critical registers require more shadow registers. The resource over-

Table 5: Benchmarks used for experiments, with resource usage and timing

Benchmark	LUT	Reg	Mem	Mult	f_{sta}(MHz)
fpadd64	5403	5078	222b	0	138.4
fpexp32	1619	1454	18kb	4	79.8
fpexp64	4333	3839	88kb	44	84.1
fplog32	2295	2089	29kb	18	98.2
fpmult32	2330	2275	0b	8	142.2
DCT	2229	2034	0b	0	188.9
IIR	1105	852	0b	0	102.7

Table 6: Overhead of slack measurement for each benchmark with a 10% CDM

Bench.	RUM	ΔLUT	ΔReg	f_{sta}(MHz)	Δf_{sta}
fpadd64	15	15	30	138.3	-0.0%
fpexp32	19	19	38	78.4	-1.6%
fpexp64	34	34	68	83.0	-1.4%
fplog32	45	45	90	93.9	-4.3%
fpmult32	19	19	38	137.0	-3.7%
DCT	19	19	38	188.1	-0.5%
IIR	19	19	38	101.7	-0.9%

head is given for the shadow registers, discrepancy checkers and discrepancy registers. Discrepancy counters are not included since only a boolean indication is needed and they can be reduced to a single-bit latch replacing the discrepancy register. Controller functionality is also excluded because it is application-dependent. In many systems it would run on a soft or hard CPU as a background task. The controller in our experiments was partially implemented in FPGA logic with the remainder running in software on a host PC.

The timing overhead of DVFS is also given by comparing f_{sta} of the design before and after the addition of shadow registers. Since placement and routing are fixed following compilation of the bare application the change is small. However, there is nonetheless a difference. This occurs because the tool is unable to preserve every original routing path when adding the extra fan-out to the shadow registers. There are also changes due to the test framework that is added to collect, store and communicate experimental results.

4.2 Characterisation

To show that timing slack measurement can track changes due external factors, we have conducted experiments with temperature and voltage sweeps. Fig. 8 shows calibrated slack measurements $t_{\text{sR},i}$ for the 19 RUMs in the fpmult benchmark over the operating temperature range. As expected, slack decreases as the circuit slows down with increasing temperature. The total change is fairly modest — the critical path has slowed by around 400ps and at this scale the quantisation caused by the measurement resolution is quite apparent. Fig. 9 shows the same measurements taken over a voltage sweep. Voltage has a dramatic influence on timing slack and once it has dropped below 1.0V all of the slack at the most critical RUMs has been eroded. In both experiments f_{clk} is set to f_{sta}.

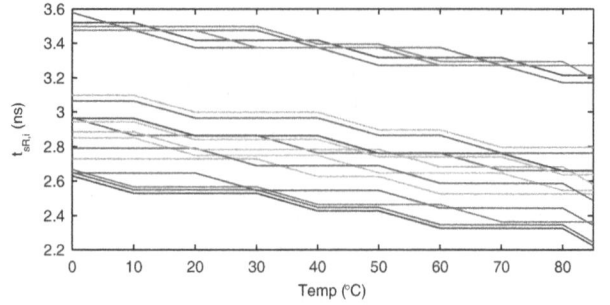

Figure 8: Slack measurement response to temperature variation in fpmult32

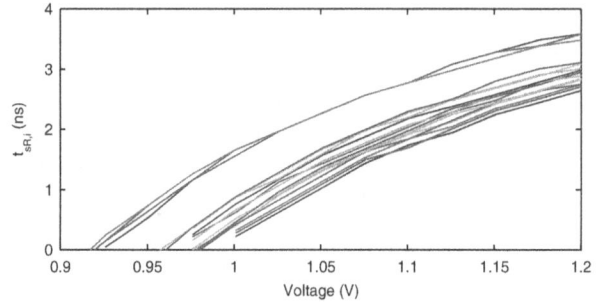

Figure 9: Slack measurement response to voltage variation in fpmult32

4.3 Voltage & Frequency Scaling

The main goal of performing closed-loop DVFS with timing slack measurement over STA-based methods is to reduce the overheads associated with timing model margins. In Figs. 10 and 11 we show how throughput and power respectively can be improved using our technique. First, in Fig. 10 we fix voltage at the nominal 1.2V assumed by the timing model and scale clock frequency to optimise timing slack. Throughputs from the timing model output (STA) are compared to throughputs under DFS at two temperature points. For this particular device, there is a substantial increase in throughput possible for all benchmarks. Delay is slightly lower at 27°C than 85°C, and the DFS controller is able to adapt to this.

Fig. 11 shows corresponding data in DVS mode. This time, clock frequency is fixed at f_{sta} of the original circuit,

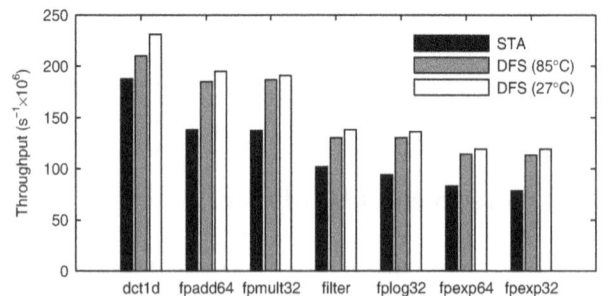

Figure 10: Throughput comparison between nominal and DFS. Benchmarks achieve a geomean improvement of **38.9%** at **27°C** and **30.7%** at **85°C**

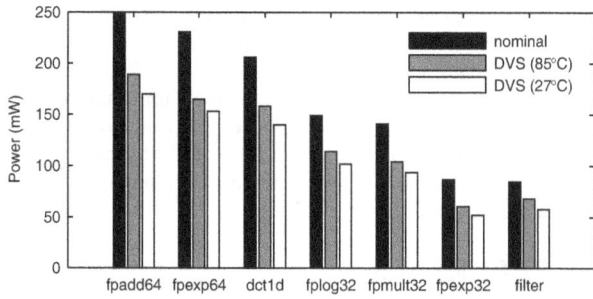

Figure 11: Operating power comparison between nominal and DVS. Benchmarks achieves a geomean improvement of 33.5% at 27°C and 24.9% at 85°C

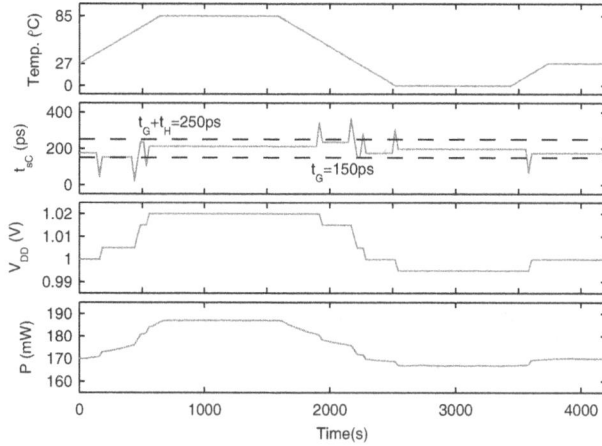

Figure 12: Transient response to temperature fluctuation in DVS with `fpmult32` at 27°C

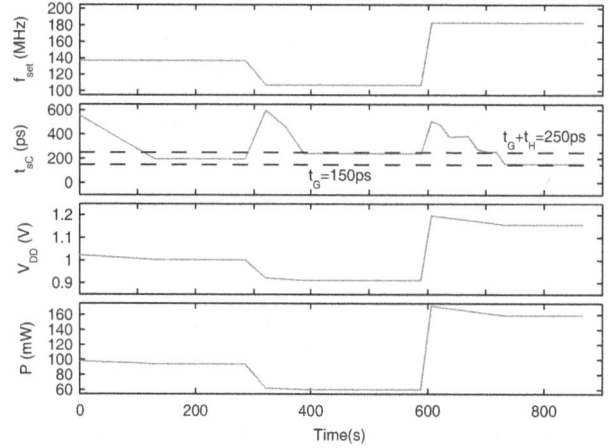

Figure 13: Transient response to throughput requirements in DVFS with `fpmult32` at 27°C

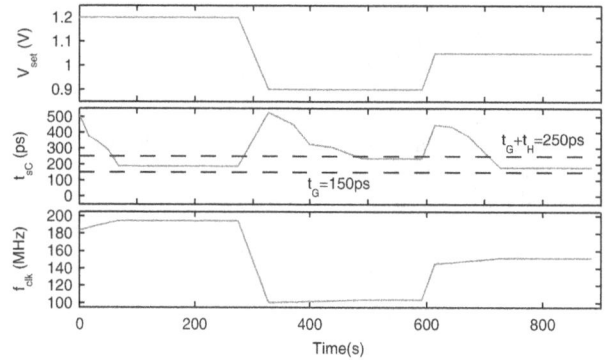

Figure 14: Transient response to voltage requirements in DVFS with `fpmult32` at 27°C

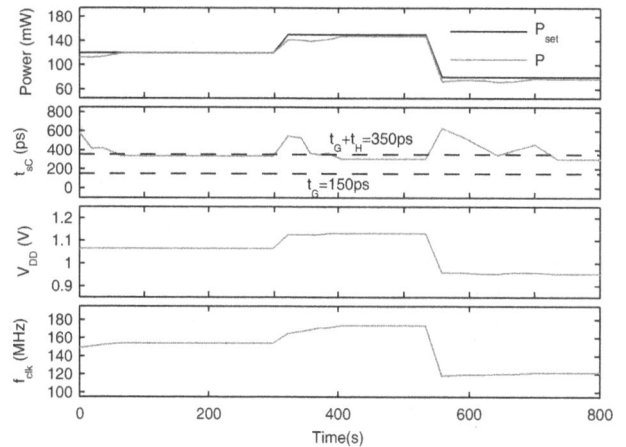

Figure 15: Transient response to power requirements in DVFS with `fpmult32`

before the addition of shadow registers and control logic and voltage is scaled to optimise timing slack. The chart displays the power consumption of benchmarks under V_{nom} (1.2V) and under dynamically-scaled voltage. There are significant reductions in power using DVS. Like throughput, power scales with temperature — some correlation would be expected anyway due to leakage current but the effect is amplified by voltage scaling.

4.4 Adaptive Scaling

In this section we test the ability of the DVS controller to adapt to changing external conditions. First, we look at a static-throughput DVS controller. Clock frequency is set to the timing model frequency f_{sta} and the voltage is adjusted to optimise timing slack. Fig. 12 shows the transient response of the system. Temperature is ramped up and down over the full operating range according to an external schedule. As temperature increases, timing slack t_{sC} drops below the guardband t_{sG}. Immediately, the controller responds by increasing voltage and slack is restored. The reverse happens as temperature falls: voltage drops and slack is kept constant. By setting voltage to the minimum required for safe operation, power is reduced and a saving is made. The controller would respond in a similar way to ageing, which can, incidentally, also cause a circuit to speed up in certain circumstances.

Next, we look at the response of systems with dynamic throughput and voltage constraints. Fig.13 shows a system responding to a changing throughput constraint. Each time there is a step in the input constraint, the DVFS table is consulted to set the voltage to a conservative level. Then, slack measurements are used to back off the voltage until optimal timing is reached. This way, the minimum power is used for each throughput level. Fig.14 shows the converse system where voltage is set according to an external schedule. Here, frequency is set to the conservative value read from the table, then it is increased to achieve maximum throughput while respecting the timing slack guardband.

Finally, we focus on the most complex DVFS controller mode: dynamic power constrained. Like the previous two modes, an external constraint — this time for power — is set according to an arbitrary schedule. At each requested power step the table is consulted to find a voltage and a frequency that are conservative for both power and timing slack. Then, following the decision process shown in Fig. 6 voltage and frequency are adjusted to maximise throughput while respecting the timing slack guardband and the power constraint.

All of the DVFS modes demonstrate that our technique is able to safely maximise throughput or power efficiency under changing external conditions and operating constraints. However, despite using a lookup table to accelerate large steps in operating points, the controller can still take some time to converge on optimum settings. There are two improvements that could be made to our controller to address this. Firstly, the slack measurement controller is currently configured for experimental purposes and gathers more data than is necessary for this application — for example, discrepancy counts are taken at all phase steps whereas only a few are needed to establish if the guardband or hysteresis slacks are violated. Secondly, the fixed-step control algorithm results in a system that is over-damped. A more advanced control technique would reach optimal operation in fewer steps.

5. CONCLUSION

This paper has demonstrated dynamic voltage and frequency scaling using online timing slack measurement in FPGAs. This method can better reduce operating margins than scaling techniques that rely on static timing analysis or tunable replica circuits, yet it requires a far smaller overhead than intrusive schemes like Razor and asynchronous design. We have shown techniques for calibration and guardbanding the slack measurements to ensure optimised and safe operation, and developed controllers that use timing information feedback to maximise circuit throughput or efficiency. This DVFS system has a range of applications including power efficiency improvement, lifespan extension and systems with dynamic operating constraints. The method has been demonstrated on a number of benchmark circuits running on a Altera Cyclone IV FPGA.

Single-variable DFS and DVS show the potential to yield significant improvements in throughput and power respectively, even at worst-case temperature corners. It is expected that even greater yields could be achieved on devices using a smaller, high-performance process node. The controllers can also adapt to changes in voltage or throughput constraints and achieve optimal operation under varying workload conditions. A more advanced system, power-constrained DVFS,

provides optimised operation within a defined and variable power envelope by scaling both the voltage and frequency.

An interesting extension of this work would be its implementation on systems with multiple clock domains. With independent slack measurement and clock (and possibly voltage) control, a power budget could be distributed by a runtime algorithm to best match the variation in computational load across a system.

6. REFERENCES

[1] Enhanced Intel SpeedStep technology for the Intel Pentium M processor. Technical report, Intel Corporation, 2004.

[2] C. Chow, L. Tsui, P. Leong, W. Luk, and S. Wilton. Dynamic voltage scaling for commercial FPGAs. In *Proc. Int. Conf. on Field Programmable Logic and Applications (FPL)*, 2005.

[3] D. Ernst, et al. Razor: a low-power pipeline based on circuit-level timing speculation. In *Proc. IEEE/ACM Int. Symp. on Microarchitecture (MICRO)*, 2003.

[4] F. de Dinechin, C. Klein, and B. Pasca. Generating high-performance custom floating-point pipelines. In *Proc. Int. Conf. on Field Programmable Logic and Applications (FPL)*, 2009.

[5] A. Gacic, M. Püschel, and J. M. F. Moura. Fast automatic implementations of fir filters. In *Proc. Int. Conf. on Acoustics, Speech, and Signal Processing (ICASSP)*, 2003.

[6] J.M. Levine, E. Stott, G.A. Constantinides, and P.Y.K. Cheung. Online measurement of timing in circuits: For health monitoring, dynamic voltage frequency scaling. In *Proc. IEEE Int. Symp. on Field-Programmable Custom Computing Machines (FCCM)*, 2012.

[7] J.M. Levine, E. Stott, G.A. Constantinides, and P.Y.K. Cheung. SMI: Slack measurement insertion for online timing monitoring in FPGAs. In *Proc. Int. Conf. on Field Programmable Logic and Applications (FPL)*, 2013.

[8] J.S.J. Wong and P.Y.K. Cheung. Improved delay measurement method in FPGA based on transition probability. In *Proc. ACM/SIGDA Int. Symp. on Field Programmable Gate Arrays (FPGA)*, 2011.

[9] J. Nunez-Yanez, V. Chouliaras, and J. Gaisler. Dynamic voltage scaling in a FPGA-based system-on-chip. In *Proc. Int. Conf. on Field Programmable Logic and Applications (FPL)*, 2007.

[10] E. Stott, J.S.J. Wong, P. Sedcole, and P.Y.K. Cheung. Degradation in FPGAs: Measurement and modelling. In *Proc. ACM/SIGDA Int. Symp. on Field Programmable Gate Arrays (FPGA)*, 2010.

[11] P. Zuchowski, P. Habitz, J. Hayes, and J. Oppold. Process and environmental variation impacts on ASIC timing. In *Proc. IEEE/ACM Int. Conf. on Computer Aided Design (ICCAD)*, 2004.

This work was supported by the Engineering and Physical Sciences Research Council [grant numbers EP/K034448/1, EP/I012036/1, EP/H013784/1]. See www.prime-project.org for more information about the PRiME programme.

CAD and Routing Architecture for Interposer-Based Multi-FPGA Systems

Andre Hahn Pereira
Computer and Digital Systems Engineering
Department - Escola Politécnica
University of São Paulo
São Paulo, SP
Brazil
andre.hahn@usp.br

Vaughn Betz
Department of Electrical and Computer
Engineering
University of Toronto
Toronto, ON
Canada
vaughn@eecg.utoronto.ca

ABSTRACT

Interposer-based multi-FPGA systems are composed of multiple FPGA dice connected through a silicon interposer. Such devices allow larger FPGA systems to be built than one monolithic die can accomodate and are now commercially available. An open question, however, is how efficient such systems are compared to a monolithic FPGA, as the number of signals passing between dice is reduced and the signal delay between dice is increased in an interposer system vs. a monolithic FPGA.

We create a new version of VPR to investigate the architecture of such systems, and show that by modifying the placement cost function to minimize the number of signals that must cross between dice we can reduce routing demand by 18% and delay by 2%. We also show that the signal count between dice and the signal delay between dice are key architecture parameters for interposer-based FPGA systems. We find that if an interposer supplies (between dice) 60% of the routing capacity that the normal (within-die) FPGA routing channels supply, there is little impact on the routability of circuits. Smaller routing capacities in the interposer do impact routability however: minimum channel width increases by 20% and 50% when an interposer supplies only 40% and 30% of the within-die routing, respectively. The interposer also impacts delay, increasing circuit delay by 34% on average for a 1 ns interposer signal delay and a four-die system. Reducing the interposer delay has a greater benefit in improving circuit speed than does reducing the number of dice in the system.

Categories and Subject Descriptors

B.7.1 [**Integrated Circuits**]: Types and Design Style—*VLSI*; B.7.2 [**Integrated Circuits**]: Design Aids—*Placement and Routing*

General Terms

Algorithms, Design

Keywords

FPGA; Silicon interposer; 2.5D ICs

1. INTRODUCTION

Interposer-based multi-FPGA systems are composed of multiple FPGA dice, which are connected through a silicon interposer. The interposer is fabricated with an older technology than that used for the dies, and links between dice include both a micro-bump on each FPGA die and a metal wire on the interposer [11]. This results in a reduced connectivity between dice and increased delay for connections between dice, as compared to the total routing connectivity and the delay one can achieve within a single die. In this paper we present an architecture study of silicon interposer-based FPGAs that analyzes how the reduced connectivity and increased delay impact their performance.

The silicon interposer FPGA technology is interesting because it enables the creation of large FPGAs composed of small dies and also of very large FPGAs, with higher logic capacity than one can achieve with a single die. Such FPGA systems are sometimes called 2.5D FPGAs, since they make use of vertical stacking of dies on an interposer to enable higher integration levels.

Being able to make large FPGAs with multiple smaller dies is particularly interesting at the beginning of a new manufacturing process, when defect densities are high. In such a case, good-die yield drops dramatically as the die size increases, and this drastically impacts the availability of large FPGAs early in the process lifetime.

The idea of using 3 dimensions to design FPGAs is not new. [1] proposed the creation of 3D FPGAs by stacking 2D FPGAs and connecting them with solder bumps. Lin et al also studied 3D FPGAs, but using a different approach [8], proposing multiple active layers, with different FPGA functions in each. While promising, both approaches have manufacturing challenges: [1] requires a higher density of through-silicon vias than can currently be manufactured and the multiple active layers required by [8] are not yet widely available. In contrast, silicon interposers linked to dies via microbumps are now manufacturable.

Chaware et al presented Xilinx's approach to silicon interposer FPGAs [4]. They describe the physical characteristics of their implementation, including the bump pitch and estimates of the amount of die-to-die connectivity and the die-to-die delay. However [4] does not analyze the architecture question of the routability of the resulting system, nor describe possible CAD optimizations, which are the questions we investigate.

The main contributions of our work are as follows:

- A detailed study of how the multi-FPGA system routability is impacted by the amount of connectivity between dice provided by the interposer.

- An Analysis of the impact of the interposer on timing.

- Modification of the VPR CAD tool to model and target 2.5D silicon interposer-based FPGAs, as well as CAD changes to optimize for 2.5D FPGAs.

- Analysis of the commercially available Xilinx Virtex-7 silicon interposer FPGAs [13][14]. We measure the connectivity reduction and delay increase between dies caused by the interposer on such FPGAs in order to see where these devices lie within the architcture space we explore.

The paper is organized as follows. Section 2 gives more information about silicon interposer technology. Section 3 describes the changes made to the FPGA architecture description and to VPR to target 2.5D FPGAs. Section 4 describes optimizations made to the VPR placement algorithm to improve quality on such FPGAs and Section 5 presents architectural results for 2.5D FPGAs.

2. SILICON INTERPOSER BACKGROUND

As mentioned in the previous section, interposer-based FPGAs allow the creation of chips larger than a single die, making a "More than Moore" improvement on the size and number of logic elements possible, and with chips combined far more tightly and with more connectivity than if they were on separate boards connected through conventional means.

The improvement in the number of logic elements of 2.5D FPGAs over conventional ones is very significant. Xilinx's largest interposer-based FPGA, the Virtex-7 XC7V2000T, has 4 dies (which Xilinx calls Super Logic Regions) and 1.954 million logic elements [14], while the largest non-interposer Virtex-7 die (the XC7VX980T), has 979k logic elements and Altera's largest FPGA, the Stratix V 5SGXBB, has 952k logic elements [2]. Even though all these FPGAs use a 28 nm process, silicon interposer technology allows the creation of FPGAs with twice the resources possible on even an extremely large single die.

Another major advantage of interposer-based FPGAs comes at the beginning of a new manufacturing process, when the defect density is high [11]. Bigger dice suffer a much reduced yield compared to smaller dice, and this greatly affects the supply and cost of top-of-the-line FPGAs to early adopters.

To illustrate this impact, consider a new process in which the defect density is $1/cm^2$, which is a reasonable value early in the process lifecycle, and the die area is $6cm^2$, which roughly matches the size of the largest member of a high-end FPGA family such as Virtex 7. Using the Poisson Yield Model [6], the yield is only 0.25% of die. If instead the chip is composed of four $1.5cm^2$ dies, the yield is 22%. This means that a 12 inch silicon wafer with $730cm^2$ of area would produce on average 0.3 working $6cm^2$ dies, while the same wafer would produce on average 107 working $1.5cm^2$ dies. Therefore, as a $6cm^2$ chip would be composed of four $1.5cm^2$ dies, the wafer would yield 26.75 systems on average, as the "assembly yield" of placing these four die on an interposer is very high [4]. Hence the number of interposer-based FPGAs created from the same silicon wafer would be almost $100\times$ greater than a monolithic FPGA of the same size.

When the process matures and the defect density decreases this advantage drops significantly. Consider a mature process with defect density of $0.1/cm^2$. The yield for a $6cm^2$ die is 55% and the yield for a $1.5cm^2$ die is 86%. Hence the number of single die FPGAs created from a $730cm^2$ silicon wafer would be 66.9 and the number of interposer-based FPGAs created would be 104.6. While the interposer-based FPGA still has a yield advantage it might not lead to a major cost advantage, particularly when the cost of the interposer and assembling the die to it are included. For the large, state-of-the-art FPGAs that are built early in a process cycle and heavily used for prototyping, however, there is clearly a compelling cost advantage to an interposer-based solution.

2.1 Virtex-7 Interposer-based FPGAs

The Xilinx 2.5D FPGAs from the Virtex-7 family are currently the only commercially available silicon interposer-based FPGAs. As described in Section 3 we are studying the impact of several key interposer parameters on the performance of the multi-FPGA system, including (i) the percentage of the wiring normally present between rows of the FPGA which are cut when crossing between dice, and (ii) the extra delay (vs. a normal connection between adjacent rows) added when one must traverse the interposer. To locate where Virtex-7 lies in this architecture space, we combined published information on the implementation of Xilinx's interposer-based FPGAs [4] with a detailed analysis of the *XC7V2000T* FPGA routing resources visible in the *Vivado Device View*.

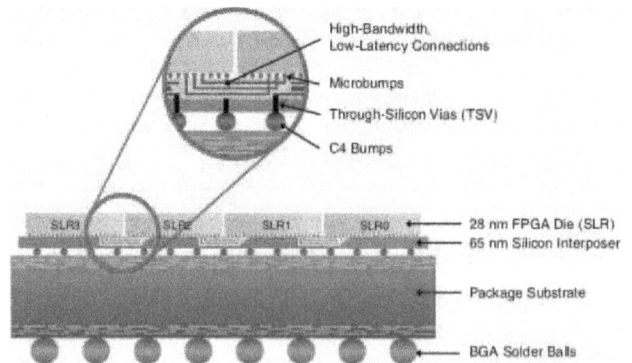

Figure 1: Lateral view of an interposer-based FPGA[13]. The FPGA dice are at the top, and are connected to the silicon interposer through microbumps. The interposer is then connected to the substrate through C4 bumps.

The *XC7V2000T* is composed of four identical dice arranged such that the vertical routing crosses between the dice. Each horizontal edge of each die has 280 groups of

48 length-12 wires crossing the interposer, which sums to a total of 13440 wires between dice. There are also 40 clock wires crossing the interposer. The average number of wires per vertical channel of this FPGA is 210 and there are approximately 280 vertical channels on the FPGA, resulting in approximately 58800 vertical wires crossing a horizontal cutline within a die. Hence the number of wires which cross the interposer is about 23% of the total number of within-die vertical wires.

The 28nm dies are connected to the 65nm silicon interposer through microbumps with a $45\mu m$ pitch. Hence the area occupied by microbumps at one edge of one die is $13440 \times (45\mu m)^2 = 27mm^2$. If we assume each die is $7 \times 12mm$, as presented by Chaware et al. in [4], the bumps have to be spread out near the edge and need to go as far as $2.25mm$ away from the edge of the die. This greater distance from the border increaes the length of the inter-die connections, and along with the presence of the micro-bumps and their capacitance, leads to an increased delay for these crossing wires vs. that of a typical on-die routing wire. Chaware et al. state that the latency to cross the interposer is approximately $1ns$. For comparison, a typical medium length 28 nm FPGA routing wire (e.g. spanning four logic blocks) has a delay of approximately 125 ps, while a longer wire (e.g. spanning 12 logic blocks) has a delay of approximately 250 ps.

Overall, these interposer-based FPGAs have increased delay and reduced connectivity between dies, with approximately 23% of the usual number of vertical wires crossing between dies and approximately $1ns$ of increased delay to cross the interposer.

3. ARCHITECTURE MODELS

To properly model a silicon interposer FPGA, the popular FPGA exploration toolset, Verilog-to-Routing (VTR) [12], was used. The logic synthesis portions of the flow (ODIN II and ABC) were left untouched, while the placement and routing portion of the flow (VPR [3]) was modified to model and optimize for interposer-based FPGAs. The modifications were made in such a way that they require no changes to any of the input files, so one can experiment with interposer-based FPGAs with any existing benchmark circuits and any existing VPR-format FPGA architecture description simply by specifying appropriate command-line parameters.

Three parameters were added to VPR: *% wires cut*, *increased delay* and *number of cuts*. These three parameters describe the interposer portion of the 2.5D FPGA as detailed below.

3.1 % wires cut

This variable describes and models the reduced connectivity between different dice by specifying the fraction of routing wires that are removed at the border between dice. For example, if a channel had 200 wires and *% wires cut* was 70, 140 of them would be cut and only 60 would pass through the interposer. Higher values of *% wires cut* make an interposer easier to manufacture, and can reduce the interposer delay by allowing all the microbumps linking dice to be placed near the die edge. However, the higher *% wires cut* is, the less routable the multi-die system becomes. As described in 2.1, the Virtex 7 family has *% wires cut* = 77%.

3.2 Increased delay

Interposer wires are longer and wider than on-die wires and have microbumps on each end. *Increased delay* models the resulting larger delay when compared with wires which are internal to a die. A reasonable estimate for this variable is around $1ns$, as presented by Chaware et al[4].

3.3 Number of cuts

Number of cuts describes how many cuts were made to the interposer-based FPGA versus a monolithic die. If *number of cuts* equals 1 then there are 2 dies, and so on. We investigate values of this parameter between 1 and 3 (between 2 and 4 dies), reflecting commercial practice: the Virtex 7 family has members with *number of cuts* = 2 and 3. Figure 2 shows a sample architecture with one cutline.

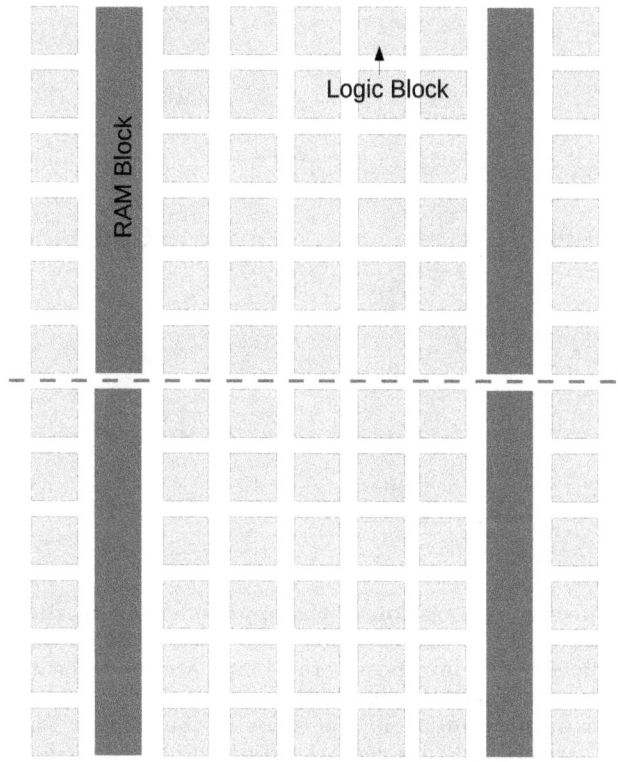

Figure 2: A sample two-die / 1-cutline architecture containing both logic blocks and RAM blocks.

3.4 Implementation

To model an interposer-based FPGA in VPR the Routing Resource Graph (*rrgraph*) must be modified. The rrgraph is the data structure that defines all the available routing wires and switches in the FPGA, as well the delay of each. Given a suitable rrgraph, the VPR router can implement circuits in the desired FPGA, and the VPR timing analyzer can estimate their delay.

The presence of multiple dice in an interposer-based FPGA was modeled by creating horizontal cuts in the FPGA, which are equally spaced vertically. Every wire that crosses one of these cuts in fact passes through the interposer. In the experiments below, we use an architecture that has only unidirectional wires [9], as these are the dominant routing architecture in modern FPGAs. Such wires can only be driven at their beginning. To control the wiring capacity between dies *% wires cut* wires of each channel segment crossing a cutline have their connections to wires and block inputs on the die opposite to their starting point removed, and the wires which aren't cut have *increased delay* added to their connections which cross the cutline. Note that the combination of a unidirectional routing architecture and a silicon interposer results in some blocks near the cutline having reduced routing connectivity as some of the routing wires driving their inputs are disconnected from the (single) wire driver, when that driver is on the other side of the cutline and the wire is one of the cut wires.

Figure 3 illustrates the approach used.

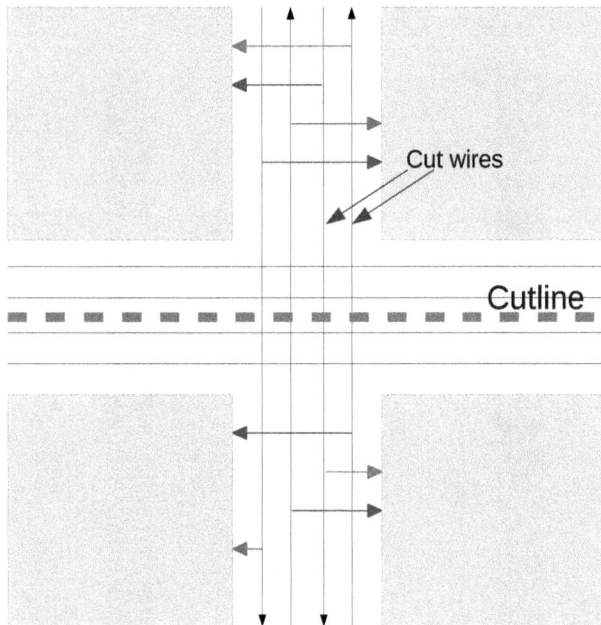

Figure 3: Illustration of the approach used to simulate crossing the interposer. The red dashed line indicates the interposer, the black arrows indicate the direction of the wires. Blue arrows indicate normal connections from the wires to the CLBs. The red arrows indicate removed connections and green arrows indicate connections with increased delay.

For all experiments in this paper, the remaining architecture parameters of the FPGA are taken from the "flagship" architecture (*k6_frac_N10_mem32K_40nm.xml*) of the VTR project. The parameters of this architecture are in line with both current commercial FPGAs and academic research into best practices. It consists of logic clusters with 10 fracturable 6-LUTs per block (N=10, k=6), and also includes 32kb RAM blocks and DSP blocks configurable to perform 9x9, 18x18 or 36x36 multipliers. The delay values in the architecture are taken from 40 nm circuit simulations and 40 nm commercial FPGAs. It uses unidirectional routing, with all wire segments having length L = 4.

4. CAD ENHANCEMENTS

Once the routing resource graph was modified as detailed in Section 3, the VPR router adapted automatically to the interposer architecture. Placement, however, is crucial in

mitigating the impact of the reduced wiring and increased delay when crossing between dice; a good placement should minimize the number of signals crossing between dice, particularly time-critical ones. We investigated several enhancements to VPR's placement cost function to improve result quality.

VPR uses 2 different costs as the metrics for its placer algorithm: the timing cost and the bounding box (wiring) cost. The usual VPR timing cost is a (criticality-weighted) summation of the estimated delay (given the current placement) of every connection required by the circuit [10]:

$$Timing\_Cost = \sum_{\forall i,j \subset circuit} delay(\Delta x_{ij}, \Delta y_{ij}) \times \\ criticality(i,j) \tag{1}$$

where ij denotes a connection from block i to block j that exists in the circuit netlist. The bounding box cost estimates the amount of wiring required for a net, based on the number of pins and size of the net's bounding box. VPR's original formulation is [3]:

$$wiring\_cost_{orig} = \sum_{n=1}^{N_{nets}} q(n) \times [\frac{bb_x(n)}{avg\_chanx\_W(n)} + \\ \frac{bb_y(n)}{avg\_chany\_W(n)}] \tag{2}$$

where $bb_x(n)$ and $bb_y(n)$ are the dimensions of the bounding box of net n in the x and y directions, respectively. avg_chanx_W and avg_chany_W are the average x-directed and y-directed channel widths over this bounding box. Finally, $q(n)$ is a function obtained from [5] which models the fact that bounding boxes underpredict the required routing for high fanout nets. $q(n)$ slowly increases with the fanout of net n, rising from 1 for nets with 3 or fewer terminals to 2.79 for nets with 50 terminals.

We modified both the placer's bounding box and timing costs to account for the increased latency to cross the interposer and for the reduced wire capacity close to the cutlines, as the wire availability becomes more sparse.

4.1 Placer timing cost

The standard placer timing cost in VPR assumes that the FPGA is homogeneous and consequently the delay between 2 points (x_1, y_1) and (x_2, y_2) only depends on $(\Delta x, \Delta y)$. This is obviously not true for interposer-based FPGAs, as the cutlines make them heterogeneous in the y direction.

To solve this problem and improve the quality of the results, an extra term was added to the delay function. The delay function becomes:

$$delay(i,j) = delay(\Delta x_{ij}, \Delta y_{ij}) + \\ times\_crossed(i,j) \times delay\_increase \tag{3}$$

where $times\_crossed(i,j)$ is the number of times this path has to cross the interposer to go from (x_i, y_i) to (x_j, y_j) and $delay\_increase$ is the timing penalty of crossing the interposer.

4.2 Placer wiring cost

VPR's wiring cost also considers the FPGA to be homogeneous, and uses only the number of nets, the size of the net's bounding box and the average number of wires per channel to calculate the cost. Thus, to account for the reduced connectivity near the cutlines an extra cost term, *cut_cost*, was created. This new cost is added to (2) to create the total wiring cost.

$$wiring\_cost = wiring\_cost_{orig} + cut\_cost \qquad (4)$$

We tested several different *cut_cost* formulations, as well as different weighting (C values) for each. For all of the formulations the variable C' was defined as:

$$C' = \frac{C \times ratio\_wires\_cut}{avg\_chany\_W(n)} \qquad (5)$$

where *ratio_wires_cut* is the ratio of wires cut at the cutline. This formulation of C' ensures that when we choose a C value of 1, the new term cost term is of roughly the same magnitude as *wire_cost_{orig}* in (2) and that it is weighted more heavily for interposer architectures in which the wiring between dice is more scarce.

The first *cut_cost* term we tested was:

$$cut\_cost = \sum_{n=1}^{N_{nets}} C' \times times\_crossed(n) \qquad (6)$$

which penalizes the net according to the number of cutlines the bounding box spans; this directly penalizes each signal crossing between dice. Surprisingly this extra term did not result in significant improvements to the quality of results and in some cases even made them worse. We believe this is due to the discontinuous, non-smooth, nature of this cost function – it does not guide placement optimization well as a bounding box shrinks toward a cutline. Placement changes that make bounding boxes "almost not cross" a cutline are not given any gain; only a sudden change in the placement that moves a bounding box entirely to one side or the other of the cutline yields a cost reduction. This insight led us to the other proposed functions, which give gradual gains as bounding boxes change in their size and come closer to avoiding a cutline crossing.

The other tested terms were:

$$cut\_cost = \sum_{n=1}^{N_{nets}} C' \times bbWidth(n) \times times\_crossed(n) \qquad (7)$$

$$cut\_cost = \sum_{n=1}^{N_{nets}} C' \times bbHeight(i) \times times\_crossed(n) \qquad (8)$$

$$cut\_cost = \sum_{n=1}^{N_{nets}} C' \times minDist(i) \times times\_crossed(n) + \\ C' \times times\_crossed(n) \qquad (9)$$

$$cut\_cost = \sum_{n=1}^{N_{nets}} C' \times bbHeight(n) \qquad (10)$$

where *bbWidth(n)* and *bbHeight(n)* are the width and height of the bounding box of the net n, respectively, and *minDist(n)* is the minimum distance from the top or bottom of the bounding box to a cutline.

4.3 Effectiveness of the enhancements

We used VPR 7.0, with the enhancements we detailed above, and the architecture file *k6_frac_N10_mem32K_40nm* in the experiments below. All experiments targeted the smallest FPGA (with number of rows equal to number of columns) which could accomodate a benchmark circuit; this represents a very full FPGA with little white space left, and hence presents a difficult case to an interposer-based FPGA as no die can be left mostly empty.

Figures 4 and 5 show the efficacy of the five placer wiring cost modifications as their weight, C varies. Each point in the graphs is the geometric mean of the results with *% wires cut* = 60 and 80, and the results for 60% and 80% are themselves geometric means of the results of 6 circuits from the VTR benchmark suite [12]: *stereovision0, stereovision1, mkDelayWorker32B, mkSMAdapter4B, or1200* and *blob_merge*. These values for *% wires cut* were chosen because they in the likely range of wires which can cross the interposer without exceeding the microbump capacity, as described in Section 2.1. The *area-delay product* is the product of the *minimum channel width* and the *critical path delay*. To obtain the *critical path delay* the circuits were run with a low stress routing with a channel width, $W = 1.3 \times minW$, where *minW* is the minimum channel width for which the circuit is still routable.

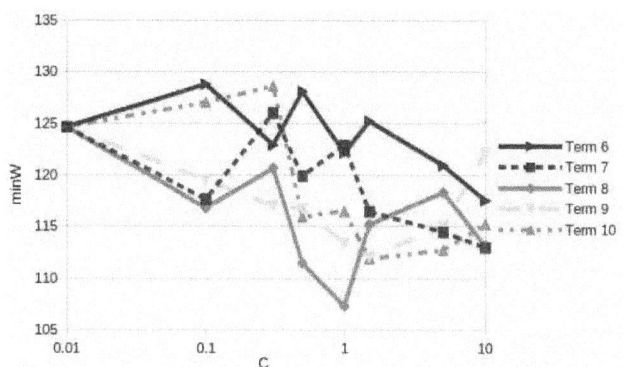

Figure 4: **Minimum channel width vs. weighting for different *cut_cost* terms.**

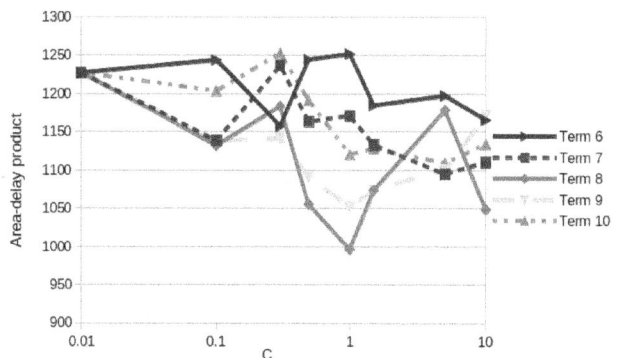

Figure 5: **Area-delay product vs. weighting for different *cut_cost* terms.**

The best C value and the resulting performance for each term is summarized in Table 1. Note that cost term (8)

Term	Best C	minW	crit_path(ns)	Area-delay
None	-	124.636	9.844	1226.955
6	0.3	122.929	9.413	1157.09
7	5	114.444	9.565	1094.68
8	1	107.303	9.285	996.26
9	1	113.381	9.280	1052.16
10	5	112.703	9.841	1109.11

Table 1: Best weighting and performance for each *cut_cost* term.

with weighting $C = 1.0$ has the best performance; this is the configuration used in the rest of our experiments.

We believe the key to the good performance of this cost function is that it produces gradual gains as bounding boxes crossing the cutline shrink to be closer and closer to being captured entirely on one side of the cutline. Consider for example the 3 bounding boxes shown in Figure 6. Note that bounding box (a) and (b) both cross the cutline and hence are penalized equally by (6), while bounding box (c) does not cross a cutline and hence is not penalized. However, bounding box (b) is mostly on the lower side of the cutline; it is more likely that later smaller placement changes will result in the bounding box moving entirely below the cutline, reducing interposer wiring demand. Cost function terms (8) and (9) will both penalize bounding box (a) more than bounding box (b) to guide placement to gradually move bounding boxes to one side or the other of a cutline. Figure 5 shows that these are the two best performing *cut_cost* terms.

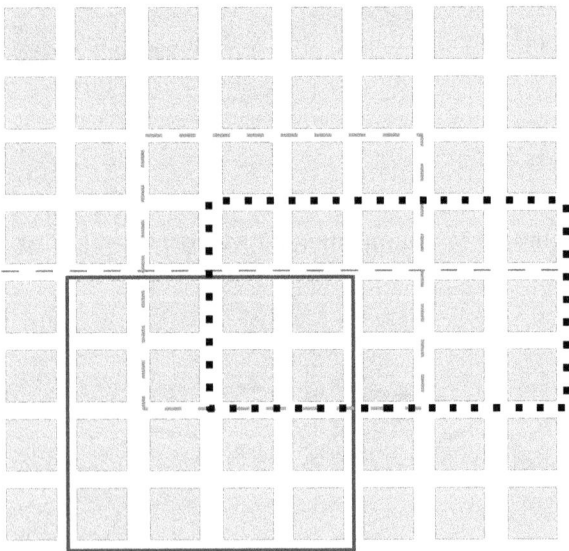

Figure 6: Illustration of three different scenarios for the wiring cost. The dashed green box shows a case where *(a)* it crosses the interposer, the dotted black box shows a case where *(b)* it barely crosses the cutline, and the solid blue one shows a case where *(c)* the bounding box does not span the cutline.

Figure 7 shows the minimum channel width for different values of *% wires cut* when there are no optimizations and

when *cut_const* (8) is used. Figure 8 compares result quality with both enhanced timing and wiring cost functions. These experiments were run with term (8), and are the geometric means of the runs with *% wires cut = 60, 70, 80*.

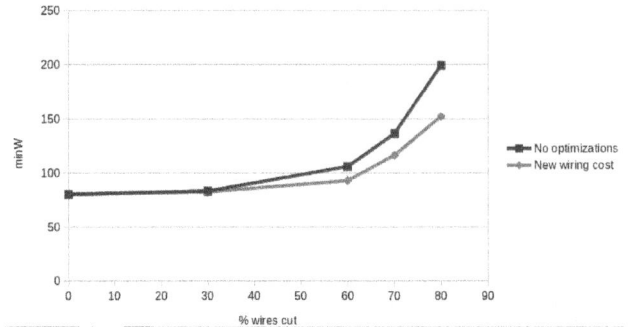

Figure 7: Minimum channel width vs. *% wires cut*.

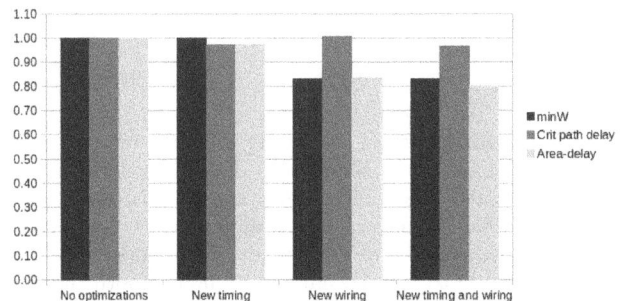

Figure 8: Performance of different placer optimizations, relative to the original VPR results. The area-delay product is calculated as the product $minW \times criticalpathdelay$.

The graphs show that combining the timing with the bounding box optimizations led to an average of 20% improvement on the area-delay product and the most significant contribution was made by incorporation of *cut_cost* into the wire cost function.

5. ARCHITECTURE RESULTS

Using the best CAD settings found in Section 4 we analyzed the impact of three key architecture parameters: *% wires cut, delay increase* and *number of cuts*. All the experiments were run with the eight largest circuits from the VTR benchmark [12], namely: *bgm, LU8PEEng, LU32PEEng, mcml, mkDelayWorker32B, stereovision0, stereovision1* and *stereovision2*. The size of these circuits ranges from 9, 100 to 153, 000 primitives (LUTs, FFs, etc.), with an average size of 52, 600 primitives. All results are the geometric mean over all circuits for a given interposer architecture.

5.1 Interposer Wiring Capacity (% wires cut)

To analyze the impact of the number of cut wires we ran experiments varying only this parameter while leaving the number of cuts and the increased delay constant. The values used for these parameters were *number of cuts = 3* (corresponding to four dice) and *increased delay = 1ns*, as these values are similar to those of the *XC7V2000T* device.

Figure 9 shows the graph of minimum channel width versus *% wires cut*. It can be noted from this graph that the minimum channel width increases slowly up to 60% of wires cut, indicating that the placement engine is able to avoid saturating the interposer routing until that point. When more than 60% of the wires are cut however (i.e. the interposer provides less than 40% of the usual within-die routing capacity), the minimum channel width grows rapidly indicating that the interposer routing bandwidth has become a limiting factor. The minW value at 60% is 20% greater than with no wires cut, while at 70% it is 52% above and at 80% it is 125% larger than the minW with no cut wires.

The critical path delay, depicted in Figure 10, on the other hand, is not strongly influenced by the percentage of wires cut, as the critical path delay at 60% of the wires cut is essentially the same as at 0% wires cut. At 80% of the wires cut the critical path delay does rise somewhat, by 6%; this is due to two factors: the placement is being modified to improve routability at the expense of timing, and some circuitous routes are occuring due to saturated interconnect across the interposer.

Tables 2 and 3 show the minimum channel width and critical path delay for each circuit. The trends for individual circuits follow those of the averages quite closely.

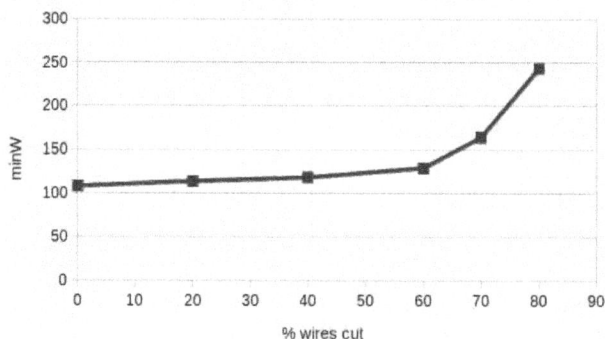

Figure 9: Minimum channel width vs. *% wires cut* for 3 cuts and 1ns of *delay increase*.

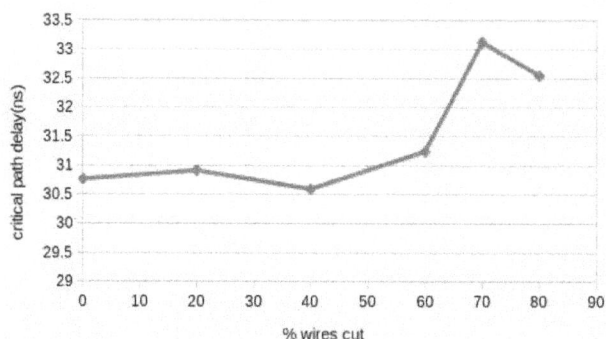

Figure 10: Critical path delay vs. *% wires cut* for 3 cuts and 1ns of *delay increase*.

Figure 11 provides an alternative way to visualize the relationship between interposer routing supply and routability. This figure shows how the geometric average minimum

% wires cut	0	20	40	60	70	80
bgm	114	128	124	132	152	226
LU32PEEng	172	178	182	218	304	426
LU8PEEng	110	116	118	128	158	236
mcml	108	124	128	116	152	218
mkDelayWorker32B	76	80	82	88	100	132
stereovision0	62	60	70	88	110	166
stereovision1	104	108	116	120	178	312
stereovision2	162	164	168	194	244	360
Geometric mean	108	114	118	129	164	243

Table 2: Minimum channel width when *number of cuts = 3* and *increased delay = 1ns*.

% wires cut	0	20	40	60	70	80
bgm	35.1	33.6	32.2	32.9	37.8	40.3
LU32PEEng	115	114	114	114	115	113
LU8PEEng	118	117	119	116	117	124
mcml	82.3	82.9	84.0	83.4	88.3	85.7
mkDelayWorker32B	11.0	12.3	12.0	12.3	14.4	12.8
stereovision0	6.9	7.8	7.0	7.4	7.6	7.0
stereovision1	11.6	9.2	10.4	11.0	11.6	11.8
stereovision2	23.3	25.4	23.9	24.9	25.6	24.8
Geometric mean	30.8	30.9	30.6	31.2	33.1	32.6

Table 3: Critical path delay (in *ns*) when *number of cuts = 3* and *increased delay = 1ns*.

channel width required within the FPGA dice varies as the geometric average of the *absolute* number of wires crossing the interposer in each channel varies, again for 4-die system. When 108 tracks cross the interposer, the interposer channels have the same capacity as the vertical routing channels within each FPGA die. As fewer wires cross the interposer, the channel width required within the FPGA dice increases to compensate for the routing difficulty in crossing the interposer. The increase is gradual as the interposer routing is reduced from 108 tracks per channel to 52 tracks per channel; over this range the routing per channel required in the FPGA dice increases from 108 tracks per channel to 129 tracks per channel. As the routing crossing the interposer is further reduced however, it becomes very difficult to increase the within-die routing sufficiently to compensate. At 49 tracks crossing the interposer channels, for example, the within-die routing must have a channel width of *243* tracks to successfully route the designs. Clearly the CAD tools have the ability to trade-off interposer routing for within-die routing over a reasonable range but below a certain level (48% of the original within-die minimum channel width in our experiments) routability becomes almost solely limited by the wiring crossing the interposer and further reduction in interposer routing is not productive.

5.2 Circuit Speed vs. Interposer Delay

To investigate the impact of the interposer delay (*delay increase*), we kept the *number of cuts* constant at 3 while *delay increase* was swept between 0 and 1.5ns.

Figure 12 shows critical path delay versus *% wires cut* for 4 different values of *delay increase*. The penalty in critical path delay is significant, ranging between 5 and 9 times the interposer *delay increase*, when compared to the case where

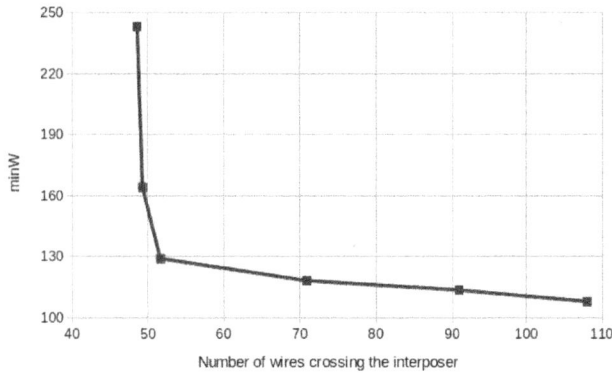

Figure 11: Geometric mean of required intra-die minimum channel width vs. geometric mean of the number of wires crossing the interposer for 3 cuts and 1*ns* of *delay increase*.

the interposer adds no delay. Note that the 0% wires cut with a 0 ns *delay increase* in Figure 12 corresponds to a traditional monolithic FPGA. The speed of an interposer-based FPGA is strongly correlated to *delay increase*: a 0.5*ns* interposer delay increases the critical path delay by 20%, while a 1*ns* interposer delay increases critical path delay by approximately 35% vs. a monolithic FPGA. Once again, the critical path increase shows little correlation to the % *wires cut*, however. Tables 4, 5, 3 and 6 show the critical path delay for each circuit for each of the different values of *delay increase*. Once again the results for individual circuits closely parallel the overall averages.

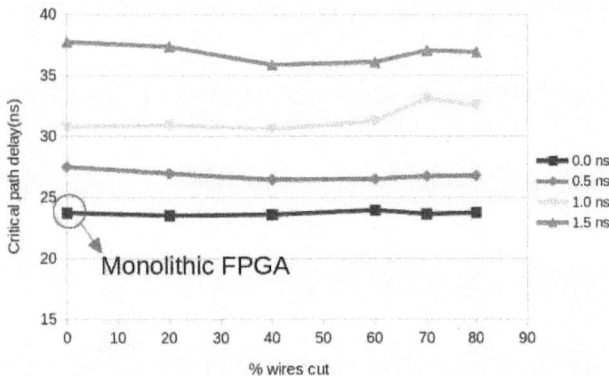

Figure 12: Critical path delay vs. *% wires cut* for 3 cuts and 0.0, 0.5, 1.0 and 1.5*ns* of *delay increase*.

5.3 Impact of Number of Dice

To examine the impact of the number of die used to construct an interposer-based FPGA, we varied the number of cuts from 1 to 3 (which varies the number of die from 2 to 4). In these experiments, the *delay increase* was kept constant at 1*ns*.

As shown in Figure 13, the number of cuts does have an impact on the minimum channel width, but not a very large or constant one. At 80% of wires cut the experiments with 2 and 3 cuts had the minimum channel width only 8% and 10%, respectively, greater than the scenario with only 1

% wires cut	0	20	40	60	70	80
bgm	25.9	26.3	25.8	26.1	25.8	26.7
LU32PEEng	113	113	117	118	113	114
LU8PEEng	115	114	116	115	118	115
mcml	77.2	78.7	79.5	80.5	77.3	76.7
mkDelayWorker32B	7.8	7.6	7.5	7.7	7.5	7.6
stereovision0	4.5	4.3	4.5	4.5	4.5	4.5
stereovision1	6.0	6.2	5.9	6.3	6.2	6.2
stereovision2	18.0	17.1	17.1	17.5	17.6	17.7
Geometric mean	23.7	23.5	23.6	23.9	23.6	23.7

Table 4: Critical path delay (in *ns*) when *number of cuts = 3* and *increased delay = 0ns*.

% wires cut	0	20	40	60	70	80
bgm	31.6	30.3	29.2	29.2	29.9	31.6
LU32PEEng	119	114	115	114	115	115
LU8PEEng	118	116	119	117	114	115
mcml	82.6	82.7	79.6	81.9	84.5	82.6
mkDelayWorker32B	9.8	10.6	10.4	9.6	10.2	9.1
stereovision0	5.7	5.3	4.8	4.9	4.9	4.8
stereovision1	8.0	7.5	7.4	8.2	7.9	8.0
stereovision2	20.1	19.7	20.3	19.9	20.2	21.6
Geometric mean	27.5	26.9	26.4	26.5	26.7	26.8

Table 5: Critical path delay (in *ns*) when *number of cuts = 3* and *increased delay = 0.5ns*.

% wires cut	0	20	40	60	70	80
bgm	47.2	52.4	43.1	42.7	44.8	48.3
LU32PEEng	115	112	117	114	116	113
LU8PEEng	161	159	122	146	118	129
mcml	94.0	86.0	93.9	88.7	77.3	87.5
mkDelayWorker32B	15.3	13.8	14.3	15.3	17.9	15.4
stereovision0	7.5	9.4	8.9	7.8	9.6	8.3
stereovision1	14.6	12.0	13.1	12.7	14.6	14.8
stereovision2	29.9	30.3	28.7	30.3	30.1	29.8
Geometric mean	37.7	37.3	35.9	36.1	37.0	36.9

Table 6: Critical path delay (in *ns*) when *number of cuts = 3* and *increased delay = 1.5ns*.

cut. At lower values of *% wires cut* the difference was even smaller.

Figure 14 shows that the number of dice in an interposer-based FPGA impacts circuit speed significantly, as the critical path delay rises significantly as systems have more cuts. Recall that a monolithic FPGA has a geometric average critical path delay of 23.7*ns* for our test architecture. With *number of cuts* = 1 the critical path delay increases by 3 to 4 ns, while with *number of cuts* = 2 the critical path delay increases by 5 to 6 ns. With *number of cuts* = 3, the critical path delay is typically 7 ns higher than that of a monolithic FPGA.

Tables 7, 8, 9, 10, 2 and 3 show the minimum channel width and critical path delay for each circuit for each of the different scenarios. The critical path results for individual circuits again follow the overall averages well. Some of the minimum channel widths for individual circuits show anomalous trends as the number of cutlines increase, however. For example, *mcml* often has a smaller minimum channel width with 2 cuts than with 1 cut. This may be due to a circuit structure that leads to easier division into thirds than halves, but also likely indicates room for further CAD optimization.

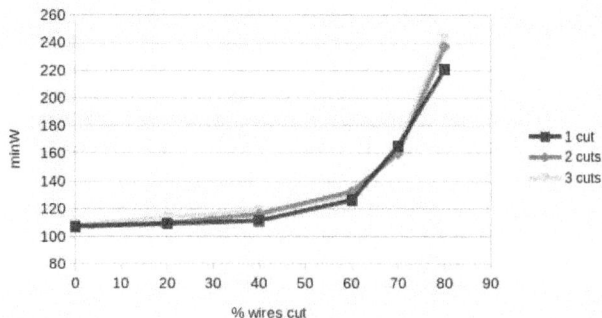

Figure 13: Minimum channel width vs. *% wires cut* for 1, 2 and 3 cuts and 1*ns* of *delay increase.*

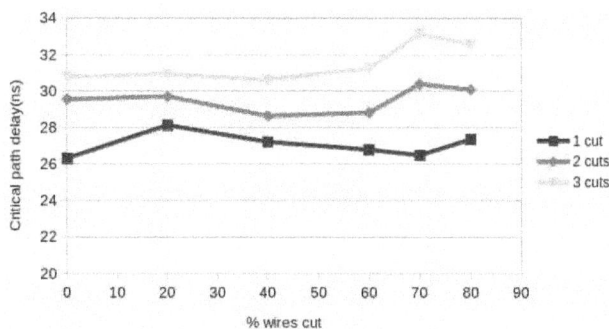

Figure 14: Critical path delay vs. *% wires cut* for 1, 2 and 3 cuts and 1*ns* of *delay increase.*

6. CONCLUSIONS AND FUTURE WORK

We have extended VPR to model and optimize for interposer-based multi-FPGA systems. While such systems are now a commercial reality, we do not know of any prior study of their key architectural parameters. We found that by

% wires cut	0	20	40	60	70	80
bgm	114	114	122	126	142	156
LU32PEEng	170	176	182	206	318	396
LU8PEEng	110	114	116	138	164	236
mcml	108	114	106	124	150	238
mkDelayWorker32B	74	78	80	88	98	138
stereovision0	62	60	62	76	132	146
stereovision1	102	104	106	108	144	186
stereovision2	160	158	164	200	264	432
Geometric mean	107	109	111	126	165	221

Table 7: Minimum channel width when *number of cuts* = 1 and *increased delay* = 1*ns*.

% wires cut	0	20	40	60	70	80
bgm	26.5	32.1	28.3	30.2	27.5	30.0
LU32PEEng	113	113	113	115	114	111
LU8PEEng	117	118	116	114	114	116
mcml	82.5	82.0	83.0	84.5	83.2	77.9
mkDelayWorker32B	11.2	11.4	11.2	9.9	10.6	11.5
stereovision0	4.5	5.1	5.0	4.9	4.9	5.4
stereovision1	7.4	8.2	8.4	7.2	7.2	7.9
stereovision2	21.3	23.1	20.9	22.3	21.6	20.9
Geometric mean	26.3	28.1	27.2	26.8	26.5	27.3

Table 8: Critical path delay (in *ns*) when *number of cuts* = 1 and *increased delay* = 1*ns*.

% wires cut	0	20	40	60	70	80
bgm	114	116	130	140	172	272
LU32PEEng	170	180	186	198	264	426
LU8PEEng	110	114	116	124	158	246
mcml	108	110	126	138	114	150
mkDelayWorker32B	76	80	82	88	100	132
stereovision0	62	58	60	88	114	166
stereovision1	104	108	116	136	184	296
stereovision2	160	156	162	188	246	362
Geometric mean	108	109	116	132	160	237

Table 9: Minimum channel width when *number of cuts* = 2 and *increased delay* = 1*ns*.

% wires cut	0	20	40	60	70	80
bgm	31.0	30.3	28.3	36.1	35.9	37.5
LU32PEEng	113	113	119	113	117	112
LU8PEEng	118	118	117	116	118	114
mcml	82.9	86.3	81.3	80.9	82.4	82.8
mkDelayWorker32B	12.3	12.1	9.8	11.1	13.5	11.3
stereovision0	6.4	5.7	6.3	5.3	5.3	5.9
stereovision1	9.3	10.4	9.5	9.6	10.2	9.9
stereovision2	22.9	24.2	24.0	21.6	24.2	25.5
Geometric mean	29.5	29.7	28.6	28.8	30.4	30.1

Table 10: Critical path delay (in *ns*) when *number of cuts* = 2 and *increased delay* = 1*ns*.

modifying VPR's placement cost function we could improve the routability (reduce minW) by 18%, while simultaneously improving speed by 2%. Interestingly, we found that a smooth cost function that less precisely models the interposing wiring demand outperformed direct monitoring of the number of required interposer connections during annealing.

We defined three key architecture parameters for interposer-based FPGAs, and used this extended VPR to analyze their impact on minimum channel width and critical path delay. We found that the *minimum channel width* increases steeply after more than 60% of the within-die wires are cut at the interposer, and when 80% of wires are cut the *minimum channel width* is more than double that required by a monolithic FPGA. The Xilinx *XC7V2000T* FPGA has 77% of the normal wiring cut at the interposer, indicating that commercial interposer-based FPGAs will require high-quality CAD optimization to maintain good routability. The *critical path delay* is not strongly influenced by the *% wires cut* but is strongly influenced by the interposer delay and the number of cuts. Our results show that the critical path usually crosses the interposer cutline more than once, as the *critical path delay* is increased by more than the interposer *delay increase*. Increasing the number of dice in an interposer-based FPGA does not significantly impact the *minimum channel width*, but does lead to a larger *critical path delay*.

There are many interesting CAD and architecture questions for interposer-based FPGAs which we plan to investigate. Currently the wires that cross the interposer are accessed with the same switch structure as other wires in the FPGA. Since interposer wires are more scarce, possibly these wires should have larger multiplexers feeding them, which would make them easier to use; this may help routability of the system. Such changes will have to be carefully considered however, to make sure the FPGA can still be laid out as an array of regular tiles. Alternative CAD flows to improve the interposer routability are also possible. For example, instead of following the synthesize, place and route CAD flow of a conventional FPGA, we could add a partitioning step before placement which would divide the circuit into one partition per die. Such a flow may improve routability, as a partitioner's main focus is minimizing the number of cut signals. Enhanced partitioners will be required, as current partitioners such as hMetis [7] cannot model the heterogeneous balance constraint (i.e. use no more than the available device logic, RAM, DSP and I/O blocks in any die) present in FPGAs. Additionally, by dividing the placement problem into two pieces – partitioning and within-die placement – we may increase the critical path delay as we can no longer globally optimize the placement of timing critical paths in one unified placement step. Nonetheless, this is a viable alternative approach and a comparison to the approach taken in this paper would be very interesting.

7. ACKNOWLEDGMENTS

This work was supported by a Ciência sem Fronteiras scholarship from CNPq - Brazil and the NSERC/Altera Industrial Research Chair in Programmable Silicon.

8. REFERENCES

[1] M. Alexander, J. Cohoon, J. Colflesh, J. Karro, and G. Robins. Three-Dimensional Field-Programmable Gate Arrays. In *IEEE Int. ASIC Conference and Exhibit*, pages 253–256, 1995.

[2] Altera. Stratix V Device Overview. *www.altera.com*, 2013.

[3] V. Betz and J. Rose. VPR: A New Packing, Placement and Routing Tool for FPGA Research. In *Int. Workshp on Field-Programmable Logic and Applications*, pages 213–222. Springer, 1997.

[4] R. Chaware, K. Nagarajan, and S. Ramalingam. Assembly and Reliability Challenges in 3D Integration of 28nm FPGA Die on a Large High Density 65nm Passive Interposer. In *IEEE Electronic Components and Technology Conference (ECTC)*, pages 279–283, 2012.

[5] C. Cheng. RISA: Accurate and Efficient Placement Routability Modeling. In *IEEE/ACM Int. Conf. on Computer-Aided Design*, pages 690–695, 1994.

[6] J. Cunningham. The Use and Evaluation of Yield Models in Integrated Circuit Manufacturing. *IEEE Trans. on Semiconductor Manufacturing*, 3(2):60–71, 1990.

[7] G. Karypis, R. Aggarwal, V. Kumar, and S. Shekhar. Multilevel Hypergraph Partitioning: Applications in VLSI Domain. *IEEE Trans. on VLSI*, 7(1):69–79, 1999.

[8] M. L., A. El Gamal, Y. Lu, and S. Wong. Performance Benefits of Monolithically Stacked 3-D FPGA. *IEEE Trans. on Computer-Aided Design of Integrated Circuits and Systems*, 26(2):216–229, 2007.

[9] G. Lemieux, E. Lee, M. Tom, and A. Yu. Directional and Single-Driver Wires in FPGA Interconnect. In *IEEE Int. Conf. on Field Programmable Technology*, pages 41–48, 2004.

[10] A. Marquardt, V. Betz, and J. Rose. Timing-Driven Placement for FPGAs. In *ACM/SIGDA Int. Symp. on Field Programmable Gate Arrays*, pages 203–213, 2000.

[11] K. Namhoon, D. Wu, D. Kim, A. Rahman, and P. Wu. Interposer Design Optimization for High Frequency Signal Transmission in Passive and Active Interposer using Through Silicon Via (TSV). In *IEEE Electronic Components and Technology Conference (ECTC)*, pages 1160–1167, 2011.

[12] J. Rose, J. Luu, C. Yu, O. Densmore, J. Goeders, A. Somerville, K. Kent, P. Jamieson, and J. Anderson. The VTR Project: Architecture and CAD for FPGAs from Verilog to Routing. In *ACM/SIGDA Int. Symposium on Field-Programmable Gate Arrays*, pages 77–86, 2012.

[13] Xilinx. Xilinx Stacked Silicon Interconnect Technology Delivers Breakthrough FPGA Capacity, Bandwidth, and Power Efficiency. *www.xilinx.com*, 2012.

[14] Xilinx. 7 Series FPGA Overview. *www.xilinx.com*, 2013.

Memory Block Based Scan-BIST Architecture for Application-Dependent FPGA Testing

Keita Ito, Tomokazu Yoneda, Yuta Yamato, Kazumi Hatayama, Michiko Inoue
Nara Institute of Science and Technology, Nara, Japan
Japan Science and Technology Agency, CREST, Tokyo, Japan
{keita-i, yoneda, yamato, k-hatayama, kounoe}@is.naist.jp

ABSTRACT

This paper presents a scan-based BIST architecture for FPGAs used as application-specific embedded devices for low-volume products. The proposed architecture efficiently utilizes memory blocks, instead of logic elements, to build up BIST components such as LFSR, MISR and scan chains for test points. It also provides enhanced scan functionality for test points and performs a hybrid test application of LOC and enhanced scan to improve delay test quality. Experimental results show that the proposed BIST architecture achieves high delay test quality with efficient resource utilization.

Categories and Subject Descriptors

B.8.1 [**Performance and Reliability**]: Reliability, Testing, and Fault-Tolerance

Keywords

built-in self-test; delay test; test point

1. INTRODUCTION

Continuous advances in silicon manufacturing technologies allow us to design large, high-speed and low power products. Among the many challenges imposed by the technologies, high in-field reliability is major concern and periodical online self-test is essential for overcoming reliability issues such as transistor aging. FPGAs are manufactured with most advanced technologies and are also used as mission-critical and application-specific embedded devices, instead of ASICs, for low-volume products due to their low development cost and short time-to-market. However, advanced technologies are more vulnerable to transistor aging and therefore it is important to ensure in-field reliability of application-specific circuits implemented on FPGA devices.

For ASIC products, several approaches have been proposed for circuit failure prediction [8, 6, 7, 11] to overcome reliability issues. Circuit failure prediction anticipates the occurrence of a circuit failure before the appearance of any error and the basic principle is to capture the gradual delay shift caused by the transistor aging using delay test schemes. For the purpose, they usually utilize scan-based

BIST architecture, which is extensively studied and widely used infrastructure for manufacturing test of ASIC products.

There is no doubt that scan-based BIST is most promising and well-established architecture for high quality delay test of ASIC products. However, it is not efficient to adopt ASIC scan-based BIST architecture as it is for FPGA devices in term of resource utilization. FPGAs are not scan-ready devices (no scan cell and no scan chain) and scan cells/chains must be implemented using general resources such as Look-Up-Tables (LUTs), registers in Logic Elements (LEs) and local/global interconnects. It was reported that scan insertion for an application-dependent circuit introduces 50% increase in LE usage [9]. Even though many approaches have been proposed for testing of application-dependent circuits implemented on FPGAs [12, 13, 1, 10], only a few approach adopt scan-based architecture [9, 3] due to high area overhead.

In this paper, we assume that intended circuits for scan-based BIST are logic-intensive circuits and require LE resources rather than memory resources, which are another resources embedded on FPGAs and can be configured to provide various memory functions. This paper presents an efficient scan-based BIST architecture for application-dependent circuits on FPGAs using shift register configurations of memory blocks. To the best of authors' knowledge, this is the first paper that discusses efficient implementation of scan-based BIST on FPGA devices. The contributions of the paper are summarized as follows.

- It presents FPGA-specific and area-efficient architecture for *Linear Feedback Shift Register (LFSR)/Multiple Input Signature Register (MISR)* [2] using shift register configurations of memory blocks.

- It presents a scan chain architecture for test point FFs. The proposed test point chain architecture is also implemented using memory blocks for area efficiency and provides *enhanced scan* [5] functionality that can improve delay test quality.

- Experimental results show the effectiveness of the proposed architecture in terms of area and fault coverage of transition delay faults compared to a conventional scan-based BIST architecture used for ASIC designs.

The rest of the paper is organized as follows. Section 2 describes the proposed BIST architecture and its test application scheme. Experimental results are shown in Section 3. Finally, Section 4 concludes this paper.

2. PROPOSED BIST ARCHITECTURE

2.1 Overview

Figure 1 shows a conventional scan-based BIST architecture with test point insertion which is widely used for ASIC products. An

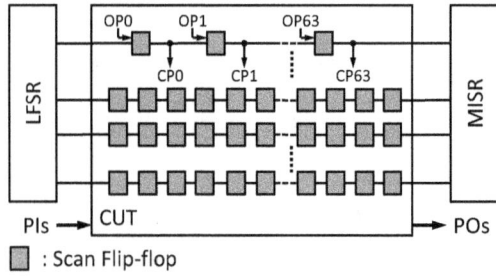

Figure 1: Conventional BIST architecture.

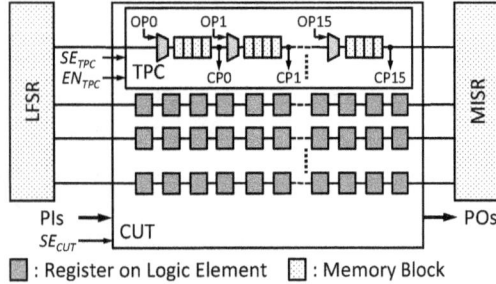

Figure 2: Proposed BIST architecture.

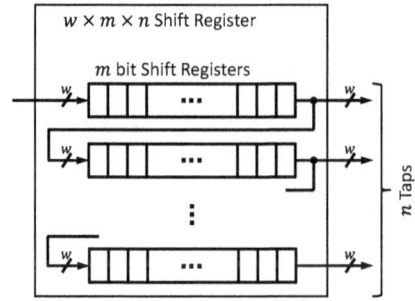

Figure 3: Shift register mode configuration of Cyclone III device family.

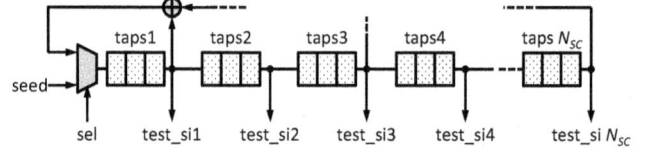

Figure 4: Proposed LFSR architecture and implementation.

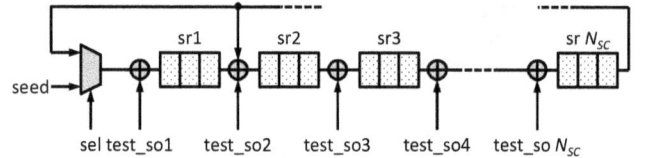

Figure 5: Proposed MISR architecture and implementation.

LFSR and a MISR are used as a test pattern generator and a test response compactor, respectively. FFs in Circuit-Under-Test (CUT) are replaced with scan cells and several scan chains are constructed. Moreover, control points (CPs) and observation points (OPs) are added to improve random pattern testability. In the target BIST architecture, we assume that each CP and OP share one FF as a test point and these test points are stitched to form independent scan chains. We call the scan chain for test points as *test point chains (TPCs)* to distinguish from other scan chains in CUT. We also assume *Launch-On-Capture (LOC)* [5] test application scheme which is widely used in industry for delay fault testing.

In this paper, we assume that intended circuits for scan-based BIST insertion are logic-intensive circuits. In other words, the application-dependent circuits targeted in this paper require LE resources rather than memory resources, which are another resources embedded on FPGAs and can be configured to provide various memory functions such as RAM, ROM, FIFO buffers and shift registers without using LEs. The main idea is to efficiently utilize unused memory blocks, instead of LEs, to implement BIST components such as LFSR, MISR and TPCs. The overall of the proposed BIST architecture is shown in Fig. 2. The detailed architectures of LFSR, MISR and TPCs and its test application scheme will be explained in the following subsections. The unique characteristics are summarized as follows.

- Shift register mode of memory blocks is efficiently configured to implement LFSR, MISR and TPCs.
- TPCs and normal scan chains are controlled by independent scan enable signals, SE_{TPC} and SE_{CUT}, respectively. TPCs remain unchanged during half of the test application cycles.
- TPCs naturally fit enhanced scan cell implementation that can improve delay test quality in LOC test application scheme.

2.2 LFSR, MISR and TPCs

As we explained in Section 3.1, memory blocks can be configured to provide shift register functions without using LEs. However, there are several design constraints to be satisfied to implement a shift register on memory block. For example, memory

blocks embedded on Altera devices provide the shift register configuration shown in Fig. 3. The shift register configuration is determined by the input data width w, the length of the taps m and the number of taps n, and the size of a $w \times m \times n$ shift register must be less than or equal to the maximum number of memory bits. In addition, the length of the taps m must be more than or equal to 3.

In order to implement the shift register part of LFSR on a memory block, we select the configuration: (1) $w = 1$, (2) $m = 3$ (minimum length of the taps) and (3) $n = N_{sc}$ where N_{sc} is the total number of scan chains including TPCs, as shown in Fig. 4. All the n bits output of the n-tap 3-bits shift register on memory block are connected to scan-in ports to feed pseudo-random patterns to CUT.

Similarly, a MISR is implemented using a shift register configuration of memory block as shown in Fig. 5. In MISR case, we select the following configuration: (1) $w = 1$, (2) $m = 3$ (minimum length of the taps) and (3) $n = 1$, and prepare N_{sc} 1-tap 3-bits shift registers. The N_{sc} 1-tap 3-bits shift registers are connected in serial by way of XOR gates, which are implemented by LEs, to form MISR.

A TPC is also implemented using a shift register configuration of memory block as shown in Fig. 6. We select the following configuration for each test point (i.e., a pair of CP and OP): (1) $w = 1$, (2) $m = 4$ and (3) $n = 1$. Each 1-tap 4-bits shift register is connected to a single CP and OP. They are also connected in serial by way of the multiplexers, which are implemented on LEs, to form a TPC. If the length of a TPC is larger than normal scan chains, then the TPC must be divided into several TPCs which does not exceed the length of normal scan chains. The 1-tap 4-bits shift register can store two 2-pattern delay tests (i.e., 4 bits) for each CP and works as an enhanced scan cell during test application to improve delay test quality.

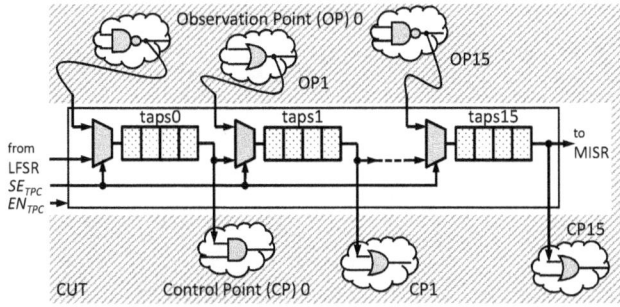

Figure 6: Proposed TPC architecture and implementation.

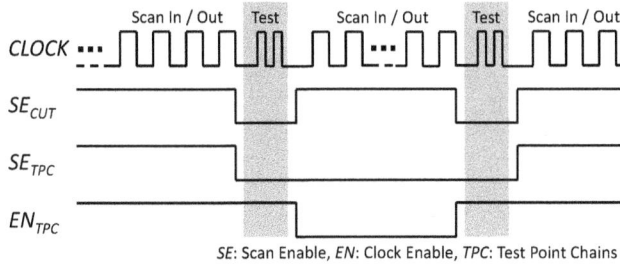

SE: Scan Enable, EN: Clock Enable, TPC: Test Point Chains

Figure 7: Timing diagram of control signals for proposed BIST.

As you can observe from the figures, the size of LFSR/MISR/TPC becomes m (3 and 4 for LFSR/MISR and TPC, respectively, in the FPGA device used in this paper) times larger than those used in the conventional BIST architecture to satisfy the design constraints. However, most part of the LFSR is implemented on memory block and there is not so much increase in LE usage.

2.3 Test Application Scheme

Figure 7 shows a timing diagram of the proposed BIST architecture during test application. Basically, it follows LOC-based at-speed delay test application scheme controlled by scan enable signal SE_{CUT}, and only TPCs have unique behavior controlled by SE_{TPC} and EN_{TPC} explained as follows.

Only when an even-numbered test pattern (i.e., pattern id is $i \times 2$) is scanned in, TPCs are active and work as a single shift register in between LFSR and MISR (i.e., $EN_{TPC} = 1$ and $SE_{TPC} = 1$). At the end of scan-in cycles for the even-numbered test pattern, each 1-tap 4-bits shift register in TPCs contains *two* 2-pattern delay tests (i.e., 4 bits) for a CP. Then, SE_{TPC} is de-activated before the launch cycle and TPCs are switched to work as independent 1-tap 4-bits shift registers to capture test responses from OPs. When the next test pattern (odd-numbered pattern) is scanned in, EN_{TPC} is de-activated and TPCs become in-active to avoid consuming unnecessary power. Finally, EN_{TPC} is again activated and it performs launch and capture operation. This process is repeated until the BIST test application process is completed.

3. EXPERIMENTAL RESULTS

In this section, we present experimental results for two ITC'99 benchmark circuits b12 and b17 [4]. They were synthesized with 8 scan chains of length 8 and 20 scan chains of length 65, respectively. We refer the designs as "Org. w/ scan" and use them as baseline for our comparison shown in Table 1.

In our experiments, we randomly added 16 and 128 CP/OP test point pairs to b12 and b17, respectively. After the test point insertion, we implemented two BIST architectures, conventional BIST

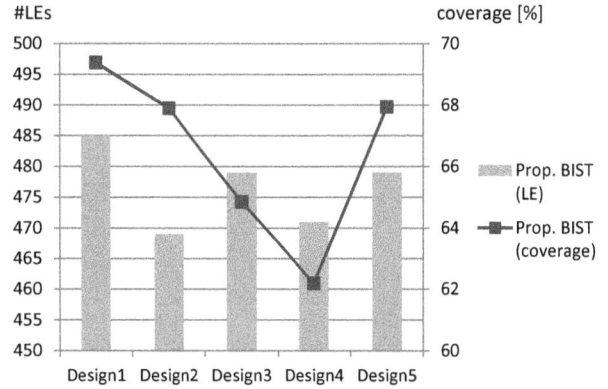

Figure 8: Impact of random test point insertion for b12.

"Conv. BIST" and the proposed BIST "Prop. BIST" on an FPGA device. In the conventional BIST architecture, we prepare one FF per each CP/OP test point pair and the size of LFSR/MISR is equal to the total number of scan chains including TPCs. In contrast, we used 3-bits and 4-bits shift register configurations for LFSR/MISR and TPCs, respectively, to satisfy the design constraints for shift register realization on memory blocks. Consequently, the number of FFs and chains for TPCs in the proposed BIST is 4 times larger and the size of LFSR and MISR is much larger than those in the conventional BIST as shown in Table 1.

The designs were implemented on Altera Cyclone III using Quartus II 13.0 Web Edition, and area overhead is evaluated in terms of "Total logic elements", "Total Combinational Functions", "Total registers" and "Total memory bits". Furthermore, fault simulations were also performed to evaluate delay test quality for the two BIST architectures. 500 and 20,000 pseudo-random patterns are used for the fault simulations of b12 and b17, respectively. The results for area and fault coverage are also included in Table 1. Note that the fault coverages are not so high since the test points are randomly inserted without considering controllability/observability in CUT and the BIST does not adopt complemental approaches such as phase shifter and reseeding [2] which are widely used to improve fault coverage.

First, we compared two results in columns "Memory" and "LE" of "Prop. BIST". These two designs have exactly the same architecture (as the proposed architecture). Only the difference is that "Memory" implemented the architecture using memory blocks while "LE" implemented the architecture with LEs only. Therefore, the results for these two columns are identical except for area related items. This comparison concludes that the proposed architecture and its implementation using memory blocks can drastically reduce the LE utilization, and users do not need to worry about how much LE resources can be used for application and how much LE resources should be kept for BIST implementation.

Then, we compared two results in columns "Prop. BIST (Memory)" and "Conv. BIST". Despite the proposed BIST architecture has larger LFSR/MISR and includes more TPCs, the difference in LE usage is very small since the proposed BIST architecture efficiently replaces LE resources with memory bits. On the other hand, the difference in delay test quality is remarkable. The proposed method can achieve 5% and 6.3% higher fault coverage than the conventional method. The differences become more visible when we compare the number of pseudo-random patterns to reach the same fault coverage. For example in b17, the proposed BIST architecture only requires 6,120 patterns to reach 49.43% fault coverage which is the final coverage of the conventional BIST architecture

Table 1: Results for b12 and b17.

Design	b12 (#scan_chains=8, length=16)				b17 (#scan_chains=20, length=65)			
	Org. w/ scan	Conv. BIST LE	Prop. BIST Memory	Prop. BIST LE	Org. w/ scan	Conv. BIST LE	Prop. BIST Memory	Prop. BIST LE
Test point	-	16 CP/OP test point pairs			-	128 CP/OP test point pairs		
Number of flip-flops for TPCs	-	16	64		-	128	512	
LFSR/MISR size	-	$9(8+1)$	$36((8+4) \times 3)$		-	$22(20+2)$	$84((20+8) \times 3)$	
Resource for shift register	-	LE	Memory	LE	-	LE	Memory	LE
Total logic elements	411	472	485	550	9334	9493	9550	9911
Total combinational functions	405	455	474	432	9126	9278	9350	9268
Total registers	121	155	133	257	1317	1489	1333	1997
Total memory bits	0	0	104	0	0	0	424	0
Delay test	-	LOC	LOC + enhanced scan		-	LOC	LOC + enhanced scan	
Fault coverage [%]	-	63.01	69.38		-	49.43	54.47	

after applying 20,000 pseudo-random patterns. This shows that the proposed method can obtain around 70% reduction in pattern count for the same fault coverage. These gains come from the two reasons: (1) the proposed BIST architecture efficiently implemented larger size LFSR and MISR and (2) TPCs have enhanced scan cell capability for LOC-based delay test application scheme.

We further analyzed the impact of test point insertion on the proposed BIST architecture for b12. Random test point insertion (16 CP/OP test point pairs) was performed for 5 times and the proposed BIST architecture was implemented for each design. Figure 8 shows the results of area overhead (the number of LEs) and fault coverage for the 5 designs. It is noticeable that the area overhead depends on the location where the test points are inserted. This trend is unique for FPGA devices and cannot be observed from test point insertion for ASIC products. It is also interesting to note that area overhead and fault coverage are not correlated so much (the correlation coefficient is 0.49). For example, "Design2" provides high fault coverage (68%) with low area overhead (the number of LEs is 469). In this case, the proposed BIST architecture can achieve 5% higher fault coverage with lower area overhead compared to the conventional BIST architecture shown in Table 1. The analysis tells us that a new test point insertion method is required for scan-based BIST on FPGA devices even though it is extensively studied for ASIC products.

4. CONCLUSIONS

We have presented a scan-based BIST architecture for application-dependent FPGA testing. The main idea is to utilize shift register configurations of memory blocks on FPGAs to efficiently implement BIST components such as LFSR, MISR and TPCs. Moreover, the proposed TPC architecture provides an enhanced scan capability and improves test quality of LOC-based delay test application scheme. One of the future works is to investigate a method for test point insertion based on the proposed BIST architecture to optimize delay test quality as well as LE usage.

5. ACKNOWLEDGMENTS

This work was supported in part by Japan Society for the Promotion of Science (JSPS) under Grants-in-Aid for Scientific Research (B)(No.25280015).

6. REFERENCES

[1] M. Abramovici and C. Stroud. BIST-based test and diagnosis of FPGA logic blocks. *IEEE Transactions on Very Large Scale Integration Systems*, 9(1):159–172, 2001.

[2] M. L. Bushnell and V. D. Agrawal. *Essentials of Electronic Testing for Digital, Memory & Mixed-Signal VLSI Circuits*. Kluwer Academic Publishers, 2000.

[3] A. Cilardo, N. Mazzocca, and L. Coppolino. Virtual scan chains for online testing of FPGA-based embedded systems. In *Proc. Euromicro Conference on Digital System Design Architectures, Methods and Tools*, pages 360–366, Sep. 2008.

[4] F. Corno, M. S. Reorda, and G. Squillero. Rt-level itc 99 benchmarks and first atpg results. *IEEE Design & Test of Computers*, 17(3):44–53, July–September 2000.

[5] P. Girard, N. Nicolici, and X. Wen. *Power-Aware Testing and Test Strategies for Low Power Devices*. Springer-Verlag, 2009.

[6] H. Inoue, Y. Li, and S. Mitra. VAST: Virtualization-assisted concurrent autonomous self-test. In *Proc. International Test Conference*, Paper 12.3, Oct. 2008.

[7] O. Khan and S. Kundu. A self-adaptive system architecture to address transistor aging. In *Proc. Design, Automation, and Test in Europe*, pages 81–86, Mar. 2009.

[8] Y. Li, S. Makar, and S. Mitra. CASP: Concurrent autonomous chip self-test using stored test patterns. In *Proc. Design, Automation, and Test in Europe*, pages 885–890, Mar. 2008.

[9] M. Renovell, P. Faure, J. Portal, J. Figueras, and Y. Zorian. IS-FPGA: A new symmetric FPGA architecture with implicit SCAN. In *Proc. International Test Conference*, pages 924–931, Nov. 2001.

[10] M. Rozkovec, J. Jenicek, and O. Novak. Application dependent FPGA testing method. In *Proc. Euromicro Conference on Digital System Design: Architectures, Methods and Tools*, pages 525–530, Sep. 2010.

[11] Y. Sato, S. Kajihara, T. Yoneda, K. Hatayama, M. Inoue, Y. Miura, S. Ohtake, T. Hasegawa, M. Sato, and K. Shimamura. DART: Dependable VLSI test architecture and its implementation. In *Proc. International Test Conference*, Paper 15.2, Nov. 2012.

[12] M. Tahoori. Application-dependent diagnosis of FPGAs. In *Proc. International Test Conference*, pages 645–654, Oct. 2004.

[13] M. Tahoori and S. Mitra. Interconnect delay testing of design on programmable logic devices. In *Proc. International Test Conference*, pages 635–644, Oct. 2004.

FPGA-based Biophysically-Meaningful Modeling of Olivocerebellar Neurons

Georgios Smaragdos[1], Sebastian Isaza[2], Martijn Van Eijk[3], Ioannis Sourdis[4] and
Christos Strydis[1]

[1]Dept. of Neuroscience, Erasmus Medical Center, Rotterdam, The Netherlands
[2]Dept. de Ingeniería Electrónica, Universidad de Antioquia UdeA, Medellín, Colombia
[3]Faculty of Electrical Engineering, Mathematics & Computer Science, Delft University of Technology,
Delft, The Netherlands
[4]Dept. of Computer Science & Engineering, Chalmers University of Technology, Gothenburg, Sweden
{g.smaragdos, c.strydis}@erasmusmc.nl
sisaza@udea.edu.co   M.F.vanEijk@student.tudelft.nl   sourdis@chalmers.se

ABSTRACT

The Inferior-Olivary nucleus (ION) is a well-charted region of the brain, heavily associated with sensorimotor control of the body. It comprises ION cells with unique properties which facilitate sensory processing and motor-learning skills. Various simulation models of ION-cell networks have been written in an attempt to unravel their mysteries. However, simulations become rapidly intractable when biophysically plausible models and meaningful network sizes ($\geq$100 cells) are modeled. To overcome this problem, in this work we port a highly detailed ION cell network model, originally coded in Matlab, onto an FPGA chip. It was first converted to ANSI C code and extensively profiled. It was, then, translated to HLS C code for the Xilinx Vivado toolflow and various algorithmic and arithmetic optimizations were applied. The design was implemented in a Virtex 7 (XC7VX485T) device and can simulate a 96-cell network at real-time speed, yielding a speedup of $\times$700 compared to the original Matlab code and $\times$12.5 compared to the reference C implementation running on a Intel Xeon 2.66GHz machine with 20GB RAM. For a 1,056-cell network (non-real-time), an FPGA speedup of $\times$45 against the C code can be achieved, demonstrating the design's usefulness in accelerating neuroscience research. Limited by the available on-chip memory, the FPGA can maximally support a 14,400-cell network (non-real-time) with online parameter configurability for cell state and network size. The maximum throughput of the FPGA ION-network accelerator can reach 2.13 GFLOPS.

Categories and Subject Descriptors

J.3 [**LIFE AND MEDICAL SCIENCES**]: [Biology and genetics]

General Terms

Design, Performance, Experimentation

Keywords

Spiking Neural Networks; Computational Neuroscience; Inferior Olive; Cerebellum; Hodgkin Huxley

1. INTRODUCTION

Artificial Neural Networks (ANNs) have been successfully used in robotics and artificial-intelligence applications on numerous occasions in the past [7]. Contrary to the typical, Von-Neumann-based computing model, a biologically-inspired ANN does not execute explicit sequential instructions to solve its computational problems. In such a network, functions across nodes (or neurons) are evaluated concurrently and the relation between the input and output of the ANN is determined by the network topology and method of interconnectivity. This topology can also be dynamically adaptive, subject to the ongoing neural computations, thus mimicking biological behavior known as plasticity.

Advances in neuroscience and greater understanding of the brain have gradually led to the creation of mathematical models of neurons and whole networks that do not simply mimic biological behavior in an abstract way but simulate it with significant detail. Such an example is the Spiking Neural Network (SNN). Here, information is not just transferred by the firing rate of each neuron in the network as is the case in classical ANNs but by the transfer of spikes [19]. Due to the SNNs' ability to model additional neuron characteristics and adapt them according to spike-train amplitude, frequency and precise arrival times, SNNs can have greater computational and predictive power than Artificial-Neural-Networks (ANNs) [14]. This, alongside with the advances of technology in computer science and engineering, has opened the possibility of implementing larger-scale NNs that have the ability to more accurately simulate brain behavior.

The United-States-National-Academy of Engineers has classified brain simulation as one of the Grand Engineering Challenges [16]. Biologically accurate brain simulation is a highly relevant topic for *neuroscience* for a number of reasons: *(1) Accelerated brain research:* Neuroscientists plan to gain greater understanding of brain behavior by simulations based on biologically accurate models. Depending on the complexity of the model, it can provide insights ranging from single-cell behavior to network dynamics of whole brain regions without having to perform in-vivo experiments. *(2) Brain rescue:* If brain functions can be simulated accurately enough and in real-time, this can lead (a) Medium-turn, to seamless brain-rescue devices with various medical and other applications; and (b) long-term, to robotic prosthetics and implants for restoring lost brain functionality in patients. *(3) Advanced A.I.:* ANNs have already been successfully used in this field even though they have not even remotely reached the computational capacity of biological systems. It is believed that greater understanding of biological systems and their richer computational dynamics can lead to more advanced, bio-inspired, artificial-intelligence (AI) models for autonomous and robotic applications. *(4) New computer-architecture paradigms:* Alternatives to the typical Von-Neumann architectures can be very useful for massively parallel applications and could potentially provide defect-tolerant systems emulating the brain's adaptability.

The main challenge in building complex, biologically accurate SNNs lies largely in the computational and communication load of the network simulations. Furthermore, biological NNs execute these computations with massive parallelism, something that conventional CPU-based execution cannot cope with very well. As a result, the neuron-population size and interconnectivity are quite low when running on PCs (with models implemented in MATLAB or neuromodeling languages such as NEURON and GENESIS). This greatly impedes the efficiency of brain research in relation to the goals of brain simulation stated above.

A good alternative would be the execution of neuron models in *GPUs*. GPUs can exploit application parallelism better and, thus, can be more efficient in running neuron models. Yet, in the case of complex models or very large-scale networks, they may not be able to provide real-time performance (i.e. to produce results for every network cell within the time allotted by the model simulation step) due to the high rates of data exchange between the neurons [8]. Moreover, GPUs are inefficient in terms of energy and power.

Another alternative would be the use of *supercomputers*. Although these systems can emulate the behavior and parallelism of biological networks with sufficient speed, the sheer size and complexity of these solutions makes them useful only for behavioral simulations. Supercomputer deployments require immense space, implementation, maintenance and energy costs while lacking any kind of mobility.

Mixed-signal VLSI is another option for simulating SNNs. Such designs achieve adequate simulation speeds while simulating the biological systems more accurately since they model neurons through analog signals, just like their biological counterparts. However, mixed-signal VLSI designs are much more difficult to implement, lack flexibility and often suffer from problems typical in analog design; for instance, accuracy issues and reduced reproducibility of results due to transistor mismatching, leakage currents, crosstalk etc. [3].

Implementing the neural network in parallel, digital hardware can efficiently match the parallelism of biological models and provide real-time or hyper-real-time performance useful for simulations, prosthetics and robotics applications. While ASIC design is certainly an option, it is expensive, time-consuming and – most importantly – inflexible: An ASIC cannot be altered after fabrication, yet model changes often required in *fitting* novel neuron models would require a new development cycle, just like mixed-signal VLSI.

Most of these issues can be tackled through the use of FPGAs. FPGAs, although slower than ASICs, still provide enough performance for real-time and hyper-real-time neuron simulations, exploiting the inherent parallelism of hardware. Besides requiring a lot less energy and, in some cases, less space than most of the above solutions for the same computational power, the reconfiguration property of FPGAs provides the flexibility of modifying brain models on demand. This flexibility is substantially enhanced by the use of high-level synthesis tools which speed up the development process; manually developing the hardware description every time a new brain model is released or an existing one is re-calibrated would be impractical and time-consuming. Besides, dynamic reconfigurability can provide a way to emulate the plasticity of biological neural networks in ways other solutions cannot.

In this paper we present an FPGA-accelerated application for a specific, biophysically-meaningful NN model, using single-precision floating-point (FP) arithmetic computations. The application models the network of one of the essential areas for the function of the cerebellum, the Inferior Olive. Concisely, the contributions of this work are:

- The analysis of the Inferior Olive model to recognize characteristics and possible performance bottlenecks.

- The optimization of the original model algorithm achieving ×2 performance improvement in hardware.

- The design, implementation and validation of the FPGA-based accelerator, achieving ×45 speedup compared to C and 96 neurons simulated at real-time.

- The performance evaluation of the designed accelerator and evaluation of precision error, issued by design optimizations, to guarantee preservation of the biological behavior reflected in the original model.

The rest of the paper is organized as follows: Section 2 presents background information necessary to tackle the neuromodeling problem at hand. Section 3 gives an overview of related works in the field. Section 4 covers the description of the Inferior Olive Model and presents application profiling results. Section 5 describes the FPGA-based Inferior Olive design and architecture. Section 6 presents the area, performance and error evaluation, while also presenting a comparison to other FPGA-based SNN applications. Finally, Section 7 concludes this paper.

2. BACKGROUND

In this section, background information on the biological structures of interest and the modeling approaches thereof will be presented. This information will help to better grasp the implementation and evaluation phases of this work.

2.1 The Biological Neuron

Neurons are electrochemically excitable cells[1] that process and transmit signals in the brain. The biological neuron comprises in general (although, in truth is a much more complicated system) three parts (called compartments in neuromodeling jargon): The *Dendrites*, the *Soma* and the *Axon*. The dendritic compartment represents the cell input stage. The dendrites pick up electrochemical stimuli from other cells and transfer them to the soma. In turn, the soma processes the stimuli and translates them into a cell *membrane potential*, which evokes a cell response called an *action potential* or, simply, a *spike*. This response is transferred through the axon, which is the cell output stage, to

---

[1] We will use the terms *neuron* and *(neural) cell* interchangeably throughout the paper.

other cells. An electrochemical connection between two cells (axon-dendrite) is referred to as a *synapse*.

2.2 The Cerebellum and the Inferior Olive

The cerebellum is one of the most complex and tightly packed regions in the brain, playing an important role in sensorimotor control. It does not initiate movement but influences the sensorimotor region in order to precisely coordinate the body's activities and motor learning skills. It also plays an important role in the sensing of rhythm, enabling the handling of concepts such as music or harmony.

The Olivocerebellar circuitry – of which the Inferior Olivary Nucleus (ION) is a part – is a relatively well-charted region of the cerebellum [6]. The ION (comprising the so-called ION cells) provides one of the two main inputs to the cerebellar system: the climbing fibers. ION cells are also interconnected by purely electrical connections between their dendrites, called *gap junctions*, considered to be important for the synchronization of activity within the nucleus and, thus, greatly influencing movement and motor learning.

2.3 Neural Modeling

There is a number of mathematical models describing the behavior of spiking-neuron compartments and neuron networks [13]. The more complex the model, the better it can emulate biological dynamics and can more accurately represent its biological counterpart. The simplest models are the Integrate-and-Fire (IaF) which model very basic spiking behavior. An IaF model essentially implements a spike-integrator function. When the membrane potential surpasses a certain threshold the neuron fires an output spike.

A more advance neuron model is the Izhikevich [12] neuron. With only 2 equations and 4 parameters the model can recreate all main behavioral neuron patterns in terms of input/output behavior. But if the goal is to simulate and study the neuronal behavior in greater detail (like details of the ionic and chemical channels of the cell) or create multi-compartmental models, one has to use **biophysically-meaningful** models, like conductance-based models.

Conductance-based models are complex and dynamic representations of neurons that can even be biophysically meaningful; that is, models that can accurately model the internal mechanisms and state of a cell. The most important such model is the so-called Hodgkin-Huxley (HH) model dating back in 1952 [11]. The model uses 4 equations and dozens of parameters to describe in detail the electrical activity in the cell. This activity results from the combination of external changes in the membrane potential and in the internal concentrations of the main chemical components involved in the transmission of neural-signals: calcium, potassium and sodium. However, this high modeling accuracy comes at the cost of complexity. HH models tend to be orders of magnitude more computationally intensive compared to other types, making efficient simulation a challenge. As explained in the next sections, in this work we accelerate an extended HH model for Inferior-Olive neurons.

3. RELATED WORK

In the past, a number of designs have been proposed for the implementation of neuron and network models in FPGAs. In this section, we present some of the most notable past works in the field.

Shayani et al. [18, 17] proposed a neuron model using a Quadratic IaF model [10, 9] which enabled simulating extra dendritic and axonal properties. The system supported on-line network-topology adaptation. Each neuron had 16 synapses and the maximum network size was 161 neurons. The simulation ran at $\times 4210$ faster than real-time on a Virtex 5 FPGA. The authors estimated that they could simulate a little above 1000 neurons at real-time, provided that they utilized the whole FPGA chip.

Two of the most notable implementations using Izhikevich neurons are the designs proposed by Cheung et al. [5, 4] and by Moore et al. (Bluehive [15]). Each approach proposed an FPGA architecture for very large-scale SNNs which is event-driven for optimizing the network traffic and the assorted memory-bandwidth needs. This optimization is based on the fact that new neuron states do not need to be calculated at every single time step but only in the instances that a new input arrives at the neuron, as otherwise the neuron state would not change. To improve on their initial memory-bandwidth requirements [4], Cheung et al. replaced the FPGA board with a Maxeler Dataflow Machine [5]. This FPGA-based device features state-of-the-art memory systems that increase the bandwidth capabilities greatly compared to simple FPGA boards. As a result, the size of the implemented network achieved was 64K neurons, each having about 1000 synaptic connections to neighboring neurons. In the Bluehive device, Moore et al. took another approach: They used external DDR2 RAMs and built custom-made SATA-to-PCI connections for stacking FPGA devices for facilitating large SNN simulations. Only a small portion of data was stored on-board the FPGAs. In a Stratix IV FPGA, the authors simulated 64K Izhikevich neurons with 64M simple synapses at real-time performance.

These works (as most others in the field) have incorporated fixed-point arithmetic to implement the computation of their neuron models. Zhang et al. [20] have proposed a somatic and dendritic HH-accelerator processor using dedicated FP units. The FP units were custom-designed to provide better accuracy, resource usage and performance. The 32-bit FP arithmetic used in the model produced a neuroprocessor architecture which met a real-time-performance demand. The architecture also included advanced synapses. The system could simulate 4 complete cells (synapse, dendrite, soma) at real-time speed.

Beuler et al. [2] proposed a system for studying firing synchronization of NNs through gap junctions. They used a custom-made simplified model of a HH neuron. The main hardware component was the NepteronCore, also using 32-bit FP arithmetic. The system achieved real-time simulation speeds and included a simple GUI for parameter setup. The maximum size of the network was 400 neurons.

4. APPLICATION DESCRIPTION

The application studied in this paper models the behavior of the ION neurons as an important module of the olivocerebellar circuit. We have chosen this state-of-the-art model as a first step towards building a high-performance olivocrebellar simulation platform. The model not only divides the cells in multiple compartments but also creates a network onto which neurons are interconnected. Although the single-cell model is described first, the rest of the paper deals with the cell-network model, also described in the coming sections.

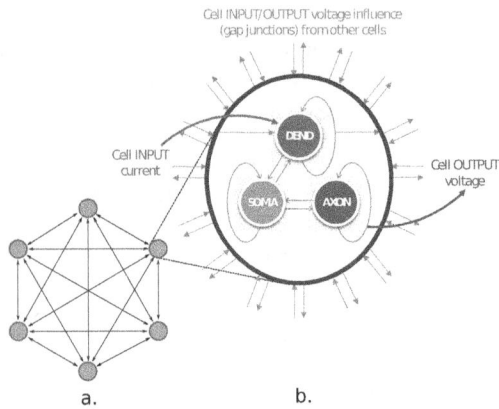

Figure 1: Illustration of (a) a 6-cell network-model example and (b) the 3-compartmental model of a single ION cell.

4.1 The ION-cell model

The ION cell model we have implemented has been originally developed by de Gruijl et al. [1]. The model is an extension of the original HH-based model [11] and divides the neuron into three computational compartments – closely resembling their biological counterparts – as shown in Figure 1(b). For every compartment, a few chemical channels are present in the model so as to contribute to the total compartment potential. Every compartment has a state that holds the electrochemical variables and, on every simulation step, the state is updated based on: i) the previous state, ii) the other compartments' previous state, iii) the other neuron's previous state and iv) the externally evoked input.

The computational model operates in a fashion that allows *concurrent* execution of the three compartments. The model is calibrated to produce every per-neuron output value with a 50 μsec time step. This means that, in order to support real-time simulations, all neurons are required to compute one iteration of compartmental calculations within 50 μsec. Due to the realistic electrochemical variables handled by the model, most of the computations require FP arithmetic.

4.2 The ION-network model

Figure 1(a) illustrates the network-model architecture with an example size of 6 cells. Every cell receives, through the dendritic compartment, the influence of all other cells in the network, thus modeling the massive biological gap junctions present in the Inferior Olive. For the analysis in the coming sections, we divide the dendritic compartment further into two parts to separate the gap-junction modeling from that of the pure dendritic computations. As illustrated in Figure 1(b), the dendrites in every cell also receive an externally evoked input current while the axonal voltage of all cells is considered the external output. The system works in lock-step computing discrete output values (with a 50 μsec time step) that, when aggregated in time, contribute to form the electrical waveform response of the system. The ION network must be synchronized in order to guarantee the correct exchange of cell state data when multiple cells and compartments are being computed simultaneously.

4.3 C-code profiling

The ION-network model was initially available to us in

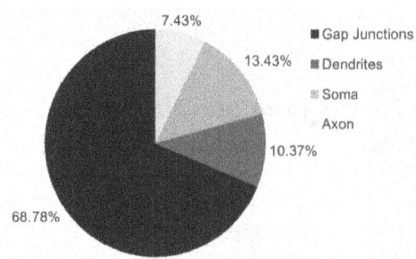

Figure 2: Software profiling of the computation time taken by the various compartments in the ION-cell model.

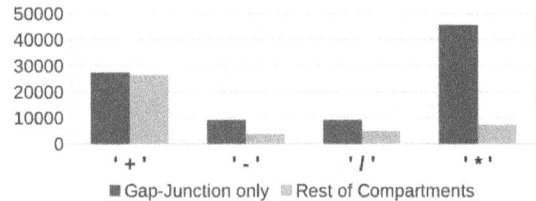

Figure 3: Software profiling of the arithmetic operations in the model for a 96-cell, fully interconnected network.

Matlab but was re-written in C for various analysis purposes and so as to be used in a High-Level Synthesis (HLS) tool. Next, we present profiling results that give insights on the distribution of computations performed in the model.

Figure 2 shows the execution-time distribution of the various model compartments (program functions). The numbers presented were obtained with GProf on an Intel Core i7 3770 (3.4 GHz, 8GB RAM, Ubuntu 12.04 OS). The gap-junction computations are shown separately from the dendrites. This division has been made in order to stress the fact that, in this fully connected ION-network model, gap-junctions computations take up most of the execution time. The reason is that they need to be repeated as many times as the network size for every individual neuron being simulated. Moreover, it should be noted that the total amount of gap-junction computations in the network grows exponentially with the number of cells. Next in terms of computational load is the Soma compartment due to the multiple and complex electrochemical channels that are modeled. Last is the Axon compartment because it only models two such channels.

Figure 3 shows the profiling of the arithmetic operations performed in the model, for one iteration of the whole ION-network. We differentiate the operations belonging to the gap-junction compartment from the rest again, to show its importance. Results show that (FP) multiplications performed in the gap-junction compartment dominate the distribution. Finally, we can see that the gap junctions contain the largest fraction of operations for all operation types and will, therefore, consume more FPGA resources.

5. FPGA-BASED OLIVOCEREBELLAR NEUROMODELING

After profiling the C code based on the Matlab model, we used it as the basis for generating the proposed hardware solution using the Vivado HLS tool. The resulting hardware accelerator simulates the behavior of multiple ION-cells *step by step* based on the aforementioned model. The hardware accelerator is designed to work alongside a softcore or host CPU that controls the total number of simulation steps and handles the I/O of the accelerator. The CPU feeds the accelerator with initialization data (initial state) and with evoked-current inputs (external stimuli of neurons) and outputs the result of the computations at every simulation step. Output data can be stored in on-board memory (e.g., SD cards) or sent to an off-board PC host.

Both, neuron states and evoked inputs – required at every simulation step – are stored in on-chip BRAMs, so as to avoid incurring off-chip latency. The performance benefit of using on-chip storage is substantial compared to going off-chip, especially for complex models such as ours, which require handling large amounts of data to represent the network state. On the other hand, this creates a constraint on the maximum network size that can be simulated, which depends on the storage capacity of the FPGA BRAMs.

The remainder of this section offers the details of our FPGA-based approach and the optimizations performed to improve the performance and area efficiency of our design.

5.1 Overview of the hardware design

The general block diagram of the proposed system can be seen in Figure 4. The actual execution is performed at the "ION Network" component, which consists of multiple identical parallel neuron-processing modules, each modeling the dendrite, soma and axon parts of a single ION cell. Our design further includes a set of BRAMs for storing the evoked inputs to the neurons as well as their state, which is updated after each simulation step. The execution flow of the ION network is controlled by a – local to the accelerator – kernel control unit. Our actual implementation of the ION network consists of eight hardware neuron-processing modules, which are able to simulate eight ION-cells in parallel.

The accelerator was designed to give run-time control over a number of simulation parameters, providing flexibility and the ability for more complex experiments. During execution, each neuron state parameter can be modified. Interconnectivity density is also adjustable during simulation.

Next, we describe the functionality of our FPGA-based accelerator. First, the neurons in the network are initialized with data streamed from the CPU to the FPGA. The initialization data are either produced by the CPU itself or read by on- or off-board resources. This introduces a delay (discussed in Section 6) which is however paid only once at the ION-network simulation onset.

After initialization, the actual execution of the network simulation is performed. Each simulation step begins with storing new evoked inputs of the neurons in BRAM, representing the network external input vector. Following the storing of this vector, the kernel-control copies to dedicated BRAM banks part of the other cells' state (the dendritic voltages) needed for computing the gap-junction effect. Each hardware neuron-processing module has a separate dual-port, BRAM bank to store its respective gap-junction data. By making this design choice, we improve the memory bandwidth during the gap-junction processing and allow the HLS-tool scheduling techniques to maximize parallelism. This would not be possible if both compartment and gap-junction logic shared the same memory banks.

With all input data ready, the next state of each neuron is computed. Each hardware neuron-processing module

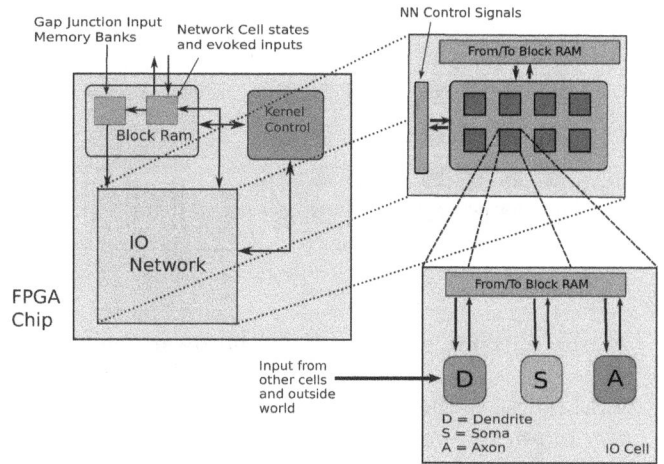

Figure 4: Block diagram of the Olivocerebellar neuromodeling hardware design.

executes in parallel. It is worth noting that all three compartments (dendrite, soma, axon) within a neuron module could execute in parallel, as they have no dependencies with each other. In practice, the axon and soma execute sequentially (soma first, axon second) to save on resources, while the dendrite compartment executes concurrently with the axon and the soma. That is due to the execution time of the dendrite which is longer than that of the axon and soma compartments combined. The final phase of the execution involves storing the newly produced ION-cell states in the BRAMs, to be used in the next simulation step, and streaming the output values needed by the experiment outside the accelerator. For our test cases, this output is the axon voltage of each neuron for every simulation step, representing the ION-network response. Presumably, the output could be any part of the neuron states, depending on the requirements of the neuroscientific experiment.

5.2 Time-multiplexing execution

For the accelerator to achieve real-time performance, each simulation step must be completed within the same time window of 50 μsec. Obviously, such a "real-time" constraint does not have a counterpart in biological neurons (that feature continuous function). It is imposed by our ION network simulator which is a self-contained, fixed-timestep, transient simulator – similar to most HH-based simulators – with a constant step $\Delta t = 50 \mu sec$ in our case. Respecting this time-step duration is essential for generating biologically-plausible signals that can be interfaced to living tissue.

Of course, our hardware neuron network (and hardware modules in general) runs significantly faster than the real-time constraint at hand. We exploit this *latency slack* by using our hardware resources more efficiently and maximizing the number of simulated neurons by *time-multiplexing* of hardware blocks. More precisely, we use the same hardware neuron-processing module multiple times within a simulation step to compute states of different simulated neurons. As illustrated in Figure 5, each hardware neuron-processing module evaluates multiple simulated neurons that together comprise the total simulated network. By online adjusting the number of simulated cells each hardware neuron is simulating (i.e. the time-multiplexing factor), the net-

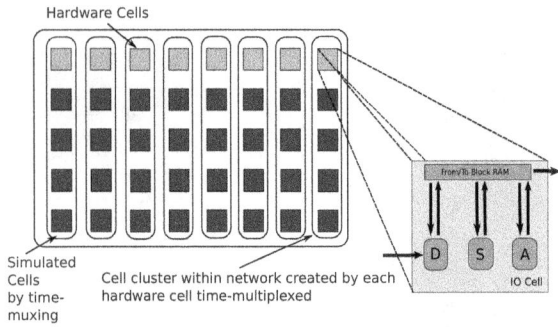

Figure 5: Time multiplexing of hardware neurons.

work size can be altered without re-synthesizing the hardware kernel, even during the simulation, if experiments indeed require it (for instance, to emulate synaptic plasticity). This is achieved by storing different input vectors and cell states for each simulated neuron evaluated in each hardware neuron-processing module. However, the input vectors and cell states need to be stored in the BRAM; this ultimately means that the maximum network size shall be *constrained by the amount of available of on-chip memory*. The BRAMs are statically allocated before synthesis to support the maximum number of possible simulated cells at runtime.

5.3 HLS C-Code Optimizations

A number of optimizations for increasing the efficiency and performance of the hardware design were implemented in the C code, motivated by code inspection and the profiling information presented in Section 4.3. According to profiling results of the reference C code, the most computationally intensive compartment in the model is the dendrite, more specifically, the gap-junction computations. These are responsible for accumulating the influence of all other neurons in the network and include complex arithmetic operations such as FP exponents and divisions performed for every other cell state, as shown in Listing 1. In such an all-to-all interconnected network, the amount of gap-junction computations increases *exponentially* with the network size.

Listing 1: Original gap-junction code.

```
for (i=0; i<ION_N_INPUT; i++) {
  V = prevVdend - neighVdend[i];
  f = 0.8 * exp(-1 * V * V/100) + 0.2;
  Ic = Ic + (CONDUCTANCE * f * V);
}

return Ic ;
```

Without changing the actual functionality described in Listing 1, we rewrote and simplified the gap-junction code. As shown in Listing 2, we removed from the for-loop any operations that are common for all iterations, thus reducing the required computations substantially. More precisely, the mathematical expression implemented by the code in Listing 1 was modified as shown in Formula (1). In other words, we removed computations simulating the total gap-junction influence (Ic) from the accumulation loop, saving three multiplications and one addition per for-loop iteration. In the optimized code, the gap junctions accumulate only the input parameters of Ic and computes the total influence only once, after the accumulation has been completed. This modification yielded a notable increase in the network size supported by our design for real-time simulations.

Design	Area	Real-Time Network Size	One Cell Latency
Baseline	99% of LUTs	48 cells	603 cycles
Opt1	99% of LUTs	84 cells	347 cycles
Opt2	96% of LUTs	96 cells	333 cycles
Opt3	91% of LUTs	96 cells	323 cycles

Table 1: Synthesis Estimation for each optimization case with Vivado HLS 2013.2 for a Virtex 707 evaluation board. Opt1: Gap-junction calculations' optimizations. Opt2: Division-by-constant replacement in dendritic compartment. Opt3: Division-by-constant replacement in all 3 compartments.

Listing 2: Optimized gap-junction code.

```
for (i=0; i<ION_N_INPUT; i++) {
  V = prevVdend - neighVdend[i];
  f_new = V * exp(-1 * V * V/100);
  F_acc =+ f_new;
  V_acc =+ V;
}

Ic = CONDUCTANCE * (0.8*F_acc + 0.2*V_acc);
   return Ic ;
```

$$
\begin{aligned}
Ic &= \sum_{i=0}^{i=N-1} (C * f_i * V_i) \\
&= C * \sum_{i=0}^{i=N-1} (0.8 * \exp(-1 * V_i * \frac{V_i}{100}) + 0.2) * V_i) \\
&= C * (0.8 * \sum_{i=0}^{i=N-1} [V_i * \exp(-1 * V_i * \frac{V_i}{100})] + 0.2 * \sum_{i=0}^{i=N-1} *V_i) \\
&= C * (0.8 * \sum_{i=0}^{i=N-1} f\_new_i + 0.2 \sum_{i=0}^{i=N-1} *V_i)
\end{aligned}
$$

where C is the CONDUCTANCE and N the ION_N_INPUT.
(1)

A second modification in the original code that helped increase both performance and area efficiency was the replacement of any division-by-constant with an arithmetic equivalent (but less computationally intensive) multiplication-by-constant (e.g. $\frac{A}{100} \Leftrightarrow A * 0.01$). In computer arithmetic, the above modifications can introduce precision error in the computations performed; in the evaluation section we measure the effect of our optimization in the quality of the simulations. As shown next, the ION-model computations have a large number of divisions-by-constant operations the replacement of which can influence both area and performance without introducing a significant precision error that would affect correct model behavior. This optimization had to be performed manually as the HLS tool does not support it automatically so as to avoid introducing potential precision error without the developer's consent.

In Table 1, we can see the performance and area benefits for the application, for each code modification. Opt1 denotes the gap-junction code modifications. The other two optimizations refer to the replacement of divisions-by-constant with multiplications-by-constant. Opt 2 replaces divisions only in the slowest part of the model (dendrite compartment), while Opt3 in the entire code. We initially attempted replacing the divisions only in the dendrite, since our main concern is performance while making sure that the arithmetic error would not be significant. As Opt1 and Opt2 had

Design	Speed-up
C Code – Double Floats	×58.64
C Code – Single Floats	×60.82
FPGA Accelerator	×731.23

Table 2: Speed-up of C implementations and the FPGA-based accelerator compared to original Matlab code for simulating a real-time network.

only favored the dendrite/gap-junction compartments, Opt3 was eventually also deemed useful as the balance changed and it lead to an extra performance benefit.

Overall, these modifications achieved an almost 50% decrease in single-neuron execution latency, doubling the maximum network size able to be simulated at real-time speed. There is also some area improvement which is not substantial due to the fact that both multiplications and divisions use in – most cases – the same number of DSP slices.

6. EVALUATION

We evaluate, next, the performance and area cost of our proposed approach and measure its speedup compared to a software implementation. Moreover, we estimate the precision error after our modifications and, finally, discuss the efficiency of our approach compared to other related works.

6.1 Experimental methodology

The development of the Inferior-Olive design was performed using the Xilinx Vivado High Level Synthesis Tool (HLS v2013.2). The tool gives the ability to describe hardware IPs using a subset of ANSI C and then automatically handles production of the IP control logic, hardware scheduling of the operations and translation of the described design in SystemC, VHDL or Verilog code. Vivado HLS also supports algorithm validation using the C code, as well as integration with RTL simulators for validation of the produced HDL code. The tool actually provides the RTL simulation with the correct input vector according to C test-benches. This allows for explicit RTL hardware validation with test-benches simulating the complete CPU/IP system operation.

The ION-network design was translated to VHDL code using HLS and validated using QuestaSim 10.1 in RTL. Our testbench highlighted the basic behavior of the ION-model. All neurons are initialized with identical states, and left without any outside stimuli, remain synchronized with their axon voltage values oscillating. After 20,000 simulation steps, evoked current signals are issued to all neurons for 500 simulation steps. The ION neurons respond to these stimuli by producing a complex spike as seen in Figure 9(a) before returning back to their oscillating steady state. The testbench simulates 6 seconds of real brain time, taking 120,000 simulation steps to complete.

6.2 Experimental Results

The accelerator achieves *real-time execution* for a 96-neuron network with 100% (full) interconnection ratio at an operating frequency of 100 MHz[2] using a Virtex 7 XC7VX485T FPGA. In Table 2 we can see a performance comparison of the C code and the hardware accelerator against the original Matlab implementation; both the C-code and Matlab model

[2]The operating frequency is limited by the Xilinx IP blocks used in the design.

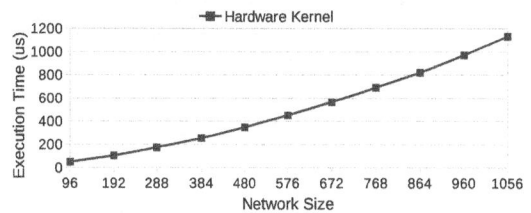

Figure 6: Accelerator step execution time for different network sizes.

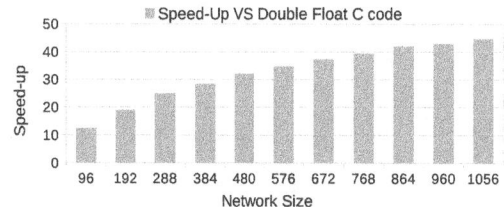

Figure 7: Accelerator performance comparison to double-FP C implementation.

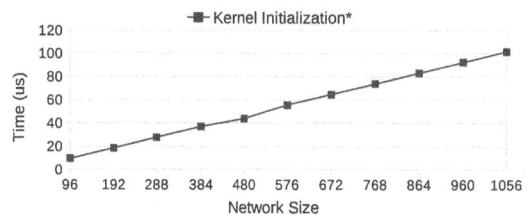

Figure 8: Initialization delay for different network sizes.

run on a Xeon 2.66GHz machine with 20GB RAM. The double-FP C implementation is about ×58 faster that Matlab, while the use of single-FP arithmetic gives a speedup of almost ×61. The FPGA ION-network kernel achieves an impressive ×731 speedup compared to the Matlab version and ×12.5 compared to the C implementation.

The on-chip memory (BRAM) resources available allow for *maximally* simulating a 14,440-cell network (non-real-time). Figure 6 plots the execution time of our designs for different network sizes. It can be observed that the execution time scales with the network size slightly worse than linearly due to the gap-junction computations which increase exponentially with the network size for an all-to-all interconnected network. However, this is still significantly better than execution-time trends in software. This point is better illustrated in Figure 7 which plots the FPGA-based speedup compared to the double-FP C implementation. As the network size increases above 96 cells, our FPGA-based simulation becomes slower than real-time, however it achieves an increasingly better speedup compared to the C implementation. This shows that the increasing gap-junction computations scale more gracefully in our parallel FPGA-based solution than in software. For a network of 96 cells, the speedup is about ×12.5 compared to the C code implementation and goes up to ×45 for a network size of 1,056 neurons.

Finally, the initialization delay also increases for higher network sizes, but in a linear fashion (Figure 8). It reaches a little over 100 μsec for a 1,056-neuron simulation. It should be noted that this time becomes proportionally smaller and even negligible for longer simulation times. Naturally, it

Area Component	Utilization	% of Available
LUTs	251485	83%
BRAMs	804	78%
FF	162217	27%
DSPs	1600	57%

Table 3: Area utilization for the Virtex 707 evaluation board.

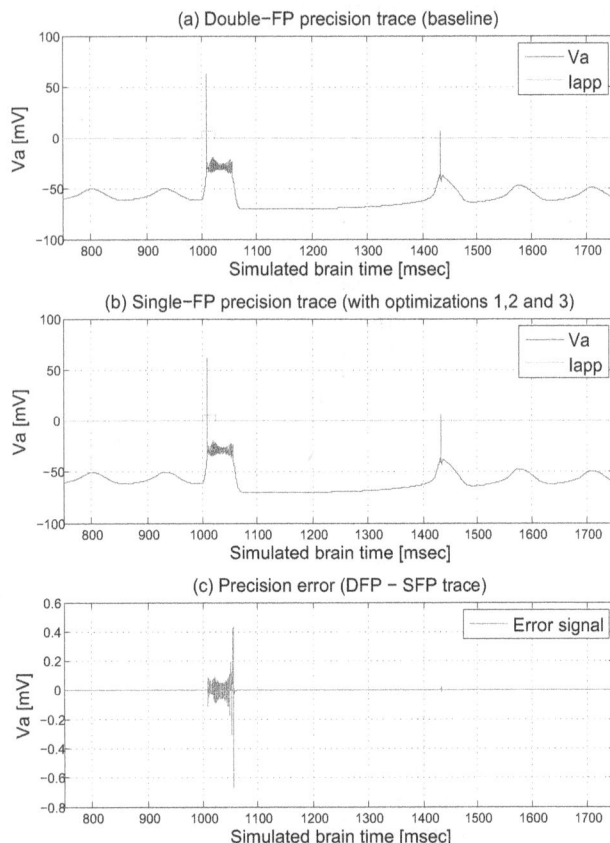

Figure 9: Graphical comparison of numerical-precision error. Externally evoked input current (Iapp) in green, axonal voltage in blue and error signal in red (Va). (a) Reference trace in double-FP precision. (b) The same trace generated with single-FP precision and all three code optimizations. (c) The error signal (i.e. difference) between the two traces. Observe the amplitude units of the error.

also represents the time penalty incurred for re-initializing the cell-states at runtime.

Place-&-Route area results are retrieved using Vivado IDE 2013.2 (Table 3). Our accelerator has been designed to utilize the maximum of the FPGA resources; in practice, it uses 83% of available LUT logic, 78% of BRAMs, 27% of Flip-Flops and 57% of the available DSPs on the FPGA chip.

6.3 Error Estimation

As previously mentioned, the original ION-network model performed all computations with double-FP precision. The main reason was that its modelers (as so many peers in the neuromodeling field) have arbitrarily opted for double-FP precision since this is the highest intrinsically supported precision in many modern programming languages (here: Mat-

lab). However, early in our design effort, we realized that double-FP precision would tax the FPGA with such high performance and area costs that no significant acceleration of the application could be achieved. We, therefore, resorted to switching to single-FP precision calculations for the hardware version of the ION-network model.

To make such a decision, we had to first make sure that single-FP precision would be sufficient for the application at hand. Due to the fact that correct, "reference" brain-simulation traces do not exist (in fact, this is one of the goals of model simulators like the one we are porting in this work), only empirical metrics of correctness can be given by neuro-scientists at the moment. That is, over a practically infinite amount of simulation time – for instance 1 day of real-time brain simulation (amounting to approx. 1.73 billion simulation steps) – the double-FP and single-FP simulation traces should not exhibit any biophysically different results.

Multiple tests have been run. As a simple illustration, in Figure 9 both the dynamic (complex spike) and steady-state (subthreshold oscillations) behavior of a single ION cell between 700 and 2000 msec of a simulation trace have been captured. Figures 9(a) and (b) illustrate runs with double-FP and single-FP precision, respectively. In the single-FP case are also included the 3 code optimizations discussed in Section 5.3 which contribute an additional precision error. In Figure 9(c), the error signal (i.e. difference of the two signals) is plotted over the same simulation period. Analysis of the error reveals that there is *no phase error*. A *very low amplitude error* is observed which ranges from 0.0%, at cell resting state (when most internal cell variables change rapidly), to about 2.1%, at cell firing state. Such a low error signal does not affect the simulator functionality, especially since the model itself cannot guarantee such high accuracy to the real biological system. In conclusion, computations in single-FP precision along with the 3 performed optimizations are considered to *not* compromise the ION-network simulation correctness and are permanently adopted. It is, of course, conceivable that a more constrained numerical range could also be used (i.e. fixed-point precision), but extensive precision analysis of the mathematical model would be required to identify such an (integer) range with certainty.

6.4 Comparison to Related Work

We discuss next the efficiency of our design and related SNN FPGA-based approaches and attempt to analyze and compare them. A direct comparison is not possible as different works consider different neuron-models with radically different characteristics, which potentially change completely the requirements of each design. Moreover, despite its complexity, each model type has its own merits for neuroscience and potential usefulness in applications. Depending on application constraints or the subject of simulation experiments different models can be of use.

Table 4 summarizes related FPGA-based brain-modeling works. Designs using the Quadratic IaF model such as the work in [18, 17] can implement spike latencies, activity-dependent thresholds and bistability properties of resting and tonic[3] spiking. This model requires only 7 FP operations per 1ms for each neuron making it useful for the exploration of large neuron integrator networks. The Izhike-vich neuron is a more advanced model, which emulates all

---

[3]Neuron fires continuously while receiving stimuli.

Design	[18, 17]	[4][5]	[15]	[20]	[2]	ION Design
Model	Quadratic IaF	Izhikevich	Izhikevich	HH	simplified HH	Extended HH
Time Step (ms)	1	1	1	-	0.1	0.05
Real-Time Network Size	1000	64000	64000	4	400	96
Arithmetic Precision	Fixed Point	Fixed Point	Fixed Point	Floating Point	Floating Point	Floating Point
Operations per Neuron in 1ms	>7	>13	>13	>1200	<1200	22200
Neuron Model OPs * Net. Size (MFLOPS)	>7*	>832*	>832*	>4.8	<480	2131.2
Interconnectivity Density	1% (10 per neuron)	1.5% (1000 per neuron)	1.5% (1000 per neuron)	100%	100%	100%
Speed-up vs. CPU	-	-	x162 (C code) 4-FPGA System	x12 (C Code)	-	x12.5 (C Coce) x731.23 (Matlab)
FPGA Chip	Virtex 5 XC5VL330T	Virtex 6 SX475T Maxeler Machine	Stratix IV 230	Spartan 3 XC3SD1800a	Virtex 4	Virtex 7 XC7VX485T
Device Capacity (LUTs/ALMs)	207360 6-input LUTs	297600 6-input LUTs	91200×4 ALMs 2 ALM≈4 6-in LUT	33280 4-input LUTs	-	303600 6-input LUTs
Performance density (FLOPS/LUT**)	34*	2796*	1140*	576	-	7019

* Fixed-point operations ** 6-input LUTs

Table 4: Overview of FPGA SNN Implementations on achievable real-time network sizes. CPU Speed-up for [15] is compared to a Xeon 2.80GHz/48GB RAM, for [20] compared to a Pentium 4 3GHz/3GB RAM and for the ION design to a Xeon 2.66GHz/20GB RAM.

known input/output behavior in a spiking neuron. Izhikevich models are useful for researching the dynamics of large neural networks. Their simplicity also allows for the implementation of very large network sizes in FPGA devices, as described in [5] and [15], achieving sizes already significant to actual brain subsystems (tens of thousands of neurons). A little more costly than the IaF, each Izhikevich neuron model requires 13 operations per 1ms. On the other hand, biophysically-meaningful models such as the HH models used in [20, 2], are one to two orders of magnitude more costly in terms of operations, which is one of the main reasons why real-time network sizes achievable in such designs are much smaller. Another interesting observation is that HH models have a much shorter simulation timestep (tens of μseconds) compared to Quadratic IaF and Izhikevich models (1 msec), which increases their complexity and their accuracy. The ION-model used in the present work has a simulation step of 50 μsec, ×2-×20 shorter than other models, making it have the tightest real-time constraint among the related works reported.

Especially for the ION-cell model considered in this paper, the complexity is even greater than the other HH models. The design accurately models 3 compartments and the gap junctions that account for more than 22,000 FP operations per 1 msec, about ×19 more than the second most complex related model. Moreover, the use of simpler models to increase efficiency is not an option when modeling the Inferior Olive. Izhikevich and IaF models only have two basic output responses for their neuron: resting and firing states. The biological behavior of the Inferior Olive requires greater resolution, since neurons are constantly oscillating even in their resting state and have the property to synchronize. Such behavior could not be simulated with such simpler models.

A strategy that improved performance in some of the related works, however not applicable in the ION-model, is the event driven execution, e.g., in [5] and [15]. Due to the fact that the response of the Inferior Olive neurons oscillates, for the network to retain the ability to synchronize, the neuron needs to compute compartment states and transmit its data through the network connections in every simulation step; consequently event driven simulation is not appropriate.

Another important performance advantage that the designs of simpler models have is the use of fixed-point arithmetic. In such models, precision errors can be insignificant for correct behavior. That is not self-evident in HH models such as the one dealt with here, as they are much more sensitive to both amplitude and phase precision errors. For this reason our design needs to deal with the complexity and cost of FP operations.

Although the above approaches are radically different, in Table 4 we attempt to quantify their complexity and evaluate their efficiency. We take into account the amount of computations per neuron in 1 msec and the network size to estimate the performance of each work in FP operations per second (FLOPS) and properly marking those that use fixed-point. It must be noted that estimations for the computing capabilities of each design are based on data presented in [13] and cannot account for the computations due to the extra custom-made characteristics in the network models of each design, as we do not have this information available. We assume that the majority of the computations come from the simulation of the main neuron model. Our design achieves 2,131.2 MFLOPS, when matching the real-time constraints, while [2] achieves 480 MFLOPS; in both cases computations are mostly due to the complexity of the models. Then, [5] and [15] support 832 million fixed-point operations per second mostly due to the size of the simulated networks. It is worth noting that the highest connectivity (in absolute numbers) is provided by [5] and [15], connecting 1,000 neurons all-to-all, however, the amount of data exchanged is expected to be significantly lower (and less frequent) compared to [2] and compared to our design, which connect 400 and 96 neurons, respectively. Taking into account the area resources used in each work, we define a metric for performance density and measure operations per second per unit area (LUT). Our design has the highest performance density, with second best being at least ×2.5 lower (without taking into account the difference between fixed- and floating-point) [5]; the higher number of DSP-slices in our FPGA device (2,800 vs. 2,015) is however in our advantage.

Finally, interesting conclusions can be derived when comparing the speedup of each approach over software implementations. Compared to a CPU, [2] achieves a ×12 speedup, while the Bluehive device reaches an impressive ×162 using, however, four FPGA devices. Our design achieves a ×731.23 speedup compared to the original Matlab code and ×12.5 compared to the double-FP C code. This speedup reaches almost ×45 for higher network sizes.

7. CONCLUSIONS

We presented an efficient FPGA design for a biophysically-meaningful model of the Inferior Olive, an important part of the olivocerebellar subsystem in the brain responsible for motor coordination and learning. Through a detailed analysis of the application and optimization of the original algorithm, our ION-model design achieves real-time performance as well as sufficient speedup for use in neuroscience experiments. Our FPGA accelerator managed to simulate a network of 96 ION-neurons in real-time being more than ×700 faster than the original Matlab model and ×12.5 faster than the C implementation. The speedup can reach ×45 for a 1,056-cell network, showing substantially better scalability with increasing network sizes compared to software. Although our accelerator implements an ION-network which is ×19 more computationally intensive and has ×2-×20 tighter real-time constraints compared to related models, it achieves at least ×2.5 better performance density supporting 2.13 GFLOPS with a single FPGA device. The empirical precision-error analysis revealed that using our optimizations and single-FP arithmetic creates a very slim amplitude error and no phase errors, preserving the correct biological behavior while benefiting in performance. Our design, implemented in a Virtex 7 XC7VX485T FPGA, can maximally support a 14,400-cell network with online parameter configurability for neuron state and network size.

8. ACKNOWLEDGMENTS

This work has been partially funded by the DeSyRe project (EC 7th Framework Programme, Grant Agr. Nr. 287611). We are also grateful to Drs. S. Koekkoek, J. de Gruijl, R. van Leuken and M. Negrello for all their help.

9. REFERENCES

[1] P. Bazzigaluppi, J. R. De Gruijl, R. S. Van Der Giessen, S. Khosrovani, C. I. De Zeeuw, and M. T. G. De Jeu. Olivary subthreshold oscillations and burst activity revisited. *Frontiers in Neural Circuits*, 6(91), 2012.

[2] M. Beuler, A. Tchaptchet, W. Bonath, S. Postnova, and H. A. Braun. Real-Time Simulations of Synchronization in a Conductance-Based Neuronal Network with a Digital FPGA Hardware-Core. In *Artificial Neural Networks and Machine Learning – ICANN 2012*, September 2012.

[3] D. Brüderle. PyNN and the FACETS Hardware. www.neuralensemble.org/media/slides/CodeJam2_Bruederle_FacetsHardware.pdf, [Online; accessed 18-December-2013] 2008.

[4] K. Cheung, S. R. Schultz, and P. H. W. Leong. A Parallel Spiking Neural Network Simulator. In *Int. Conf. on FPT*, pages 47–254, Dec. 2009.

[5] K. Cheung, S. R. Schultz, and W. Luk. A large-scale spiking neural network accelerator for FPGA systems. In *Int. conf. on Artificial Neural Networks and Machine Learning*, ICANN'12, pages 113–120, 2012.

[6] C.I. De Zeeuw, F.E. Hoebeek , L.W.J. Bosman, M. Schonewille, L. Witter, and S.K. Koekkoek. Spatiotemporal firing patterns in the cerebellum. *Nat Rev Neurosci*, 12(6):327–344, jun 2011.

[7] H. de Garis, M. Korkin, and G. Fehr. The CAM-Brain Machine CBM: An FPGA Based Tool for Evolving a 75 Million Neuron Artificial Brain to Control a Lifesized Kitten Robot. *Auton. Robots*, 10(3):235–249, May 2001.

[8] H. Du Nguyen. GPU-based simulation of brain neuron models. Master's thesis, Delft Technical University, Aug. 2013.

[9] G. Ermentrout and N. Kopell. Parabolic Bursting in an Excitable System Coupled With a Slow Oscillation. *SIAM J on Applied Mathematics*, 46:233–253, 1986.

[10] G. B. Ermentrout. Type I membranes, phase resetting curves, and synchrony. *Neural Computation*, 83:979–1001, 1996.

[11] A. L. Hodgkin and A. F. Huxley. Quantitative description of membrane current and application to conduction and excitation in nerve. *Journal Physiology*, 117:500–544, 1954.

[12] E. Izhikevich. Simple Model of Spiking Neurons. *IEEE Trans. on Neural Networks*, 14(6), 2003.

[13] E. Izhikevich. Which Model to Use for Cortical Spiking Neurons? *IEEE Trans on Neural Net.*, 15(5), 2004.

[14] W. Maass. Noisy Spiking Neurons with Temporal Coding have more Computational Power than Sigmoidal Neurons. In *Neural Information Processing Systems*, pages 211–217, 1996.

[15] S. W. Moore, P. J. Fox, S. J. Marsh, A. T. Markettos, and A. Mujumdar. Bluehive — A Field-Programable Custom Computing Machine for Extreme-Scale Real-Time Neural Network Simulation. In *IEEE Int. Symp. on FCCM*, pages 133–140, 2012.

[16] National Academy of Engineering (nae.edu). Grand Challenges for Engineering, 2010.

[17] H. Shayani, P. Bentley, and A. M. Tyrrell. A Cellular Structure for Online Routing of Digital Spiking Neuron Axons and Dendrites on FPGAs. In *ICES '08, Int. Conf. on Evolvable Systems: From Biology to Hardware*, pages 273–284, 2008.

[18] H. Shayani, P. Bentley, and A. M. Tyrrell. Hardware Implementation of a Bio-plausible Neuron Model for Evolution and Growth of Spiking Neural Networks on FPGA. In *NASA/ESA Conf. on Adaptive Hardware and Systems*, pages 236–243, June 2008.

[19] G. Wulfram and W. Werner. *Spiking Neuron Models*. Cambridge University Press, 2002.

[20] Y. Zhang, J. P. McGeehan, E. M. Regan, S. Kelly, and J. L. Nunez-Yanez. Biophysically Accurate Floating Point Neuroprocessors for Reconfigurable Logic. *IEEE Trans on Computers*, 62(3):599–608, march 2013.

Square-Rich Fixed Point Polynomial Evaluation on FPGAs

Simin Xu
Xilinx Asia Pacific
Singapore
siminx@xilinx.com

Suhaib A. Fahmy
School of Computer
Engineering
Nanyang Technological
University, Singapore
sfahmy@ntu.edu.sg

Ian V. McLoughlin
School of Information Science
and Technology
University of Science and
Technology of China
ivm@ustc.edu.cn

ABSTRACT

Polynomial evaluation is important across a wide range of application domains, so significant work has been done on accelerating its computation. The conventional algorithm, referred to as Horner's rule, involves the least number of steps but can lead to increased latency due to serial computation. Parallel evaluation algorithms such as Estrin's method have shorter latency than Horner's rule, but achieve this at the expense of large hardware overhead. This paper presents an efficient polynomial evaluation algorithm, which reforms the evaluation process to include an increased number of squaring steps. By using a squarer design that is more efficient than general multiplication, this can result in polynomial evaluation with a 57.9% latency reduction over Horner's rule and 14.6% over Estrin's method, while consuming less area than Horner's rule, when implemented on a Xilinx Virtex 6 FPGA. When applied in fixed point function evaluation, where precision requirements limit the rounding of operands, it still achieves a 52.4% performance gain compared to Horner's rule with only a 4% area overhead in evaluating 5th degree polynomials.

Categories and Subject Descriptors

B.2.4 [**Arithmetic and Logic Structures**]: High-Speed Arithmetic—*Algorithms*; F.2.1 [**Analysis of Algorithms and Problem Complexity**]: Numerical Algorithms and Problems—*Computations on polynomials*

Keywords

Fixed point; field programmable gate arrays; polynomial evaluation.

1. INTRODUCTION

Polynomials are commonly used in high-performance DSP applications to approximate the computation of functions, or to model systems parametrically. They are found inside

many basic digital circuits including high-precision elementary functional evaluation circuits [1] and advanced digital filters [2].

Simple polynomials can be evaluated using lookup tables. However, when the degree and wordlength increases, lookup tables become infeasible and thus computation is more appropriate for polynomial evaluation. Work on software and hardware approaches for speeding up polynomial evaluation is numerous. The simplest scheme for computing polynomials is Horner's rule, which is an inherently serial process. Parallel schemes for software implementation, such as Estrin's method [3], have been shown to offer a significant speed improvement. With more resources available, polynomial evaluation can be accelerated significantly. For example, Estrin's method takes $2\lceil log_2(k+1)\rceil$ iterations with $\lceil k/2 \rceil$ processing units to evaluate a kth order polynomial. More recently, fully parallel hardware architectures have been more commonly investigated [4].

Field programmable gate arrays (FPGAs) offer an ideal architecture for such systems due to their fine-grained customisability in terms of datapath wordlength and pipelining. Numerous FPGA-based polynomial evaluation architectures have been presented [5, 6], and various methods have been proposed to speed up polynomial evaluation [7, 8, 9, 10, 11].

In this paper, polynomial evaluation methods are first reviewed, followed by the proposal of a novel evaluation algorithm that takes advantage of the reduced complexity of squaring compared to general multiplication. The new method is then evaluated against both Horner's rule and Estrin's method. The novel algorithm has two variations, suited to different implementations, called the Square-Rich method and Modified Square-Rich method. While this approach can be applied to both floating and fixed point evaluation, we discuss the latter in this paper.

2. BACKGROUND

2.1 Polynomial Evaluation

The general format for k^{th} degree polynomial is,

$$f(x) = \sum_{i=0}^{k} a_i x^i \qquad (1)$$

The fixed point number x is the input of the polynomial with a set of coefficients a_i. These coefficients are defined by the application, and are computed in various ways. We assume that the coefficients do not change frequently, although they can be updated from time to time, as is the case in most

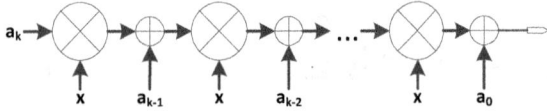

Figure 1: Architecture of polynomial evaluator using Horner's rule.

systems. In other words, we consider a system in which the computation *using* fixed a_i is the limiting factor, rather than the computation *of* a_i values themselves.

Polynomial evaluation procedures have been the subject of investigation since the 1950s. Apart from directly computing the polynomial, which is only practical for low degree polynomials [12], a few prominent methods have emerged.

2.1.1 Horner's Rule

Horner's rule is a basic and widely used method for computing polynomials, and is used in numerous complex applications [13, 14, 15, 16]. It works by transforming the polynomial into a series of multiply-add operations. Considering the polynomial equation stated in (1), Horner's rule re-writes the formula as:

$$f(x) = \{...((a_k \cdot x + a_{k-1}) \cdot x + a_{k-2}) \cdot x + ... + a_0\} \quad (2)$$

Horner's rule has been proven in [17] and [18] to use the minimal number of iterations to evaluate a particular polynomial, i.e. it is optimal in terms of the number of computational steps. Furthermore, it also has a regular structure which is easily implemented, and these factors have lead to its widespread adoption.

In a hardware context, where a custom pipelined datapath can be built, the required amount of hardware resources for polynomial evaluation increases linearly as the degree of the polynomial increases. k multiply-add computations are needed (generally k multipliers and k adders) in a parallel implementation. Figure 1 shows the structure of a polynomial evaluator using Horner's rule.

While the structure is simple, Horner's rule suffers from a long latency due to the serial arrangement of operations. If we denote multiplier latency as T_{mul}, squarer latency as T_{sq}, and adder latency as T_{add}, the latency for k^{th} order polynomial is $k \cdot T_{mul} + k \cdot T_{add}$, which increases linearly with the degree of the polynomial.

2.1.2 Parallel Methods

For applications with low latency requirements, such as communications or cryptography, parallel evaluation is desirable. Dorn [19] proposed a parallel scheme for Horner's Rule. Tree structure approaches have also been presented [20, 21, 22] for ultra-high degree polynomial evaluation ($k > 20$). Among parallel schemes, Estrin's method has been preferred due to its short latency [23].

Estrin's method has since been adopted in many applications [5, 24] for fast evaluation of polynomials. It works by reforming (1) as follows:
If k is even:

$$f(x) = a_k \cdot x^k + \sum_{i=0}^{(k-2)/2} (a_{2i+1}x + a_{2i}) \cdot x^{2i}, \quad (3)$$

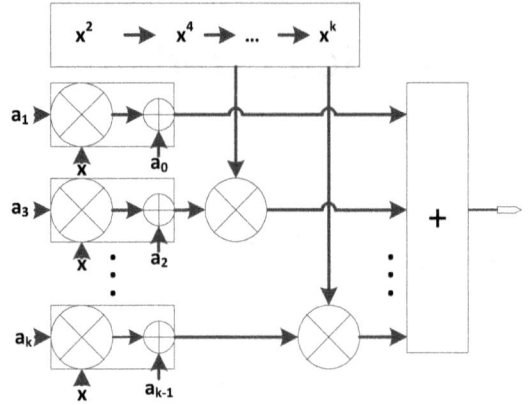

Figure 2: Architecture of polynomial evaluator using Estrin's method.

else if k is odd:

$$f(x) = \sum_{i=0}^{(k-1)/2} (a_{2i+1}x + a_{2i}) \cdot x^{2i} \quad (4)$$

Each sub expression can be computed in parallel and the results summed together at the end. The worst case latency is determined by the exponential function x^k and it can be computed in a total of $\lceil log_2(k) \rceil$ steps, which consists of a series of multiplication and/or squaring operations. This is followed by the multiplication of its coefficient and the final additions. Estrin's method is shown pictorially in Figure 2.

The overall latency for polynomials up to $k = 6$ is summarized in Table 1. Generally, the latency increases at a slower rate than Horner's Rule with increasing degree, and hence, for higher degree polynomials the latency is shorter.

Degree	T_{mul}	T_{sq}	T_{add}
2	1	1	
3	2	0	2
4	1	2	1
5	1	2	1
6	2	2	1

Table 1: Latency for evaluating k^{th} degree polynomials using Estrin's method.

This performance is enabled by increased hardware cost. Although the same number of additions is required as for Horner's rule, as many as $\lfloor k/2 \rfloor$ more multiplications/squares are required in Estrin's method to compute each even degree of x^k and this leads to $\lfloor log_2(k) \rfloor$ more squarers and $\lfloor k/2 \rfloor - \lfloor log_2(k) \rfloor$ more multipliers needed in hardware. Overall implementation costs are summarized for polynomials up to $k = 6$ in Table 2.

2.2 FPGA Computation

Modern FPGAs include hard DSP blocks that enable fast and area efficient multiplication and addition. In the Xilinx Virtex 6, and all subsequent 7 Series FPGAs from Xilinx, the DSP48E1 blocks support 25×18 bit signed multiplication, followed by a programmable ALU in the datap-

Degree	Mults	Squarers	Adders
2	2	1	2
3	3	1	3
4	4	2	4
5	5	2	5
6	7	2	6

Table 2: Hardware cost for evaluating k^{th} degree polynomials using Estrin's method.

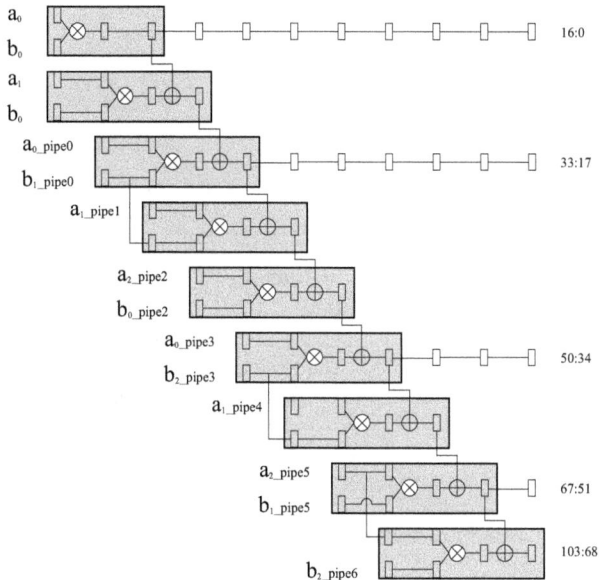

Figure 3: Pipelined 52-bit multiplier built using DSP blocks.

ath. These blocks can also be efficiently cascaded to support wider arithmetic. The DSP48E1 primitives also support dynamic modification of their datapath functions [25], which can be leveraged for iterative implementations of fundamental computational blocks [26]. For polynomial evaluation, the basic functions of multiplication and squaring can be efficiently built using DSP blocks. In order to obtain maximum performance, it is important to consider the structure of the DSP block when building a computational datapath [27].

Fast, wide multipliers are built by cascading together chains of DSP blocks using dedicated hard wires that do not add significantly to the routing delay. This allows for wide operations to be computed at near full frequency, as long as all the stages are pipelined. A 52-bit multiplication using three DSP blocks is shown in Figure 3. Each shaded block is a single DSP block, with the cascade chains between the blocks shown. The only extra resources needed are registers to maintain alignment in the datapath between subsequent DSP block stages. The pipeline stages before DSP blocks are indicated by the names of the input bus for simplicity while the alignment of pipeline stages within and after DSP blocks are illustrated using small rectangles.

While a squarer can be implemented using multiplication with its inputs tied together, it is also possible to build wide squarers more efficiently. The number of DSP blocks re-

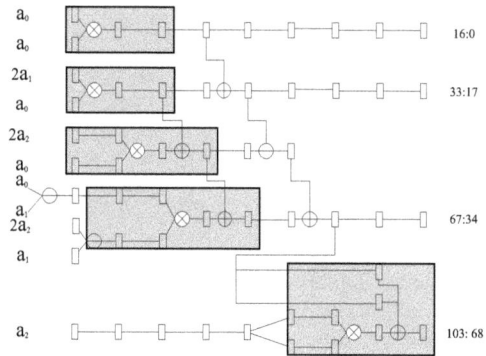

Figure 4: Pipelined 52-bit squarer using DSP blocks.

quired for a squarer grows more slowly than for a general multiplier, as operand wordlength increases [28]. Hence, where it is possible to use a squarer instead of a multiplier, efficiency gains are possible in terms of both area and performance. In our previous work [28], an efficient squarer was proposed which consumes up to 50% less hardware resources than an equivalent width multiplier. It can use 1 fewer DSP block than the method in [29] at a cost of only 127 additional LUTs. The architecture for a 52-bit squarer is shown in Figure 4.

The squarer design also benefits in terms of latency. After pipelining the circuit to meet the maximum frequency of the DSP blocks, a 52 bit squarer has a pipeline 23% shorter than an equivalent multiplier. For a 64 bit squarer, this advantage increases to 31%. Note that in order to achieve maximum DSP block frequency, it is necessary to add an additional register stage any time a DSP block output is passed to LUTs (for implemented small adders for example). This has not been taken into account in [29] and [13], but is done by default in this work.

3. SQUARE-RICH METHOD

In this section, we present the novel polynomial evaluation algorithm. It involves transformation of the general form of a polynomial into a "square rich" format and so we name it the "Square-Rich" (SR) method. The main benefit of the algorithm is to achieve faster evaluation with minimum hardware overhead. Although the total number of operations is more than for Horner's rule, the hardware implementation can be more efficient than the "optimum method in theory", thanks to the efficiency gains achieved by using squarers instead of multipliers. The latency of this method will be shown to be close to that of Estrin's method but using fewer hardware resources. Although this paper only presents results for polynomials up to the 6th degree, the approach can be applied to polynomials of arbitrary degree.

3.1 Algorithm

The SR method is based on the following hypothesis, illustrated by a 2nd degree polynomial example:

HYPOTHESIS 1.

To evaluate the 2nd degree polynomial,

$$f(x) = a_2 x^2 + a_1 x + a_0 \qquad (5)$$

it is advantageous to reform the equation as,

$$f(x) = a_2 \cdot ((x + m_2)^2 + n_2) \qquad (6)$$

Where m_2 and n_2 are defined as,

$$m_2 = \frac{a_1}{2a_2} \qquad (7)$$

$$n_2 = \frac{a_0}{a_2} - \frac{a_1^2}{4a_2^2} \qquad (8)$$

The new format completes the square and converts the original polynomial into its vertex form. In (6), m_2 and n_2 are coefficients derived from a_1 and a_0, thus they can be considered precomputed values. It can be seen that four steps are needed to compute (6): one addition, one square followed by another addition, and a final multiplication. The same number of steps is needed using Horner's rule but with two multipliers and two adders. The latency is thus $T_{mul} + T_{sq} + 2T_{add}$ for the proposed method, compared to $2T_{mul} + 2T_{add}$ for Horner's rule. If $T_{sq} < T_{mul}$, this represents a saving. The SR method also results in reduced hardware cost since the resources required for a squarer are fewer than for a multiplier.

To apply Hypothesis 1 to the general k^{th} degree polynomial in (1), we define an integer number j, which is the binary logarithm of k:

$$j = \lfloor log_2 k \rfloor \qquad (9)$$

and define

$$p_t(x) = (a_{k-t}x^{k-t} + a_{k-j-t}x^{k-j-t} + a_{k-2j-t}x^{k-2j-t}), \qquad (10)$$

where t ranges from $[0, j-1]$. Then the equation can be divided into the following groups:

$$f(x) = \sum_{t=0}^{j-1} p_t(x) + f'(x), \qquad (11)$$

where $f'(x)$ only exists if $k - 3j \geq 0$ and is

$$f'(x) = \sum_{i=0}^{k-3j} a_i x^i. \qquad (12)$$

In $p_t(x)$, a common divisor of $a_{k-t}x^{k-2j-t}$ can be extracted so that the equation becomes

$$p_t(x) = a_{k-t}x^{k-2j-t}(x^{2j} + \frac{a_{k-j-t}}{a_{k-t}}x^j + \frac{a_{k-2j-t}}{a_{k-t}}) \qquad (13)$$

Completing the square in (13), it becomes

$$p_t(x) = a_{k-t}x^{k-2j-t}[(x^j + m_{k-t})^2 + n_{k-t}], \qquad (14)$$

where

$$m_{k-t} = \frac{a_{k-j-t}}{2a_{k-t}} \qquad (15)$$

$$n_{k-t} = \frac{a_{k-2j-t}}{a_{k-t}} - \frac{a_{k-j-t}^2}{4a_{k-t}^2} \qquad (16)$$

Equation (11) with (14) are the general forms of the SR method for evaluating polynomials of arbitrary degree. The same iteration process from (10) to (14) is applied on $f'(x)$ with degree k' and for $f'(x)$, the degree k' is now $k-3j$. This continues until the lowest degree of polynomial has been computed.

The latency required for the SR method applied in 2th to 6th degree polynomial is shown in Table 3. It is clear that the SR method has shorter latency than Horner's rule for parallel evaluations of higher degree terms and a gain from an increased number of square operations instead of multiplications shown in Hypothesis 1. The latency is no longer limited by the computation of x^k as the highest power exponential that must be computed is only x^j. Therefore, the SR method can at least equal, or potentially improve upon the performance of Estrin's method. This will be discussed in more detail when FPGA implementation results are presented in Section 5.

deg	T_{mul}	T_{sq}	T_{add}
2	1	1	2
3	1	1	3
4	1	2	3
5	1	2	3
6	1	2	4

Table 3: Latency for evaluating k^{th} degree polynomials using SR method.

The hardware resource requirements for the SR method are shown in Table 4 and a diagram of the architecture is shown in Figure 5. The hardware requirements are smaller than for Estrin's method since fewer multipliers and fewer squarers are used. Compared to the Horner's rule, which needs the minimum number of computational steps, the SR method can have reduced hardware overhead as a result of the more efficient squarer (compared to multiplication). This comparison, in the context of FPGA implementation, is presented in Section 5.

deg	Multiplier	Squarer	Adder
2	1	1	2
3	2	1	3
4	3	2	4
5	3	3	5
6	4	3	6

Table 4: Hardware cost for evaluating k^{th} degree polynomials using SR method.

3.2 Coefficients

The SR method needs a new set of coefficients, which are a one-off derivation from the original polynomial coefficients. For an application such as an adaptive filter, this may result in an additional overhead every time the polynomial adapts, however the generation process can be performed when deriving the polynomial. Even when the coefficients are computed on the fly, compared to the actual polynomial evaluation process, this overhead is small and tends to be negligible as the number of evaluations performed using each new coefficient set increases. In this paper, the coefficients are pre-computed and stored in block RAMs at design time. This is considered to be a typical real-world scenario; the polynomial is generated during system setup or programming rather than on the fly.

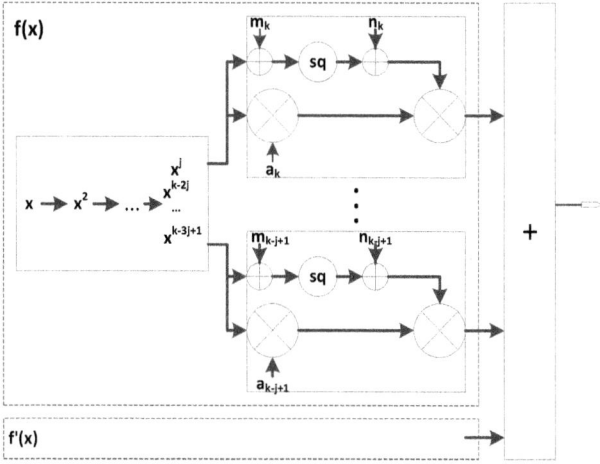

Figure 5: Architecture of polynomial evaluator using SR method.

4. ERROR ANALYSIS

In real applications, like function approximation, the complexity and latency of polynomial evaluation is often traded-off against accuracy. A certain tolerance of error, including evaluation error and other errors may be allowed and the designer can implement faithful rounding for coefficients and perform truncation in intermediate computations while controlling the total error. In this paper, as we are only interested in the process of polynomial evaluation, we assume that all other error factors involved are the same among all the evaluation algorithms except for evaluation error caused by rounding. The error contributed by the coefficient generation process in previous sections is negligible and we assume that the new coefficients themselves are computed without additional errors being introduced.

Two types of wordlength optimization for fixed-point implementation in FPGA will be discussed in this paper and the error analysis will performed differently in the individual contexts.

4.1 Fixed Point Implementation

First, we consider a general fixed point implementation where each computation will only truncate its result to the same wordlength as the input operands, which is common practice in many signal processing systems. In this case, as the error is mainly associated with the multiplications, different evaluation algorithms will have different evaluation error, due to the differing structures. Generally, as Horner's rule requires the least number of computational steps, it is more accurate than any other evaluation scheme in this context. Take a 3rd degree polynomial as example. The total evaluation error using Horner's rule can be calculated from

$$\epsilon_{total}f(x) = \sum_{i=0}^{2} \epsilon_{eval}(q_i \cdot x + a_i) \cdot x^i \qquad (17)$$

In (17), q_i is the multiply-add result for the $i+1$th term except for the highest degree, which is a_k. Each multiply-add evaluation error only depends on the previous multiply-add result. Assuming x is in the range of $[0, 1]$, for higher degree terms, each multiply-add evaluation error is multiplied

by the exponential of x and thus it is less significant in the overall error than the lower degree terms.

For Estrin's method, as more multiplication steps (including squares) are required, it naturally has larger error than Horner's rule in this context. For the same 3rd degree polynomial, the total evaluation error has four terms rather than three and it can be represented as,

$$\epsilon_{total}f(x) = \epsilon_{eval}(a_1 \cdot x + a_0)$$
$$+ (a_3 x + a_2) \cdot \epsilon_{trunc}(x^2)$$
$$+ x^2 \cdot \epsilon_{eval}(a_3 \cdot x + a_2)$$
$$+ \epsilon_{trunc}((a_3 x + a_2) \cdot x^2) \qquad (18)$$

The first and third error term refer to the evaluation errors of the multiply-add computation and they are comparable with Horner's rule. However, the other two error components may contribute to a larger total error than Horner's rule, depending on the value of the coefficients. The second error term $\epsilon_{trunc}(x^2)$, which refers to the truncation error of the square and is comparable with $\epsilon_{eval}(q_1 \cdot x + a_1)$ in (17), is multiplied by $a_3 x + a_2$ which can be larger than x. The last error term $\epsilon_{trunc}((a_3 x + a_2) \cdot x^2)$, which refers to the truncation error of the multiplication indicated by $\cdot$, is due to the additional multiplication that Horner's rule does not require. For higher degree polynomials, Estrin's method is worse in terms of total evaluation error with the current wordlength optimization. There will be more error components for Estrin's method than Horner's rule due to a larger number of operations and the error from the exponential computation is significant as well, however, we do not detail them here due to space constraints.

In contrast, the SR method has smaller error than Estrin's method due to fewer multiplication operations. For the same 3rd degree polynomial, the total evaluation error can be represented as,

$$\epsilon_{total}f(x) = \epsilon_{eval}(a_0 + p_0)$$
$$+ a_3 x \cdot \epsilon_{eval}((x + m_3)^2 + n_3)$$
$$+ ((x + m_3)^2 + n_3) \cdot \epsilon_{trunc}(a_3 \cdot x_3) \qquad (19)$$

The first error term $\epsilon_{eval}(a_0 + p_0)$ refers to the evaluation error of the final multiplication in p_0 and the addition with a_0, which is the same amount as the first error term in Estrin's method (18). The second error term refers to the evaluation error for computing the square and the addition of n_3 while the last error term refers to the truncation error of $a_3 \cdot x_3$. Depending on the value of the coefficients, these two terms have similar values to the second and third error terms in (18). Therefore, the SR method is better in terms of evaluation error than Estrin's method as it has three comparable error components instead of four. For higher degree polynomials, as the SR method has much fewer multiplication operations and does not require a large degree exponentiation of x, it can be more accurate than Estrin's method generally.

However, the SR method is not always as accurate as Horner's rule. In fact, with the current optimization scheme, the SR method has the same number of evaluation error components for a 3rd degree polynomial, but the total evaluation error could potentially be larger than Horner's rule, depending on the value of the coefficients. For higher degree polynomials, the SR method has more error components than Horner's rule due to the number of computations being higher and this difference increases as the degree increases. Therefore, a modified formulation, we call the "Modified Square-Rich" (MSR) method can be created and applied to reduce the total evaluation error. The new format is

$$p'_t(x) = x^{k-2j-t}(a_{k-t} \cdot (x^j + m_{k-t})^2 + n'_{k-t}), \qquad (20)$$

where

$$n'_{k-t} = a_{k-2j-t} - \frac{a_{k-j-t}^2}{4a_{k-t}} \qquad (21)$$

To implement the MSR method in hardware, the same amount of hardware resources are needed as for the SR method, as the total number of operations is the same. However, MSR has slighly increased latency, where one more multiplication must be serially computed for 3rd, 5th and 6th degree polynomials, as summarized in Table 5. The structure of the MSR method is shown in Figure 6.

deg	T_{mul}	T_{sq}	T_{add}
2	1	1	2
3	2	1	3
4	1	2	3
5	2	2	3
6	2	2	4

Table 5: Latency for evaluating k^{th} degree polynomials using MSR method.

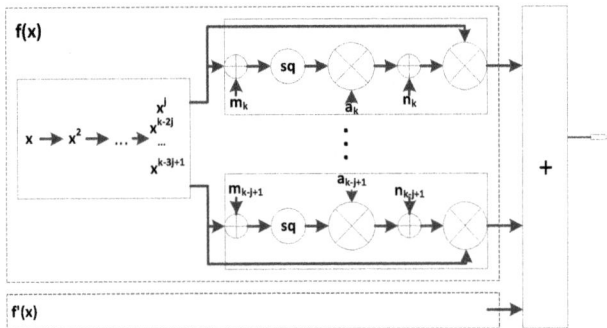

Figure 6: Architecture of polynomial evaluator using MSR method.

Although one more multiplication must be performed serially, the MSR method reduces the total evaluation error. Without the common factors to be taken out, the total evaluation error for the same 3rd degree polynomial now becomes,

$$
\begin{aligned}
\epsilon_{total} f(x) = {} & \epsilon_{eval}(a_0 + p'_0) \\
& + a_3 x \cdot \epsilon_{trunc}((x + m'_3)^2) \\
& + x \cdot \epsilon_{eval}(a_3 \cdot (x + m'_3)^2 + n'_3) \qquad (22)
\end{aligned}
$$

Similarly, the first error term refers to the evaluation error including final multiplication of p'_0 and the final addition. The second error term multiplies the same $a_3 x$ coefficient as (19) while the last error term has a much smaller coefficient which leads to smaller total error.

The MSR method shows its advantages further when a_{k-t} is small, which is usually the case in high degree polynomial

applications. In this case, n_{k-t} tends to be large and the total evaluation error using the SR method will be large. In contrast, as the evaluation error is not related to the value of n_{k-t}, the MSR method retains its small evaluation error.

In summary, with the above general fixed point error analysis, Horner's rule remains the most accurate method. For lower degree polynomials, the SR method is more accurate than using Estrin's method and close to the accuracy of Horner's rule. However, for higher degree polynomials, the evaluation error from the SR method is much larger than for Horner's Rule and using the MSR method can reduce the gap. Section 5 presents the implementation results for the SR method and MSR method with general wordlength optimization along with results for Estrin's method and Horner's rule as reference designs.

4.2 Faithful Rounding in Specific Application

Another optimization is faithful rounding of coefficients and other operands, which is only possible in the context of a specific application, like fixed point function evaluation using polynomials. Typically, implementation in FPGAs is more flexible than architectures that enforce a fixed wordlength for each computation as each operand can be freely optimized according to requirements. Computational complexity can be reduced by reducing the wordlength of each operand bit by bit, as long as the total evaluation error is no worse than the error target. FloPoCo [13] includes an automated design generator with such optimization for a function evaluator using Horner's rule. For a fair comparison to the FloPoCo design, we apply a similar rounding strategy for function evaluation using Estrin's method, the SR method and the MSR method and our target is to achieve evaluation error no worse than the FloPoCo designs in each specific interval. We assume no overflow/underflow occurs in each computational step.

Gappa [1] is used to verify that the optimized designs are within the evaluation error bounds. Gappa is a tool that helps verify and formally prove properties of numerical programs dealing with floating-point or fixed-point arithmetic [30] and has been used to verify fixed point polynomial evaluations previously [5, 8, 13]. It computes the range of a given function based on the constraints of using interval arithmetic. In this case, each rounding trail of a particular algorithm will be verified by Gappa. If the verification shows the evaluation error for the SR method, MSR method or Estrin's method are not within the same bound as the FloPoCo design, rounding is modified for the next iteration and verified once more by Gappa. The verification scripts are not presented due to space constraints, though the optimized design details are presented in Section 6.

5. IMPLEMENTATION IN FPGA

In this section, a series of evaluators using the SR method and MSR method are built in Verilog and synthesized, placed and routed using Xilinx ISE 13.4 on a Virtex 6 XC6VLX240T-1 FPGA as found on the ML605 evaluation board. These evaluators are built for 52 and 64 bit arithmetic with polynomial degree ranges from 2 to 6 and equal input and output wordlengths. Each intermediate step truncates its result to 52 or 64 bits after the maximum wordlength has been computed. Evaluators using Horner's rule and Estrin's

---

[1]Version 0.16.4 gappa.gforge.inria.fr

method with the same wordlengths and degrees are built as references. Fixed point multiplications used in the evaluator are built using multipliers provided by Xilinx CoreGen and squarers are built using the method in [28]. Adders are synthesized to use carry chain resources in CLBs automatically. The designs are all pipelined and targeted to achieve the maximum frequency of DSP blocks for the targeted -1 speed grade device, which is 450MHz [31]. The same approach can be used on higher speed grade devices and result in higher frequencies. We have chosen the slowest speed grade to prove the baseline performance gain of the proposed methods, which can be applied across any FPGA containing the DSP48E1 primitive. DSP block pipelining is done by instantiating Xilinx primitives and turning on all the optional register stages to maximize performance. Adders with data flowing from or to DSP blocks are pipelined using flip flops or shift registers in CLBs.

A comparison of the cost in DSB blocks for all the evaluators is shown in Table 6.

bits	deg	MSR/SR	Estrin's	Horner's
	2	14	23	18
	3	23	32	27
52	4	37	46	36
	5	42	55	45
	6	51	73	54
	2	24	40	32
	3	40	56	48
64	4	64	80	64
	5	72	96	80
	6	88	128	96

Table 6: DSP block usage for all evaluators.

Both the SR and MSR methods use same number of DSP blocks since the number of operations is the same. They require at least 3 fewer DSP blocks than Horner's Rule for a wordlength of 52 bits and 8 fewer blocks for a wordlength of 64 bits except for the 4th degree evaluators. Compared to the Estrin's method, they are much smaller with up to 22 and 40 fewer DSP blocks for wordlengths of 52 and 64 bit respectively. Hence, both novel methods are more efficient in terms of DSP usage.

The equivalent hardware cost for all the evaluators is shown in Figure 7. Cost is determined in terms of the equivalent number of LUTs, which we use as a metric to combine the DSP block count and LUT count. The equivalent number of LUTs for one DSP block is defined as the total number of LUTs in the device divided by the total number of DSP blocks. Hence, a circuit that uses an additional DSP block should save at least that number of LUTs for it to be considered an overall area saving. While this metric is not universally applicable, it serves as a useful proxy here. For the specific target FPGA, with 150720 LUTs and 768 DSP blocks, this ratio is 196 (it ranges from 160 to 240 for most general purpose Xilinx Virtex FPGAs).

For 52 and 64 bit polynomials, both novel methods use up to 20.9% fewer equivalent LUTs than Horner's rule for 2nd and 3rd degree polynomials and no more than 5% more for higher degrees. Considering that Horner's rule has the fewest operations, the novel methods are very efficient in terms of resource requirements, mainly as a result of the ef-

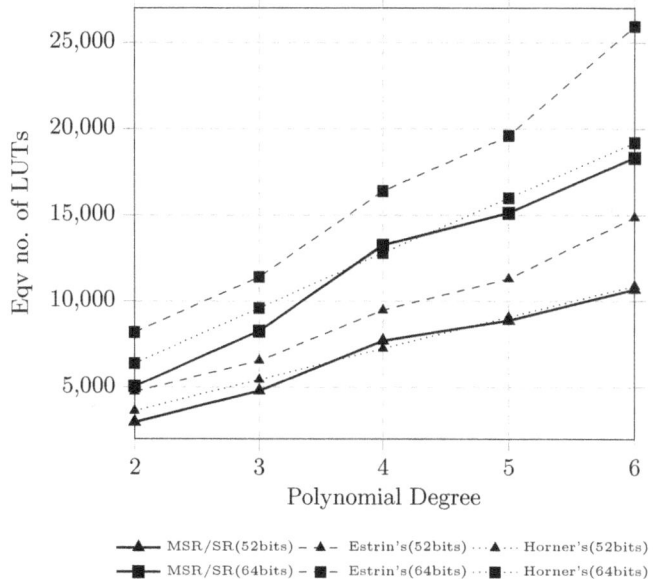

Figure 7: Equivalent hardware cost for all evaluators.

ficient squarer design. Compared to Estrin's method, the novel methods use up to 38.3% fewer equivalent LUTs for 2nd degree polynomials. The equivalent LUT count for 3rd degree polynomials is 18.6% less and up to 29.3% less for higher degrees. The hardware savings become more significant as the polynomial degree increases.

Although other FPGA devices have different equivalent LUT counts, the novel methods still shows an advantage in terms of overall hardware cost as savings are dominated by the use of fewer DSP blocks. The SX series DSP-rich FPGAs from Xilinx, with a different LUT to DSP block ratio, give a 3% reduction in area savings against Estrin's method and Horner's rule, for example.

Meanwhile, the SR and MSR methods also show a benefit in terms of latency compared to Horner's rule, as shown in Table 7. The evaluator using the SR method can achieve up to 54.4% shorter latency for a wordlength of 52 bits and up to 57.9% shorter latency for a wordlength of 64 bits. For the MSR method, the figures are 40.0% and 42.9% less than Horner's rule.

bits	deg	SR	MSR	Estrin's	Horner's
	2	27	27	25	30
	3	29	42	30	45
52	4	39	39	35	60
	5	39	52	35	75
	6	41	54	48	90
	2	36	36	34	42
	3	38	57	42	63
64	4	51	51	47	84
	5	51	70	47	105
	6	53	72	66	126

Table 7: Latency comparison for all evaluators with F_{max} all above 400MHz.

Comparing to Estrin's method, the SR method is as fast in terms of latency for both 52 and 64 bit wordlength polynomials below degree 4. For 4th and 5th degree polynomials, the SR method is four stages or 11.4% longer than Estrin's method, as it can only compute two groups of terms in parallel while the other is able to compute three at the same time. With a 14.6% shorter latency for 6th degree polynomials, the SR method shows its benefit in higher degrees where Estrin's method is limited by the slow computation of x^6. Although the details of implementation are not presented here, the latency benefit for the SR method is sustained for polynomials with degree higher than 6 and below 15, as the worst case path for the SR method does not change while the worst case path for Estrin's method becomes longer.

On the other hand, the MSR method increases latency by 34.5% on average compared to the SR method for 3rd 5th and 6th degree polynomials and therefore the latency is longer than Estrin's method (but still much shorter than Horner's). There is no penalty in latency for 2nd and 4th degree polynomials evaluated using the MSR method.

6. APPLICATION TO FUNCTION EVALUATION

Function evaluation is one of the most important applications for polynomials. In this section, we present function evaluators using the SR/MSR method and compare the performance with designs generated by the FloPoCo fixed point function evaluator module [13], which uses Horner's Rule, as well as function evaluators using Estrin's method that we have built.

The function evaluators built in this section are used to approximate the function $log_2(x + 1)$ in the range of $x \in [0, 1]$. $3^{rd}, 4^{th}, 5^{th}$ and 6th degree polynomials are used in the designs with input/output precisions of 36, 52, and 64 bits. The same amount of range reduction is applied for all the evaluators, which divides the range of x into sub intervals to achieve higher precision. Coefficients generated from the approximation process for each interval are shared among all the methods to minimize approximation error.

We implemented evaluators with the SR and MSR methods as well as the reference designs targeting the same Xilinx Virtex 6 FPGA (XC6VLX240T-1) using ISE 13.4 with default settings. Note that the FloPoCo designs are pipelined by the tool using the default strategy. We additionally enable the DSP optional registers and add one register stage after the DSP blocks to achieve higher frequency. The other parallel evaluators evaluated are pipelined manually using a similar pipelining strategy.

Table 8 summarizes the hardware results for all evaluators. The latencies are in clock cycles, with the DSP blocks fully pipelined. After each optimization iteration, a new set of coefficients must be applied to both Estrin's and the SR method. For Estrin's method, it is a simple rounding for reducing complexity while for the SR method, the coefficients are re-generated and then rounded to the optimized wordlength. Coefficients are stored in BRAMs after being generated and optimized. Although final coefficients may not have exactly the same wordlengths, they all fit into same number of BRAM blocks. Therefore, the BRAM count is not included in the results.

With effective optimizations, all of the methods are able to reduce DSP block usage. Note that the wordlengths of the operands are sometimes either too large to fit into a smaller multiplier or too small to fully utilize the DSP blocks in a larger multiplier. Therefore, LUTs are used to complete the multiplication rather than wasting DSP resources. This is reflected in the LUT usage increases in all the evaluators.

The SR method is extremely efficient for the 3rd degree polynomial evaluator with a wordlength of 36 bit. It is 24.2% smaller in terms of equivalent LUTs and 36.8% faster in terms of latency than the FloPoCo design. Compared to Estrin's method, where both evaluators have 12 pipeline stages, it is 35.2% smaller in terms of area. The performance gain and area savings are mainly as a result of the faster and smaller squarers used in place of multipliers.

It is also efficient for the 5th degree polynomial evaluator with a wordlength of 52 bits, where the SR method is 52.4% faster in latency than FloPoCo at the cost of only 4% more equivalent LUTs. Compared to Estrin's method, which can also achieve the same latency gain for the same polynomial, the SR method saves two DSP blocks and 49 LUTs.

For the 4th degree evaluators with wordlengths of 36 and 52 bits, the SR method has a 45.8% reduced latency compared to the FloPoCo design on average. However, the equivalent LUT overhead is larger, averaging 17.6%. Evaluators using Estrin's method for these two polynomials do not have significantly reduced latency compared to the SR method, but require 6.6% more hardware resources.

When the degree is as high as 6 and the precision requirement is up to 64 bits, the SR method needs 38.3% more hardware resources than the FloPoCo designs to maintain equal evaluation error. Meanwhile, due to the large multiplication, the latency gain reduces to 34.6%. Estrin's method can only achieve a similar latency gain with two more DSP blocks and 119 more LUTs.

On the other hand, the MSR method is 14.1% faster in terms of latency than FloPoCo while it uses only 8 more DSP blocks but less than half the number of LUTs compared to the FloPoCo 6th degree evaluator. Although it has more computations and the latency is 12.8% longer than the SR method, it saves 17.2% in terms of resources due to smaller multipliers. Interestingly, the MSR method is also efficient for 5th degree polynomial evaluation, where the MSR method is only 3 stages slower than SR method, but reduces the equivalent LUT usage by 15.4%. This translates into a 45.2% latency gain and 11.9% area saving compared to the FloPoCo design. As the MSR method has a smaller evaluation error by design, it can be used with fewer operand bits compared to the SR method, reducing area and minimising the latency overhead. Thus it is useful in high precision, large degree polynomial evaluation. For lower degrees, although it is smaller than the SR method, the MSR method has a longer latency.

After pipelining, all the parallel evaluators can achieve an operating frequency in the range of 375MHz to 385MHz, agains the FloPoCo designs which only achieve a frequency below 334MHz, representing more than a 12% throughput improvement. Further pipelining on top of the FloPoCo default pipeline strategy could increase the frequency, however, it would increase latency. Note that as the coefficient BRAM sizes are the same, the latency for the BRAM reads is identical for all the evaluators and so is not detailed here.

We have also implemented both Estrin's method and the SR method to approximate other functions, including $sin(x)$ and $\sqrt{1 + x}$. For lower degree polynomials, the SR method

		FlopoCo					Estrin's Method				
bits	deg	LUTs	DSPs	eq. LUTs	Latency	F (MHz)	LUTs	DSPs	eq. LUTs	Latency	F (MHz)
36	3	314	6	1490	19	320	174	8	1642	12	392
36	4	280	7	1652	26	319	214	10	2174	13	395
52	4	665	14	3409	33	332	189	20	4109	18	384
52	5	901	18	4429	42	334	350	24	5054	20	378
64	6	1215	26	6311	52	322	615	44	9239	33	380

		Square-Rich					Modified Square-Rich				
bits	deg	LUTs	DSPs	eq. LUTs	Latency	F (MHz)	LUTs	DSPs	eq. LUTs	Latency	F (MHz)
36	3	149	5	1129	12	394	149	5	1129	17	390
36	4	190	9	1954	14	388	212	8	1780	19	385
52	4	259	19	3983	18	381	259	17	3591	21	380
52	5	301	22	4613	20	380	375	18	3903	23	375
64	6	496	42	8728	34	379	563	34	7227	39	376

Table 8: Performance and hardware cost for all evaluators when used to approximate $log_2(x + 1)$.

demonstrates that, with faithful rounding, it is able to outperform both Estrin's method and Horner's rule similarly to the results shown in Table 8. However, to achieve 64 bit precision or higher where a 6th degree polynomial is required, Estrin's method, the SR method and the MSR methods are all unable to match the evaluation error of Horner's rule. The solution to this problem would be to further increase the number of intervals, and reduce the range of each to compensate for the loss of precision due to evaluation error. The hardware overhead would be more BRAMs and the latency penalty would be negligible. However this refinement is beyond the scope of this paper.

7. CONCLUSION

In this paper, an efficient polynomial evaluation algorithm is presented. It can achieve a 57.9% latency reduction over Horner's rule or a 14.6% latency reduction over Estrin's method in general fixed point implementation without faithful rounding of the coefficients on a Xilinx Virtex 6 FPGA, with the help of an efficient squarer design. It can achieve hardware savings over Horner's rule implementations and over 38.3% area reduction compared to Estrin's method.

When the novel method is applied to a function evaluation application on FPGA, using the SR method can be 52.4% faster in latency than design generated by FloPoCo using Horner's rule with 4% equivalent LUT overhead. For higher precisions, although the latency of the SR method is still 34.6% shorter than the FloPoCo design at a cost of 38.3% more hardware resources, the MSR method is more efficient as the latency is only 12.8% longer than using SR method but with a 17.2% reduction in area overhead. Both the SR and MSR methods are much smaller than Estrin's method in terms of area and have lower latency than designs using Horner's rule. We aim to demonstrate more function evaluators, and larger polynomial degrees, before releasing the source code for our generator tool.

8. REFERENCES

[1] J.-M. Muller, *Elementary functions: algorithms and implementation.* Birkhauser Boston, Inc., 1997.

[2] L. Rabiner, J. McClellan, and T. Parks, "FIR digital filter design techniques using weighted Chebyshev approximation," *Proceedings of the IEEE*, vol. 63, no. 4, pp. 595–610, 1975.

[3] G. Estrin, "Organization of computer systems: the fixed plus variable structure computer," in *Proceedings of Joint IRE-AIEE-ACM Computer Conference*, 1960, pp. 33–40.

[4] J. Duprat and J.-M. Muller, "Hardwired polynomial evaluation," *J. Parallel Distrib. Comput.*, vol. 5, no. 3, pp. 291–309, 1988.

[5] A. Tisserand, "Hardware reciprocation using degree-3 polynomials but only 1 complete multiplication," in *Proceedings of Midwest Symposium on Circuits and Systems*, 2007, pp. 301–304.

[6] J. A. Pineiro, J. D. Bruguera, and J. M. Muller, "FPGA implementation of a faithful polynomial approximation for powering function computation," in *Proceedings of Euromicro Symposium on Digital Systems Design*, 2001, pp. 262–269.

[7] D.-U. Lee, A. A. Gaffar, O. Mencer, and W. Luk, "Optimizing hardware function evaluation," *IEEE Trans. Comput.*, vol. 54, no. 12, pp. 1520–1531, 2005.

[8] A. Tisserand, "High-performance hardware operators for polynomial evaluation," *Int. J. High Perform. Syst. Archit.*, vol. 1, no. 1, pp. 14–23, 2007.

[9] N. Brisebarre, J. M. Muller, and A. Tisserand, "Sparse-coefficient polynomial approximations for hardware implementations," in *Conference Record of Asilomar Conference on Signals, Systems and Computers*, 2004, pp. 532–535.

[10] M. Wojko and H. ElGindy, "On determining polynomial evaluation structures for FPGA based custom computing machines," in *Proceedings of Australasian Computer Architecture Conference*, 1999, pp. 11–22.

[11] B. Rachid, S. Stephane, and T. Arnaud, "Function evaluation on FPGAs using on-line arithmetic polynomial approximation," in *Proceedings of IEEE North-East Workshop on Circuits and Systems*, 2006, pp. 21–24.

[12] F. Curticpean and J. Nittylahti, "Direct digital frequency synthesizers of high spectral purity based on quadratic approximation," in *Proceedings*

International Conference on Electronics, Circuits and Systems, 2002, pp. 1095–1098.

[13] F. de Dinechin, M. Joldes, and B. Pasca, "Automatic generation of polynomial-based hardware architectures for function evaluation," in *Proceedings of IEEE International Conference on Application-specific Systems Architectures and Processors*, 2010, pp. 216–222.

[14] F. Haohuan, O. Mencer, and W. Luk, "Optimizing logarithmic arithmetic on FPGAs," in *Proceedings of IEEE Symposium on Field-Programmable Custom Computing Machines (FCCM)*, 2007, pp. 163–172.

[15] J. C. Bajard, L. Imbert, and G. A. Jullien, "Parallel montgomery multiplication in GF(2k) using trinomial residue arithmetic," in *Proceedings of IEEE Symposium on Computer Arithmetic*, 2005, pp. 164–171.

[16] D. De Caro and A. G. M. Strollo, "High-performance direct digital frequency synthesizers using piecewise-polynomial approximation," *IEEE Transactions on Circuits and Systems I*, vol. 52, no. 2, pp. 324–337, 2005.

[17] V. Y. Pan, "Methods of computing values of polynomials," *Russ. Math. Surv*, vol. 21, p. 105, 1966.

[18] S. Winograd, "On the number of multiplications required to compute certain functions," *Proceedings of the National Academy of Sciences of the United States of America*, vol. 58, no. 5, pp. 1840–1842, 1967.

[19] W. S. Dorn, "Generalizations of Horner's rule for polynomial evaluation," *IBM J. Res. Dev.*, vol. 6, no. 2, pp. 239–245, 1962.

[20] K. Maruyama, "On the parallel evaluation of polynomials," *IEEE Transactions on Computers*, vol. 22, no. 1, pp. 2–5, 1973.

[21] I. Munro and M. Paterson, "Optimal algorithms for parallel polynomial evaluation," *J. Comput. Syst. Sci.*, vol. 7, no. 2, pp. 189–198, 1973.

[22] Y. Muraoka, "Parallelism exposure and exploitation in programs," Ph.D. dissertation, 1971.

[23] M. Abbas and O. Gustafsson, "Computational and implementation complexity of polynomial evaluation schemes," in *Proceedings of NORCHIP*, 2011.

[24] M. Bodrato and A. Zanoni, "Long integers and polynomial evaluation with Estrin's scheme," in *Proceedings of International Symposium on Symbolic and Numeric Algorithms for Scientific Computing*, 2011, pp. 39–46.

[25] H. Y. Cheah, S. A. Fahmy, and D. L. Maskell, "idea: A dsp block based fpga soft processor," in *Proceedings of the International Conference on Field Programmable Technology (FPT)*, Dec. 2012, pp. 151–158.

[26] F. Brosser, H. Y. Cheah, and S. A. Fahmy, "Iterative floating point computation using FPGA DSP blocks," in *Proceedings of the International Conference on Field Programmable Logic and Applications (FPL)*, 2013.

[27] B. Ronak and S. Fahmy, "Evaluating the efficiency of DSP block synthesis inference from flow graphs," in *Proceedings of the International Conference on Field Programmable Logic and Applications (FPL)*, 2012, pp. 727–730.

[28] S. Xu, S. A. Fahmy, and I. V. Mcloughlin, "Efficient large integer squarers on FPGA," in *Proceedings of the IEEE International Symposium on Field Programmable Custom Computing Machines (FCCM)*, 2013, pp. 198–201.

[29] F. de Dinechin and B. Pasca, "Large multipliers with fewer DSP blocks," in *Proceedings of Interenational Conference on Field Programmable Logic and Applications (FPL)*, Sep. 2009, pp. 250–255.

[30] G. Melquiond. (2013) Gappa. [Online]. Available: http://gappa.gforge.inria.fr/

[31] Xilinx Inc, "Virtex-6 FPGA Data Sheet: DC and Switching Characteristics," Xilinx Inc, 2012.

Accelerating Frequent Item Counting with FPGA

Yuliang Sun[1], Zilong Wang[1], Sitao Huang[1], Lanjun Wang[2],
Yu Wang[1], Rong Luo[1], Huazhong Yang[1]
[1]E.E. Dept., TNLIST, Tsinghua University; [2]IBM Research-China
{sunyuliang13, wang-zl11, hst10}@mails.tsinghua.edu.cn, {wangljbj}@cn.ibm.com,
{yu-wang, luorong, yanghz}@mail.tsinghua.edu.cn

ABSTRACT

Frequent item counting is one of the most important operations in time series data mining algorithms, and the space saving algorithm is a widely used approach to solving this problem. With the rapid rising of data input speeds, the most challenging problem in frequent item counting is to meet the requirement of wire-speed processing. In this paper, we propose a streaming oriented PE-ring framework on FPGA for counting frequent items. Compared with the best existing FPGA implementation, our basic PE-ring framework saves 50% lookup table resources cost and achieves the same throughput in a more scalable way. Furthermore, we adopt SIMD-like cascaded filter for further performance improvements, which outperforms the previous work by up to 3.24 times in some data distributions.

Categories and Subject Descriptors

B.7.1 [Integrated Circuits]: Types and Design Styles – Algorithms implemented in hardware

H.2.8 [Database Management]: Database application – Data mining

General Terms

Algorithms, Design, Performance.

Keywords

Frequent item counting, FPGA, time series

1. INTRODUCTION

Frequent item counting focuses on the operation to pick up items which occur most frequently in a given sequence. It is one of the most basic and important operations in many domains, such as data mining [1] and natural language processing [2]. A wide variety of operations in practical applications can be abstracted into this problem, for example, finding the most popular destinations on the Internet [3]. Moreover, the frequent item counting provides intermediate results or acts as a 'subroutine' for many streaming applications, such as frequent item set mining [4]. With the rapid rising of data input speeds, it is important to find a method to implement an efficient and scalable frequent item counting system.

In recent years, researchers have tried parallel multi-core or computer-cluster frameworks for frequent item counting. For example, Roy et al. proposed a sequence of 'cascaded filters' in the preprocessing of skew input data, and made the final core only face a small volume of data [5]. Roy et al. considered a kind of

skew data distribution as known as Zipfian distribution, which is widely used to describe many types of data studied in the physical and social sciences. However, their framework loses effectiveness for general data distributions. Moreover, it suffers from the memory wall problem of von Neumann architecture, which causes a time, power and resource waste of CPUs.

Meanwhile, the existing best field programmable gate arrays (FPGAs) implementation [6] achieves a data-independent result, which is 4 times faster than the best software. However, the resource consumption increases linearly with the problem size (i.e., k in the top-k query), which may cause the scalability problem. The reason is that all the counting results are stored in the registers rather than the block RAMs in FPGA. The existing implementation cannot support a large top-k query, especially when k is larger than 1000. In addition, the utilization ratio of their processing elements (PEs) is only 50%, which means there is quite a waste of resources.

In this paper, an FPGA framework is proposed for frequent item counting to reduce resources cost while maintaining the performance. Moreover, the optimizations of cascaded filter and SIMD-like method are applied to the basic framework for further performance improvements. The major contributions of our study are as follows:

1) Our proposed PE-ring framework for frequent item counting fixes the positions of the input tuples, while transfers parameters and temporary counting results to achieve scalability. Compared with the previous framework, the PE-ring framework reduces 50% of lookup table resources cost with similar performance.

2) We combine the advantages of cascaded filter and SIMD-like method to improve the performance. The throughput of improved framework is 242 million tuples per second in some data distributions (for 1024 bins whose α is larger than 2 in Zipfian distribution).

2. FRAMEWORK

2.1 Space Saving Algorithm and its FPGA Implementations

The frequent item counting problem is defined as follows. Assume a stream S of size N is drawn from an alphabet A, the Φ-frequent items are those tuples x that occur at least ΦN times in S ($\Phi \in (0,1)$). The number of counting for a tuple x in S is termed the frequency f_x.

If the frequent item counting requires absolute accuracy, the occurrences of all tuples have to be counted in memory. This resource consumption would be totally unrealistic. Usually, practical applications can tolerate a small error ε in the counting result. The counting result may include some additional tuples for which $(\Phi-\varepsilon)N < f_x < \Phi N$. The space saving algorithm is proposed to meet the requirement of limit space consumption [7]. In the space saving algorithm, k bins are set to only count the most frequent tuples in stream S. Each bin is composed of two parameters: item and count. To achieve an error no more than ε, k should be larger than $1/\varepsilon$.

```
1:  for each x in Stream S do
2:      for i = 1 : k do
3:          if b_i.item == x then
4:              b_i.count = b_i.count +1;
5:              x = Null;
6:          end if
7:          if b_i.count > b_{i-1}.count then
8:              swap( b_{i-1}, b_i );
9:          end if
10:     end for
11:     if x ≠ Null then
12:         b_k.item = x;
13:         b_k.count = b_k.count + 1;
14:     end if
15: end for
```

Figure 1 Space saving customized for PE-ring

The space saving algorithm customized for PE-ring is shown in Figure 1. In step 1, the input tuple x is compared with $bin_i.item$. Corresponding addition operation is executed if they match (line 3~6). In step 2, the bin swaps its contents with its neighbor if their counts are reversed (line 7~9), which is similar as the bubble sort algorithm. The next bin is pushed in after all these operations are done in step 3 (line 2). In addition, the last bin will be replaced if there is no bin matches the tuple (line 11~14).

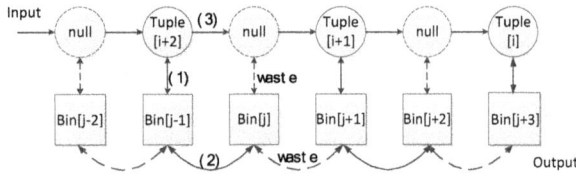

Figure 2 Pipelining array on FPGA [6]

A previous framework for FPGA based frequent item counting is shown in Figure 2 [6]. Bins are arranged by their count. The tuple is the current input data that waits to be considered, and each of them needs to be compared with the bins in order. For every input tuple, a counter is allocated. Along with the flowing from the first counter to the last one, an increment operation is triggered if the tuple matches the item of the current bin (step 1). If the adjacent bins are not in order, their contents are exchanged (step 2). Another delivery of tuples starts when all these operations are done (step 3). When matching and swapping are executed in one counter, its neighboring counters are idle, which is a waste of resources.

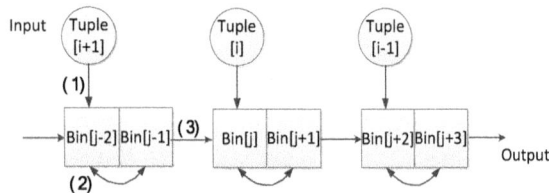

Figure 3 Stream oriented PE-ring on FPGA

A stream oriented PE-ring framework is proposed in which bins rather than input tuples are flowing in Figure 3. Both frameworks accomplish the same function in the space saving algorithm. Matching and swapping operations are fixed in independent

elements to avoid redundant resource consumption. The PE-ring framework is adapted to a full utilization of the advantage in fine-grained parallelism on FPGA.

2.2 PE-ring Framework

A PE is the smallest structure executing the operations for one input tuple shown in Figure 4. In each PE, two bins are recorded in the registers. The neighbor input is the bin from the last PE. The global input is a tuple from time series, distributed by a time series router. The neighbor output bin is passed to the next PE.

The operation in each PE corresponds to the algorithm in line 4~14 in Figure 3. Two neighbor bins are recorded in each PE. In every cycle, PE compares the input *tuple* and the item of the input bin_j, and the count of the input bin will be accumulated if the input *tuple* matches $bin_j.item$. In order to pick up the bin with minimum count value at the end of the bin series, an adjustment of the storage position of two bins in the same PE is executed. Moreover, every bin has a tab to record whether it is the last bin in the bin series. The item of the last bin will be updated by the input *tuple* in case the input tuple has not matched.

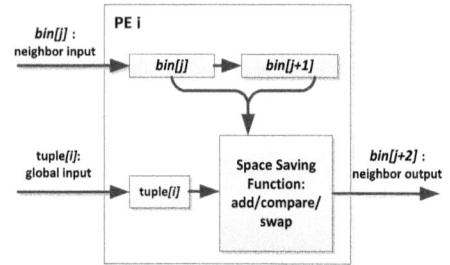

Figure 4 Architecture of PE

This PE structure ensures that in the PE-ring, the storage of input tuple is fixed and the bins are delivered forward to the neighbor PE. The framework exactly matches the operations in the algorithm. In a single PE, one tuple and two bins are handled in every cycle to fully use the resources without any idle time. In Section 4.1, experimental results show that compared with [6], 50% lookup table resources cost is saved for the whole system.

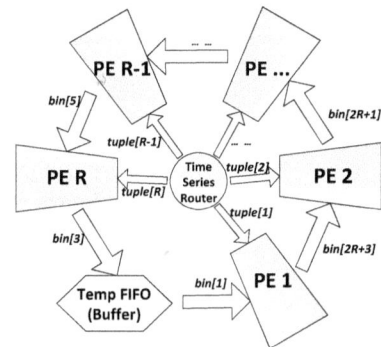

Figure 5 Architecture of PE-ring

Based on the experience from our previous work [8], PEs are linked as a ring in Figure 5, which is called the PE-ring. PEs communicate with their neighbors by the flowing bins in the PE-ring. Moreover, a distribution of a new input tuple is executed through global routing after finishing the comparison of current tuples. According to the mobility of bins in the PE-ring, the sequential output bins from a certain PE are the current accumulated result by the end of the tuple in this PE.

As introduced in Section 2.1, the amount of bins needs to be large enough to achieve high precision in space saving. The number of PEs in a PE-ring is very large and limited by resources on FPGA. To solve this problem, a buffer is inserted to the architecture. The output bin from the last PE is pushed into the buffer for temporary storage, which can be achieved by using a temp FIFO. This bin can be later delivered to the first PE again to start a new circulation if the number of PEs in the PE-ring is less than k.

A PE-ring with a proper buffer can save a lot of on-chip resources cost compared with the situation that all the bins are stored in PEs. The temp FIFO uses the space on the block RAMs rather than the registers on FPGAs. Besides, the buffer also guarantees the scalability for PE-ring. The limited on-chip resources can be a strict restriction for the scale of the PE-ring without a buffer. If frequent item counting requires high accuracy, the number of bins would be too large for an FPGA to afford it. Therefore, a buffer in the PE-ring which stores those redundant bins that cannot be put into the PE-ring would be very beneficial.

3. OPTIMIZATIONS

3.1 Cascaded Filter

In many domains, especially in linguistics [9] and social sciences [10], many types of data are approximated with a Zipfian distribution and can be called skew tuples. Skewness means a measure of the asymmetry of a probability distribution. Skew tuples have a feature that most of the tuples find their matches at the first several bins in space saving. Zipfian distribution is described in the equation below, where N is the number of tuples, r is the tuple's rank in the frequency table of the dataset, and α is the value of the exponent parameter in the distribution. The bigger α is, the skewer this distribution becomes.

$$f(r, \alpha, N) = \frac{1/r^{\alpha}}{\sum_{n=1}^{N}(1/n^{\alpha})} \qquad (1)$$

Cascaded filter is suitable to accelerate frequent item counting for skew tuples. The intention of cascaded filter is to place a filter which picks up those input tuples with high frequencies. By routing those most frequent tuples through a shortcut code path, the workload in the module of space saving can get a significant relief [5].

There are two parts of bins in the cascaded filter strengthened PE-ring. Part I is stored in the cascaded filter and part II on in PE-ring. Part I, which is in a small scale, contains the bins with highest frequencies and corresponds to the shortcut path processing. Part II is used for the exact space saving implementation. Tuples will be sent into PE-ring only after their flowing through the cascaded filter without a match. Especially when the input tuples are skew enough, the cascaded filter is able to catch most of the tuples so that the workload in PE-ring for space saving can be greatly reduced.

In our software simulation of the cascaded filter algorithm, tuples with different α values in Zipfian distribution are tested. Figure 6 shows the ratio that tuples are caught in the filter over streams. If over a half tuples find their matches in the cascaded filter, the workload for the PE-ring is halved. In this scenario, a PE-ring with a same length of buffer can complete this work which saves half resources cost compared with a single PE-ring.

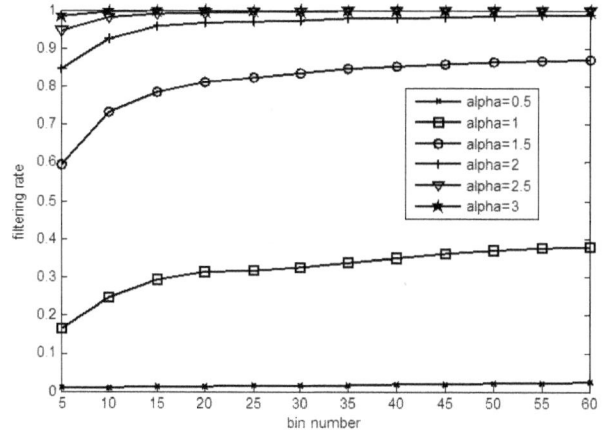

Figure 6 Filtering rate with different number of bins

3.2 SIMD-like method

For the cascaded filter strengthened PE-ring, all the input tuples pass through the cascaded filter. The performance of the cascaded filter determines the performance of the frequent item counting system. A SIMD-like method is applied in the filter to improve the performance. The SIMD-like method is analogous to single instruction multiple data (SIMD) from the multi-core implementation [5]. If m tuples are compared with one bin in every cycle, then the throughput of the whole system can be about m times over before. The SIMD-like method focuses on the step of comparison between tuples and bins and tries to parallelize this step to speed up.

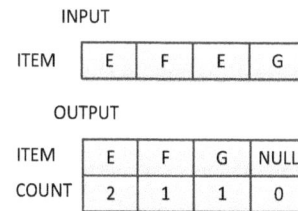

Figure 7 Data collation for SIMD

As shown in Figure 7, the same tuples should be aggregated together before the cascaded filter. To make such collation or not is crucial for the circuit structure design. If the tuple collation is not implemented, uncertain times of accumulation have to be considered in PE and m counters are required. The circuit structure in each PE would become more complex without the tuple collation.

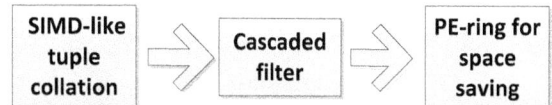

Figure 8 Framework for SIMD-like cascaded filter

The overall framework for PE-ring combined with cascaded filter and SIMD-like method is shown in Figure 8. After coming in, the input tuples move through three modules: tuple collation, cascaded filter and PE-ring. Based on the scalability of PE-ring, the cascaded filter and SIMD-like method are inferred for further performance improvements for data with skew distributions.

4. EXPERIMENT

We choose the platform Virtex-6 XC6VLX550T to make rational comparison with the previous work that uses the same device [6]. The word width of tuples and counting results are 32 bits.

4.1 PE-ring Framework

Table 1 Pipelining array [6] and PE-ring implementation

Bins	LUT		Register		Clock (MHz)		Throughput (M items/s)	
	array	PE-ring	array	PE-ring	array	PE-ring	array	PE-ring
64	4%	2%	1%	1%	110	267	110	133
128	9%	4%	1%	1%	115	255	115	127
256	20%	7%	3%	3%	105	246	105	123
512	39%	15%	6%	6%	110	217	110	108
1024	78%	31%	12%	12%	95	224	95	·112
2048	-	64%		24%	-	202	-	101

Table 1 shows the results of the previous work [6] and the PE-ring framework. For example, for 256 bins, both of these two methods uses 3% register. However, our method only uses 7% LUTs, which is less than half of previous one. Meanwhile, it is note that PE-ring processes one tuple in every two cycles, so that our throughputs are over 100M items/s, which are comparable to the previous work. That is to say, PE-ring achieves a similar performance with reducing 50% of lookup table. Furthermore, since we balance the utilization of registers and LUTs, our PE-ring achieves 2048 bins, which means a high accuracy in frequent item counting.

4.2 SIMD-like Cascaded Filter Framework

Table 2 PE-ring with FIFO and filter implementation (16 bins in filter)

Bins in PE-ring	LUT	Register	Filter clk (MHz)	PE-ring clk (MHz)	Throughput (M items/s)
256	11%	4%	200	100	400
1024	35%	14%	121	60	242

We implement a SIMD-like cascaded filter to pursuit a higher performance, especially for skew data. We set 4 tuples processed in the cascaded filter at the same time. The input data is with a Zipfian distribution with a parameter α no less than 2. Table 2 shows the results of framework. Comparing with the results from Table 1, for the same precision (bin size), the throughput of improved framework outperforms the basic framework. For example, as 256 bins, the optimized method achieves a throughput as 400M items/s which is more than three times of the basic implementation.

In addition, it is note that the existing per-line bandwidth of Peripheral Component Interconnect Express (PCIe) is 1 GB/s. The throughput here requires the memory bandwidth from off-chip is 968 MB/s, almost approaching the bandwidth limitation.

5. CONCLUSION

In this paper, we propose a novel FPGA framework for frequent item counting to achieve scalability and save 50% lookup table resources cost. Unlike the traditional framework that makes input tuples flowing through, our PE-ring structure passes through parameters and operations to implement space saving algorithm. In addition, we leverage the idea of cascaded filter and SIMD-like method to achieve higher performance for skew input tuples.

6. ACKNOWLEDGMENTS

This work was supported by IBM Research China University Relationship Program, National Natural Science Foundation of China (No. 61373026, No. 61261160501, No. 61028006), 973 project 2013CB329000, National Science and Technology Major Project (2013ZX03003013-003), and Youth Talent Development Plan of Beijing (YETP0099).

7. REFERENCES

[1] Liu J, Pan Y, Wang K, et. al. Mining frequent item sets by opportunistic projection. Proceedings of the eighth ACM SIGKDD international conference on Knowledge discovery and data mining. ACM, 2002: 229-238.

[2] Beil F, Ester M, Xu X. Frequent term-based text clustering. Proceedings of the eighth ACM SIGKDD international conference on Knowledge discovery and data mining. ACM, 2002: 436-442.

[3] Cormode G, Hadjieleftheriou M. Finding frequent items in data streams. Proceedings of the VLDB Endowment, 2008, 1(2): 1530-1541.

[4] Chakrabarti A, Cormode G, McGregor A. A near-optimal algorithm for computing the entropy of a stream. Proceedings of the eighteenth annual ACM-SIAM symposium on Discrete algorithms. Society for Industrial and Applied Mathematics, 2007: 328-335.

[5] Roy P, Teubner J, Alonso G. Efficient frequent item counting in multi-core hardware Proceedings of the 18th ACM SIGKDD international conference on Knowledge discovery and data mining. ACM, 2012: 1451-1459.

[6] Teubner J, Muller R, Alonso G. Frequent item computation on a chip. Knowledge and Data Engineering, IEEE Transactions on, 2011, 23(8): 1169-1181.

[7] Metwally A, Agrawal D, Abbadi A E. An integrated efficient solution for computing frequent and top-k elements in data streams. ACM Transactions on Database Systems (TODS), 2006, 31(3): 1095-1133.

[8] Wang Z, Huang S, Wang L, et al. Accelerating subsequence similarity search based on dynamic time warping distance with FPGA. Proceedings of the ACM/SIGDA international symposium on Field programmable gate arrays. ACM, 2013: 53-62.

[9] Montemurro M A. Beyond the Zipf–Mandelbrot law in quantitative linguistics. Physica A: Statistical Mechanics and its Applications, 2001, 300(3): 567-578.

[10] Gabaix X. Zipf's Law and the Growth of Cities. The American Economic Review, 1999, 89(2): 129-132.

A Power Side-Channel-Based Digital to Analog Converter for Xilinx FPGAs

Brad L. Hutchings, Joshua Monson, Danny Savory and Jared Keeley
Department of Electrical and Computer Engineering, Brigham Young University
Provo, UT, USA
hutch@ee.byu.edu

ABSTRACT

A novel Digital to Analog Converter (DAC) modulates the overall power consumption of an FPGA by disabling/enabling short circuits programmed into the interconnect. The power pin of the FPGA serves as the output of the DAC. The DAC achieves high linearity and can be used to implement applications in communications, security, etc. The short-circuit-based DAC consumes 1/3 the area of an alternative shift-register-based DAC that is presented for the sake of comparison.

Categories and Subject Descriptors

B.4.1 [**Data Communications Devices**]: Transmitters

Keywords

FPGA; power; side channel; DAC

1. INTRODUCTION

The variations in global power consumption that occur during normal circuit operation can be exploited as a form of "side-channel" communication. In the most common scenario, the power side-channel attack, an attacker carefully measures the dynamic power consumption at the chip as the chip performs specific operations to extract otherwise secret data. For example, researchers have shown that it is feasible to extract the otherwise secret key used to encrypt/decrypt FPGA configuration data directly from the device [6]. It is also possible to purposely transmit data via the device power pin by actively modulating power consumption specifically for the purpose of transmitting data.

This paper introduces a novel way to modulate *static* power consumption by creating a Digital-Analog Converter (DAC) implemented using user-controllable short circuits. By way of review, remember that a DAC functions by generating a unique voltage or current level at its output for each binary input vector applied to it [2]. DACs are often

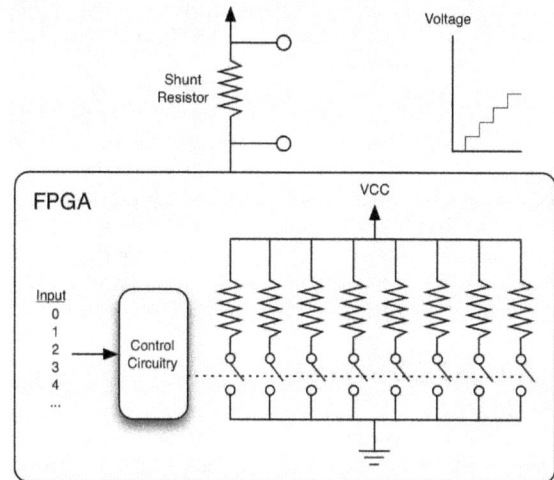

Figure 1: Schematic View of the Short-Based DAC

used to convert a digital stream of data into a continuous analog voltage in audio applications, for example.

In the example presented here and illustrated in Figure 1, the DAC contains a fixed number of user-controllable short circuits. Each short circuit has a fixed resistance and consumes a fixed amount of power when it is enabled. Numeric values are accepted by the DAC and converted by control circuitry to enable and disable short circuits. The number of short circuits that are enabled at any given time is typically proportional to the magnitude of the input values. The output of the DAC is measured as the voltage drop across a 0.1 ohm, 3 watt, shunt resistor that is connected between the power supply and the power input pin on the FPGA. The actual current value can be found by dividing the supply voltage by the shunt resistance according to Ohm's law. Note that shunt resistors are commonly used in situations like this, e.g., side-channel attacks, etc., where power consumption needs to be measured. For example, the SASEBO board is a purpose-built FPGA board commonly used for side-channel attack experiments in the security community and it provides a shunt resistor for measuring the voltage drop near the power pin [4]. Also note that while shunts are convenient, voltage drops can be measured near the FPGA power pin without them [12].

The goal of this paper is to demonstrate a feasible technique to implement a useable Power Side-channel DAC (PS-DAC) circuit inside an FPGA. Two different versions of the

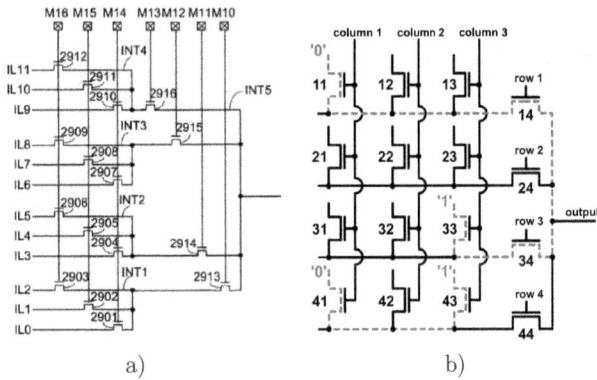

Figure 2: Diagrams of routing multiplexers. a) Partial Figure 29 from Patent 7,279,929, and b), Examples of a row and column short.

PS-DAC were implemented and tested. One version consumes static power and is based upon shorts that are inserted into switch-boxes. The second version consumes dynamic power and is based on the shift-register approach that was previously discussed [12]. These two approaches were compared to determine differences in area, power consumption, output waveforms, and ease of implementation.

2. RELATED WORK

The fluctuations in power-supply current that occur during circuit operation can be exploited both passively and actively. The most common passive application is the side-channel attack, where an attacker "eavesdrops" on circuit behavior by carefully measuring its dynamic power consumption. The target of such attacks are the encryption keys of cryptographic algorithms running in integrated circuits. Successful side-channel attacks have been reported on smart cards [8], FPGA configuration logic [5] [6], circuits operating in an FPGA's programmable logic [3], and an ASIC [9].

Active applications employ application-specific circuitry to actively modulate power consumption. Ziener, Baueregger and Teich report on using the power side channel as a communication link that can be used for monitoring, debugging and power watermarking using banks of shift registers preloaded with an alternating bit vector [12]. Others have explored the idea of modulating system power to counter side-channel attacks, such as Güneysu and Moradi, who obfuscated the power signature of an AES encryption algorithm [3]. The authors used two different methods to actively consume power: shift-register based methods and short-circuit based methods. They found that noise generators made side-channel attacks slightly more difficult by requiring more measurements, but did not render side-channel attacks infeasible. No details regarding the electrical nature of the short circuits, nor how much additional power was required to generate noise was discussed.

3. PS-DAC IMPLEMENTATION STRATEGIES

3.1 Using Short-Circuit Elements to Consume Power

Although Xilinx does not publish the details of the switch-box tile in user guides, the general switch-matrix architec-

ture can be surmised from Patent 7,279,929 authored by Steven Young [11]. Figure 2a contains part of a figure from the Young patent that illustrates a switchbox architecture.

As shown in the figure, each interconnect tile contains a switch matrix that is constructed of numerous programmable routing multiplexers. These routing multiplexers are composed of several Programmable Interconnect Points (PIPs) that are typically implemented with a single N-channel Field-Effect Transistor (FET). Sets of PIPs within a routing multiplexer can be configured to select a specific input and route that input to the multiplexer output. The inputs are labeled "M16", "M15", etc., and represent the configuration bits that are used to configure the switch.

Several experiments (somewhat similar to those conducted by Beckoff et al. [1]) confirmed that the switchbox in the Virtex-4 interconnect tile is similar to that described in the patent. Figure 2b is a routing multiplexer essentially redrawn from the Young patent depicting different types of short circuits to be described in the following discussion[1].

Short circuits can be created in a switch-box by driving two separate routing multiplexer inputs with complementary values (e.g. '1' and a '0') and then setting the configuration bits to allow current to flow between the pass transistors. Depending on which routing multiplexer inputs are driven, different types of shorts will be created. If the two inputs are on the same row, a *column short* is created. Fig. 2b displays this type of short between PIP_{41} and PIP_{43}. For this to occur, the column 1 and column 3 inputs of the multiplexer would have to be driven '1'. If, instead, a short circuit exists from multiplexer inputs being driven on different rows, a *row short* is created. An example of a row short is depicted in Fig. 2b between PIP_{11} and PIP_{33}.

3.2 Using Shift Registers to Consume Power

Dynamic power consumption is largely determined by switching signals and their activity factors in relation with clock frequency [7].

$$P_{dynamic} = \alpha C V_{DD}^2 f \qquad (1)$$

Equation 1 is a well-known equation for dynamic power, where α is the activity factor of the signal in relation to the clock signal, C is the capacitance of the wire carrying the signal, V_{DD} is the switching voltage, and f is the clock frequency [7]. Shift registers, initialized with an alternating pattern of bits (e.g."...101010...") and configured with feedback paths, are ideal for dynamic power consumption [12]. Xilinx Unified Libraries come with a 16-bit shift register that compactly fits within a single LUT (SRL16E [10]). Note that shift-register elements require a clock signal to modulate power, whereas short-circuit-based methods do not.

An overview of these two different power-consuming elements is shown in in Figure 3.

3.3 PS-DAC Organization

Figure 4 shows the basic block diagram of both types of PS-DACs implemented in this paper. The input bit-vector is directed to a special decoder, whose output select signals activate corresponding power elements. These power elements are either shift-registers or short-circuit components, and the select signals are shift-register clock enable signals or switchable short-circuits. Numerous output select signals

---

[1] Also note that Beckhoff et al. [1] provide similar illustrations of their view of the Xilinx switch matrix for Virtex-II and Spartan-3.

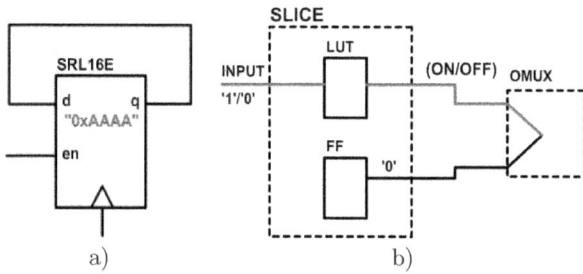

Figure 3: Basic power elements in PS-DACs. a) An SRL16E shift register primitive, b) A short-circuit element.

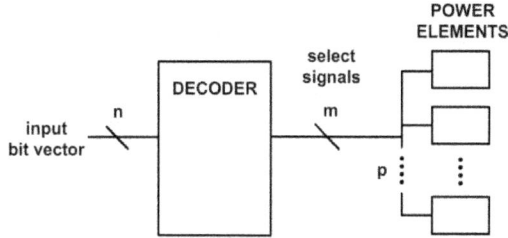

Figure 4: Basic PS-DAC block diagram.

Design name	3-bit DAC			
	c_1	c_2	R-square	SSE
500 SRL16E	0.002721	0.02408	0.9998	8.428e-09
256 shorts	0.00266	0.0198	1.0000	5.9902e-10
68 SRL16E	0.0003912	0.01748	0.9986	1.453-09
32 shorts	0.0003244	0.01667	0.9961	2.446e-09

Table 1: DAC Linearity

Design	Slices	LUTs	$V_r(mV)$	σ	Power
500 SRL16	1,156	1,710	8.54	3.91e-04	3.4 mW
256 shorts	289	576	8.56	1.30e-05	2.9 mW
68 SRL16	125	179	1.12	5.86e-04	26 μW
32 shorts	38	75	1.04	3.00e-05	27 μW

Table 2: Comparison of DAC Implementations

of the decoder may be driven high at the same time based on the number of active power elements that are required to achieve a given DAC output voltage.

3.4 Short Circuit PS-DAC Implementation

Design Rule Checks (DRC) in the Xilinx tools detect short-circuit configurations in a design and will generally refuse to generate a bit-stream that contains them. It was necessary to circumvent these DRC checks for the purposes of this paper, and special bit-stream "patching" tools were developed for this project.

Construction of the short-circuit based DAC began with creating a hard macro design in Xilinx FPGA Editor, consisting of a single CLB (four slices). The CLB slices were configured to have each LUT pass an input signal to the X and Y LUT outputs of the slice. Signals intended to create short circuits were routed to the hard macro's inputs. The design was then synthesized, placed and routed using conventional Xilinx tools. After a valid bit-stream is generated, it is subsequently modified so that the FFs within the hard macro instances output constant logical '0' signals. PIPs are also modified in the bitstream to route the LUT and FF outputs together. In this fashion, a short-circuit is created every time a logical '1' signal is input to a hard macro.

One short circuit PS-DAC design was constructed with 32 hard macro instances, for a maximum of 256 short circuit configurations. Another smaller PS-DAC design was constructed with 4 hard macro instances, allowing a maximum of 32 short circuit configurations.

3.5 Shift Register PS-DAC Implementation

The shift register PS-DAC designs were constructed using numerous instantiations of SRL16E components from the Xilinx Unisim library [10]. These registers were loaded with an alternating bit-vector (0xAAAA) and configured with a

feedback path so that when enabled, stored logic values alternate every clock cycle. As previously discussed, switching logical values every clock cycle increases the signal's activity factor, maximizing the dynamic power consumed. To have the same approximate output voltage range, V_r, as the short circuit PS-DACs with 256 and 32 shorts, the SRL16E PS-DACs contained 500 and 68 SRL16E instances respectively.

3.6 Equipment

The DAC designs were implemented on a Xilinx Virtex-4 device (XC4VLX60). Xilinx ISE version 14.4 was used to synthesize design HDL and generate bitstreams. Power was indirectly calculated using the voltage measured across a 0.1 Ω resistor in series with the target device's power supply. A National Instruments NI PCI-6132 2.5 MS/s Simultaneous Sampling Multifunction DAQ was used with a BNC-2110 Shielded Connector Block to measure the voltage across the 0.1 Ω resistor.

4. COMPARATIVE RESULTS

This section reports on a comparison of the shift-register and short-based PS-DACs with regard to area efficiency relative to power consumption, signal generation, total power consumption, and linearity.

4.1 Linear Performance

Linearity and monotonicity are key properties of DAC performance. The Curve-Fitting Toolbox, available in Matlab software (ver. R2012a), was used to find the least-squares best-fit lines through output plots of the different PS-DACs. Fig. 5 shows the output plots and best fit lines of a 3-bit PS-DAC. The best fit line of the plot follows the form of Equation 2, where c_1 and c_2 are approximate parameters.

$$f(x) = c_1 * x + c_2 \qquad (2)$$

Table 1 contains these metrics for the different PS-DAC designs. The R-square and Sum of Squares due to Error (SSE) values of Table 1 indicate that the PS-DAC output is very linear.

4.2 Area and Power

Table 2 displays size metrics and V_r ranges of the different PS-DACs. These ranges were obtained from averaging over 1,000 waveforms on each PS-DAC. The standard deviations of these means are listed under the σ column of the table. The power listed in the table is the power difference between maximum voltage output and the zero value voltage output. The 500 shift-register-based PS-DAC design consumes more power than the 256 short-circuit-based PS-DAC because of the extra control circuitry required to maintain the shift register instances. Short-circuit-based PS-DACs occupy less area than their shift-register-based DAC counterparts while offering comparable V_r ranges. Examining the larger designs (256 short circuit PS-DAC and 500 SRL16E PS-DAC) reveals the SRL16E PS-DAC is 2.96 times larger than the short-circuit-based PS-DAC with regard to the number of occupied 4-LUTs. A study of the smaller PS-DAC designs reveals similar results; the 68 SRL16E PS-DAC is approximately 2.38 times larger than the 32 short circuit PS-DAC in the number of occupied 4-LUT primitives.

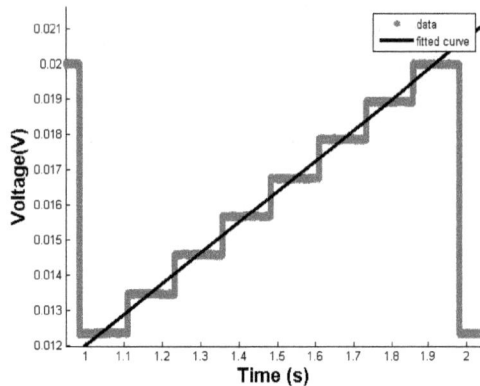

Figure 5: a) A 3-bit PS-DAC cycling through each output level (red), the black line is the best-fit line from the regression parameters.

5. FUTURE WORK

There are several potential future directions for this work, including characterizing PS-DAC behavior on other, newer devices, since process size has decreased. Heat and device reliability also warrants further investigation. Additional effort should be made to investigate the application of PS-DACs for use as a side-channel attack countermeasure. Also, the PS-DAC may have future application in frequency watermarking of IP designs [13]. Thermal properties of PS-DACs may also make it potentially suitable for application as a device kill-switch, since short-circuits in routing interconnect consume much more power than do shift registers.

6. CONCLUSION

In this paper, we have evaluated a novel PS-DAC design based on short-circuits inserted into the routing interconnect of the FPGA. Our short-circuit PS-DAC was also highly linear; meaning that the output voltage divisions were evenly spaced and the PS-DAC generates predictable output. This PS-DAC was also found to be highly area efficient when compared to a shift register-based PS-DAC. Potential applications of PS-DACs include IP watermarking and programmable device kill-switches.

7. REFERENCES

[1] C. Beckhoff, D. Koch, and J. Torresen. Short-circuits on fpgas caused by partial runtime reconfiguration. In *Field Programmable Logic and Applications (FPL), 2010 International Conference on*, pages 596–601, 2010.

[2] I. Grout. *Digital Systems Design with FPGAs and CPLDs*, chapter 8, pages 537–565. Newnes, Burlington, MA, first edition, 2008.

[3] T. Güneysu and A. Moradi. Generic side-channel countermeasures for reconfigurable devices. In *CHES*, volume 6917 of *Lecture Notes in Computer Science*, pages 33–48. Springer, 2011.

[4] T. Katashita, A. Satoh, T. Sugawara, N. Homma, and T. Aoki. Development of side-channel attack standard evaluation environment. In *Circuit Theory and Design, 2009. ECCTD 2009. European Conference on*, pages 403–408, 2009.

[5] A. Moradi, M. Kasper, and C. Paar. Black-box side-channel attacks highlight the importance of countermeasures: an analysis of the xilinx virtex-4 and virtex-5 bitstream encryption mechanism. In *Proceedings of the 12th conference on Topics in Cryptology*, CT-RSA'12, pages 1–18, Berlin, Heidelberg, 2012. Springer-Verlag.

[6] A. Moradi, D. Oswald, C. Paar, and P. Swierczynski. Side-channel attacks on the bitstream encryption mechanism of altera stratix ii: facilitating black-box analysis using software reverse-engineering. In *Proceedings of the ACM/SIGDA international symposium on Field programmable gate arrays*, FPGA '13, pages 91–100, New York, NY, USA, 2013. ACM.

[7] D. M. H. Neil H. E. Weste. *CMOS VLSI Design*, chapter 5, pages 185–194. Addison-Wesley, Boston, MA, fourth edition, 2010.

[8] E. Oswald, S. Mangard, C. Herbst, and S. Tillich. Practical second-order dpa attacks for masked smart card implementations of block ciphers. In *Proceedings of the 2006 The Cryptographers' Track at the RSA Conference on Topics in Cryptology*, CT-RSA'06, pages 192–207, Berlin, Heidelberg, 2006. Springer-Verlag.

[9] T. Sugawara, N. Homma, T. Aoki, and A. Satoh. Differential power analysis of aes asic implementations with various s-box circuits. In *Circuit Theory and Design, 2009. ECCTD 2009. European Conference on*, pages 395–398, 2009.

[10] Xinlinx Inc. *Virtex-4 Libraries Guide for Schematic Designs, UG620*, 14.1 edition, April 2012.

[11] S. P. Young. Integrated circuit with programmable routing structure including straight and diagonal interconnect lines. US Patent, 2007. Patent 7,279,929.

[12] D. Ziener, F. Baueregger, and J. Teich. Using the power side channel of fpgas for communication. In *Field-Programmable Custom Computing Machines (FCCM), 2010 18th IEEE Annual International Symposium on*, pages 237–244, 2010.

[13] D. Ziener and J. Teich. Fpga core watermarking based on power signature analysis. In *Field Programmable Technology, 2006. FPT 2006. IEEE International Conference on*, pages 205–212, 2006.

Soft Vector Processors with Streaming Pipelines

A. Severance †, ‡   J. Edwards †
aaronsev@ece.ubc.ca jedwards@vectorblox.com

† VectorBlox Computing Inc.
Vancouver, BC

H. Omidian ‡   G. Lemieux †, ‡
hosseino@ece.ubc.ca lemieux@ece.ubc.ca

‡ Univ. of British Columbia
Vancouver, BC

ABSTRACT

Soft vector processors (SVPs) achieve significant performance gains through the use of parallel ALUs. However, since ALUs are used in a time-multiplexed fashion, this does not exploit a key strength of FPGA performance: pipeline parallelism. This paper shows how streaming pipelines can be integrated into the datapath of a SVP to achieve dramatic speedups. The SVP plays an important role in supplying the pipeline with high-bandwidth input data and storing its results using on-chip memory. However, the SVP must also perform the housekeeping tasks necessary to keep the pipeline busy. In particular, it orchestrates data movement between on-chip memory and external DRAM, it pre- or post-processes the data using its own ALUs, and it controls the overall sequence of execution. Since the SVP is programmed in C, these tasks are easier to develop and debug than using a traditional HDL approach. Using the N-body problem as a case study, this paper illustrates how custom streaming pipelines are integrated into the SVP datapath and multiple techniques for generating them. Using a custom pipeline, we demonstrate speedups over 7,000 times and performance-per-ALM over 100 times better than Nios II/f. The custom pipeline is also 50 times faster than a naive Intel Core i7 processor implementation.

1. INTRODUCTION

Although capable of high performance, FPGAs are also difficult to program. Exploiting both wide and deep custom pipelines typically requires a hardware designer to design a custom system in VHDL or Verilog. Recently, the emergence of ESL tools such as Vivado HLS and Altera's OpenCL compiler allow software programmers to produce FPGA designs using C or OpenCL. However, since all ESL tools translate a high-level algorithm into an HDL, they share common drawbacks: changes to the algorithm require lengthy FPGA recompiles, recompiling may run out of resources (eg, logic blocks) or fail to meet timing, debugging support is very limited, and high-level algorithmic features such as dynamic

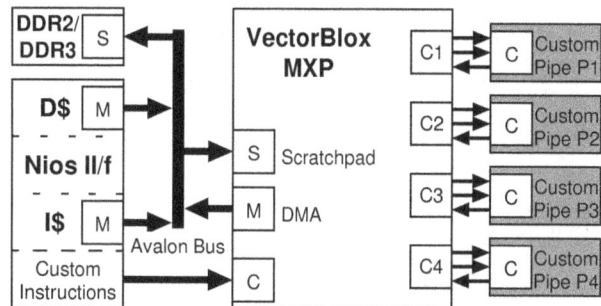

Figure 1: System view of VectorBlox MXP

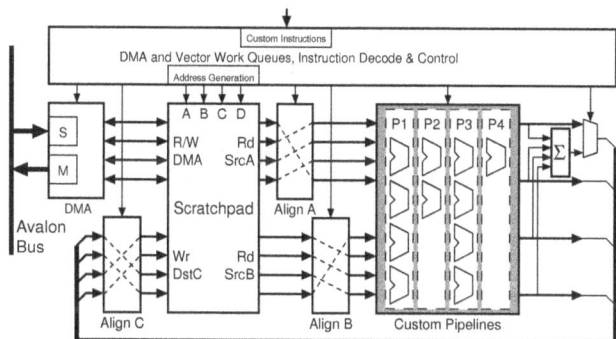

Figure 2: Internal view of VectorBlox MXP

memory allocation and recursion are unavailable. Hence, ESL tools are not the most effective way to make FPGAs accessible to software programmers.

Another approach to supporting programmers is to provide a soft vector processor (SVP). A SVP achieves high performance through wide data parallelism, efficient looping, and prefetching. The main advantages of a SVP are scalable performance and a traditional software programming model. Performance scaling is achieved by adding more ALUs, but beyond a certain point (eg, 64 ALUs) the increases in parallelism are eroded by clock frequency degradation. This ultimately limits performance scaling.

To increase performance of SVPs even further, they must also harness deep pipeline parallelism. For example, most types of encryption (such as AES) need deep pipelines to get significant speedup. Although processors (and SVPs) are not built to exploit deep pipeline parallelism, FPGAs support it very well.

The natural questions then become: How can a SVP be interfaced with deep pipelines to exploit both wide and deep parallelism? What kind of performance can be achieved? What types of problems arise, and how can they be solved?

To investigate these questions, we developed the Vector-Blox MXP, shown in Figure 1 and devised a way to add deep custom pipelines to the processor, shown in Figure 2. The interface is kept as simple as possible so that software programmers can eventually develop these custom pipelines using C; we also show that a simple high-level synthesis tool can be created for this purpose. To demonstrate speedups, we selected the N-body gravity problem as case study. In this problem, each body exerts an attractive force on every other body, resulting in an $O(N^2)$ computation. The size and direction of the force between two bodies depends upon their two masses as well as the distance between them. Solving the problem requires square root and divide, neither of which are native operations to the MXP. Hence, we start by implementing simple custom instructions for the reciprocal and square root operations. Then, we implement the entire gravity equation as a deep pipeline.

It is important to note that we view the problem of adding floating-point units (FPUs) as a special case of adding deep, custom pipelines. FPUs are large in area, so many applications will not need one FPU for every integer ALU. In fact, many floating-point applications would find a single f-p divide unit or f-p square root unit to be sufficient, along with several f-p adders and f-p multipliers. Also, FPUs are deeply pipelined, so they need very long vectors to keep their pipelines utilized, especially when many units are instantiated in parallel. So, for both area and performance reasons, the programmer should control the number of integer units separately from the number of f-p adders, the number of f-p multipliers, etc. Hence, this paper is not just proposing a method for connecting specialized pipelines, but also for connecting general floating-point operators to SVPs.

The main contribution of this work is introducing a modular way of allowing users to add streaming pipelines into SVPs as *custom vector instructions* to get huge speedups. On the surface, this appears to be a simple extension of the way custom instructions are added to scalar CPUs such as Nios II. However, there are unique challenges to be able to stream data from multiple operands in a SVP. Also, scalar CPU custom instructions are often data starved, limiting their benefits. We show that SVPs can provide high-bandwidth data streaming to properly utilize custom instructions.

2. BACKGROUND

Vector processing has a long tradition in high performance computing, with designs originating in the 1960s. The canonical example (and the first commercially successful) is the Cray-1 [1]. The Cray-1 used a RISC-like load/store model, processing vector operands from a vector register file (VRF) of 8 named registers that were each 64-bits wide and 64 elements deep. Vector operations were streamed through the execution units at a rate of one per clock cycle.

2.1 FPGA-based Soft Vector Processors

The VIRAM [2] project demonstrated that vector processing could be more efficient than traditional processor architectures for embedded multimedia ASIC designs. Following this path, two FPGA-based projects implemented a VIRAM-like soft vector processor in FPGAs: VESPA [3] and

VIPERS [4]. All three processors employed a hybrid vector-SIMD model, where vectors are streamed sequentially over time through replicated (parallel) execution units.

VESPA included support for heterogeneous vector lanes [5], e.g. there are fewer multipliers than general-purpose ALUs. Due to the mismatch between vector register file width and execution unit width, a parallel load queue was used to buffer a vector for heterogeneous operations, and a separate output queue was used to buffer results before writeback. This required additional memory and multiplexers. In contrast, this paper uses pre-existing alignment networks and requires no additional buffering to solve the width mismatch problem for 2-input/1-output custom instructions. We show how to add custom vector instructions that require more operands using minimal additional buffering.

VEGAS [6] and VENICE [7] are refinements of the VIPERS processor, further tailoring the architecture for FPGAs. Improvements include replacing the VRF with a scratchpad memory to allow for arbitrary data packing and access, removing vector length limits, enabling sub-word SIMD (four packed bytes or two packed shorts) within each lane, simplified conditionals and flags to fit within FPGA BRAMs, and a DMA-based memory interface rather than a traditional vector load/store approach.

Work by Cong et al. [8] created composable vector units. At compilation time, the DFG of a vector program was examined for clusters of operations that can be composed together to create a new streaming instruction that uses multiple operators and operands. This was done by chaining together existing functional units using an interconnection network and multi-ported register file. This is similar to traditional vector chaining, but it was resolved statically by the compiler (not dynamically the architecture) and encoded into the instruction stream. This provided pipeline parallelism, but was limited by the number of available operators and available register file ports. It is not easily extended to support wide SIMD-style parallelism. The reported speedups were less than a factor of two.

The FPVC, or floating point vector coprocessor, was developed by Kathiara and Leeser [9]. It adds a floating-point vector unit to the hard Xilinx PowerPC cores which can exploit SIMD parallelism as well as pipeline parallelism. The FPVC fetches its own VIRAM-like instructions and has its own private register file. Unlike most other vector architectures, it can also execute its own scalar operations separate from the host PowerPC.

Convey's HC-2 [10] is a vector computer built using several FPGAs. The FPGAs can adopt one of several 'personalities', each of which provides a domain-specific vector instruction set. User-developed personalities are also possible. Designed for high-performance computing, the machine includes a high bandwidth, highly interleaved, multi-bank DRAM array to reduce strided access latency.

2.2 VectorBlox MXP

The VectorBlox MXP [11], or MXP for short, is a new SVP that somewhat resembles VENICE [7]. It is designed for embedded systems that use a simple memory system. Figure 1 gives a high-level system view of MXP on Altera FPGAs; there is also a Xilinx version.

The host processor, Nios II/f, runs C code compiled with Altera's gcc. MXP instructions are inserted as Nios *custom instructions* using inline C functions. There are two types of

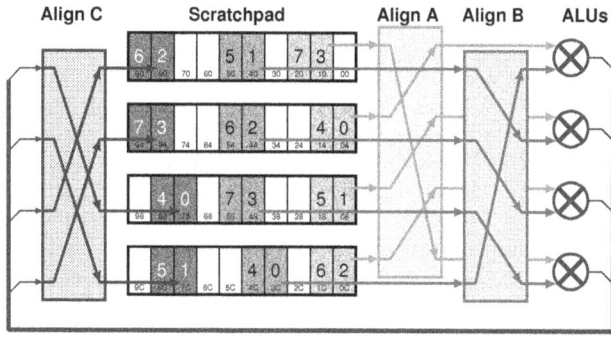

Figure 3: Alignment of data operands during vector instruction execution

MXP instructions: DMA operations and vector operations. Nios, DMA and vector operations all run concurrently, providing 3-way parallelism. Hardware interlocks resolve dependencies between the DMA and vector engines without software intervention.

In addition, the user can add custom operators or pipelines by connecting them in Altera's Qsys tool using a 'conduit' interface connection. These conduits are indicated in Figure 1 using the letter 'C', as opposed to Avalon masters (M) or slaves (S).

Figure 2 provides an internal view of the processor. The 2D DMA engine fetches data from the external Avalon system, typically from a DRAM controller. This efficiently copies data from external DRAM to a scratchpad memory built using on-chip block RAM. The scratchpad is double-clocked to provide four access ports. The DMA engine uses one of these ports; the vector engine uses the other three to fetch operands and store results. Internally, the scratchpad is organized as a wide, byte-addressable multibanked memory to provide concurrent, high-bandwidth data access.

Source and destination vectors are specified by a pointer into the scratchpad. These vectors can be unaligned with respect to each other. Data alignment networks ensure that any starting address can be issued to any port. Unaligned vectors naturally occur with sliding window algorithms such as convolutions; at each iteration the starting location of the vector to be processed will advance by one element. For these cases MXP has three separate alignment networks as shown in Figure 3: networks A and B align the source operands to the ALUs, while network C aligns the writeback results. Data is read out from the scratchpad in waves, where one wave is a full-width set of data that requires just one clock cycle. Back-to-back waves form a data stream.

Networks A and B shift the data to ensure that the first vector element of operands A and B, respectively, appears at the 'top' position of the wave, regardless of which bank it is actually stored in. Successive data elements are also shifted, forming a contiguous fully packed wave. The waves stream through the ALUs, which are followed by an optional summation stage (for accumulation reductions), and finally into network C to align the writeback. Figure 3 shows an alignment example where the first wave of 4 elements are read out from two vectors, and written back to a third vector, where all three vectors have differing alignments. Execution of a vector instruction on all 8 elements fits into two waves and fills two back-to-back pipeline cycles. A following vec-

tor instruction can issue its own operands with completely different alignments and have its waves packed back-to-back with the preceeding instruction.

The regular integer ALUs for MXP are located between the front-end alignment networks A and B and the back-end alignment network C. These are not directly shown in Figure 2, but they should be assumed to coexist with the 'custom pipelines' stage. The regular ALUs have a 3-stage pipeline, while custom pipelines can be of arbitrary length and have an arbitrary number of internal operators. The figure shows four different custom pipelines in the processor.

The number of parallel lanes (scratchpad banks/execution units) is configurable at synthesis time, but software does not need to be rewritten for different configurations thanks to the vector paradigm. Vector operations may execute over multiple cycles depending on the vector length and number of parallel lanes. Multiple instructions may be in the pipeline at a time. When hardware detects a hazard, e.g. when a vector instruction attempts to read a value currently in the pipeline, pipeline bubbles are inserted until the values are written back to the scratchpad.

The MXP natively supports integer and fixed-point data types. Every instruction can operate on bytes, shorts, or 32-bit integers in either signed or unsigned mode. Operations include traditional ALU instructions, including multiply, rotate and shift instructions, plus a move and several conditional move instructions. Also, fixed-point multiply can be done with a fixed decimal position. Note that divide or modulo operations and floating-point data types are missing, as these require complex logic.

3. CUSTOM VECTOR INSTRUCTIONS

3.1 Minimal Core Instructions

The VectorBlox MXP was designed to have a minimal core instruction set. It is very important to keep this instruction set minimal with a SVP because the area required by an operation will be replicated in every vector lane, thus multiplying its cost. In MXP, multiplication/shift/rotate instructions are included as core instructions because they share use of the hard multipliers in the FPGA fabric. However, divide and modulo are not included as core instructions because they require more than 3 pipeline stages and more logic than all other operators combined.

In addition to the minimal core instruction set, there are a large number of simple, stateless 1- or 2-input, single-output operators with no state that can be created. This includes arithmetic (e.g. divide, modulo, reciprocal, square root, reciprocal square root), bit manipulation (e.g. population count, leading-zero count, bit reversal), and encryption acceleration (e.g. s-box lookup, byte swapping, finite field arithmetic). Some of these operators require very little logic, while others demand a significant amount of logic. However, supporting all such operators is prohibitively expensive in FPGAs. Also, it is hard to imagine a single application that makes use of almost all of these specialized instructions. Finally, even when they are used by an application, they may not appear very frequently in the dynamic instruction mix.

For this reason, we have excluded many operations that could potentially be useful, but we felt are too specialized. Instead, we have devised a way for users to add these operations to the processor using custom vector instructions. Also, we allow the user to decide how many of these opera-

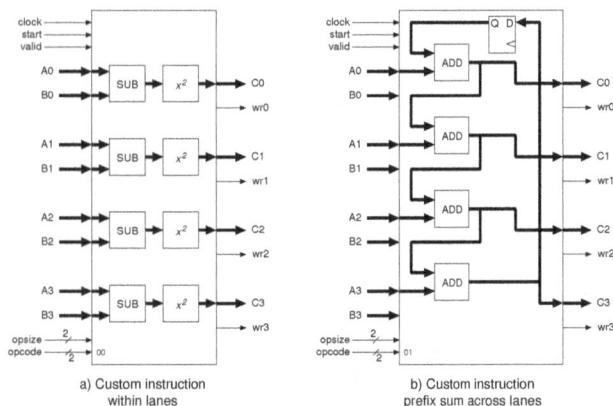

Figure 4: Examples of custom vector instructions

a) Custom instruction within lanes

b) Custom instruction prefix sum across lanes

tors should be added to the pipeline, since it may not make sense to replicate large operators in every lane.

3.2 Custom Vector Instructions (CVIs)

For applications that require more complex operations, where software emulation is too difficult or slow, users can add their own application-specific *custom vector instructions*, also known as CVIs, into the pipeline.

Our add-on CVI approach is different from the VESPA approach [3], which allows selective instruction subsetting from a master instruction set. Subsetting allows very fine-grained control but it typically saves only a small amount of logic. Because no core set of instructions are defined, it also leads to derivative SVPs with incompatible instruction sets.

In contrast, the MXP approach defines a core set of instructions to increase software portability, while user-specified CVIs can be added to accelerate application-specific operations that are rarely needed by other applications. CVIs use an external conduit port interface to MXP, allowing the addition to be done without modifying the processor source HDL. This modularity will also make it easier to add CVIs using run-time reconfiguration. The user can create CVIs or take advantage of our current library of CVIs. This library includes count leading zeroes, compress, divide, square root, and prefix sum operations.

3.3 CVI Interface

A typical CVI is executed in MXP like a standard arithmetic instruction, with two source operands and one destination operand. The main difference is that data is sent out of MXP, through the conduit to the CVI and back again, then multiplexed back into the MXP pipeline before writeback. One individual CVI may consist of many parallel execution units, processing data in both a parallel and a streaming fashion.

In Altera's Qsys environment, CVIs are implemented as Avalon components with a specific conduit interface. Vector data and control signals are exported out of the top level of MXP and connected to the CVI automatically through the conduit. The conduit interface to a CVI designer can be seen in Figure 4. The left side (Figure 4a) shows an example of a simple CVI, the 'difference-squared' operation. This CVI does the same action on all data, so its individual execution units are simply replicated across the number of CVI lanes.

In the simplest case, the number of CVI lanes will match the number of MXP lanes. This is adequate if the CVI is small, or there is plenty of area available. Later, we will consider the area-limited case when there must be fewer CVI lanes than MXP lanes.

The right side (Figure 4b) shows a more complicated example, a prefix sum, where data is communicated across lanes. The prefix sum calculates a new vector that stores the running total of the input vector appearing on operand A. Even if expressed as a tree, its complexity scales faster than $O(N)$. This makes it a very different type of operation than the difference-squared operation, which does not have communication between lanes. As a result, computing a prefix sum is a difficult operation for wide vector engines; it is best implemented in a streaming fashion. Since a vector may be longer than the width of the SVP, it is important to accumulate the value across multiple clock cycles in time. To support this, the CVI interface provides a clock and vector start signal. Furthermore, a data valid signal indicates when each wave of input data is provided, and individual data-enable input signals (not shown for clarity) are provided for each lane.

Additional signals in the CVI interface include an opsize (2 bits) that indicates byte/short/word data. Also, output byte-enable signals allow writing back only partial vector data, or to implement conditional-move operations, or when writing back a last (incomplete) wave. Finally, an opcode field is provided to allow the selection of multiple CVIs. Alternatively, the opcode can be passed to a single CVI and used as a mode-select for different functions, such as sharing logic for divide and modulo, or to implement different rounding modes. The opcode field is shown as two bits, but this can be easily extended.

We have found this interface capable of implementing a wide array of CVIs. We are considering extending this interface with a few additional control signals, such as signed/unsigned, scalar load, and pipeline status information, but we wish to keep the interface as simple as possible.

3.4 Heterogeneous Lane Support

Custom operators may be prohibitively large to add to each vector lane. For example, a fully pipelined Q16.16 fixed-point divider requires 2,652 ALMs to implement in a Stratix IV FPGA. This is more logic than an entire vector lane in the MXP. Thus, it can be desirable to use fewer dividers than the number of lanes (depending upon the portion of divides in the dynamic instruction mix). MXP supports using narrower CVIs with minimal overhead by reusing existing address generation and data alignment logic.

Figure 5 shows how CVIs with a different number of lanes are added to the existing MXP datapath. During normal operation, the address generation logic increments each address by the width of the vector processor each cycle. For the example shown, i.e. an MXP with four 32-bit lanes (written as a 'V4'), each source and destination address is incremented by 16 bytes, until the entire vector is processed. As discussed in Section 2, the input alignment networks align the start of both source vectors to lane 0 before the data is processed by the ALUs. After execution, the destination alignment network is used to align the result to the correct bank in the scratchpad for writeback.

During a CVI, the address generation logic only increments the source and destination addresses by the number

a) Funneling elements 0, 1, 2 through three custom ALUs

b) Funneling elements 3, 4, 5 through three custom ALUs

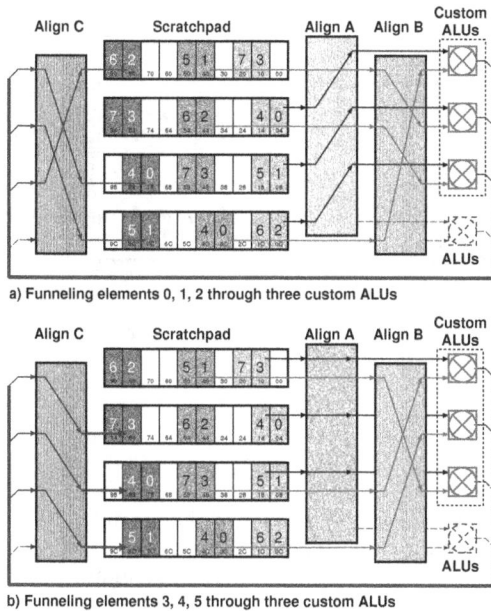

Figure 5: Custom vector instructions with fewer lanes than the SVP

of CVI lanes times the 4-byte width of each lane. In the example shown, the addresses are incremented by 12 bytes for each wave, regardless of the SVP width. As in normal execution, the alignment networks still align source data to start at lane 0 before data is processed in the custom ALUs. In this case, the fourth lane would not contain any data, so its data-enable input would be inactive. After execution, the CVI result is muxed back into the main MXP pipeline, and finally the resulting data is aligned for writeback into the scratchpad. On CVI writeback, the output byte enables are then used to write out data for only the first 12 bytes of each wave; the destination alignment network then repositions the wave to the correct target address.

3.5 CVIs with Deep Pipelines

MXP uses an in-order, stall-free backend for execution and writeback to achieve high frequencies. The CVIs are inserted in parallel to the regular 3-stage execution pipeline of MXP, which means they can also have 3 internal register stages. If fewer stages are needed, it must be padded to 3 stages. This is usually sufficient for combinations of small operators, bit twiddling, and reductions.

Some operations, such as divide or floating point, require much deeper pipelines. If the user naively creates a pipeline that is longer than 3 cycles, the first wave of data would appear to the writeback stage later than the writeback address, and the last wave of data would not reach the writeback stage at all.

To address the latter problem, we have devised a very simple strategy for inserting long pipelines. In software, we extend the vector length to account for the additional pipeline stages (minus the 3 normal stages). This solves part of the problem, allowing the last wave of vector data to get flushed out of the pipeline and appear at the writeback stage. During the last cycles, the pipeline will read data past the end of the input operands, but their results will never be written

back. However, the beginning of the output vector will have garbage results.

To eliminate this waste of space, the MXP could simply delay the writeback address by the appropriate number of clock cycles. However, another way is to allow the CVI itself to specify its destination address for each wave. This requires the MXP to inform the CVI of the destination addresses, and rely upon the CVI to delay them appropriately. We have chosen this latter technique, as it allows for more complex operations where the write address needs to be controlled by the CVI, such as vector compression. Because this can write to arbitrary addresses, any CVI using this mode must set a flag which tells the SVP to flush its pipeline after the CVI has completed.

4. MULTI-OPERAND CVI

The CVIs described in the previous section are intended for 1 or 2 input operands, and 1 destination operand. This can be useful for some applications, but it is not very flexible. Certainly, the DAGs of most large compute kernels require multiple inputs and outputs, and require both scalar and vector operands. In this section, we describe how to to support multiple-input, multiple-output CVIs. As a motivating example, we have chosen the N-body gravitational problem. We modified the problem slightly to produce a pleasing visual demonstration: we restrict calculations to only 2 dimensions, we use a repelling force rather than an attracting force, and we allow collisions with the screen boundary.

4.1 N-Body Problem

The traditional N-body problem simulates a 3D universe, where each celestial object is a body, or particle, with a fixed mass. Over time, the velocity and position of each particle is updated according to interactions with other particles and the environment. In particular, each particle exerts a net force (i.e., gravity) on every other particle. The computational complexity of the basic all-pairs approach we use is $O(N^2)$. Although advanced methods exist to reduce this time complexity, we do not explore them here.

In our modified version, we consider a 2D screen rather than a 3D universe. The screen is easier to render than a 3D universe, but it also has boundaries. Also, we change the sign of gravity so that objects repel each other, rather than attract. (Attractive forces with screen boundaries would result in the eventual collapse into a moving black hole, which is not visually appealing.) Like the traditional N-body problem, we also treat particles as point masses, i.e. there are no collisions between particles. We have also adjusted the gravitational constant to produce visually pleasing results.

The run-time of the N-body is dominated by the gravity force calculation, shown below:

$$\vec{F_{i,j}} = G\frac{M_i M_j}{r^2} = 0.0625\frac{M_i M_j}{|\vec{P_i} - \vec{P_j}|^3}(\vec{P_i} - \vec{P_j})$$

where $\vec{F_{i,j}}$ is the force particle i imposes on particle j, $\vec{P_i}$ is the position of particle i, and M_i is the size or 'mass' of particle i. When computing these forces, we chose a fixed-point Q16.16 fixed-point representation, where the integer component of $\vec{P}$ represents a pixel location on the screen.

When a particle reaches the display boundary, its position and velocity are adjusted to reflect off the edge (towards the center) after removing some energy from the particle. These checks do not dominate the run-time as they are only $O(N)$.

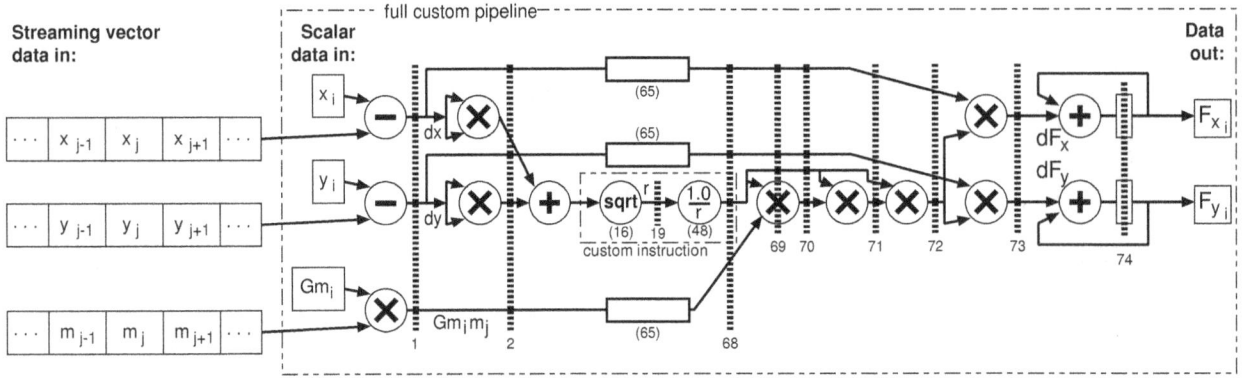

Figure 6: Force summation pipeline

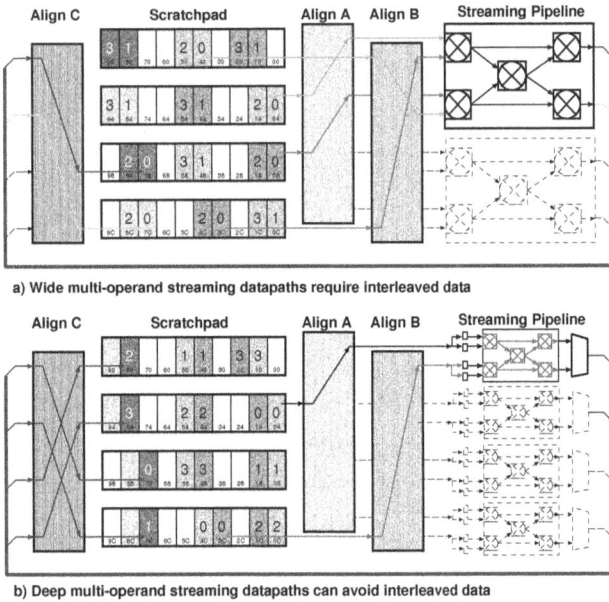

a) Wide multi-operand streaming datapaths require interleaved data

b) Deep multi-operand streaming datapaths can avoid interleaved data

Figure 7: Multi-operand custom vector instructions

An implementation of the gravity computation as a streaming pipeline is shown in Figure 6. This is a fixed-point pipeline with 74 stages; the depth is dominated by the fixed-point square root and division operators at 16 and 48 cycles, respectively.[1] For each particle, its x position, y position, and mass (premultiplied by the gravitational constant) is loaded into scalar data registers within the instruction. This is the reference particle. Then, three vectors representing the x position, y position and mass of all particles are streamed through the vector pipeline. The pipeline integrates the forces exerted by all these particles, and computes a net force on the reference particle.

Overall, the pipeline requires 3 scalar inputs (reference particle properties) and 3 vector inputs (all other particles). It also produces 2 vector outputs (an x vector and a y vector), although the output vectors are of length 1 because

---

[1]We used Altera's LPM primitives for these operators. The pipeline would benefit from a combined reciprocal square root operator, but it does not exist in the Altera library.

of the accumulators at the end of the pipeline. Hence, this gravity pipeline is a 3-input, 2-output CVI.

All of the MXP vector instructions, including the custom type, only have 2 inputs and 1 output. This is a limitation in the software API, where only 2 inputs and 1 output can be specified, as well as the hardware dispatch, where only two source vector addresses and one destination vector address can be issued. Hence, programming a CVI with an arbitrary number of inputs and outputs requires a different way of looking at things.

Loading of scalar data can be accomplished by using vector operations with length 1, and either using an opcode bit to select scalar loading versus vector execution, or by fixed ping-ponging between scalar loading and vector execution. We use the ping-pong approach to save opcodes.

Supporting multiple vector operands is not as simple, however, and will be discussed below.

4.2 Multi-Operand CVI Dispatch

The wide approach requires data to be laid out spatially, such that operand A appears as vector element 0, operand B appears as vector element 1, and so forth. This is shown in Figure 7a. In other words, the operands are laid out consecutively in memory as if packed into a C structure. To stream these operands as vectors, an array-of-structs (AoS) is created. Ideally, the input operands would precisely fit into the first wave; with two read ports, the amount of input data would be twice the vector engine width. If more input data is required, then multiple waves will be required, which will be similar to the depth approach below. If less input data is required, then the CVI does not need to span the entire width of the SVP. In this case, it may be possible to provide multiple copies of the pipeline to add SIMD-level parallelism to the CVI.

The main drawback of the wide approach is that the data must be interleaved into an AoS. In our experience, SVPs work better when data is arranged into a struct-of-arrays (SoA). The SoA layout assures that each data item is in its own array, so SVP instructions can operate on contiguouly packed vectors.

For example, suppose image data is interleaved into an AoS as {r,g,b} triplets. With this organization, it is difficult to convert the data to {y,u,v} triplets because each output data item requires a different equation. When the image data is blocked as in a SoA, it is easy to compute the {y}

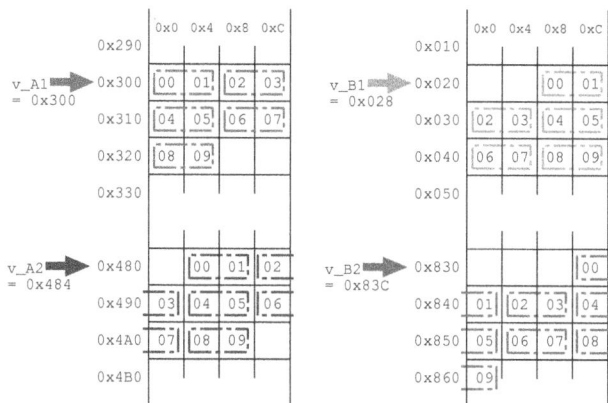

```
VL = 2 (number of elements to keep together)
num1 = (number of arrays to interleave)
     = 2
num2 = (number of elements/VL)
     = 10/VL = 5

srcAStride1 = (v_A2 - v_A1)
            = 0x184
srcAStride2 = (v_A1[VL] - v_A1[0])
            = 0x08

srcBStride1 = (v_B2 - v_B1)
            = 0x814
srcBStride2 = (v_B1[VL] - v_B1[0])
            = 0x08
```

Interleaved read-out order:			
Cycle	Operand A		Operand B
1	A1 00 01		B1 00 01
2	A2 00 01		B2 00 01
3	A1 02 03		B1 02 03
4	A2 02 03		B2 02 03

```
vbx_set_vl( VL );
vbx_set_2D( num1, dstStride1, srcAStride1, srcBStride1 );
vbx_set_3D( num2, dstStride2, srcAStride2, srcBStride2 );
vbx_3D( VVW, VCUSTOM1, v_dest, v_A1, v_B1 );
```

```
vbx_interleave_4_2( VVW, VCUSTOM1, num_elem, VL,
    v_D1, v_D2, v_A1, v_A2, v_B1, v_B2 );
```

```
vbx_interleave_4_2( int TYPE, int INSTR, int NE, int VL,
  int8 *v_D1, int8 *v_D2,
  int8 *v_A1, int8 *v_A2, int8 *v_B1, int8 *v_B2 )
{
  vbx_set_vl( VL );
  vbx_set_2D( 2, v_D2-v_D1, v_A2-v_A1, v_B2-v_B1 );
  vbx_set_3D( NE/VL, v_D1[VL]-v_D1[0],
              v_A1[VL]-v_A1[0], v_B1[VL]-v_B1[0] );
  vbx_3D( TYPE, VINSTR, v_D1, v_A1, v_B1 );
}
```

Figure 8: Using 3D vector operations for multi-operand dispatch

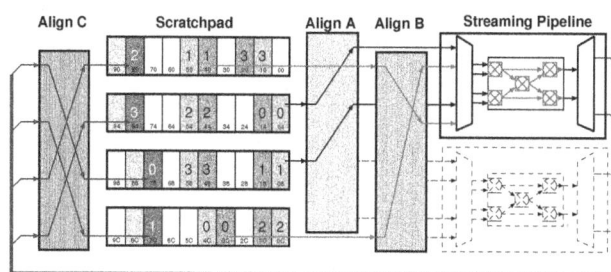

Figure 9: Multi-operand custom vector instructions with funnel adapters

matrix based upon the {r}, {g}, and {b} matrices. Furthermore, converting between AoS and SoA on the fly requires data copying and can take a long time. Hence, it is better for regular SVP instructions to use SoA format.

An alternative depth approach to multiple-operand CVIs requires data to be interleaved in time. This is shown in Figure 7b, where a streaming datapath only has access to two physical ports, operands A and B of one vector lane. This can be combined with wide parallelism by replicating the deep pipeline. It is not desirable to simply fully read two input vectors and then read the third input, though, as the CVI would have to buffer the full length of the instruction. In MXP, vector lengths are limited only by the size of the scratchpad, so the buffering could be costly. Rather, it is desirable to only buffer a single cycle's worth of inputs.

We accomplish this in MXP by using its 2D and 3D instruction dispatch to issue a single wavefront of data from each input on alternating cycles. The 2D instructions work by first executing a normal (1D) vector instruction, then applying a different stride to each of the input addresses and output address and repeating this operation multiple times. The strides and repetitions can be set at runtime using a separate set_2D instruction. The 3D instructions are an ex-

tension of this, where 2D instructions are repeated using another set of strides.

Figure 8 illustrates how these 2D/3D ops are used to dispatch CVIs with multiple operands. In this example, a CVI with 4 inputs (A1, A2, B1, and B2) and 2 outputs (D1 and D2) is to be executed. The desired result is that the CVI will alternate A1/B1 and A2/B2 inputs each cycle, and alternate D1/D2 outputs each cycle.

To get this outcome, first the 1D vector length (VL) is set to the number of CVI lanes, and the 2D strides are set to the difference between input addresses (A2-A1, B2-B1) and output addresses (D2-D1). Since the inner vector length is the same as the number of custom instruction lanes, each row is dispatched as one wave in a single cycle, followed by a stride to the next input. The 2D vector length is set to the total number of cycles required (max(inputs/2, outputs/1)). Note that if more than 2 cycles (4 inputs or 2 outputs) are needed, sets of additional inputs and outputs will need to be laid out with a constant stride from each other.

Since a 2D operation merely alternates between sets of inputs (and outputs), a 3D instruction is used to stream through the arrays of data. Each 2D instruction processes one wavefront (of CVI lanes) worth of data, so the 3D instruction is set to stride by the number of CVI lanes. The number of these iterations (the 3D length) is set to the data length divided by the number of CVI lanes.

In Figure 8, the complex setup routine (top) can be abstracted away to a single function call, `vbx_interleave_4_2()` (middle). One possible implementation of this call is shown at the bottom of the figure.

On the hardware side, data is presented in wavefronts and needs to be multiplexed into a pipeline. Because a new set of inputs only arrives every max(inputs/2, outputs) cycles, the pipeline would be idle part of the time if it had the same width and clockrate as the CVI interface. We can recover the lost performance, and save area, by interleaving two or more logical streams into one physical pipeline. To do this, we have created 'funnel adapters' which are used to accept the spatially distributed wave and feed it to the pipeline over time. This is illustrated in Figure 9.

The funnel adapter for our 3-input, 2 output particle physics pipeline, which has inputs arriving every 2 cycles (and outputs leaving every 2 cycles), allows two MXP lanes worth of data to share a single physical streaming pipeline.

4.3 Face Detection CVI Example

As another example, we have also designed a multiple-input/output CVI for Viola-Jones face detection. The face detection pipeline is shown in Figure 10. Unlike the gravity

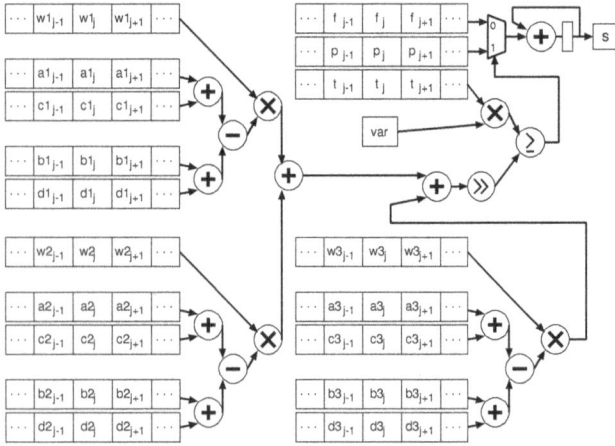

Figure 10: Face detection pipeline

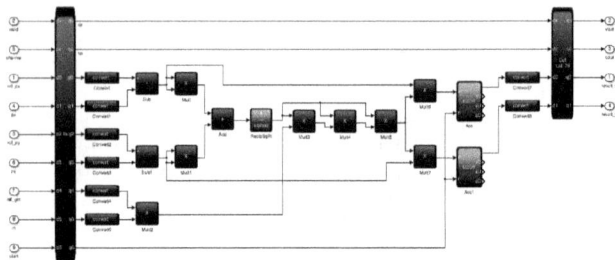

Figure 11: FLOAT Custom Vector Pipeline in Altera's DSP Builder

pipeline, the face detection requires far more inputs – a total of 18 vector inputs and 1 scalar input. It produces a single vector output.

Using regular SVP instructions, this face detection requires a total of 19 instructions, requiring 19 clock cycles per wave of data. In contrast, due to the large number of vector input operands, the face detection pipeline takes 9 clock cycles per wave of data. Hence, the best-case speedup expected from this custom pipeline is $\frac{19}{9}$, or roughly 2 times. Even though face detection contains a large number of operators, the number of input operands limits the overall speedup. Hence, not all applications will benefit significantly from custom pipelines.

5. CVI DESIGN METHODOLOGIES

While implementing a CVI to accelerate a SVP program is much easier than writing a complete accelerator, implementing them in HDL is not desirable for our target users, software programmers. Hence, we have explored two alternatives for generating CVI pipelines.

5.1 Altera's DSP Builder Pipelines

Altera's DSP Builder [12] (ADSPB) is a block-based toolset integrating into Matlab and Simulink to allow for push-button generation of RTL code. Figure 11 shows a floating-point version of our physics pipeline implemented in ADSPB. ADSPB was able to create the entire pipeline, including accumulation units, and design was significantly faster than manually building the fixed-point version in VHDL. Although we were not able to create a fixed-point version of

```
#define CVI_LANES 8 /* number of physical lanes */
typedef int32_t f16_t
f16_t ref_px, ref_py, ref_gm;
f16_t px[CVI_LANES], py[CVI_LANES], m[CVI_LANES];
f16_t result_x[CVI_LANES], result_y[CVI_LANES];

void force_calc()
{
  for( int glane = 0 ; glane < CVI_LANES ; glane++ ) {
    f16_t gmm = f16_mul( ref_gm, m[glane] );
    f16_t dx  = f16_sub( ref_px, px[glane] );
    f16_t dy  = f16_sub( ref_py, py[glane] );
    f16_t dx2 = f16_mul(dx,dx);
    f16_t dy2 = f16_mul(dy,dy);
    f16_t r2  = f16_add(dx2,dy2);
    f16_t r   = f16_sqrt(r2);
    f16_t rr  = f16_div(F16(1.0),r);
    f16_t gmm_rr   = f16_mul(rr,gmm_68);
    f16_t gmm_rr2  = f16_mul(rr,gmm_rr);
    f16_t gmm_rr3  = f16_mul(rr,gmm_rr2);
    f16_t dfx = f16_mul(dx,gmm_rr3);
    f16_t dfy = f16_mul(dy,gmm_rr3);
    f16_t result_x = f16_add(result_x[glane],dfx);
    f16_t result_y = f16_add(result_y[glane],dfy);
    result_x[glane] = result_x;
    result_y[glane] = result_y;
  }
}
```

Figure 12: Gravity pipeline C code for HLS (retiming registers omitted for clarity)

our pipeline in ADSPB because it lacks fixed-point reciprocal and square root, we were happy to generate a floating-point version as an additional data point of interest.

Some glue logic was needed to integrate the pipeline into a CVI, however, because our CVI pipelines require a clock enable signal, which ADSPB generated logic does not have. Rather than attempt to modify the generated code (including libraries used), we built a FIFO buffer to retime data appropriately, which adds minimal logic and uses one additional M9K memory per lane. This glue logic is sufficiently generic to allow any ADSPB-generated pipeline to be integrated into a CVI.

5.2 High Level Synthesis

Additionally, we have started to develop a High-level Synthesis (HLS) tool to implement CVIs in C. The goal is to show that only very simple HLS features are required to produce functional CVIs. For this reason, we started with bare LLVM rather than a more advanced HLS tool such as LegUp [13].

The user writes a function in C that produces the desired dataflow behaviour. This function has a standard API interface that matches the physical CVI interface shown in Figure 4. The input and output data are presented as global variables, and the user reads and writes to these variables to achieve the desired streaming behaviour. At the moment, our compiler recognizes specific global variable names, but this can be modified to use pragmas.

Like LegUp, our compiler converts C code into Verilog RTL output. However, since we are only attempting to generate dataflows, not complex sequential behaviour, only simple translation steps are required. For example, we unroll all loops as if they are for-generate hardware statements.

In our current implementation, the user manually inserts pipeline registers for retiming using a special function, `reg()`. For example, `a_3 = reg(a,3);` tells our LLVM compiler to

Table 1: Results with MXP compared to Nios II/f, Intel, and ARM Processors

Processor	Area (ALMs)	DSP 18-bit	F_{max} (MHz)	s/frame	GigaOp/s	pairs/s	Speedup
Nios II/f (fixed)	1,223	4	283	231.6	0.004	0.3M	1.0
Cortex A9 (zedboard) (fixed)	–	–	667	52.1	0.02	1.3M	4.5
Cortex A9 (zedboard) (float)	–	–	667	14.0	0.07	4.8M	16.6
Intel Core i7-2600 (fixed)	–	–	3400	6.5	0.15	10.3M	35.6
Intel Core i7-2600 (float)	–	–	3400	1.6	0.63	41.9M	144.8
MXP V32 (fixed)	46,250	132	193	73.8	0.14	9.1M	31.4
MXP V32+16FLOAT	115,142	644	122	0.041	24.6	1,326M	5,669
MXP V32+16FIXED	86,642	740	153	0.032	31.3	2,087M	7,203

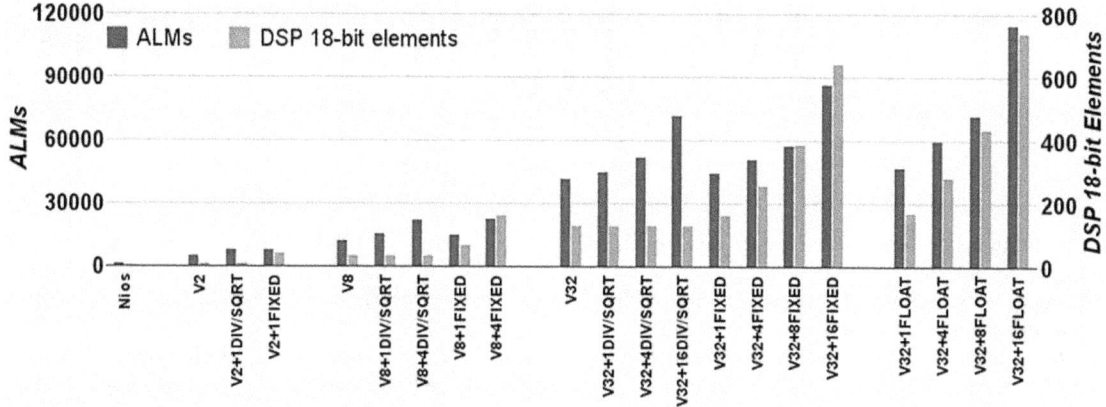

Figure 13: Area of gravity pipeline systems

create signal a_3 after adding 3 pipeline stages. Apart from this function, our C code is naturally readable by a software programmer. Later, we plan to add automatic retiming heuristics.

Although our compiler is limited in scope, we are able generate Verilog that is cycle-accurate with the fixed-point gravity pipeline described earlier in this paper. A portion of our C code using a Q16.16 fixed-point data type is shown in Figure 12. For clarity, we have removed the retiming registers and not shown the fixed-point function definitions.

6. RESULTS

All FPGA results are obtained using Quartus II 13.0 and a Terasic DE4 development board which has a Stratix IV GX530 FPGA and a 64-bit DDR2 interface. For comparison, Intel Core i7-2600 and ARM Cortex-A9 (from a Xilinx Zynq-based ZedBoard) performance results are shown. Both fixed-point (fixed) and floating-point (float) implementations were used. MXP natively supports fixed-point multiplication in all lanes. The Nios II/f contains an integer hardware multiplier and hardware divider; additional instructions are to operate on fixed-point data. The Intel, ARM and Nios II versions are written with the same C source using libfixmath [14]. We developed a vectorized version of this library for use with MXP. Nios II/f and MXP results use gcc-4.1.2 with '-O2'. The Core i7 results use gcc-4.6.3 and '-O2 -ftree-vectorize -m64 -march=corei7-avx'. ARM results use gcc-4.7.2 and reports the best runtime among '-O2' and '-O3'.

The MXP results vary the number of SVP lanes (V2, V8, and V32) and the number of CVI lanes. Three types of CVIs are generated: one containing separate fixed-point divide and square root instructions (DIV/SQRT), one containing a

manually generated fixed-point gravity pipe (FIXED), and an ADSPB pipe (FLOAT). The LLVM pipeline results are omitted because they are nearly identical to (FIXED).

Figure 13 shows the area, in Adaptive Logic Modules (ALMs) on the left and DSP Block 18-bit elements on the right. The DIV/SQRT configurations take roughly the same area (in ALMs) as the FIXED pipeline. However, FIXED requires more multipliers. The FLOAT pipelines require about 5,500 ALMs and 38 DSP elements per lane versus 3,000 and 32 per lane for FIXED.

Running the N-body problem with 8,192 particles, Figure 14 shows the speedup relative to a Nios II/f soft processor for the various MXP configurations as well as a 3.4GHz Intel Core i7-2600 and a 667MHz ARM Cortex A9. The processor implementations are naive, but typical of what a C programmer might start with. A highly optimized single-core AVX implementation for i7-2600 matches our best MXP performance at 2×10^9 pairs per second [15]. However, that code was painstakingly hand-written in assembly language.[2] Overall, this is over 7,200 times faster than Nios II/f.

7. CONCLUSIONS AND FUTURE WORK

This work has demonstrated a way to reuse existing structures in SVPs to attach a variable number of streaming pipelines with minimal resource overhead. These can be accessed in software via *custom vector instructions* (CVIs). Logic-intensive operators, such as fixed-point divide, should not be simply replicated across all vector lanes. Doing so wastes FPGA area unnecessarily. Instead, it is important

---

[2]The AVX-optimized version also solves the 3D problem. Our 2D pipeline can be converted into a 3D version, with no expected loss in performance, with just 3 more additions and 2 more multiplications.

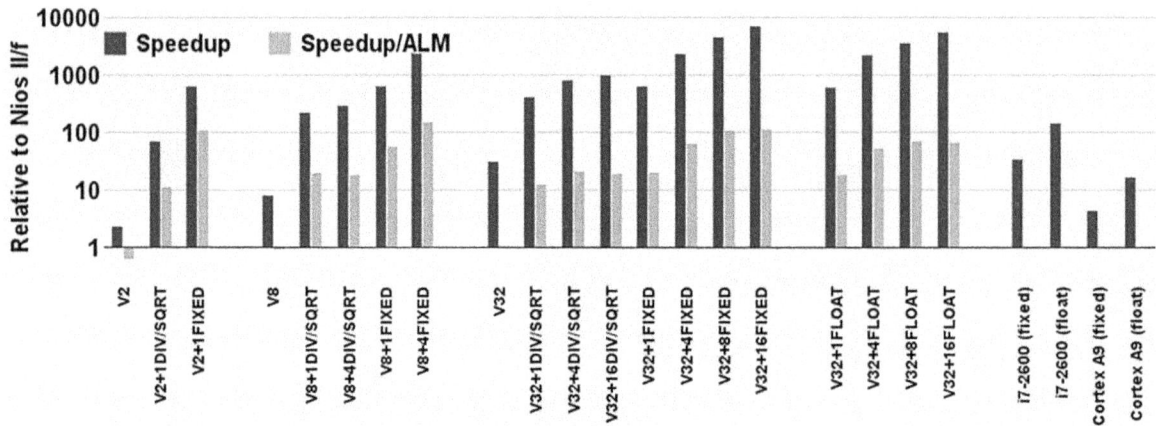

Figure 14: **Performance and performance-per-area of gravity pipeline**

to consider the frequency of use of the specialized pipeline, and add enough copies to get the most speed-up with minimal area overhead. Methods for dispatching complex CVIs were presented, including a time-interleaved method that allows an arbitrary number of inputs and outputs using funnel adapters.

The performance results achieve speedups far beyod what a plain SVP can accomplish. For example, a 32-lane SVP achieves a speedup of 31.4, whereas a CVI-optimized version is another 230 times faster, with a net speedup of 7,200 versus Nios II/f. This puts the MXP at par with an AVX-optimized Intel Core i7 implementation.

One area of future work is to make a repository of common operations and data types, such as min, max, power, and log for fixed-point, floating-point and even complex numbers. Also, we plan to continue exploring high-level synthesis options so that programmers can easily generate custom CVIs. Finally, allowing the programmer to dynamically reconfigure the CVIs will help when an FPGA must run several different applications.

As limitations of our work, some read and write bandwidth of the scratchpad is not utilized during the execution of our CVIs. Also, more advanced instruction dispatch strategies could be used to overlap execution of multiple CVIs. Alternatively, regular vector instructions could also overlap with a CVI.

8. ACKNOWLEDGMENTS

The authors would like to thank Martin Langhammer for his encouragement and advice on using Altera's ADSPB. We would also like to thank Altera for donating hardware and software licenses used in this research.

9. REFERENCES

[1] R. M. Russel, "The CRAY-1 computer system," *Communications of the ACM*, vol. 21, no. 1, pp. 63–72, 1978.

[2] C. Kozyrakis and D. Patterson, "Vector vs. superscalar and VLIW architectures for embedded multimedia benchmarks," in *Microarchitecture*, 2002, pp. 283–293.

[3] P. Yiannacouras, J. G. Steffan, and J. Rose, "VESPA: portable, scalable, and flexible FPGA-based vector processors," in *CASES*, 2008.

[4] J. Yu, C. Eagleston, C. H. Chou, M. Perreault, and G. Lemieux, "Vector processing as a soft processor accelerator," *ACM TRETS*, vol. 2, no. 2, pp. 1–34, 2009.

[5] P. Yiannacouras, J. G. Steffan, and J. Rose, "Fine-grain performance scaling of soft vector processors," in *CASES*, 2009, pp. 97–106.

[6] C. H. Chou, A. Severance, A. D. Brant, Z. Liu, S. Sant, and G. Lemieux, "VEGAS: Soft vector processor with scratchpad memory," in *FPGA*, 2011, pp. 15–24.

[7] A. Severance and G. Lemieux, "VENICE: A compact vector processor for FPGA applications," in *FPT*, 2012, pp. 261–268.

[8] J. Cong, M. A. Ghodrat, M. Gill, H. Huang, B. Liu, R. Prabhakar, G. Reinman, and M. Vitanza, "Compilation and architecture support for customized vector instruction extension," in *ASP-DAC*, 2012.

[9] J. Kathiara and M. Leeser, "An autonomous vector/scalar floating point coprocessor for FPGAs," in *FCCM*, 2011, pp. 33–36.

[10] "The Convey HC-2 computer: Architectural overview," http://www.conveycomputer.com/files/4113/5394/7097/Convey_HC2_Architectual_Overview.pdf.

[11] "Embedded supercomputing in FPGAs with the vectorblox MXP matrix processor," in *ACM International Conference on Hardware/Software Codesign and System Synthesis*, Sept. 2013.

[12] "DSP builder," http://www.altera.com/technology/dsp/advanced-blockset/dsp-advanced-blockset.html.

[13] A. Canis, J. Choi, M. Aldham, V. Zhang, A. Kammoona, J. Anderson, S. Brown, and T. Czajkowski, "LegUp: High-level synthesis for FPGA-based processor/accelerator systems," in *FPGA*, 2011, pp. 33–36.

[14] "libfixmath - cross platform fixed point maths library," http://code.google.com/p/libfixmath/.

[15] A. Tanikawa, K. Yoshikawa, K. Nitadori, and T. Okamoto, "Phantom-GRAPE: numerical software library to accelerate collisionless *n*-body simulation with SIMD instruction set on x86 architecture," *arXiv.org*, Oct. 2012.

MORP: Makespan Optimization for Processors with an Embedded Reconfigurable Fabric

Artjom Grudnitsky, Lars Bauer, Jörg Henkel
Karlsruhe Institute of Technology (KIT), Karlsruhe, Germany
{grudnitsky, lars.bauer, henkel}@kit.edu

ABSTRACT

Processors with an embedded runtime reconfigurable fabric have been explored in academia and industry started production of commercial platforms (e.g. Xilinx Zynq-7000). While providing significant performance and efficiency, the comparatively long reconfiguration time limits these advantages when applications request reconfigurations frequently. In multi-tasking systems frequent task switches lead to frequent reconfigurations and thus are a major hurdle for further performance increases. Sophisticated task scheduling is a very effective means to reduce the negative impact of these reconfiguration requests. In this paper, we propose an online approach for combined task scheduling and re-distribution of reconfigurable fabric between tasks in order to reduce the makespan, i.e. the completion time of a taskset that executes on a runtime reconfigurable processor. Evaluating multiple tasksets comprised of multimedia applications, our proposed approach achieves makespans that are on average only 2.8% worse than those achieved by a theoretical optimal scheduling that assumes zero-overhead reconfiguration time. In comparison, scheduling approaches deployed in state-of-the-art reconfigurable processors achieve makespans 14%–20% worse than optimal. As our approach is a purely software-side mechanism, a multitude of reconfigurable platforms aimed at multi-tasking can benefit from it.

Categories and Subject Descriptors

C.1.3 [**Other Architecture Styles**]: Adaptable architectures

Keywords

Reconfigurable Processor; Area Allocation; Task Scheduling

1 Introduction and Motivation

Reconfigurable processors allow hardware adaption to the computational profile of running applications, resulting in a platform which – unlike a processor with an application

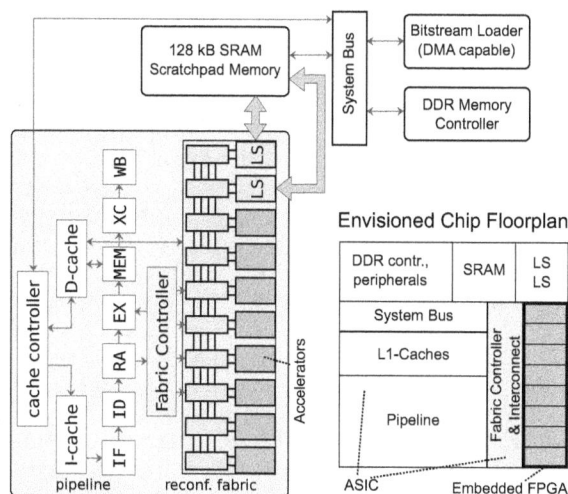

Figure 1: Architecture of a System-on-Chip processor with an embedded reconfigurable fabric.

specific instruction set (ASIP) [13] – is capable of accelerating a wide range of applications [8]. A widespread approach is to extend a non-reconfigurable general-purpose processor (core processor) with a reconfigurable fabric, onto which application-specific accelerators can be loaded at runtime (e.g. [26, 18, 5, 7, 17, 2]). The fabric is implemented on an embedded FPGA [23], while the core processor and other SoC components are implemented as an ASIC on the same chip. Figure 1 shows a typical architecture for such a reconfigurable processor and a possible floorplan with the embedded FPGA. A commercial example of such a reconfigurable platform is the Xilinx Zynq-7000 processor [27], which uses a dual-core ARM Cortex-A9 connected to 7-Series reconfigurable fabric on the same chip.

The instruction set architecture (ISA) of the core processor is extended with Special Instructions (SIs), which are typically used in computationally intensive kernels of the applications and provide access to the accelerators on the fabric. The latency (execution speed in cycles) of an SI typically ranges from a few cycles up to a few hundred cycles and an SI is typically executed several hundreds to thousands times per kernel (depending on the application and input data).

The high performance and flexibility of fine-grained reconfigurable accelerators comes at the cost of a considerable reconfiguration time which is typically in the range of milliseconds for complex accelerators [21]. Reconfiguration is performed using a DMA transfer from the memory location where the accelerator bitstream is stored to the reconfiguration port of the fabric, thus the processor can continue executing applications while an accelerator is loaded. Until reconfiguration of an accelerator is complete, the application cannot use that accelerator but has to fallback on a slower SI implementation. The SI functionality can be emulated in software by using the normal ISA of the core processor, triggered either by an unimplemented instruction trap or by a conditional branch that queries whether the accelerator finished reconfiguration. That means that at least two implementations are available per SI.

We call the latency difference between the fastest possible SI implementation (selected by the runtime system of the reconfigurable processor but not necessarily reconfigured yet) and the fastest currently reconfigured SI implementation (potentially the software emulation) *Reconfiguration-induced Cycle Loss* (RiCL). An application exhibiting a high cumulative RiCL will take longer to finish than when running with a low cumulative RiCL. RiCL depends on the time required to complete the reconfiguration of an accelerator. The slower reconfigurations are performed, the higher RiCL.

Figure 2 presents a motivational case study that shows the RiCL over time for an H.264 Video Encoder focusing on one outer loop iteration that encodes one video frame. For each frame, the application executes three kernels after each other and each kernel uses a different set of SIs (9 different SIs are used in this example and each SI is typically executed several hundreds to thousands times per kernel). Therefore, each kernel triggers reconfigurations of multiple accelerators when it starts. In Figure 2, the starting time of the three kernels is indicated as ①, ②, and ③ and all times on the X-axis are relative to the first kernel when the application starts encoding the frame. The height of the bar at a particular point on the X-axis corresponds to the RiCL of the SIs that execute during that time (potentially zero, e.g. when no SI executes or all reconfigurations are completed) averaged over a sliding time window of 1000 cycles. Right at the beginning of the first kernel (see ① in Figure 2), RiCL is high as several accelerators that are beneficial for this kernel are not yet reconfigured, because the third kernel of the preceding frame just finished and the reconfigurable fabric still contains the accelerators beneficial for that kernel. As more accelerators are reconfigured for the first kernel of the new frame, RiCL reduces to zero until the second kernel starts and requests different accelerators.

Summarizing, applications that are composed out of multiple kernels always face a reconfiguration-induced cycle loss when they switch from one kernel to another (unless the reconfigurable fabric is large enough to accommodate all accelerators at the same time, which is not the case for complex applications as H.264). The green dashed line in Figure 2 shows the theoretical time when frame encoding would be finished, if the cumulative RiCL were zero ($1.35\times$ faster for this frame). This is the potential that can be exploited by reducing RiCL.

If the system does not support multi-tasking, or only one task is executable, then RiCL can only be reduced by further improving the reconfiguration speed (we assume 66 MB/s average bandwidth for reconfiguration). However, if the task scheduler has multiple candidates that are executable, then the reconfiguration overhead of a task A can be *hidden*, by running a different task B while the accelerators for task A are reconfigured. But simply switching to a different task

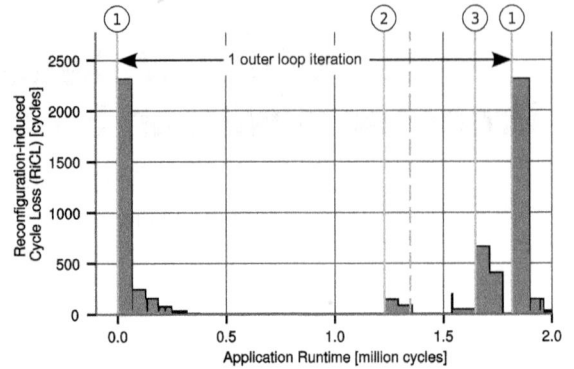

Figure 2: Case study: performance loss due to reconfiguration overhead; the green dashed line shows when processing would be finished if RiCL were zero.

does not necessarily improve overall performance. For instance, if task A has been granted the entire reconfigurable fabric, switching to task B would actually worsen overall performance, as B would run without any accelerators and thus with a very high RiCL.

We therefore propose a novel combined task-scheduling and fabric-distribution approach called MORP (*M*akespan *O*ptimizer for *R*econfigurable *P*rocessors), that minimizes the makespan, i.e. the completion time of a taskset that executes on a runtime reconfigurable processor. To do so, upon anticipation of a drop in execution speed of the currently executing *primary task* (when switching from one kernel to another) our combined approach dynamically selects a suitable *secondary task*, grants it a small share of the reconfigurable fabric (fabric re-distribution), and switches execution to the secondary task (task scheduling) until the primary task completed most of its reconfigurations. This effectively hides the reconfiguration latency of the primary task at a reasonable performance (and thus reasonable RiCL) of the secondary task, thus reducing the overall RiCL of the taskset. The challenge is to identify suitable primary and secondary tasks and to identify when to switch between them and which share of the reconfigurable fabric shall be granted to the secondary task.

2 Related Work

Surveys about reconfigurable processors are available that provide good introductions as well as classifications [8, 25, 10]. Whereas early reconfigurable processors focused on accelerating single-tasking applications, recent approaches target multi-tasking scenarios. A recent survey categorizes them into reconfigurable processors with implicit, explicit, and no architectural support for multi-tasking [28].

Several reconfigurable processors with support for multi-tasking implement entire tasks either in hardware or in software. The hardware tasks execute in parallel whereas the software tasks execute sequentially on the core CPU without acceleration. A hierarchical approach to dynamically decide which task shall execute on the reconfigurable fabric is proposed in [19]. An infrastructure for transparent inter-task communication – independent on whether a task executes in hardware or software – is presented in [16]. [20] proposes OS extensions for support of reconfigurable processors, among them a hardware module that performs thread scheduling. Tang et al. [24] present a scheduler that assigns periodic tasks to heterogeneous processing elements (including a reconfigurable fabric) offline and that integrate sporadic tasks by extending the resulting schedule at runtime. However, all these approaches perform a binary decision whether to implement a task entirely in hardware or software without acceleration, i.e. some tasks are significantly accelerated and other tasks are not accelerated at all. Additionally, they perform a fixed fabric distribution per task. Each task that shall execute in hardware obtains a fixed share of the reconfigurable fabric that is typically reconfigured once when the task starts rather than being adapted to the requirements of a task that may change when executing different kernels.

Due to the limited flexibility and efficiency of such a binary decision, several reconfigurable processors use software tasks with a focus on the performance-critical parts of computational kernels that are accelerated by Special Instructions (SIs), e.g. [26, 18, 5, 7, 2]. This allows for a high efficiency as it provides several options for hardware acceleration, i.e. the decision whether an SI shall be implemented in hardware or software can be determined independent of other SIs and other tasks.

RISPP [5] presents an adaptive reconfigurable processor where a runtime system selects among different compile-time prepared SI implementations at runtime depending on the application requirements. However, it does not support multi-tasking. Proteus [7] proposes a mechanism that allows to preempt SIs during their executions (e.g. to handle interrupts or to switch to another task) and resume their execution later. However, they do not propose how to optimize the task schedule or the fabric distribution to reduce the reconfiguration-induced cycle loss. [15] presents an online task-scheduler and fabric allocator for a reconfigurable processor. The authors formulate the scheduling and allocation problem as a 2D model, where a task is defined by its runtime and required fabric area. This approach requires knowing the runtime of a task before it starts and only supports tasks that perform all their reconfigurations at the start of a task, which limits its applicability.

The reconfigurable multi-core processor presented in [2] does not use a task scheduler as at most one task executes per core. The reconfigurable fabric is allocated based on the deadlines of the parallel executing applications. Frequent fabric re-distributions are performed whenever any of the applications proceeds to its next kernel, which leads to frequent reconfigurations and thus exacerbates the need to reduce the reconfiguration-induces cycle loss. [6] proposes a runtime mapping approach of multiple tasks to a runtime-reconfigurable system, aiming to reduce reconfiguration latency. The approach aims to reuse existing configurations and thus reduce the amount of configurations during deployment of a new application, focusing mainly on the allocation/mapping of fabric, not on task scheduling. Reconfiguration latency reduction is also the goal of [21], where a design-time approach is used to map multiple applications onto the fabric. A kind of reconfiguration hiding has been explored in [11] and [4] for soft real-time systems, thus their main goal was minimizing deadline misses or tardiness (i.e. accumulated time by which tasks miss their deadlines). None of these approaches aim at minimizing the makespan of a taskset or aim at reducing the reconfiguration-induced cycle loss.

A compiler-assisted scheduling approach for the MOLEN reconfigurable platform [26] is presented in [22]. The compiler provides information about the temporal distance be-tween kernels to the runtime system, a technique which is also utilized by our approach. For the actual task scheduling, the approach in [22] uses Round Robin and we compare our approach with [22] in the results. For a non-reconfigurable single-core processor, Shortest Processing Time (SPT) scheduling is optimal for makespan minimization [14]. This is not the case for reconfigurable processors as we demonstrate with our comparison in the results.

3 System Definition

3.1 Architecture & Application Assumptions

This work targets reconfigurable processors, capable of loading hardware **accelerators** at runtime onto a reconfigurable fabric. The fabric is partitioned into **reconfigurable containers**, i.e. designated regions on the fabric where accelerators can be loaded. Figure 1 shows a simplified example of such an architecture where the processor pipeline and the reconfigurable fabric are tightly coupled to accelerate applications. The containers are interconnected using the 1D fixed-size area model [12] and they are implemented on an embedded FPGA. Loading an accelerator takes a considerable amount of time (in the order of milliseconds, depending on accelerator complexity), but can be performed without stalling the pipeline using a DMA transfer.

Applications that are implemented for reconfigurable processors typically have computationally intensive **kernels** that benefit from hardware acceleration. They are accelerated by invoking **Special Instructions (SIs)** that are implemented in multiple alternatives: one software implementation and at least one hardware implementation (using the reconfigurable accelerators). In general, applications run faster when more reconfigurable fabric is allocated to them (until a certain amount of parallelism is utilized).

The operating system (also called runtime system) is taking care of task scheduling and management of the reconfigurable fabric. The decision which SIs shall be implemented in hardware (given a certain amount of reconfigurable containers) is performed at runtime and can be determined automatically by a runtime system (as in [17, 5, 2]) or explicitly by the application (as in [26, 18]).

3.2 Task Properties

We assume the following task properties and requirements to the system (for in-depth details on scheduling background, see [14]): The problem is to schedule a taskset T, consisting of tasks T_i. Each task T_i has a finite **Completion Time** C_i, i.e. the time when T_i finishes its execution. The optimization goal of MORP is to minimize the **makespan** (see Eq. (1)), i.e. the time when all tasks of the taskset completed.

$$makespan := \max\{C_i \mid \forall \text{ Tasks } T_i \in T\} \qquad (1)$$

We assume that the system supports task **preemption**, i.e. that the currently executing task can be interrupted at any time by the operating system, so that the task scheduler can decide which task to run next, and switch to a different task if required.

Before a task can use the reconfigurable fabric, the application issues a **prefetch** system call that triggers the reconfigurations of the accelerators. Prefetches are used to inform the runtime system about the SIs the application is about to execute. The runtime system can then decide which SI implementation (software or one of the hardware implementations) to use and start loading the corresponding accelerators as in [5]. Alternatively, prefetches can directly contain the information which accelerators shall be reconfigured as in [26]. Once a task has finished all its hardware accelerated kernels, it can use a designated prefetch called **last prefetch** to inform the runtime system that it will not execute further SIs. This last prefetch can be added to the application in the same manner as regular prefetches, e.g. by the compiler or a profiling tool.

Depending on the kernel execution behavior, MORP assigns tasks into one of the following three task categories. This categorization is done offline using a profiling tool.

Multi-Kernel Task (MKT): An MKT executes more than one hardware accelerated kernel (i.e. kernels that are accelerated by invoking SIs) over its lifetime. The kernel execution can happen periodically, e.g. the H.264 Video Encoder example in Figure 2 executes three different kernels sequentially to process a frame.

Single-Kernel Task (SKT): An SKT executes one single hardware accelerated kernel and issues one prefetch for it (typically short time after the application starts).

Zero-Kernel Task (ZKT): A ZKT (or "Software" task) does not issue any prefetches or SIs. After an MKT or SKT executes its dedicated last prefetch, it behaves like a ZKT.

3.3   Required Metrics

In addition to the task category, MORP uses further task-specific metrics for its decisions. Tasks benefit to a different degree from the reconfigurable fabric. ZKTs run at the same speed for all fabric sizes (i.e. number of reconfigurable containers), SKTs and MKTs will benefit from increasing fabric sizes up to a saturation point (as is shown in Figure 5 in Section 5). This fabric-size dependent characteristic is called **Task Performance**. Task performance is profiled offline by executing the task alone (i.e. no multi-tasking) on different fabric sizes (i.e. allocating different numbers of containers to it). The relative task performance $RTP_{i,n}$ of task T_i on a fabric of size n is defined as shown in Eq. (2), where $C_{i,j}$ is the completion time of T_i executing in single-tasking mode on a fabric of size j.

$$RTP_{i,n} = C_{i,n}/C_{i,0} \qquad (2)$$

The relative task performance is normalized into the range $[0, 1]$ once the task enters the system to allow comparing performances of different tasks. The normalized task performance $TP_{i,n}$ is shown in Eq. (3), where N is the fabric size of the actual system.

$$TP_{i,n} = \begin{cases} 1.0 & \text{if } n \geq N \\ RTP_{i,n}/RTP_{i,N} & \text{otherwise} \end{cases} \qquad (3)$$

Tasks that use accelerators (i.e. MKT and SKT) run at different speeds depending on how many of the prefetched accelerators already finished reconfiguration. When no prefetched accelerators are available (e.g. short time after the prefetch was issued) the speed is low which leads to a large RiCL as shown in Figure 2. To make these different speeds comparable among different tasks, we use the relative **Task Efficiency** metric, which is defined as follows: When the current prefetch for a task is completed, i.e. there are no pending reconfigurations for this task, then the task efficiency for this task is defined to be 1.0. If some reconfigurations are not yet completed for this task, then not all SIs of the currently executing kernel can be executed in the targeted implementation (decided by the runtime system or directly determined by the prefetch instruction) and thus the task efficiency is lower. Let $SI_i.C$, $SI_i.T$, and $SI_i.SW$ be

the latency (i.e. execution time in cycles) of the current, target, and software implementation of SI_i, respectively, then the following relation holds: $SI_i.T \leq SI_i.C \leq SI_i.SW$. The SI latencies are weighted by the average number of executions for this SI w_i (from offline profiling). To compute the task efficiency for kernel K_x, first ΔL is computed as the accumulated weighted difference between the latency of the current SI implementations and the target SI implementations for all $SI_i \in K_x$. The worst possible latency for the prefetched SI, i.e. the latency of their software implementations, constitutes L_{worst}. The task efficiency TE is then defined as in Eq. (4).

$$\begin{aligned} \Delta L &= \sum_{SI_i \in K_x} w_i(SI_i.C - SI_i.T) \\ L_{worst} &= \sum_{SI_i \in K_x} w_i SI_i.SW \qquad (4) \\ TE &= 1.0 - \frac{\Delta L}{L_{worst}} \end{aligned}$$

The concept of task efficiencies is inspired by [4]. The difference between task performance and task efficiency is that task performance is a static characteristic (usually implemented as a lookup table), while task efficiency is a dynamic value, changing with each prefetch and with each reconfiguration that loads or removes accelerators beneficial for the currently executing kernel.

If a task does not run at an efficiency of 1.0, then ΔL is larger than 0. We call ΔL the **Reconfiguration-induced Cycle Loss (RiCL)**, compared to the task running at maximal efficiency. The RiCL metric denotes how many cycles a task looses accumulated over all its SIs over all its execution time due to reconfiguration delays compared to a hypothetical situation where the accelerators that are requested by a prefetch would be immediately available (i.e. under the assumption that the reconfiguration would happen instantaneously). Reducing the RiCL is the goal of our proposed scheduling approach.

For each kernel K_x that performs a prefetch, the **Average Time Between Prefetches (ATBP)** determines the time between that prefetch and the following prefetch. The ATBP is determined offline by a profiling tool.

4   MORP: Scheduling and Fabric Allocation

The overall idea is to hide the prefetches of a *primary task* by executing a *secondary task*, while the reconfigurations for the primary task are performed. To do so, the system selects a secondary task when the primary task is approaching its next kernel, i.e. its next prefetch. Tasks that do not execute SIs (i.e. ZKTs) or tasks that reach a high task efficiency with only few reconfigurable containers are good candidates for secondary tasks. They may also receive a small amount of reconfigurable containers (called *reallocation*) before the primary task reaches its next kernel to run much more efficiently, at the cost of slightly reduced performance of the primary task. When the primary task issues its next prefetch, the system switches to the secondary task while the prefetch for the primary task is performed. The RiCL of the primary task is reduced (because its reconfiguration time is hidden) without significantly increasing the RiCL of the secondary task, thus a net reduction of RiCL is achieved and thereby the makespan is reduced.

Figure 3 shows the flow-chart of our approach, MORP. The system is usually either in the *Primary Task Execution* state or the *Secondary Task Execution* state.

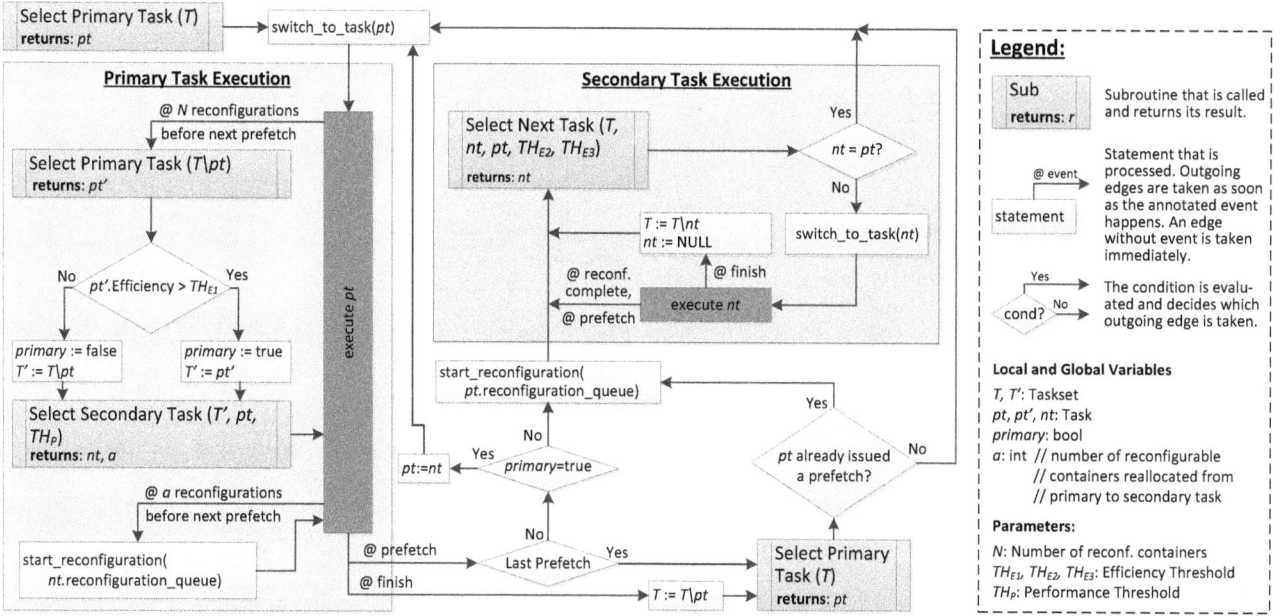

Figure 3: Overview of Task Scheduling, Reconfiguration Sequence, and Dynamic Fabric Re-Distribution for Primary and Secondary Tasks.

First, a primary task pt is selected from the current taskset T. The primary task is preferably a MKT, characterized by a high RiCL and is selected using the following method:

1. Select MKT with highest RiCL from T. If no MKTs are left in T, then
2. Select SKT with highest RiCL from T. If no SKTs are left in T, then
3. Select any ZKT from T. If no ZKTs are left in T, then Taskset T has been finished, exit.

The system allocates the entire fabric to pt, starts it, and enters the *Primary Task Execution* state (see Figure 3).

During compilation and profiling, each program has been annotated with ATBP (see Section 3.3), which is used to start selection of the secondary task. MORP uses the average time required to load one accelerator as the basic time unit. In the following, time specifications such as "N reconfigurations" (see also Figure 3) mean "the time required to load N accelerators".

N reconfigurations before the next prefetch of the primary task pt, the system decides what to do after that prefetch. It either continues executing pt as primary task (potentially switching to a secondary task for a short time to hide the reconfiguration latency of the prefetch) or it switches to a different primary task pt'. N is chosen as half the size of the reconfigurable fabric, i.e. when deciding to switch to a new primary task pt', then there is sufficient time to reconfigure half of the reconfigurable fabric towards pt' to reduce its RiCL. MORP selects the task with the highest efficiency as the next primary task. A good candidate for a pt' with high efficiency is a task that can utilize accelerators that are currently loaded on the fabric.

If the efficiency of pt' is higher than the threshold TH_{E1}, pt' is provided as the only input candidate to the "Select Secondary Task" function (see Figure 3). Due to its already high efficiency, pt' will be selected by the "Selected Secondary Task" function, and additional fabric will be reallocated to pt' to improve its efficiency.

TH_{E1} needs to be fairly high, as primary tasks tend to use a lot of accelerators (in general equal to the number of reconfigurable containers). Switching to a new primary task with low efficiency would require multiple reconfigurations until the new task reaches full efficiency. During this time RiCL would be high, thereby increasing the makespan. If the efficiency of pt' is lower than the threshold TH_{E1}, a secondary task is selected out of all MKTs and SKTs (except the current primary task) to hide the reconfiguration latency of the primary task.

Secondary task selection is shown in Algorithm 2. The goal is to select the next task nt (along with the number of accelerators a that shall be reallocated to it) that provides the highest total performance for the primary task pt and the secondary task nt. Taking performance for both tasks into account is crucial, as reconfigurations for nt start while pt still executes, thus pt will run with reduced efficiency for a short time until switching to nt. The performance of all kernels of all tasks for different fabric sizes is known from offline profiling and is used in Algorithm 2 to search an appropriate secondary task. The task that maximizes performance is returned as the secondary task nt, along with the number of accelerators a that are required for providing that performance. If reallocation would cause the performance of either the secondary or the primary task to drop below the threshold TH_P, reallocation of reconfigurable fabric is not considered an option. A secondary task may still be used later, but without reallocation.

If the parameter TH_P is chosen too high, it would discard most secondary task candidates, e.g. if set to 1.0, no efficiency loss for the primary task would be tolerated, thus only very few (if any) containers would be considered for reallocation to the secondary task. The secondary task would have to reach maximum performance with those few containers. Meeting such tough constraints is almost impossible, thus the system would not perform any reallocation at all. Setting TH_P too low would allow for reallocation of too many containers to the secondary task. The primary task usually

Algorithm 1: Select Next Task

input:
> Taskset T
> Previously/initially selected secondary task nt
> Originally executed primary task pt
> Efficiency Threshold for primary task TH_{E2}
> Efficiency Threshold for secondary task TH_{E3}

output : next task to execute
// *Resume to the primary task pt when its efficiency is good*
if *no outstanding reconfigurations or pt.efficiency* $> TH_{E2}$
then return pt

// *Execute those tasks that are awaiting their first prefetch*
$next\_task := \text{MAX}\{t.ricl \mid t \in T.MKT \cup T.SKT$ **and not**
$t.issued\_prefetch\}$
if $next\_task \neq NULL$ **then return** $next\_task$

// *Execute secondary task, if available*
if $nt \neq NULL$ **then if** $nt > TH_{E3}$ **then return** nt

// *Execute ZKT*
$next\_task := T.ZKT.pop()$

// *Execute low-efficiency secondary task, if no ZKT left*
if $next\_task = NULL$ **then** $next\_task := nt$

return $next\_task$

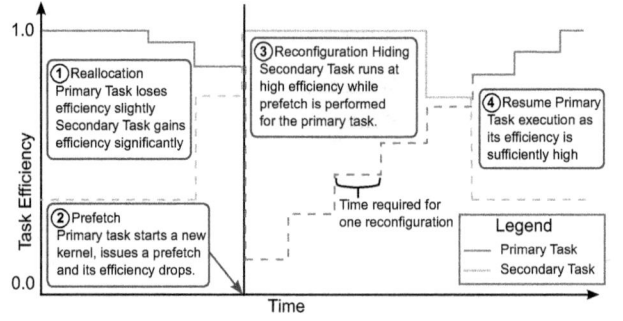

Figure 4: Efficiency of primary and secondary tasks in the proximity of a primary task prefetch.

turns to the *Primary Task Execution* state, and finishes any outstanding reconfigurations for the new primary task, if required. Otherwise (if the selected next task is not a primary task), reconfigurations for the primary task are started, and the system enters the *Secondary Task Execution* state.

Algorithm 2: Select Secondary Task

input:
> taskset T',
> currently running task pt,
> Performance Threshold TH_P

output : reallocation amount a, secondary task nt
$nt = NULL$, $a = 0$, $best = 0$
foreach *amount i in Fabric.size/2* **do**
> **foreach** *task t in* T' **do**
>> **if** $t \in T.ZKT$* *or not* $t.issued\_prefetch$ **then**
>>> **continue**
>>
>> // *Performance of primary task if i containers of*
>> *fabric are taken away*
>> $P = pt.current\_kernel.Perf(\text{Fabric.size} - i)$
>> // *Performance of secondary task if i containers of*
>> *fabric are provided*
>> $N = t.current\_kernel.Perf(i)$
>> **if** $P < TH_P$ *or* $N < TH_P$ **then continue**
>> // *Score if i reconfigurable containers are reallocated*
>> *to task t*
>> **if** $P + N > best$ **then**
>>> $best = P + N, a = i, nt = t$

return (nt, a)

---

has more time-consuming kernels than the secondary task, thus reduced performance of the primary task has a strong negative impact on the makespan, more than can be made up for by improved secondary task performance.

After Secondary Task Selection the system resumes executing pt until 'a reconfigurations' before its next prefetch. Reconfigurations for nt are then started and the system resumes executing pt until it issues its next prefetch.

The events before and after the prefetch are sketched in Figure 4 for illustration. Task efficiency of the currently running task (sometimes primary, sometimes secondary) is shown with a solid line, while a dashed line is used for the non-running task. Ideally, reconfiguration for the secondary task (see ① in Figure 4) is finished immediately before the primary task issues its next prefetch. Due to input-data dependent behavior of the primary task, its prefetch may be issued earlier or later than expected (differences between expected prefetch time from offline profiling and actual prefetch time are evaluated in the results) and thus reconfigurations of the secondary task may be finished earlier or later than the prefetch of the primary task. If the reconfigurations are finished earlier, RiCL for the primary task *before* the prefetch will be increased more than expected by Algorithm 2 due to the longer time the primary task runs with less reconfigurable fabric. If reconfigurations for the secondary task are not yet finished at the time the primary task issues its prefetch, its pending reconfigurations are aborted (to start the new reconfigurations for the primary task), and the secondary task executes with reduced efficiency until switching back to the primary task.

Once the primary task issued its prefetch, its efficiency will drop as it requires accelerators that are not yet loaded on the reconfigurable fabric (see ② in Figure 4). MORP now exits the *Primary Task Execution* state (see Figure 3). Before *Secondary Task Execution* can start, the system handles the following special cases: If the primary task issued its *Last Prefetch* or terminates, then a new primary task needs to be selected and its pending reconfigurations need to be started before proceeding to the *Secondary Task Execution* state. If the next task nt that was selected during the *Primary Task Execution* state was a primary task, then the system directly switches to the new primary task, re-

In the *Secondary Task Execution* state, the next task is selected using Algorithm 1. If the primary task efficiency is above the threshold TH_{E2}, it is considered sufficiently high and the system switches back to the *Primary Task Execution* state. Otherwise, tasks that have not yet issued their first prefetch (e.g. that are still in their initialization phase) are selected as the next task. We call this preferred selection of not yet initialized tasks '*task warm up*'. The goal of this warm up is to have a prefetch ready for all tasks (where possible), as without a prefetch the system does not know which accelerators are needed for the task and therefore no reallocation can be performed. If all tasks are already warmed up, the secondary task is scheduled, if such a task is available and its efficiency is higher than TH_{E3}. Otherwise a ZKT (Software-task) is scheduled, and if none are available, the secondary task is scheduled even if its efficiency is lower than TH_{E3}.

The system proceeds with the *Secondary Task Execution*, hiding the reconfiguration latency of the primary task (see ③ in Figure 4), until the primary task has sufficiently high

Parameter	Value
Fabric Size [# Reconf. Containers]	$1 - 15$
Evaluated Schedulers	SPT, RR, MORP
Number of Tasksets	3
Number of Tasks per Taskset	$3 - 5$
TH_{E1}, TH_{E2}, TH_{E3}	0.9
TH_P	0.8
Total Number of Simulations	135

Table 1: Benchmarking Setup

	Taskset 1	Taskset 2	Taskset 3
MKT	H.264 SUSAN	H.264 SUSAN	H.264
SKT		AdPCM Rijndael	
ZKT		SHA	SHA SHA SHA

Table 2: Tasksets used during evaluation

efficiency. At this point the system returns to the *Primary Task Execution* state.

If parameter TH_{E2} is too low, RiCL reduction after a prefetch will be minor, if it is very large (near 1.0), secondary task will be wasted reducing minuscule amounts of RiCL and will likely no longer be available during later prefetches where they could be used to reduce large amounts of RiCL. TH_{E3} values near 1.0 would cause ZKTs to be used even though fabric has been reallocated to a SKT. Low TH_{E3} would allow secondary tasks with a low efficiency (e.g. due to misprediction of the prefetch, reconfigurations for the secondary could not be started) to be used, and RiCL reduction would not occur.

5 Results

Evaluation was done with our cycle-accurate SystemC-based simulator, which models the reconfigurable processor shown in Figure 1 and described in Section 3.1. We envision that such a reconfigurable processor is implemented using an embedded FPGA for the reconfigurable fabric and the core processor is implemented as an ASIC on the same chip, similar to the Xilinx Zynq-7000 (with the difference that the fabric is loosely coupled in the Zynq, while we assume that the fabric is tightly-coupled to the core CPU).

As a proof-of-concept, we have implemented the reconfigurable processor as an FPGA-only prototype, based on a Gaisler SoC, consisting of a LEON 3 [1] SPARC V8 CPU with MMU, DDR Controller and peripherals. The pipeline of the LEON CPU is connected to our runtime-reconfigurable fabric. Special Instructions executing in the fabric can receive input data from the register file, the memory hierarchy, or an on-chip Scratchpad Memory that is connected to the fabric with two 128-bit wide ports (see Figure 1). We used a Xilinx Virtex-5 LX110T based evaluation board for the implementation. Running Linux 2.6.36.4 on the prototype, we have measured the reconfiguration time required for loading one accelerator to be $0.6 - 0.7$ ms and context switching time approximately 12.5 μs. Depending on accelerator complexity, the number of FPGA Slices required to implement one accelerator was between 12 and 147 with a median of 51 slices. The simulator configuration parameters for the benchmarks are summarized in Table 1.

We have evaluated 3 different tasksets, shown in Table 2. The tasksets comprise applications from the MiBench-suite [9] and an H.264 video encoder. The tasks H.264 (video

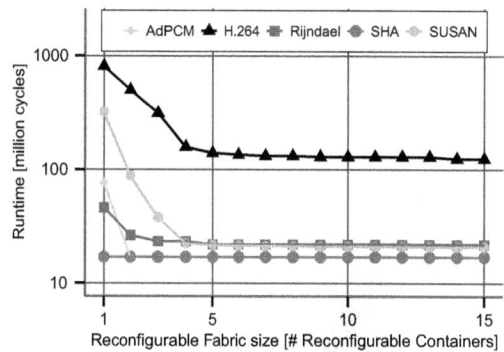

Figure 5: Runtime of tasks (logarithmic scale) when executed alone on the system.

encoding) and SUSAN (image recognition) are multi-kernel tasks, i.e. for each outer loop iteration, multiple distinct prefetches are performed. AdPCM (audio encoding) and Rijndael (cryptography) are single-kernel tasks, i.e. only one prefetch at the start of the program is performed. SHA (cryptographic checksum) is a software task, i.e. no prefetches are performed an thus no reconfigurable fabric is used. Although SHA is a good candidate for hardware-accelerated execution, we chose to use a software-only version to show how our system handles heterogeneous tasksets. Figure 5 shows the single-tasking execution time of the tasks when executed on systems with different fabric sizes. A normalized version of these curves is provided to MORP for making scheduling decisions.

For task scheduling policies we use Shortest Processing Time (SPT, optimal for makespan minimization of non-reconfigurable single-core processor [14]), Round Robin (RR, used in the reconfigurable Molen processor [22]), MORP and Optimal. We define "Optimal" as SPT scheduling with a RiCL of 0 and no overhead apart from context switching time. We can obtain such results from our simulator by configuring it to assume zero-overhead reconfiguration time. However, makespans produced by the "Optimal" scheduler are not achievable in most cases, and should be only regarded as a lower bound for the makespan.

In addition to scheduling, the distribution of the reconfigurable containers, i.e. the share of the reconfigurable fabric assigned to a task at a given point in time, needs to be determined. SPT runs a task to completion, therefore during the time a task runs, all reconfigurable containers are assigned to this task. This policy is not beneficial for RR, as it switches frequently between different tasks and would have to reconfigure potentially all containers after each context-switch (multiple ms additionally, which is an infeasible overhead). Instead, for RR it is beneficial to divide the reconfigurable fabric between the currently executing tasks, i.e. a particular task T_i has a certain share of the reconfigurable fabric where it can reconfigure. Another task T_j has its own share that it can reconfigure, but it can not overwrite the share of T_i. RR partitions the fabric equally among the tasks, however, not exceeding the amount of accelerators a task can make use of, e.g. AdPCM achieves its highest performance with 2 reconfigurable containers, while performance of H.264 just saturates at 19 containers. MORP uses its integrated fabric distribution, described in Section 4.

For accurate overhead analysis, the C implementation of MORP was fed with test input data and the execution time

133

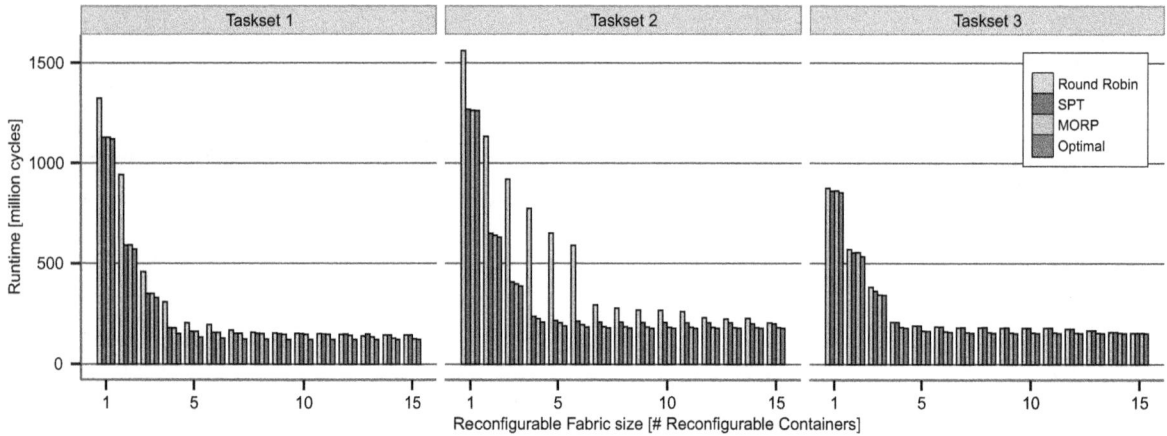

Figure 6: Makespan of 3 tasksets when scheduled by different schedulers.

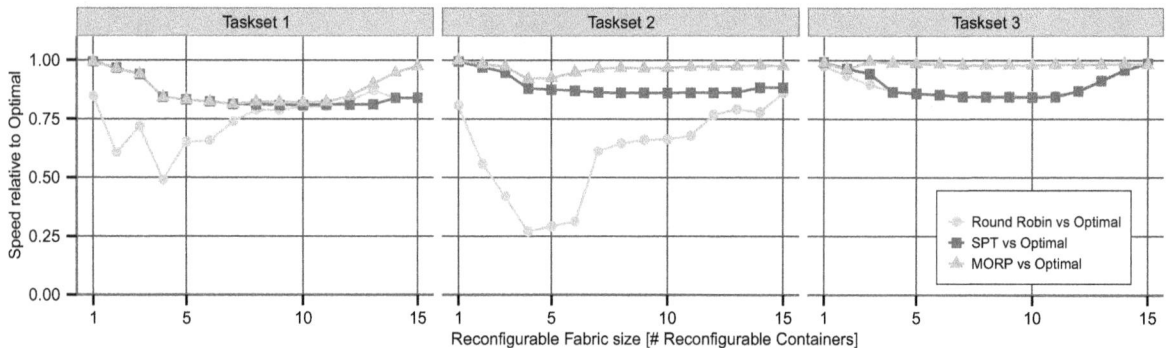

Figure 7: Relative speed of MORP, Round Robin and SPT schedulers compared to Optimal.

(in cycles) of its functions was measured using the ArchC SPARC V8 instruction set simulator [3]. Our SystemC-based full system simulator uses execution counters to determine how often the functions of MORP are executed. This allows us to simulate the total overhead of using MORP for each benchmark. Context switching duration was measured on our FPGA-based runtime reconfigurable system running Linux. Over all simulations, FIFO performed 3.6, MORP 272.9 and SPT 488.9 context switches per taskset on average. Context switch duration and MORP overhead is included in all of the following results.

5.1 Evaluation & Discussion

The makespan results of the benchmarks characterized by Table 1 are shown in Figure 6. Figure 7 shows the results of the benchmark as relative speed of MORP, Round Robin; and SPT when compared to Optimal. Makespans scheduled by MORP are 2.8% slower than Optimal (median; mean: 5.8% slower), whereas makespans of SPT and Round Robin are 13.8% and 19.6% slower than Optimal (median: 12.2% and 19.6%), respectively. Scheduler performance varies with the taskset. MORP achieves its best results with Taskset 3, as does Round Robin, while SPT favors Taskset 2. For each of the 3 tasksets for all sizes of the reconfigurable fabric MORP yields better results than SPT and Round Robin in 35 out of 45 benchmark configurations. In the cases where MORP does not yield the best makespan, its result is on average 1% worse than that of the best scheduler for the particular configuration. Most of

the configurations where MORP did not achieve the best result were in Taskset 1, which is disfavorable to MORP, as explained further below. In the remaining configurations in Tasksets 2 and 3 where MORP does not yield the best makespan, RiCL was already very low, thus the RiCL reduction by MORP could not offset the makespan increase due to its overhead.

The following two non-scheduler related effects can be observed: (i) The more reconfigurable fabric is available for accelerators, the faster the taskset is completed – this is due to more kernels being executed in hardware, as more fabric is available. (ii) As the fabric size increases, the makespans of all schedulers converge. The reason is that once sufficient reconfigurable containers are available, a task will have all accelerators for all of its kernels loaded on the fabric and will no longer perform any reconfigurations. Once this fabric size is reached, RiCL is nearly 0 and the scheduler no longer has an effect on the makespan (apart from its overhead).

For very small fabric sizes (1–2 reconfigurable containers) MORP and SPT produce similar results, as reallocating from the already small fabric would slow down the primary task significantly, thus MORP behaves similar to SPT. Round Robin will generally yield a worse makespan for small fabric sizes. If multiple tasks would benefit from hardware acceleration, then RR will force some of them to execute in software as not enough reconfigurable containers are available for all of them. For instance, in Taskset 3 only the H.264 task is hardware accelerated when using RR. On larger fab-

Scheduling Strategy	Transferred Configuration Data
Round Robin	24,022 kB
SPT	25,800 kB
MORP	28,318 kB

Table 3: Average amount of reconfiguration data transferred.

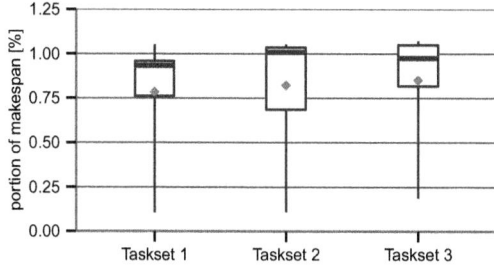

Figure 8: Overhead of MORP as share of the total makespan.

rics (8–12 reconfigurable containers), MORP has more opportunities to reduce RiCL and thus improve the makespan.

The potential for improvement depends on the set of executable tasks from which secondary tasks can be selected. Taskset 1 has two MKT tasks, which are both good candidates for primary tasks, but not very suitable for secondary tasks. They also have a rather long runtime and with that a high total RiCL. As there is no suitable candidate for a secondary task, no reallocation is performed and MORP behaves comparable to SPT until the taskset is finished. That is also the reason why MORP did not always achieve the best result in Taskset 1. Taskset 2 offers better possibilities, as there are enough SKTs and ZKTs for hiding prefetches of both H.264 and SUSAN MKTs. MORP has the best performance when used on Taskset 3, as hiding prefetches with ZKTs incurs no performance loss on the primary task, due to no reallocation of reconfigurable containers of the primary task. The reason is that RR does some amount of prefetch hiding (although not intentionally): when it switches to another task, the prefetches for the first task continue. In the other tasksets this effect is also present but dominated by the negative performance impact due to the fabric distribution strategy used by RR.

The overhead required for MORP (already included in the benchmark measurements) is approximately 1% of the total makespan. Figure 8 shows boxplots for the overhead for each of the 3 tasksets. The runtime of the MORP components mainly depends on the number of tasks in the tasksets and the size of the reconfigurable fabric. Table 3 shows the amount of bytes transferred through the reconfiguration port per simulation run. MORP keeps the reconfiguration port busier than the other schedulers, as it deliberately performs prefetches when from a primary to a secondary task to reduce the total makespan. The increased utilization of the reconfiguration port may have a negative impact on power utilization, however, as the makespan of a taskset is reduced, the energy consumption may still be lower.

5.2 In-Depth Analysis

In this section we focus on one run of Taskset 2 on a fabric with 10 containers. In Figure 9, the top stripes marked "Reconfiguration Trace" show the reconfigurations performed by the system and the areas marked "Scheduling Trace" show the scheduled task. The colors indicate which task recon-

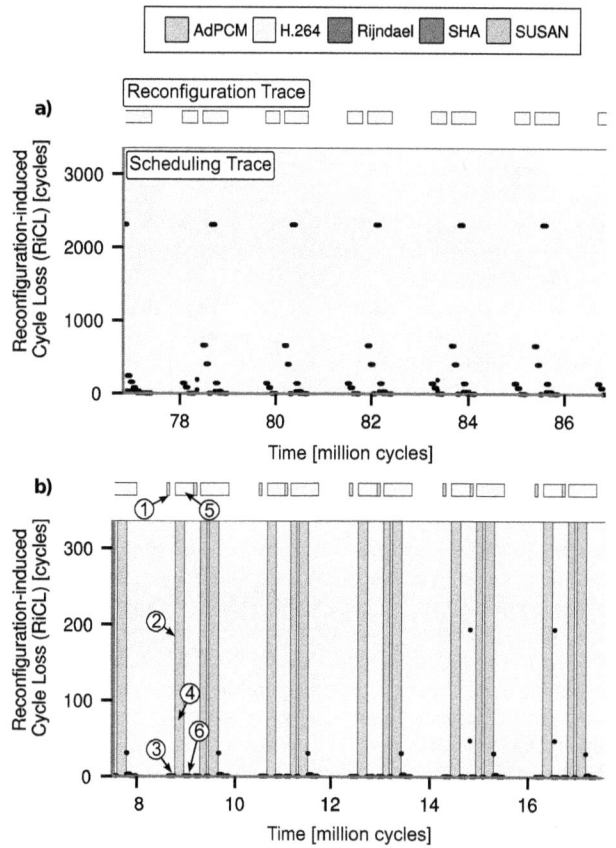

Figure 9: Scheduling and reconfiguration traces and RiCL of Taskset 2 using **a)** SPT, and **b)** MORP scheduling. Note that the y-scale in a) is different than in b).

figures or is currently running, respectively. Black dots are plotted whenever RiCL is greater than 0.

Figure 9a) shows an excerpt of 10 million cycles from the H.264 task scheduled with SPT. As motivated in Figure 2, traditional schedulers (such as SPT) disregard RiCL, resulting in a larger makespan. The repetitive sequence of the H.264 Encoder (encoding each frame and executing 3 kernels per frame) can be seen in the periodic pattern of the RiCL values. RiCL rises after each prefetch (start of small stripes at the top), and takes some time to reach 0.

The same taskset on the same reconfigurable fabric scheduled by MORP is shown in Figure 9b). As both MORP and SPT schedule the tasks at different points in time, showing an excerpt in the same timerange as in Figure 9a) would have shown the trace of a different task, thus we have chosen a different range where the H.264 task is scheduled by MORP. Note that the y-scale, which shows the RiCL, ranges only to 300, unlike in Figure 9a), where it ranges to 3000.

Shortly before each prefetch, the AdPCM task is selected as secondary task, and 2 reconfigurable containers are reallocated to AdPCM to improve its performance. The reconfiguration for AdPCM ① is finished a short time before H.264 issues its prefetch ②, thus RiCL before the prefetch is marginally increased ③. After the prefetch of H.264, MORP switches to the AdPCM task ④, and executes it while the accelerators for H.264 are being loaded ⑤. Once H.264 has a high enough efficiency (greater than TH_{E2}), the system schedules H.264 and the RiCL after the prefetch is significantly lower ⑥ than for H.264 when scheduled with SPT.

In the direct comparison in Figure 9, MORP reduced the RiCL value down to only 6% of the SPT RiCL value. RiCL in Figure 9b) at ③ is due to the difference between the Average Time Between Prefetches (ATBP) from offline profiling (see Section 3.3) and the actual time between prefetches during the execution of the taskset. ATBP is provided for each kernel, and is only of interest for MKTs (as SKTs only issue one prefetch). For the H.264 MKT in Taskset 2 on a fabric with 10 reconfigurable containers, offline determined ATBP for the first kernel is off by 13%, for the second kernel by 21% and for the third kernel even by 72%. The third kernel has a very short duration, compared to the other two, thus RiCL reduction and execution time variation due to input data have a stronger effect. As evidenced by the overall RiCL reduction and the resulting makespan improvement, MORP is quite robust against these mispredictions in ATBP.

6 Conclusion

In this work we present an approach for reducing makespan on reconfigurable processors. To achieve this goal, our proposed approach, MORP, tackles both scheduling and allocation of the reconfigurable fabric. We identify the Reconfiguration-induced Cycle Loss (RiCL) as the main contributor to makespan on reconfigurable processors. RiCL occurs after a task has issued a reconfiguration prefetch, thus our technique focuses on improving system performance at these particular points during task execution. We reduce RiCL through hiding reconfiguration latency of a primary task by choosing a fitting secondary task and re-allocating fabric between both tasks in a way as to optimize performance of both tasks.

Our MORP scheduler achieves an average makespan reduction by 6.5% and 20.3%, when compared to the SPT scheduler (Shortest Processing Time, optimal for makespan minimization of non-reconfigurable single-core processor) and Round Robin (used in the reconfigurable Molen processor), respectively. Compared to the makespan of an optimal schedule, MORP produces results which are only 2.8% (median; mean: 5.8%) worse than optimal, while other evaluated schedulers produce schedules with makespans that are 14%–20% worse than optimal.

7 Acknowledgments

This work was partly supported by the German Research Foundation (DFG) as part of the Transregional Collaborative Research Center "Invasive Computing" (SFB/TR 89).

References

[1] Aeroflex Gaisler. Leon 3. http://www.gaisler.com.

[2] W. Ahmed, M. Shafique, L. Bauer, and J. Henkel. Adaptive resource management for simultaneous multitasking in mixed-grained reconfigurable multi-core processors. In CODES+ISSS, pages 365–374, 2011.

[3] R. Azevedo, S. Rigo, M. Bartholomeu, G. Araujo, C. Araujo, and E. Barros. The ArchC architecture description language and tools. International Journal of Parallel Programming, 33(5):453–484, 2005.

[4] L. Bauer, A. Grudnitsky, M. Shafique, and J. Henkel. PATS: a performance aware task scheduler for runtime reconfigurable processors. In FCCM, pages 208–215, 2012.

[5] L. Bauer, M. Shafique, and J. Henkel. Run-time instruction set selection in a transmutable embedded processor. In Conference on Design Automation (DAC), pages 56–61, 2008.

[6] I. Beretta, V. Rana, D. Atienza, and D. Sciuto. A mapping flow for dynamically reconfigurable multi-core system-on-chip design. TCAD, pages 1211–1224, 2011.

[7] M. Dales. Managing a reconfigurable processor in a general purpose workstation environment. In Design Automation and Test in Europe (DATE), pages 980–985, 2003.

[8] P. Garcia, K. Compton, M. Schulte, E. Blem, and W. Fu. An overview of reconfigurable hardware in embedded systems. EURASIP Journal on Embedded Systems, 2006:1–19, 2006.

[9] M. Guthaus, J. Ringenberg, D. Ernst, T. Austin, T. Mudge, and R. Brown. MiBench: A free, commercially representative embedded benchmark suite. In International Workshop on Workload Characterization, pages 3–14, 2001.

[10] H. P. Huynh and T. Mitra. Runtime adaptive extensible embedded processors – a survey. In SAMOS, pages 215–225, 2009.

[11] H. P. Huynh and T. Mitra. Runtime reconfiguration of custom instructions for real-time embedded systems. In Design Automation and Test in Europe (DATE), pages 1536–1541, 2009.

[12] H. Kalte, M. Porrmann, and U. Rückert. System-on-programmable-chip approach enabling online fine-grained 1d-placement. In RAW, page 141, 2004.

[13] K. Keutzer, S. Malik, and A. R. Newton. From ASIC to ASIP: The next design discontinuity. In International Conference on Computer Design (ICCD), pages 84–90, 2002.

[14] J. Y.-T. Leung. Handbook of scheduling: algorithms, models, and performance analysis. 2004.

[15] Y. Lu, T. Marconi, K. Bertels, and G. Gaydadjiev. Online task scheduling for the FPGA-Based partially reconfigurable systems. In ARC, page 216–230, 2009.

[16] E. Lübbers and M. Platzner. ReconOS: An RTOS supporting hard- and software threads. In FPL, pages 441–446, 2007.

[17] R. Lysecky, G. Stitt, and F. Vahid. Warp processors. TODAES, 11(3):659–681, 2006.

[18] C. Mucci, M. Bocchi, M. Toma, and F. Campi. A case-study on multimedia applications for the XiRisc reconfigurable processor. In ISCAS, pages 4859–4862, 2006.

[19] V. Nollet, J. y. Mignolet, T. A. Bartic, D. Verkest, S. Vernalde, and R. Lauwereins. Hierarchical run-time reconfiguration managed by an operating system for reconfigurable systems. In ERSA, pages 81–87, 2003.

[20] W. Peck, E. Anderson, J. Agron, J. Stevens, F. Baijot, and D. Andrews. Hthreads: A computational model for reconfigurable devices. In FPL, pages 1–4, 2006.

[21] V. Rana, S. Murali, D. Atienza, M. D. Santambrogio, L. Benini, and D. Sciuto. Minimization of the reconfiguration latency for the mapping of applications on FPGA-based systems. In CODES+ISSS, page 325–334, 2009.

[22] M. Sabeghi, V.-M. Sima, and K. Bertels. Compiler assisted runtime task scheduling on a reconfigurable computer. In FPL, pages 44–50, 2009.

[23] T. v. Sydow, B. Neumann, H. Blume, and T. G. Noll. Quantitative analysis of embedded FPGA-architectures for arithmetic. In ASAP, pages 125–131, 2006.

[24] H.-K. Tang, P. Ramanathan, and K. Compton. Combining hard periodic and soft aperiodic real-time task scheduling on heterogeneous compute resources. In International Conference on Parallel Processing (ICPP), pages 753–762, 2011.

[25] S. Vassiliadis and D. Soudris. Fine- and Coarse-Grain Reconfigurable Computing. 2007.

[26] S. Vassiliadis, S. Wong, G. Gaydadjiev, K. Bertels, G. Kuzmanov, and E. Panainte. The MOLEN polymorphic processor. Transact. on Computers (TC), 53(11):1363–1375, 2004.

[27] Xilinx, Inc. Zynq-7000 All Programmable SoC Overview. http://www.xilinx.com/support/documentation/data_sheets/ds190-Zynq-7000-Overview.pdf, 2013.

[28] P. G. Zaykov, G. K. Kuzmanov, and G. N. Gaydadjiev. Reconfigurable multithreading architectures: A survey. In SAMOS, pages 263–274, 2009.

OmpSs@Zynq All-Programmable SoC Ecosystem

Antonio Filgueras[1], Eduard Gil[2]
Daniel Jimenez-Gonzalez*[1,2]
Carlos Alvarez[1,2],Xavier Martorell[1,2]
Barcelona Supercomputing Center[1]
Universitat Politecnica de Catalunya[2]
*djimenez@ac.upc.edu

Jan Langer, Juanjo Noguera*
Kees Vissers
Xilinx Research Lab
*juanjo.noguera@xilinx.com

ABSTRACT

OmpSs is an OpenMP-like directive-based programming model that includes heterogeneous execution (MIC, GPU, SMP, etc.) and runtime task dependencies management. Indeed, OmpSs has largely influenced the recently appeared OpenMP 4.0 specification. Zynq All-Programmable SoC combines the features of a SMP and a FPGA and benefits DLP, ILP and TLP parallelisms in order to efficiently exploit the new technology improvements and chip resource capacities. In this paper, we focus on programmability and heterogeneous execution support, presenting a successful combination of the OmpSs programming model and the Zynq All-Programmable SoC platforms.

Categories and Subject Descriptors: D.1.3 [Concurrent Programming]: Parallel programming B.6.3 [Design Aids]: Automatic synthesis

Keywords: Heterogenous Parallel Programming model; Task dataflow models; Automatic Hardware Generation

1. INTRODUCTION

Power efficiency is nowadays one of the main objectives of high performance computing, where heterogeneous parallel computing appears as the right approach. In particular, those heterogeneous architectures that combine FPGA and general-purpose processors seem to be key to overcome the problem of chips hitting a power wall because of slowed supply voltage scaling [11, 12, 20], that is, breaking the Dennard scaling [9].

The hardware specialization of part of the application within the FPGA, as well as the low power consumption of the FPGA, can significantly contribute to improve the power efficiency of high performance computing. As a matter of fact, an embedded heterogeneous architecture SMP/FPGA SoC was presented: the Zynq-7000 family of devices [22]. The Zynq All-Programmable SoC is a shared memory machine with a snoop cache coherence protocol that combines (1) a traditional SMP with two Cortex-A9 cores, with a 512KB shared L2 cache, and (2) a Xilinx FPGA, on a modern SoC processor. The ARM based SMP can run Linux with FPGA device support, increasing the usability and flexibility for the programmers. That SoC combines the features of a SMP and a FPGA and benefits DLP, ILP and TLP parallelisms in order to efficiently exploit the new technology improvements and chip resource capacities.

However, easy high level language programmability continues being a challenge and a necessity on programming FPGAs, and in particular, this lack of tools is becoming worse with the recent SMP/FPGA SoCs. To the best of our knowledge, there is no embedded solution to this problem for high level language applications. In this paper we focus on those programmability and heterogeneous execution support challenges. We present a successful combination of the OmpSs programming model and the Zynq All-Programmable SoC platforms as the first step towards power efficient high performance systems.

OmpSs is a task dataflow programming model that includes heterogeneous execution support as well as data and task dependency management [2] and has significantly influenced the recently appeared OpenMP 4.0 specification. In the current available implementation of OpenMP the programmer can specify tasks, and later ensure that all the tasks defined up to some point have finished. Tasks are generated in the context of a team of threads, while the **parallel** construct creates such team. A task is created when the code reaches the *task construct*.

OmpSs extends the task mechanism of the current OpenMP implementation to allow the specification of dependencies between tasks and to map the execution of certain tasks to a type of hardware accelerator (a device). OmpSs considers each accelerator (e.g., a MIC, a GPU, a FPGA) as a *single* execution unit, which can efficiently execute specialized pieces of code. The runtime implementation of the model isolates the user from all the complexities related to task scheduling and offloading. The OmpSs extensions are orthogonal to other possible extensions to generate efficient input and output dependencies to be copied to/from the device code by a compiler (e.g., vectorization width, number of threads running on accelerators and code transformations).

In this paper, we present the OmpSs@Zynq ecosystem that allows to easily and efficiently exploit the capabilities of the Zynq family of devices. With it, programmers can parallelize and accelerate their applications using all the resources of the Zynq device in just **"one-click"** (two OmpSs pragmas). In addition, programmers can automatically generate an executable with instrumentation so that they can trace and analyze the parallel and heterogeneous execution. That helps to understand possible bottlenecks in the communication with the accelerator, task dependency problems, etc.

Overall, our main contributions of this work are:

- We propose a new and unique programming ecosystem framework to easily program a Zynq All-Programmable SoC, a heterogeneous and parallel power efficient system consisting of a SMP with two ARM Cortex-9 and a FPGA fabric. The framework is able to automatically generate the bitstream (accelerated part of the application) from C using Vivado HLS extensions. This bitstream will contain the hardware accelerators that the host binary will use.

- We propose an easy way of programming the Zynq All-Programmable SoC platform using C with OmpSs directives (two pragmas). With only two pragmas, the programmers can run their applications on the Zynq SoC[1] using one or more SMPs, one or more hardware accelerators or ANY combination of them. Indeed, our framework guarantees portability since the same C code annotated with OmpSs directives can be compiled and run on other SMP platforms.

- We propose a runtime system with a fast task dependency management to support very fine-grained task heterogeneous executions on the Zynq All-Programmable SoC.

- Our framework can transparently instrument the OmpSs binaries in order to generate execution traces to perform analysis of the applications. The instrumentation should be activated by the programmer at compile time. That instrumentation allows the analysis of the different levels of the runtime system, the FPGA management libraries, and the task level heterogeneous execution: number of times executed in each device, the amount of time spend in each task execution, etc.

- We present performance results of our framework using state-of-the-art Xilinx Tools to program the Zynq All-Programmable SoC. For simplicity, we present results for well-known numerical codes, although we can use our framework ecosystem for heterogeneous execution on the Zynq for any C code that is supported by Vivado HLS.

The rest of paper is organized as follows. In Section 2 the related work is presented. Section 3 describes the OmpSs programming model directives that helps to exploit the heterogeneous parallel execution. In Section 4, we explain the operational flow of our framework. Section 6 show the results for four applications that has been accelerated: 32x32 Matrix Multiply, 64x64 Matrix Multiply, Cholesky and Covariance. Finally, we conclude in Section 7.

2. RELATED WORK

OpenMP [16] grew out of the need to standardize the explosion of parallel programming languages and tools of the 90s. It was initially structured around parallel loops and

---

[1]We can include Vivado HLS pragmas in the code for optimizing the automatic bitstream generation

was meant to handle dense numerical applications. The simplicity of its original interface, the use of a shared-memory model, and the fact that the parallelism of a program is expressed with annotations loosely-coupled to the code, all have helped OpenMP become well-accepted. While additions to OpenMP 3.0 [3] accommodate for task parallelism, making it more suitable for irregular codes, OpenMP was not ready for the challenges posed by the new generation of multi-core heterogeneous architectures until the OpenMP 4.0 specification appeared last July 2013.

In the origins of this challenge, Cell B.E. [18] was likely one the most challenging heterogeneous architectures to program. IBM developed an OpenMP prototype compiler that generates parallel programs under the master-slave programming model. Data transfers between master (PPE) and slaves (SPEs) were transparently introduced employing a software cache, although the compiler tried to optimize for very regular access patterns. Other programming solutions for the Cell B.E. like Sequoia, MPI microtasks, and a Cell B.E. specific earlier version of OmpSs (CellSs) were more promising than the original approach in that they target task parallelism, employing higher-level information to perform more complete optimizations.

GPUs have traditionally been programmed using specific-domain graphics libraries such as OpenGL or DirectX. Nvidia was one of the pioneering graphics companies to realize the potential of general-purpose graphics processors, and the benefits which could be gained by offering a general-purpose application programming interface (API). The result was CUDA [15], a "unified" architecture design featuring a programmable graphics pipeline, and an API to develop parallel programs that exploit data-parallelism on this architecture. Unfortunately, in order to develop efficient codes, CUDA programmers (as well as those of Brook+ [7], the data-parallel language for AMD/ATI GPUs) still need to be aware of the underlying architecture. A promising approach that may solve this problem consists in automatically transforming existing OpenMP code into CUDA. Some recent works have also studied frameworks that enable efficient performance porting from existing CUDA programs to programs that exploit the Zynq All-programmable SoC [17]. In our approach, that can be done from any C/C++ code with just two pragmas.

Hardware description languages (e.g., Verilog or VHDL) are employed to develop FPGA-accelerated computational kernels. In order to solve the programmability problem for these devices, extensions to the C language have appeared. Usually, there are two strategies to compile these extensions. In the first strategy, the section of code to be offloaded to the FPGA is translated from C to VHDL. The second strategy is to map a soft processor (e.g. Xilinx Microblaze) into the FPGA, and translate the source code to be executed to the code that this soft processor understands. In both cases, a host/device communication library, such as the RASClib for the SGI RASC architecture, is necessary to offload the execution to one of the FPGAs available, including data movement. Other tools try to reduce the FPGA programmability problem by offering the possibility of generating HDL code from C or C-like languages like ROCCC[21, 14] or generating systems with an embedded soft processor connected to the generated hardware accelerators like LegUp[8] and C2H tool[1]. In this sense, the present work is similar to those since it includes support to automatically generate the hardware accelerators (relying on the Vivado HLS and Xilinx tools for the HDL and bitstream generation). However, with the new SMP/FPGA SoCs, new strategies are required in order to exploit those current heterogeneous *and* parallel platforms. Our ecosystem also covers runtime support for parallel execution of heterogeneous tasks on those SoCs.

PGI [19] and HMPP [10] programming models are two other approaches quite related to OmpSs. PGI uses compiler technology to offload the execution of loops to the accelerators. HMPP also annotates functions as tasks to be offloaded to the accelerators. We think that OmpSs has higher potential in that it shifts part of the intelligence that HMPP and PGI delegate in the compiler to the OmpSs runtime system. Although these alternatives do support a fair amount of asynchronous computations expressed as futures or continuations, the level of lookahead they support is limited in practice. In these approaches, synchronization requests (waiting for a given future or selecting among some list of them when the result is needed) have to be explicitly inserted in the main control flow of the program. Besides the additional complexity of the code, this approach implies that certain scheduling decisions are made statically and hardwired in the application code. The approach followed in OmpSs exploits much higher levels of lookahead (tens of thousands of tasks) without requiring the programmer to schedule the synchronization operations explicitly and giving much higher flexibility to the runtime to respond to the foreseeable variability of application characteristics and resource availability.

A recent attempt to unify the programming models for general-purpose multi-core architectures and the different types of hardware accelerators (Cell B.E., GPUs, FPGAs, DSPs, etc.) is OpenCL [13]. The participation of silicon vendors (e.g., Intel, IBM, NVIDIA, and AMD) in the definition of this open standard ensures portability, low-level access to the hardware, and supposedly high performance. We believe, however, that OpenCL still exposes much of the low-level details (i.e. explicit platform and context management, kernel special intrinsic functions, explicit program, kernel and data transfer management, etc.), making it cumbersome to use by non-experts.

Finding the appropriate interoperability between the OmpSs extensions to OpenMP and OpenCL can be a viable solution. Thus, OmpSs can target the exploitation of task-parallelism by mapping/scheduling the execution of tasks to the hardware accelerators in the system, and can automatically use OpenCL to express, in a portable way, the data-level parallelism to be exploited in the applications, and then, obtain better performance.

3. OMPSS PROGRAMMING MODEL

OpenMP has been traditionally employed to exploit loop-based parallelism present in most regular scientific and engineering applications on shared-memory multiprocessors. OpenMP 3.0 was extended with *tasks*, or deferrable units of work, to accommodate irregular applications as well. In particular, with current available OpenMP implementations the programmer can specify tasks, and later ensure that all the tasks defined up to some point have finished. Tasks are generated in the context of a team of threads, while the **parallel** construct creates such team. A task is created when the code reaches the *task construct*, defined as follows:

```
#pragma omp task [clause-list]
    structured-block
```

Recently (July 2013) the OpenMP 4.0 specification was released and new extensions to specify task dependencies and heterogeneous computing have been included, significantly influenced by OmpSs programming model. Therefore, under the point of view of task dependency management and heterogeneous execution, and by the time of accepting this paper, OmpSs can be considered the current available version of the OpenMP 4.0.

The OmpSs programming model allows the specification of dependencies between tasks and to map the execution of certain tasks to a specific type of hardware accelerator (a device). OmpSs considers each accelerator as a *single* execution unit, which can efficiently execute specialized pieces of code. The runtime implementation of the model isolates the user from all the complexities related to task scheduling and offloading. The OmpSs extensions are orthogonal to other possible extensions to generate efficient code by a compiler (e.g., vectorization width, number of threads running on accelerators and code transformations).

OmpSs can specify that a function should be executed as a task. To allow this, the OpenMP **task** construct has been extended to annotate functions:

```
#pragma omp task [clause-list]
    {function-declaration| function-definition|
     structured-block}
```

Whenever the program calls a function annotated in this way, the runtime will create an explicit task.

This construct can have clauses **in**, **out** and **inout**. This information is used to derive dependencies among tasks at runtime, and schedule/fire a task. Tasks are fired when their inputs are ready and their outputs can be generated. The syntax of these clauses is:

- **in(data-reference-list)**
- **out(data-reference-list)**
- **inout(data-reference-list)**

Dependencies are expressed by means of *data-reference-lists*, which are a superset of a *variable-list*. A *data-reference* in such a list can contain a variable identifier, but also references to subobjects. References to subobjects include array element references (e.g., **a[4]**), array sections (**a[3:6]**), field references (**a.b**), and elaborated shaping expressions (**[10][20] p**).

Figure 1 illustrates the use of the extended **task** construct to parallelize a sequential code that computes the matrix multiplication $OUT = A \cdot B$. The annotations are placed on the original sequential version of the code, with no transformations applied to identify the specification of the inherent parallelism available. The runtime creates the data dependency graph at runtime as the tasks, with their data dependency information, are created, and uses it transparently to the user/programmer, to extract task parallelism while satisfying the dependencies among tasks. In Figure 1, due to the pragma in line 2, the three matrix multiply calls will be created as tasks and the runtime will create the data dependency graph. Therefore, the first two **matrix_multiply** instances will be executed in parallel since there are not dependencies between them, and the third call will have to wait until the first task finishes. Finally, the program waits for the all tasks to finish with the directive **taskwait**.

To target heterogeneous systems composed of general-purpose processors and hardware accelerators, OmpSs construct **target device** may precede an existing **task** pragma

```
1  #pragma omp target device(fpga, smp) copy_deps
2  #pragma omp task in(a[0:64*64-1], b[0:64*64-1]) \
3                            out(c[0:64*64-1])
4  void matrix_multiply(float a[64][64],
5                       float b[64][64],
6                       float out[64][64]) {
7      for (int ia = 0; ia < 64; ++ia)
8          for (int ib = 0; ib < 64; ++ib) {
9              float sum = 0;
10             for (int id = 0; id < 64; ++id)
11                 sum += a[ia][id] * b[id][ib];
12             out[ia][ib] = sum;
13         }
14 }
15 ...
16 int main( void ){
17 ...
18  matrix_multiply(A,B,C1);
19  matrix_multiply(A,B,C2);
20  matrix_multiply(C1,B,D);
21 ...
22  #pragma omp taskwait
23 }
```

Figure 1: Matrix multiplication annotated with OmpSs directives.

to OpenMP, as can be seen in Figure 1, line 1. The **target** construct specifies that the execution of the task could be off-loaded to any of the (types of) devices specified in **device-name-list** (and as such its code must be handled by the proper compiler backend).

```
#pragma omp target device(device-name-list) \
                [clause-list]
```

If the task is not preceded by a **target** directive, then the default **device-name**, which is **smp** and corresponds to a homogeneous shared-memory multicore architecture, is used. In Figure 1 we are specifying that **matrix_multiply** can be executed in two different devices: **fpga** and **smp**.

Three additional clauses can be used with the **device** pragma:

- copy_in(data-reference-list)
- copy_out(data-reference-list)
- copy_deps

Those three clauses, which are ignored for the **smp** device, specify data movement for **shared** variables used inside the task. The **copy_in** clause specifies those variables that must be moved from host memory to device memory. The **copy_out** clause specifies those variables that need to be moved back from device memory to host memory. The **copy_deps** clause makes input and output dependencies to be copied to/from the device.

For all the devices, the runtime takes care of moving the needed data before and after the execution of the task.

4. OMPSS@ZYNQ ECOSYSTEM

The OmpSs@Zynq Ecosystem consists of infrastructure for compilation, runtime execution and instrumentation, in addition to an easy-to-use command line. The compilation infrastructure will help to (1) generate ARM binary code from OmpSs code, that can run in the ARM-based SMP of the Zynq All-Programmable SoC, (2) extract the kernel of the part of the application to be accelerated into the FPGA and (3) automatically generate a bitstream that includes the IP cores of the accelerator/s, the DMA engine IP/s, and the necessary interconnection. The runtime infrastructure

should allow heterogeneous tasking on any combination of SMPs and accelerators, depending on the availability of the resources and the target devices specified. An instrumentation and analysis infrastructure is also part of our ecosystem since we want to understand and detect possible bottlenecks of the heterogeneous execution, allowing the programmer to easily generate traces and visualize them. Finally, a command line to compile and execute a code that should be accelerated is key to motivate the Zynq All-Programmable SoC usage.

4.1 Compilation Infrastructure

Figure 2 shows the high level compilation flow using our OmpSs@Zynq ecosystem. The OmpSs code is passed through the source-to-source compiler Mercurium [6], that includes a specialized **fpga** compilation phase to process annotated **fpga** tasks. For each of those tasks, it generates two C codes. One of them is a **Vivado HLS**[2] annotated code for the bitstream generation branch ("accelerator codes" box in Figure 2). The other is an intermediate host source code with OmpSs runtime (Nanos++) calls that is generated for the software generation branch ("Host C code + Nanos++ runtime call" box in Figure 2). Both the hardware and the software generation branches are transparent to the programmer.

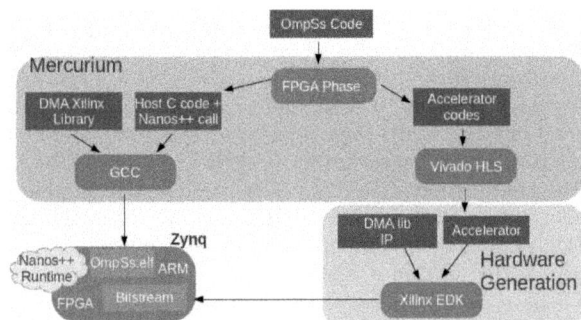

Figure 2: OmpSs@Zynq Ecosystem Compilation Flow

For the bitstream generation branch, the C/C++ code generated by the **fpga** phase should include the necessary code for **scatter/gather** operations to receive/send data through the DMA engine. Input data parameters sent to the task are automatically gathered by the DMA engine system as one single input data port to the IP accelerator core, in addition to some control signals for data management. Therefore, the C/C++ code generated in this branch should scatter those parameters before calling the original task kernel C code; as a wrapper. The wrapper function only has one input parameter and one output parameter. Figure 3 shows the wrapper code generated by the **fpga** phase for the matrix multiply of Figure 1. the input parameter is scattered in two parameters, and the output parameter is only copied to the output stream of the wrapper. Note that there is an **HLS pipeline II=1** pragma (II stands for Initiation Interval) in each inner loop of the wrapper code. That helps to increase the throughput of the copies (one data per cycle). The code of the **matrix_multiply** is not changed.

The wrapper will become the top module of the hardware design, which communicates to the memory through an AXI DMA engine as shown in Figure 4. In particular, the first

---
[2]Source to HDL Xilinx tool

```
1  void mmult_wrapper (hls::stream<float> &in, \
2                      hls::stream<float> &out) {
3  #pragma HLS interface ap_ctrl_none port=return
4  #pragma HLS resource variable=in  core=AXI4Stream
5  #pragma HLS resource variable=out core=AXI4Stream
6
7    //Start Scatter Code
8    float a[Dim][Dim];
9    for (int i = 0; i < Dim; i++)
10     for (int j = 0; j < Dim; j++)
11   #pragma HLS pipeline II=1
12       a[i][j] = in.read();
13
14   float a[Dim][Dim];
15   for (int i = 0; i < Dim; i++)
16     for (int j = 0; j < Dim; j++)
17   #pragma HLS pipeline II=1
18       b[i][j] = in.read();
19   //End Scatter Code
20
21   float c[Dim][Dim];
22   matrix_multiply(a,b,c);
23
24   for (int i = 0; i < Dim; i++)
25     for (int j = 0; j < Dim; j++)
26   #pragma HLS pipeline II=1
27       out.write(c[i][j]);
28 }
```

Figure 3: Wrapper code for interconnection purposes, automatically generated by the framework.

three HLS pragmas in Figure 3 indicate how the top module will be connected to the AXI interconnection that will connect the AXI DMA engine and the top module.

Once the wrapper and the original codes are passed through the Vivado HLS tool, the EDK Xilinx tool is used in order to create the complete integrated system consisting of the hardware accelerators generated by Vivado HLS and the interconnection to the Processing System of Zynq. In the current implementation, each accelerator is connected to an AXI DMA engine (provided as a standard Xilinx IP core) as it is shown in Figure 4. The generated bitstream can be easily loaded into the programmable logic fabric of the Zynq, redirecting it to the linux device file representing the FPGA.

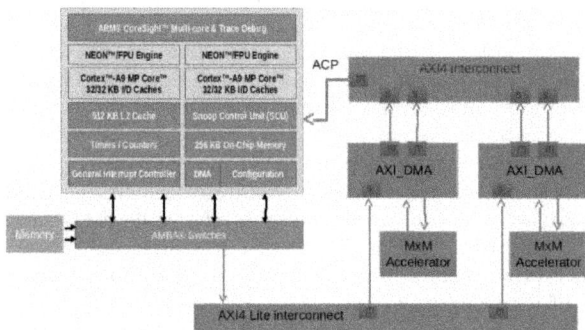

Figure 4: System connection overview of the accelerators

For the software part, an intermediate C code is generated with the necessary OmpSs runtime calls. Nanos++ is the OmpSs runtime and provides the support for task management, data dependency management, data coherence, task scheduling, etc. for different hardware devices (smp, gpu, fpga, etc.).

4.2 Runtime Infrastructure

The Nanos++ abstraction layers are shown in Figure 5. In this work we have added the necessary FPGA support to deal with all the features of the Zynq All-Programmable SoC and the Xlinx DMA library characteristics. Therefore, in addition to the FPGA-Host communication support, we have included new features to the Nanos++ runtime system. First, the Nanos++ task scheduling mechanism has been modified for the fpga device to allow the submission of several tasks to the FPGA if no dependencies exists among them, exploiting the double buffering and pipeline features of the accelerators running in the FPGA. That feature necessarily means that the thread executing those fpga tasks cannot stall waiting for the output of each task since it has to keep sending fpga tasks to the FPGA. Then, waiting for the output data of a task is postponed until another task needs that data, or until a certain limit of resource usage is reached. That delay on waiting the output data of tasks submitted to the FPGA helps to overlap the communication time between the FPGA and the host, and the computation time in the host.

Second, in this version, the number of Nanos++ helper threads in charge of the fpga device can be limited to a certain number of threads to better exploit the SMP resources of the Zynq All-programmable SoC. Depending on the number of cores, NUMA nodes, devices, etc. different configurations of the threads assigned to the different devices may influence the final performance of the applications. By default, Nanos++ runtime would create as many threads as the NX_THREADS environment variable indicates, and one per device.

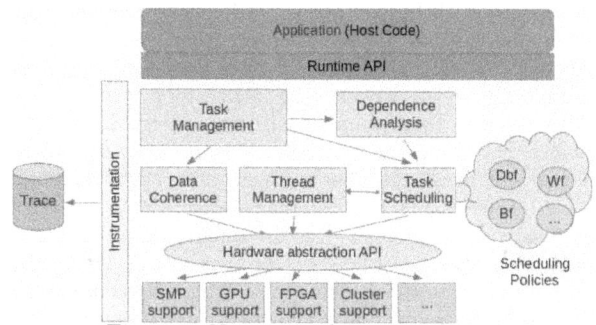

Figure 5: Nanos++ abstraction layers

4.3 Instrumentation Infrastructure

Nanos++ includes trace instrumentation support (w/ Extrae library [4]) along the different abstraction layers. We have included the necessary support for the fpga device. With this support, the programmer can have a detailed idea of the task execution and Zynq resource usage, as the programmer will have in other devices. Indeed, we have added instrumentation in order to know when a task is scheduled to the fpga device, which are the accelerators in use at any time and the DMA transfers between the FPGA and the HOST (inputs and outputs). The generated traces can be visualized with the Paraver tool [5]. Note that the extrae library also allows to instrument the user code so that the programmer can have information of the running code.

4.4 Command line usage

The compilation command line is:

```
$ fpgacc -omps -o main.elf main.c
```

and if instrumentation required:

```
$ fpgacc -omps -instrument -o main.elf main.c
```

The output of this compilation is an ARM elf that can be run in the Zynq All-Programmable SoC and, with the `fpga` wrapper HLS code, an FPGA bitstream will be automatically generated. The bitstream can be generated with one or two accelerators for the same task to exploit the implicit task parallelism in the program. Once we have the ARM elf binary and the bitstream, the program can be easily executed using:

```
$ ./main.elf
```

for the non instrumented execution, and:

```
$ NX_ARGS="-instrumentation=extrae" ./main.elf
```

for the instrumented one. Indeed, to specify the number of threads decicated to execute tasks in the FPGA device the programmer can use the `NX_FPGA` environment variable.

5. EXPERIMENTAL SETUP

Results in Section 6 have been obtained on a Zynq All-Programmable SoC 702 board, connected to a PC through ethernet network and managed using a remote terminal. Timing of the applications has been obtained by instrumenting with `gettimeofday` the part of the code that calls several times the kernel code. Results show the average elapsed execution time of 10 application executions on the Zynq 702 board under linux.

The current OmpSs@Zynq ecosystem has been developed with Mercurium 1.99.0, Nanos++ 0.7a, and instrumentation support with Extrae Library 2.3.4. The Paraver 4.3.5. version was used to analyze the execution traces. For the hardware compilation branch we have used the Xilinx ISE Design 14.6 and the Vivado HLS 2013.2 tools.

All codes have been compiled with the `arm-xilinx-linux-gnueabi-g++` (Sourcery CodeBench Lite 2011.09-50) 4.6.1 and `arm-xilinx-linux-gnueabi-gcc` (Sourcery CodeBench Lite 2011.09-50) 4.6.1 compilers, with "-O3" optimization flag. No hand made vectorization neither optimization has been done on the code running on the ARMs. We cross-compile the applications on a 64-bit linux processor with enough memory and CPU resources to generate the bitstreams.

We show results for 4 applications of different `fpga` task granularities: 32x32 single-precision floating point Matrix multiply (very fine-grained tasks), 64x64 single-precision floating point Matrix Multiply, 64x64 double-precision complex Cholesky decomposition and 32-bit integer complex Covariance (*big* tasks). All real data generated by the Vivado HLS are synthesized with IEEE-754 standard compliance. We have implemented three different versions of each code: sequential code, pthread code and OmpSs code. OmpSs versions of the codes consider the full Matrix Multiply, the full Cholesky, and the full Covariance as tasks. For each application, we have run 128 independent instances of a task.

In order to understand the task execution time in the hardware accelerators, we analyze each of the generated accelerators by using the Vivado HLS reports and simulator.

Application	Seq - DMA version	pthread version	OmpSs version
Cholesky	71	26	3
Covariance	94	29	3
64x64	95	39	3
32x32	95	39	3

Table 1: Total number of additional lines of code for the sequential code using the hardware accelerators through the DMA lib (Seq-DMA), the pthread version using the SMP, and the OmpSs version, for the four benchmarks.

6. RESULTS

6.1 Programmability Analysis

First, we want to remark the programmability facilities of our proposal. With this objective, we show in Table 1 the total number of additional lines of code for each of the different versions of the applications: a pthread version *only* running tasks in one or two ARMs, a sequential version using one or two hardware accelerators via direct library calls to the Xilinx DMA library (`Seq-DMA`), and the OmpSs version.

The non-Ompss versions require more additional lines than the OmpSs version, specially the sequential versions using the hardware accelerators. Sequential versions use hardware accelerators via Xilinx DMA lib calls to manage all the data DMA transfers from/to memory and the wait synchronizations of all those DMA transfers. In the case of the `pthread` versions, those should manage the creation, execution and joining of the threads, but there are not Xilinx DMA library calls. On the other hand, in the case of the OmpSs version, the thread management is intrinsic to Nanos++ runtime and all the intrinsics of the Xilinx DMA lib management are hidden to the programmer in the device dependent layer of Nanos++. Therefore, the programmer can save time and programming errors, and then, testing and debugging time. Indeed, the current compilation and runtime infrastructure of the OmpSs programming model allows to exploit the heterogeneous characteristics of the Zynq All-Programmable SoC with the only effort of two directive lines. Note however that Table 1 indicates that the OmpSs version needs an additional third line. This line is a `taskwait` before the program ends. For the non-OmpSs versions, no code can be developed to perform heterogeneous executions in a reasonable amount of time, as we would have to develop a complete task scheduler.

Finally, our compilation infrastructure can easily extract the kernel to be accelerated in hardware, generating a bitstream with up to two instances of the same accelerator. That bitstream generation feature saves time and effort to understand all the Xilinx ISE Design tools and other intrinsics of hardware generation.

6.2 Execution Analysis

Figure 6 shows the average execution time of the four applications: 32x32 Matrix Multiply, 64x64 Matrix Multiply, Cholesky and Covariance. They have been sorted by their average execution time. For each application, we have run 9 different experiments. From the leftmost to the rightmost bar: two 1 SMP bars that are a pthread version and an OmpSs version using 1 ARM core, two 2 SMP bars that are a pthread version and an OmpSs version using 2 ARM cores, two 1 ACC bars that are a sequential version and an

OmpSs version using 1 hardware accelerator, two 2 ACC bars that are a sequential version and an OmpSs version using 2 hardware accelerators, and the heterogeneous bar, which is an OmpSs version that runs tasks on both the SMP and the two hardware accelerators. Note that the OmpSs code is the same for any of the bar versions, independent of the devices the tasks should be run on. For non-OmpSs codes, no results are shown for the heteronegeous execution because it does not make sense to implement a pthread task scheduler from scratch as we explained above.

We are not showing results for 2 ARM cores and 2 hardware accelerators. That is due to the fact that the performance of this combination is worse than the 1 ARM core and 2 hardware accelerators alternative, and it needs more resources. We would need at least three active helper threads running in the SMP with only two ARM cores, significantly increasing the number of context switches.

In general, non-OmpSs and OmpSs versions scale in the same way and have similar results for each of the experiments.

For the SMP experiments (only ARM cores), Figure 6 shows that Ompss versions present a small overhead compared to the pthread versions, which is insignificant for coarse-grained tasks.

For the ACC experiments (only hardware accelerator cores), although OmpSs versions include some overhead that the sequential version does not have, the performance of the OmpSs version, *using only one helper thread to run tasks on the hardware accelerators*, is similar to the sequential version. That is due to the fact that Nanos++ OmpSs runtime has been significantly specialized to efficiently deal with different task granularities and characteristics.

Results show that the ACC and heterogeneous experiments are much faster than the pure SMP experiments. Figure 7 shows the speedups of the OmpSs versions using 1 hardware accelerator (1 ACC in the Figure), 2 hardware accelerators (2 ACC in the Figure) and heterogeneous execution compared to the OmpSs version running on 1 ARM core (1 SMP in the Figure). For 1 and 2 hardware accelerators (ACC experiments), results show 6.6x and 13.5x speedup, in average, respectively. On the other hand, the heterogeneous execution speedup result is very similar to that of the 2 ACC. That is due to the fact that hardware accelerators are completely exploited by the OmpSs code and there are not more chances of improvement running tasks on the ARM cores, since SMP tasks are much slower. Heterogeneous execution will benefit, for instance, on applications with tasks where some of them are only FPGA tasks and other are SMP/FPGA tasks. In this case, when the hardware accelerators are busy, the SMP can be used in order to advance in the execution of the application. Thus, Table 2 shows the distribution of tasks among the different devices in the heterogeneous version: 1 SMP and two hardware accelerators: 1 or 2, for each application. In general, we can see that the number of tasks executed in the SMP is much smaller than the number of tasks executed in the accelerators. In the case of the 32x32 Matrix Multiply benchmark the number of tasks executed in the SMP increases but is less than 1/3 of the tasks executed in the accelerators.

Trace Execution Analysis

Our OmpSs@Zynq ecosystem includes trace execution support, allowing a detailed analysis of the heterogeneous par-

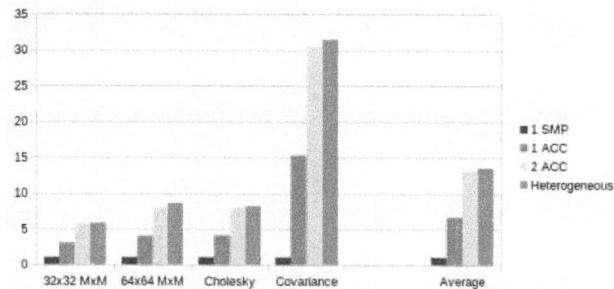

Figure 7: Speedup of the 1ACC, 2ACC and heterogeneous OmpSs versions compared to the 1 SMP OmpSs version.

Heterogeneous Execution	# SMP tasks	# Acc 1 tasks	Acc 2 tasks	Real Time
Covariance	4	62	62	2.3582s
Cholesky	7	61	60	0.0471s
64x64 MxM	10	59	59	0.0416s
32x32 MxM	31	49	48	0.0087s

Table 2: Number of task executions in each device, SMP or accelerators, during the heterogeneous execution of Covariance, Cholesky, 64x64 Matrix multiply and 32x32 Matrix multiply

allel execution of the tasks on the Zynq system. That instrumentation can help to detect bottlenecks on: (1) the parallelization strategy, (2) the OmpSs runtime and (3) the Xilinx DMA library. The generated traces can be visualized by the Paraver tool. For instance, Figure 8 shows the details of previous executions with a Paraver visualization of the execution traces for the OmpSs version of the applications when using heterogeneous resources. From top to bottom, results are for 32x32 MxM, 64x64 MxM, Cholesky and Covariance. Each execution trace visualization has two time horizontal bars (one per each thread in the application) with different colors that, in general, can identify user defined and OmpSs runtime instrumented code, and application or thread states. The one on the top is for the master thread, that is in charge of the task management, and also executes tasks in the SMP. The one on the bottom is for the helper thread that takes care of the tasks executed on the accelerators. On the left of the Figure 8, the Paraver `thread state` view of Nanos++ threads is shown. On the right, we have the `In task` view for the same execution. That view represents when a task is executed in the SMP (top bar) or start executing in the accelerators (bottom bar) in dark blue. We can see that there is an heterogeneous execution pattern when executing independent tasks. For the master thread, there is a task creation phase (pink color) and then, it starts executing tasks (yellow in the trace). On the other hand, the helper thread states show that the helper thread is scheduling tasks to the accelerators from the very beginning. We can see that task executions in the accelerators and in the SMP are overlapped during all of the execution trace but the last SMP task execution. Therefore, only the task granularity will determine the load balance between both devices. Note that the three phases correspond to the execution of several independent tasks. Otherwise, the creation

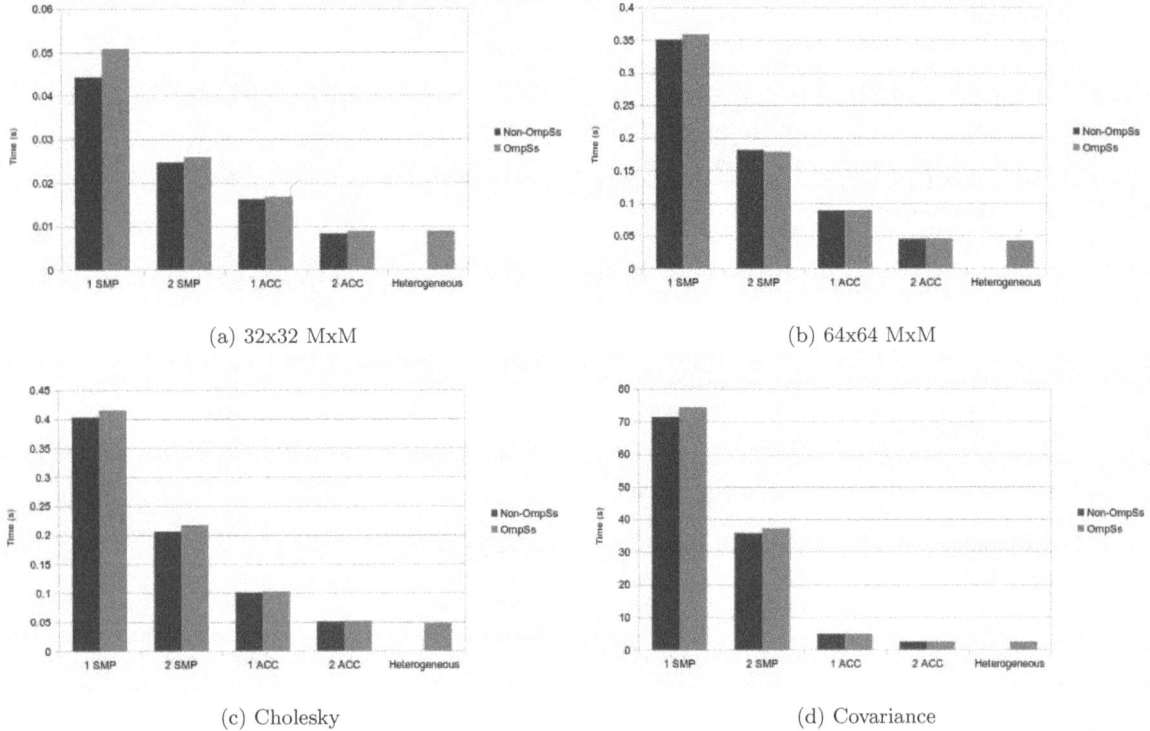

(a) 32x32 MxM

(b) 64x64 MxM

(c) Cholesky

(d) Covariance

Figure 6: Execution time for 128 independent task executions where a task is a 32x32 MxM, a 64x64 MxM, a Cholesky and a Covariance.

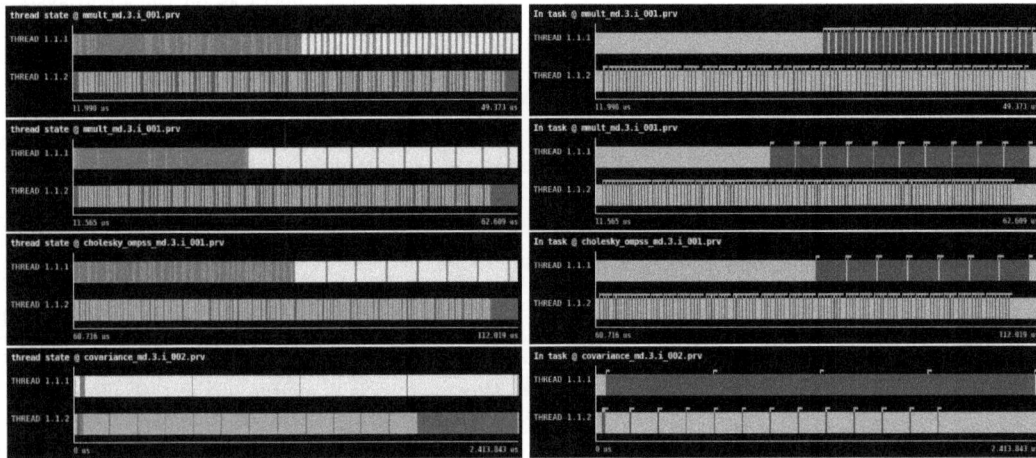

Figure 8: Heterogeneous execution pattern: 1 SMP + 2 hardware accelerators. From top to bottom: 32x32 Matrix Multiply, 64x64 Matrix Multiply, Cholesky and Covariance. Thread state view on the left and task execution view on the right.

of tasks may occur along all the master thread execution, depending on the task data dependencies.

Next, we will analyze in detail the execution of the Cholesky application. With Paraver, we can synchronize different views so that they show the same period of time, with the same size of the window, so that the programmer can easily analyze them. Figure 9 shows the execution trace of the Cholesky application using four different views, from top to bottom: thread state of Nanos++ threads, FPGA DMA management, In task execution and accelerator number. As mentioned above, there are three different phases on the heterogeneous execution of this OmpSs application. Figures 10-12 zoom in those three phases.

Figure 10 shows the phase where the master thread is creating all tasks. Meanwhile master thread is creating tasks (up to a certain Nanos++ runtime internal limit) it does not execute any task. On the other hand, the helper thread can start running tasks (see Figure 9), and performing DMA submissions. In Figure 10, bottom bar, the helper thread submits one in (dark red vertical lines) and two out (light green vertical lines) parameters for each task execution. In order to guarantee that those submissions have finished, the helper thread, or any other thread that requires those submissions to finish, has to perform a DMA wait operation using the corresponding handler. Therefore, helper thread and master thread can continue until there is a dependency

144

Figure 9: Execution traces for 128 independent Cholesky task executions. From top to bottom: thread state view, DMA call view, task execution view and accelerator running view.

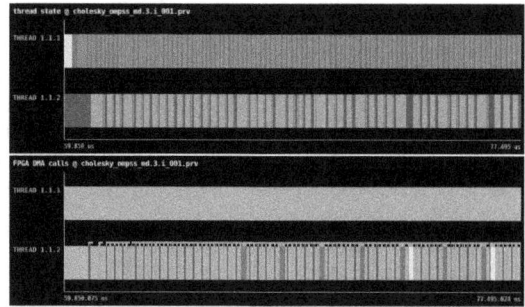

Figure 10: Creation phase of the execution trace for 128 independent Cholesky task executions. Thread state view on the top. FPGA DMA call view on the bottom.

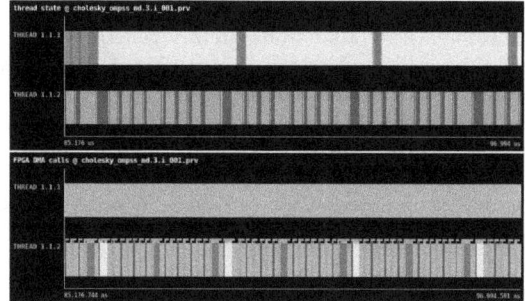

Figure 11: Intermediate phase of the execution trace for 128 independent Cholesky task executions. Thread state view on the top. FPGA DMA call view on the bottom.

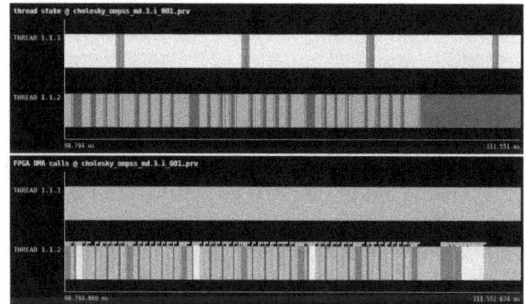

Figure 12: Last phase of the execution trace for 128 independent Cholesky task executions. Thread state view on the top. FPGA DMA call view on the bottom.

or the limit of the resources of the system has been reached. In this case, they have to do the corresponding DMA wait. In the figure, the helper thread starts doing DMA waits of the in parameters (wide and vertical light red lines in the figure) and out parameters (yellow lines), only once the resource limit has been reached.

Once the master thread finishes creating tasks, it starts running tasks. Figure 11 shows this moment in the execution trace. Each task execution in the master thread is shown in yellow. Between two task executions there are different states in which the master thread looks if there are more tasks to be created or run. In the case of the helper thread, there is a pattern of task scheduling. The helper thread is performing runtime operations in order to submit the in and out parameters, shown in dark red and light green respectively in the FPGA DMA views. We can also observe that every couple of submissions of in and out parameters, a DMA wait operation is performed to free resources.

Finally, Figure 12 shows the moment when both master thread and helper thread, finish executing tasks. In the case of the helper thread it has to DMA wait for all the pending DMA transfers, guaranteeing that all tasks have ended at this point. This is shown in the execution trace with two very wide red and yellow areas, guaranteeing that all tasks have ended at this point.

6.3 Hardware Accelerators

Our framework is able to generate the hardware accelerator of any C code that Vivado HLS supports. The performance of the generated hardware accelerator depends on the application itself, how the C code has been annotated with Vivado HLS directives and the requested synthesis clock fre-

quency. In our case we have not automatically annotated the original C code with Vivado HLS directives, only using the already existing programmer annotations. In addition, in the case of our four applications, the hardware accelerators of Covariance and Cholesky are running at 166MHz, meanwhile both versions of Matrix Multiply are running at 41MHz. We wanted to evaluate different frequencies in order to show how our system deals with different scenarios.

		Benchmark Elapsed Execution Time (s)			
		Covariance	Cholesky	64x64 MxM	32x32 MxM
#	1	4.8675	0.1015	0.0893	0.0167
Acc	2	2.4342	0.0513	0.0450	0.0088

Table 3: Elapsed execution time for 128 executions of the kernel w/ one or two accelerators.

Table 3 shows, for each application, the execution time used by each application to run 128 independent executions of the kernel application when using one or two accelerators of the same kernel. Results are similar to those obtained for the RTL simulation results, showing that the overhead introduced by the OmpSs runtime and programming model is not significant for any of the benchmarks. That means that we are perfectly exploiting the Zynq All-Programmable FPGA resources with a simple and easy programming model, independently of the granularity of the tasks.

7. CONCLUSIONS

In this paper we have shown that OmpSs provides an easy way for the programmer to efficiently exploit all the resources of the Zynq All-Programmable SoC in just one click: only adding two OmpSs pragmas to the source code.

Our OmpSs@Zynq ecosystem proposal allows the programmer to automatically and transparently generate the ARM elf executable and the bitstream containing the accelerators for the `fpga` tasks specified in the source code.

Results show that the OmpSs code version is, for a given number of resources, as fast as the hand coded pthread and sequential equivalent versions, solving the heterogeneity execution and programmability challenges of using hardware accelerators and/or generating bitstreams.

Acknowledgment

We thank the anonymous referees for their valuable feedback and suggestions. This work is supported by the Ministry of Science and Technology of Spain and the European Union (FEDER funds) under contract TIN2012-34557, by the Generalitat de Catalunya (contract 2009-SGR-980) and HiPEAC3 Network of Excellence (FP7/ICT 287759).

8. REFERENCES

[1] Altera, Corp. *Nios II C2H Compiler User Guide*, 2009.

[2] E. Ayguade and et. al. A proposal to extend the openmp tasking model for heterogeneous architectures. In *Proceedings of the 5th International Workshop on OpenMP: Evolving OpenMP in an Age of Extreme Parallelism*, IWOMP '09, pages 154–167. Springer-Verlag, 2009.

[3] E. Ayguadé and et. al. The Design of OpenMP Tasks. *IEEE Trans. Parallel Distrib. Syst.*, 20(3):404–418, 2009.

[4] Barcelona Supercomputing Center. *Extrae Instrumentation Library*, Sept. 2013. http://www.bsc.es/computer-sciences/extrae.

[5] Barcelona Supercomputing Center. *Paraver Visualization Tool*, Sept. 2013. http://www.bsc.es/computer-sciences/performance-tools/paraver.

[6] Barcelona Supercomputing Center. *Programming Models @ BSC*, Sept. 2013. http://pm.bsc.es/mcxx.

[7] I. Buck, T. Foley, D. Horn, J. Sugerman, K. Fatahalian, M. Houston, and P. Hanrahan. Brook for GPUs: stream computing on graphics hardware. In *SIGGRAPH '04: ACM SIGGRAPH 2004 Papers*, pages 777–786, New York, NY, USA, 2004. ACM Press.

[8] A. Canis, J. Choi, M. Aldham, V. Zhang, A. Kammoona, J. H. Anderson, S. Brown, and T. Czajkowski. Legup: High-level synthesis for fpga-based processor/accelerator systems. In *Proceedings of the 19th ACM/SIGDA International Symposium on Field Programmable Gate Arrays*, FPGA '11, pages 33–36, New York, NY, USA, 2011. ACM.

[9] R. H. Dennard, F. H. Gaensslen, H. Yu, V. L. Rideout, E. Bassous, and A. R. LeBlanc. Design of ion-implanted MOSFET's with very small physical dimensions. *IEEE Journal of Solid-State Circuits*, 9:256–268, Oct. 1974.

[10] R. Dolbeau, S. Bihan, and F. Bodin. HMPP: A hybrid multi-core parallel programming environment. In *First Workshop on General Purpose Processing on Graphics Processing Units*, October 2007.

[11] H. Esmaeilzadeh, E. Blem, R. St. Amant, K. Sankaralingam, and D. Burger. Dark silicon and the end of multicore scaling. In *Proceedings of the 38th annual international symposium on Computer architecture*, ISCA '11, pages 365–376, New York, NY, USA, 2011. ACM.

[12] R. Hameed and et. al. Understanding sources of inefficiency in general-purpose chips. In *Proceedings of the 37th annual international symposium on Computer architecture*, ISCA '10, pages 37–47, New York, NY, USA, 2010. ACM.

[13] Khronos OpenCL Working Group. The OpenCL Specification. Aaftab Munshi, Ed., 2009.

[14] W. A. Najjar and J. R. Villarreal. Fpga code accelerators - the compiler perspective. In *DAC*, page 141, 2013.

[15] Nvidia. *CUDA Compute Unified Device Architecture - Programming Guide*, 2007.

[16] OpenMP Architecture Review Board. OpenMP 3.0 Specification. http://www.openmp.org, May 2008.

[17] A. Papakonstantinou, D. Chen, W.-M. Hwu, J. Cong, and Y. Liang. Throughput-oriented kernel porting onto fpgas. In *Proceedings of the 50th Annual Design Automation Conference*, DAC '13, pages 11:1–11:10, New York, NY, USA, 2013. ACM.

[18] D. C. Pham and et. al. Overview of the architecture, circuit design, and physical implementation of a first-generation cell processor. *Solid-State Circuits, IEEE Journal of*, 41(1):179–196, 2006.

[19] The Portland Group. *PGI Accelerator Programming Model for Fortran & C*.

[20] G. Venkatesh, J. Sampson, N. Goulding, S. Garcia, V. Bryksin, J. Lugo-Martinez, S. Swanson, and M. B. Taylor. Conservation cores: reducing the energy of mature computations. volume 38, pages 205–218, New York, NY, USA, Mar. 2010. ACM.

[21] J. R. Villarreal, A. Park, W. A. Najjar, and R. Halstead. Designing modular hardware accelerators in c with roccc 2.0. In R. Sass and R. Tessier, editors, *FCCM*, pages 127–134. IEEE Computer Society, 2010.

[22] Xilinx. Zynq-7000 All Programmable SoC, Sept. 2013. http://www.xilinx.com/products/silicon-devices/soc/zynq-7000/.

A FPGA Prototype Design Emphasis
on Low Power Technique

Xu Hanyang
Fudan University
No.825 Zhangheng Rd, shanghai,
China
11110720012@fudan.edu.cn

Wang Jian*
Fudan University
No.825 Zhangheng Rd, shanghai,
China
wjian@fudan.edu.cn

Lai Jinmei*
Fudan University
No.825 Zhangheng Rd, shanghai,
China
jmlai@fudan.edu.cn

ABSTRACT

In this paper, we propose a fully-functional Nanometer FPGA prototype chip. Compared to traditional single supply voltage, single threshold voltage design, we explore low power nanometer FPGA design challenges with Multi-Vt, Static Voltage Scaling and sleep mode technique. Compared to Dynamic Voltage Scaling (DVS), we make a table of Voltage-Delay parameter pairs under different voltage conditions so that timing information can be calculated by a Static Timing Analysis (STA) tool. Thus a lowest supply power is chosen among all results which meet the timing requirements. This approach would simplify the hardware design since we don't need a complex workload detection circuit compared to DVS system. By separating supply voltages, we can directly shutdown power supply of the unused circuits. Compared to inserting sleep transistor in pull-up or pull-down networks, we can eliminate the speed penalty cased by the additional sleep transistor. We implement a tile-based heterogeneous architecture with island style routing and embedded specific blocks such as DSP and memory. The array size is 64×31 (Row×Col) including 64×24 CLBs. The final design is fabricated using a 1P10M 65-nm bulk CMOS process. Test results show a 53% reduction in static power compared to a commercial FPGA device which is also fabricated in 65nm process and has a similar array size.

Categories and Subject Descriptors

B.7.1 [**Integrated Circuits**]: Types and Design Styles – *Gate arrays, VLSI.*

General Terms

Design, Theory.

Keywords

FPGA, Multi-Vt, Voltage scaling, multiple supply voltage, sleep mode, leakage, dynamic, LUT.

1. INTRODUCTION

With the continuous progressing in process, feature size of transistor continues scaling down. In consequence of short-channel effect, lower threshold voltage and thinner gate oxide, static power has become more dominant in total power dissipation of the chip [1]. So low power design have become more and more important, especially for static power. There have been lots of low

power techniques in ASIC design [2, 3]. For FPGA chip, power efficiency is usually much lower than ASIC since its programmability. FPGA's dynamic power is roughly 7.1~14 times higher and static power is roughly 5.4~87 times higher than ASIC [4, 5]. This greatly limits FPGA's usage in low power application. To overcome the above shortcomings, a series of low power techniques suited for FPGA chips have been proposed.

An effective method to reduce static power is by implementing Multi-Vt transistors. While placing low-Vt transistor on critical path and high-Vt transistor on non-critical path, static power can be reduced without any effect on performance [6]. To adjust threshold voltage, one way is by adjusting process parameters like doping concentration and gate oxide thickness during fabrication. The disadvantage of this approach is once the chip has been fabricated, threshold voltage is fixed and cannot be adjusted anymore [7]. Another way is by controlling the substrate voltage [8, 9], by adjusting the body bias voltage, threshold voltage can still be adjusted even though the chip has been fabricated. So it is more flexible. But transistor's well-separate margin and the additional control circuits would bring an area overhead. Power gating is also an effective way to reduce static power [10], by inserting NMOS in pull-down or PMOS in pull-up network, power supply and circuit can be isolated when the circuit is in idle state. But sleep transistors occupy excess layout area, and when the circuit is in active state, the on resistance of sleep transistor would lead to a speed penalty. Dynamic Voltage Scaling technique is also an effective way to reduce power consumption, [11] proposed a self-adaptive voltage control scheme. To detect workload, a 4-phase dual-rail encoding asynchronous architecture is implemented. But 2N+1 wires are required to transfer N bits data using a dual-rail encoding. Compared to synchronous logic, the asynchronous architecture takes up more resources and chip area.

This paper proposes a fully-functional low power FPGA prototype chip design with Dual-Vt transistors. The high-Vt transistor is mainly used in configuration SRAM since the static power of SRAM cell takes a large proportion of total static power dissipation, approximately 38% according to [13]. Another reason is once the configuration data is downloaded completely, SRAM cells do not flip anymore, so performance of SRAM cell will only affect the download speed. We also implement a Dual supply voltage to support sleep mode, by separating power supply of configuration SRAM and power supply of the rest array elements, we can shutdown most logic when the chip enters sleep mode while keep the power supply of configuration SRAM to retain configuration information. By doing this, we can minimize static power dissipation when the chip is in idle state without the speed penalty cased by sleep transistor. To support voltage scaling, we design an on chip Low-Dropout regulator (LDO). By recording delay parameters of each kind of cells under different voltage conditions, we make a table of Voltage-Delay parameter pairs. Then the STA tool takes the table to calculate timing information. Finally, among all results which meet the timing requirements, a lowest supply power is chosen. Compared to the DVS method mentioned in [11, 12], the voltage scaling method proposed in this paper is a static voltage scaling technique, the benefit of this approach is we can simplify hardware design and eliminate the waste of resources compared to an asynchronous design.

The final design is fabricated in 1P10M 65nm bulk CMOS process, Test results show a 53% reduction in static power compared to a commercial FPGA device. At last, the entire chip consumes only 2.03mW power in sleep mode, which is only 1.37% of the normal mode.

2. FPGA CIRCUITS AND FABRICS

This paper presents a tile-based heterogeneous architecture with island style routing and embedded specific blocks. Main components in the array including CLB, DSP, Block RAM (BRAM), IO, LDO, Phase-Locked Loops (PLL) and Configuration module (CFG) as shown in Figure 1. The array size is 64×31 (Row$\times$Col). Elements in array connect each other through Global Routing Matrix (GRM).

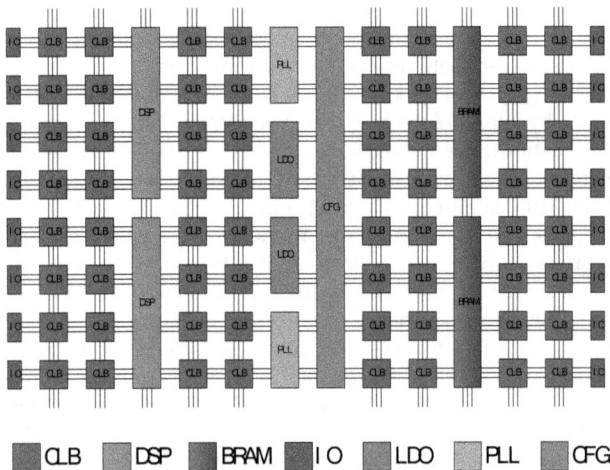

Figure 1. Array Structure

The main components of CLB are Look-Up Table (LUT), Fast Carry Chain, Multiplexer and Register. Except for function generators, The CLB proposed in this paper can also be configured as Distributed RAM, Read Only Memory (ROM) and Shift Registers. In the design of LUT, we adopt CMOS Transmission Gate (TG) instead of the traditional LUT structure with NMOS TG [5]. Since in 65nm process with 1V nominal voltage, a high level signal's voltage loss can be up to 360mV only through one-stage of NMOS TG, the situation will get worse when voltage scaling is implemented. CMOS TG can avoid voltage loss and asymmetry between rise time and fall time. But the static power of CMOS TG is 10.4% higher than the NMOS TG.

There are 4 columns of specific blocks in the array including DSPs and BRAMs. As for some specific functions like multiplier, accumulator and memory, these specific blocks are much more efficient than CLBs, providing faster speed and less power

consumptions [5]. We also implement LDOs in the array. By controlling the configuration bits in the LDO, supply voltage of other logics in the array can be adjusted to support voltage scaling.

3. LOW POWER TECHNIQUE

3.1 Static Voltage Scaling

This paper proposes a static voltage scaling method. The main advantage of this method is its simplicity compared to a dynamic voltage scaling technique. Usually a DVS system needs a dynamic frequency and voltage scaling unit. A slack analysis and scheduling algorithm is also needed to control the voltage-frequency scaling unit. This increases design complexity significantly.

In our design, we scale the supply voltage from 0.8V to 1V with a 500mV step. Test results show that the minimum voltage to make the chip work stably is 740mV, and we leave a margin of 60mV in case of ripples of the supply power. Then we measured the delay information of different elements under the voltage of 0.8V, 0.85V, 0.9V, 0.95V and 1V respectively. Since the delay of some elements in the chip is hard to test, we implement several ring oscillators, so the delay information can be read directly from the frequency of the ring oscillator. Delay of the rest elements is measured by subtracting the delay value of two similar path, for example, we measure the 16to1 MUX delay by implementing two path denoted as path A and path B, routings of the two path is all the same except for path B containing the 16to1 MUX, then delay information of the MUX can be obtained by simply subtracting delay of path A from path B. After the delay parameters have been measured, we make a table of voltage-delay parameter pairs under different voltage conditions so timing information can be calculated by a Static Timing Analysis (STA) tool. Finally a lowest voltage is chosen among all results which meet the timing requirements, and the voltage is scaled by changing the configuration bit of the LDO. The disadvantage of this approach is once the circuit is downloaded, the voltage is fixed. So it is not as flexible as the DVS technique.

3.2 Multiple Threshold Voltage

To realize programmability, FPGA chip contains a large amount of configuration SRAM cells to control the logic functions and interconnection structures. Since these SRAM cells do not flip after configuration process is completed, the speed of SRAM cells will only impact the download speed. Thus the main object of SRAM design is to limit its static power. We employ the traditional 6T structure in SRAM design and all the 6 transistor is implemented with high threshold voltage. Except for implementing High-Vt transistors, we can further reduce leakage current by increasing transistor's channel length. Figure 2 shows the leakage current of an inverter with different threshold voltage and transistor's channel length.

As increasing channel length will also increase the layout area, and there are a great many of SRAM cells in the chip (4.6 millions in our design), so we have to select elaborately to avoid too much area overhead. Besides, long channel length may induce programming and reading problem since it increases the on resistance and capacitance of the word-line transistor.

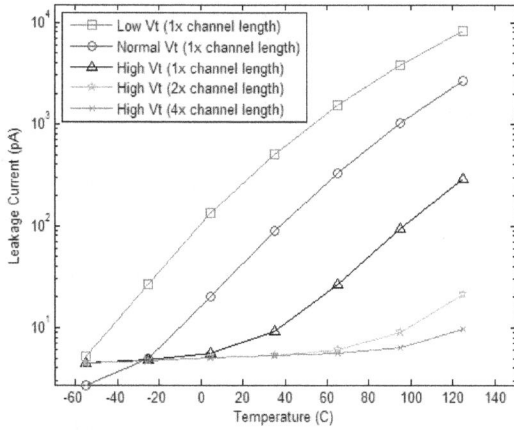

Figure 2. Leakage current with different channel length

We chose channel length of each transistor based on evaluations on various combinations of transistor's size. Table 1 lists some of the combinations, and the corresponding leakage current, area, leakage area product results under 27℃, TT corner simulation conditions. In Table 1, BP denotes the back-to-back PMOS, BN denotes the back-to-back NMOS while WN denotes the NMOS controlled by word line signal. Finally we chose size D since the leakage is relatively small while the layout area of size D is only 2.3% more compared to size A (the minimum size).

Table 1. Different combinations of channel length in SRAM

Size	Channel length of BP(nm)	Channel length of BN(nm)	Channel length of WN(nm)	Leakage (pA)	Area ($_{um^2}$)	Product
A	60	60	60	18.73	1.33	24.91
B	70	60	65	18.06	1.33	24.02
C	90	65	70	16.79	1.35	22.67
D	120	70	85	16.52	1.36	22.47
E	150	80	100	16.44	1.50	24.66

3.3 Sleep Mode

In practical applications, FPGA chip may not always in active mode, so we can turn off some parts of the chip to save power when the chip is in idle state. Inserting sleep transistor in the pull-up or pull-down network is an effective way to achieve this goal. But sleep transistor lead to a speed penalty due to its on resistance, simulation result shows that a PMOS sleep transistor in pull-up network increases the delay of LUT cell by 7% with an area overhead of 20%. In our design, we implement LDOs in the array to power all the cells with an area overhead of 4.8%, the power supply is separated into two parts: core logics are powered by VCC_INT, and the configuration SRAM is powered by VCC_SRAM. When the chip is in idle state, VCC_INT can be easily removed by disabling the corresponding LDO while VCC_SRAM is retained to keep the configuration information. Compared to inserting sleep transistors, LDO can eliminate the speed penalty since its feedback mechanism. For the case of sleep transistor, there exists a large voltage drop when the load current is large.

Since the power supply of registers and BRAMs is not separated from other core logics, so the sleep mode only support combinational circuits in this design, in a future work, the power supply of all memory cells can be further separated to support a sleep mode of sequential circuits.

4. TEST RESULTS
The layout of entire chip is shown in Figure 3.

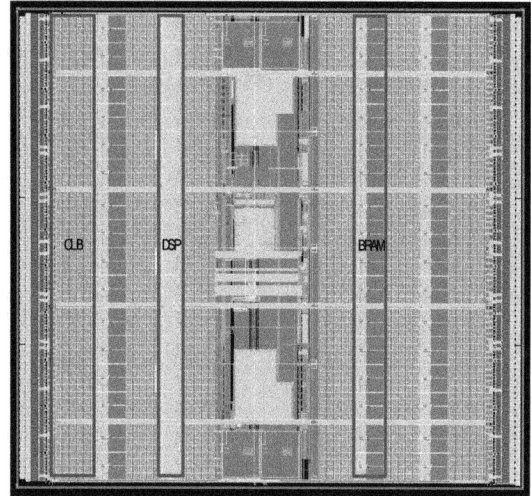

Figure 3. Layout

Layout area is 33.79 mm^2. The final design is fabricated in a 1P10M 65nm bulk CMOS process. Test results are compared to Xilinx's XC5VLX20T which is also fabricated in 65nm process and have a similar array size.

Table 2. Comparisons between Our Design and XC5VLX20T

	Process	Array Size	Number of LUT	Nominal Voltage
Our Design	65nm	64×31	12288	1V
XC5VLX20T	65nm	60×26	12480	1V

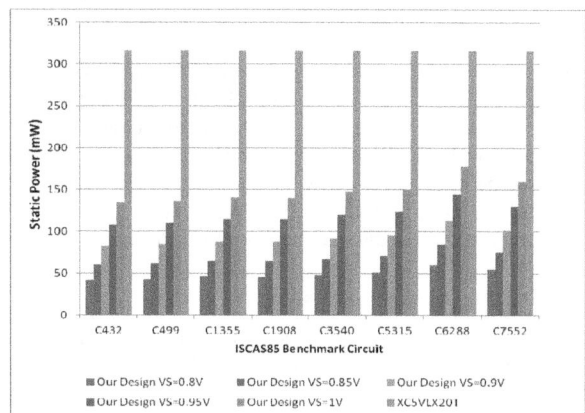

Figure 4. Static Power

We implement 8 combinational benchmark circuits from ISCAS'85 to test the static power. Since the test is for static power, we fix all input pins to high level. Then we get the current value of our design by measuring the current on the power pins of the chip directly. For XC5VLX20T, we get the current value from Xilinx's power analysis tool - XPower Analyzer.

Test results show that under a nominal voltage condition, we have a 53% reduction in static power, while the LUT delay in our design increases by 46.8% and the fast carry chain delay increases by 4% compared to XC5VLX20T under nominal voltage.

Table 3. Static Power of ISCAS85 Benchmark Circuit

	Our Design (mW)					XC5VLX20T (mW)
	Voltage Scaling (V)				Nominal Voltage	Nominal Voltage
	0.8	0.85	0.9	0.95		
C432	41.6	60.4	82.8	108.3	134.6	316
C499	43.2	62.1	84.6	110.2	136.4	316
C1355	46.4	64.6	88.2	115.0	141.2	316
C1908	45.6	64.6	87.3	114.9	140.0	316
C3540	48.0	67.2	91.8	119.7	147.6	316
C5315	51.2	71.4	95.4	123.5	150.8	316
C6288	60.0	85.0	113.4	144.4	178.6	316
C7552	54.4	75.7	101.7	130.2	160.4	316
Average	48.8	68.9	93.15	120.8	148.7	316

By further scaling the voltage, a 67% reduction in static power can be achieved compared to a nominal voltage condition. But the delay of LUT and Double Length Interconnections also increases by 81.7% and 217.6% respectively. The results show that Interconnections tend to be more sensitive to voltage scaling compared to logics like LUT. So in a future work, supply power of Logics and interconnections can be further separated, thus a higher voltage can be applied to interconnections to compensate excessive speed degradation under a low voltage condition

5. CONCLUSIONS

This paper proposes a low power FPGA prototype chip. Under nominal voltage condition, our design can achieve a 53% reduction in static power compared to a commercial FPGA device which is also fabricated in 65nm process and has a similar array size. By further scaling the supply voltage, more power reduction can be achieved. At last, the proposed design can support sleep mode when configured as combinational logic, the power dissipation in sleep mode is 2.03mW, which is only 1.37% compared to the power dissipation in normal mode.

6. ACKNOWLEDGMENTS

This Work is supported by the National High Technology Research and Development (863) Thematic Program of China, No. 2012AA012001.

7. REFERENCES

[1] 2011 International Technology Roadmap for Semiconductors (ITRS).

[2] Puri, R., Stok, L., Bhattacharya, S., 2005, keeping hot chips cool, Design Automation Conference, 285 – 288.

[3] Roy, K., Mukhopadhyay, S., Mahmoodi-Meimand, H., 2003, leakage current mechanisms and leakage reduction techniques in deep-submicrometer CMOS Circuits, Proceedings of the IEEE, 305 – 327.

[4] Ian Kuon, Rose, J., 2007, Measuring the Gap Between FPGAs and ASICs, IEEE Transactions on Computer-Aided Design of Integrated Circuits and Systems, 203 – 215.

[5] Ian Kuon, Russell Tessier, Jonathan Rose, 2008, FPGA Architecture: Survey and Challenges, Foundations and Trends in Electronic Design Automation, 135-253.

[6] Arifur Rahman, Vijay Polavarapuv, 2004, Evaluation of low-leakage design techniques for field programmable gate arrays, Proceedings of the ACM/SIGDA international symposium on Field programmable gate arrays, 23-30.

[7] Fei Li, Yan Lin, Lei He, etc. 2004, Low-power FPGA using pre-defined dual-Vdd/dual-Vt fabrics, Proceedings of the ACM/SIGDA international symposium on Field programmable gate arrays, 42-50.

[8] Masakazu Hioki, Toshihiro Sekigawa, Tadashi Nakagawa, etc. 2013, Fully-functional FPGA prototype with fine-grain programmable body biasing, Proceedings of the ACM/SIGDA international symposium on Field programmable gate arrays, 73-80.

[9] David Lewis, Elias Ahmed, David Cashman, etc. 2009, Architectural Enhancements in Stratix-III™ and Stratix-IV™, Proceedings of the ACM/SIGDA international symposium on Field programmable gate arrays, 33-42.

[10] Krishnan, N.Rajagopala, Sivasuparamanyan, K., 2013, A reconfigurable low power FPGA design with autonomous power gating and LEDR encoding, International conference on intelligent systems and control (ISCO), 221-226.

[11] Sreenivaas, V.L., Prasad, D.A., Kamalanathan, M., 2010, A novel dynamic voltage scaling technique for low-power FPGA Systems, International Conference on Signal Processing and Communications (SPCOM), 1-5.

[12] Atukem Nabina, Jose Luis Nunez-Yanez, 2012, Adaptive Voltage Scaling in a Dynamically Reconfigurable FPGA-Based Platform, ACM Transactions on Reconfigurable Technology and Systems, Volume 5, Issue 4.

[13] Tuan, T., Lai, B., 2003, Leakage Power Analysis of a 90nm FPGA, Proceedings of the IEEE on Custom Integrated Circuits Conference, 57 – 60.

Hardware Acceleration of Database Operations

Jared Casper and Kunle Olukotun
Pervasive Parallelism Laboratory
Stanford University
{jaredc, kunle}@stanford.edu

ABSTRACT

As the amount of memory in database systems grows, entire database tables, or even databases, are able to fit in the system's memory, making in-memory database operations more prevalent. This shift from disk-based to in-memory database systems has contributed to a move from row-wise to columnar data storage. Furthermore, common database workloads have grown beyond online transaction processing (OLTP) to include online analytical processing and data mining. These workloads analyze huge datasets that are often irregular and not indexed, making traditional database operations like joins much more expensive.

In this paper we explore using dedicated hardware to accelerate in-memory database operations. We present hardware to accelerate the selection process of compacting a single column into a linear column of selected data, joining two sorted columns via merging, and sorting a column. Finally, we put these primitives together to accelerate an entire join operation. We implement a prototype of this system using FPGAs and show substantial improvements in both absolute throughput and utilization of memory bandwidth. Using the prototype as a guide, we explore how the hardware resources required by our design change with the desired throughput.

Categories and Subject Descriptors

C.1.3 [**Processor Architectures**]: Other Architecture Styles

Keywords

Database; FPGA; Hardware Acceleration; Join; Sort

1. INTRODUCTION

Database systems have historically been largely constrained by disk performance. Now, with advances of memory technology, the amount of main memory available in large database systems has grown enough that many large database tables now reside entirely in main memory. While Moore's law continues to hold and the number of transistors available

Permission to make digital or hard copies of all or part of this work for personal or classroom use is granted without fee provided that copies are not made or distributed for profit or commercial advantage and that copies bear this notice and the full citation on the first page. Copyrights for components of this work owned by others than the author(s) must be honored. Abstracting with credit is permitted. To copy otherwise, or republish, to post on servers or to redistribute to lists, requires prior specific permission and/or a fee. Request permissions from permissions@acm.org.

FPGA'14, February 26–28, 2014, Monterey, CA, USA.
Copyright is held by the owner/author(s). Publication rights licensed to ACM.
ACM 978-1-4503-2671-1/14/02 ...$15.00.
http://dx.doi.org/10.1145/2554688.2554787.

to chip architects continues to increase, power constraints limit the number of logic transistors that can be active at any given time on a chip [3]. It is unlikely that general purpose processing elements will ever be able to fully utilize the amount of memory bandwidth available to a chip while performing all but the most basic database operations. As an example, studies have increased join performance into the 100s of million tuples per second [7, 6], with 64-bit tuples this corresponds to a data bandwidth of one to five gigabytes per second. Modern chips, conversely, can achieve memory bandwidth over 100 GB/s [1]. Clearly using general purpose compute is leaving performance on the table.

To achieve maximum performance for in memory database operations, it will thus be necessary to move to special purpose processors. The move to heterogeneity is not a new idea. Researchers at Intel have proposed that architectures move from optimizing for the 90% case, the traditional 90/10 approach, to spending new transistors on dedicated accelerators for multiple 10% cases, the "10x10" approach. [5, 2].

In this paper we propose hardware designs that accelerate three important primitive database operations: selection, merge join, and sorting. These three operation can be combined to perform one of the most fundamental database operations: the table join. The primary goal in our designs is to build hardware that fully utilizes any amount of memory bandwidth available. To that end our designs have as few limiters to scaling as possible, such that as logic density increases more hardware can be added to increase the throughput of the design with very little redesign of the architecture. Contribution of this this work include:

- We detail hardware to perform a selection on a column of data streamed at peak memory bandwidth.
- We describe hardware to merge two sorted data columns.
- We present hardware to sort a data column using a merge sort algorithm.
- We describe how to combine these hardware blocks to perform an equi-join entirely in hardware.
- We prototype all three designs on an FPGA platform and discuss issues faced when building the prototype.
- We analyze the performance of our prototype and identify key bottlenecks in performance.
- For each hardware design, we explore the hardware resources necessary and how those resources requirements grow with bandwidth requirements.

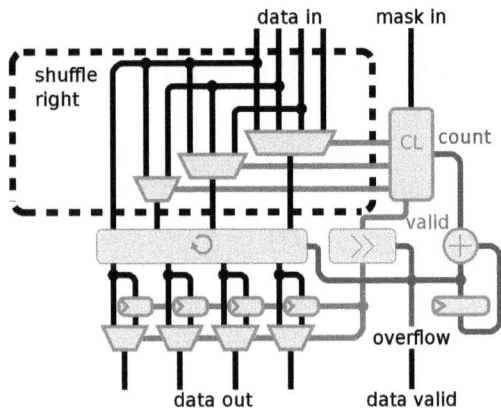

Figure 1: Data and control paths for selection of four elements.

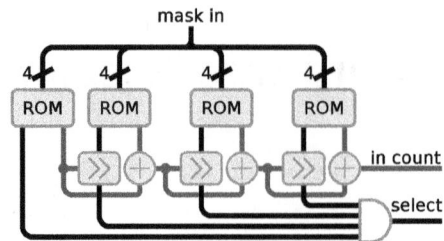

Figure 2: Control logic for the selection unit.

2. HARDWARE DESIGN

2.1 Selection

In this paper we define the selection operation to take two inputs, a bit mask of selected elements and a column of data stored as an array of equal width machine data types. The inputs can either come from arrays laid out linearly in memory, or be produced by another operation which may be looking at a different column of data. In some cases the bit mask may be RLE compressed and must be decompressed before being used by the selection unit. A common case would have the bit mask coming from another operation and the data column being read from memory. The output of the operation is values from the input column that correspond to the true bits in the bit mask, in the same order that they appear in the original column. Like the input, the output data can be streamed to another processing unit or written sequentially into memory.

There are many ways to implement selection in software. One efficient implementation fills a SIMD register with the next values from the input column. A portion of the bit mask is used as an index into a look up table which contains indices for the SIMD shuffle operation to shuffle the selected data to one end of the SIMD register. The resulting SIMD register is written to the output array and the output pointer is incremented by the number of valid data elements that were written. This store is thus an unaligned SIMD memory access, which was added in SSE4, and has little performance impact when writing to the L1 cache. These unaligned stores are used to incrementally fill the output with compacted data. Parallel algorithms must first scan through the bit mask counting bits to determine the proper offset to begin writing each portion of the result. Once those offsets are calculated, the column can be partitioned for multiple threads to work on in parallel.

Hardware to perform this selection is presented in Figure 1. We call the number of elements consumed each pass through the hardware the "width" of the selection block. Assuming a fully pipelined implementation, the bandwidth of the block is fully determined by the width of the block and the clock speed. A barrel shifter can be efficiently implemented using multiple stages of multiplexors; however, such large barrel shifters must be pipelined to achieve high clock frequencies, so the datapath in Figure 1 was care-fully designed to avoid feedback paths containing large barrel shifters which would necessitate pipeline stalls. As is, the only feedback path in the design is a very small addition (with width $log_2(W)$), allowing for a deeply pipelined design to achieve a high clock rate.

The first step is to produce a word array in which all selected words from the input are shuffled next to each other at one end of the array (in this case, the right side). A combinational logic block takes in a segment of the mask stream and produces a count of the number of selected elements in the segment, a bus of valid lines, and an index vector which specifies which word should be selected for each position in the shuffled word array.

For small input widths, this combination logic can simply be implemented as a single ROM. Such a ROM would have depth 2^W. This is clearly not feasible for any realistic input width. Using pure-combinational logic, such as a cascade of leading-1-detectors, would also not be feasible for larger input widths. We thus use smaller sections of the mask as addresses into multiple smaller ROMs. So for example, instead of using all 16 bits of a mask segment to address a 64k deep ROM, we can use each 4-bit nibble of the mask to address four 16 element ROMs. It is then necessary to shift the output of each ROM into the correct position of the final index vector, based on the accumulated count from the adjacent ROM. Figure 2 shows an implementation of this for an input width of 16. This datapath has no feedback paths and can thus be efficiently pipelined to achieve full throughput. Decreasing the size of the ROMS and including more of them results in lower total ROM space but higher latency and more adders, barrel shifters, and pipeline registers.

Once the selected values are shuffled to the right side, they are rotated left to a position indicated by the current number of saved values ready to be output. Values in the input that complete a full output are sent directly to the output and values that will make up a partial output are saved in registers. For example, if two values were previously saved in the registers, and three values are selected in the input, the input will be rotated right by two, such that the lowest (furthest right) two values fill the left two positions in the output, and the third input word is saved in the register furthest to the right, ready to be added to selected values from the next input.

2.2 Merge Join

The merge join operation takes two sorted columns of fixed-width keys as input, each with an associated payload column, and produces an output column which contains all the keys that the two columns have in common, together with the associated payload values. When there are duplicate matching keys, the cross product of all payload values

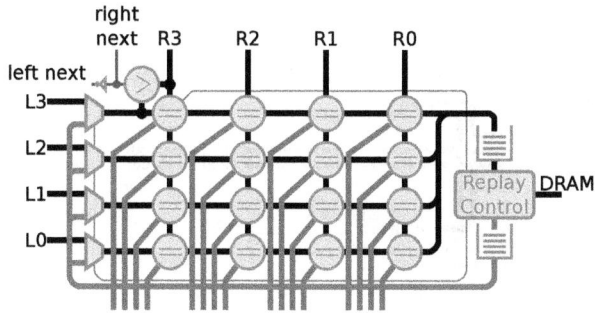

Figure 3: Hardware to perform the merge join operation. The green lines exiting diagonally from each comparator encompass the key, both values, and the result of the comparison.

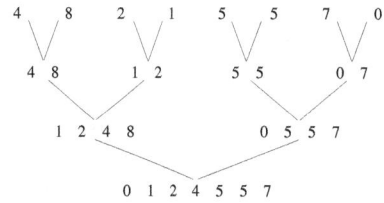

Figure 4: Sorting using a sort merge tree.

2.3 Sorting

Sorting an array, or column, of numbers has been and will continue to be a very active area of research and is an essential primitive operation in many application domains, including databases. Quicksort based algorithms have traditionally been considered to have the best average case performance among software sorting algorithms. However, recent advances in both CPU and GPU architectures have brought merge sort based algorithms, such as bitonic sort and Batcher odd-even sort, to the forefront of performance as they are able to exploit new architectures more effectively and better utilize a limited amount of bandwidth [4, 15, 17, 9]. Satish et.al.[16] provide a comprehensive overview of state of art sorting algorithms for general purposes CPU and GPU processors.

We present here a dedicated hardware solution to perform a merge sort entirely in hardware. The goal of this design is to sort an in-memory column of values while streaming the column to and from memory at full memory bandwidth as few times as possible. Figure 4 depicts the essence of a merge sort. We call the merge done at the individual node a "sort merge", which is distinguished from a "merge join" presented in Section 2.2. To accomplish this we implement a merge tree directly in hardware, stream unsorted data from memory into the merge tree and write out sorted portions of the column. Those sorted portions then become the input to each input leaf of the merge tree again, generating much larger sorted portions. This process is repeated until the entire column is sorted. The number of passes required through the tree is dependent on the width of the merge tree. Thus, if the width of the tree is relatively large, the number of passes required grows extremely slowly with the size of the input table and very large tables can be sorted in just two or three passes of the data.

Before we describe the design of the merge tree itself, we first look at an individual node in the merge tree. The maximum throughput of data through the merge tree will be ultimately limited by the throughput of data through the final node at the bottom of the tree. Depending on the data, other nodes of the tree can also become a bottleneck. For example, if the far left input on a second pass contains all of the lowest elements of the full column, then only the far left branches of the tree will be used until the entire portion is consumed. It is thus not practical to move only the lowest single value of the two inputs of a node to the output. This would result in the throughput of the tree being only one element per cycle. Multiple values must be merged every cycle.

Figure 6 gives a logical overview of how multiple values from the input are merged at a time. Each iteration, the lowest value of each input are compared and some number of values, in this case four, are removed from the input queue

are produced. For example, if there are four entries of a key x in one input column, and six entries of x in the other input, there will be 24 entries in the output with key x.

This operation can be performed in software by sequentially moving through each input column and advancing the pointer of the column with the lower value. When two keys match, an output row is written to the output array and the output pointer incremented. Care must be taken to handle the case of multiple matching keys and produce the correct cross-section output. The resulting code has a large number of unpredictable branches that result in a very low IPC and quickly becomes processor bound, not able to keep up with the memory bandwidth available to even a single core.

Our hardware design to perform this operation is laid out in Figure 3. The basic design is rather straightforward; all combinations of a section of keys from each of two inputs ("left" and "right") are compared. An array of possible output combinations with a bit mask indicating which should be used is produced. This output can then be sent into the selection unit from Section 2.1 to produce the actual output rows. The highest value from each input is compared, the input with the lower highest value is advanced, while the same selection from the other input remains. This ensures that any combination of input keys that could potentially match are compared.

Complications arise, however, when the highest value of each input selection is equal. In this case it is necessary to buffer the keys from the left input and advance through the left input until the highest keys no longer match. When that happens, it is guaranteed that the highest right input is lower than the highest left input, and the right input can be advanced. Any values buffered are then replayed and compared against the new selection from the right. When the replay buffer is empty, execution continues as normal.

Because the number of comparators grows quadratically with the width of input, it is difficult to implement hardware with a wide input array. An optimization to help increase the throughput of the design looks at a much wider selection of each input than the actual comparator grid. The input is partitioned into sections that fit into the comparator grid and the highest and lowest values are compared. Using those comparisons, only those cross sections with potential matches are sent into the comparator grid sequentially while the others are skipped.

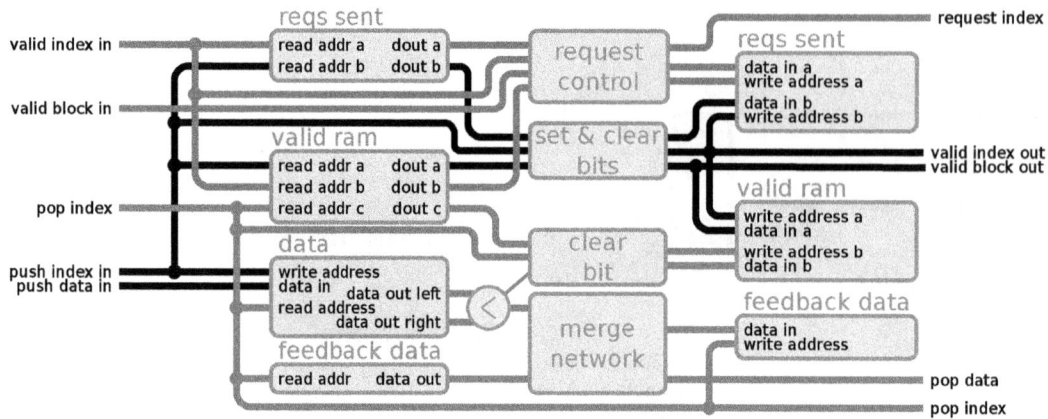

Figure 5: Sort merge unit. Note that for simplicity, ports to the same memory are separated.

with the lower lowest value. These four values are merged with the highest four values from the previous iteration. The four lowest values resulting from that merge are guaranteed to be lower than any other value yet to be considered since any values lower than the fourth would already have been pulled in. The highest four values, however, may be higher than and must therefore be fed back and merged with the next set of input values. In this way, four values are produced and four values are consumed from one of the inputs each iteration.

It is not necessary, however, to put a merge network like that in Figure 6 at each node of the tree. Each level of the tree need only supply values as fast as the level below it can consume values. Thus, each level need only match the throughput of the final node of the tree, which need only match the write memory bandwidth to keep up with memory. Figure 5 presents the hardware that encompasses a single level of a merge tree, which we call a "sort merge unit". A data memory buffers the input data to the level. It is only necessary to hold as a single value for each input leaf to the level. The data memory is partitioned into "left" and "right" data so that both inputs to a particular node can be read at once, but each can be written separately. Another memory holds the feedback data from the previous merge of values for each node in the level. A valid memory holds a bit for each input leaf to indicate that the data for that leaf is valid, and a bit for each entry in the feedback memory. These valid bits are blocked in chunks, so a single read or write works on multiple values at once. Finally, a "request sent" memory, which is blocked like the valid memory, holds a single bit for each input leaf to indicate that a request has been sent up the tree to fill the data for that leaf. Note that there are no output buffers, as the outputs are buffered at the next level in the tree.

We now describe three operations performed on a sort merge unit: a push, a request, and a pop. A push, whose data path is black in Figure 5, is performed when input data comes from above the unit in the tree. First, the data is written to the data memory, which is known to be invalid because it was previously requested, and the valid and request outstanding blocks are read. The corresponding valid bit is set and the request outstanding bit is cleared, and the new blocks are written back. The new block of valid bits is also sent down to the lower level along with the index. If

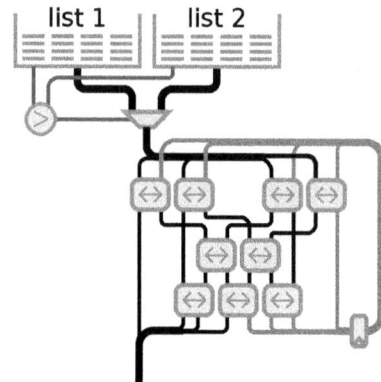

Figure 6: Merging multiple values at once.

nothing is being pushed in a particular cycle, a valid block (determined by an internal counter) is still read and sent down to the lower level, this is not shown in the figure and prevents deadlock in some cases.

When the valid block and associated index are sent to a sort merge unit, it initiates a request operation, which follows the green data path in Figure 5. First, the level's own valid and request outstanding blocks corresponding to the valid bits received are read. The incoming valid block, which represent data valid at nodes above, and the local valid and request outstanding blocks are examined to to find invalid elements that have two valid parents and have not been requested. One such element is selected, a bit for it is set in the request outstanding memory, and the request is sent up to the parent.

Finally, an incoming request from below results in a pop operation, which follows the orange data path. Both data values, the feedback data, and corresponding valid block are read. The lowest values in each data buffer are compared. The block with the lowest is sent to the merge network along with the feedback data (if valid) and the valid bit corresponding to the consumed leaf is cleared while the valid bit for the feedback data is set. The lower values from the merge network are sent to the next level to pushed and the higher values are written back into the feedback memory.

As mentioned previously, the throughput of the entire merge tree is limited by the throughput of the final node

154

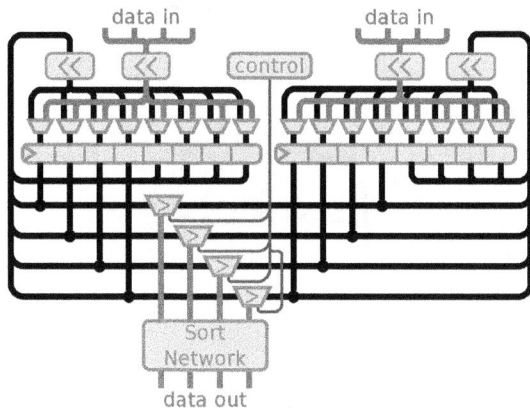

Figure 7: High bandwidth sort merge unit.

in the tree. The design in Figure 5 works well when there are plenty of inputs and outputs to fill the pipeline; merges of multiple nodes in the level are happening simultaneously. However, the final node of the tree has only two inputs. That means that an entire iteration must complete before the next merge can begin. It is thus insufficient for use in the final nodes of the tree.

Figure 7 presents a higher bandwidth sort merge unit which implements a single node of the tree, not an entire level with multiple nodes like Figure 5. Instead of consuming and merging a set number of values from one of the inputs, shift registers are used to consume a variable number from each input and new values are shifted in as space becomes available. Let W be the number of values to output each iteration. Let L_i and R_i be the values in the left and right shift registers, respectively, with i ranging from 0 to $2W - 1$. To determine the four lowest value from across both shift registers, each L_x is compared with $R_{(W-1-x)}$ for x between 0 and $W - 1$. The lower of the two in each case is advanced to the sort network while the higher remains in the shift register. For example, if $L_0 < R_3$, then at least one from the left and no more than three from the right are among the lowest, so L_0 is necessarily one of the lowest and R_3 is necessarily not. Likewise for L_1 and R_2, L_2 and R_1, and L_3 and R_0. The number taken from each side is counted and the shift register is shifted by that amount. If there is enough free space in the shift register, an input section is consumed, shifted, and stored into the correct position. The four lowest values are then sent into a full sort network and passed down to the next level. A merge network like that in Figure 6 is insufficient here since the input is not necessarily split into two equally sized, already sorted arrays.

The datapath in Figure 7 still has feedback paths which prevent a pipelined implementation from being fully utilized; the critical feedback path is a bit count, barrel shifter, and 2:1 multiplexor. This path is much shorter and grows much less quickly as the width increases than the feedback path of Figure 5 which include a full merge network.

Finally, Figure 8 shows the datapath for a full merge tree. A "tree filler" block has the same interface as a sort merge unit, but fulfills requests by fetching from DRAM. It continually sends blocks of "valid" bits which indicate that data is still available for a particular input, turns requests from the top level of the merge tree into DRAM requests, and turns

replies from DRAM into pushes into the top sort merge unit. During the initial pass through the memory, the data for an input can come from anywhere, so the input column is read linearly and sent through a small initial bootstrap sort network since the sort merge units expect blocks of sorted data as input. To prevent very wide levels that make routing more difficult, the top levels of the tree are split into four sub-trees, which operate independently of each other. The final two levels of the tree are the high bandwidth merge sort unit to maintain the total throughput of the tree and merge the output of the four lower bandwidth trees to produce a single sorted output.

On passes after the initial pass through data, the tree filler must obtain data from the particular sorted portion that matches the tree input of the request. Depending on the number of portions remaining to be merged, the tree filler maps some number of inputs of the tree to each of the remaining portions. For example, if the full tree is 16k inputs wide and there are four portions remaining to be merged, the first portion is mapped to the first 4k inputs, the second to the next 4k, etc. This means that some values of the portion are re-merged, but also has the effect of using sections of the tree as an input buffer for each of the portions. The fewer portions that remain to be merge, the larger the "input buffer" for each portion is and the larger the requests to DRAM can be. When the number of portions remaining to be sorted is equal to the number of inputs to the tree, only a single chunk of a portion can be requested at a time, leading to inefficient use of the DRAM bandwidth. We see the results of this in Section 3.3.

To support using portions of the merge tree as an input buffer in subsequent passes, the tree filler keeps a bit mask of tree inputs that it has received a request for. When enough of the inputs mapped to a particular portion have been requested, a single large request for the next values in that portion are requested and all of the requests are fulfilled in bulk.

2.4 Sort Merge Join

A full join operation is the same operation as a merge join, described in Section 2.2, but does not require the input columns to be sorted. Two main algorithms are most often used to perform joins, a hash join and sort merge join [7]. A hash join builds a hash table of one of the two input columns, then looks each element of the other column up in the hash table to find matches. Modern hash join implementation use sophisticated partitioning schemes to parallelize the operation and utilize a processors cache hierarchy. A sort merge join simply sorts both input columns then performs a merge join on the sorted columns. Implementations leverage the massive amount of research to improve the performance of sorting.

Figure 8 shows how each of the three blocks previously described can be combined to perform an entire sort merge join in hardware. Two independent sort trees are used to sort each of the two input columns. On the final pass through each column, the sorted data is sent to the merge join block instead of back to DRAM. The merge join output is sent to the select block as before and only the result of the join operation is written back into DRAM. The design also include data paths that allow the sort, merge join, and select blocks to be used independently of each other.

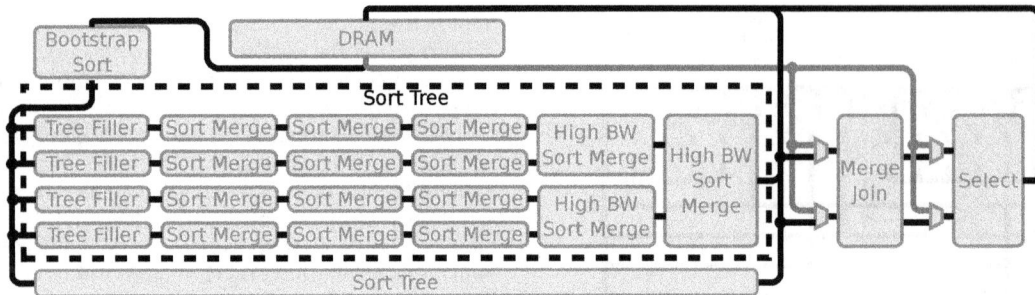

Figure 8: Full system block diagram and data paths.

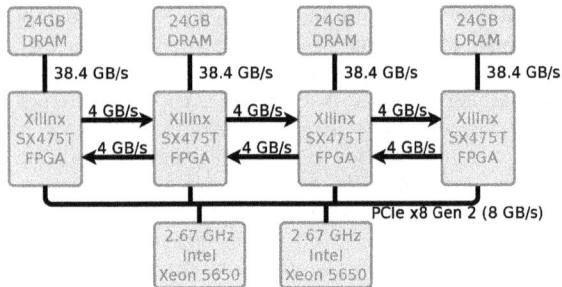

Figure 9: Block diagram of prototyping platform from Maxeler Technologies.

3. IMPLEMENTATION AND RESULTS

To prototype the design we used a system from Maxeler Technologies described in Figure 9. This system features four large Xilinx Virtex-6 FPGAs (XC6VSX475T). Each FPGA has 475k logic cells and 1,064 36 Kb RAM blocks for a total of 4.67 MB of block memory. Each FPGA is connected to 24 GB of memory via a single 384 bit memory channel capable of running at 400 MHz DDR, for a line speed of 307.2 Gbps, or 38.4 GB/s per FPGA. This gives a total line bandwidth between the FPGAs and memory of 153.6 GB/s, comparable to modern GPUs. The FPGAs are connected in a line with connections capable of 4 GB/s in each direction. For each design, we clocked the FPGA fabric at 200 MHz. Finally, each FPGA is connected via PCIe x8 to a host processor which is two 2.67 GHz Xeon 5650s, each containing 6 multi-threaded cores. These processor each have a line memory bandwidth of 32 GB/s.

Our purpose in prototyping the design was not entirely to determine the performance of the design, although we do provide performance numbers. As long as the components are able to match or exceed the memory bandwidth, the performance is largely determined by the memory system of the design, and thus many of the performance results are as much a test of Maxeler's memory system as they are of the acceleration design. Our main purpose in building the prototype was to drive the design using a real world implementation instead of what are often inaccurate simulations, and to be able to determine the challenging issues that arise as the hardware scales to higher bandwidths. Indeed, the final designs we have presented are fairly different from the original designs we came up with based on early simulations.

We chose the Maxeler platform for the large amount of memory capacity and bandwidth available to the FPGAs;

we wanted to ensure that our prototype handled a sufficient amount of bandwidth to prevent masking any scalability issues. The largest performance bottleneck we faced using the platform is the relatively narrow intra-FPGA links, which prevented us from effectively emulating a single chip with a full 153.6 GB/s of memory bandwidth. Thus, for all but Section 3.4, we use a single FPGA, since using the narrow intra-FPGA links skews the results in terms of the memory bandwidth utilization.

Since many of the performance numbers are dominated by the performance of the memory system on the Maxeler platform, we also present percentage of the maximum memory throughput (by which we mean the line bandwidth of the memory interface) as a metric of comparison. Since our hardware is designed to scale with available bandwidth, these percentages give an idea of how the design would perform with different memory systems. They also provide a metric of comparison with previous work, as it is difficult to make a true "apples-to-apples" comparison when the hardware is so vastly different. We also give some intuition as to how the resource requirements of each design will scale to platforms with different memory bandwidths.

3.1 Selection

We implemented the software algorithm described in Section 2.1 and optimized at the assembly language level. On our system's host processor, this implementation is able to achieve a maximum throughput using 8 threads, with an average throughput of 7.4 GB/s and 6.0 GB/s as the selection cardinality moves from 0% to 100%. This corresponds to 23.1% to 18.8% of the 32 GB/s maximum memory throughput of the Xeon 5650. For reference, the STREAM benchmark[10] also achieves the maximum bandwidth with 8 threads and is able to copy memory at a maximum speed of 11.8 GB/s[1], about 36.8% of the line rate memory bandwidth of the Xeon 5650. Results reported on the STREAM benchmark website [10] indicate that this utilization of maximum memory bandwidth is typical for modern processors.

Our implementation uses three SIMD registers, one to hold the data to be shuffled, one to hold the bit mask, and one to hold the shuffle indices loaded from memory. Thus, the lack of available SIMD registers accounts for the inability of the processor to fully pipeline the selection process and achieve the throughput of STREAM. The Xeon's in our

---

[1]The STREAM benchmark reported 23.6 GB/s, but counts bytes both read and written, or the "STREAM" method; the number here is for the "bcopy" method, which counts total bytes moved, which is more aligned with our use of bandwidth in this work.

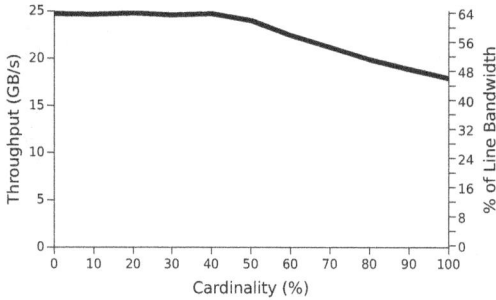

Figure 10: Measured throughput of the select block prototype.

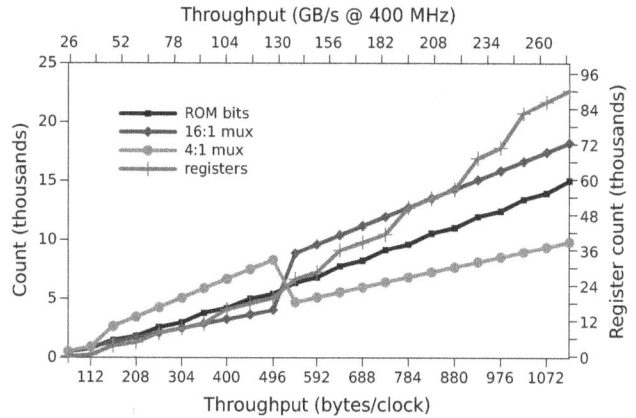

Figure 11: Amount of resources needed as the desired throughput of the select block increases.

test system support 16 byte wide SIMD instructions; using the 32 byte wide AVX2 integer instructions in the Haswell processors we would expect better performance and a highly tuned software selection algorithm to match the throughput of STREAM.

The design in Section 2.1 maps almost directly to the FPGA platform and we built a block that processes 72 64-bit values per clock cycle, for a maximum throughput of 14.4 billion values per second, or 115.2 GB/s. This is much more than the memory bandwidth available to a single chip; we will see in Section 3.2 why we made it that wide.

Figure 10 shows the measured throughput of the prototype. Throughout Section 3, bandwidth numbers are measured as the number of input bytes processed per second [2]. We could alternatively use total number of bytes read and written. This is pertinent here because a selection with cardinality of 0% transfers half the amount data as one with cardinality of 100%. With a constant amount of memory bandwidth that can be used for either reading or writing data, the 100% case will take longer to execute, but would have higher throughput if bytes both read and written were counted. Counting only bytes read, the cardinality of 100% case shows lower bandwidth since it takes longer to process the same amount of input data. This explains the nearly linear drop from 24.7 GB/s down to 17.8 GB/s as the cardinality moves from 40% to 100%. Below 40% the limits of a single port of the DRAM controller are reached and the full line rate of the memory interface is not realized. At 100% cardinality, the memory controller is more efficient with two streams of data (in and out) and is able to utilize 93% of the 38.4 GB/s of line bandwidth. This high utilization is achieved because of the very linear nature of the data access pattern and by putting the source and destination columns in different ranks of the DRAM, preventing them from interfering with one another.

At low cardinalities, the 24.7 GB/s achieved is 64.3% of the 38.4 GB/s maximum memory throughput of the FPGA. This represents a 2.8x increase in the memory bandwidth utilization over the 23.1% utilization of the software, and a 1.7x increase over the STREAM benchmark, which is as high as any software implementation could possibly achieve.

We now look at the number of resources required to scale the design. Figure 11 shows the resources used by the implementation as the width, and thus bandwidth, of the block

increases (note the different scale for registers and the other components). We present throughput as bytes per clock to decouple the results from any particular frequency, but also present GB/s at 400 MHz for reference. The range in throughput represents the range in width from 8 to 144 64-bit words. In choosing the number of stages used in the initial shuffle control (see Section 2.1), we experimentally found a good number of stages to use is $W/4$, where W is the width in words of the selection block.

Note that the numbers in Figure 11 present resources at the bit level. So a multiplexor that select between 4 64-bit words requires 64 4:1 multiplexors. For convenience, we lump 2:1 multiplexors in with 4:1 multiplexors and 8:1 multiplexors in with 16:1 multiplexors. Any multiplexor wider than 16 inputs is split into multiple stages to ease routing congestion and maintain clock speed. The swap that occurs at 496 bytes/block (or 62 to 68 words) results from the second stage of an 68:1 multiplexor requiring 16:1 multiplexors instead of the 4:1 second stage of smaller widths ($W/16 > 4$ when $W > 64$).

The most dramatic increase in resources as throughput increases comes from the number of registers. This results from the additional pipeline stages needed as the width increases. In addition to addition stages in the shuffle multiplexor and barrel shifter, we added duplicate registers to reduce fanout for each 16 inputs to help with the routing on the FPGA.

3.2 Merge Join

The prototype of the design presented in Section 2.2 is designed to merge two streams of elements composed of 32-bit keys and 16-bit values. Because of the high demand for routing resources, the structure did not map well to the FPGA fabric and we were able to achieve a block with a width of eight words for each input. The output combinations, which are a 32-bit key and two 16-bit values, and equality bit vector are sent into a selection block, which is wide enough to accept all 64 64-bit inputs.

The throughput of the prototype for varying amounts of output vs the input table size is presented in Figure 12. The line labeled "m=1" is the raw comparison grid without the optimization of not examining unnecessary cross sections. The other line, "m=8" shows the throughput for looking at 8 chunks of each input and only actually comparing

___
[2] Also note that "GB" is here is really gigabyte, not gibibyte, making percentage of line bandwidth, which is also in GB, not GiB, make sense

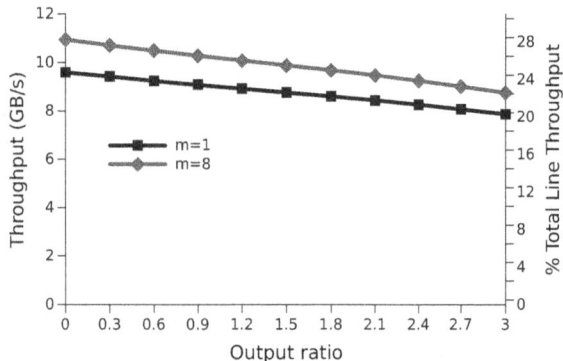

Figure 12: Throughput of the merge join prototype.

Memory	Port	Read Cycle	Write Cycle
valid copy 1	A	Read for push	Write for push
	B	Read for pop	Write for pop
valid copy 2	A	Read for request	Write for push
	B	Idle	Write for pop
request outstanding	A	Read for push	Write for push
	B	Read for request	Write for request

Table 1: Memory port usage in sort merge unit.

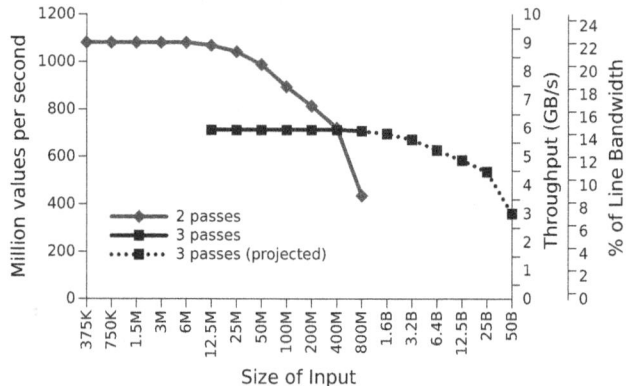

Figure 13: Throughput of the sort tree prototype.

chunks with potential matches. The output ratio is the size of the output compared to the input table size (which is two equally sized tables). The keys are uniformly distributed within a range that is changed to vary the output ratio.

At low output ratios, the throughput is contrained by the throughput of the hardware block itself (eight six byte values at 200 MHz is 9.6 GB/s). As the output ratio increases, it is necessary to "replay" portions of the input more often (see Section 2.2) and the throughput decreases. Above a ratio of 1.5 (i.e. the output is 1.5 times the size of the input), the throughput is entirely limited by the write memory bandwidth. We looked at non-uniform distributions, but saw no variance in the throughput for any given output ratio. Most skewed data, such as data with a Zipf distribution used in the literature, produced a very large amount of output and were all limited by the write memory bandwidth.

We do not plot the required resources for the merge join block because it is dominated entirely by the comparators and routing resources and is simply a quadratic function of the bandwidth required. To consume N values from either input every cycle required N^2 comparisons. Higher bandwidth could be obtained by replicating the merge block and partitioning the data, but doing so is left for future work.

3.3 Sorting

Section 2.3's implementation handles 12 64-bit values every other 200 MHz cycle, providing a maximum throughput of 19.2 GB/s, which is able to keep up with the memory bandwidth of an individual FPGA (assuming a column is being read and written). One of the major challenges faced in implementing the low bandwidth merge sort unit was the number of memory ports needed. In particular, it was necessary to access five different addresses of the valid memory in any given cycle. The local memories on the FPGA have two full RW ports. To solve the issue we duplicated each valid memory and time multiplexed the ports, alternating between reading and writing (thus handling a new input every other cycle). Table 1 details how each port was used to achieve a virtual 5-port memory. Note that each copy must perform the same operation on the write cycle to maintain coherent duplication.

All the other structures mapped directly to the FPGA logic. To maintain 19.2 GB/s through the entire tree, the three high bandwidth sort merge units at the bottom of the tree were built to accept 24 values every four cycles to accommodate the feedback path. The most challenging aspect was getting the control for the fine grained communication

between levels correct. As an example, the pop operation is pipelined to take six cycles: 1) start the read of data and valid blocks; 2) decode the index; 3) start the read of the feedback data; 4) the reads complete, compare the data; 5) multiplex the data based on the comparison result; 6) merge decoded index with read valid blocks, update the valid block, and send the feedback data and selected data to the merge network. At every other pipeline stage the index being pushed is compared with the incoming index and if the two fall within the same block, the decoded index, which indicates the valid bit to set, is updated and the incoming push is considered complete. The pipelines for the request and push operations are similar.

The memories on the FPGA provided enough space for 12 levels in the merge tree, with a top level 8k inputs wide. The data buffering alone for the merge tree (including the feedback data) occupied 18.6 Mbits, or 50%, of the 37.4 Mbits of block ram available on the device.

Figure 13 shows the throughput of the prototype as the size of the input column grows. Note that when performing two passes over the entire data set, the theoretical maximum throughput is one quarter of the maximum memory throughput (each value needs to be both read and written twice), or 9.7 GB/s in our case. At small input sizes, we achieve 8.7 GB/s, which is 22.7% of the maximum memory bandwidth, or 89% of the theoretical maximum with two passes. This high utilization is possible because there are fewer partially sorted portions to merge in the second pass and as a result each portion has a large virtual input buffer and the requests to memory can be large (see Section 2.3). For reference, recent work on sorting values on both CPUs and GPUs achieved rates as high as 268 million 32-bit values per second [16]. This corresponds to 1 GB/s of throughput, which is 3.9% of the 25.6 GB/s available to the Core i7 used (GPU performance was worse). We thus see a 5.7x improvement in terms of memory bandwidth utilization.

158

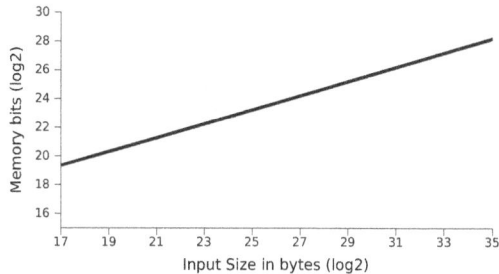

Figure 14: Memory bits required to achieve optimal throughput for a given input size. Note the log/log scale.

As the size of the input increases, the number of portions that must be merged on the second pass increases and the size of the requests to memory decrease. At an input size of 25M values, the memory requests are too small to fully utilize the memory bandwidth and performance begins to degrade. When the input size reaches 400M values, there are enough portions in the second pass that it is advantageous to perform a third pass. In this case, the portions from the first pass are partitioned into groups small enough that large memory requests can be used. Above 800M values, there was insufficient memory to hold both the input and output columns, we therefore projected the performance for larger columns using predictions based on the throughput seen on the second pass of smaller columns.

Unlike the previous sections, the interesting resource metric is not how the resource usage grows with desired bandwidth, but how the resource usage grows with input size, keeping bandwidth constant. A very small merge tree could maximize bandwidth for small inputs, but performance would rapidly decrease as input size grows. For example, our prototype was able to use the maximum amount of memory bandwidth until the input was over 12.5 million values. To see where this limit comes from, let N be the size of the input, in bytes, and let W be the width of the top level of the tree in bytes (in our prototype $W = 8k * 12 \; records * 8 \; bytes/record = 786432 \; bytes$). The number of portions left after the first pass through the data is $L = N/W$ and the maximum size of each read on the second pass is W/L, or W^2/N. If the minimum read size for optimal memory throughput is M, the maximum input size that achieves optimal memory performance is W^2/M. For the Maxeler platform, M is measured to be 6144 bytes, which gives a maximum size of 100 MB, or 12.5M 64-bit values. Likewise, W must be $\sqrt{M * N}$ for a table of size N to fully utilize the memory bandwidth on the second pass. Figure 14 provides the number of memory bits needed to achieve maximum memory bandwidth efficiency for given input sizes, provided a minimum read size of 6144 bytes.

To obtain the highest throughput possible using our platform, we tested a prototype where one quarter of the input column was split onto FPGAs 0 and 2, while the remaining three quarters were put on FPGA 1. With this configuration, the two smaller portions were individually sorted then streamed to the FPGA with the bulk of the data, and we achieved a throughput of 1.4 billion values per second, or 11.2 GB/s. With the narrow intra-FPGA links in play, this is a much lower percentage of the memory bandwidth available to the three chips used (9.7%).

System	Clock Freq	Throughput/ Mem BW (GB/s)	% of BW
Multi FPGA	200 MHz	6.45 / 115.2	5.6%
Single FPGA	200 MHz	6.25 / 38.4	16.3%
Kim [7] (CPU)	3.2 GHz	1 / 25.6	3.8%
Kaldewey [6] (GPU)	1.5 GHz	4.6 / 192.4	2.3%

Table 2: Summary of sort merge join results.

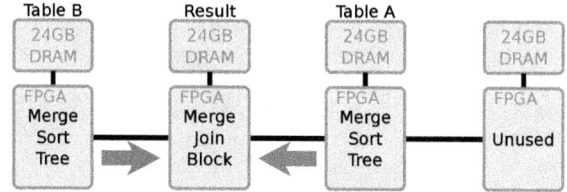

Figure 15: Full multi-FPGA join process. Each table is first sorted separately on the respective FPGA. Finally, both tables are sent to the FPGA containing the merge join block to be merged.

3.4 Sort Merge Join

Finally, we combine the selection, merge join, and sorting blocks to prototype the full design in Figure 8. The resources of a single FPGA were too constrained to fit all three blocks on a single FPGA, so we put the merge join and selection blocks on one FPGA and sort trees on the two adjacent FPGAs. Figure 15 outlines the process used to perform a full join. Each of the columns to be joined is held entirely on a seperate FPGA. Each table is individually sorted, except the output of the sort tree on the final pass is sent across the intra-FPGA links to the merge join block described in Section 3.2. These blocks are sufficiently wide to keep up with the bandwidth of the intra-FPGA links. Since the first sorting pass through the table has a constant throughput limited by the memory bandwidth, and the second and final pass through the data is limited by the intra-FPGA link, the end-to-end throughput of the whole design is a consistent 6.45 GB/s across all table sizes and output cardinality, or just over 800 million key/value pairs a second. This is slightly under the aggregate intra-FPGA bandwidth of 8 GB/s due to the initial pass through the data for sorting. The achieved 6.45 GB/s is 5.6% of the 115.2 GB/s of memory bandwidth available to the three chips. This lower utilization is due to the narrow intra-FPGA links.

If all three blocks were able to fit on a single chip, the second pass through the data would be constrained by the throughput of the merge-join block. In this case, the end-to-end throughput would be 6.25 GB/s, which is lower absolute throughput than the multi-FPGA design due to using only one FPGA's memory bandwidth, but is 16.3% of that FPGA's maximum memory throughput.

Table 2 summarizes our results and compares with other recent work on join processing. In Kim et. al.'s work [7], they used a Core i7 965 with 25.6 GB/s to achieve a join throughput of 128 million 64-bit tuples per second, or 1 GB/s and 3.9% of memory bandwidth. Our multi-FPGA design achieved a 40% increase over this utilization, and a single-chip design would provide a 4.1x increase in utilization. More recent work by Kaldewey et. al. [6] uses a GTX 580 GPU with 192.4 GB/s of memory bandwidth to achieve 4.6 GB/s of aggregate throughput. These results used UVA memory access over a PCIe link since their experiments showed that the computational throughput of the GPU was less then the PCIe data transfer throughput. This, even if the tables were contained in device memory, the join throughput would remain at 4.6 GB/s, or 2.3% of memory bandwidth of the device.

4. RELATED WORK

There has been a growing interest in using dedicated acceleration logic to accelerate database operations, specifically using FPGAs as an excellent platform to explore custom hardware options. Mueller et.al. proposed an FPGA co-processor that performs a streaming median operator which utilizes a sorting network [12]. This work performs a different operation and is directed at much smaller data sets and lower bandwidths than our work. In their design, it was only necessary to have single merge unit that data flowed through, sorting small eight word blocks in a sliding window independent of each other. Our design incorporates a full sorting tree that has many merge units coordinating the sorting of the entire memory stream. This same team has also proposed Glacier, a system which compiles queries directly to a hardware description [11, 13]. This is complimentary to our work as it looks at ways to incorporate accelerators into an overall database system.

Koch and Torrenson also propose an architecture for sorting numbers using FPGAs [8]. The design in this work has similarities to the sorting implementation presented here; however, they were constrained to a system with much lower memory bandwidth and capacity and thus achieve results on the order of 1 to 2 GB/s of throughput. They do not discuss scaling their results to higher bandwidths, which requires fundamental design changes as illustrated in our work. Our work builds on top of this work by presenting new designs that make use of a modern prototyping system with a large amount of memory capacity and bandwidth.

Researchers at IBM proposed an architecture to accelerate database operations in analytical queries using FPGAs [18]. Their work focuses on row decompression and predicate evaluation and concentrates on row based storage. Netezza, now part of IBM, provides systems that use FPGA based query evaluators that sit between disks and the processor [14]. Like Glacier, this work is complimentary and shows the possibilities of incorporating accelerators like those presented here into real database systems.

5. CONCLUSION

In this work we have presented three new hardware designs to perform important primitive database operations: selection, merge join, and sorting. We have shown how these hardware primitives can be combined to perform an equi-join of two database tables entirely in hardware. We described an FPGA based prototype of the designs and discussed challenges faced. We showed that our hardware designs were able to obtain close to ideal utilization of available memory bandwidth, resulting in a 2.8x, 5.7x, and 1.4x improvement in utilization over software for selection, sorting, and joining, respectively. We also present the hardware resources necessary to implement each hardware block and how those hardware resources grow with bandwidth.

6. ACKNOWLEDGEMENTS

This research is supported by DARPA Contract, SEEC: Specialized Extremely Efficient Computing, Contract # HR0011-11-C-0007; Army contract AHPCRC W911NF-07-2-0027-1; NSF grant, SHF: Large: Domain Specific Language Infrastructure for Biological Simulation Software, CCF-1111943; Stanford PPL affiliates program, Pervasive Parallelism Lab: Oracle, AMD, Intel, NVIDIA, and Huawei. Authors also acknowledge additional support from Oracle and the Maxeler University Program.

7. REFERENCES

[1] M. Bauer, H. Cook, and B. Khailany. CudaDMA: optimizing GPU memory bandwidth via warp specialization. In *High Performance Computing, Networking, Storage and Analysis*, SC '11.

[2] S. Borkar and A. A. Chien. The future of microprocessors. *Commun. ACM*, 54(5):67–77, May 2011.

[3] S. Borkar, T. Karnik, S. Narendra, J. Tschanz, A. Keshavarzi, and V. De. Parameter variations and impact on circuits and microarchitecture. In *Design Automation Conference*, June 2003.

[4] J. Chhugani, A. D. Nguyen, V. W. Lee, W. Macy, M. Hagog, Y.-K. Chen, A. Baransi, S. Kumar, and P. Dubey. Efficient implementation of sorting on multi-core SIMD CPU architecture. *Proc. VLDB Endow.*, August 2008.

[5] A. A. Chien, A. Snavely, and M. Gahagan. 10x10: A general-purpose architectural approach to heterogeneity and energy efficiency. *Procedia Computer Science*, 4(0):1987 – 1996, 2011.

[6] T. Kaldewey, G. Lohman, R. Mueller, and P. Volk. GPU join processing revisited. In *Workshop on Data Management on New Hardware*, DaMoN '12.

[7] C. Kim, T. Kaldewey, V. W. Lee, E. Sedlar, A. D. Nguyen, N. Satish, J. Chhugani, A. Di Blas, and P. Dubey. Sort vs. hash revisited: fast join implementation on modern multi-core CPUs. *Proc. VLDB Endow.*, August 2009.

[8] D. Koch and J. Torresen. FPGASort: a high performance sorting architecture exploiting run-time reconfiguration on fpgas for large problem sorting. In *Field Programmable Gate Arrays*, FPGA '11.

[9] N. Leischner, V. Osipov, and P. Sanders. GPU sample sort. In *Parallel Distributed Processing*, IPDPS '10.

[10] J. D. McCalpin. STREAM: Sustainable memory bandwidth in high performance computers. http://www.cs.virginia.edu/stream/.

[11] R. Mueller, J. Teubner, and G. Alonso. Glacier: a query-to-hardware compiler. In *Conference on Management of data*, SIGMOD '10.

[12] R. Mueller, J. Teubner, and G. Alonso. Data processing on FPGAs. *Proc. VLDB Endow.*, August 2009.

[13] R. Mueller, J. Teubner, and G. Alonso. Streams on wires: a query compiler for FPGAs. *Proc. VLDB Endow.*, August 2009.

[14] Netezza. The Netezza FAST engines framework.

[15] N. Satish, M. Harris, and M. Garland. Designing efficient sorting algorithms for manycore GPUs. In *Parallel Distributed Processing*, IPDPS '09.

[16] N. Satish, C. Kim, J. Chhugani, A. D. Nguyen, V. W. Lee, D. Kim, and P. Dubey. Fast sort on CPUs and GPUs: a case for bandwidth oblivious SIMD sort. In *Conference on Management of data*, SIGMOD '10.

[17] E. Sintorn and U. Assarsson. Fast parallel GPU-sorting using a hybrid algorithm. *Journal of Parallel and Distributed Computing*, 68(10), 2008.

[18] B. Sukhwani, H. Min, M. Thoennes, P. Dube, B. Iyer, B. Brezzo, D. Dillenberger, and S. Asaad. Database analytics acceleration using FPGAs. In *Parallel Architectures and Compilation Techniques*, PACT '12.

A Scalable Sparse Matrix-Vector Multiplication Kernel for Energy-Efficient Sparse-Blas on FPGAs

Richard Dorrance
EE Department, UCLA
Los Angeles, CA 90095 USA
rdorrance@ucla.edu

Fengbo Ren
EE Department, UCLA
Los Angeles, CA 90095 USA
renfengbo@ucla.edu

Dejan Marković
EE Department, UCLA
Los Angeles, CA 90095 USA
dejan@ee.ucla.edu

ABSTRACT

Sparse Matrix-Vector Multiplication (SpMxV) is a widely used mathematical operation in many high-performance scientific and engineering applications. In recent years, tuned software libraries for multi-core microprocessors (CPUs) and graphics processing units (GPUs) have become the status quo for computing SpMxV. However, the computational throughput of these libraries for sparse matrices tends to be significantly lower than that of dense matrices, mostly due to the fact that the compression formats required to efficiently store sparse matrices mismatches traditional computing architectures. This paper describes an FPGA-based SpMxV kernel that is scalable to efficiently utilize the available memory bandwidth and computing resources. Benchmarking on a Virtex-5 SX95T FPGA demonstrates an average computational efficiency of 91.85%. The kernel achieves a peak computational efficiency of 99.8%, a >50x improvement over two Intel Core i7 processors (i7-2600 and i7-4770) and showing a >300x improvement over two NVIDIA GPUs (GTX 660 and GTX Titan), when running the MKL and cuSPARSE sparse-BLAS libraries, respectively. In addition, the SpMxV FPGA kernel is able to achieve higher performance than its CPU and GPU counterparts, while using only 64 single-precision processing elements, with an overall 38-50x improvement in energy efficiency.

Categories and Subject Descriptors

B.7.1 [**Integrated Circuits**]: Types and Design Styles— *Algorithms implemented in hardware*; G.1.3 [**Numerical Analysis**]: Numerical Linear Algebra—*Sparse, structured, and very large systems (direct and iterative methods)*

General Terms

Algorithms, performance

Keywords

SpMxV, sparse-BLAS, FPGA, CPU, GPU, energy-efficiency, computational efficiency, benchmarking

FPGA'14, February 26–28, 2014, Monterey, California, USA.
Copyright © 2014 ACM 978-1-4503-2671-1/14/02...$15.00.
http://dx.doi.org/10.1145/2554688.2554785

1. INTRODUCTION

Sparse matrices arise in a wide variety of computational disciplines, including image reconstruction, circuit and economic modeling, industrial engineering, compressive sensing, neural networks, and algorithms for least squares and eigenvalue problems [1-3]. As such, Sparse Matrix-Vector Multiplication (SpMxV) is the main computational kernel that dominates the performance of many of the aforementioned applications. Unfortunately, the performance of SpMxV algorithms tends to be much lower than that of dense matrices, mostly due to the mismatch between the memory access patterns of sparse matrices and the compression formats required to efficiently store them [3,4].

Numerous efforts have been made to accelerate the performance of SpMxV on multi-core microprocessors (CPUs) [5,6] and graphics processing units (GPUs) over the years [7-9]. Recently, field-programmable gate arrays (FPGAs) have become an attractive option for accelerating SpMxV [1-4,10-14]. FPGAs have high floating-point performance, large amounts of on-chip memory, and an abundant number of high-speed I/O pins capable of providing large amounts of off-chip memory bandwidth. The flexible nature of FPGAs also allows architectural adaptations to satisfy the needs of different problems.

In this paper, we propose a scalable architecture for SpMxV with higher computational efficiency than traditional CPU/GPU-based approaches. Computational efficiency is a measure of the percentage of the total hardware resources available that are actively being used by an algorithm. An implementation of an algorithm with a higher computational efficiency will therefore be more energy-efficient. We leverage the structure of conventional sparse matrix compression formats for general sparse matrices in order to regularize their memory access patterns. The benchmarking results based on the FPGA implementation show that the proposed SpMxV kernel can reach significantly higher computational efficiency than state-of-the-art solutions using CPUs and GPUs, with more than a 50x and 300x improvement respectively. Even for very large, irregular, sparse matrices, our design can achieve performance comparable to that of dense matrices.

The remainder of the paper is organized as follows. Section 2 introduces SpMxV and discusses the inefficiencies present in existing software (powered by CPUs and GPUs) and hardware (FPGA) implementations. Section 3 details the proposed architecture to address these short comings. Benchmarking results on computational throughput and energy efficiency are presented in Section 4. Section 5 concludes the paper.

(a)

$$A = \begin{bmatrix} 1 & 4 & 0 & 0 & 0 \\ 0 & 2 & 3 & 0 & 0 \\ 5 & 0 & 0 & 7 & 8 \\ 0 & 0 & 9 & 0 & 6 \end{bmatrix}$$

(b) $COO \begin{cases} data = \begin{bmatrix} 1 & 4 & 2 & 3 & 5 & 7 & 8 & 9 & 6 \end{bmatrix} \\ row = \begin{bmatrix} 0 & 0 & 1 & 1 & 2 & 2 & 2 & 3 & 3 \end{bmatrix} \\ col = \begin{bmatrix} 0 & 1 & 1 & 2 & 0 & 3 & 4 & 2 & 4 \end{bmatrix} \end{cases}$

(c) $CSR \begin{cases} data = \begin{bmatrix} 1 & 4 & 2 & 3 & 5 & 7 & 8 & 9 & 6 \end{bmatrix} \\ ptr = \begin{bmatrix} 0 & 2 & 4 & 7 & 9 \end{bmatrix} \\ col = \begin{bmatrix} 0 & 1 & 1 & 2 & 0 & 3 & 4 & 2 & 4 \end{bmatrix} \end{cases}$

(d) $CSC \begin{cases} data = \begin{bmatrix} 1 & 5 & 4 & 2 & 3 & 9 & 7 & 8 & 6 \end{bmatrix} \\ row = \begin{bmatrix} 0 & 2 & 0 & 1 & 1 & 3 & 2 & 2 & 3 \end{bmatrix} \\ ptr = \begin{bmatrix} 0 & 2 & 4 & 6 & 7 & 9 \end{bmatrix} \end{cases}$

Figure 1. The sparse matrix representation for (a) an example matrix A in the (b) COO, the (c) CSR, and the (d) CSC formats.

2. SPARSE MATRIX-VECTOR MULTIPLICATION

SpMxV is a mathematical kernel that takes the form of:

$$y \leftarrow Ax, \tag{1}$$

where A is an M×N sparse matrix (the majority of the elements are zero), y is an M×1 vector, and x is an N×1 vector. More generally, SpMxV can be represented as:

$$y \leftarrow \alpha Ax + \beta, \tag{2}$$

where α and β are scalars.

The performance of sparse-matrix algorithms tends to be much lower than that of dense matrices due to two key factors: (1) the way the sparse matrix is represented in memory and (2) the computation architecture of the target platform.

2.1 Sparse Matrix Representation

There are a variety of ways to represent the sparse matrix for storage purposes. However, the few computationally efficient formats are restricted to highly structured matrices, such as diagonal or banded matrices. In this paper, we focus on boosting the efficiency of SpMxV for generic sparse matrices. Therefore, we only present general sparse storage schemes in this section.

Figure 1 illustrates a sample sparse matrix and three different schemes to represent it. The simplest storage scheme, shown in Fig. 1(b), is the coordinate (COO) format. The row indices, column indices, and values of the nonzero matrix entries are explicitly stored in 3 separate arrays: *row*, *col*, and *data*. The compressed sparse row (CSR) format (Fig. 1(c)) is the most commonly used sparse storage scheme, which also stores the column indices and nonzero values into the arrays: *col* and *data*.

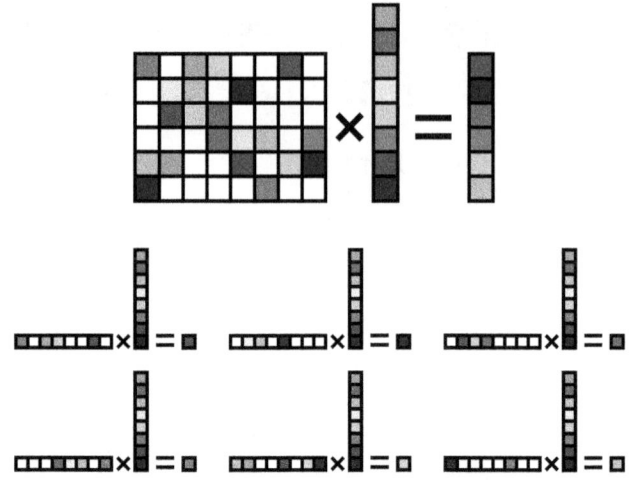

Figure 2. A graphical representation of how SpMxV is performed using the CSR format on CPUs and GPUs. Each element in y is calculated as the dot product between the appropriate row of A and the vector x.

Unlike the COO format, the row indices are not explicitly stored, but rather as an array of row pointers, *ptr*. The ith element of *ptr* corresponds to the offset of the ith row into the *col* and *data* arrays. For example, in Fig.1(c) the first element of *ptr* is 0, indicating that the first element in row 0 is 1 and is located in column 0; the second element of *ptr* is 2, indicating that the first element in row 1 is 2 and is located in column 1; the third element of *ptr* is 4, indicating that the first element in row 2 is 5 and is located in column 5; and so on. For an M×N matrix, *ptr* has M+1 elements in the CSR format, with the final element indicating the total number of nonzero entries in the matrix. The compressed sparse column (CSC) format, used in our SpMxV kernel, is a variation of the CSR format (Fig. 1(d)). Instead of storing the column indices and an array of row pointers, the CSC stores the row indices and an array of column pointers. For any matrix A, the CSR storage of A is exactly the same as the CSC storage of A^T.

2.2 Existing SpMxV Architectures

Specialized software libraries for solving dense and sparse linear algebra problems are very popular for high-performance computing. These libraries, such as MKL [5] for CPUs, and cuBLAS [7] and cuSPARSE [8] for GPUs, provide a standardized programming interface, with subroutines optimized for the target platform.

For SpMxV on CPUs and GPUs, the ith element of y is typically calculated as the dot-product of the ith row of A and the vector x (Fig. 2). This is because each computing core usually contains only a handful of general purpose registers and a single floating-point unit (FPU). Therefore, CSR is one of the most computationally efficient storage options for sparse matrices on CPUs and GPUs. It has the added benefit of being easily parallelizable: each computing core can be independently assigned a different value of y to calculate.

Improving the parallel performance of SpMxV via blocking (splitting up the matrix into several sub-matrices) and modifications to the CRS format is a very active area of study

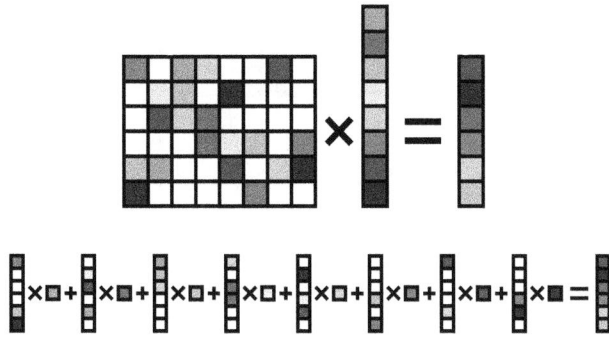

Figure 3. A graphical representation of how SpMxV is performed using the CSC format. The entire vector *y* is calculated as a series of vector additions of the columns of *A* weighted by the appropriate element from *x*.

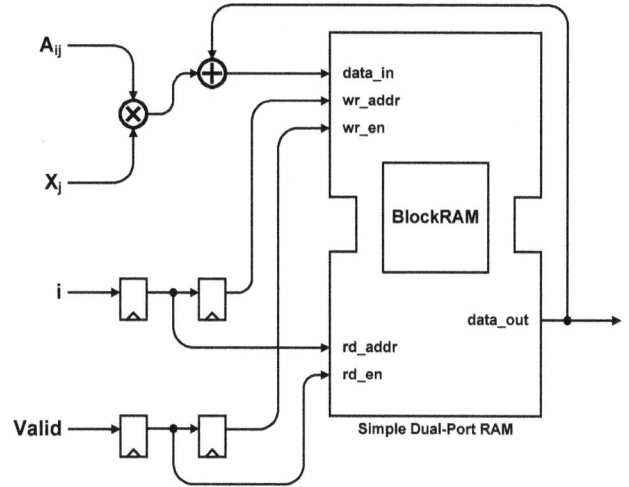

Figure 4. Schematic of a single PE using a simple dual-port RAM, floating-point adder, and a floating-point multiplier.

[3,6,9]. Unfortunately, the use of CSR, and its variants, for SpMxV have several drawbacks on CPUs and GPUs that hurts its overall computational efficiency [3]:

(1) The SpMxV kernel is memory-bounded. CPUs and GPUs typically have much larger computational throughput than available memory bandwidth. This leads to a very low utilization rate for the computing resources, and subsequently, poor energy efficiency.

(2) The indirect (global) memory references for the vector *x* present in *col* adds uncertainty to the memory access pattern, ultimately delaying the computation. Each element of *col* must first be loaded from memory and added to the address of *x* as an offset. Only then can the correct value of *x* be loaded into the FPU for computation.

(3) Irregular memory access of vector *x* causes a large number of cache misses. In CPUs, this cache miss can add tens of cycles of latency. In GPUs, a cache miss can add hundreds of cycles of latency. GPUs typically try to hide these large latencies by interleaving dozens of threads on a single computational core. This works well for computation-bounded algorithms, but not memory-bounded algorithms like SpMxV.

(4) Short row lengths (i.e. very few nonzero elements per row) can cause serious performance degradation. When rows are short, the overhead associated with calculating each element of *y* becomes significant.

Due to these drawbacks, CPUs and GPUs reach less than 5% of their theoretical peak processing throughput and utilize less than 50% of their available memory bandwidth for SpMxV [6,9].

Previous FPGA implementations have attempted to alleviate these inefficiencies by introducing several architectural changes. In some designs, several processing elements (PEs) work together to compute a single element of *y* in parallel [1,4,12]. These designs employ various reduction circuits in order to combine the intermediary results. Other designs have each PE calculate several elements of *y* in a sequential manner in order to mitigate the effect of short rows [2,10,12]. In both cases, the entirety of the *x* vector, or a large subsection (in the case of blocking), is buffered in on-chip Block RAM (BRAM) to reduce the effects of irregular memory accesses [1-4,10-13]. However, these prior implementations primarily focus on reducing the total number of

adders and their resource usage in the design. As such, they only average less than 50% of their theoretical peak processing throughput and memory bandwidth [1-4,10-14].

3. PROPOSED ARCHITECTURE

Our architecture abandons the idea of calculating each element of *y* separately as the row-wise dot product between *A* and *x*. Instead, the entirety of *y* is calculated as the column-wise vector additions of *A* weighted by each element of *x*, as shown in Fig. 3. Fundamentally, this allows us to directly address the major limitations present in the SpMxV algorithm when implemented on an FPGA:

(1) A dedicated co-processor allows for much better balancing of system resources. The number of processing elements (PEs) can be efficiently scaled to match the available memory bandwidth.

(2) What used to be indirect (global) memory references for *x* in *col* vector (for the CSR format) are now direct (local) memory references for *y* in the *row* vector. In other words, when a column of *A* is multiplied by an element of *x*, in the manner shown in Fig. 3, we know exactly which elements of *y* the partial product contributes to. This allows us to halve the number of require memory accesses, the largest bottleneck in the SpMxV algorithm.

(3) Memory access to the *x* vector is no longer irregular, but sequential. By using the CSC format to store *A*, both *A* and *x* can be placed in a large off-chip memory and sequentially streamed into the DSP co-processor (eliminating the time and energy overheads of a cache miss).

(4) Short row or column lengths have much less impact on the performance of SpMxV, since the PEs are rarely idled thanks to the balanced memory bandwidth and computing capability. However, performance is degraded as the memory bandwidth of *x* approaches that of *A* for extremely sparse matrices. In the rare case of M ≫ N, the performance of CSC is no better than that of CSR.

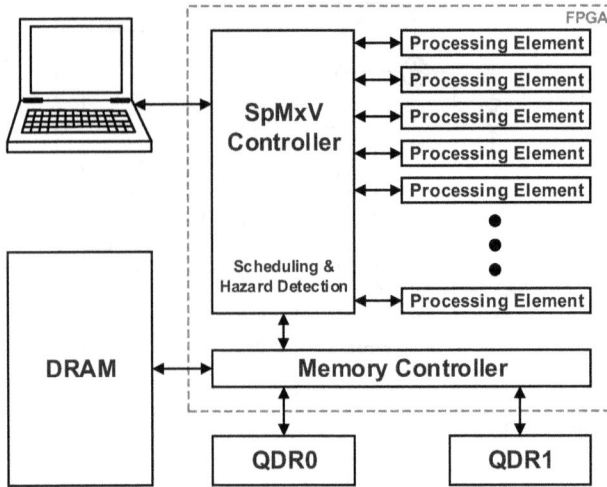

Figure 5. Top-level schematic of the SpMxV kernel, with 8 processing elements, running on the ROACH FPGA platform. The SpMxV kernel acts as a coprocessor for a networked computer running a MATLAB environment.

Table 1. Resource usage for the SpMxV kernel (64 PEs).

Resource	Used	Available	Percent
Registers	31,621	58,880	53.70%
LUTs	27,958	58,880	47.48%
BRAMs	160	244	65.57%
DSP48Es	320	640	50.00%

First, the reduction circuit adds a large amount of overhead in terms of latency and additional hardware (even if existing adders are used, more resources are needed for configurability). Second, by splitting up computation along the columns, we lose some of the sequential nature of the memory accesses we had gained with the CSC format. The memory accesses for each PE are still sequential, but globally the memory accesses for all PEs are irregular. To mitigate this, a more complicated memory controller is required to ensure a balanced load across all of the PEs. Third, if there are fewer columns than PEs, this approach is effectively no different than prior FPGA implementations.

The second option for computing the final vector is to assign a subset of rows of A to each PE (i.e. blocking along the rows of A). Each PE computes a subset of the final vector, which are then concatenated together at the end (requiring no additional latency). Additionally, this preserves the property of sequential memory accesses across all PEs, allowing for a much simpler memory controller (at the cost of a slightly more complicated SpMxV controller to handle additional scheduling and hazard detection). Finally, with minor modifications to the SpMxV and memory controllers, our SpMxV kernel can also support a sparse matrix dense matrix multiplication (SpMxM): each column of the dense matrix is assigned to a PE, which each PE computing a single column of the resulting matrix. Our SpMxV kernel uses this option, with the modifications to support SpMxM, in its implementation.

Computing the SpMxV column-wise also allows for an extremely simple PE (Fig. 4). Each PE contains a single-precision floating-point adder and multiplier, as well as a simple dual-port RAM. Each simple dual-port RAM utilizes the large amounts of BRAM resources available on FPGAs and can accommodate several hundred to several thousand elements of y. Figure 5 shows the overall experiment setup, in which the SpMxV kernel (implemented on an FPGA) serves as a co-processor attached to an external computer. A dedicated memory controller allows the elements of A and x to be continuously streamed into the FPGA, while the SpMxV controller's primary function is scheduling and hazard detection. Hazard detection avoids the conflict between two partial products that contribute to the same element of y overlapping due to the latency of the floating-point adder. If such a hazard is detected, we must either stall or provide alternative data to ensure that the result of y is calculated correctly.

3.1 Processing Element

As stated previously, each PE (Fig. 4) contains a single-precision floating-point adder and multiplier, as well as a simple dual-port RAM. To perform the SpMxV, each PE multiplies an element of the *data* vector (A_{ij}) and the corresponding element of the x vector (X_j) together. The resulting partial product is then added to address in the *row* vector (i), before being stored back into the BRAM of the dual-port RAM. Due to the latency of the multiplication and addition operations, a *Valid* signal is used to prevent data corruption due to hazards. Using this strategy, data can be continuously streamed into each PE (directly from the CSC format) with a small startup overhead latency equal to that of the adder and the multiplier.

Since each PE has its own working copy of the vector being computed, there are two possible strategies for assembling the final vector. The first option is to assign a subset of the x vector to each PE (i.e. blocking along the columns of A). Each PE computes a partial sum of the final vector and an adder tree (which can be built from the existing adders in each PE) is used to combine them at the end. Similar to prior FPGA implementations [1-4,10-13], this straightforward approach has several drawbacks.

3.2 SpMxV and Memory Controller

The primary purposes of the SpMxV controller are scheduling and hazard detection. The memory controller acts as a slave to the SpMxV controller, ensuring a continuous stream of data into the PEs. Hazards arise when two or more partial products want to write to the same memory address of the dual-port RAM in a short period of time. Due to the latency of the floating-point adder in Fig. 4, the existing sum of the partial products in the dual-port RAM must be prefetched. If two partial products that contribute to the same term are allowed to proceeded, the second product will prefetch a sum that does not include the first product. The result is that the final sum of products will not include the first conflicting partial product. The SpMxV controller detects these hazards and corrects them in one of two ways. It first attempts to shuffle the partial products to increase their distance in time. If this is not possible, or would result in additional hazards, the SpMxV controller issues a stall command to the PE (by deasserting the *Valid* signal, and holding the values of A_{ij}, X_j, and i).

Figure 6 shows the stalling behavior for a single processing element performing SpMxV between the example A matrix from Fig. 1(a) and the vector $x = [0.1\ 0.2\ 0.3\ 0.4\ 0.5]^T$. In the example, the latency of the floating-point multiplier and adder are both 2

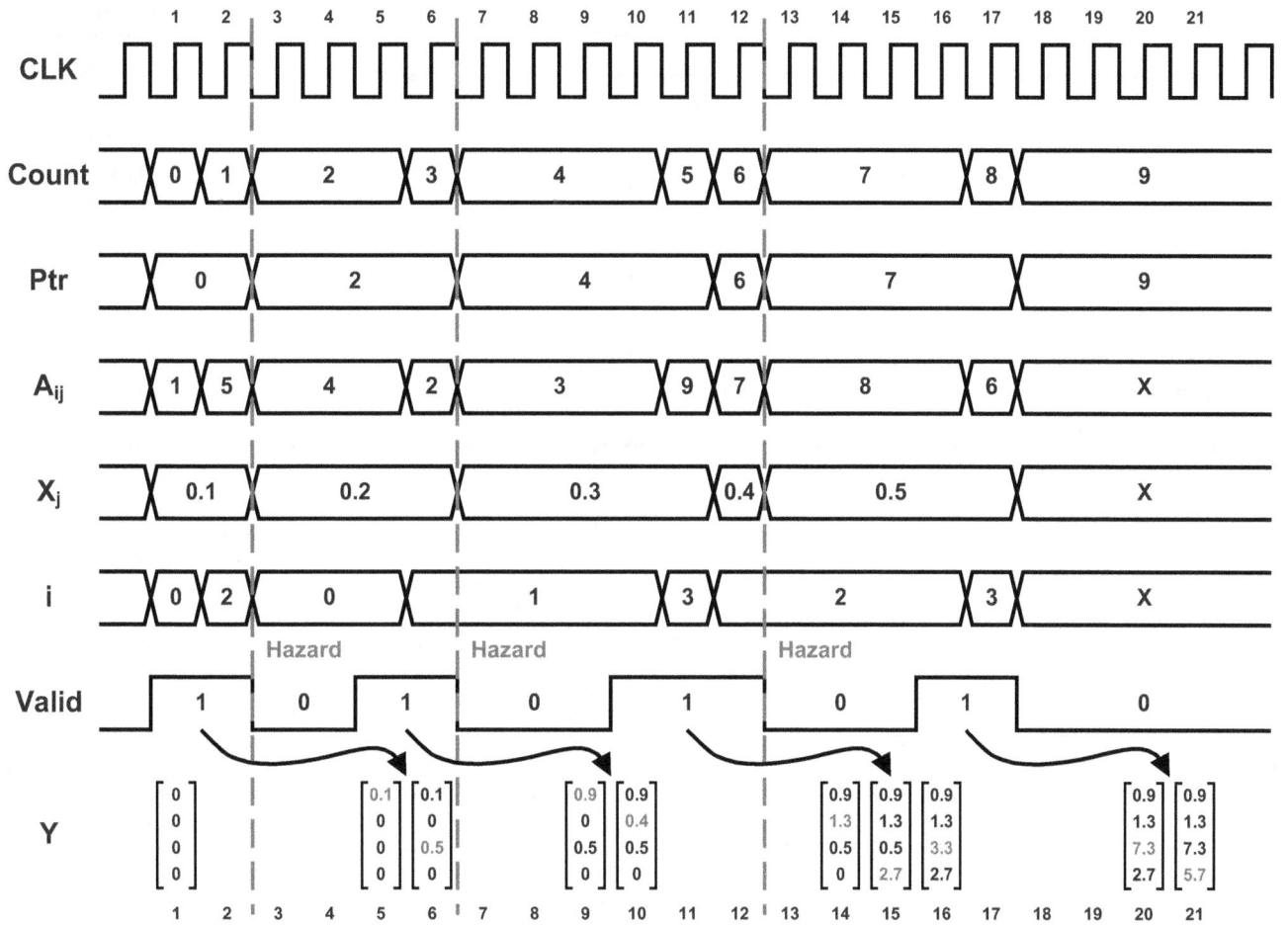

Figure 6. Timing diagram for calculating the SpMxV of the example *A* matrix from Fig. 1(a) and *x* = [0.1 0.2 0.3 0.4 0.5]^T using a single PE. For this example, the floating-point adder and multiplier both have a latency of 2 clock cycles and the simple dual-port memory (*Y*) has a latency of 1 clock cycle.

clock cycles. Additionally, the simple dual-port memory (*Y*) has a latency of 1 clock cycle. In cycle 2, a hazard is detected due to the proximity of the partial product of 1×0.1 and the partial product of 4×0.2. We must stall for 2 cycles—by deasserting *Valid* and holding the values of A_{ij}, X_j, and *i*—to ensure that partial product of 1×0.1 is added to *Y* before continuing. If co-processor had not stalled, the partial product of 4×0.2 would have added itself to the current value of *Y*, 0, producing an incorrect final value of 0.8 (instead of 0.9). Computation resumes in cycle 5, after the hazard has passed. Additional hazards are detected in cycles 6 and 12, with each hazard resulting in 3 clock cycles of stalling.

4. PERFORMANCE EVALUATION

The SpMxV kernel was evaluated on the open-source academic research platform "ROACH" (Reconfigurable Open Architecture Computing Hardware) [15]. The ROACH platform is equipped with a Virtex-5 SX95T FPGA for DSP applications, a PowerPC running Linux, two 36Mb QDRII+ SRAMs, and 2GB of DDR2 SDRAM for a combined peak memory bandwidth of 35.74 GB/s. The PowerPC allows a computer running MATLAB to interface with "software registers," BRAMs, and FIFOs on the FPGA, as well as to load data in and out of the board-level QDRs and DRAM (Fig. 5).

Table 1 show the total resource usage of the SpMxV kernel implemented with 64 PEs using a single-precision floating-point format. The SX95T FPGA can support up to 96 single-precision PE (using 98.4% of the available BRAM), but is ultimately limited by our available memory bandwidth. The CSC *A* matrix is stored in the SDRAM, while the *x* and *y* vectors are stored in the two QDRs. The QDRs are accessed in parallel to effectively create a single memory with twice the bit width. The ROACH board can operate up to 150MHz (limited by the QDR memory controller), resulting in a peak performance of 19.2 GFLOP/s with a thermal design power (TDP) of 25W.

4.1 Comparison to CPUs and GPUs

We use a collection of 10 unstructured matrices used by both Williams et al. [6] and Bell et al. [9] in our performance benchmarking study. Table 2 details the size and overall sparsity structure of each matrix. All of the matrices are publically available online from the University of Florida Sparse Matrix Collection [16]. For comparison, the same benchmarks are run on both a 64-bit Linux machine and a 64-bit Windows machine.

The Linux machine has 16GB of memory and an Intel Core i7-2600 processor (4 physical cores with hyper-threading, for a total of 8 virtual cores), using the MKL sparse-BLAS library [5]. The Core i7-2600 processor has a peak memory bandwidth of 21GB/s

Table 2. Summary of unstructured matrices used for benchmarking performance (publically available from [16]).

Matrix	Rows	Columns	Nonzeros	Nonzeros/Column	Density
Dense	2,000	2,000	4,000,000	2000.00	100.00000%
Protein	36,417	36,417	4,344,765	119.31	0.32761%
FEM/Spheres	83,334	83,334	6,010,480	72.13	0.08655%
FEM/Cantilever	62,451	62,451	4,007,383	64.17	0.10275%
Wind Tunnel	217,918	217,918	11,524,432	52.88	0.02427%
FEM/Harbor	46,835	46,835	2,374,001	50.69	0.10823%
QCD	49,152	49,152	1,916,928	39.00	0.07935%
FEM/Ship	140,874	140,874	3,568,176	25.33	0.01798%
Economics	206,500	206,500	1,273,389	6.17	0.00299%
FEM/Accelerator	121,192	121,192	2,624,331	21.65	0.01787%

with a peak performance of 108.8GFLOP/s and a TDP of 95W [17]. The benchmarks were also run on an NVIDIA GeForce GTX 660 graphics card (960 CUDA cores), installed on the same Linux machine, using the cuSPARSE library [8]. The GPU has a peak memory bandwidth of 144.2GB/s and a peak performance of 1881.6GFLOP/s with a TDP of 140W [18].

The Windows machine has 32GB of memory and an Intel Core i7-4770 processor (4 physical cores with hyper-threading, for a total of 8 virtual cores), using the MKL sparse-BLAS library [5]. The Core i7-4770 processor has a peak memory bandwidth of 25.6GB/s and a peak performance of 217.6GFLOP/s with a TDP of 84W [19]. The benchmarks were also run on an NVIDIA GeForce GTX Titan graphics card (2688 CUDA cores), installed on the same Windows machine, using the cuSPARSE library [8]. The GPU has a peak memory bandwidth of 288.4GB/s and a peak performance of 4,500GFLOP/s with a TDP of 250W [20].

Figure 7 compares the raw computational performance (in GFLOP/s) of the CPU, GPU, and FPGA SpMxV kernels for all of the matrices tested. SpMxV on the two CPUs showed a performance drop of 20-50% compared to dense matrices, while the two GPUs showed a performance drop of 30-60%. Figure 8 compares the computational efficiency of the CPU, GPU, and FPGA SpMxV kernels for all of the matrices tested. For a memory bound algorithm like SpMxV, the computational efficiency is strongly determined by the memory hierarchy (i.e. the cache structure and size). The computational efficiency is calculated as the ratio of the measured SpMxV performance, in GFLOP/s, over the theoretical peak GFLOP/s achievable for each platform.

The Core i7-2600 and Core i7-4770 processors achieved an average performance of 2.01 and 4.59GFLOP/s, respectively, across all 10 test matrices. The resulting computational efficiencies were 1.84% and 2.11%. Overall, the computational efficiency of both CPUs was 1-2% for all of the test matrices. The Core i7-4770 processor was able to achieve a 2.28x speedup over the Core i7-2600, despite only having 22% more memory bandwidth, due to its more efficient memory accesses with its larger vector processing cores.

The largest drops in performance for the CPUs were recorded using the sparsest matrices: FEM/Ships, Economics, and FEM/Accelerator. These matrices had a significantly higher rate of cache misses due to their large size and overall sparsity. The relativity small number of nonzero elements per row (especially for the Economics matrix) also added significant overhead by having to flush the pipeline more often.

Similarly, the GTX 660 and GTX Titan GPUs achieved an average performance of 5.79 and 14.86 GFLOP/s, respectively across all 10 matrices. The resulting computational efficiencies were 0.31% and 0.33%. Overall, the computational efficiency of both GPUs was between 0.2-0.5% for all of the test matrices. The GTX Titan had an average speed up of 2.57x over the GTX 660 GPU, which is consistent with the GTX Titan having 2x the memory bandwidth and 2.39x the number of processing cores as the GTX 660. Because individual process threads are organized differently on the GPU, each CUDA core had to be flushed far less often than the CPU for the FEM/Ships, Economics, and FEM/Accelerator matrices, leading to more even performance.

On the Linux test setup, the GTX 660 had an average speedup of 2.93x over the i7-2600 processor, and on the Windows setup, the GTX Titan had a 3.23x speedup over the i7-4770 processor. Despite the roughly 3x performance increase by the GPUs (Fig. 6), the CPUs are about 6x more computationally efficient than the GPUs (Fig. 7). The GPUs use 100-300x more processing cores to achieve a total, theoretical peak performance roughly 20x greater than that of the CPU, but only have about 8x more memory bandwidth. The cache structure of a GPU is smaller and has higher latency that of a CPU [18,19]. GPUs are designed to mask random memory accesses for computationally intensive algorithms, leading to much larger penalties in efficiency for cache misses when compared to a CPU.

The SpMxV kernel running on the Virtex-5 SX95T FPGA achieved an average performance of 17.64GFLOP/s, for a computational efficiency of 91.85%, across all 10 matrices. The Dense matrix achieved a peak performance of 19.16GFLOP/s for a computational efficiency of 99.8%. This performance represents an average speedup of 9.55x and 4.18x over the i7-2600 and i7-4770 CPUs and a 3.31x and 1.28x speedup over the GTX 660 and GTX Titan GPUs. Moreover, the computational efficiency of the FPGA SpMxV kernel had an average improvement of 54x and 322x over the CPUs and GPUs, respectively.

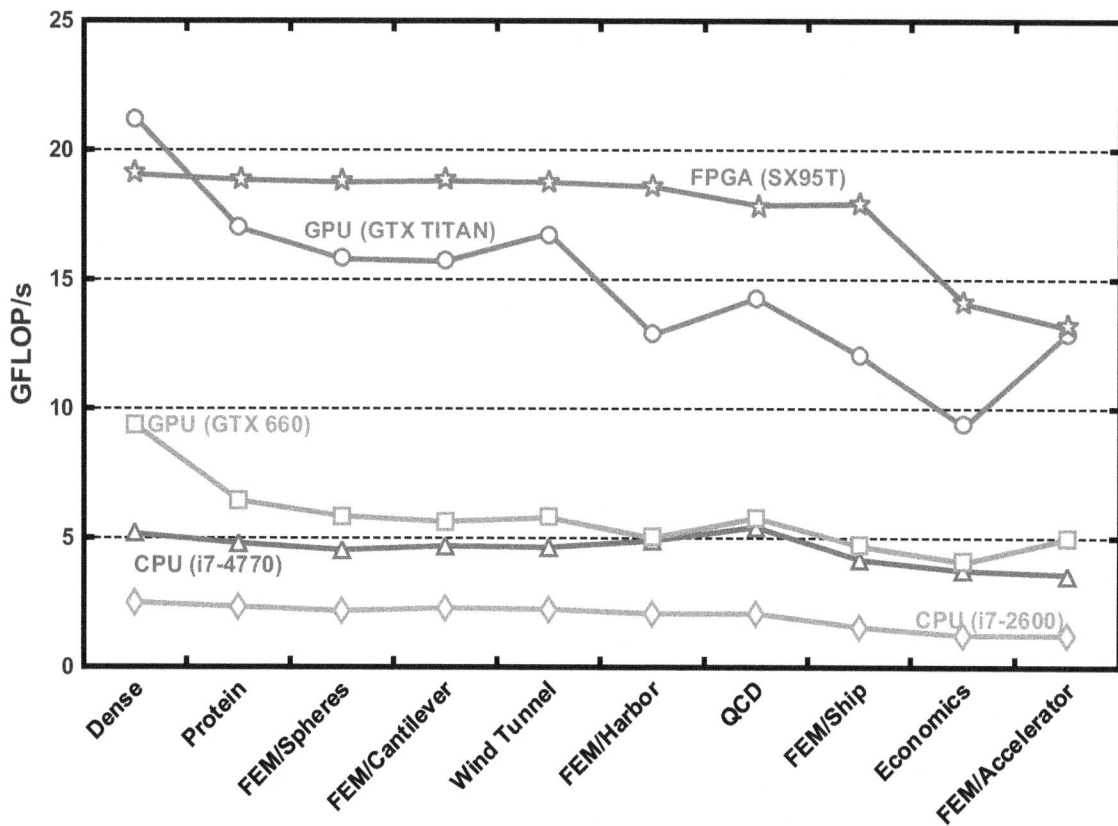

Figure 7. Raw computational performance of the CPU, GPU, and FPGA SpMxV kernels.

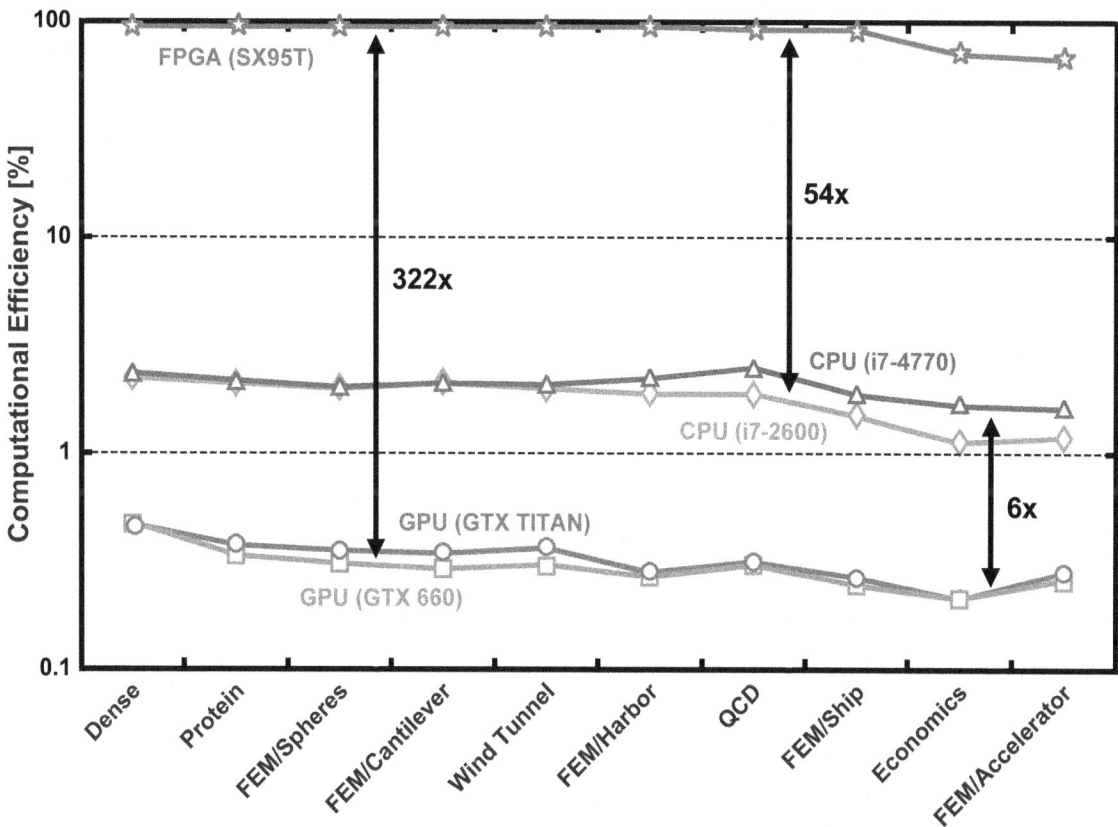

Figure 8. Computational efficiency of the CPU, GPU, and FPGA SpMxV kernels.

Table 3. Comparison of FPGA SpMxV Architectures

	[1]	[2]	[11]	[12]	[13]	This Work
FPGA	Virtex-5 LX155T	Stratix-III EP3SE260	Virtex-II Pro 70	Virtex-II Pro 100	Virtex-II 6000	Virtex-5 SX95T
Frequency [MHz]	100	100	200	170	95	150
Memory Bandwidth [GB/s]	6.5	8.5	8	8.5	1.6	35.74
Number of PE	16	6	4	5	3	64
Peak Performance [GFLOP/s]	3.2	1.2	1.6	1.7	0.57	19.2
Matrix Format	CVBV†	COO	CSR	CSR	SPAR*	CSC
Sparse Test Matrix Density						
MIN-MAX [%]	0.01-5.48	0.51-11.49	0.04-4.17	0.04-0.39	0.01-1.10	0.003-0.33
Average [%]	1.41	3.34	0.87	0.16	--	0.09
Computational Efficiency						
MIN-MAX [%]	1-7	5-7	20-79	50-98.4	1-74	69-99.8
Average [%]	4.48	5.63	42.6	79.4	55.6	91.9

†Variant of CSR.   *Variant of CSC.

The average power consumption of the i7-2600 and i7-4770 processors was measured to be 77.2W and 66.3W, respectively. The resulting power efficiencies are 26MFLOP/s/W and 69MFLOP/s/W. Similarly, the average power of the GTX 660 and GTX Titan were measured to be 99W and 163W, respectively. The resulting power efficiencies are 58MFLOP/s/W and 91MFLOP/s/W. The worst case power of the SX95T FPGA was measured to be 5.1W, resulting in a power efficiency of 3,460 MFLOP/s/W. This represents more than a 50x and 38x improvement in energy efficiency over the CPU and GPU implementations, respectively.

4.2 Comparison to Existing FPGA Art

In Table 3, we compare our proposed architecture to several published SpMxV FPGA architectures. The architectures can be categorized into 3 distinct groups. The first is to either re-encode, reorder, or preprocess the sparse matrix in such a way as to reduce data hazards [1,2]. Kestur et al. [1] re-encode the matrix into the Compressed Variable-Length Bit Vector (CVBV) format (a variation of the CSR format) on the fly to reduce the required memory bandwidth. However, re-encoding the matrix insures a significant overhead penalty, resulting in marginal efficiency improvements over CPU and GPU implementations (only 3-10x). Sun et al. [2] preprocess the matrix to reorganize and optimize the datapath to eliminate hazards. After preprocessing, the matrices achieve a computational efficiency of 96-99% on the FPGA. Unfortunately, the preprocessing overhead (datapath optimization, FPGA reconfiguration, and buffering the matrix on BRAM) is about 20 times greater than that of the SpMxV calculation. This results in an effective computational efficiency of only 5-7%.

The second approach is to use several PE (each with its own working copy of x) in parallel with a reduction circuit or adder tree to accumulate a single element of y [11,12]. In Zhuo et al. [11], the partial product of 4 multipliers are added together via a tree of 3 adders. The resulting sum is then fed into a novel reduction circuit (accumulator) that handles the potential read-after-write data hazards. The drawback of this approach is that it requires zero padding to achieve a minimum row size. Combined with blocking along the columns of A, the design is sensitive to

the sparsity structure of the matrix. The computational efficiency ranges from 20% to 79%, performing particularly poorly for extremely sparse matrices (<0.1% density). Zhang et al. [12] improves upon this design by having each PE calculate a different element of y. Their accumulator requires a minimum row length of 8, zero padding when necessary, but can switch between any of several different rows if it encounters a data hazard. This roughly doubles the computational efficiency of the design as compared to Zhuo et al. [11]. However, it still performs quite poorly for extremely sparse matrices.

The final approach is to use the method outlined is Section 3 to stream CSC matrix data through several PEs. Gregg et al. [13] use a variant of CSC called the sparse matrix architecture and representation (SPAR) format. In the SPAR format, *row* and *ptr* are combined into a single vector with zero padding introduced at the start of each column of the *data* vector. Each PE only buffers a small portion of the y vector (32 elements vs. 3,456 elements in our design) in a local cache. A y-cache miss requires a write-back to high latency DRAM, incurring a 109 clock cycle penalty. With such a small cache, the design is very highly sensitive to the sparsity structure of the matrix. Computational efficiency ranges from as low as 1% to as high as 74%.

Our architecture improves upon Gregg et al. [13] by buffering much larger sections of the y vector (removing the need for a costly write-back scheme) and the elimination of unnecessary stalling due to zero padding (due to the SPAR format). Our design is able to handle matrix densities below 0.01% (10x sparser than prior FPGA designs) with computational efficiencies as high as 99.8%. Our drop in performance (and efficiency) for the Economics matrix on the ROACH platform is due to the very small number of nonzeroes per column, causing the x vector to need more memory bandwidth than the QDRs can deliver. This results in about 25% of the PEs being idled during any given cycle. The FEM/Accelerator matrix, while similar in density to the FEM/Ship matrix, alternates between being extremely dense and extremely sparse along its columns, causing about 30% of the PEs to be idled during any given clock cycle. This particular issue can be alleviated by buffering the x vector on-chip like previous

FPGA designs. We estimate that this would increase the sustained (average) computational efficiency from 91.85% to 98.29%.

5. CONCLUSIONS

This paper describes a SpMxV kernel using a CSC sparse-matrix format, and demonstrates its computational efficiency using an FPGA. The efficiency advantage of the kernel results from transforming irregular random memory accesses into a regularized stream of serial memory accesses. The benchmarking results show that the proposed architecture achieves a peak computational efficiency of 99.8% when performing SpMxV, which is over 54 and 322 times more efficient than an Intel Core i7-4770 processor and over an NVIDA GTX Titan GPU performing the same tasks, respectively. Implemented on a Virtex-5 SX95T FPGA, our design is able to achieve higher performance than its CPU and GPU counterparts running optimized sparse-BLAS software libraries, while only using 64 single-precision processing elements, with a 38-50x improvement in energy efficiency.

6. ACKNOWLEDGMENTS

The authors would like to thank Yuta Toriyama and Fang-Li Yuan of UCLA for their helpful discussions.

7. REFERENCES

[1] S. Kestur, J.D. Davis, and E.S. Chung, "Towards a Universal FPGA Matrix-Vector Multiplication Architecture," *Int. Symp. Field-Programmable Custom Comp. Mach. (FCCM 2012)*, pp. 9–16, May 2012.

[2] S. Sun, M. Monga, P.H. Jones, and J. Zambreno, "An I/O Bandwidth-Sensitive Sparse Matrix-Vector Multiplication Engine on FPGAs," *IEEE Trans. Circuits Syst. I, Reg. Papers*, vol. 59, no. 1, pp. 113–123, Jan. 2012.

[3] G. Goumas, K. Kourtis, N. Anastopoulos, V. Karakasis, and N. Koziris, "Understanding the Performance of Sparse Matrix-Vector Multiplication," *Euromicro Conf. Parallel, Distributed and Network-Based Process. (PDP 2008)*, pp. 283–292, Feb. 2008.

[4] J. Sun, G. Peterson, and O. Storaasli, "Mapping Sparse Matrix-Vector Multiplication on FPGAs," *Reconfigurable Systems Summer Institute (RSSI 2007)*, July 2007.

[5] "Intel Math Kernel library." [Online]. Available: http://software.intel.com/en-us/intel-mkl

[6] S. Williams, L. Oliker, R. Vuduc, J. Shalf, K. Yelick, and J. Demme, "Optimization of sparse matrix-vector multiplication on emerging multicore platforms," in *Proc. ACM/IEEE Conf. Supercomputing (SC 2007)*, pp.1–12, Nov. 2007.

[7] "Nvidia cuBLAS." [Online]. Available: http://developer.nvidia.com/cublas

[8] "Nvidia cuSPARSE." [Online]. Available: http://developer.nvidia.com/cusparse

[9] N. Bell and M. Garland, "Implementing sparse matrix-vector multiplication on throughput-oriented processors," in *Proc. ACM/IEEE Conf. Supercomputing (SC 2009)*, pp. 18:1–18:11, Nov. 2009.

[10] G. Kuzmanov and M. Taouil, "Reconfigurable sparse/dense matrix-vector multiplier," *Int. Conf. Field-Programmable Tech. (FPT 2009)*, pp. 483–488, Dec. 2009.

[11] L. Zhuo and V.K. Prasanna, "Sparse Matrix-Vector multiplication on FPGAs," in *Proc. ACM/SIGDA Int. Symp. Field-Programmable Gate Arrays (FPGA '05)*, pp. 63-74, Feb. 2005.

[12] Yan Zhang, Y.H. Shalabi, R. Jain, K.K. Nagar, and J.D. Bakos, "FPGA vs. GPU for sparse matrix vector multiply," *Int. Conf. Field-Programmable Tech. (FPT 2009)*, pp. 255–262, Dec. 2009.

[13] D. Gregg, C. McSweeney, C. McElroy, F. Connor, S. McGettrick, D. Moloney, and D. Geraghty, "FPGA Based Sparse Matrix Vector Multiplication using Commodity DRAM Memory," *Int. Conf. Field Programmable Logic Applicat. (FPL 2007)*, pp. 786-791, Aug. 2007.

[14] C.Y. Lin, H. K.-H. So, and P.H.-W. Leong, "A Model for Matrix Multiplication Performance on FPGAs," *Int. Conf. Field Programmable Logic Applicat. (FPL 2011)*, pp.305–310, Sept. 2011.

[15] "ROACH." [Online]. Available: https://casper.berkeley.edu/wiki/ROACH

[16] T. A. Davis and Y. Hu., "The university of Florida sparse matrix collection.," *ACM Trans. Math. Softw.*, vol. 38, no. 1, pp. 1:1–1:25, Dec. 2011.

[17] P. Gepner, D. L. Fraser, and V. Gamayunov, "Evaluation of the 3rd generation Intel Core Processor focusing on HPC applications," *Int. Conf. Parallel Distrib. Process. Techn. Applicat. (PDPTA 2012)*, pp. 818–823, July 2009.

[18] "NVIDIA GeForce GTX 680: The fastest, most efficient GPU ever built." [Online]. Available: http://www.geforce.com/Active/en_US/en_US/pdf/GeForce-GTX-680-Whitepaper-FINAL.pdf

[19] "Intel® Core™ i7-4770 Processor." [Online]. Available: http://ark.intel.com/products/75122/Intel-Core-i7-4770-Processor-8M-Cache-up-to-3_90-GHz

[20] "Introducing the GeForce GTX TITAN." [Online]. Available: http://www.geforce.com/whats-new/articles/introducing-the-geforce-gtx-titan

Binary Stochastic Implementation of Digital Logic

Yanzi Zhu   Peiran Suo   Kia Bazargan

Electrical and Computer Engineering Department
University of Minnesota
4-178 Keller Hall, 200 Union St SE, Minneapolis, MN 55455
{zhuxx405, suoxx009, kia}@umn.edu

ABSTRACT

Stochastic computing refers to a mode of computation in which numbers are treated as probabilities implemented as 0/1 bit streams, which essentially is a unary encoding scheme. Previous work has shown significant reduction in area and increase in fault tolerance for low to medium resolution values (6-10 bits). However, this comes at very high latency cost. We propose a novel hybrid approach combining traditional binary with unary stochastic encoding, called *binary stochastic*. Similar to the binary representation, it is a positional number system, but instead of only 0/1 digits, the digits would be fractions. We show how simple logic such as adders and multipliers can be implemented, and then show more complex function implementations such as the gamma correction function and functions such as *tanh*, *absolute* and *exponentiation* using both combinational and sequential binary stochastic logic. Our experiments show significant reduction in latency compared to unary stochastic, while using significantly smaller area compared to binary implementations on FPGAs.

Categories and Subject Descriptors

B.2 [**ARITHMETIC AND LOGIC STRUCTURES**]: B.2.1 Design Styles, B.2.3 Reliability, Testing, and Fault-Tolerance (*Redundant design*).

General Terms

Algorithms, Performance, Design, Reliability.

Keywords

Stochastic Computing, Binary Stochastic, Bernstein Coefficients.

1. INTRODUCTION

Stochastic computing is an alternative digital approach to real arithmetic. A stochastic computing system requires stochastic bit streams to represent real values. A real value x [0,1] is encoded as a stochastic bit-stream, where the probability of a bit in the stream to be at logic 1 equals x. We call such an encoding *unary stochastic* in this paper. The idea of performing arithmetic using stochastic bit streams has been discussed in [1][2] and was motivated by the simplicity of stochastic computational elements, especially useful in systems that can tolerate small amounts of

inaccuracies, such as many image and signal processing applications. For example, when performing contrast enhancement before doing edge detection, the final result would not change in a meaningful way if we have one percent random fluctuation error in the contrast enhancement step. In the past few years, there has been renewed interest in stochastic computing, showing significant benefits including remarkable hardware cost reductions and high degrees of fault tolerance to as large as 20% bit flips [3][4][5]. Stochastic computing has been successfully used in LDPC decoding [6][7], FIR filter design [8], and digital image processing [9]. It is especially appealing for FPGA implementations due to the limited logic resources of FPGAs compared to ASICs.

As simple examples showing the elegance of stochastic computing, we consider the multiplication and addition operations. Assume X and Y are independent random Bernoulli bit-streams representing probabilities x and y, respectively. Figure 1 shows how the two stochastic values can be multiplied and added (scaled). Since each bit i in stream X is independent from its corresponding bit in stream Y, the probability of the output of the AND gate being one at that clock cycle is $P(X_i=1) \times P(Y_i=1)$, which is $x.y$ (multiplication operation). Similar analysis shows that the output of the MUX is $s.x + (1-s)y$, which is the scaled addition operation. The beauty of the stochastic implementation is that it performs these operations with no carry propagation or unwrapping the multiplier bits, generating partial products and adding them to generate the final multiplication result, resulting in significantly smaller area, and higher clock frequency (but *not* overall lower latency).

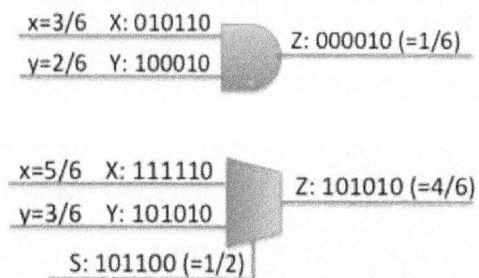

Figure 1 Multiplication (top) and scaled addition (bottom) in unary stochastic computing.

Stochastic computing can also perform signed operations. A simple linear transformation of $z=(2x-1)$ to map the range [0..1] to [-1..1] can be used to represent signed numbers (also called bipolar). Scaled addition is done similarly to the unsigned (unipolar) method, but multiplication is done using an XNOR gate instead of an AND gate [12].

Note that the hardware cost for multiplication and scaled addition in unary stochastic is drastically smaller than that of the binary operations[1]. However, this comes at a potentially high price in latency. Figure 2 compares the binary and unary representations for a number with a fixed accuracy. Binary uses $log_2 N$ bits sent in one clock cycle to represent a number with a resolution of $1/N$, whereas unary stochastic requires N bits to achieve the same resolution, which is *exponentially* higher than binary. As noted in [1] and [5], a resolution of 1/1024 seems to be the limit where unary stochastic is useful. This is a serious limitation for stochastic computing which we will address in this work.

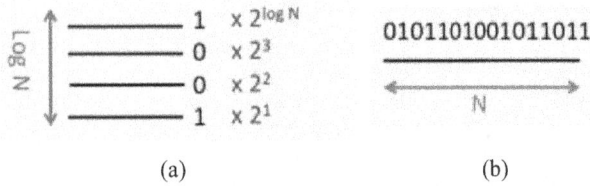

Figure 2. Assuming a resolution for representing numbers between 0 and N=16, number 9 is shown in (a) Binary requiring *log N=4* bits, and (b) Unary stochastic encoding requiring *N=16* bits. The positional power weights *2^i* are implicit in the binary representation.

In terms of tolerance to soft errors, unary stochastic is shown to significantly outperform binary [5]. In a binary number, if a bit flip happens on the most significant bit, it changes the value by *half* the range of the number (8 out of 16 in Figure 2-a, assuming K=4, and 512 out of 1024 assuming K=10). Assuming the same percentage of bit flips happen in unary stochastic, we get much smaller error rates (4 out of 16 for K=4, and 102.4 out of 1024 on average for K=10). The authors in [5] show very good tolerance of the stochastic method in the presence of bit flips that range from 1% to 20%.

We propose a novel encoding that we have called *binary stochastic*, which combines the ideas of unary stochastic and the classic binary number system (Section 2). We show how scaled addition and multiplication can be done with small hardware costs and latencies (Section 2.2). As a case study for a complex function implemented in combinational stochastic logic, we implement the Gamma Correction function and compare binary stochastic to unary stochastic and traditional binary implementations in terms of accuracy, latency and area (Section 3). We also present sequential circuits that use reversible Markov chains to implement approximations of a number of functions, and compare the performance of binary stochastic to unary stochastic in Section 4. Experimental results are presented in Section 5. We discuss future plans in Section 6.

2. BINARY STOCHASTIC ENCODING

In the previous section we highlighted the difference between (unary) stochastic and the traditional binary encoding systems. Here we introduce a hybrid encoding called *Binary Stochastic*, which is an encoding combining the ideas of binary and unary stochastic. It is flexible and allows designers to trade-off area with latency, while still being able to perform basic arithmetic operations using simple hardware.

---

[1] One has to consider the overhead associated with generating the bit streams for stochastic computing: good random number generators are needed for each independent input required in the computation. For example for $y=x^2$, we need two sources of independent random streams for *x*.

2.1 The Basic Idea

The main advantage of the binary positional number system is its compact representation of data, which requires only $\lceil log_2 N \rceil$ bits to represent a variable that can take values in the range [0..N]. However, as noted in Section 1, it suffers from higher area and high sensitivity to bit flips, especially when such faults happen on the most significant bit[2].

The binary stochastic approach tries to take advantage of the attractive properties of both unary stochastic and traditional binary. Similar to unary stochastic, it uses lean hardware and avoids carry propagation both in the addition operation and when adding partial products in multiplications. On the other hand, it cuts down on the number of bits required to represent a unary stochastic number by an exponential factor of 2^K by using K positional digits, similar to binary. Compared to binary, though, it has fewer number of digits and hence smaller weight differences between the most significant digits and the least significant ones. Furthermore, the "digits" in the binary stochastic representation would be fractional numbers instead of 0/1 used in binary. We will first use an example to explain the idea and then show the formal definition. The concept can be better explained when we consider numbers between 0 and 1, which essentially means we are dividing all values by N. Using this convention, the number represented in Figure 2 is 9/16 in the unary format and the positional weights are $2^{-1}, 2^{-2}, 2^{-3}, ..., 2^{-log N}$.

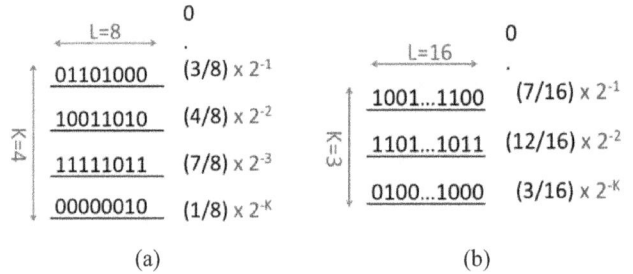

Figure 3 Binary stochastic representation of the number 0.43 with a resolution of 2^{-7}. (a) using four binary stochastic wires, (b) using three binary stochastic wires.

Suppose we want to represent the number 0.43 with a resolution of 2^{-7}. We would need L=128 bits to represent it in the unary stochastic format, because we need to be able to distinguish numbers that are different by as little as $2^{-7}=1/128$. Figure 3 shows two examples of representing the same number 0.43 in the binary stochastic representation with an overall resolution of 2^{-7}. In Figure 3-a, we have used K=4 parallel streams of unary stochastic each with a bit stream length of 8. The four streams represent *digits* 3/8, 4/8, 7/8 and 1/8 from top to bottom. Similar to the binary representation, these digits are positional and have weights $2^{-1}, 2^{-2}, 2^{-3}$ and 2^{-4}. We can use the notation $0.43_{10} = 0 . (3/8) (4/8) (7/8) (1/8)_{L=8,K=4}$ where the subscripts indicate the base in which the number is represented. Part (b) of the figure shows the same number with the same resolution but with fewer binary stochastic

---

[2] As the number of bits increase, the weight of the most significant bit gets exponentially larger than the weight of the least significant bit, leading to exponentially higher sensitivities to more significant bits. For example, if *N=1024*, the most significant bit has a weight of *512*, which is 2^9 times higher than the least significant bit, and hence a bit flip on the most significant bit has *512* times the impact compared to a bit flip on the least significant bit.

digits. Note that the bit-stream length increases exponentially as the number of binary digits decreases. It is important to mention that using binary stochastic with K digits, the range of the numbers we can represent would be between $0..1\text{-}2^{-K}$ as opposed to $0..1$ in unary stochastic. But that is not a major issue, as we can interpret all data to be a scaled value of the original numbers (e.g., in image processing, we map pixel values $0..255$ to $0..1$ for unary stochastic. Now we have to map them to $0..0.75$ for K=2).

Definition 1: *Binary Stochastic Representation*. Given a resolution of $1/2^N$ and a positive integer $K \leq N$, a real number $0 \leq X \leq 1$ is represented in the binary stochastic format using unary bit-streams b_i, where $1 \leq i \leq K$, and

$$X = \sum_{i=1}^{K} 2^{-i} \times b_i.$$

Theorem 1: Binary Stochastic Bit-Stream Length. To maintain the resolution $1/2^N$, bit-streams must be of length $L = 2^{N-K}$.

Proof: A bit-streams b_i has a resolution of $1/L$ (because it has L bits and by changing one 0 in the stream to a 1, we get a number that is $1/L$ larger than the first number). Note that in the binary stochastic representation, bit-stream b_i's value is weighted by the factor 2^i. The smallest weighted value bit-stream b_K can represent is $(1/L) \times 2^{-K}$, which has to be equal to 2^{-N} to satisfy the resolution constraint. Solving for L we get $L = 2^{N-K}$. $\square$

A corollary to the above theorem is that as we increase the number of binary stochastic digits K, the required bit-stream length, and hence the latency for sending a value, decreases exponentially. This is a powerful property of binary stochastic that allows designers to take a middle road between the traditional binary number system and unary stochastic[3]. This is especially important as arithmetic operations such as scaled addition and multiplication can be done with linear latency, as opposed to super-linear latencies associated with addition and multiplication in binary (see Sec. 2.2).

An important property of binary stochastic encoding, which we will explore in our future work, is its non-canonical representation for any number X. For example, 0.6_{10} can be represented as $0.(0.7)(1.0)_{K=2,L=10}$ and three more including $0.(0.9)(0.6)_{K=2,L=10}$. As L increases, the number of representations increases. Although non-canonical representations are not desired in deterministic calculus, such as binary operations, it would be an advantage in stochastic computing. If our encoding of a variable can change dynamically, it has better potential for tolerating permanent faults. For example, if the wire carrying digit 2 is shorted to ground, representation $0.(0.7)(1.0)$ will take a large hit in terms of representation error, whereas a dynamic representation sometimes shifts more of the value to digit 1 and show less sensitivity to the permanent fault.

2.2 Scaled Addition and Multiplication

One of the reasons unary stochastic is appealing is its very low hardware cost for single bit calculations. When adding two values

using the scaled addition mux (see Figure 1), there are no carry bits to propagate from one bit to the next as is needed in binary addition. Similarly, when multiplying two bit-streams, no partial products are created and no carry propagation is required to add partial results. Fortunately, we can maintain a similar simplicity in hardware when performing multiplication and scaled addition in binary stochastic: no carry propagations are needed[4].

To illustrate how scaled addition and multiplication can be done in binary stochastic, we use K=2 and arbitrary values of L, but our method is general and can extend to any K and any L values. Scaled addition of two binary stochastic numbers $A = 0.(a_1)(a_2)$ and $B = 0.(b_1)(b_2)$ can be done by performing pair-wise scaled additions on $\{a_1,b_1\}$ and $\{a_2,b_2\}$ to get c_1 and c_2 respectively. It can be easily shown that $C=0.(c_1)(c_2) = \frac{1}{2}(A+B)$.

To perform multiplication $C = A \times B$, we first write:

$$0.(c_1)(c_2)=0.(a_1)(a_2)\times 0.(b_1)(b_2) = (2^{-1}a_1 + 2^{-2}a_2) \times (2^{-1}b_1 + 2^{-2}b_2)$$

$$= 2^{-1}\,0 + 2^{-2}a_1b_1 + 2^{-3}(a_1b_2 + a_2b_1) + 2^{-4}a_2b_2 \qquad (1)$$

To reduce the number of digits to two to match the format required by $0.(c_1)(c_2)$, we can perform the following *rank increase* operations, as also shown in Table 1: we can move the term a_2b_2 from digit 2^{-4} to digit 2^{-3} by applying a scaled addition between 0 and a_2b_2:

$$2^{-4}a_2b_2 = 2^{-3}\left[\tfrac{1}{2}(0 + a_2b_2)\right] \qquad (2)$$

Similarly, the term a_1b_2 can move to digit 2^{-2}, and finally the remaining terms in digits 2^{-3} and 2^{-2} can increase ranks to fill digits 2^{-1} and 2^{-2}. The final result is:

$$c_1 = \tfrac{1}{2}(a_1b_1 + \tfrac{1}{2}(0+a_1b_2)) \quad , \quad c_2 = \tfrac{1}{2}(a_2b_1 + \tfrac{1}{2}(0+a_2b_2)) \qquad (3)$$

2^{-1}	2^{-2}	2^{-3}	2^{-4}
0	a1.b1	a1.b2 + a2.b1	a2.b2
0	a1.b1 ½ {0+a1.b2}	a2.b1 ½{0+a2.b2}	
c1	c2		

Table 1 Binary Stochastic Multiplication

Each row in Table 1 corresponds to one step with a latency of a mux. Note that the rank increase operations can be done in parallel resulting in a general architecture shown in Figure 4. It is important to note that given K binary stochastic digits, the area of the circuit is proportional to K^2, and its latency to only K.

---

[3] Although we did not perform experiments to measure it, we expect the fault tolerance of binary stochastic to be between unary and binary: it *could* be worse than unary because the bits in b_1 are weighted 2^{K-1} more than the bits in b_K, hence a bit flip in b_1 *could have* 2^{K-1} more impact on the overall error compared to a bit flip in b_K ; on the other hand, the ratio of the bits b_1 and b_K is smaller than the maximum ratio in binary, which is 2^{N-1}, and we choose $K < N$.

---

[4] Note that even if we had to do carry propagation in the addition and multiplication operations, the hardware cost had been lower than binary, because K<N.

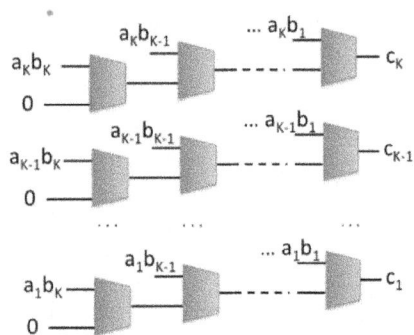

Figure 4 Binary Stochastic Multiplication Circuit

3. CASE STUDY: GAMMA CORRECTION

We showed simple binary stochastic arithmetic operations in Sec. 2.2. One can imagine that for straightforward applications that involve additions and multiplications, chains of (binary) stochastic operations could be used to implement the function efficiently. However, there are cases in which a direct and simple synthesis of a function mapped to scaled addition and multiplication cannot be found. In this section we look at one such case representing a general framework for synthesizing complex functions. We use the application of Gamma Correction as a case study and compare our binary stochastic results to the unary stochastic presented in [5].

The architecture in [5] first approximates the Gamma Correction Function $y=x^\gamma$ using Bernstein Polynomials. A degree n Bernstein polynomial is of the form:

$$ \tag{4} $$

in which b_i values are real numbers called Bernstein coefficients, and each $B_{i,n}$ is a Bernstein basis polynomial:

$$ \tag{5} $$

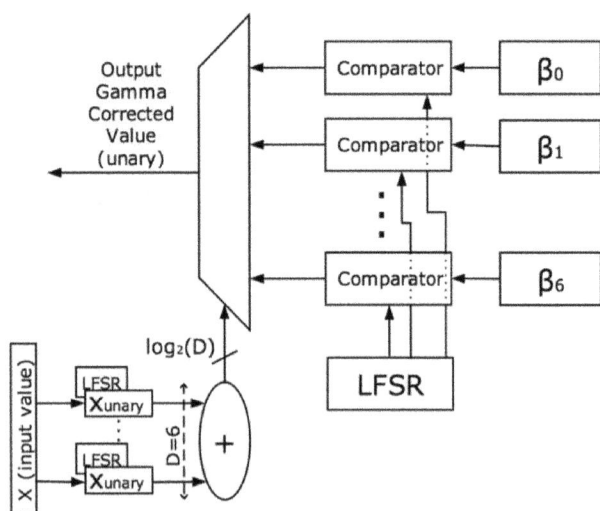

Figure 5 Gamma correction architecture from [5]. D=6 is the degree of the Bernstein Polynomial.

The reason Bernstein polynomials are useful for stochastic computing is that one can guarantee that a degree n polynomial that maps the unit interval to the unit interval (regardless of the values of its coefficients which may be greater than one) can be transformed to a Bernstein polynomial with coefficients in the unit interval.

The authors in [5] used a Bernstein polynomial of degree 6 to approximate a non-polynomial, which is the Gamma Correction function $y=x^\gamma$. A constrained quadratic optimization problem is solved to minimize the mean square error of the Bernstein approximation and the gamma correction function. They made very efficient use of 6 independent copies of the unary stochastic x stream to generate a binomial distribution involving the terms $x^j(1-x)^{6-j}$. The binomial distribution was used to pick the right mix of Bernstein coefficients, which in turn means multiplying the powers of $x^j(1-x)^{6-j}$ to the Bernstein coefficients. The architecture from that work is shown in Figure 5 for ease of comparison to our work.

The architecture basically does two things: (1) generate the "histogram" of the binomial distribution corresponding to the value of X, and (2) using the MUX, indirectly multiplying the Bernstein coefficients $\beta 0 .. \beta 6$ to the weights generated by the histogram, and adding them up. The output of the adder in Figure 5 is responsible for task (1) over a period of L clock cycles (L is the bit stream length), and the multiplexer does the weighted addition of the $\beta 0 .. \beta 6$ values over the course of the L cycles. To better understand the architecture, we can consider a case in which the output of the adder is, say, 2. In that case, 2 out of the D=6 streams of X had a value of 1, while the other 4 had a value of 0, but it is not clear which 2 out of the 4. It is not hard to imagine the choice of 2 out of 6 would make the first term in the right hand side of Eq. 5, and the fact that we had two 1's and four 0's means there was a probability $x^2 (1-x)^4$, which would be the second part of the right hand side of Eq. 5.

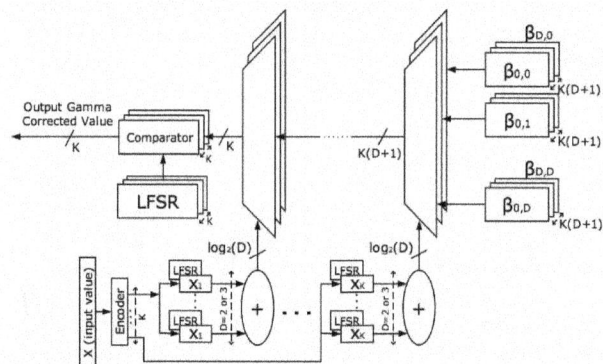

Figure 6 The Binary Stochastic Architecture. D is the degree of the Bernstein polynomial, and K is the number of binary stochastic digits.

The block labeled "X (input value)" contains the N-bit binary value of the input. N-bit Random number generators (LFSR in the figure – Linear Feedback Shift Register) paired with N-bit comparators are used to generate unary bit streams with probability X (if the LFSR value is less than or equal to X, output 1, otherwise output 0). Note that since the degree of the polynomial is D=6, we need six LFSR/comparator pairs. The output of the adder is a binary number between 0 and 6. The inputs to the mux are seven unary stochastic streams. Note that only one LFSR is enough to compare against all seven beta values, because they are selected exclusively and hence there is no fear of correlations between them further downstream. The circuit has to run for 2^N cycles to match the resolution of an N-bit binary system.

Our binary stochastic architecture is shown in Figure 6. There are a number of notable differences compared to the unary stochastic architecture: **(1)** Each input X is now replaced by two (or three) variables: $X = 2^{-1} X_1 + 2^{-2} X_2$ when K=2, and $X = 2^{-1} X_1 + 2^{-2} X_2 + 2^{-3} X_3$ when K=3. **(2)** Instead of one output bit stream, we now have K weighted output bit streams. **(3)** The Bernstein polynomial has two (three) variables and instead of an array of beta values, it has a two-dimensional table of beta values. The table is (D+1) × (D+1) entries. **(4)** Because we have two (three) variables and their power combinations to use, we can approximate the original function using a polynomial with much smaller degree. In our experiments, we can achieve approximation errors in mapping K=2 and K=3 binary stochastic functions with Bernstein polynomials of degree D=2 or 3, as opposed to D=6 in unary. The two MUXes in Figure 6 together with the collection of the beta values are essentially implementing a two-dimensional array lookup, which is suitable for embedded memory blocks in FPGA architectures.

Area, clock period and approximation error values of the binary stochastic architecture are compared to unary stochastic and are presented in Section 5.

4. CASE STUDY: SEQUENTIAL LOGIC

Stochastic logic can also be used in sequential logic that implements reversible Markov chains to approximate functions that cannot be approximated well with Bernstein Polynomials. The authors in [3] and [12] show a number of examples of such functions. They use deterministic finite state machines (FSMs) that use stochastic input values to make state transitions in the FSM. A Markov chain is a discrete-time stochastic process modeled as an FSM that satisfies the Markov property, which asserts that given the present state of a stochastic system, the probability of transition to the next state depends only on the present state and not on any past history of the system. The probability of transition from state i to state j is known as the transition probability P_{ij}.

When analyzing a Markov chain, we are interested in the probability that the state machine visits each state during the lifetime of its transitions. At equilibrium, the probability of the Markov chain to be in a particular state i is independent of the initial state and is a constant, called the stationary probability. The stationary probabilities of a finite state Markov chain are unique if the Markov chain is ergodic. Ergodicity implies that any state of the Markov chain is accessible from any other state (irreducibility) at irregular time instants (aperiodicity). The Markov chains we use in our designs are ergodic with unique stationary probabilities. We omit the details of the calculations of stationary (or steady state) probabilities and refer interested readers to in [3] and [12].

It is not hard to imagine that once stationary probabilities of an FSM topology are calculated as functions of input probability x, we can assign output values to states so that a particular function is approximated by the FSM. In the general case the output values could be real-valued numbers in the unit interval (e.g., the state number could be used as an array index to read probability values similar to the beta values used in Section 3). In this paper we only focus on the 0/1 output values.

Figure 7 shows a generic linear FSM that is a reversible Markov chain, that is, its stationary probabilities can be calculated in polynomial time. The FSM is similar to an up/down counter with saturation states at the two ends. Assigning different patterns of 0's and 1's to the state outputs would result in different functions.

For example, the *tanh* function is implemented by setting the outputs of the first half of states to 0 and output of the other half to 1. Exponentiation function, $y = e^{-2.G.x}$, is implemented by setting the output of the last G states to 0 and the rest to 1. The *absolute* function is implemented by setting the output of the first half states to alternating 1 and 0, starting with 1, and mirroring the first half to the second half.

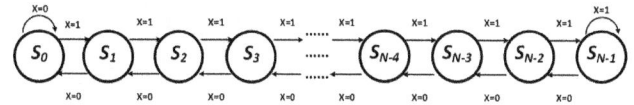

Figure 7 A generic unary stochastic linear FSM

We improve unary stochastic FSMs with input bit stream x, by employing two bit streams x_1 and x_2 that do a 3:1 compression of the latency. The governing equation is slightly different from the combinational logic case: $x = (2 x_1 + x_2) / 3$, but still bit stream x_1 has twice the weight of x_2. The table to the right shows different combinations of bit values of the x_1 and x_2 bit

If (x1,x2) is:	It is equivalent to three bits of x
(0,0)	0 0 0
(0,1)	1 0 0 OR 0 1 0 OR 0 0 1
(1,0)	1 1 0 OR 1 0 1 OR 0 1 1
(1,1)	1 1 1

streams at a certain clock and what unary bits they are equivalent to. If for example x_1 is 1 and x_2 is 0, they represent a value of 2, which means two bits out of three consecutive bits of an equivalent unary stream must have been either 110, 101, or 011. As a result, if one were to only look at the unary state machine every three clock cycles, s/he can observe similar transitions in a binary stochastic FSM with three times slower clock speed. In other words, every pair of (x_1,x_2) presented in one clock of the binary stochastic are equivalent to three consecutive bits in the unary stochastic implementation.

Given that the state transitions behave similarly, we can derive an (almost) equivalent state machine to unary stochastic FSM by using both x1 and x2 values to determine the next state transition. Given that in our generic unary stochastic FSM a value of x=1 moves to the state to the right of the current state and a value of x=0 moves to the left, we can determine the net effect of each of the four cases listed in the table above on state transitions. Figure 8 shows the binary stochastic FSM that is (almost) equivalent to the one shown in Figure 7. They are not exactly the same because of the way the boundary nodes saturate. Even though Figure 8 might look complicated, it is basically created using a simple rule: if both x_1 and x_2 are zero, move three states to the left. If they are both one, move three states to the right. If $x_1=1$ and $x_2=0$, then move one state to the right (unary would have moved two steps to the right and one step to the left), otherwise, move one state to the left. If the transition results in a state number that is less than zero or greater than N-1, fall back to 0 and N-1 respectively.

The elegance of this binary stochastic FSM approach is that we do not need to recalculate the stationary probabilities or the output values that were calculated for the unary stochastic. In the next section we provide experimental results comparing our binary stochastic method to unary stochastic method.

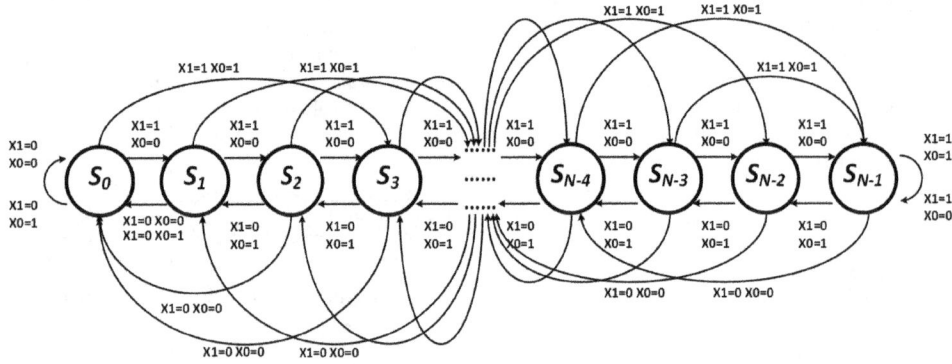

Figure 8 A generic linear binary stochastic FSM

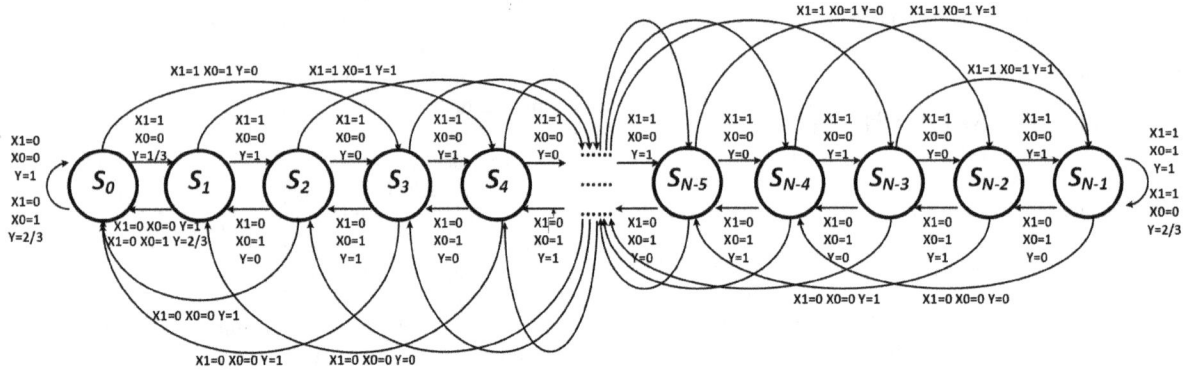

Figure 9 Binary stochastic FSM for the absolute function. Y values are the output values assigned to states.

5. EXPERIMENTAL RESULTS

We present comparisons between unary stochastic, binary stochastic and traditional binary implementations of the functions discussed in the previous sections. Figure 10 shows the output value of the bit streams generated by unary and binary stochastic implementations for a selection of architectural parameters. We chose only a selection of the architectures because the error bars would not be distinguishable if we add more graphs. Instead, we chose the best and the worst performing architectures in terms of standard error in this figure. Figure 11 shows the standard error of a wider selection of architectures, including the best (binStoch K=3,D=3) and the worst (unary D=6) which were also depicted in Figure 10.

In these experiments we used an equivalent of 10-bit binary resolution, which translates to L=1024 bits for unary with degree D=6, L=512 for binary stochastic with K=2, and L=256 for binary stochastic with K=3. We chose the degrees of binary stochastic polynomials such that their approximation errors are close to unary stochastic. It can be observed from the standard error graph that indeed binary stochastic is able to deliver the same (or slightly better) accuracy compared to unary but with half or a quarter of the latency required for unary stochastic.

In order to see if one can simply take the unary stochastic architecture and duplicate it to reduce the latency by half while maintaining the same number of bits (2 × L=512 bits), we implemented the "parallel unary D=6" version too. It can be seen in Figure 11 that although the parallel unary version is better than

unary (less random fluctuations), but it does not beat the best of binary stochastic implementations *and* it has higher area (see Table **2**).

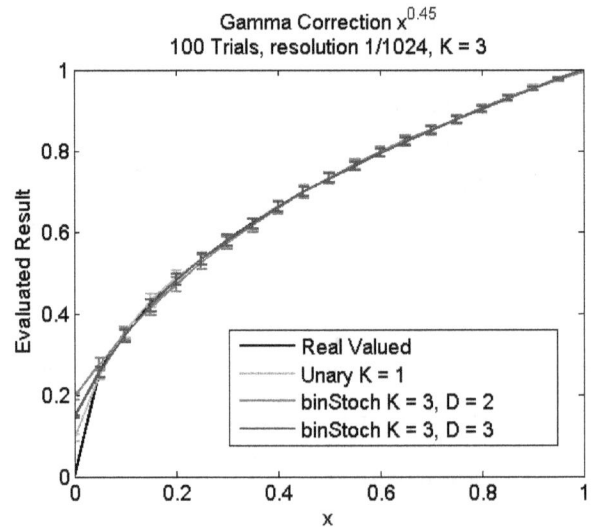

Figure 10 Gamma correction function results on a selection of implementations.

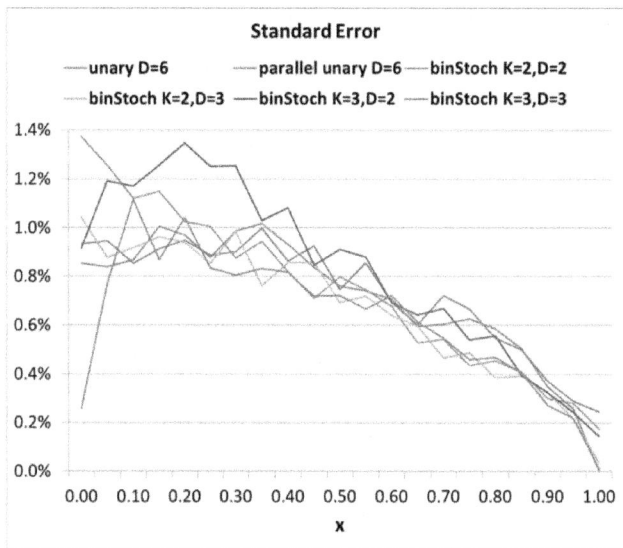

Figure 11 Standard error values for different implementation of the Gamma correction function.

To study the area and delay overheads of the binary stochastic scheme, we synthesized different configurations of the architecture on a Xilinx Virtex 5 XC5VLX20T FPGA using the normal optimization options in the Xilinx ISE WebPack tool flow. We did not try optimizing the designs, e.g., by mapping the beta values to block RAMs, so the results are meant to provide a basis for comparison of different architectures and not necessarily as final area / delay numbers. Table 2 shows the results of the implementation. The results are reported both with randomization units (LFSR) and without (the core only) for all the stochastic implementations. The reason for reporting the core only numbers is to show how much area and delay contributions are due to the LFSR units and how much due to the rest of the logic. One could argue that better random number generators such as Mersenne Twister could significantly reduce the resource usage by allowing different shuffling orders

of the bits generated in one clock to be used by different comparators in the circuit to generate independent random bit streams. Given the high correlation between neighboring bits at different clocks in an LFSR, such resource sharing is not possible in our current implementation. Furthermore, if there are cascades of computations, we only need random number generators at the inputs and amortize their area overhead over all cascaded units.

The first row shows the results of conventional, non-stochastic implementation. The second row shows the unary implementation with a Bernstein polynomial of degree 6 (as in [5]). The third row "2x parallel…" is the same as the row above, but with duplicate hardware. The output is considered to be the total bits coming out of the two output bit streams. The rest of the rows correspond to different binary stochastic implementations. The columns labeled "area" show the total number of slices used, some of which only used flip-flops and no logic. Area-Delay Product per bit is calculated for one bit of computation. That number is multiplied to the number of bits required for the configuration to meet the 10-bit binary accuracy. For example, in the row "unary D=6", we need 1024 bits to represent the output value, hence $872 \times 1024 = 893,497$. But in the case of 2x parallel unary, we only need 512 clock cycles to get 1024 bits total, hence $1386 \times 512 = 709,798$. The column labeled "Approx Error" is the approximation error between the real-valued function $y=x^\gamma$, and the real-valued polynomial function (e.g., Bernstein) that approximates it. We tried different degrees of polynomials to get similar approximation errors across all architectures.

The table shows that increasing K does not drastically increase area and even with K=3,D=3, the area is smaller than the unary with D=6. When we consider the required bit stream length, we can see that binary stochastic has a much better area delay product compared to unary or parallel unary in both with and without LFSRs. It is also important to note that for the Gamma correction function, stochastic cannot compete with traditional binary implementation, at least not for 8 bits of accuracy. The authors in [5] also reported this but were able to show better stochastic implementations compared to binary for other applications. The main advantage of stochastic as reported in [5] is its far superior tolerance to input errors.

Table 2 Area and delay report for the Gamma correction function for an accuracy of 8-bit binary values.

8-bit	With LFSRs				Core only (no LFSRs)				Approx Error
	Area	Delay	Area-Delay Product	Area-Delay Product	Area	Delay	Area-Delay Product	Area-Delay Product	
		(ns)	per bit (ns)	for all bits (ns)		(ns)	per bit (ns)	for all bits (ns)	
Binary (conventional, non-stochastic)					226	1.819	411	411	9.77E-04
unary D=6	178	4.902	872	893497	11	1.817	20	20467	1.98E-05
2x parallel unary D=6	291	4.764	1386	709798	20	1.941	39	19876	4.27E-06
binStoch K=2,D=2	161	4.764	767	392706	18	1.702	31	15686	3.38E-05
binStoch K=2,D=3	193	4.764	919	470759	16	1.602	26	13124	6.02E-06
binStoch K=3,D=2	198	3.769	746	191043	24	1.959	47	12036	3.38E-05
binStoch K=3, D=3	245	3.769	923	236392	18	1.489	27	6861	6.03E-06

The unary and binary stochastic implementations of the absolute, exponentiation, tanh and exponentiation of absolute $y=e^{-2G|x|}$ functions using 32 state FSMs are shown in Figure 12 through Figure 15. The functions use the bipolar interpretation of stochastic values, i.e., x is in the range [-1,+1], as discussed in the introduction. In all these figures, unary bit streams of length L=3072 are used. The binary stochastic implementations use K=2 and L=1024 bit stream lengths. It can be seen that binary stochastic performs as well as, or in cases such as the tanh function better than unary even though it is using three times fewer bits.

In terms of area usage, the authors in [12] provide back of the envelope calculations comparing unary stochastic FSM to traditional binary implementation of these functions (see Table 4 in that paper). If we assume an accuracy of 8-bit binary values, then their area delay product numbers calculate as in Table 3. It can be seen that even though unary stochastic needs to perform 256 bit operations per one byte operation of traditional binary, its very small footprint area results in considerable reduction in overall area delay product for the first three functions. However, since there is a trivial implementation for the absolute function in traditional binary, the area delay product of unary stochastic is about 50x worse than that of a traditional binary implementation. We expect our binary stochastic implementations to be similar to unary in terms of area delay product. Part of our future work is to implement binary stochastic FSMs with K=2 and K=3 and compare to exact area delay products of traditional binary and also unary stochastic systems.

Table 3 Rough area delay calculations comparing traditional binary to unary stochastic.

	Area × Delay unary stoch	Area × Delay trad binary	Unary stoch / trad binary
Tanh	26880	305490	0.088
Exp	76800	254575	0.302
expAbs	129024	255151	0.506
Abs	30720	576	53.33

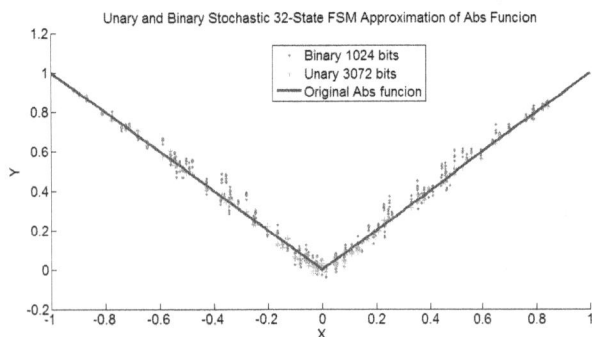

Figure 12 Absolute function results. The green dots represent unary outputs and the red dots show binary stochastic.

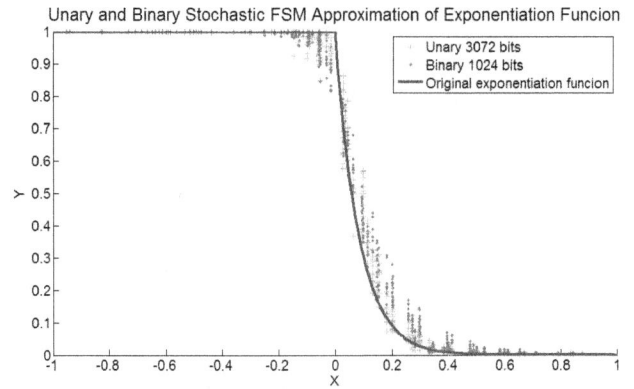

Figure 13 exponentiation function results

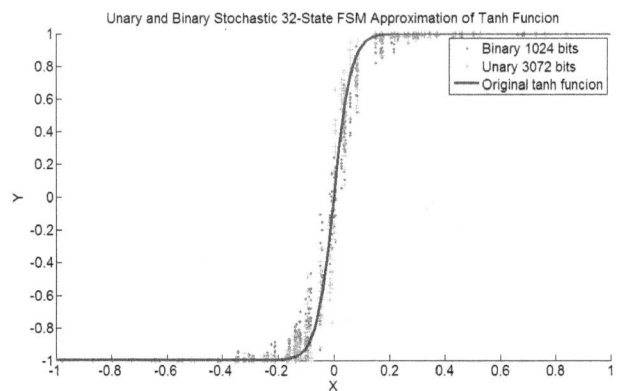

Figure 14 The tanh function results.

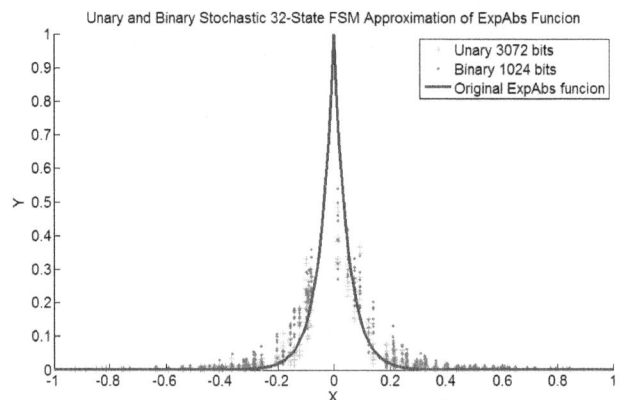

Figure 15 The ExpAbs function results

6. CONCLUSIONS

We presented a novel encoding called binary stochastic, which allows designers to trade-off latency for accuracy and fault tolerance. The proposed approach outperforms unary, especially in terms of latency at an exponential rate. Multiplication and scaled addition operations can be performed in linear time, as opposed to super-linear times in binary. We also demonstrated two general synthesis approaches for approximating polynomial and non-polynomial functions using stochastic logic.

Our future work includes studying the fault tolerance of the proposed binary stochastic approach, which is expected to be between unary and conventional binary implementations. Another area of exploration would be to harness the redundancy in the encoding of binary stochastic numbers. Values closer to 1 have fewer binary stochastic representations (e.g., 1.0 has only one representation), whereas numbers closer to zero have more representations. We are in the process of developing an encoding scheme that minimizes the random fluctuation error when generating the K bit streams. Furthermore, computational blocks should allow bits to move across the K digits. For example, if $x=0.(1/2)(0.0)(0.0)...(0.0)$, then our current multiplication scheme computes $y=x^P$ as $y=0.(0.5^P)(0.0)(0.0)...(0.0)$. However, solutions such as $y=0.(0.0)(0.0)...$ $(0.0)(0.5)(0.0)...(0.0)$, or $y=0.(0.0)$ $(0.0)...(0.0)(1.0)(0.0)...(0.0)$ might result in better encodings.

7. ACKNOWLEDGEMENTS

This work was funded in part by the National Science Foundation under Grant CCF-1241987, and in part by the Undergraduate Research Opportunities Program (UROP) at the University of Minnesota. We would like to thank Kevin Krile (formerly an undergraduate researcher at the Univeristy of Minnesota) and Yokesh Ramasamy (graduate student at the UofM) for their valuable feedback and their efforts during the early phases of the development of the binary stochastic idea. Their implementations were not used in this paper but were useful in developing better encodings and circuit designs. We would also like to thank the reviewers for their valuable comments that helped improve the quality of the paper.

8. REFERENCES

[1] B.R. Gaines, "Stochastic Computing Systems," Advances in Information Systems Science, J.F.Tou, ed., vol.2, chapter 2, pp.37-172, New York: Plenum, 1969.

[2] J. vonNeumann, "Probabilistic logics and the synthesis of reliable organisms from unreliable components," Automata Studies, pp. 43-98, Princeton University Press, 1956.

[3] B.D. Brown, H.C. Card, "Stochastic neural computation I: Computational elements," IEEE Transactions on Computers, vol.50, pp. 891-905, September 2001.

[4] P. Li, W. Qian, M.D. Reidel, K. Bazargan, D. Lilja, "The synthesis of linear finite state machine based stochastic computational elements," ASPDAC 2012.

[5] Xin Li, Weikang Qian, Marc D. Riedel, Kia Bazargan, and David J. Lilja, "A Reconfigurable Stochastic Architecture for Highly Reliable Computing", Great Lakes Symposium (GLSVLSI), 2009.

[6] G. Sarkis and W. J. Gross, "Efficient Stochastic Decoding of Non-Binary LDPC Codes with Degree-Two Variable Nodes", IEEE Communications Letters, Vol. 16, No. 3, March 2012, pp. 389-391.

[7] Jienan Chen, Jianhao Hu: Sliding Window Method for stochastic LDPC decoder. ISCAS 2011: 1307-1310.

[8] Jienan Chen, Jianhao Hu, Shuyang Li: Low power digital signal processing scheme via stochastic logic protection. ISCAS 2012: 3077-3080.

[9] Peng Li and David J. Lilja, "Using Stochastic Computing to Implement Digital Image Processing Algorithms," IEEE International Conference on Computer Design (ICCD), 2011.

[10] Thinh Nguyen, "Robust Data-Optimized Stochastic Analog-to-Digital Converters", IEEE Transactions on Signal Processing, vol. 55, issue 6, pp. 2735-2740, 2007.

[11] Majzoobi, M, Koushanfar F, Devadas S., "FPGA-based True Random Number Generation using Circuit Metastability with Adaptive Feedback Control", Workshop on Cryptographic Hardware and Embedded Systems (CHES), 2011.

[12] Peng Li, David Lilja, Weknag Qian, Marc Riedel and Kia Bazargan, "Logical Computation on Stochastic Bit Streams with Linear Finite State Machines", IEEE Transactions on Computers, 19 Sept. 2012.

Accelerating Parameter Estimation for Multivariate Self-Exciting Point Processes

Ce Guo
Department of Computing
Imperial College London
United Kingdom
ce.guo10@imperial.ac.uk

Wayne Luk
Department of Computing
Imperial College London
United Kingdom
w.luk@imperial.ac.uk

ABSTRACT

Self-exciting point processes are stochastic processes capturing occurrence patterns of random events. They offer powerful tools to describe and predict temporal distributions of random events like stock trading and neurone spiking. A critical calculation in self-exciting point process models is parameter estimation, which fits a model to a data set. This calculation is computationally demanding when the number of data points is large and when the data dimension is high. This paper proposes the first reconfigurable computing solution to accelerate this calculation. We derive an acceleration strategy in a mathematical specification by eliminating complex data dependency, by cutting hardware resource requirement, and by parallelising arithmetic operations. In our experimental evaluation, an FPGA-based implementation of the proposed solution is up to 79 times faster than one CPU core, and 13 times faster than the same CPU with eight cores.

1. INTRODUCTION

The study of random processes is attracting attention from researchers and practitioners in various areas. These processes serve as powerful tools to analyse stochastic mechanisms. A self-exciting point process is a random process that describes the occurrences of repeatable momentary random events. This point process is particularly useful in modelling random events whose occurrence patterns do not follow obvious temporal distributions. Applications of self-exciting point process models include crime detection [6], high-frequency trading [1], earthquake analysis [4] and neurone spiking analysis [2].

We focus on self-exciting point process models for multivariate data. To build such a model, one needs to estimate an appropriate parameter set from data. This calculation is computationally expensive for a data set with a long occurrence sequence or high dimensionality. On the other hand, to adapt a model to a rapidly changing environment, one needs to repeat the estimation frequently to incorporate newly arrived data. As a result, an acceleration solution for this parameter estimation problem is in great demand.

Reconfigurable computing is a promising acceleration technology for this problem, but the best acceleration solution we know in existing work [3] can only handle univariate data. It is challenging to design a solution for the multivariate case. The most time-consuming calculation in parameter estimation, log-likelihood estimation, involves complex data dependency. It is necessary and challenging to develop novel and hardware-specific mathematical methods to eliminate this data dependency.

In this paper, we address this challenge and propose the first acceleration solution to the parameter estimation problem. The major contributions of this paper are as follows.

- An acceleration strategy for log-likelihood evaluation which eliminates complex data dependency.
- A pipelined hardware accelerator for maximum likelihood estimation based on the proposed strategy.
- An implementation of the proposed architecture on a commercial FPGA acceleration card.

2. SELF-EXCITING POINT PROCESSES

In this section we provide a short introduction to multivariate self-exciting point processes and the parameter estimation problem.

A sequence of random variables, $\{t_i\} = (t_1, t_2, t_3, \dots)$, is a *univariate point process* if and only if $t_i > 0$ and $t_i < t_{i+1}$ for all $i \in \mathbb{N}^+$. The *intensity* of a point process $\{t_i\}$ at a time point t is mathematically defined by

$$\lambda(t) = \lim_{h \to 0^-} E\left(\frac{C(t+h) - C(t)}{h}\right) \quad (1)$$

where

$$C(t) = \sum_{t_i \leq t} 1_{i \in \mathbb{N}^+} \quad (2)$$

A *multivariate point process* with M dimensions is a collection of M univariant point processes. In this research we focus on the *multivariate self-exciting point process* whose intensity functions satisfy

$$\lambda_m(t) = \lambda_m^\perp + \sum_{m'=1}^{M} \int_0^t \alpha_{m,m'} e^{-\beta_{m,m'}(t-w)} dC_{m'}(w) \quad (3)$$

The property of such a point process is uniquely given by a parameter set $\theta = \langle \Lambda^\perp, A, B \rangle$ where $\Lambda^\perp = \{\lambda_m^\perp : m \in [1..M]\}$, $A = \{\alpha_{m,m'} : (m, m') \in [1..M] \times [1..M]\}$ and $B = \{\beta_{m,m'} : (m, m') \in [1..M] \times [1..M]\}$.

FPGA'14, February 26–28, 2014, Monterey, CA, USA.
Copyright 2014 ACM 978-1-4503-2671-1/14/02 ...$15.00.
http://dx.doi.org/10.1145/2554688.2554765.

Parameter estimation for self-exciting point process models is the computation of a reasonable parameter set that fits a model to a data set. This calculation is the critical part in various applications related to point processes.

Parameter estimation can be achieved by maximum likelihood estimation [7] where we compute at least one member of the following set:

$$\Theta_{\text{MLE}} = \{\theta : (\forall \theta')[L(\theta, D(T)) \geq L(\theta', D(T))]\} \quad (4)$$

where $L(\theta, D(T))$ is the log-likelihood value calculated given a parameter set θ and a data set $D(T)$. The log-likelihood of a multivariate self-exciting point process can be computed by

$$L(\theta, D(t)) = \sum_{m=1}^{M} L_m = Q + R + S \quad (5)$$

where

$$Q = \sum_{m=1}^{M} \sum_{k=1}^{C_m(T)} \log \lambda_m(t_{m,k}) \quad (6)$$

$$R = T \sum_{m=1}^{M} \lambda_m^{\perp} \quad (7)$$

$$S = \sum_{m=1}^{M} h_m(T) \quad (8)$$

The search of parameters can be conducted by any general-purpose optimisation algorithm. However, no matter what algorithm is used, it needs to evaluate log-likelihood frequently. This evaluation process can be computationally expensive if the number of data points is large or the data dimension is high [3]. Hardware acceleration solution to the parameter estimation problem for multivariate self-exciting point processes has not been developed. There are only partial solutions [3, 5] based on simplified problem settings.

3. STRATEGY OF ACCELERATION

Log-likelihood evaluation is the most computationally expensive subroutine in parameter estimation. In this section, we describe an acceleration strategy for log-likelihood evaluation.

3.1 Log-Likelihood Evaluation

Each observation in the data set is recorded in the form $o_i = (t_i, m_i)$ where t_i is the occurrence time and m_i is the corresponding dimension label.

For ease of discussion, we denote the number of data points in the data set as N. If o_i corresponds to $t_{m,k}$, then we let $\lambda(o_i) = \lambda_m(t_{m,k})$. As we have discussed, a log-likelihood value can be computed by adding up three components by Equation (5). By Equation (7), we know that it is easy to compute R directly in $O(M)$ time. $(S+Q)$ can be computed by

$$S + Q = \sum_{i=1}^{N} (s_i + q_i) \quad (9)$$

where

$$s_i = \sum_{m=1}^{M} \frac{\alpha_{m,m_i}}{\beta_{m,m_i}} \left(e^{-\beta_{m,m_i}(T-t_i)} - 1 \right) \quad (10)$$

$$q_i = \log \lambda(o_k) \quad (11)$$

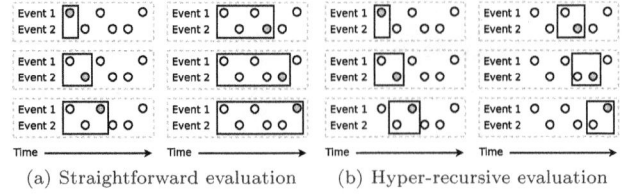

(a) Straightforward evaluation   (b) Hyper-recursive evaluation

Figure 1: Data dependency pattern in different intensity evaluation methods

In other words, one may obtain $(S + Q)$ by adding up $(s_i + q_i)$ for all $i \in [1..N]$. The effort to compute $(S + Q)$ depends on the efficiency of intensity evaluation. We need to evaluate $\lambda(o_i)$ for all observations o_i for all $i \in [1..N]$. Moreover, to evaluate $\lambda(o_i)$, one needs to collect a piece of statistical information from o_1 to o_i. The data dependency pattern of this method is shown in Figure 1(a).

3.2 Hyper-Recursive Intensity Evaluation

We propose *hyper-recursive intensity evaluation* which enables the log-likelihood to be computed without complex data dependency. The key insight of this method is that we introduce a group of intermediate variables that (i) contain all necessary statistical information of all past points for intensity computation and (ii) can be computed with a hardware resource requirement that does not scale up with data size N.

Finding such a group of intermediate variables is a very difficult task from the perspective of statistics, information theory and algorithm design, because this variable set needs to be compact, informative and easy to compute. In this study, we manage to find a set of variables that meet all these requirements. We propose to use the following equations to calculate intensities in a hardware-friendly manner:

$$\lambda(o_i) = \lambda_{m_i}^{\perp} + \sum_{m'=1}^{M} \alpha_{m_i, m'} r_{i, m'} \quad (12)$$

where

$$r_{i,m'} = u_{i,m'} + v_{i,m'} \quad (13)$$

$$u_{i,m'} = e^{-\beta_{m^*, m'}(x_i - x_{\iota(i,m^*)})} \omega_{i, m', m_i} \quad (14)$$

$$v_{i,m'} = e^{-\beta_{m_i, m'}(x_i - x_{\iota(i,m_i)})} \psi_{i, m', m_i} \quad (15)$$

$$\iota(i, m^*) = \sup\{i' : m_{i'} = m^* \text{ and } i' < i\} \quad (16)$$

$$\omega_{i,m',m^*} = \begin{cases} r_{i-1,m'} & \text{if } m_{i-1} = m^* \\ \omega_{i-1,m',m^*} & \text{if } m_{i-1} \neq m^* \end{cases} \quad (17)$$

$$\psi_{i,m',m^*} = \begin{cases} 0 & \text{if } m_{i-1} = m^* \\ \psi_{i-1,m',m^*} + \tilde{\phi}_{i-1,m',m^*} & \text{if } m_{i-1} \neq m^* \end{cases} \quad (18)$$

$$\tilde{\phi}_{i-1,m',m^*} = \begin{cases} e^{-\beta_{m^*,m'}(x_{\iota(i,m^*)} - x_{i-1})} & \text{if } m_{i-1} = m' \\ 0 & \text{if } m_{i-1} \neq m' \end{cases} \quad (19)$$

Equation (14) to (19) suggest that the variables ω_{i,m',m^*} and ϕ_{i,m',m^*} for all $(m', m^*) \in [1..M] \times [1..M]$ provide sufficient information for intensity computation without involving complex data dependency.

We name this method *hyper-recursive intensity evaluation* because the intensity is obtained from a two-layer recursive computation. The mathematical derivation of this method will be provided in a future publication.

This method is an excellent candidate for hardware implementation. One reason is that the requirement for arithmetic resources scales linearly with the dimensionality of the problem M. Another reason is that the data dependency, shown in Figure 1(b), is not related to the size of the data set N. Moreover, updating operations for $\omega_{i,m',m*}$ and $\psi_{i,m',m*}$ can easily be parallelised.

Hyper-recursive intensity evaluation is arguably the most general hardware-oriented algorithmic optimisation for parameter estimation, as there is no theoretical constraint in the number of data dimensions. An existing work about hardware-oriented adoption of univariate log-likelihood evaluation for self-exciting point process described in [3] is merely a special case of hyper-recursive intensity evaluation when $M = 1$. A detailed discussion of how our proposed method relates to existing work will be provided in a future publication.

Moreover, hyper-recursive intensity evaluation can be used with any likelihood-based parameter searching algorithm, because it produces the same results as the straightforward intensity evaluation.

4. PIPELINED ACCELERATOR FOR LOG-LIKELIHOOD EVALUATION

In this section, we develop a pipelined architecture for the hyper-recursive log-likelihood evaluation strategy described in the previous section.

4.1 Hardware Design

We propose a basic hardware module called the *intensity evaluation cell* to compute $r_{i,m'}$, $\psi_{i,m',m*}$ and $\omega_{i,m',m*}$ for a data point o_i and a dimension m' following the hyper-recursive intensity evaluation strategy discussed in the previous section. In other words, an intensity evaluation cell does not provide the intensity value directly, but it collects statistical information from data so that the intensity value can easily be computed.

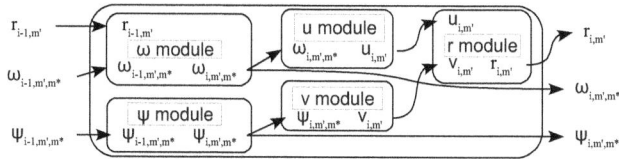

Figure 2: Intensity evaluation cell

The structure of the intensity evaluation cell is shown in Figure 2. The data input and the parameter set are omitted for brevity. As shown in the figure, an intensity evaluation cell contains five modules. The ω module and ψ module compute Equation (17) and (18) respectively for $\omega_{i,m',m*}$ and $\psi_{i,m',m*}$. The u module and v module take the outputs of the $\omega_{i,m',m*}$ and $\psi_{i,m',m*}$ respectively, and then evaluate Equation (14) and (15) to produce $u_{i,m'}$ and $v_{i,m'}$. The r module calculates $r_{i,m'}$ by adding up $u_{i,m'}$ and $v_{i,m'}$.

We design a pipelined accelerator to finalise the log-likelihood evaluation by combining multiple intensity evaluation cells. The structure of the accelerator is shown in Figure 3.

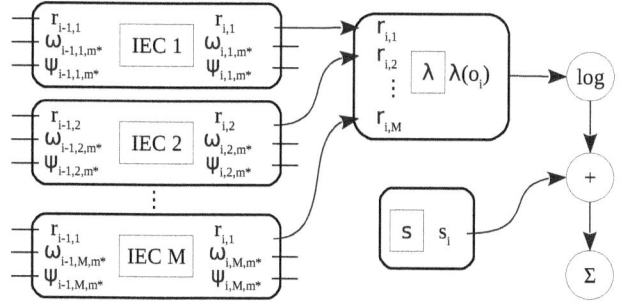

Figure 3: Log-likelihood evaluation accelerator

Each block marked with 'IEC' represents an intensity evaluation cell. In this architecture, we deploy M intensity evaluation cells to compute $r_{i,1}, r_{i,2}, \ldots, r_{i,M}$ for each data point o_i. These results are passed to a λ module which computes the intensity $\lambda(o_i)$ by Equation (12). In addition, we design the s module which computes s_i according to Equation (10). By accumulating the sum of $\log(o_i)$ and s_i in an accumulator, we can finally harvest the value of $(S + Q)$ by Equation (9).

4.2 An FPGA Implementation

We build an FPGA implementation of the proposed accelerator. The hardware platform we use is a Maxeler MAX3 acceleration card. This card is equipped with a Xilinx Virtex-6 V6-SX475T FPGA. The card is installed in a host computer with eight Intel i7-870 CPU cores running at 2.93GHz and 16GB DDR3 memory. The acceleration card communicates with the host computer via an 8-lane PCI Express 2.0 interface. The hardware design is described in the MaxJ language and compiled to VHDL with Maxeler MaxCompiler.

The occurrence times of data points are represented in IEEE single precision floating point numbers. The dimension labels are represented in 8-bit unsigned integers. We validate the correctness and precision of the system by comparing its results with a MATLAB implementation using simulated data sets with known parameters. The maximum relevant error is less than 1.1 percent.

We deploy 14 intensity evaluation cells in the FPGA to maximise resource usage. This implementation takes around 71 percent fine-grained logic, 38 percent of DSPs and 45 percent of block memory on the FPGA. Although the fine-grained logic is the resource usage bottleneck in this particular implementation, we believe that the block memory consumption will become the bottleneck when the number of intensity evaluation cells increases. This is because such resource consumption theoretically grows quadratically with the number of intensity evaluation cells while the consumption of other resources grows linearly.

The clock frequency of the FPGA is set to 120MHz. The memory bandwidth of our acceleration platform is around 4GB/s. The actual consumption of our accelerator is only around 0.56GB/s. This bandwidth consumption only depends on the clock frequency and the number representation scheme. If these two factors do not change, the memory consumption will not change even if we deploy more intensity evaluation cells in the system.

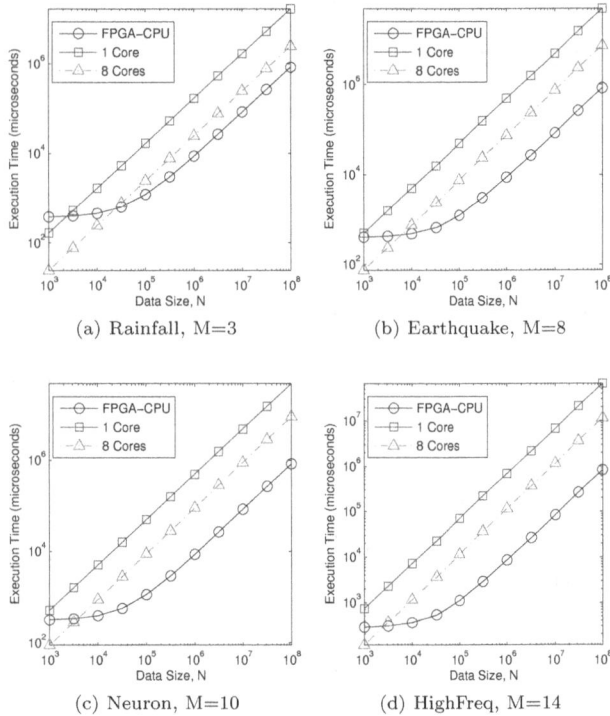

(a) Rainfall, M=3   (b) Earthquake, M=8

(c) Neuron, M=10   (d) HighFreq, M=14

Figure 4: Experimental Results

5. EXPERIMENTAL EVALUATION

We use four data sets in the experiments, namely 'Rainfall', 'Earthquake' , 'Neuron' and 'HighFreq'. These data sets are sampled from four different real-world problems: 'Rainfall' is collected from three rainfall monitors; 'Earthquake' is based on the log of a micro-earthquake detector; 'Neuron' is extracted from a neuron spiking train data; and 'HighFreq' is adapted from a high-frequency currency trading log. The numbers of dimensions of these four data set are 3, 8, 10, and 14 respectively.

We build a CPU-only implementation that runs exclusively on the host computer of the acceleration card. This implementation is programmed with the OpenMP library. To make a fair comparison, we apply a series of optimisations to this implementation, including avoiding redundant memory access and selecting appropriate parallelisation scheme. Both the host code for the FPGA accelerator and the CPU-only implementation are written in the C programming language and compiled with the Intel C compiler with the highest compiling optimisation.

The performance measure of the experiments is the execution time of log-likelihood evaluation. This performance measure is independent of the selection of searching algorithm. Experimental results for log-likelihood evaluation are shown in Figure 4. We record the data size in log scale with base 10 in these figures. To reflect the trend of the increment of the execution time, we also record the execution time in log scale. Note that a small difference along the vertical axis in each figure means a huge difference in execution time due to the properties of the logarithm function.

The FPGA-CPU system demonstrates higher speedup for large data in general. The maximum speedup is achieved

when $M = 14$ and the data size reaches 10^7. In this case, the FPGA implementation is respectively 79 times and 13 times faster than a single-core CPU and an eight-core CPU for log-likelihood evaluation. Moreover, we find that the FPGA-CPU implementation consumes 31 times less energy than the CPU-only implementation during the computation. A detailed analysis of the experimental results will be provided in a future publication.

6. CONCLUSION AND FUTURE WORK

This paper presents the first hardware acceleration solution to the parameter estimation problem of multivariate self-exciting point processes. We first develop an acceleration strategy for log-likelihood evaluation. The core method of the strategy is the hyper-recursive intensity evaluation which eliminates complex data dependency. This strategy enables log-likelihood values to be computed in a pipelined manner. By mapping the proposed strategy into reconfigurable hardware, we design an accelerator for log-likelihood evaluation which works for all likelihood-based parameter searching algorithms. This accelerator evaluates log-likelihood values efficiently, and its resource requirement does not grow with the data size. One possible direction of future work is to further improve the performance by applying application-specified optimisations. Another possible direction is to develop point process models which natively support hardware acceleration.

7. ACKNOWLEDGEMENT

This work is supported in part by the China Scholarship Council, by Maxeler University Programme, by the European Union Seventh Framework Programme under grant agreement number 257906, 287804 and 318521, by UK EPSRC, and by Xilinx.

8. REFERENCES

[1] C. G. Bowsher. Modelling security market events in continuous time: Intensity based, multivariate point process models. *Journal of Econometrics*, 141(2):876–912, 2007.

[2] R. Dahlhaus, M. Eichler, and J. Sandkühler. Identification of synaptic connections in neural ensembles by graphical models. *Journal of neuroscience methods*, 77(1):93–107, 1997.

[3] C. Guo and W. Luk. Accelerating maximum likelihood estimation for Hawkes point processes. In *International Conference on Field Programmable Logic and Applications*, 2013.

[4] Y. Y. Kagan. Statistical distributions of earthquake numbers: consequence of branching process. *Geophysical Journal International*, 180(3):1313–1328, 2010.

[5] S. W. Linderman and R. P. Adams. Discovering structure in spiking data. In *New England Machine Learning Day*, Cambridge, MA USA, 2013.

[6] G. O. Mohler, M. B. Short, P. J. Brantingham, F. P. Schoenberg, and G. E. Tita. Self-exciting point process modeling of crime. *Journal of the American Statistical Association*, 106(493):100–108, 2011.

[7] Y. Ogata. On Lewis' simulation method for point processes. *IEEE Transactions on Information Theory*, 27(1):23–31, 1981.

Energy-Efficient Multiplier-Less Discrete Convolver through Probabilistic Domain Transformation

Mohammed Alawad, Yu Bai, Ronald DeMara, and Mingjie Lin
Department of EECS, University of Central Florida, USA.

ABSTRACT

Energy efficiency and algorithmic robustness typically are conflicting circuit characteristics, yet with CMOS technology scaling towards 10-nm feature size, both become critical design metrics simultaneously for modern logic circuits. This paper propose a novel computing scheme hinged on *probabilistic domain transformation* aiming for both low power operation and fault resilience. In such a computing paradigm, algorithm inputs are first encoded through probabilistic means, which translates the input values into a number of random samples. Subsequently, light-weight operations, such as simple additions will be performed onto these random samples in order to generate new random variables. Finally, the resulting random samples will be decoded probabilistically to give the final results.

To validate the effectiveness of this proposed computing scheme, we presents a high-performance reconfigurable discrete convolver specifically designed for FPGA-based image and video processors. While the conventional multiplier-based architecture can only achieve $\mathcal{O}(N^2)$, the proposed architecture, through the proposed probabilistic domain transformation, can achieve approximately $\mathcal{O}(N)$ in algorithmic complexity, therefore highly scalable and energy efficient. In addition, the PDT methodology makes the proposed architecture highly fault-tolerant because information to be processed is encoded with probability density function instead of its binary forms. As such, the local perturbations of its computing accuracy or signal values are inconsequential to its overall results. The convolver prototype implemented with Virtex 6 FPGA devices (XC6VLX550t) requires just 4.09 μs to perform a 128×128 convolution and dissipates only 166.63 nJ in dynamic energy consumption at 250 MHz. This new architecture can be exploited in all the real-time applications in which energy-efficient convolutions are required and it can be realized with many other FPGA device families.

Keywords

Discrete Convolution, Stochastic Logic.

1 Introduction

Digital signal processing (DSP) plays a central role in modern image processing and computer vision algorithms. Among many DSP techniques, domain transformation, especially the spatial temporal domain transfer, is particularly important. For example, advanced techniques, such as Radon transformation, Fourier transformation, and Hankel transformation, etc., are widely used in medical imaging techniques like Computed Tomography (CT) and Magnetic Resonance Imaging (MRI). Unfortunately, these transformation methods are often quite computationally intensive. As such, conventional domain transformations become in-

creasingly more challenging to perform because both the volume of imagery data and the algorithmic complexity of image processing are expected to increase exponentially in the coming years [1]. Therefore, it is imperative to design new methodology for domain transformation in DSP, which not only have high performance but also can achieve high algorithmic robustness.

2 Probabilistic Domain Transformation

In DSP, domain transformations can yield equivalent results to input signals that would be hard to obtained if its original domain is used. For example, Fourier transform, maybe the most importance domain transformation in DSP, considers the representation and analysis of analog signals and systems in the frequency domain. This is because the frequency domain can reveal further characteristics of signals and systems, i.e., the frequency content of an arbitrary aperiodic (or non-periodic) signal often referred to as the spectrum.

Inspired by the Fourier transform, we propose a new domain transformation called *Probabilistic Domain Transformation*(PDT). In this method, the input discrete signal $x[n]$ will be first converted into a serial of random samples $\mathbf{T}_x[m]$) through the transform $\mathcal{P}(\cdot)$. Corresponding to the system function $H[j\omega]$ in the Fourier transform, the random samples $\mathbf{T}_x[m]$) are processed by $\mathcal{F}(\cdot)$, subsequently generating new random samples $\mathbf{T}_y[m]$. Finally, these newly generated random samples $\mathbf{T}_y[m]$) can be decoded as the final results $y[n]$ by $\mathcal{P}^{-1}(\cdot)$. Obviously, in order to successfully perform the proposed PDT, we need to clearly define what $\mathcal{P}(\cdot)$, $\mathcal{P}^{-1}(\cdot)$, and $\mathcal{F}(\cdot)$ represent, respectively.

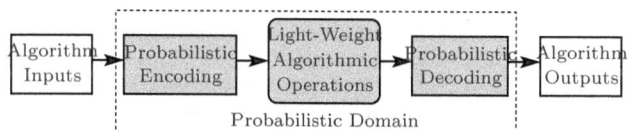

Figure 1: Conceptual picture of our proposed probabilistic computing paradigm. All operations within gray blocks will be realized by leveraging basic stochastic operations.

Fig. 1 conceptually illustrates the scheme of using probabilistic domain transformation. In such a computing scheme, algorithm inputs are first encoded through probabilistic means, which translates the input values into a number of random samples. Subsequently, light-weight operations, such as simple additions will be performed onto these random samples in order to generate new random variables. Finally, the resulting random samples will be decoded probabilistically to give the final results. In Fig. 1, all these three steps enclosed in gray boxes are conducted within the probabilistic domain.

The expected benefits of our proposed probabilistic domain transformation are three-fold. First, because the probabilistic operations will be performed using light-weight operations, the needed hardware usage will be significantly reduced. Second, because most operations performed in the probabilistic domain are quite primitive, the total power consumption will be low. Finally, maybe more importantly, because all signal values will be represented and computed probabilistically, the circuit implementation will be very robust because local signal corruption can not easily destroy the overall probabilistic patterns [2, 3, 4, 5].

3 Stochastic Convolution through Adding Random Variables

Suppose $\mathbf{X}$ and $\mathbf{Y}$ are two independent discrete random variables with distribution functions $m_{\mathbf{X}}[n]$ and $m_{\mathbf{Y}}[n]$. Let $\mathbf{Z} = \mathbf{X} + \mathbf{Y}$. According to the basic principle of probability, the distribution function $m_{\mathbf{Z}}[n]$ can be proved to be

$$m_{\mathbf{Z}}[n] = \sum_{k=1}^{N} m_{\mathbf{X}}[k] m_{\mathbf{Y}}[n-k] = m_{\mathbf{X}}[n] * m_{\mathbf{Y}}[n], \quad (1)$$

where $n = 1, 2, \cdots, N$. The fully derivation can be found in [6]. In the following, we exploit this result to compute the discrete convolution probabilistically.

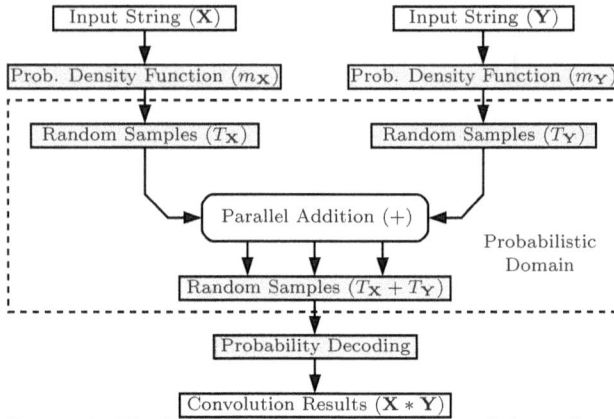

Figure 2: Block diagram of the key steps and flow of our proposed probabilistic convolution algorithm. Two steams of inputs are both treated as PDFs. Subsequently, random samples are generated according to these PDFs. Adding these random samples pairwise can mimic the addition of random samples. Finally, the PDF of the resulting random samples is computed as the final result.

Fig. 2 depicts our basic idea of evaluating convolution probabilistically. Two input signals X and Y are first converted into two sequence of random samples $T_{\mathbf{X}}$ and $T_{\mathbf{Y}}$ respectively with the conditions $m_{\mathbf{X}} = \text{PDF}(\mathbf{X})$ and $m_{\mathbf{Y}} = \text{PDF}(\mathbf{Y})$ to be satisfied. Subsequently, $T_{\mathbf{X}}$ and $T_{\mathbf{Y}}$ are added sample by sample to obtain $\mathbf{Z} = \mathbf{X} + \mathbf{Y}$. Finally, the PDF of $\mathbf{Z}$ is computed as the final output. Because it is well known that the PDF of the sum of two independent random variables equals to the convolution of their individual PDFs, we therefore conclude $\mathbf{Z} = \mathbf{X} * \mathbf{Y}$.

Both input vectors $\mathbf{X}$ and $\mathbf{Y}$ come in the form of N integers. The first step of our probabilistic convolution algorithm is to treat these streams of integer numbers as the histogram of index numbers, which is an approximation of the probability density function. Subsequently, we use these two histograms to generate random samples ($T_{\mathbf{X}}$ and $T_{\mathbf{X}}$)that satisfy these probability density functions, i.e., $\text{PDF}(T_{\mathbf{X}}) = \mathbf{X}$ and $\text{PDF}(T_{\mathbf{Y}}) = \mathbf{Y}$. In other words, the numerical value of each input value roughly represents the frequency for its index value to appear in the generated random samples. Next, we add these random samples pairwise to produce a number of new random samples $T_{\mathbf{Z}} = T_{\mathbf{X}} + T_{\mathbf{Y}}$. Finally, we compute the histogram or PDF of the random samples of $T_{\mathbf{Z}}$, which automatically results in the convolution result $\mathbf{Z} = \mathbf{X} * \mathbf{Y}$.

4 Prototype Implementation

Figure 3 depicts the overall hardware architecture for our proposed discrete convolution through probalistic domain

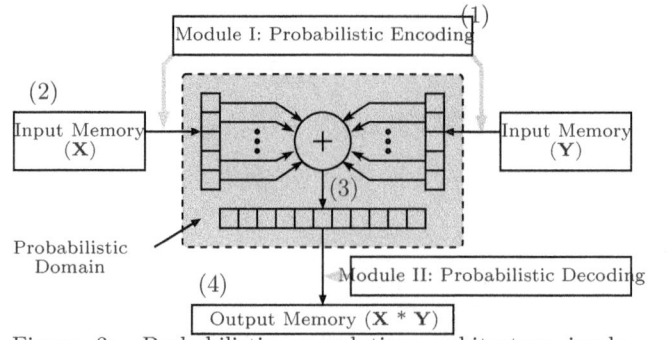

Figure 3: Probabilistic convolution architecture implemented with FPGA. Four hardware techniques are marked: (1) Stochastic Mixing Scheme. (2) Segmented Memory Swapping. (3) Scalable Adder Extension. (4) Virtual Indexing Scheme.

transform. Input values $\mathbf{X}$ and $\mathbf{Y}$ are saved in two pieces of memory. We use gray color to denote the probabilistic domain. There are two important components in the whole system. The first component, Module I, transforms the input vector values into random samples, whose Probability Density Functions (PDFs) mirror these input stream values. Next, these random samples are added pairwise, thus producing a new stream of random samples. According to Equation 1, the PDF of these random values will be exactly the convolution of $\mathbf{X}$ and $\mathbf{Y}$, which can be computed by the Module II. Note that, within the probabilistic domain, our proposed architecture relies solely on registers and adding procedure. In this way, the traditional convolution method with many multiplications can be easily achieved by parallel adders, hence the name of "multiplier-less".

Two operations are critical to the success of above scheme. First, given any sequence of input values, how to extract its PDF. Second, given a pdf, how to generate random samples that match it. As shown in Fig. 3, when the input value sequence arrives, we shift them into a chain of registers. At the same time, the randomizer will randomly pick one of the register and emit a number of random samples with the value determined by the position of the chosen register. Further more, the number of output samples will be decided by the value in the chosen register. Clearly, the sequence of random samples will have a PDF or histogram approximated by the values in all shift registers. Similarly in Fig. 3, when the random samples arrive sequentially, they will be counted according to its signal value. In other words, each register will hold a counter value of how many arriving samples fall in its value range.

To fully implement our proposed architecture and enable our architecture to convolute extremely long input vectors in a scalable way, we need four hardware techniques in order to overcome various challenges. Specifically, 1) when the size of input vector is large, most of the input data has to be stored in external memory, therefore can only be read from and written to at relatively slow speed relative to the logic computation or on-chip registers. 2) To mimic the independence of random numbers, theoretically, we need a large number of random number generators (such as LFSRs) to pair with all parallel adders. However, LFSR is costly in hardware usage. 3) In theory, increasing the number of parallel adders can significantly improve the overall performance. However, more adders create performance bottleneck for counter updating. 4) Assuming the input size N to be large, during each round, only a small portion of inputs can be placed in the buffer of parallel adders.

5 Results and Analysis

To validate our proposed architecture for probabilistic convolution, we have various prototypes using the Xilinx Virtex 4 FPGA device. As a reference, we implemented a multiplier-based convolver using the same FPGA device. In the following, for different configurations, we compare our proposed probabilistic convolver against the conventional convolver in terms of hardware usage, computing through-put, and energy consumption. In all of our studies, we assume all input numbers are 32-bit long and the resulting output numbers are 64-bit long. One unique property of our proposed probabilistic convolution is that its solution can only achieve close-to-100% accuracy to the corresponding accurate solution. Given the fact that our proposed proba-bilistic convolver is mainly used in FPGA-based image and video processors, such accuracy poses no negative impact to the final results of our target applications. In the follow-ing comparisons, to be fair, we always choose $\sigma \leq 0.001$ to be the termination criterion for our probabilistic convolu-tion. We define the relative error σ as $\sigma = \frac{\|Z^* - Z\|}{\sum_i Z_i/N}$, where Z^* and Z are the probabilistic and conventional convolution results, respectively. In addition, $\|Z^* - Z\|$ denotes the Euclidean norm of $Z^* - Z$, which is defined by the formula $\|Z^* - Z\| = \sqrt{\sum_i |z_i^* - Z_i|^2}$.

6 Scalable Probabilistic Convolvers

In order to convolute large-scale input vectors, we have to store the input data and some intermediate data in the off-chip memory, thus posing a big challenge to achieve high per-formance for long input vectors because of the relatively long latency and small bandwidth between the external mem-ory and on-chip block RAMs. Using Virtex 6 FPGA de-vices, we have implemented three different configurations of both conventional and probabilistic convolvers: 8×8, 16×16, and 32×32. In order to be scalable, additional architectural structures have to be implemented in our probabilistic con-volver. For the same 16×16 configuration of probabilistic convolver, the hardware usage of scalable version (1284 Slice LUTs) is almost 2 times larger than the non-scalable version (547 Slice LUTs), but still 1/3 smaller in hardware usage when compared with the conventional 16×16 convolver.

When comparing performance, for all three configurations (8×8, 16×16, and 32×32), the clock period of our scalable probabilistic convolver is about two times smaller than the conventional case.This difference is largely due to the fact that relatively slow multipliers have been completely re-placed with relatively fast adders. As for the total execution time for a problem size $N = 128$, on average, our probabilis-tic convolver is only about 10% faster than the conventional one mainly because the large number of total clock cycles is needed in the probabilistic convolution.

Finally, we consider the power consumptions of both con-volvers. In all three different configurations, our proposed probabilistic convolver consistently achieve about 3 to 4 times less dynamic power consumption than the conventional con-volver. This significant reduction is mostly caused by the significantly less hardware usage. Because of the roughly same total execution time between these two kinds of con-volvers, this directly translates into about 3.5 times less total energy consumed when convolving two 128-element vectors.

Our results have shown that, although dynamic power consumption increases with the number of adders, the mag-nitude of these increases is relatively small, merely a 15% total increase. This is because, from $K = 8$ to 128, although the total hardware usage is increased by about 2 times, the clock frequency is actually decreased by about 55%. For a $N = 128$ discrete convolution, the $K = 128$ probabilis-tic convolver consumes only 11.49% of the total energy of a conventional convolver, an near 10 times improvement in energy efficiency.

For a probabilistic convolver consisting of $K = 16$ adders, how will the total execution time change as the problem size

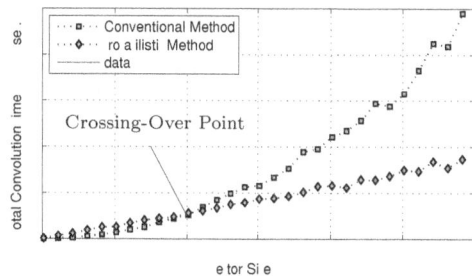

Figure 4: Execution time of a $K = 16$ scalable probabilistic convolver for different problem size N.

N increases? In Figure 4, we plotted the total execution time for different problem sizes N. These two curves represent conventional and probabilistic convolvers, respectively. Our results clearly show that the execution time of conventional method increases almost quadratically, while the execution time of probabilistic convolution increases almost linearly. At first, when the problem size $N \leq 110$, the conventional convolver outperforms the probabilistic convolver, i.e., has short execution time. However, as soon as N exceeds 110, the probabilistic convolver starts to outperform the conven-tional one. Moreover, the performance gap between these two convolvers grows exponentially.

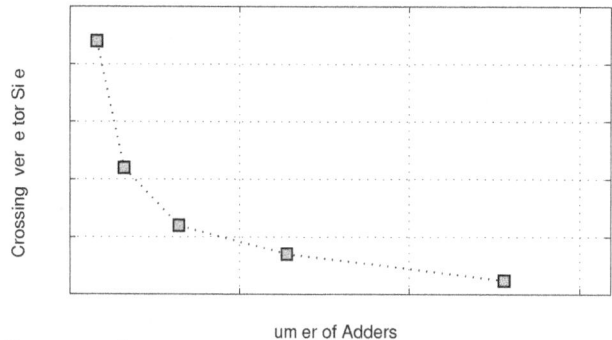

Figure 5: Crossing-over points vs. Number of adders (K). As K increases, the crossing-over point decreases. This means that for large K, a probabilistic convolver can out-perform the conventional convolver even for small problem size.

To further investigate the relative performance between our probabilistic convolver and the conventional one, we de-fine the crossing-over vector size as the N value at which the relative performance between these two convolvers changes. We have collected the crossing-point vector sizes for K val-ues ranging from 8 to 128 and presented them in Figure 5. It is clear that, while the number of adders K increases, the crossing-over vector size decreases precipitously from about 220 to about 10. In other words, the larger the problem size N is, the higher performance advantage of our probabilistic convolver will have.

Computing Complexity Analysis

According to Equation 1, convolving two N-sized vec-tors X and Y needs N^2 multiplications and N^2 additions. Therefore, the computing complexity of conventional con-volver is $\mathcal{O}(N^2)$. For the discrete convolution in this study, we assume w bits in each integer number, therefore the largest numerical value of all inputs is 2^w. As discussed in Section 2, we compute the discrete convolution by mim-icking the addition of two independent random variables. In theory, the total number of random samples M can be $\sum_{i=1}^{N} X_i + \sum_{i=1}^{N} Y_i \approx 2N \cdot 2^w$. Assuming there are K adders, as shown in Figure 4, during each iteration, each adder will independently and randomly select one memory element from $X_1, \cdots, X_K$ and $Y_1, \cdots, Y_K$, respectively. Therefore, each memory element X_i has $1/K$ probability to be chosen by one particular adder during each iteration. Because all adders are completely independent and there are K in total, on average, each memory element X_i or Y_i will be decremented by $1/K \cdot K = 1$. Moreover, there are K memory elements to be operated on, thus during each iteration, in total, the total numerical values will be reduced by $K \cdot 1 = K$. Finally, the total number of iterations can be computed as $\frac{N \cdot 2^w}{2K}$. Because both w and K are user-chosen design parameters, we conclude that the computing complexity of our proposed probabilistic convolution is $\frac{N \cdot 2^w}{2K} = \mathcal{O}(N)$. The results in the above sections also validated this conclusion.

7 Real-World Application

(a) σ=1%, $P = 69$.   (b) σ=1%, $P = 89$.

(c) σ=5%, $P = 43$.   (d) σ=5%, $P = 88$.

(e) σ=10%, $P = 24$.   (f) σ=10%, $P = 85$.

Figure 6: Two methodologies. (a)(c)(e) Conventional Computing. (b)(d)(f) Probabilistic Computing.

To illustrate the utility of our proposed probabilistic convolver, we choose computing the image correspondence as our test bench. We replaced the convolution module in its original implementation with our probabilistic one. We then inject the same percentage of computing errors σ to both implementations. We then measure their quality of results (the number of detected features P) as shown in Fig. 6. When σ increases from 1% to 10%, the conventional method can only detect 1/3 of available features, whereas our probabilistic method can still recover more than 95%. This clearly shows the huge advantages in reliability for our probabilistic method.

8 Conclusion

Deviating from the conventional multiplier-based convolution methods, this paper presents a novel multiplier-less probabilistic convolution, where the hardware-expensive multipliers can be replaced with light-weight adders through probabilistic domain transformation. Our study can be viewed as one design instance of a new probability-based computing paradigm, in which computing information is encoded with probabilistic means such as Probability Density Function (PDF), therefore enabling more primitive operations to be performed to achieve higher energy-efficiency and low hardware cost.

In addition to the fundamental contribution of probabilistic convolution method, this paper also developed numerous novel reconfigurable hardware techniques, such as Segmented Memory Swapping, Stochastic Mixing Scheme, Virtual Indexing Scheme, and Scalable Adder Extension, to minimize hardware usage and mitigate memory bandwidth bottleneck. Compared with the conventional convolver implemented with the identical FPGA device, our new multiplier-less probabilistic convolver has shown more than three times of improvements in energy efficiency for nominal test cases. Maybe the most important advantage, our new probabilistic convolver can reduce the algorithmic complexity of conventional convolution ($\mathcal{O}(N^2)$) to a significantly less one ($\mathcal{O}(N)$). This discovery makes our probabilistic convolver even more advantageous when the problem size N becomes larger.

Although not discussed in this paper, we believe the new probabilistic convolve is significantly more robust or fault tolerant than the conventional architecture because, through our proposed probabilistic domain transformation, all signal values will be represented and computed probabilistically, and local signal corruption can not easily destroy the overall probabilistic patterns, therefore achieving much higher tolerance to local errors. We currently are investigating this line of research.

9 References

[1] Microsystems Technology Office, "Unconventional processing of signals for intelligent data exploitation (UPSIDE)," Aug. 2012.

[2] D. Wilhelm and J. Bruck, "Stochastic switching circuit synthesis," in *Information Theory, 2008. ISIT 2008. IEEE International Symposium on*, pp. 1388 –1392, july 2008.

[3] P.-L. Loh, H. Zhou, and J. Bruck, "The robustness of stochastic switching networks," in *Information Theory, 2009. ISIT 2009. IEEE International Symposium on*, pp. 2066 –2070, 28 2009-july 3 2009.

[4] H. Zhou and J. Bruck, "On the expressibility of stochastic switching circuits," in *Information Theory, 2009. ISIT 2009. IEEE International Symposium on*, pp. 2061 –2065, 28 2009-july 3 2009.

[5] W. Qian, X. Li, M. Riedel, K. Bazargan, and D. Lilja, "An architecture for fault-tolerant computation with stochastic logic," *Computers, IEEE Transactions on*, vol. 60, pp. 93 –105, jan. 2011.

[6] W. Feller, *AN INTRODUCTION TO PROBABILITY THEORY AND ITS APPLICATIONS, 2ND ED.* No. v. 1 in Wiley publication in mathematical statistics, Wiley India Pvt. Limited, 2008.

Wordwidth, Instructions, Looping, and Virtualization
The Role of Sharing in Absolute Energy Minimization

André DeHon

Department of Electrical and Systems Engineering, University of Pennsylvania
200 S. 33rd St., Philadelphia, PA 19104
andre@acm.org

ABSTRACT

When are FPGAs more energy efficient than processors? This question is complicated by technology factors and the wide range of application characteristics that can be exploited to minimize energy. Using a wire-dominated energy model to estimate the absolute energy required for programmable computations, we determine when spatially organized programmable computations (FPGAs) require less energy than temporally organized programmable computations (processors). The point of crossover will depend on the metal layers available, the locality, the SIMD wordwidth regularity, and the compactness of the instructions. When the Rent Exponent, p, is less than 0.7, the spatial design is always more energy efficient. When $p = 0.8$, the technology offers 8-metal layers for routing, and data can be organized into 16b words and processed in tight loops of no more than 128 instructions, the temporal design uses less energy when the number of LUTs is greater than 64K. We further show that heterogeneous multicontext architectures can use even less energy than the $p = 0.8$, 16b word temporal case.

Categories and Subject Descriptors

B.7.1 [**Integrated Circuits**]: Type and Design Styles—*VLSI*; C.0 [**General**]: Modeling of Computer Architecture; C.2.1 [**Computer Communication Newtorks**]: Network Architecture and Design

Keywords

Energy; Energy Modeling; Low Power; FPGA; Rent's Rule; Locality; Instructions; Multicontext; SIMD

1. INTRODUCTION

As we enter the era of mobile devices and *dark silicon* [4], minimizing energy becomes the dominant concern when engineering computations. Battery life and power-density envelopes limit the performance we can extract, not critical

path delay or area. Under these constraints, architectures that reduce the energy per operation are the most beneficial.

In prior work [2], we established that spatial (FPGA-like) computations can use asymptotically lower energy than sequential (processor-like) computations. However, this analysis did not estimate when these asymptotic effects would begin to dominate. The goal of this paper is to estimate when the asymptotic effects are large enough to have a practical impact and to refine the comparison to account for common optimizations that allow processors to save energy. Consequently, this paper builds absolute energy models including constant terms and scale factors. To make the model results general, we introduce parameters for key technology factors (*e.g.*, relative size of memory bits compared to wire pitch, metal layers available for routing). To balance model complexity with accuracy, we use a wire-dominated energy model suitable for modern VLSI processes (Sec. 3.2).

To better characterize absolute energy in processors, we observe that processors reduce the overhead of instruction energy by sharing instructions using single-instruction, multiple data (SIMD) control of multibit words and looping (Sec. 4). The energy reduction is sufficient to allow the processor to use less energy for a computation than spatial (FPGA-like) designs (Sec. 5) when the design has little interconnect locality such that its Rent Exponent, p (Sec. 2.1), is greater than 0.75. When the Rent Exponent is less than 0.75, even with these optimizations, the FPGA uses less energy than the processor, but the optimizations reduce the absolute advantage. For the cases where the Rent Exponent is large, we identify architectural points between the FPGA and processor extremes that achieve lower energy than either (Sec. 6). Our analysis provides parameterized models that allow relative area and energy comparisons across a wide range of design and technology parameters.

Our contributions include:

1. parameterized, wire-dominated energy models for a programmable structure that can be tuned to represent single and multiple context FPGAs and processors
2. identified energy crossover points as a function of design size and a wide range of technology (*e.g.*, metal layers) and application characteristics including locality, word width, and loop size
3. optimized heterogeneous, synchronous, multicontext architecture and identification of the energy-minimizing architectural parameters
4. comparison of relative energies for select organizations across this design space

2. BACKGROUND

Before developing our detailed energy models, we first review Rent's Rule, the hierarchical network style we will use for interconnect, and the asymptotic results from [2] that leverage Rent's Rule and the hierarchical networks.

2.1 Rent's Rule

Typical circuits do not look like random graphs. Rather, they have local clusters that can be physically placed to minimize the number of nets that enter and exit a region. First identified by E. F. Rent and published by Landman and Russo [8], Rent's Rule says that the number of wires that must cross into or out of a region of N components is reasonably modeled by:

$$BW = cN^p \qquad (1)$$

where p is the Rent Exponent, which is typically in the range 0.5–0.7. The Rent Exponent can be used as a measure of locality. Designs with a smaller fraction of wires exiting a region, smaller BW, are characterized by a smaller p. Rent's Rule has been used to estimate wiring requirements in FP-GAs (*e.g.* [7] used $p = 0.78$). As Hutton notes, both the circuit netlists and the FPGA substrate can each be characterized with their own Rent Parameters. For the scope of this paper, we make the simplifying assumption that the design and substrate Rent Parameters are matched.

Rent locality directly implies the wire length distributions in a design [3]. If the circuit has a Rent Exponent less than 0.5, the average wirelength is a constant independent of the number of gates, N. When the circuit has a Rent Exponent greater than 0.5, the average wirelength scales as $N^{p-0.5}$.

2.2 Hierarchical Network Review

Lieserson observed that excessive wiring in VLSI designs could lead to area inefficient implementations. As a result, he developed the Fat Tree interconnection network that has limited wiring bandwidth that grows according to Rent's Rule and, like Rent's Rule, can be parameterized by p [10]. The Butterfly Fat Tree (BFT) variant of the Fat Tree uses simple, constant size switches at the tree stages [6] (See. Fig. 1a). In this paper, we use a version of the BFT based on directional wiring [12, 11].

In these networks, the bandwidth into each subtree grows toward the root in accordance with Rent's Rule. The growth can be programmed discretely by selecting the use of bandwidth preserving 2:1 stages (2 parent links for 1 child link in each of the two sibling subtree) and bandwidth reducing 1:1 stages. By alternating 2:1 and 1:1 stages as shown in Fig. 1a, the bandwidth increase by a factor of 2 across two stages where the number of gates in the subtree has increased by a factor of 4. This corresponds to a p of 0.5 ($4^{0.5} = 2$). By changing the selection of 2:1 and 1:1 stages, we can configure networks for different p's. A $p = \frac{2}{3}$ network is realized by repeating a sequence of 2:1, 2:1, and 1:1 switches ($(2^3)^{0.67} = 4$).

In the heterogeneous multicontext design, we allow the tree to have a different set of Rent parameters ($c' = \frac{c}{C_t}$, $p' = p_t$) from the design it supports and place configuration memories local to the switches. To route the design, we time multiplex the original wiring requirements over this reduced physical network. When $p_t < p$, the time multiplexing factor, and hence the size of the memories, grows toward the root of the tree giving rise to the heterogeneous

multicontext interconnect. At the root of a subtree of size N, the instruction memories are of depth $C_t N^{p-p_t}$. Fig. 1b shows a $C_t = 2$, $p_t = 0.25$, network used to implement the $c = 2$, $p = 0.5$ network shown in Fig. 1a. It realizes the $p = 0.25$ network by repeating the stage sequence of 2:1, 1:1, 1:1, and 1:1 switches ($(2^4)^{0.25} = 2$). The switch at the top of the 16-gate tree shown has memories of depth $C_t N^{p-p_t} = 2 \times (2^4)^{0.25} = 4$.

2.3 Asymptotic Review

To implement a computation sequentially, we must store the intermediate state of the computation in a memory. A circuit with N gates, stores each of the N gate outputs in a large memory. The size N memory has a side length of $O(\sqrt{N})$, meaning every input read or value stored will cost $O(\sqrt{N})$ energy. In contrast, if we spatially layout the circuit for the graph, we can try to minimize the average wirelength between producers and consumers. If the design has a Rent Exponent less than 0.5, the average wirelength is constant, and the energy per operation is $O(1)$. If we have an unlimited number of wire layers, we immediately know that the wires between gates will be at most $O(\sqrt{N})$ and, consequently, energy is no greater than $O(\sqrt{N})$. The wirelength relation above suggests the wirelength will only grow as $O(N^{p-0.5})$, meaning the energy will always be less than $O(\sqrt{N})$—less than the sequential energy—until $p = 1.0$. This wirelength phenomena largely explains the spatial and sequential asymptotic results from [2].

When we are limited to a constant number of metal layers, the side length grows as $O(N^p)$, and energy per gate can grow as $O(N^{2p-1})$, which is greater than the sequential energy $O(\sqrt{N})$ when $p > 0.75$. This larger area and energy is driven by the wiring required to support a large p design. However, [2] also shows that, by using a $p_t < 0.5$ heterogeneous multicontext BFT (previous section), we can bring the energy per operation below $O(\sqrt{N})$ for any $p < 1$.

While the spatial design has lower energy, asymptotically, it is not clear when the asymptotic effects begin to matter. Furthermore, while the asymptotic analysis points to the inefficiency of a sequential processor with a single memory, it does not rule out the possibility that sequential processors of some limited, fixed capacity could be less energy than fully spatial designs. The asymptotic results do not address how to organize the computation to minimize absolute energy.

3. MODELS

3.1 Computational Graph Model

Our computational model is a graph of interconnected operators that must all be evaluated on each cycle of operation. The graph could be a circuit netlist or a homogeneous synchronous dataflow (SDF) graph [9]. The graph may include state elements such as SDF delay elements or registers in a circuit netlist. The graph may contain cyclic paths as long as they are valid synchronous cycles, meaning there must be one or more registers or delay elements on each cyclic path. The operators are nodes in the graph. Nodes take in a fixed set of inputs, perform some logical operation on the inputs, and produce a fixed set of outputs. The node could be a logical gate or a flip flop in a circuit netlist or an arithmetic operation or delay element in an SDF graph. The edges in the graph describe how outputs from one graph node be-

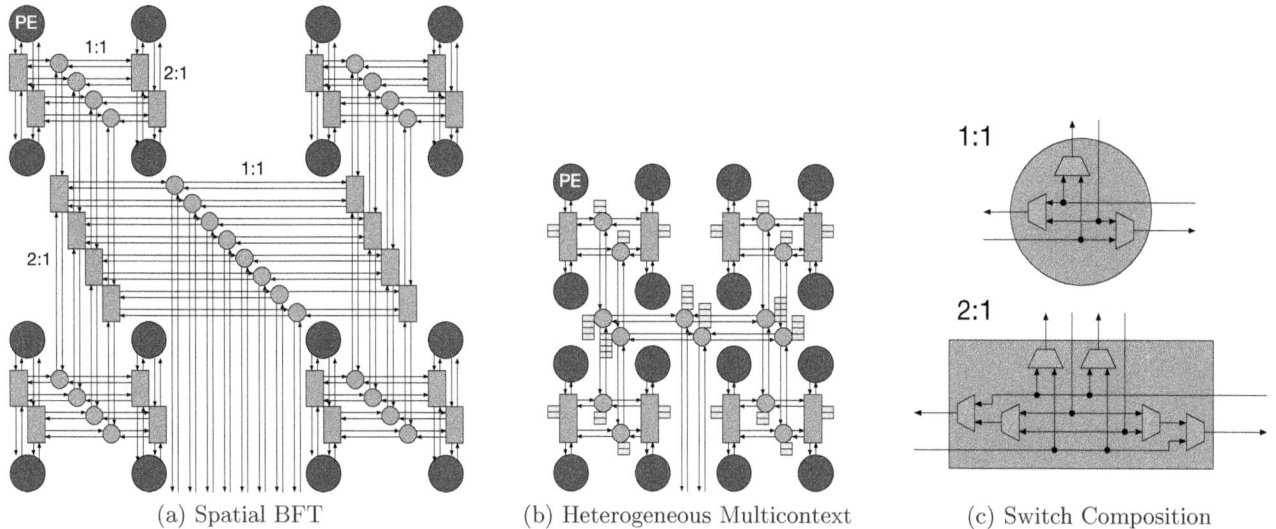

(a) Spatial BFT　　　　(b) Heterogeneous Multicontext　　　　(c) Switch Composition

Figure 1: Directional Butterfly Fat Tree (BFT) with $c = 2$, $p = 0.5$

come inputs to others. Each edge has a single source and may have multiple destinations. Since the graph is a valid synchronous graph, a cycle of computation can be computed by ordering the nodes topologically and evaluating each node once based on its inputs. As a simplifying assumption, we assume every node switches on every evaluation cycle and leave the issue of non-homogeneous node switching or low activity to future work (Sec. 7).

3.2 Wire-Dominated Energy Model

To limit the complexity of the models and to improve their generality, we use a wire-dominated energy model. Assuming a fixed voltage for operation, dynamic switching energy is proportional to the capacitance switched. The capacitance switched will come from both the gates driven by each net and the capacitance of the wiring. In modern processes the capacitance in the wiring is the dominant component. At 32nm, the capacitance per unit wire of length one minimum feature width, F, is 6.4×10^{-18} Farads, while the capacitance of a transistor gate per minimum transistor width unit is 29×10^{-18} Farads (From [1], INTC2 and PIDS3-LOP). A dense SRAM cell is $140F^2$. Crossing the $12F$ width of the cell is $\frac{12\times6.4}{29} \approx 2.6\times$ more wire capacitance than the gate. Other gates are packed less densely than SRAM cells and have wiring that extends across multiple cells. As a consequence, we can reasonably focus on the wire capacitance to get an adequate approximation for dynamic capacitance switched. For this paper, we calculate the total wire lengths switched in order understand dynamic switching energy, E_{dyn}.

$$E_{dyn} \approx 0.5V^2 \sum_{\text{all wires i}} \alpha_i L_{wire_i} \times C_u \qquad (2)$$

L_{wire_i} is the length of wire component i, and α_i is its switching activity. C_u is the capacitance per unit length of wire.

3.3 Memory Energy Models

Our memory energy model is based on and illustrates the wire-dominated model. For a random access memory with a W-bit wide interface containing M W-bit words, the total

capacitance switched on a read or write operation is:

$$C_{rmem}(W, M) = (\log(M) + 2(2W + 2))\sqrt{WMA_{bit}}C_u \qquad (3)$$

To minimize energy, the core array is organized into a square of length $\sqrt{WM}$ bit cells on a side. We must drive the $\log(M)$ address lines across the width of the array either for the word-line decoders or for the final mux selection. We must drive the bit-lines that run the height of the array for the W bits selected. The W selected bits will then run the width of the array in multiplexer selection. These two are captured in the $2W$ term. The bit-line and a word-select line run the width and height of the array, hence the "+2" term. We assume the bit-line and word-lines switch on and off for each memory operation and multiply those terms by two. The area for this memory is:

$$A_{rmem}(W, M) = \left(\sqrt{WMA_{bit}} + FP\left(\frac{\log(M)}{2}\right)\right)^2 \qquad (4)$$

FP is the full wire pitch. CACTI [14] estimates at 32nm and below confirm the wire dominated energy assumption. Since CACTI is optimized more for performance than energy, the absolute CACTI results are uniformly $2.5\times$ larger than the estimate above. At the risk of being generous to the sequential designs where the energy is dominated by memories, we use our smaller energy estimate as the main comparison point. In select places (Fig. 3, 4, and 11), we also report the larger memory energy case to illustrate the sensitivity of results to the ratio of memory energy to wire energy.

Sequentially accessed memories, as are appropriate for the instruction memories, can avoid the cost of addressing. A simple shift register can activate the appropriate rows and control the output multiplexer. The capacitance switched for a sequentially accessed memory is:

$$C_{smem}(W, M) = (2(2W + 1))\sqrt{WMA_{bit}}C_u \qquad (5)$$

The area of the sequential memory is:

$$A_{smem}(W, M) = WMA_{bit} + \sqrt{WM}A_{shift} \qquad (6)$$
$$+\sqrt{\frac{M}{W}}A_{shift} + \left(\sqrt{WM} - W\right)A_{mux}$$

4. SEQUENTIAL PROCESSOR

We start with a simple sequential architecture composed of a 4-LUT to perform the computation, an instruction memory to specify the behavior of each logical 4-LUT in the netlist graph, and a data memory to hold the value on each edge, or net, in the netlist graph (Fig. 3 in [2]). We use a 4-LUT because previous work showed it to be the least energy for spatial designs [15, 13]; for the sake of this paper, we take the LUT size as a constant and do not explore it as an optimization parameter. For the wire-dominated energy model, we ignore the gate energy for the 4-LUT and control and focus on the memory energy. For each LUT evaluation, we must read the instruction, read 4 data values from the data memory, and write one value to data memory. This means a total of five memory operations on the random-access memory that holds data. The total capacitance switched when evaluating an N node graph is:

$$
\begin{aligned}
C_{seq} = \ & 5NC_{rmem}(1,N) \\
& + I_{bits}(N,p)C_{smem}(1,I_{bits}(N,p))
\end{aligned} \tag{7}
$$

The instruction bits, I_{bits}, depend on the size of the graph and the Rent Exponent, p. As [2] notes, a naive version would spend $\log(N)$ bits for each of the read addresses, but exploiting a Rent's-Rule style recursive bisection, we can use fewer bits to specify nodes that are "closer" in the recursive bisection tree. Only the nets that are cut at the root of the tree require $\log(N)$ bits; with $p < 1$, most require fewer. Examining the recursive bisection tree, we can account for the number of nets crossing at each tree level to understand the total number of bits to specify addresses, B_{src}:

$$
B_{src} = \sum_{l=0}^{\log(N)} \left(2^{lp} \times \frac{N}{2^l} \right) = N \sum 2^{l(p-1)} = \frac{N}{1-2^{p-1}} \tag{8}
$$

l is the height in the recursive bisection tree from the leaves $(l = 0)$ to the root $(l = \log(N))$. Each instruction needs to specify 4 inputs and one output, so we multiply this value by 5. Each instruction must also specify the 4-LUT function, so we add 2^4 bits for the function, giving us:

$$
I_{bits} = \left(\frac{5}{1-2^{p-1}} + 16 \right) N \tag{9}
$$

It is clear from examining Eq. 9 that the instruction memory is larger than the data memory by a significant constant factor. For $p = 0.7$, $I_{bits}/N \approx 43$. For regular graph operations, the instructions are the same for different data values and can potentially be reused. A common form of this is looping, where a set of instruction, the loop body, are reused across a large set of data. Low-level image processing or cellular automata are some of the most familiar examples of this kind of looping, applying the same set of operations to each neighborhood region of data. For a general formulation, we introduce a separate variable I for the total number of unique instructions required and allow that to be independent of N. To first order, I can also be viewed as modeling the impact of a first-level instruction cache, assuming the instruction trace is sufficiently localized that all references are effectively satisfied in this cache.

We can also reduce the number of instructions by sharing them across a wide word, W. One defining property of processors is that they do not operate on single-bit data elements, but rather operate on a set of bits (e.g., 8, 16, 32, 64) grouped into words. This allows them to read many

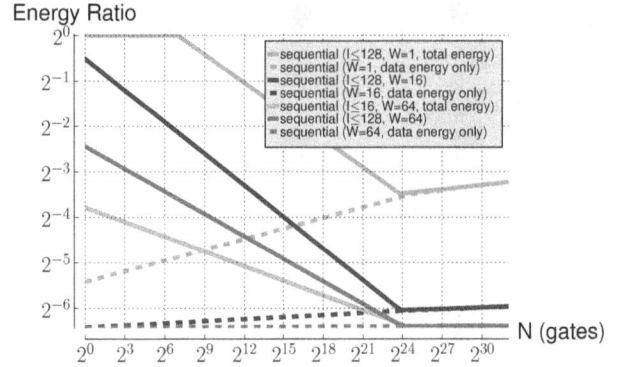

Figure 2: Sequential Energy Ratio to $W = 1$, $I = N$ for $p = 0.7$

bits from memory, both reducing the number of addresses that must be specified and amortizing out the cost of specifying the address. Assuming the data bits stay fixed, this also reduces the number of instructions, since an instruction now applies to a group of W bits. The word operations are typically applying the same operation to each bit (e.g., bitwise-AND, bitwise-XOR), and even arithmetic operations like ADD and SUBTRACT are effectively telling each bit of the datapath to act like an adder bitslice. This is known as a single-instruction, multiple-data (SIMD) operation since a single instruction is reused to control the W bits in the datapath. As a result, we can reformulate the energy for the processor in terms of the SIMD width, W and the total instructions, I.

$$
\begin{aligned}
C_{seqlw} = \ & 5 \left(\frac{N}{W} \right) C_{rmem} \left(W, \frac{N}{W} \right) \\
& + \left(\frac{I_{bits}(N,p)}{W} \right) C_{smem}(1, I_{bits}(I,p))
\end{aligned} \tag{10}
$$

Fig. 2 compares the energy ratios at $p = 0.7$ to show the impact of limited instructions, I, and SIMD word width, W. All cases are normalized to the $I = N$, $W = 1$ sequential energy case. As the "data energy only" curves show, there is a clear crossover point where data energy begins to dominate instruction memory energy.

5. SPATIAL PROCESSING

The fully spatial processing architecture builds a 4-LUT for each node in the graph along with the BFT interconnection network. Instructions (configuration bits) are stored local to each LUT and interconnect multiplexer control bits and never change, consuming no dynamic energy. Dynamic energy is consumed switching the wire capacitance routing data between LUTs. To model this capacitance, we need to know the number and lengths of the wires, which, in turn, demands we know the area of the structure.

Area is driven either by the active area for LUTs, configuration bits, and switches or the wiring area for routing interconnect. Since these use different layers, an accurate calculation might take the maximum of the area required for wiring and interconnect. To simplify analytic calculation, we will add together area for wiring and active elements. The result is potentially a conservative overestimate, by as much as a factor of two when wiring area is the same as active area. When one area component dominates, as it does for large designs, the sum becomes close to the maximum.

For simplicity, we use 2-input multiplexers as the basic building block for switching (Fig. 1c), including in the C-box connections between the network and the LUT. c is the number of base channels in the tree. Since this is a bidirectional network, there are both c inputs and c outputs from the network at each leaf (Fig. 1a). We will be using $c = 5$. The leaf area includes the LUT, its configuration bits, and the C-box multiplexers to select the LUT inputs from the tree network. C-box multiplexers can be depopulated to exploit the fact that they are feeding a 4-LUT [5]. The single output is driven into all of the network inputs at the leaf, leaving their selection to the network switches.

$$A_{leaf} = A_{4lut} + 2^4 A_{bit} + ((c-4)4)) (A_{mux2} + A_{bit}) \quad (11)$$

From Figs. 1a and 1c, we see that each directional wire pair at the top of a subtree is associated with 3 two-input multiplexers. Counting based on wiring at each tree level gives the total switch area:

$$A_{sws} = \left(c \sum \left(2^{lp} \frac{N}{2^l} \right) \right) (3A_{bit} + 3A_{mux2}) \quad (12)$$

Putting these together:

$$A_{active} = N A_{leaf} + A_{sws} \quad (13)$$

For wiring we first count the number of wire channels needed across the width of the chip by looking across all overlapping wiring channels:

$$Wires = 2 \left(cN^p + 2cN^p \left(\frac{1}{2} \right)^{2p} + 4cN^p \left(\frac{1}{2} \right)^{4p} + \ldots \right)$$
$$= 2cN^p \sum 2^{(1-2p)l} \quad (14)$$

The constant two at the beginning of Eq. 14 accounts for the separate up and down links of the bidirectional channels. The exponent increases by a factor of two since we are counting every other stage to account the contribution of wires to a single dimension. The constant in front doubles since we're doubling the number of wire channels that parallel each other at every other tree stage.

The actual width required by the wires will depend on the number of metal layers available for programmable interconnect routing in the process. We will assume half the metal layers are available for horizontal wiring and half for vertical. We further assume we can perfectly use all the metal layers in each direction. This gives:

$$L_{wire} = \frac{Wires \times FP}{M_{layers}/2} = \frac{2FP \times Wires}{M_{layers}} \quad (15)$$

FP is the full pitch of the wires, which we take as 2 to normalize to the half-pitch feature size used in defining C_u. The length of the side of the entire design is thus:

$$L_{side} \leq \sqrt{A_{active}} + L_{wire} \quad (16)$$

We then determine the total wire capacitance switched by summing up the capacitance of all the wires.

$$C_{spatial} = \sum cN^p 2^i \left(\frac{N}{2^i} \right) \left(\frac{L_{side}}{2^{\lceil i/2 \rceil}} \right) \quad (17)$$

The ceiling in the sum accounts for the fact that every other stage extends in a different dimension, so the subtree width

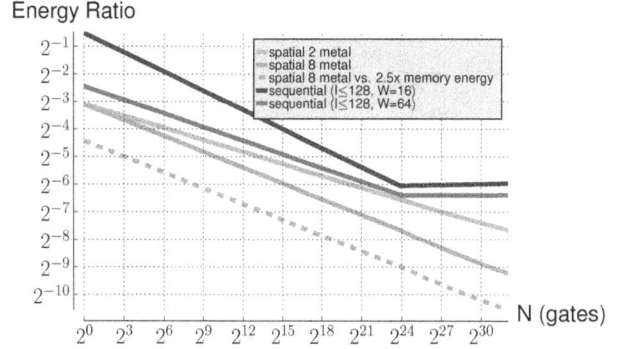

Figure 3: Energy Ratio to $W = 1$, $I = N$ Sequential for $p = 0.7$

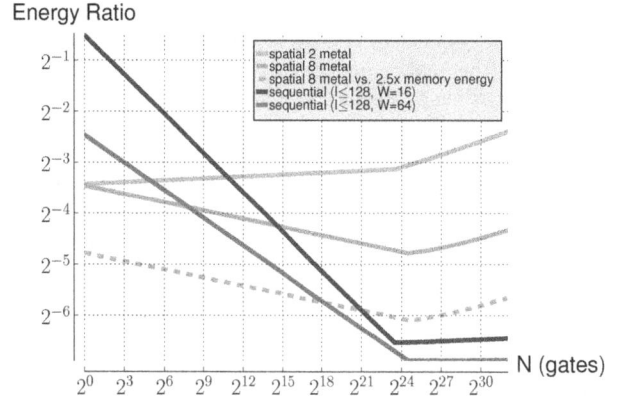

Figure 4: Energy Ratio to $W = 1$, $I = N$ Sequential for $p = 0.8$

shrinks every other stage. Computing the subtree length as a fraction of L_{side} like this is a conservative overestimate of wire length since lower level wiring runs do not need to cross upper-layer wiring.

Fig. 3 shows the energy ratios to the sequential architecture at $p = 0.7$. The spatial energy is always below the sequential energy and the benefit grows with design size, N. Large word width, W, and tight loops (small I) reduce the spatial benefit, but do not eliminate it. We include an 8-metal case as typical for current technology. At 32nm, the ITRS [1] suggests up to 13 metal layers are available, so even if some of those are dedicated to local wiring and power and clock distribution, eight metal layers may reasonable be available for network routing. If the technology or memory design is more expensive relative to wiring (e.g., $2.5\times$ as appropriate to match CACTI memories), the spatial advantage is even larger.

However, when $p > 0.75$, the benefits of the spatial design will eventually diminish or reverse, as illustrated in Fig. 4 for $p = 0.8$. Here, the spatial design is less energy for $W = 1$, $I = N$ up to billions of 4-LUTs, but the benefit is beginning to diminish. When the word width is larger and the instruction memory small, the sequential design can be more energy efficient. For 8 metal layers, $I \leq 128$, and $W = 16$, the sequential design becomes more energy efficient around 64K 4-LUTs. *Both the growing spatial benefit below $p = 0.75$ and the diminishing spatial benefits above $p = 0.75$ show that asymptotic effects do matter for this design size.* Asymp-

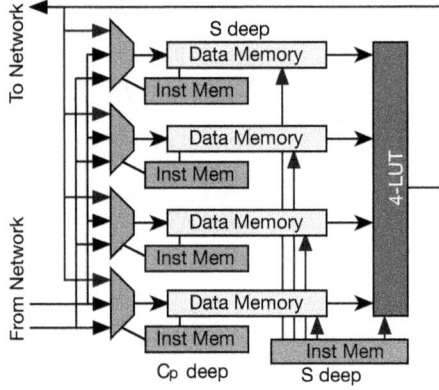

Figure 5: Multicontext Leaf Processing Element

totically, the sequential energy of $O(\sqrt{N})$ per operation is larger than the spatial energy of $O(N^{2p-1})$ when $p < 0.75$ and smaller when $p > 0.75$ (Sec. 2.3, [2]).

We do not evaluate the impact of looping and SIMD word width for the spatial design. The spatial design is already spending no switching energy on instructions, so there is no instruction energy to reduce with instruction sharing. Word grouping could reduce the number of configuration bits required. However, since the designs are wire rather than active area dominated, the savings is not significant.

6. MULTICONTEXT

The sequential and spatial designs are extremes in a larger design space. Since we see regions where each achieves lower energy, the natural question arises: is there an intermediate point in the design space that achieves even lower energy than the extremes? In this section, we extend our energy analysis to the heterogeneous multicontext design from [2].

We consider three main architectural variables S, p_t, and C_t. S is the leaf serialization. We assign S nodes to each physical leaf PE and evaluate them on a single 4-LUT. C_t is a constant serialization of the interconnect. p_t is the growth of the physical tree. As a result, the number of physical wires at the top of the hierarchical network (Fig. 1b) is $\frac{c}{C_t}N^{p_t}$ rather than cN^p when $p_t < p$, meaning there is a communication serialization of $C_t N^{p-p_t}$.

In this section, we first show the composition and resources for the leaf PE, then identify the interconnect resources, before addressing coordination. We identify the coordination challenge, examine the asynchronous proposal from [2], and introduce a synchronous version that is more efficient for typical designs. Finally, we determine the energy minimizing parameters and compare to the spatial and sequential extremes from the previous sections.

6.1 PE

Fig. 5 shows the multicontext PE. Each PE has a single 4-LUT fed by four independent data memories. Each data memory selects inputs from the incoming network wires to the PE. Independent instruction memories control each data memory write and the evaluation of the PEs. Each data memory holds S values so that the four together can provide the 4 inputs to each of the S nodes assigned to this PE. In the extreme case where there is only one PE ($S = N$), this is four times the data memory required since there are only N

different data items. The input instruction memories need to be large enough to write S values into memory that may arrive over $C_t S^{p-p_t}$ cycles, so we define their depth:

$$C_p = \max\left(S, C_t S^{p-p_t}\right) \quad (18)$$

We compute the area of the PE as:

$$
\begin{aligned}
A_{pe} &= 4A_{mux}\left(\frac{c}{C_t}S^{pt}\right) + 4A_{rmem}(1, S) + A_{4lut} \\
&\quad + 4A_{smem}\left(\log\left(\frac{c}{C_t}S^{pt} + 1\right) + \log(S), C_p\right) \\
&\quad + A_{smem}\left(4\log(S) + 16, S\right)
\end{aligned} \quad (19)
$$

We compute the capacitance contribution from the PE per node evaluated as:

$$
\begin{aligned}
C_{pe} &= 8C_{rmem}(1, S) \\
&\quad + 4\frac{C_p}{S}C_{smem}\left(\log\left(\frac{c}{C_t}S^{pt} + 1\right) + \log(S), C_p\right) \\
&\quad + C_{smem}\left(4\log(S) + 16, S\right) \\
&\quad + 2 \times 6C_{wire}\sqrt{A_{rmem}(1, S)}\left(\log(S) + 1\right)
\end{aligned} \quad (20)
$$

The eight on the random access memory captures the fact that we read and write to each data memory once for each PE evaluation. The final term captures the fact that we must route address wires over data memories that cannot all be adjacent to the associated instruction memories.

6.2 Network

The network is designed to be parameterizable between the fully spatial network used in Sec. 5 (when $p_t = p$ and $C_t = 1$) and a binary tree (when $p_t = 0$ and $C_t = c$, Fig. 5(a) in [2]). When the network is not fully spatial, the data transfer will need to be sequentialized across some of the network links. In order to support this, the switches at those data links will have instruction memories to allow them to change behavior. With $p_t < p$, the amount of sequentialization and hence the size of the switching instruction memories grow toward the root of the fat tree. This means there will be points in the tree where an upper-level switch changes behavior while a lower-level switch remains unchanging.

To understand the area for the array, we must, again, account for both active and wiring area. The total area going into switches is:

$$
\begin{aligned}
A_{sw} &= \sum_{l=\log(S)}^{\log(N)}\left(\frac{N}{2^l}\right)\left(\frac{c}{C_t}\right)\left(2^l\right)^{pt} \quad (21) \\
&\quad \times \left(3A_{mux2} + A_{smem}\left(3, C_t\left(2^l\right)^{p-p_t}\right)\right)
\end{aligned}
$$

This includes both the area of the switch and the area of the instruction memory for the switch. Three bits control each of the three multiplexers in the 1:1 switch.

$$A_{mcactive} = \left(\frac{N}{S}\right)A_{pe} + A_{sw} \quad (22)$$

We count the number of wire widths across each side of the array:

$$MCWires = 2\sum_{l=\log(S)/2}^{\log(N)/2}\left(\sqrt{\frac{N}{2^{2l}}}\right)\left(\frac{c}{C_t}\right)\left(2^{2l}\right)^{pt} \quad (23)$$

Energy Ratio

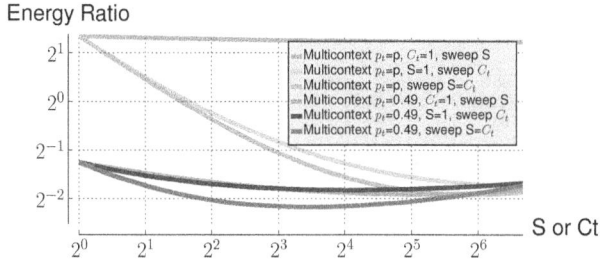

Figure 6: No Coordination Overhead Energy Ratio to Spatial for $p = 0.8$ at $N = 10^7$ and $M_{layers} = 8$

Side length due to wires is then:

$$L_{mcwire} = \frac{2 \times FP \times MCWires}{M_{layers}} \quad (24)$$

Including both wires and active area contributions:

$$L_{mcside} \leq \sqrt{A_{mcactive}} + L_{mcwire} \quad (25)$$

Interconnect energy will have contributions both from data transmission on wires and from switch instruction memories. For total wire data transmission capacitance, we compute a weighted sum based on wire length and usage.

$$C_{mcwire} = \sum_{l=\log(S)}^{\log(N)} \left(\frac{N}{2^l}\right) \left(c2^{lp}\right) \left(\frac{L_{mcside}}{2^{\lceil(\log(N)-l)/2\rceil}}\right) (26)$$

For total switch instruction memory capacitance, we compute a weighted sum of the switch instruction memory uses.

$$C_{mcimem} = \sum_{l=\log(S)}^{\log(N)} \left(\frac{N}{2^l}\right) \left(\frac{c}{C_t}\right) \left(2^l\right)^{p_t} \left(C_t 2^{l(p-p_t)}\right)$$
$$\times C_{smem}\left(3, C_t \left(2^l\right)^{p-p_t}\right) \quad (27)$$

Putting this together with the PE capacitance:

$$C_{mc} = NC_{pe} + C_{mcwire} + C_{mcimem} \quad (28)$$

Before dealing with coordination overhead, we can examine how multicontext energy compares to spatial energy assuming there is negligible overhead for coordination (Fig. 6). The multicontext designs shown here are normalized to the energy of the spatial design and achieve enough savings to drop below the sequential energy even for the $W = 64$ design (*c.f.* Fig. 4). At $S = C_t = 1$ and $p_t = p$ the multicontext design is larger than the spatial design (ratio above 2) due to memories and the PE structure in the multicontext case. We see that sequentializing the leaf alone (S) has little effect reducing energy since we still pay all the energy for the network above the sequential leaf. *Interconnect sequentialization, both through C_t and p_t, is effective at reducing energy.* These directly attack the larger area that goes into switches and wiring that is driving the wire lengths in the spatial design when $p > 0.5$.

6.3 Coordination

For multicontext evaluation, ordering of node evaluation in the graph is also an issue. For the fully sequential design, we can sequence the nodes topologically within the energy framework we've described. For the fully spatial design, all

edges have their own physical wires, allowing LUTs to evaluate and send their results as dictated by precedence without coordination between the LUTs. However, for the multicontext design, we must control when graph nodes are evaluated on each physical PE and when an edge is routed on a shared wire. Because of precedence constraints, we cannot simply divide nodes by the PE sharing factor, S, and evaluate N/S nodes on each of S cycles.

To illustrate, consider the case of a depth 2 graph on an $S = C_t = 2$, $P_t = p$ design. For some graphs, we will be lucky such that (1) half the nodes are at depth 1 from the inputs and half are at depth 2, (2) each PE is assigned one node at depth 1 and one at depth 2, (3) we can route the outputs of the first half of the PEs through the network with exactly half the wire links. In this case, we can read the first configuration, evaluate the first half of the nodes, route their outputs through the network, read the second configuration from local memories, then evaluate the second half of the nodes and route their outputs. However, (1) the simple Rent's Rule spatial bisection we took to get p did not consider dividing wires and PEs by evaluation time, (2) we can get a pair of nodes at a PE that are the same depth from the input, and (3) there are designs where significantly more than half the nodes are at depth 2. That is, in the general case, the configuration memories may need to change at more than two different times. While each configuration memory only needs to provide one of two values, some PEs and interconnect links may require both to evaluate depth one nodes, while others may require both to evaluate depths two nodes. This means we can change configurations at any of four different times.

A depth D graph could need to switch at any of $D \times \max\left(S, C_t N^{p-p_t}\right)$ times. The simplest way to handle this would be to give every PE and switch a memory of this depth and globally clock the design. However, this would add substantial energy by (1) making the design larger and hence the wires longer, (2) making the memory energy more expensive, (3) adding substantial energy for clocking.

6.4 Asynchronous

A simple way to avoid making the memories larger is to allow the switches to operate asynchronously based on data presence [2]. The mapping from a spatial design to an asynchronous, heterogeneous multicontext design is a way to use the minimum instruction memory depths identified in Sec. 6.2. The switch instruction tells each switch which input it should wait upon and route next, so the switch only acts and uses energy as data becomes available.

The downside of asynchronous control is that we must route a handshake and acknowledgment with every data signal. This means all wiring channels have three times as many wires; for the asynchronous version of $MCWires$ (Eq. 23), we must multiply the channel widths by 3. Each asynchronous link makes four transitions to transfer data rather than one, meaning, in addition to the longer wires, we must account for more switching events in the asynchronous C_{mcwire} (Eq. 26). Furthermore, we expect the asynchronous switches to be larger than the synchronous switches; driven by the 3× wiring, we assume they are 3× the area.

6.5 Synchronous

As noted above (Sec. 6.3) it would be expensive to simply make all memories deeper and clock every switch and PE at the worst-case sequentialization. Ideally, we would map the design directly for multicontext evaluation, carefully selecting which nodes can share a PE and scheduling PEs and wires to fit into a minimum number of cycles. However, for the reasons previously noted, without doing that mapping, we cannot guarantee how it will turn out. Here we describe synchronous evaluation strategies to minimize the memory depth expansion and estimate the likely range of values.

6.5.1 Heterogeneous Memory Clocking

We can clock the different tree levels proportional to their original multicontext depth ($C_t 2^{l(p-p_t)}$), meaning the tree switches closer to the root are clocked more often than the tree switches closer to the leaves. To do this, we evaluate the tree once for each leaf serialization C_t. That means, we evaluate the top of the tree N^{p-p_t} times, the next level $\left(\frac{N}{2}\right)^{p-p_t}$ times, and so forth until we clock the leaf once. At adjacent tree levels, the higher level will switch either once or twice for each time the lower level switch changes. At the level boundaries, the clock is divided where needed so that the lower level switches at half the rate of the upper level.

Fig. 7 shows the basic operation for heterogeneous clocking. Here, level $i+1$ is sequentialized at the same rate as i, which is sequentialized twice as heavily as level $i-1$. As a result, we must clock levels $i+1$ and i twice for every time we clock level $i-1$. To realize the connection set $A \to p0$, $C \to B$, $p0 \to C$, $D \to A$, $p1 \to D$, we pass $A \to p0$, $C \to B$, $p0 \to C$, on the first cycle and $D \to A$, $p1 \to D$ on the second. If $i-1$ is, itself, sequentialized, we allow it to switch on the second cycle.

To estimate clock energy, we must estimate the total capacitance switched across all the clocking required.

$$C_{clk} = CSF \cdot C_t \times (C_{tdist} + C_{sdist}) \qquad (29)$$

CSF account for the fact that the clock switches multiple times per evaluation. We assume a 2-phase clock that switches up and down each evaluation, so use $CSF = 4$. C_{tdist} deals with the wiring to distribute clock to each tree level and is weighted by the number of times the tree level is switched.

$$
\begin{aligned}
C_{tdist} &= \sum \left(2^l\right)^{p-p_t} \times L_{mcside} \left(\frac{2^{l/2}}{2\sqrt{N}}\right)\left(\frac{N}{2^l}\right) \\
&= \frac{L_{mcside}}{2} \sum 2^{l(p-p_t)} \left(\frac{\sqrt{N}}{2^{l/2}}\right)
\end{aligned}
$$

C_{sdist} deals with the wiring to distribute the clock to the individual switch memories within a tree level.

$$C_{sdist} = \sum_{l=\log(S)}^{l=\log(N)} \left(2^l\right)^{p-p_t}\left(\frac{3}{2}\right) N_{sw}(l)\sqrt{A_{sw\_w\_mem}(l)}$$
$$(30)$$

The $\frac{3}{2}$ arises from H-Tree distribution over the switch area. $N_{sw}(l)$ is the total number of switches at level l in all subtrees:

$$N_{sw}(l) = \left(\frac{N}{2^l}\right)\left(\frac{c}{C_{txt}}\right)\left(2^l\right)^{p_t} \qquad (31)$$

The area for a switch with its memory at a given level is:

$$A_{sw\_w\_mem(l)} = \sqrt{\left(A_{1:1} + A_{imem}\left(3, C_{txt}\left(2^l\right)^{p-p_t}\right)\right)} \qquad (32)$$

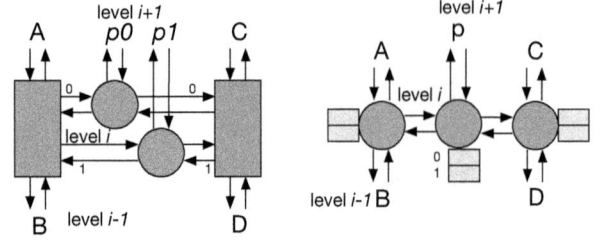

Figure 7: Heterogeneous Clocking Example

6.5.2 Context Switching

With the heterogeneous upper-level switching scheme, we route the entire interconnection pattern with C_t leaf switching cycles. Precedence constraints may prevent us from performing this route once; it may be necessary to route signals at different times. As a general formulation, we introduce a context factor, CF, as a multiplier on C_t, then define:

$$C_t' = CF \times C_t \qquad (33)$$

Our evaluation strategy can then be to make the memories CF larger and clock the leaf levels CF as many times. In estimation, we replace C_t by C_t' when calculating memory depth and evaluation cycles (e.g., Eq. 29). In the best case, $D = 1$, all results can be routed simultaneously and $CF = 1$. This may also be achievable with good packing of nodes into PEs and scheduling of wires. In the worst case, $CF = D$, and we must route the network at every graph depth. Modern designs are often pipelined to be shallow, resulting in a small D. As we will see the best values of C_t are around 8, so a typical operating regime will have $C_t \geq D$. In practice, when $C_t \geq D$, it should be possible to keep $CF \approx 2$. That is, we need at least C_t leaf routes to handle the leaf interconnect serialization, which is also enough to handle node serialization when $C_t \geq S$. Since $C_t \geq D$, we will have depths that need more than one context for routing, C_{t_i}. The routing required for nodes at a particular depth may not perfectly fill an integral number of contexts, meaning we may end up with one partially filled context per depth. So, we have:

$$C_t' = \sum_{i=1}^{D} C_{t_i} \leq C_t + D \leq 2C_t \qquad (34)$$

Local routing hotspots could make this worse. In the following we use $CF = 4$ as a likely conservative bound, expecting realistic cases to have a CF somewhere between 1 and 4.

Note that the total switching energy on the wires and memories can remain proportional to the traffic that needs to be routed; it does not need to be multiplied by this CF factor. We must arrange for the switch configurations to change *only* when a different edge must actually be routed. To achieve this, we program the unused context memory slots to return the same value as the preceding cycle so they do not switch their output causing the switch to select a different input. Since we use sequential memories for instructions, selection of sequential memory locations is based on a shift register, and we avoid paying the cost of address line toggles for these extra memory contexts. We do have to pay for the longer wires associated with these memories, which we model by making the memories C_t' deep.

Fig. 8 compares the various coordination strategies, all normalized to the fully spatial case. For designs smaller than

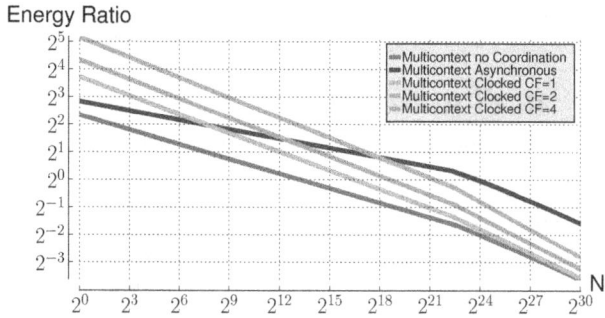

Figure 8: Energy Ratio to Spatial for $p = 0.8$ at $p_t = 0.49$, $C_t = S = 1$ and $M_{layers} = 8$

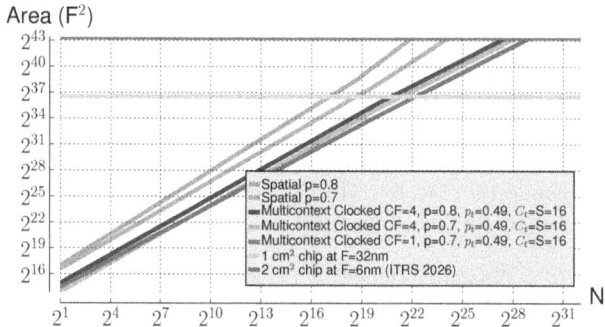

Figure 9: Area for $M_{layers} = 8$

32K 4-LUTs, the coordination energy makes all multicontext designs more expensive than spatial designs. For larger designs, the multicontext designs can be smaller. However, the asynchronous requires more energy than spatial up to 16 million 4-LUTs, by which point, even a context factor, CF, of 4 achieves less energy than the asynchronous design.

6.6 Comparisons

To understand the size of designs viable over the range of the ITRS 2012 roadmap [1], Fig. 9 plots the area of spatial and multicontext designs and marks the capacity of a moderate (1cm^2) chip at current 32nm technology and a large (2cm^2) chip at the 6nm technology predicted for 2026. This establishes that we could soon build multicontext designs with over 2 million 4-LUTs and establishes the potential viability of multicontext designs up to 512M LUTs.

Fig. 10 varies the physical tree Rent Exponent, p_t, for 100 million 4-LUT designs. This shows that p_t around 0.5 minimizes energy. *This is consistent with the asymptotic results that tell us that we need $p_t < 0.5$ to avoid wirelengths that grow faster than $\sqrt{N}$.* These absolute results shows that the binary tree ($p_t = 0$) is more expensive than a $p_t = 0.49$ tree and, more generally, the energy increases as the Rent Exponent decreases from around $p_t = 0.49$. Below $p_t = 0.5$, we can become switch and memory rather than wire dominated, such that additional interconnect sharing does not significantly reduce wire lengths. However, this sharing does increase instruction memory energy.

Fig. 11 shows how the various energy components contribute to total switching energy. Even at $p_t = 0.49$, wire energy dominates with no further sequentialization ($S = C_t = 1$). As the context and processor sharing increases,

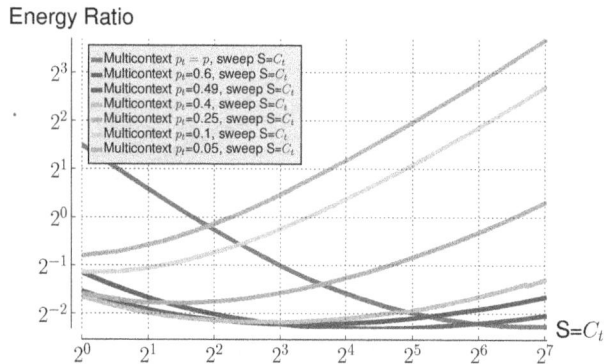

Figure 10: p_t Energy Comparison for $N = 10^8$, $p = 0.8$ and $M_{layers} = 8$ assuming $CF = 4$

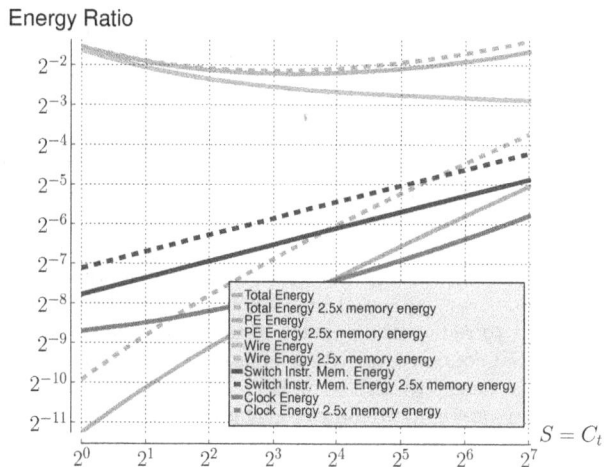

Figure 11: Energy Components for $N = 10^8$, $p = 0.8$, $p_t = 0.49$, and $M_{layers} = 8$ assuming $CF = 4$

the switch instruction memory and PE energy increase to the point where PE energy costs grow faster than the wiring energy savings, inducing an energy minimum around $C_t = S = 16$. Fig. 11 also shows the impact of memory being relatively more expensive. Since the minimum energy point is wire dominated, the impact of larger memories has a smaller effect at the energy-minimizing multicontext point than it does on a fully sequential design (*c.f.* Fig. 3).

The benefits of using a $p_t < 0.5$ tree increase with p for $p > 0.5$ as shown in Fig. 12. This savings is enough to match $W = 64$ at $p = 0.8$ for 512M 4-LUT designs. Nonetheless, at even higher p's, the multicontext design will require larger designs before it will achieve lower energy than the wide word sequential implementation—sizes that are not feasible in the next decade.

7. DISCUSSION AND OPEN ISSUES

Throughout this paper, we have assumed full activity for the communication links between nodes. This is an upper bound for absolute energy. However, activity will have a differential effect on the designs explored. The fully spatial design will directly benefit from a low activity edge—the output of a node drives a single wire, and if the node doesn't change values on a cycle, the wire does not switch.

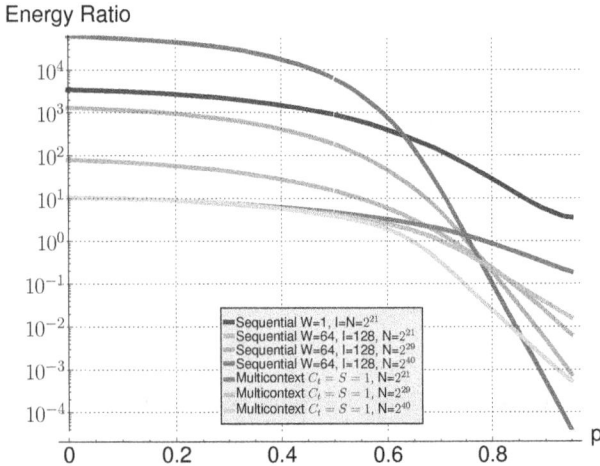

Figure 12: Energy Ratio to Spatial for $p_t = \min(0.49, p)$, and $M_{layers} = 8$ assuming $CF = 4$

A multicontext design that is sharing a wire between two different edges may switch twice on a cycle even if neither edge switches; if one node is non-active at 0 and the other at 1, when they are time multiplexed onto the same physical link, we pay two transitions on that cycle. As a result, we expect this effect to increase the advantage of spatial implementations over sequential implementations, and we expect this effect to reduce the benefits of multicontext evaluation over spatial compared to what we have shown here.

In some cases, it will be possible to exploit wordwidth optimizations for multicontext evaluation. For example, if $S = C_t = W$ and $p = p_t$ we may need no more than a single configuration like the spatial design. Even with $p_t < p$, the memories in the interconnect can be up to a factor of W smaller than in the $W = 1$ case assumed in Sec. 6. Additional development is needed to treat this properly.

8. CONCLUSIONS

With energy-limited technology, architectures that minimize energy will maximize the computational performance offered at a given power-envelope or energy budget. Communication locality, which we can quantify with Rent's Rule, is an important characteristics of computational tasks that determines how efficiently the task can be implemented. When the Rent Exponent, p, is less than 0.75, FPGAs use less energy than processors, even after considering SIMD word optimizations and tight loops that share instructions across operations. For the larger p designs, multicontext FPGAs can reduce energy compared to spatial designs (single-context FPGAs) by sharing interconnect wires to limit wire area. This allows them to reduce the energy requirements below sequential (processor) designs, at least up to $p = 0.8$, for the design sizes feasible in the next decade.

9. ACKNOWLEDGMENTS

Randy Huang and Andrew Sutherland provided valuable feedback on drafts of this work. This research was funded in part by National Science Foundation grant CCF-0904577 and DARPA/CMO contract HR0011-13-C-0005. Any opinions, findings, and conclusions or recommendations expressed in this material are those of the authors and do not reflect the official policy or position of the National Science Foundation, the Department of Defense, or the U.S. Government.

10. REFERENCES

[1] International technology roadmap for semiconductors. <http://www.itrs.net/Links/2012ITRS/Home2012.htm>, 2012. 3.2, 5, 6.6

[2] A. DeHon. Location, Location, Location—The Role of Spatial Locality in Asymptotic Energy Minimization. In *FPGA*, pages 137–142, 2013. 1, 2, 2.3, 4, 4, 5, 6, 6.2, 6.4

[3] W. E. Donath. Placement and average interconnection lengths of computer logic. *IEEE Trans. Circuits Syst.*, 26(4):272–277, April 1979. 2.1

[4] H. Esmaeilzadeh, E. Blem, R. S. Amant, K. Sankaralingam, and D. Burger. Dark silicon and the end of multicore scaling. In *ISCA*, pages 365–376, 2011. 1

[5] K. Fujiyoshi, Y. Kajitani, and H. Niitsu. Design of minimum and uniform bipartites for optimum connection blocks of FPGA. *IEEE Trans. Computer-Aided Design*, 16(11):1377–1383, Nov. 1997. 5

[6] R. I. Greenberg and C. E. Leiserson. *Randomness in Computation*, volume 5 of *Advances in Computing Research*, chapter Randomized Routing on Fat-Trees. JAI Press, 1988. Earlier MIT/LCS/TM-307. 2.2

[7] M. Hutton. Interconnect prediction for programmable logic devices. In *Proc. SLIP*, pages 125–131, 2001. 2.1

[8] B. S. Landman and R. L. Russo. On pin versus block relationship for partitions of logic circuits. *IEEE Trans. Comput.*, 20:1469–1479, 1971. 2.1

[9] E. A. Lee and D. G. Messerschmitt. Synchronous data flow. *Proc. IEEE*, 75(9):1235–1245, Sept. 1987. 3.1

[10] C. E. Leiserson. Fat-trees: Universal networks for hardware efficient supercomputing. *IEEE Trans. Comput.*, C-34(10):892–901, Oct. 1985. 2.2

[11] G. Lemieux, E. Lee, M. Tom, and A. Yu. Directional and single-driver wires in FPGA interconnect. In *ICFPT*, pages 41–48, 2004. 2.2

[12] D. Lewis, V. Betz, D. Jefferson, A. Lee, C. Lane, P. Leventis, S. Marquardt, S. McClintock, B. Pedersen, G. Powell, S. Reddy, C. Wysocki, R. Cliff, and J. Rose. The Stratix routing and logic architecture. In *FPGA*, pages 12–20, 2003. 2.2

[13] F. Li, Y. Lin, L. He, D. Chen, and J. Cong. Power modeling and characteristics of field programmable gate arrays. *IEEE Trans. Computer-Aided Design*, 24(11):1712–1724, Nov. 2005. 4

[14] N. Muralimanohar, R. Balasubramonian, and N. P. Jouppi. CACTI 6.0: A tool to model large caches. HPL 2009-85, HP Labs, Palo Alto, CA, April 2009. Latest code release for CACTI 6 is 6.5. 3.3

[15] K. Poon, S. Wilton, and A. Yan. A detailed power model for field-programmable gate arrays. *ACM Tr. Des. Auto. of Elec. Sys.*, 10:279–302, 2005. 4

Theory and Algorithm for Generalized Memory Partitioning in High-Level Synthesis

Yuxin Wang[1]
ayerwang@pku.edu.cn

Peng Li[1]
peng.li@pku.edu.cn

Jason Cong [2,3,1,*]
cong@cs.ucla.edu

[1]Center for Energy-Efficient Computing and Applications, Peking University, China
[2]Computer Science Department, University of California, Los Angeles, USA
[3]PKU/UCLA Joint Research Institute in Science and Engineering

ABSTRACT

The significant development of high-level synthesis tools has greatly facilitated FPGAs as general computing platforms. During the parallelism optimization for the data path, memory becomes a crucial bottleneck that impedes performance enhancement. Simultaneous data access is highly restricted by the data mapping strategy and memory port constraint. Memory partitioning can efficiently map data elements in the same logical array onto multiple physical banks so that the accesses to the array are parallelized. Previous methods for memory partitioning mainly focused on cyclic partitioning for single-port memory. In this work we propose a generalized memory-partitioning framework to provide high data throughput of on-chip memories. We generalize cyclic partitioning into block-cyclic partitioning for a larger design space exploration. We build the conflict detection algorithm on polytope emptiness testing, and use integer points counting in polytopes for intra-bank offset generation. Memory partitioning for multi-port memory is supported in this framework. Experimental results demonstrate that compared to the state-of-art partitioning algorithm, our proposed algorithm can reduce the number of block RAM by 19.58%, slice by 20.26% and DSP by 50%.

Categories and Subject Descriptors

B.5.2 [**Hardware**]: Design Aids—*automatic synthesis*

General Terms

Algorithms, Performance, Design

Keywords

high-level synthesis, memory partitioning, polyhedral model

*In addition to being a faculty member at UCLA, Jason Cong is also a co-director of the PKU/UCLA Joint Research Institute and a visiting professor of Peking University.

1. INTRODUCTION

To balance the requirements of high performance, low power and short time-to-market, field-programmable gate array (FPGA) devices have gained a growing market against ASICs and general-purpose processors over the past two decades. In addition to their traditional use, FPGA devices are increasingly used as hardware accelerators to speed up the performance of energy-critical applications in heterogeneous computing platforms. A major obstacle that FPGA accelerators must overcome is that of finding an efficient programming model. Traditional register-transfer level (RTL) programming requires expertise with the hardware description language (e.g., VHDL, Verilog), and more importantly, with the hardware mindset, including, the underlying concurrent hardware programming model and the trade-offs between performance and resource utilization. Manual RTL design is time-consuming, error-prone and difficult to debug. Implementing a simple algorithm often takes weeks or months, even for an expert.

High-level synthesis (HLS) is a key technology for breaking the programming wall of FPGA-based accelerators. By transforming algorithms written in high-level languages (e.g., C, C++, SystemC), HLS can significantly shorten the learning curve and improve programming productivity. After over 30 years of joint effort by academia and industry, HLS promises to be a critical bridging technology that offers high productivity and quality of results for both the semiconductor and FPGA industries. A number of state-of-art commercial tools have been developed and gradually accepted by the traditional hardware designers, such as Vivado_HLS from Xilinx [9] (based on AutoPilot [13, 23]), C-to-Silicon from Cadence [2], Catapult C from Calypto [3], Synphony from Synopsys [8], and Cynthesizer [4] from Forte.

Although off-the-shelf commercial HLS tools are capable of generating high-quality circuits, there is still a significant performance gap compared to manually customized RTL designs, even for programs with regular affine loop bounds and array accesses. One important reason for this performance gap is the redundant off-chip and on-chip memory accesses and inefficient loop pipelining with the presence of loop dependence and resource restraint. Currently, most of the tools support versatile efficient parallelization flows on a data path, such as loop pipelining and loop unrolling. FPGAs are capable of providing enough computational units for high-computation parallelism and plenty of on-chip memory resources for parallelized data accesses, while the simultaneous data access is highly restricted by the data mapping

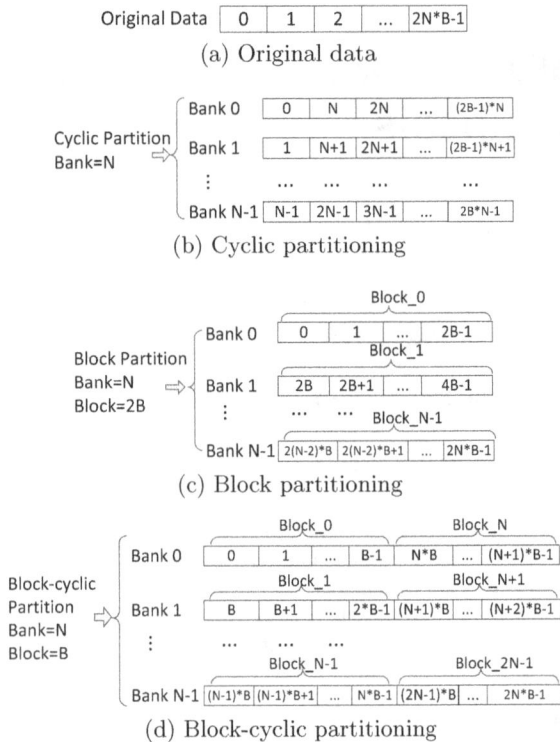

Figure 1: **Memory partitioning schemes: (a) original data (b) cyclic partitioning (c) block partitioning (d) block-cyclic partitioning**

strategy and memory port constraint. Typical block RAMs (BRAMs) in FPGAs have limited ports to feed the highly parallelized execution units. Memory becomes a crucial bottleneck that impedes performance enhancement when multiple data elements from the same array are required simultaneously. How to supply the computational units with the required high-speed data streams is a major challenge.

It is unrealistic to increase the number of ports of block RAMs on FPGAs. Even in an ASIC design, increasing the ports' number induces quadratic growth in complexity and area. Duplicating the data elements into multiple copies can support simultaneous data accesses [18], but it may have significant area and power overhead and introduce memory consistency problems.

A comparatively better approach is to partition the original array into multiple memory banks. Each bank holds a portion of the original data and serves a limited number of memory requests. This method provides the same effects as memory duplication, largely saving the storage requirement and having no problem with multiple data copies. According to the classification in [10], the regular memory partitioning methods are classified as cyclic partitioning, block partitioning, and block-cyclic partitioning. We depict them in Fig. 1(b), Fig. 1(c), and Fig. 1(d) respectively, where each square denotes a data element in the array.

Memory partitioning in high-level synthesis has been studied in several related works. A scheduling-based automated flow is proposed in [12] to support multiple simultaneous affine memory accesses. The algorithm can be extended to efficiently support memory references with modulo operations with limited memory paddings [22]. The work in [17]

schedules memory accesses in different loop iterations to find the optimal or near-optimal partitioning in a larger design exploration space. These memory-partitioning methodologies are able to find the optimal partitioning for one-dimensional arrays under different circumstances. However, many designs for FPGAs are specified by nested loops with multidimensional arrays, such as image and scientific computing. The work in [21] provides a linear transformation-based (LTB) method for multidimensional memory partitioning. However, the method is limited to cyclc partitioning. The access conflict analysis algorithm eliminates the information of iteration vectors in the index and only provides a sufficient but unnecessary condition, which may lead to suboptimality in some cases.

In this work we provide a generalized memory partitioning (GMP) method. The main contributions of this work are described as follows:

1. We formulate the memory partitioning using a polyhedral model, including various memory-partitioning schemes, and supporting partitioning for multi-port memories.

2. We transform the problem of detecting the access conflict between a pair of references to an equivalent problem of polytope emptiness testing. We also formulate the intra-bank offset generation as a problem of counting the integer points in the polytopes in lexicographic order.

To our knowledge, we are the first to use a polyhedral model to solve the bank access conflict problem in loop nest. We are also the first to use the polytope emptiness test for access conflict detection. In addition, we propose a resource estimation model, which enables the choice of an optimal partitioning automatically through design space exploration.

The remainder of this paper is organized as follows: Section 2 gives the motivational examples for our work; Section 3 formulates the problem; Section 4 introduces the bank-mapping algorithm; and Section 5 describes the theory for intra-bank offset generation. Section 6 presents the design space exploration; the experimental results is discussed in Section 7; this is followed by conclusions in Section 8.

2. MOTIVATIONAL EXAMPLES

In this section we use a motivational example to explain the limitations of previous work [21]. Our motivational example stems from a critical loop kernel of a 2D denoise algorithm derived from medical image processing [14]. As shown in Fig. 2(a), there are four accesses to a two-dimensional array in the loop nest. To improve the processing throughput of the loop kernel, we pipeline the execution of successive inner-loop iterations, which means that multiple accesses to the same array will happen in one clock cycle. We assume that only one array element can be read from a physical memory in each clock cycle (the case with multi-port memories is considered in Section 4.3). If all the array elements are stored in one physical memory, fetching all the required data elements in an iteration requires four clock cycles. Thus, the performance will be highly impacted. Memory partitioning allocates the array elements into multiple banks to reduce the access conflict.

```
int A[w_0][w_1];
for (j=1; j<w_0-1; j++)
 for (i=1; i<w_1-1; i++)
  foo(A[j][i-1], A[j-1][i], A[j+1][i], A[j][i+1]);
```

(a) Loop kernel

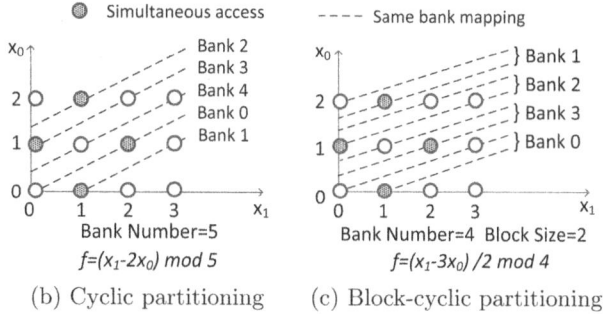

(b) Cyclic partitioning   (c) Block-cyclic partitioning

Figure 2: Denoise: (a) loop kernel, (b) cyclic partitioning, (c) block-cyclic partitioning

Table 1: Symbol table

Variables	Meaning
N	Partition factor, representing the number of logic banks used after memory partitioning
B	Partition block size
P	Memory port number
l	Level of loop nest
d	Number of dimensions of the array
m	Number of array references in the inner loop
$\mathcal{D}$	Iteration domain
$\mathcal{M}$	Data domain
$\vec{i}$	Iteration vector
$\vec{x}$	Array index vector
$\vec{\alpha}$	Partition vector
q	Padding size
i,j,k,t	Temporal variables
$\mathbb{Z}$	Integer set
w_k	The k-th dimensional size of the array

The memory-partitioning method in a previous work [21] can solve this problem by applying linear transformation-based cyclic partitioning on the multidimensional array. Using this method, we can always achieve conflict-free access with five memory banks. Fig. 2(b) illustrates the partitioning with five banks, where x_0 and x_1 are the two dimensions of array A[1]. The points represent the array elements, and the shaded points are the data elements accessed in the same loop iteration. The data elements on the same dotted line are mapped to the same memory bank. The partitioning function is $f = (x_1 - 2x_0) \bmod 5$. As we see in the figure, four simultaneous accesses are in different banks, so there is no conflict.

However in this case, the use of cyclic partitioning alone will not achieve the ideal optimal result. The ideal minimum bank number is four for Fig. 2(a), as there are only four accesses in the inner loop. Note that previous HLS memory-partitioning work [12,17,22] also use only cyclic partitioning, and thus suffer the same limitations. Block-cyclic provides a larger design exploration space and can solve this problem, as shown in Fig. 2(c). The ideal conflict-free partitioning with four banks can be achieved by using a partition block size of two.

Moreover, the current block RAMs on the real FPGA platforms always have dual ports. Previous work [12] proposes a scheduling-based method for partitioning for multi-port memory, but the mapping relationship between the ports and references is fixed. This may lead to a suboptimal partitioning result. Our generalized partitioning model based on polyhedral model can be easily extended for multi-port memory.

3. PROBLEM FORMULATION

In this section we present the definitions and problems of memory partitioning. The important variables in the following descriptions are listed in Table. 1. We introduce a polyhedral model to define the problem. The polyhedral model

is a powerful mathematical framework based on parametric linear algebra and integer linear programming. It provides a flexible representation for expressing the loop nests.

Definition 1. (Polyhedron) A set $P \in Q^d$ is a polyhedron if there exists a system of a finite number of inequalities $A \cdot \vec{x} \le b$ such that

$$P = \{\vec{x} \in Q^d | A \cdot \vec{x} \le \vec{b}\},$$

where Q denotes the set of rational numbers, $\vec{x}$ is a d-dimensional vector in d-dimensional space Q^d. A is a rational matrix and $\vec{b}$ is a rational vector. A polytope is a bounded polyhedron. We define the iteration domain, data domain and affine array references as polytopes.

Definition 2. (Iteration Domain [15]) Given an l-level loop nest, the iteration domain $\mathcal{D}$ is formed by the iteration $\vec{i} = (i_0, i_1, ..., i_{l-1})^T$ within the loop bounds.

Definition 3. (Data Domain) Given a d-dimensional array, the data domain $\mathcal{M}$ is bounded by the array size, where $\forall 0 \le k < d$, the k-th dimensional size is w_k.

Definition 4. (Affine Memory Reference) A d-dimensional affine memory reference $\vec{x} = (x_0, x_1, ..., x_{d-1})^T$ is represented as the following linear combinations

$$\vec{x} = A_{d \times l} \cdot \vec{i} + C,$$

$$A_{d \times l} = \begin{pmatrix} a_{0,0} & \cdots & a_{0,l-1} \\ \vdots & \ddots & \vdots \\ a_{d-1,0} & \cdots & a_{d-1,l-1} \end{pmatrix}, C = \begin{pmatrix} a_{0,l} \\ \vdots \\ a_{d-1,l} \end{pmatrix}$$

where $a_{k,j} \in \mathbb{Z}$ is the coefficient of the j-th iteration vector in the k-th dimension.

Example 1. An affine array reference $A[i_0][i_1 + 1]$ is represented as $\vec{x} = (i_0, i_1 + 1)^T$, where

$$\vec{x} = \begin{pmatrix} i_0 \\ i_1 + 1 \end{pmatrix} = \begin{pmatrix} 1 & 0 \\ 0 & 1 \end{pmatrix} \cdot \begin{pmatrix} i_0 \\ i_1 \end{pmatrix} + \begin{pmatrix} 0 \\ 1 \end{pmatrix}.$$

---

[1]Note that the order of the dimensions is different from that in [21].

With these definitions, we can formulate the bank mapping of the array elements in the polyhedral model. Our memory partitioning consists of two mapping problems: bank mapping and intra-bank offset mapping.

Definition 5. (Memory Partitioning) A memory partitioning of an array is described as a pair of mapping functions $(f(\vec{x}), g(\vec{x}))$, where $f(\vec{x})$ assigns a bank for the data element, and $g(\vec{x})$ generates the corresponding intra-bank offset.

A bank access conflict between two references $\vec{x}_j$ and $\vec{x}_k$ $(0 \le j < k < m)$ is represented as $\exists \vec{x} \in \mathcal{D}$, s.t.

$$f(\vec{x}_j) = f(\vec{x}_k).$$

This means the references intend to access the same bank in the same clock cycle. We use Problem 1 to formulate the bank mapping problem (for single-port memories).

PROBLEM 1. *(Bank Minimization) Given a l-level loop in the iteration domain $\mathcal{D}$ with m affine memory references $\vec{x}_0, ..., \vec{x}_{m-1}$ on the same array, find the partition factor N such that:*

$$Minimize: N = max_{\le i < m}\{f(\vec{x}_i)\} \tag{1}$$

$$\exists \vec{i} \in \mathcal{D}, 0 \le j < k < m, f(\vec{x}_j) \ne f(\vec{x}_k). \tag{2}$$

Eqn. (1) defines the objective function of memory partitioning, and Eqn. (2) ensures no access conflict between any two references. After bank mapping, a data element in the original array should be allocated a new intra-bank location. For correctness, two different array elements will be either mapped onto different banks or the same bank with different intra-bank offsets. An intra-bank offset function is valid if and only if

$$\forall \vec{x}_j, \vec{x}_k \in \mathcal{M}, \vec{x}_j \ne \vec{x}_k \Leftrightarrow (f(\vec{x}_j), g(\vec{x}_j)) \ne (f(\vec{x}_k), g(\vec{x}_k)),$$

which means either

$$f(\vec{x}_j) \ne f(\vec{x}_k), or\ f(\vec{x}_j) = f(\vec{x}_k),\ g(\vec{x}_j) \ne g(\vec{x}_k).$$

Considering storage requirement, we also want to minimize the largest offset of each bank. The intra-bank offset mapping problem is formulated as Problem 2.

PROBLEM 2. *(Storage Minimization) Given an l-level loop in the iteration domain with m affine memory references $\vec{x}_0, ..., \vec{x}_{m-1}$ on the same array and a partition factor N, find an intra-bank offset mapping function g with minimum storage requirement $\mathcal{S}$ such that:*

$$Minimize: \sum_{j=0}^{N-1} max_{\le i < m, f(\vec{x}_i)=j}\{g(\vec{x}_i)\} \tag{3}$$

$$\forall \vec{x}_j, \vec{x}_k \in \mathcal{M}, (f(\vec{x}_j), g(\vec{x}_j)), \ne (f(\vec{x}_k), g(\vec{x}_k)). \tag{4}$$

Eqn. (3) defines the objective function of partitioning with minimum storage overhead, and Eqn. (4) is responsible for the valid partition detection.

4. BANK MAPPING

In this section we describe how we automatically map a array in a loop nest into separate memory banks to enable parallelized memory access. We use a loop initiation interval (II) of loop pipelining to measure the throughput. It represents the clock cycles between the successive iterations and

reflects the parallelism of on-chip memory access. For a fully pipelined loop with all accesses parallelized, II is one. This is the performance target in this paper. For other constant loop initiation intervals, we use conflict analysis together with scheduling to find a proper partitioning (as presented in [12]).

In our GMP method, we consider the block-cyclic partitioning scheme, for it covers all three schemes mentioned in our introduction. The bank mapping function for memory reference $\vec{x}$, with a partition vector $\vec{\alpha} = (\alpha_0, \alpha_1, ..., \alpha_{l-1})$, $\alpha_i \in \mathbb{Z}$, is described as Eqn. (5).

$$f(\vec{x}) = \left\lfloor \frac{\vec{\alpha} \cdot \vec{x}}{B} \right\rfloor \ mod\ N \tag{5}$$

N is the partition factor representing the total bank number, and B is the partition block size. The bank mapping function for cyclic partitioning is $f(\vec{x}) = (\vec{\alpha} \cdot \vec{x})\ mod\ N$. From a geometrical point of view, $\vec{\alpha} \cdot \vec{x}$ represents a sequence of hyperplanes in the data domain. The mapping function $f(\vec{x})$ assigns the points on the hyperplanes to different memory banks.

Given a partition factor N, a block size B, and a partition vector $\vec{\alpha}$, the conflict detection process is executed between each pair of references. We propose a method using polytope emptiness testing. For simplicity, we first discuss the conflict detection in cyclic partitioning under a single-port memory constraint. We will introduce the algorithm for block-cyclic partitioning and partitioning for multi-port memory as extensions to the framework.

4.1 Generalized Conflict Detection

Considering the iteration domain, integer linear programming is optimal in access conflict analysis. In this section we use a polyhedral model for access conflict detection in the iteration domain with given parameters, including partition factor, block and vector. The framework is general for extending to multiple loop kernels. We introduce the concept of a conflict polytope expressing the access conflict necessarily occuring between a pair of references in any iteration in the iteration domain. We assume that two d-dimensional affine memory references are $\vec{x}_0 = A_0 \cdot \vec{i} + C_0$ and $\vec{x}_1 = A_1 \cdot \vec{i} + C_1$.

Definition 6. (Conflict Polytope) A conflict polytope of two simultaneous references $\vec{x}_0$ and $\vec{x}_1$ is a parametric polytope restricted to the iteration domain $\mathcal{D}$ as

$$\mathcal{P}_{conf}(\vec{x}_0, \vec{x}_1) = \{\vec{i}|\forall \vec{i} \in \mathcal{D}, f(\vec{x}_0) = f(\vec{x}_1)\}.$$

Obviously, if $\forall \vec{i} \in \mathcal{D}, f(\vec{x}_0) \ne f(\vec{x}_1)$, $\mathcal{P}_{conf}(\vec{x}_0, \vec{x}_1)$ is empty.

THEOREM 1. *Given two memory references $\vec{x}_0$ and $\vec{x}_1$ in the same inner-loop iteration, they are conflict free in any iteration if and only if their conflict polytope $P_{conf}(\vec{x}_0, \vec{x}_1)$ is empty.*

PROOF. Proof omitted due to the page limit. □

With the bank mapping function $f(\vec{x}) = (\vec{\alpha} \cdot \vec{x})\ mod\ N$, two distinct data elements $\vec{x}_0$ and $\vec{x}_1$ are mapped to the same bank if and only if

$$f(\vec{x}_0) = f(\vec{x}_1) \Leftrightarrow \vec{\alpha} \cdot \vec{x}_0\ mod\ N = \vec{\alpha} \cdot \vec{x}_1\ mod\ N$$
$$\Leftrightarrow \exists k \in \mathbb{Z}, s.t.\ \vec{\alpha} \cdot \vec{x}_0 + Nk = \vec{\alpha} \cdot \vec{x}_1,$$

where $k \in \mathbb{Z}$ is a variable. The conflict polytope for cyclic partitioning is formulated as

$$\mathcal{P}_{conf} : \begin{cases} \vec{\alpha} \cdot (A_0 - A_1) \cdot \vec{i} + \vec{\alpha} \cdot (C_0 - C_1) + Nk = 0 \\ \vec{i} \in \mathcal{D} \\ k \in \mathbb{Z} \end{cases}$$

where $\vec{i} = (i_0, i_1, ..., i_{l-1})^T$ and k are variables. Example 2 is a detailed example. We apply an emptiness test on the polytope [19] to detect the access conflict.

Example 2. For the references $A[i_0+1][i_1]$ and $A[i_0][i_1+1]$ with a partition vector $\vec{\alpha} = (2, 1)$ and partition factor $N = 2$, and the iteration domain $0 \leq i_0, i_1 \leq 63$, $\exists k \in \mathbb{Z}$

$$f(\vec{x}_0) = f(\vec{x}_1) \Leftrightarrow 2(i_0 + 1) + i_1 + 2k = 2i_0 + i_1 + 1$$
$$\Leftrightarrow 2k + 1 = 0$$

Thus the conflict polytope is formed by $2k + 1 = 0$ and the iteration domain as

$$\mathcal{P}_{conf} : \left(\begin{array}{cccc} 0 & 0 & 2 & 1 \\ \hline 1 & 0 & 0 & 0 \\ -1 & 0 & 0 & 63 \\ 0 & 1 & 0 & 0 \\ 0 & -1 & 0 & 63 \end{array} \right) \cdot \left(\begin{array}{c} i_0 \\ i_1 \\ k \\ 1 \end{array} \right) \begin{array}{c} = 0 \\ \hline \geq \vec{0} \end{array}$$

The polytope is empty. According to Theorem 1, no conflict exists between these two array references. For multiple references in the inner-loop, the conflict detection is executed between each pair of the references. This means for m references, C_m^2 conflict polytopes are constructed for non-conflict access among all the references. Because of the exponential complexity of the polyhedral emptiness tests, this pair-wise conflict test, which keeps a moderate numbers of dimensions at each run, is a more scalable approach.

4.2 Extension for Block-Cyclic Partitioning

In block-cyclic partitioning, a reference $\vec{x}$ is first linearized as $\vec{\alpha} \cdot \vec{x}$, and partitioned into blocks by $\lfloor \frac{\vec{\alpha} \cdot \vec{x}}{B} \rfloor$. Then the blocks are cyclically allocated to banks. The access conflict between $\vec{x}_0$ and $\vec{x}_1$ is formed as

$$f(\vec{x}_0) = f(\vec{x}_1) \Leftrightarrow \lfloor \frac{\vec{\alpha} \cdot \vec{x}_0}{B} \rfloor \bmod N = \lfloor \frac{\vec{\alpha} \cdot \vec{x}_1}{B} \rfloor \bmod N$$
$$\Leftrightarrow \exists k_0 \in \mathbb{Z}, s.t. \lfloor \frac{\vec{\alpha} \cdot \vec{x}_0}{B} \rfloor + Nk_0 = \lfloor \frac{\vec{\alpha} \cdot \vec{x}_1}{B} \rfloor.$$

As this formulation is not linear, it cannot be represented by a polyhedral model. Further linearizing is required to express the partition blocks as $\exists k_0, k_1 \in \mathbb{Z}, s.t.$

$$\begin{cases} BNk_0 + Bk_1 \leq \vec{\alpha} \cdot \vec{x}_0 \leq BNk_0 + B(k_1 + 1) - 1 \\ Bk_1 \leq \vec{\alpha} \cdot \vec{x}_1 \leq B(k_1 + 1) - 1 \end{cases}$$

With the above inequalities expressing the linearized space inside the blocks and among the banks, the conflict polytope for block-cyclic partitioning is formulated as below, where $\vec{i} = (i_0, i_1, ..., i_{l-1})^T$, k_0 and k_1 are variables.

$$\mathcal{P}_{conf} : \begin{cases} -\vec{\alpha} \cdot A_0 \cdot \vec{i} - \vec{\alpha} \cdot C_0 + B(Nk_0 + k_1 + 1) - 1 \geq 0 \\ -\vec{\alpha} \cdot A_1 \cdot \vec{i} - \vec{\alpha} \cdot C_1 + B(k_1 + 1) - 1 \geq 0 \\ \vec{\alpha} \cdot A_0 \cdot \vec{i} + \vec{\alpha} \cdot C_0 - B(Nk_0 + k_1) \geq 0 \\ \vec{\alpha} \cdot A_1 \cdot \vec{i} + \vec{\alpha} \cdot C_1 - Bk_1 \geq 0 \\ \vec{i} \in \mathcal{D} \\ k_0, k_1 \in \mathbb{Z} \end{cases}$$

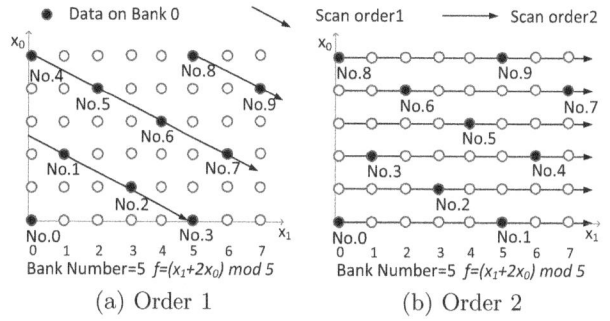

(a) Order 1 (b) Order 2

Figure 3: Examples of data ordering

Example 3 compares cyclic partitioning and block-cyclic partitioning by giving different block size.

Example 3. For two references $A[i_0][i_1 - 1]$ and $A[i_0][i_1 + 1]$, with a partition vector $\vec{\alpha} = (2, 1)$, partition factor $N = 2$, the partition block size $B = 1$, and the iteration domain $0 \leq i_0, i_1 \leq 63$, the conflict polytope is non-empty, which means conflict exists between two references when using two banks. But with a partition vector $\vec{\alpha} = (2, 1)$, partition factor $N = 2$, the partition block size $B = 2$, the conflict polytope is empty. According to Theorem 1, no conflict exists between two references.

4.3 Extension for Multi-Port Memories

The conflict polytope built for multi-port partitioning follows the same principle. Take cyclic partitioning under the port constraint $P = 2$, for example, assuming three simultaneous accesses $\vec{x}_0$, $\vec{x}_1$ and $\vec{x}_2$, where $\vec{x}_2 = A_2 \cdot \vec{i} + C_2$. The access conflict is formed by

$$f(\vec{x}_0) = f(\vec{x}_1) \; and \; f(\vec{x}_1) = f(\vec{x}_2).$$

The conflict polytope is constructed as

$$\mathcal{P}_{conf} : \begin{cases} \vec{\alpha} \cdot (A_0 - A_1) \cdot \vec{i} + \vec{\alpha} \cdot (C_0 - C_1) + Nk_0 = 0 \\ \vec{\alpha} \cdot (A_1 - A_2) \cdot \vec{i} + \vec{\alpha} \cdot (C_1 - C_2) + Nk_1 = 0 \\ \vec{i} \in \mathcal{D} \\ k_0, k_1 \in \mathbb{Z} \end{cases}$$

where $\vec{i} = (i_0, i_1, ..., i_{l-1})^T$, k_0 and k_1 are variables. Given m references and P memory ports, we need to detect the conflict among every $P + 1$ references by building C_m^{P+1} polytopes, and testing the emptiness of each of them.

5. INTRA-BANK OFFSET GENERATION

The function $g(\vec{x})$ maps a multidimensional array address to a non-negative integer as the corresponding intra-bank offset after bank mapping, following the partitioning validity principle. An optimal approach without increasing the original size is to scan and order the data elements on the same bank in a certain sequence. Fig. 3 shows an example of data ordering, where the black points are data elements assigned to Bank 0. Fig. 3(a) and Fig. 3(b) shows different scanning order. The corresponding intra-bank offset mapping functions are different as well.

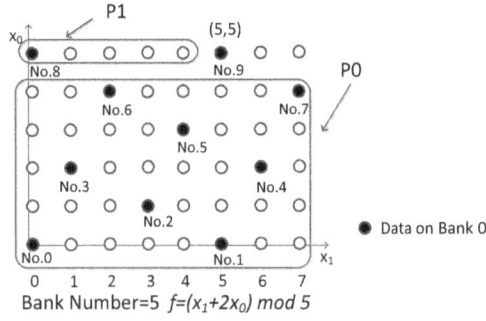

(a) Optimal approach

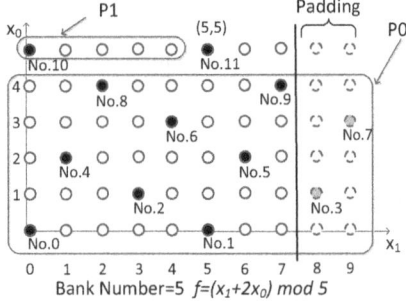

(b) Heuristic approach

Figure 4: An example of generating intra-bank offset: (a) optimal approach (b) heuristic approach

In this section we propose a method based on polytope integer points counting to generate the intra-bank offset mapping function. First, we introduce the concept of bank polytope for the references mapped to the same bank.

Definition 7. (Bank Polytope [16]) Given a d-dimensional array reference $\vec{x}$, $\mathcal{P}_{bank}(\vec{x})$ is a bank polytope of $\vec{x}$ in the data domain $\mathcal{M}$ defined as

$$\mathcal{P}_{bank}(\vec{x}) = \{\vec{y} | \forall \vec{y} \in \mathcal{M}, f(\vec{x}) = f(\vec{y})\}.$$

With a partition factor N, there are N bank polytopes in total. The minimum total storage requirement for bank $f(\vec{x})$ is $C(\mathcal{P}_{bank}(\vec{x}))$, where $C(\mathcal{P})$ is a function calculating the number of integer points in the polytope $\mathcal{P}$.

Definition 8. (Lexicographic Order) A lexicographic order $\prec_{lex}$ on a d-dimensional set $\mathcal{M}$ is a relation, where for $\forall \vec{x}, \vec{y} \in \mathcal{M}$, $\vec{x} = (x_0, x_1, ..., x_{d-1})$ and $\vec{y} = (y_0, y_1, ..., y_{d-1})$,

$$\vec{y} \prec_{lex} \vec{x}$$

$$\Leftrightarrow \exists 1 < t < d, \forall 0 \leq i < t, (x_i = y_i) \wedge (y_t < x_t).$$

We can define a valid and optimal intra-bank offset mapping function with minimum storage requirement by using the lexicographic ordering number as the intra-bank offset as

$$g(\vec{x}) = C(\{\vec{y} | \vec{y} \in \mathcal{P}_{bank}(\vec{x}), \vec{y} \prec_{lex} \vec{x}\}).$$

5.1 Integer Points Counting in Polytopes

We illustrate a two-dimensional example in Fig. 4(a). The intra-bank offset for $(5, 5)$ is generated by counting the integer points in the bank polytope $\mathcal{P}_{bank}(5, 5)$ in lexicographic

order. The data elements on Bank 0 are represented as the dark points. The polytope $\mathcal{P}_{bank}(5, 5)$ is dvided into two polytopes, $\mathcal{P}_0$ and $\mathcal{P}_1$. There are eight integer points in $\mathcal{P}_0$, and one point in $\mathcal{P}_1$. As a result, the intra-bank offset for $(5, 5)$ is nine. We define $\mathcal{P}_0$ and $\mathcal{P}_1$ together as an ordered polytopes set. Given a d-dimensional address $\vec{x} = (x_0, x_1, ..., x_{d-1})^T$ in the data domain, its ordered polytopes set $\mathcal{S}_{P_t(\vec{x})}$ is constructed by a union of polytopes as

$$\mathcal{S}_{P_t(\vec{x})} = \{\mathcal{P}_t(\vec{x}) \mid \forall 1 \leq t \leq d\}, where$$

$$\mathcal{P}_t(\vec{x}) = \{\vec{y} | \vec{y} \in \mathcal{P}_{bank}(\vec{x}), \forall 0 \leq i < t, (x_i = y_i) \wedge (y_t \prec_{lex} x_t)\}.$$

$\mathcal{P}_t(\vec{x})$ is a sub-polytope of $\mathcal{P}_{bank}(\vec{x})$. $\mathcal{S}_{P_t(\vec{x})}$ is organized by generating $\mathcal{P}_t(\vec{x})$ in lexicographic order.

THEOREM 2. *Given an ordered polytopes set $\mathcal{S}_{P_t(\vec{x})}$ of $\vec{x}$, a valid and optimal intra-bank offset generation function for $\vec{x}$ with minimum storage requirement is $\forall 0 \leq i < t, \mathcal{P}_t(\vec{x}) \in \mathcal{S}_{P_t(\vec{x})}$,*

$$g(\vec{x}) = \sum C(\mathcal{P}_t(\vec{x}))$$

PROOF. Proof omitted due to the page limit. $\square$

Thus, we can convert the intra-bank offset generation problem to an equivalent problem on counting the total number of elements in several parameterized polytopes. Counting integer points in polytopes is a fundamental mathematical problem, and has a wide application in analysis and transformations of nested loop programs. Several automatic algorithms and libraries have been previously provided, such as Ehrhart's theorem [11] and the Barvinok library [20]. In this paper we use Ehrhart's method presented by [11] for computing the parametric vertices. It generates the Ehrhart polynomial as a parametric expression of the number of integer points. Example 4 presents a detailed example for generating the intra-bank offset by using this method [11].

Example 4. Given the array reference vector $\vec{x} = (x_0, x_1)$, the data domain $0 \leq x_0, x_1 \leq 7$, a partition vector $\vec{\alpha} = (2, 1)$, a partition factor $N = 5$, and partition block size $B = 1$, the polytope $\mathcal{P}_0$ is formulated by

$$\begin{cases} 2x_0' + x_1' + 5k = 2x_0 + x_1 \\ 0 \leq x_0, x_1 \leq 7 \\ 0 \leq x_0', x_1' \leq 7 \\ x_0 \geq x_0' + 1 \end{cases}$$

The points counting result is $C(\mathcal{P}_1) = \lfloor \frac{x_1}{N} \rfloor$ and

$$C(\mathcal{P}_0) = \frac{8}{5} \times x_0 + [[0, \frac{2}{5}, -\frac{1}{5}, \frac{1}{5}, -\frac{2}{5}]x_0,$$

$$[0, -\frac{3}{5}, -\frac{1}{5}, \frac{1}{5}, -\frac{2}{5}]x_0, [0, -\frac{3}{5}, -\frac{1}{5}, -\frac{4}{5}, -\frac{2}{5}]x_0,$$

$$[0, \frac{2}{5}, \frac{4}{5}, \frac{1}{5}, \frac{3}{5}]x_0, [0, \frac{2}{5}, -\frac{1}{5}, \frac{1}{5}, \frac{3}{5}]x_0]x_1.$$

$u(n) = [u_0, u_1, ..., u_{p-1}]_n$ is equal to the item whose rank is equal to $n \bmod p$ [11], thus

$$u(n) = \begin{cases} u_0, & if\ n \bmod p = 0, \\ u_1, & if\ n \bmod p = 1, \\ ... \\ u_{p-1}, & if\ n \bmod p = p - 1. \end{cases}$$

For $\vec{x} = (5, 5)$, $C(\mathcal{P}_1) = \lfloor \frac{5}{5} \rfloor = 1$, $C(\mathcal{P}_0) = \frac{8}{5} \times 5 + 0 = 8$, $g(\vec{x}) = 8 + 1 = 9$.

5.2 Mapping to Hardware

By counting integer points in polytopes, we can generate an optimal intra-bank offset mapping function with the minimum storage overhead. However, as shown in Example 4, building the complex mapping function will cost too much in hardware resources. A trade-off between practicality and optimality is considered by using a memory-padding based heuristic approach. As shown in Fig. 4(b), padding two data elements on dimension x_1 insures that each row maintains two data elements of Bank 0. The calculation of the intra-bank offset for data (5,5) is simplified as $2 \times 5 + 1 = 11$.

Our heuristic method makes each polytope $\mathcal{P}_t$ have a constant number of data elements. Under lexicographic ordering, padding on dimension x_{d-1} is able to ensure the constant number of data elements in each $\mathcal{P}_t$. Take block-cyclic partitioning for example: the padding size q is calculated as

$$ q = N \times B \times \lceil \frac{w_{d-1}}{N \times B} \rceil - w_{d-1}. $$

The points number in the padded polytope is calculated as

$$ C(\mathcal{P}_t) = \begin{cases} \prod_{j=t+1}^{d-2} w_j \times \lceil \frac{w_{d-1}}{N \times B} \rceil \times B \times x_t & 0 \leq t < d-2 \\[2mm] \lceil \frac{w_{d-1}}{N \times B} \rceil \times B \times x_t & t = d-2 \\[2mm] \lfloor \frac{x_t}{N \times B} \rfloor \times B + x_t \bmod B & t = d-1 \end{cases} $$

Example 5. Given the array reference $\vec{x} = (5,5)$, the data domain $0 \leq x_0, x_1 \leq 7$, a partition vector $\vec{\alpha} = (2,1)$, a partition factor $N = 5$, and partition block size $B = 1$, the intra-bank offset generated by padding is $C(\mathcal{P}_1) = 1$, $C(\mathcal{P}_0) = \lceil \frac{8}{5} \rceil \times 5 = 10$, $g(\vec{x}) = 10 + 1 = 11$.

6. PARTITIONING ALGORITHM AND DESIGN SPACE EXPLORATION

The design flow is shown as Fig 5. The algorithm's input is the iteration domain and memory references information extracted from the input code. The output is a selected partition strategy $(N, B, \vec{\alpha})$, which guides the code transformation. The main partitioning algorithm is composed of two parts: one part constructs the bank-mapping function and the other constructs the intra-bank offset function. The strategies are derived by bounded enumeration and conflict detection. The enumeration of N and $\vec{\alpha}$ is the same as the method in [21]. The enumeration of the block size starts from $B = 1$, and to reduce the resource resulting from the division operations, we only consider $B = 2^k$, $k \in \mathbb{Z}$, $k \geq 0$. A resource estimation model is built for selecting an optimal partition strategy. Assuming $B = 1$, the algorithm for cyclic partitioning is described in Algorithm 1.

6.1 Resource Model

The partition strategy affects the resource usage of the hardware implementation of the transformed program. We introduce a resource estimation model and set up a standard for strategy selection. The use of resources is mainly made up of two parts: the storage and the address logic. We estimate the resource for a given partition strategy using a weighted arithmetic average, as Eqn. (6).

$$ Est = c_0 \times U_{store} + c_1 \times U_{addr} \qquad (6) $$

Algorithm 1 Partitioning algorithm (block size fixed)

1: $\mathbb{S} \rightarrow$ partition strategy set
2:
3: $\mathbb{S} = \emptyset$
4: **for** $N = m$ to $\prod_{j=0}^{d-1} w_j$ **do**
5:      **for each** $\vec{\alpha}$ in the space of N^d **do**
6:          empty=ConflictDetect$(N, \vec{\alpha})$
7:          **if** (empty) **then** add $(N, \vec{\alpha})$ in $\mathbb{S}$
8:      **end for**
9:      **if** $(\mathbb{S} \neq \emptyset)$ **break**
10: **end for**
11: CalculatePadding(q)
12: Stratey $\rightarrow s \in \mathbb{S}$, minimize$\{$ResourceEstimate$(s, q)\}$
13: CodeGen(Stratey)

---

c_0 and c_1 reflect the importance of the resource, $c_0 + c_1 = 1$. U_{store} and U_{addr} are the percentages of BRAMs and address logic resource utilization on the target platform. In our method, the resource for array storage is block RAM. Registers and distributed memories can be alternatives, but currently we don't consider them. Ideally the use of block RAMs is only influenced by the partition factor N and the padding size q. The storage is calculated as

$$ U_{store}(N, q) = \lceil \frac{(w_{d-1} + q) \times \prod_{j=0}^{d-2} w_j}{N \times BRAM_{size}} \rceil, $$

in which $BRAM_{size}$ is the block RAM's size of the target FPGA platform. However we find that the use of block RAMs in the implementation is also related to the data width and the port number P. Such dedicated estimation is platform dependent. Taking Virtex-7 from Xilinx for example, there are two block RAM modes: SDP (simple dual-port mode; one read, one write) and TDP (true dual-port; two read or write). The detailed relationship between the BRAM's mode and maximum port width is shown in Table 2. Using the method of partitioning for multi-port memory may not save BRAMs due to this relationship. Only when the width of the array is less than 18 bits, can two simultaneous accesses to one block RAM (RAMB18E1) in one cycle be achieved. The dedicated storage estimation for Virtex7 is formulated below, with N_P as the partition factor with port P ($P = 1$ or $P = 2$) and the *width* of the target array.

$$ U_{store-v7}(N_P, q, width) = \lceil \frac{(w_{d-1} + q) \times \prod_{j=0}^{d-2} w_j}{N_P \times \lceil \frac{width}{18} \rceil \times BRAM_{size}} \rceil. $$

U_{addr} estimates the resource for address generation. A template of code transformation after partitioning is given in Fig. 6. The address generation unit and data assignment unit are two pieces of code which will be repeated multiple times for generating the address logic for different references and banks. Assuming that the resource for the address generation unit is Ad_{gen} and for the data assignment unit is $Data_{assign}$, the total resource for the address logic is mainly estimated as

$$ U_{addr}(N, B, \vec{\alpha}) = (Ad_{gen} + Data_{assign}) \times N \times m. $$

The value of N and B influences the physical resource for divisions and modulo operations. The value of $\vec{\alpha}$ affects the resource used for multiplications. For example, the resource for the implementation with $N = 4$, $B = 1$, $\vec{\alpha} = (1,2)$ is less than using $N = 4$, $B = 3$, $\vec{\alpha} = (1,3)$. As a result, we intend

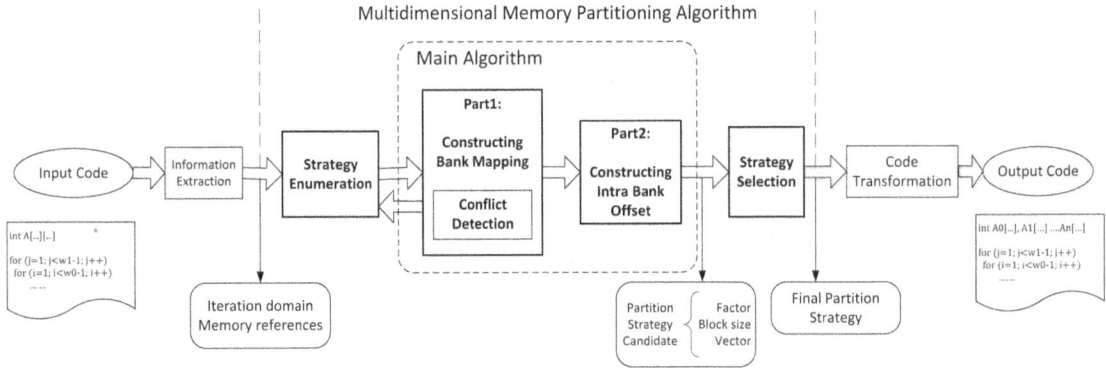

Figure 5: The design flow

Table 2: Virtex-7 BRAM mode and data width [1]

	Block RAM	Maximum port width	Simultaneous access
RAMB18E1(TDP)	1	18	2
RAMB18E1(SDP)	1	36	1
RAMB36E1(TDP)	2	36	2
RAMB36E1(SDP)	2	72	1

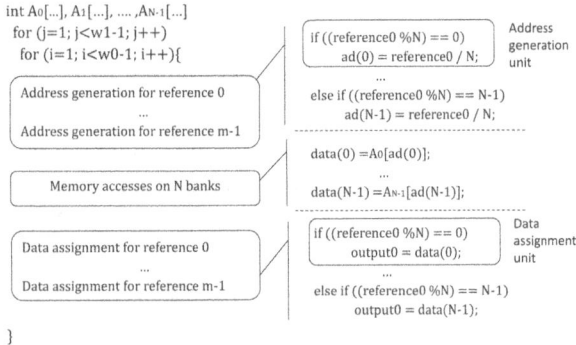

Figure 6: A template of code transformation

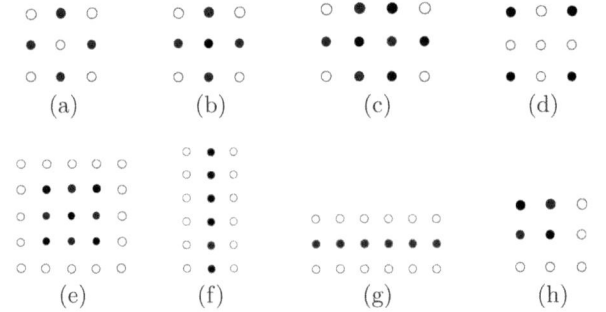

Figure 7: The access patterns of the benchmarks: (a) DENOISE (b) DECONV (c) DENOISE-UR (d) BICUBIC (e) SOBEL (f) MOTION-LV (g) MOTION-LH (h) MOTION-C

to use the number which is a power of two in the partition strategy.

7. EXPERIMENTAL RESULTS

The automatic memory-partitioning flow is implemented in C++ and is built in the open source compiler infrastructure ROSE [7]. ROSE is a flexible translator supporting source-to-source code transformation. We use Ehrhart testing provided by Polylib [6] for both polytopes emptiness testing and integer points counting, and Vivado Design Suite 2013.2 from Xilinx [9] as the high-level synthesis, logic synthesis, simulation, and power estimation tool. The RTL output targets the FPGA platform Xilinx Virtex-7. The high-level abstraction (C program) is parsed into the flow with the partition and loop pipelining directives. After memory-partitioning analysis and source-to-source code transformation, the transformed C code is synthesized into RTL through high-level synthesis and followed by logic synthesis, simulation, and power estimation tool.

Eight loop kernels with different access patterns are selected from the real applications, such as medical image processing [14] and H.264 motion compensation [5], as shown in Fig. 7. In the experiments, we mainly focus on the effects brought by different access patterns.

The detailed experimental results are shown in Table 3, Table 4, and Table 5. We re-implemented the LTB method [21], and we compare the results to our GMP method. During the experiments, although we use exhaustive enumeration, the runtime for all the benchmarks is less than 1 second. Because all the ideal minimum partition factors are achieved, the enumeration space for the partition vector, which is related to the partition factor, is not large. We implement loop pipelining in the benchmarks and set the target throughput as II=1, which requires all of the memory accesses in the same iteration to be in one clock cycle. In the experiments, all of the two partitioning methods can achieve this target throughput requirement.

7.1 A Case Study: DECONV

We use benchmark DECONV as a case study on the effect of different intra-bank offset generation algorithms, as shown in Table 3 . Two algorithms are applied: optimal (integer points counting in polytopes), and heuristic (memory padding). Although the array size is increased by 4.69% with the heuristic method, it still uses the same number of

Table 3: Intra-bank offset generation comparison

	Array size (bits)	BRAM	Slice	DSP
Optimal	640*32	5	696	20
Heuristic	670*32	5	597	5
Compare	4.69%	0.00%	-14.22%	-75.00%

Table 4: Partition factor comparison

Partition Factor	BRAM	Slice	FF	DSP
Minimum	5	597	1298	5
Power-of-2	8	457	1279	0
Compare	60%	-23.45%	-1.46%	-100.00%

BRAMs as the optimal method. Because the size of the block RAMs on FPGAs is fixed, the small padding size did not increase the use of BRAMs. We tried 140 different array sizes, and compared to the array size, the padding rate is from 0.98% to 7%. As shown in the table, the heuristic method can reduce up to 14.22% slice and 75% DSP in this case. We used memory padding as our algorithm in the rest of our experiments.

We also had a case study on the partition factor. Two partition factors are applied: minimum (due to the conflict detection algorithm), and power-of-2 (increase the minimum partition factor to a number as power of two and also perform conflict detection). As shown in Table 4, although the use of BRAM is increased from 5 to 8, other resources are reduced. However, this is only suitable for the case when the power-of-2 partition factor is close to the minimum partition factor. As our main target in this paper is to reduce the bank number, we still use the minimum partition factor for DECONV, but use a power-of-2 partition factor under the multi-port partitioning mode.

7.2 Complete Experimental Results

Table 5 shows the complete experimental results on all eight benchmarks and the comparison with the LTB method in [21]. Information is presented in the table in the following order: access number in the inner-loop, data bitwidth, partition strategies, utilization of block RAMS, slices and DSPs, clock period, and dynamic power.

The LTB method only uses cyclic partitioning for single-port memory, while our GMP method can select a multi-port memory mode and use different block sizes. The bit-width of the array affects the selection of multi-port memory modes. According to the relationship between the port width and the block RAM's mode listed in Table 2, only when the width is less than 18 bit can two data elements from one RAMB18E1 under true dual-port mode be accessed simultaneously. As a result, three benchmarks (MOTION-LV, MOTION-LH and MOTION-C) with 8-bit width select the multi-port memory mode with $P = 2$. And for the block size in the partition strategy, as shown in the table, two benchmarks (DENOISE and BICUBIC) select the partition block size $B = 2$.

We set the access number in the inner-loop as the optimal partition factor for the single-port memory mode $P = 1$. With the selected partition strategies, our GMP method can achieve this target. Although LTB can already reduce the use of BRAMs and other resources in most of the cases, an optimal partitioning with a bank number equal to the access number is still not achieved in benchmark DENOISE and BICUBIC. However, with our GMP method using a block size two, all the bank numbers are reduced to the access number. Note that under the multi-port memory partitioning mode, we intend to choose a bank number that is a power of two. Thus, in MOTION-LV and MOTION-LH, despite $\frac{Access\#}{P} = 3$, we use four block RAMs as a trade-off.

The use of DSP is highly related to the division's number in the transformed code, which is related to the bank number. When the bank number is a power of two, DSP is reduced to zero. The divisions can be implemented as shift operators. Also, the use of slice can be reduced comparatively. Among the benchmarks, the bank number of DENOISE-UR and MOTION-C can already be reduced to a power of two by using LTB, while our GMP method can further reduce the use of DSP to zero on DENOISE, BICUBIC, MOTION-LV and MOTION-LH.

In all, compared to the previous work [21], our GMP method has an average reduction of 19.58% in BRAM, 20.26% in the use of slice, 50% in the number of DSP, and 10.09% in dynamic power.

8. CONCLUSION

In this work we propose a generalized memory partitioning (GMP) method using a polyhedral model. A theory based on polytope emptiness testing and integer points counting is presented for conflict detection between array references and intra-bank offset generation. To our knowledge, we are the first to use a polyhedral model to formulate and solve the bank access conflict problem. Experimental results demonstrate that, compared to the state-of-art partitioning algorithm, our proposed algorithm can reduce the number of block RAMs by 19.58%, slices by 20.26% and DSPs by 50%.

9. ACKNOWLEDGMENT

This work was supported in part by the National High Technology Research and Development Program of China 2012AA010902, RFDP 20110001110099 and 20110001120132, and NSFC 61103028. We thank the UCLA/PKU Joint Research Institute and Xilinx for their support of our research.

10. REFERENCES

[1] *7 Series FPGAs Memory Resources.*
    http://www.xilinx.com/support/ documentation.
[2] *C-to-Silicon Compiler.*
    http://www.cadence.com/products/.
[3] *Catapult C.* http://calypto.com/.
[4] *Cynthesizer.* www.forteds.com.
[5] *JM Software.* http://iphome.hhi.de/suehring/tml/.
[6] *Polylib.* http://www.irisa.fr/polylib/.
[7] *ROSE compiler infrastructure.*
    http://rosecompiler.org/.
[8] *Synphony C Compiler.* http://www.synopsys.com.
[9] *Vivado High-Level Synthesis.* http://www.xilinx.com/.
[10] S. Chatterjee, J. R. Gilbert, F. J. E. Long,
     R. Schreiber, and S. Teng. Generating local addresses
     and communication sets for data-parallel programs.

Table 5: Experimental results

Benchmark	Access #	Bit width	Method	BRAM	Slice	DSP	CP (ns)	Dynamic Power(mw)
DENOISE	4	32	LTB [21]	5	520	4	3.729	26
			GMP (P=1), B=2	4	303	0	3.395	16
			GMP vs LTB	-20.00%	-41.73%	-100.00%	-8.96%	-38.46%
DECONV	5	32	LTB [21]	5	597	5	4.538	27
			GMP (P=1), B=1	5	597	5	4.538	27
			GMP vs LTB	0.00%	0.00%	0.00%	0.00%	0.00%
DENOISE-UR	8	32	LTB [21]	8	794	0	3.738	31
			GMP (P=1), B=1	8	794	0	3.738	31
			GMP vs LTB	0.00%	0.00%	0.00%	0.00%	0.00%
BICUBIC	4	32	LTB [21]	5	483	4	4.364	24
			GMP (P=1), B=2	4	238	0	3.169	15
			GMP vs LTB	-20.00%	-50.72%	-100.00%	-27.38%	-37.50%
SOBEL	9	32	LTB [21]	9	1523	9	4.468	53
			GMP (P=1), B=1	9	1523	9	4.468	53
			GMP vs LTB	0.00%	0.00%	0.00%	0.00%	0.00%
MOTION-LV	6	8	LTB [21]	6	538	6	3.682	25
			GMP (P=2), B=1	4	425	0	3.169	25
			GMP vs LTB	-33.33%	-21.00%	-100.00%	-13.93%	0.00%
MOTION-LH	6	8	LTB [21]	6	536	6	3.946	21
			GMP (P=2), B=1	4	334	0	3.169	23
			GMP vs LTB	-33.33%	-37.69%	-100.00%	-19.69%	9.52%
MOTION-C	4	8	LTB [21]	4	174	0	3.405	14
			GMP (P=2), B=1	2	155	0	3.169	12
			GMP vs LTB	-50.00%	-10.92%	0.00%	-6.93%	-14.29%
Average			**GMP vs LTB**	-19.58%	-20.26%	-50.00%	-9.61%	-10.09%

Journal of Parallel and Distributed Computing, 26(1):72–84, 1995.

[11] P. Clauss and V. Loechner. Parametric parametric analysis of polyhedral iteration spaces. *Journal of VLSI Signal Processing*, 19(2):179–194, 1998.

[12] J. Cong, W. Jiang, B. Liu, and Y. Zou. Automatic memory partitioning and scheduling for throughput and power optimization. *ACM Transaction on Design Automation of Electronic Systems (TODAES)*, 16, 2011.

[13] J. Cong, B. Liu, S. Neuendorffer, J. Noguera, K. Vissers, and Z. Zhang. High-level synthesis for fpgas: From prototyping to deployment. *IEEE Transactions on Computer-Aided Design of Integrated Circuits and Systems*, 30(4):473–491, 2011.

[14] J. Cong, V. Sarkar, G. Reinman, and A. Bui. Customizable domain-specific computing. *IEEE Design and Test of Computers*, 28(2):5–15, 2011.

[15] P. Feautrier. Some efficient solutions for the affine scheduling problem, part i, one dimensional time. *International Journal of Parallel Processing*, 21(6), 1992.

[16] P. Li, L. N. Pouchet, D. Chen, and J. Cong. Loop transformations for throughput optimization in high-level synthesis. *In Proceedings of the ACM/SIGDA international Symposium on Field programmable gate arrays (to appear)*, 2014.

[17] P. Li, Y. Wang, P. Zhang, G. Luo, T. Wang, and J. Cong. Memory partitioning and scheduling co-optimization in behavioral synthesis. *IEEE/ACM International Conference on Computer-Aided Design (ICCAD)*, pages 488–495, 2012.

[18] Q. Liu, T. Todman, and W. Luk. Combining optimizations in automated low power design. In *Proc. of Design, Automation and Test Europe (DATE)*, pages 1791–1796, 2010.

[19] A. Schrijver. *Theory of Linear and Integer Programming*. JohnWiley and Sons, 1986.

[20] S. Verdoolaege, R. Seghir, K. Beyls, V. Loechner, and M. Bruynooghe. Counting integer points in parametric polytopes using barvinok's rational functions. *Algorithmica*, 2007.

[21] Y. Wang, P. Li, P. Zhang, C. Zhang, and J. Cong. Memory partitioning for multidimensional arrays in high-level synthesis. *Proceedings of the 50th Annual Design Automation Conference (DAC)*, (12), 2013.

[22] Y. Wang, P. Zhang, X. Cheng, and J. Cong. An integrated and automated memory optimization flow for fpga behavioral synthesis. *Asia and South Pacific Design Automation Conference (ASP-DAC)*, pages 257–262, 2012.

[23] Z. Zhang, Y. Fan, W. Jiang, G. Han, C. Yang, and J. Cong. *High-Level Synthesis: From Algorithm to Digital Circuit*, chapter AutoPilot: a platform-based ESL synthesis system. Springer, New York, NY, USA,, 2008.

Using High-level Synthesis and Formal Analysis to Predict and Preempt Attacks on Industrial Control Systems

Lee W. Lerner, Zane R. Franklin, William T. Baumann, and Cameron D. Patterson
Bradley Department of Electrical and Computer Engineering
Virginia Tech, Blacksburg, VA 24061 U.S.A.
{lwl, zanef, baumann, cdp}@vt.edu

ABSTRACT

Industrial control systems (ICSes) have the conflicting requirements of security and network access. In the event of large-scale hostilities, factories and infrastructure would more likely be targeted by computer viruses than the bomber squadrons used in WWII. ICS zero-day exploits are now a commodity sold on brokerages to interested parties including nations. We mitigate these threats not by bolstering perimeter security, but rather by assuming that potentially all layers of ICS software have already been compromised and are capable of launching a latent attack while reporting normal system status to human operators. In our approach, application-specific configurable hardware is the final authority for scrutinizing controller commands and process sensors, and can monitor and override operations at the lowest (I/O pin) level of a configurable system-on-chip platform. The process specifications, stability-preserving backup controller, and switchover logic are specified and formally verified as C code, and synthesized into hardware to resist software reconfiguration attacks. To provide greater assurance that the backup controller can be invoked before the physical process becomes unstable, copies of the production controller task and plant model are accelerated to preview the controller's behavior in the near future.

Categories and Subject Descriptors

C.3 [**Special-purpose and Application-based Systems**]: Process control systems; D.2.4 [**Software/Program Verification**]: Formal methods

Keywords

industrial control systems; security; reconfigurable platform; high-level synthesis; formal analysis

1. INTRODUCTION

The malicious reprogramming of process control systems has become a high-profile threat in the increasingly auto-

mated physical world. Existing reliability analysis can use redundancy to mitigate faults occurring in sensors and actuators, and we assume that the adversary does not have physical access. Our threat model instead targets the implicit trust in control applications, middleware, operating systems and communication drivers. We assume that malware may already exist through insider or third party sources or through the application of malicious firmware updates.

TECEP (Trust Enhancement of Critical Embedded Processes) is our method of implementing application-specific critical system functions in a way that is beyond the reach of *any* local or remote software, regardless of the credentials [3]. This greatly reduces the attack surface. Our focus on physical control systems is mainly due to their importance, but also because precise specifications already exist for defining normal system operation. Predicting future deviation from normal operation is enabled by pre-existing accurate models for the physical process. Normally these models are used only during development, but TECEP retains them in the fielded platform.

TECEP is compatible with a traditional model-based design process. An additional but relatively small amount of independent system monitoring code is concerned only with meeting the operating specifications, and is checked with a rigorous software verification framework. The flow maintains a clean separation between application, platform, and formal analysis expertise, with the ultimate goal being semi-automatic synthesis and validation of the additional, autonomic components.

2. TECEP OVERVIEW

2.1 Platform Components

The system overview shown in Fig. 1 includes two software-implemented blocks (production controller code running on both hard and soft processors) and two hardware-targeted blocks (a *hardware monitor* synthesized from formally analyzed C code, and a *junction box* captured and validated in a hardware description language (HDL)) which are invisible to the software blocks at any level. Because the FPGA fabric is not dynamically configured, software or network access to programmable logic configuration ports can be disabled. Changes to the programmable logic requires physical access to the secure plant, and are needed only if the process specifications, plant model, stability-preserving backup controller, or switchover policies change. Routine software updates, including production control code revisions, would be performed on network-accessible, external flash memory that

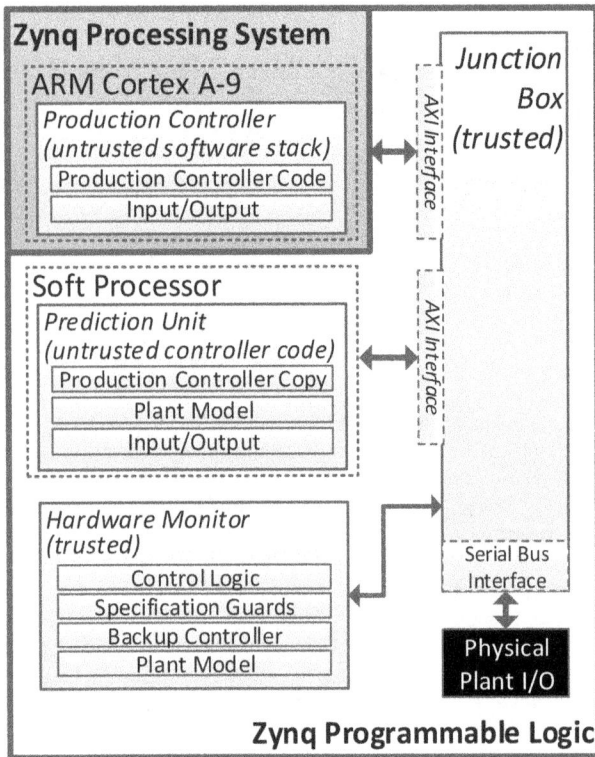

Figure 1: Platform components

can be efficiently shared by hard and soft processors with instruction caches. As in a normal system without TECEP, the production controller is implemented in software on the Zynq-7000's ARM Cortex-A9 processor.

The hardware monitor is implemented in the Zynq-7000's programmable fabric. Inputs include the $u(t)$ output of the production controller, the $y(t)$ output of the physical plant and the output of the prediction unit. A stability-preserving backup controller (possibly a high-assurance version of the production controller) is incorporated in the hardware monitor and acts on the physical plant's output. A model of the plant is also included and receives the output of the production controller. A specification guard tests whether the outputs of the physical plant, plant model and prediction unit are within an acceptable range. If any of these values are outside specifications, the output from the backup controller overrides the production controller's output.

Production to backup controller transitions may be reversed if it is determined that the production controller fault was merely temporary, such as with a glitch or denial-of-service attack. A cool down period is invoked after a fault to increase assurance and avoid a premature return to the production controller. Noise in the system, which may cause false error reporting, will be greatly reduced with the future addition of a Kalman filter. The specifics of fault tolerance and return to the production controller are application-dependent and left to the end user.

A copy of the production controller and a model of the plant running in a closed loop comprise the prediction unit, and are implemented in functions running on a soft processor in the Zynq-7000's programmable logic. In future work,

the production Cortex-A9's complete software stack will be executed on the soft processor, allowing malicious behavior in supervisory and library software to be detected.

Once the prediction unit receives a `start` signal from the junction box, the closed loop is run normally for one control cycle. The state of the plant and controller are then saved, and the closed loop is run for a predefined number of cycles into the future. Upon completion, the predicted plant output is sent to the hardware monitor, and the states of the plant and controller are restored to their previous values.

The junction box is implemented in the programmable fabric of the Zynq-7000. It passes signals between components and manages the system's flow of control, and this functionality is independent of all other system components. Verification is straightforward with conventional hardware analysis techniques such as model checking.

2.2 High-level and Interface Synthesis

Using C code rather than HDL allows the easy inclusion of a backup controller and the plant model as well as formal analysis and verification. After formal verification, the hardware monitor's software-defined functions are implemented in the programmable fabric using high-level synthesis (HLS). The `set_directive_allocation` command is applied to the C-synthesis process to restrict the number of floating-point cores generated, and the `config_bind` command reduces the resources used by those instantiated cores. An `ap_none` interface is added to each of the inputs to create simple data ports with no additional handshaking signals. An `ap_ctrl_hs` interface added to the top-level function provides basic handshaking signals such as `start` and `done` for the operation of the hardware monitor. No AXI slave adapters are needed, as the hardware monitor is connected directly to the junction box using simple 32-bit data ports. Once HLS and interface synthesis processes are complete, the hardware monitor is exported as an IP block for use in Vivado Design Suite.

3. FORMAL VERIFICATION

Formal analysis tools can be incorporated into the high-level design flow to assist in verifying functional and security specifications. We demonstrate verification of TECEP additions using Frama-C, an open source, modular static analysis framework [2]. Proof annotations are specified in the ANSI/ISO-C Specification Language (ACSL) and added to the design source code as comments. Program functions can be analyzed in isolation, which is useful in our security scheme where in order to prove properties of system security the verification space is reduced to only TECEP additions. We use the Jessie deductive verification plug-in to ensure that the hardware monitor result is driven by the appropriate controller module under all possible conditions [4]. Jessie automatically translates ACSL annotations into verification conditions in the Why language, which can then be submitted to external automatic theorem provers such as Simplify, Alt-Ergo, Z3, Yices, and CVC3.

The hardware monitor source code and Frama-C annotations are provided in Fig. 2. We use a combination of *ghost code* (code only Frama-C evaluates) and function contracts to reason about hardware monitor behaviors under valid and invalid specification conditions. The `assigns` clause simply specifies that the `hw_monitor` function does not have any side effects (i.e., does not assign any values which are not local). The first behavior, `verify_all_valid`, aims to verify that the `hw_monitor` does not trigger the backup condition whenever the specification guard does not detect an out-of-specification condition. To test this normal operating condition we assume that the plant response, plant model response, and predicted plant model response are all within stability specifications. The `assumes` clause can specify valid `y_physical` and `y_accel` value ranges directly because they are inputs of the function. To control the value ranges of `y_model`, which is local to the function, we override it within the function with a ghost code variable, `ghost_y_model`. Another ghost variable, `ghost_backup`, is used to store the value of the local `backup` variable within the function. The `ensures` clause using `ghost_backup` tests if the backup controller is ever set to active at the completion of the function. The second behavior, `verify_any_invalid`, is similarly specified and seeks to prove that the `hw_monitor` will always choose the backup, hardware-implemented controller response when any unit is out of specification. The set of behaviors is considered `disjoint` when they do not overlap and `complete` when all cases are covered, both of which properties are also tested.

The Jessie to Why translation for each function contract results in 96 total postcondition verification conditions (or proof obligations) representing various possibilities for input values and corresponding branches of the function that could be executed. All conditions must be discharged for the behaviors to be proven valid, which is accomplished using the Alt-Ergo prover with a 10 second timeout threshold within only a few minutes. The set of behaviors is also proven both disjoint and complete. Thus, Frama-C is able to provide confidence that our TECEP protections both correctly select the production controller output under normal operating conditions and select the backup controller in the event of malicious production controller behaviors or anomalous plant sensor data.

4. MOTOR CONTROLLER EXAMPLE

A simple motor controller example described in [1] is used to test and demonstrate the security features described in this work. For this example, the production controller is a proportional-integral-derivative controller while the backup controller is a proportional-only controller with a fixed reference input. The plant is a motor emulated in software functions on the ARM. This closed-loop system is run once per millisecond.

4.1 Control Flow

Each system cycle begins with the plant output being read and passed to the production controller. The junction box then signals the production controller and prediction unit to begin operation, and performs blocking reads on their respective outputs. These outputs, along with that of the physical plant, are sent to the hardware monitor with a signal to begin operation. The hardware monitor runs the backup controller and the plant model, checks the specification guards, and writes the selected controller's output to the plant. Should the production controller fail to respond within a predetermined amount of time, the backup controller is invoked each cycle based on the junction box's internal timer rather than upon the completion of the production controller and prediction unit.

```
//@ ghost float ghost_y_model, ghost_u_hw;
//@ ghost int ghost_backup;
/*@ assigns \nothing;
    behavior verify_all_valid:
        assumes y_physical >= y_min &&
                y_physical <= y_max &&
                ghost_y_model >= y_min &&
                ghost_y_model <= y_max &&
                y_accel >= y_min &&
                y_accel <= y_max;
        ensures ghost_backup == 0;
    behavior verify_any_invalid:
        assumes y_physical < y_min ||
                y_physical > y_max ||
                ghost_y_model < y_min ||
                ghost_y_model > y_max ||
                y_accel < y_min ||
                yaccel > y_max;
        ensures \result == ghost_u_hw;
    disjoint behaviors;
    complete behaviors; */

#define BACKUP_HOLD_COUNT 200

float hw_monitor(float u_sw,
                 float y_physical,
                 float y_accel) {
    static int backup_hold;
    static float y_model;
    if (reset) y_model = hw_plant_model(u_sw);
    float u_hw = hw_controller(y_physical);
    //@ ghost y_model = ghost_y_model;
    int backup = !hw_spec_guard(y_physical) ||
        !hw_spec_guard(y_model) ||
        !hw_spec_guard(y_accel);
    backup_hold = backup ? BACKUP_HOLD_COUNT
        : (backup_hold - 1);
    backup_hold = (backup_hold < 0) ? 0
        : backup_hold;
    float u = (!backup && !backup_hold) ? u_sw
        : u_hw;
    y_model = hw_plant_model(u);
    //@ ghost ghost_backup = backup;
    //@ ghost ghost_u_hw = u_hw;
    return u;
}
```

Figure 2: `hw_monitor` code annotated with Frama-C

4.2 System Behavior

In this example, the prediction unit's forecast window and the cool down counter length are 200 system cycles (i.e., 200 ms). These and other aspects of the implementation process are specific to the motor controller example used here and will differ among various control systems.

The test begins with a unit step response followed by activation of the latent malware, which attempts to drive the plant's output to its maximum (clipped) value beginning at $t = 350$ ms. With no countermeasures in place, the plant's output continues past the safe limit of 3.2, as shown in Fig. 3. When the hardware monitor is added, the plant's output approaches the acceptable limit at $t = 480$ ms before being corrected by the backup controller. With prediction included, the hardware monitor proactively invokes the backup controller at $t = 280$ ms, thereby preventing the physical plant from reaching an unsafe state. In this configuration, the backup controller will remain active until the system is reset. Fig. 4 shows the plant's output with prediction and automatic resumption of the production controller. As in Fig. 3, the prediction unit forecasts the future consequences of the malware, and the hardware monitor again preemptively switches to the backup controller at $t = 280$ ms. The hardware monitor's cool down counter expires and the production controller is reinstated when the malware ends at $t = 650$ ms since 200 ms before this time the physical plant, plant model, and predicted plant state are found to be within specifications. General mechanisms are being developed to manage transitions between controllers in order to avoid excessive overshoot caused by stale state information.

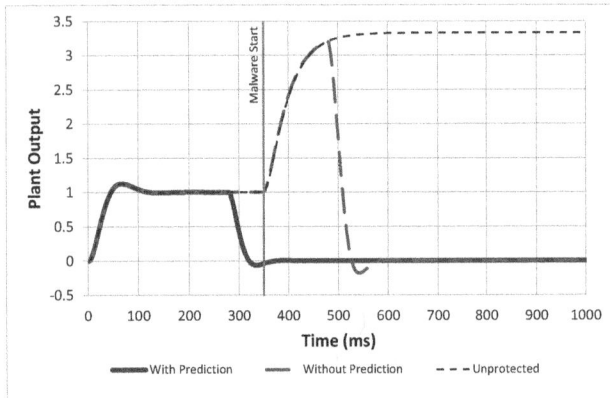

Figure 3: Unprotected and protected plant behavior with and without prediction

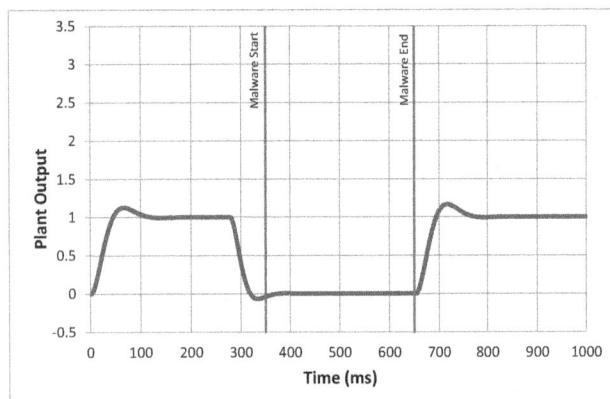

Figure 4: Protected plant behavior with return to the production controller

4.3 Time and Resource Utilization

Performance is not an objective in this work, as the system needs to operate only once per millisecond. The ARM processor operates at 667 MHz; the soft processor and other hardware components operate at 140 MHz. Both processors utilize full optimization and hardware floating point instructions. One iteration of the prediction unit requires 1.43 microseconds to complete. Considering this runtime, the comparatively minimal runtimes of the production controller and hardware monitor and all communication overheads, it is possible to forecast over 500 cycles into the future during each 1 ms system cycle. The resources consumed by the components and the overall system are shown in Table 1.

Table 1: Programmable logic resource usage

	FF	LUT	DSP	BRAM
Hardware Monitor	677	1046	5	0
HLS AXI interfaces	295	78	0	0
Junction Box	70	80	0	0
Prediction Unit	2813	3174	2	4
Total Used	3855	4378	7	4
Available	53200	106400	140	220
Percent Used	7%	4%	5%	2%

5. CONCLUSIONS AND CURRENT WORK

Rather than co-design hardware and software in tightly integrated manner, we instead increase the orthogonality of application-level software and application-specific, security-enforcing hardware at both design-time and run-time. Orthogonality is the common denominator of system reliability, security, and trust. Software, including the OS and drivers, cannot control or configure this autonomic hardware, which monitors software operation at the external I/O level, and may override software decisions if they contravene system-level operating or security specifications. TECEP hardware is developed independently of application-specific software, and is updated only when operational or security specifications change. These attributes allow the autonomic hardware to be rigorously verified without assuming the correctness of application, support, or supervisory software. Hardware synthesis from C code provides high performance, parallel operation with application software, and protection from software vulnerabilities such as buffer overflows.

We are applying TECEP to an electromechanical physical plant possessing non-ideal effects such as noise, disturbances, and actuator limitations. A Kalman filter-based technique will increase the accuracy of system state extrapolations.

6. ACKNOWLEDGMENTS

This material is based on work supported by the National Science Foundation under Grant Number CNS-1222656. Any opinions, findings, and conclusions or recommendations expressed in this material are those of the authors and do not necessarily reflect the views of the National Science Foundation. ZedBoards and tools were donated by Xilinx, Inc.

7. REFERENCES

[1] D. Bagni and D. Mackay. Floating-point PID Controller Design with Vivado HLS and System Generator for DSP, January 2013. XAPP1163 (v1.0).

[2] P. Cuoq, B. Yakobowski, and V. Prevosto. *Frama-C's value analysis plug-in: Fluorine-20130501.* CEA LIST, Software Reliability Laboratory, Saclay, F-91191, 2013. http://frama-c.com.

[3] L. W. Lerner, M. M. Farag, and C. D. Patterson. Run-time prediction and preemption of configuration attacks on embedded process controllers. In *International Conference on Security of Internet of Things (SecurIT 2012)*, Kerala, India, Aug 2012.

[4] C. Marché and Y. Moy. *The Jessie plugin for Deductive Verification in Frama-C.* INRIA Saclay - Télé-de-France and LRI, CNRS UMR 8623, 2013. http://proval.lri.fr/.

Combining Computation and Communication Optimizations in System Synthesis for Streaming Applications

Jason Cong, Muhuan Huang, and Peng Zhang
Computer Science Department, University of University of California, Los Angeles
{cong, mhhuang, pengzh}@cs.ucla.edu

ABSTRACT

Data streaming is a widely-used technique to exploit task-level parallelism in many application domains such as video processing, signal processing and wireless communication. In this paper we propose an efficient system-level synthesis flow to map streaming applications onto FPGAs with consideration of simultaneous computation and communication optimizations. The throughput of a streaming system is significantly impacted by not only the performance and number of replicas of the computation kernels, but also the buffer size allocated for the communications between kernels. In general, module selection/replication and buffer size optimization were addressed separately in previous work. Our approach combines these optimizations together in system scheduling which minimizes the area cost for both logic and memory under the required throughput constraint. We first propose an integer linear program (ILP) based solution to the combined problem which has the optimal quality of results. Then we propose an iterative algorithm which can achieve the near-optimal quality of results but has a significant improvement on the algorithm scalability for large and complex designs. The key contribution is that we have a polynomial-time algorithm for an exact schedulability checking problem and a polynomial-time algorithm to improve the system performance with better module implementation and buffer size optimization. Experimental results show that compared to the separate scheme of module select/replication and buffer size optimization, the combined optimization scheme can gain 62% area saving on average under the same performance requirements. Moreover, our heuristic can achieve 2 to 3 orders of magnitude of speed-up in runtime, with less than 10% area overhead compared to the optimal solution by ILP.

1. INTRODUCTION

A large percentage of real-world applications can be classified as streaming applications, which are becoming increasingly important and widespread. Due to the prevalence of streaming applications, there are extensive studies on system modeling and design techniques. Actor-based streaming modeling is developed to capture the intrinsic features of these applications, such as synchronous data flow models [1]. In this modeling an application is specified as a set of actors connected by communication channels. The parallelism of an application is implicitly specified within the graph model, and can be derived from the data dependencies between the actors, *i.e.*, actors that do not have data dependencies among them can work in parallel. Throughput is an important criterion for evaluating performance of streaming applications. We can implement efficient FIFO-based dedicated and low-cost communication channels on FPGAs to support pipelining and thus improve the system throughput. In addition, we can also design customized computation datapaths for the actors.

How to best utilize the parallelism and regularity of streaming application at design time has recently been a hot research topic. The first common approach to increase the system performance is replicating the actors to exploit the data parallelism. A stateless actor, whose output is fully determined by its input, offers opportunities for data parallelism — replicas of a stateless actor can be executed in parallel. This strategy has been well studied on the multi-core platforms [2, 3, 4, 5, 6, 7, 8]. The general idea is to first perform actor fission and fusion and then allocate the replicas to different processor cores. In the context of FPGA, replication optimization is more complex, because actors have different resource utilizations in terms of look-up tables (LUT) and registers, and they have to share the available on-chip resource. In [9], a heuristic method is proposed which performs maximal replication of all the stateless actors and then iteratively fuses the actors that do not affect the throughput. In general, the replication technique is an easy way to increase throughput. However by simply replicating the actors, not only are the critical computation datapaths replicated, all the non-critical datapaths and control paths are also replicated, which does not necessarily contribute to improving the system performance. To better utilize the FPGA on-chip resources, one should explore different customized actor implementations with the same functionality, rather than rely on the replication technique only. This is a typical module selection problem, as discussed below.

The second approach to increase the system performance focuses on module selection [10, 11, 12, 13, 14]. Given different implementations of each actor, one selects the proper implementations to integrate into the system and schedule the actors to meet the system requirement. A more recent work [15] explores different configurations of application specific instruction set processors (ASIPs) under throughput and latency constraints and proposes an ILP-based solution. However, most of the studies mainly focus on module selection while the design space of module replication, which is essentially useful in the case of FPGAs, is not explored. Recently a combination of module selection and replication in a throughput/area optimization problem was proposed in [16],

FPGA'14, February 26–28, 2014, Monterey, CA, USA.
Copyright 2014 ACM 978-1-4503-2671-1/14/02 ...$15.00.
http://dx.doi.org/10.1145/2554688.2554771 .

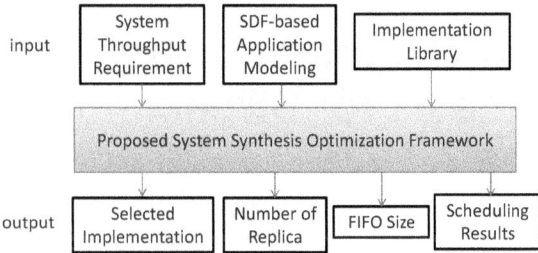

Figure 1: The proposed system synthesis framework.

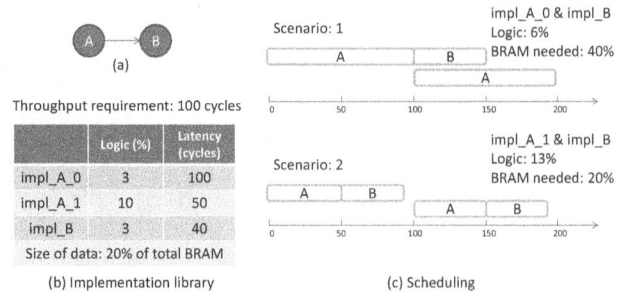

Figure 2: A motivating example. In scenario 1, buffer size is not considered during module selection. The implementation with minimum logic is selected. In scenario 2, buffer size is considered together with module selection. In both cases, these are feasible schedules that can meet the system throughput requirement. However in scenario 2 with the consideration of buffer size, the selected implementation can reduces BRAM use by 20%.

in which an ILP-based formulation is derived to achieve the optimal solution for small- or medium-sized problems.

On the other hand, communication between computation actors is also important for streaming applications in terms of system performance and resource utilization. FIFO is the common communication mechanism used to enable pipelining between actors. FIFO size is one of the key design parameters that needs to be optimized in the system synthesis. It affects the on-chip block RAM (BRAM) utilizations. More importantly, it affects the concurrency of the actor scheduling and thus has a direct impact on system performance. The buffer optimization problem is known to be NP-complete [17]. [18] formulates the buffer size constraints directly on the SDF graph. The buffer size requirement on communication channels is imposed on the SDF graph by adding additional backward channels. The number of initial tokens corresponds to the FIFO size. Thus the original application model that does not the consider the FIFO size is transformed into a new model which contains the scheduling constraints imposed by the given FIFO size.

Several approaches have been proposed to optimize the buffer utilization under certain design metrics [19, 20]. Integer linear programming is used to obtain the minimal buffer size for synchronous data flow(SDF) [19] and homogeneous synchronous data flow (HSDF) [20] respectively. But these methods are limited to the maximal throughput scheduling which is not efficient in exploring the different performance and area trade-off options. Some researchers [21, 22] use a model checking technique to efficiently explore the state-space of the SDF graph. But the complexity of these methods is relatively high, especially for the graphs with large amount of state transitions. In addition, they minimize buffer size just for a deadlock-free scheduling without considering actual performance. [18] proposed an efficient way to explore the Pareto-curve of the buffer size and throughput by pruning the design space without losing the Pareto points, where throughput is calculated by an eager simulation of the periodic execution, and buffer size distribution is incrementally explored according to the storage dependencies. A recent work [23] modeled the buffer size directly in the analytic model and proposed an efficient heuristic based on it. But it works only on acyclic SDFs and does not prove optimal or near-optimal in large graphs. In all of this set of work, actor optimizations like module selection and replication are assumed to be a separate preprocessing or postprocessing stage. This may lose the optimality in finding the scheduling for both actor and buffer optimization.

Other related work includes [24] where a simulator is adopted to evaluate different dataflow architectures for streaming applications. Our problem is a subset of their's since in our architecture we only consider FIFO interfaces. With our simplified architecture, we are able to quickly decide the selected modules without resorting to a simulator. Outside of

streaming context, a computation and communication co-optimization framework is studied in [25]. It combines data-reuse optimization using a scratchpad and loop-level parallelism optimization into a singe framework and formulate it into an integer geometric programming problem. This is a module-level optimization and does not apply to our problem directly.

Learning from the existing work, we observe that system design for streaming applications is still facing two major challenges: (1) System design results are determined by a complicated combination of different design aspects (module selection, module replication, buffer size optimization, scheduling and allocation), but current automation frameworks always take single or limited aspects into considerations. (2) Considering all these comprehensive design objectives and constraints makes the existing algorithms either non-scalable for large and complex designs, or difficult to achieve comparable quality of results with the optimal solutions.

In this paper we propose a novel system synthesis approach to tackling the above two issues. We formulate the module selection, module replication, buffer size optimization and scheduling simultaneously into one single optimization framework, considering the trade-offs among system throughput, logic and on-chip memory utilization. The proposed framework is shown in Fig. 1. It takes the system throughput requirement, application model, and an implementation library as inputs and outputs the module selection/replication results, FIFO size and a feasible schedule. Within the framework, an efficient solving algorithm is presented which achieves both high-quality design (i.e. low logic/BRAM costs within the throughput constraints) and scalability.

The remainder of this paper is organized as follows. Section 2 gives a motivation example which shows the benefit of combining computation and communication optimizations in system synthesis. Section 3 presents the abstraction model of streaming application and the concept of scheduling iteration within the model. Section 4 provides a detailed analytic formulation of the scheduling constraints and objectives for module selection, module replication and buffer size optimizations. Section 5 proposes an efficient iterative algorithm to find the solution to the combined optimization problem. Experimental results are shown in Section 6, where

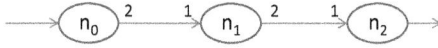

Figure 3: An example of SDFGs. Producer/consumer rates are labeled at the beginning/end of the edges.

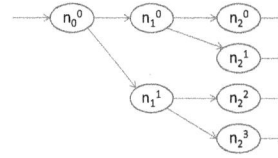

Figure 4: The HSDFG converted from SDFG in Fig. 3.

both design quality and run-time complexity are measured with streaming benchmarks.

2. A MOTIVATION EXAMPLE

Fig. 2 gives a motivational example. We show a very simple case in streaming applications in Fig. 2(a), where A is the producer actor and B is the consumer actor. A and B are executed repeatedly.

The implementation options are listed in Fig. 2(b). Actor A has two implementations, impl_A_0 and impl_A_1, which show the trade-offs between the logic cost and execution latency. Actor B has only one fixed implementation. Each of actor A's executions produce a fixed size of data to the communication channel. We assume the size is 20% of the FPGA on-chip memory. Each of actor B's executions consume the same amount of data from the communication channel. The system throughput target is set to one execution of A and B in every 100 cycles.

In Fig. 2(c) scenario 1 , we decouple the computation and communication optimizations by first considering module selection without considering buffer size. The solution with minimal logic utilization is considered to be the optimal one. Then the scheduling that has the minimum buffer size requirement is calculated afterwards. Therefore, in the optimal solution, impl_A_0 and impl_B are selected. Then in this case, we need to double the data buffer size which takes 40% BRAM resource, since a second execution of A has to be overlapped with the first execution of B in order to meet the throughput constraint. And the second execution of A has already started before the first execution of B finishes. In Fig. 2(c) scenario 2, we consider buffer size optimization together with module selection. In this case, a slightly large implementation of A is selected which can significantly improve the performance of actor A (at the cost of 7% logic increase compared to scenario 1). Then we do not have to execute A and B in parallel. When the second execution of A starts, the first execution of B has finished and the communication channel is empty. Thus, the needed buffer size is only 20% of total BRAM.

From the example we see that we cannot take computation optimizations (module selction/replication) and communication (buffer size) optimizations as two separate steps. Thus, in this work we propose to combine computation and communication optimizations together during system synthesis.

3. APPLICATION MODEL

In this section we present synchronous data flow graphs and homogeneous synchronous data flow graphs which are used to model streaming applications, and we define system throughput from the graphs.

3.1 Synchronous Data Flow Graph

Synchronous data flow graphs (SDFGs) [1] have been traditionally used to model streaming applications. In an SDFG $G(V, E)$, each node $v \in V$ (also called an actor) represents a computation kernel. Each edge $u \to v$ represents a data communication channel from node u to v. The amount of data tokens consumed and produced by a computation kernel is determined at design time, and is usually referred to

as the producer rate and the consumer rate. For example, in Fig. 3, the producer rate and consumer rate for actor n_1 is 2 and 1 respectively. When an actor starts its firing/execution, it removes the number of tokens that equals the consumer rate from its input channels. At the end of a firing/execution, the actor produces the number of tokens that equals the producer rate to its output channels. We model the data consumption and production process as an atomic process where the number of tokens on a channel will only be changed at the beginning or at the end of an actor firing. Such a fixed producer rate and consumer rate make it easier to analyze and predict the timing behavior of complex streaming applications, and this is the main reason that SDFGs are used.

The execution of an SDFG is defined in terms of actor firings:

DEFINITION 1. *A **periodic execution schedule** or iteration of an SDFG is a set of actor firings such that after all these firings, the SDFG returns to the same state, i.e., the number of tokens on each channel remains the same before or after an iteration.*

The number of actor firings in one periodic execution schedule is called the repetition factor vector q [26]. In Fig. 3, actors n_1, n_2 and n_3 fire 1, 2 and 4 times respectively to maintain a data balance between producer and consumer actors. Therefore, the corresponding repetition factor vector q is [1;2;4]. Note that it is possible that the execution of SDFGs results in deadlock or an infinite number of accumulated tokens on the channels. Such a system is called an inconsistent system, and it is beyond the scope of this work.

The *periodic execution schedule* is very important in analyzing system throughput for streaming applications. Streaming applications usually perform computation on a very long data sequence (which is typically assumed to be infinite). It is costly to adopt an irregular scheduling for each of the repeated actor firings. Since SDFG has a periodic behavior in actor firings, it's reasonable to have a periodic scheduling.

Note that in the context of SDF, communication channels are often referred to as buffers. In the context of FPGA implementations, communication channels are often referred to as FIFOs. In this paper we do not distinguish between these two.

3.2 Homogeneous Synchronous Data Flow Graph

An SDFG can be transformed into an equivalent single-rate data flow graph, which is called a homogeneous synchronous data flow graph (HSDFG) [1]. In HSDFG, all the actor firings in one iteration are explicitly enumerated. Fig. 4 shows the HSDFG converted from the SDFG in Fig. 3. There are two firings of actor n_1 (n_1^0 and n_1^1) and four firings of actor n_2 ($n_2^i, 0 \le i < 4$). Edges in HSDFG represent data dependency between producers and consumers. For example, n_1^0 and n_1^1 can start to work only after n_0^0 finishes and produces one data to each of them, so there are data dependency edges between them.

We find it easier to start from the HSDFG (instead of the SDFG) when modeling scheduling constraints since all the actor firings have been enumerated in the graph. Thus, given an application that is modeled in an SDFG, we will first transform it into an HSDFG by using the conversion algorithm in [27]. As detailed in Sec. 4.2 , we will add a new set of edges onto HSDFGs later to reflect the scheduling constraints.

3.3 Throughput Definition

In this work throughput is viewed as a constraint for streaming applications. Denote n_i^j as the jth firing of actor n_i in the first iteration. We associate each actor firing n_i^j in the scheduling graph with a start firing time t_i^j, which denotes when the firing can start. We also refer to t_i^j as scheduling variables.

Throughput is defined as how often the actor firing n_i^j can start a firing again. Particularly in the scheduling graph, throughput is defined as follows:

$$Throughput = \frac{1}{t'^j_i - t_i^j}, \qquad (1)$$

where t'^j_i denotes the start firing time of the jth firing of actor t_i in the following iteration.

4. SYSTEM MAPPING

Table 1: Denotation of variables

parameters	meaning
n_i^j	jth firing of actor n_i
n'^j_i	jth firing of actor n_i in 2nd iteration
Lib_n	implementation library for actor n
P_n^s	implementation in library Lib_n
$A(P_n^s)$	area cost of P_n^s
$et(P_n^s)$	execution time of P_n^s
$\delta(P_n^s)$	initiation interval of P_n^s
Thr_{tar}	throughput target
variables (unknown)	meaning
t_i^j	start firing time of n_i^j, scheduling variables
t'^j_i	start firing time of n_i^j in 2nd iteration, scheduling variables
b_n^s	if implementation P_n^s is selected
rep_n	number of replicas for each module

With the modeling of application behavior in the HSDF graph, our system mapping problem can be defined as the following:

Given application modeling in an HSDF graph consisting of actor firings n_i^j as nodes and data dependencies between actor firings as edges, the target throughput requirement Thr_{tar}, and implementation options P_n^s for each actor with the logic cost $A(P_n^s)$, execution latency $et(P_n^s)$, and pipeline initial interval $\delta(P_n^s)$, we find the optimized module selection results P_n^{sel} and replication factors rep_n for each actor, the total FIFO size, and the periodic scheduling t_i^j for each actor firing. The BRAM and logic utilization on FPGA is minimized under the given system throughput constraint.

A list of the denotations used in the following sections of the paper can be found in Table. 1.

In this section we discuss the problem of mapping HSD-FGs onto FPGAs. First, we generate an FPGA implementation library for each actor which realizes the functionality of streaming application kernels. Second, given the selected

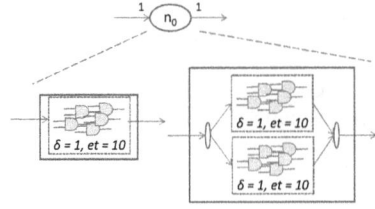

Figure 5: An example of module replication. Module throughput can be further improved by duplicating the modules and adding the corresponding split and join logic.

modules, we formulate all the scheduling constraints and delineate them as new edges on the HSDFG. We refer to the HSDFG with scheduling constraints as the scheduling graph. Last, we formally state the whole system synthesis framework, which contains module selection/replication, buffer size optimization and scheduling. An ILP formulation is presented throughout this section to capture the optimal solution. We present a scalable and efficient near-optimal algorithm in Sec. 5.

4.1 Implementation Library Constraints

In realizing streaming applications onto FPGAs, by setting different optimization configurations we can generate a set of "functionally equivalent" implementations that differ in area and performance. Usually a significant area saving can be achieved by using slower implementations. In terms of performance, hardware implementations can differ in initiation interval (δ) and latency (et). Initiation interval specifies to what extent the hardware module can be pipelined. Latency specifies execution time of the hardware module. It is the time interval between the time point when an actor starts firing and the time point when the actor finishes its firing and produces data tokens to its output channels.

In streaming applications, initiation interval means the number of cycles that the two consecutive firings, which are mapped to the same module, need to be separated by. An initiation interval $\delta = 1$ indicates a fully pipelined module with a new firing initiated every clock cycle. Hardware modules with a smaller δ, and thus with a higher throughput, are usually achieved at a larger area cost because a smaller δ reduces many resource-sharing opportunities. For the same reason, hardware modules with a smaller et require more logic for parallel computing since the logic can not be shared if they are used in parallel.

Module replication techniques can further improve the module throughput even when δ has decreased to 1. Fig. 5 shows an example of module replication. The actor consumes one data token and produces one data token on each firing. Assume we already have a module that achieves $\delta = 1$ and $et = 10$ and we replicate it into two copies. Then from a system point of view, such an implementation consumes and produces two data tokens on each firing in every clock cycle. Note that additional split and join logic is needed here to distribute the data to different modules in a round-robin fashion.

Several commercial C-to-FPGA high-level synthesis tools now provide the ability to synthesize hardware modules with a specified pipeline level and parallelism level. For example, the initiation interval and loop unrolling factor can both be specified for a loop. FPGA synthesis tools can also provide an estimation of area usage, initiation interval and latency of the current synthesized hardware modules. Thus, given a C program for streaming applications, we can quickly generate different hardware implementations by altering the design

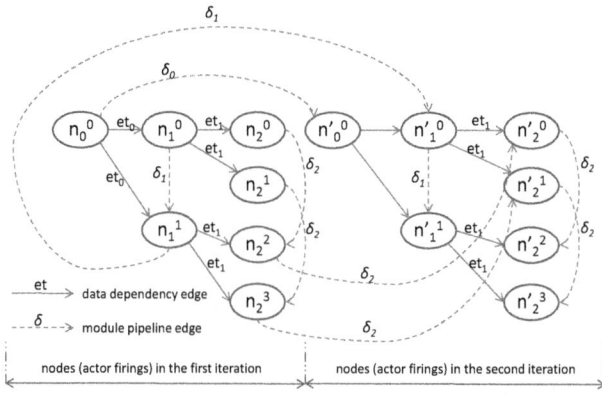

Figure 6: Scheduling graph for SDFG in Fig. 3. It contains all the actor firings in two iterations. Detailed explanations of the edges can be found in Sec. 4.2.

configurations, and build up a library of implementations. In addition, to save development cost, we can also adopt IPs (*e.g.* FFT) cores provided by FPGA vendors into our implementation library. In this work, granularity of a module is defined by users — it can be a few instructions for the smallest module or multiple loops for a large module.

The implementation alternatives are formulated as the following: For each actor n, the implementation library is Lib_n ($P_n^1, P_n^2, ...P_n^{S_n}$), where each implementation P_n^s in Lib_n can perform the functionality of n with area cost $A(P_n^s)$, initiation interval $\delta(P_n^s)$, and execution time $et(P_n^s)$. S_n denotes the number of implementations we have for actor n. P_n^{sel} denotes the selected implementation from the library. A binary variable b_n^s is introduced to denote if P_n^s is selected. Thus, $A(P_n^{sel})$, $\delta(P_n^{sel})$ and $et(P_n^{sel})$ (area costs, initiation interval and latency of the selected modules respectively) can be formulated as the following:

$$A(P_n^{sel}) = rep_n \cdot \sum_s b_n^s \cdot A(P_n^s)$$

$$\delta(P_n^{sel}) = \sum_s b_n^s \cdot \delta(P_n^s)$$

$$et(P_n^{sel}) = \sum_s b_n^s \cdot et(P_n^s)$$

$$\sum_s b_n^s = 1,$$

where rep_n denotes the number of replicas for the selected implementation.

4.2 Scheduling Constraints

In order to model a periodic scheduling, [16] proposed to depict the throughput constraint on two consecutive SDF iterations. Therefore, we unfold the HSDFG twice to include all the actor firings in two iterations, as shown in Fig. 6. We also add edges to delineate the hardware dependencies and communication buffer constraints. We call this type of graph a **scheduling graph**.

DEFINITION 2. *A **scheduling graph** is a graph $G(V, E)$, consisting of a set of actor firings in two iterations and a set of edges including data dependency edges, module pipeline edges and buffer-constrained edges(explained in detail below).*

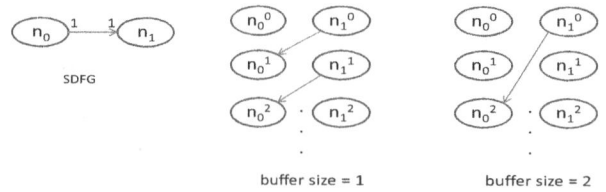

Figure 7: An example of buffer-constrained edges. An SDFG is shown on the left. Buffer-constrained edges are shown in the scheduling graph when buffer size is 1 and 2 respectively. The producer rate and consumer rate is 1.

In the scheduling graph, node n_i^j denotes the jth firing of the actor n_i. We would map each actor firing to a hardware module. Actor firings that perform the same computation can share the same hardware implementation. For example, actor firings n_2^j and $n_2'^j$ ($j = 0, 1, 2, 3$) are all performing the same computation task, and thus can be mapped to the same module.

We associate a weight for each edge in the scheduling graph. The weight denotes the number of cycles that the two firings connected by this edge need to be separated by. The edges can be divided into three categories:

Data dependency edges: Edge weight equals execution latency (et) of the hardware module that the predecessor[1] of this edge is mapped to. These are the edges between the firings of different actors. They reflect the producer-consumer relations where the successor cannot start firing until the predecessor has finished its firing. For example, the weight of the edge between n_1^0 and n_2^0 is the execution time of the hardware module for n_1^0, since n_2^0 cannot start firing until n_1^0 produces the data to the communication channel. We use FIFOs as data communication channels.

Module pipeline edges: Edge weight equals initiation interval (δ) of the hardware module. These are the edges between the firings that are mapped to the same hardware module. They need to be separated by δ cycles since a hardware module can only start to process a new firing every δ cycles. When the number of replicas for an actor is more than one, we adopt the cyclic scheduling policy to assign firings to the hardware module. The cyclic scheduling policy works in a round-robin fashion that always assigns a firing to the first available hardware module. For example, if the number of replicas is two, then all the even-numbered firings are assigned to the first module and all the odd-numbered firings are assigned to the second module. In Fig. 6, we assume two copies of hardware modules are selected for actor n_2; thus firings n_2^0, n_2^2, $n_2'^0$ and $n_2'^2$ are mapped to one module, and the other firings of n_2 are mapped to the other module. In Fig. 6, the corresponding edges are added between n_2^0, n_2^2, $n_2'^0$ and $n_2'^2$ with weight equal to δ_2.

Similar to [16], the detailed formulations of the module pipeline edges are as follows:

$$t_i^{j_2} - t_i^{j_1} \geq \begin{cases} \delta(P_{n_i}^{sel}), \, if \, j_2 - j_1 = rep_n \\ 0, \quad otherwise \end{cases} \quad (2)$$

where $t_i^{j_2}$ and $t_i^{j_1}$ denote the j_2th and j_1th firings of actor n_i.

Buffer-constrained edges: In the representation of constraints in [16], the impact of buffer size on scheduling is not modeled. Here we model the scheduling constraints imposed

---
[1]If there exists a directed edge e from u to v, we call u the predecessor, and v the successor of edge e.

by buffer size as buffer-constrained edges. The edge weight of a buffer-constrained edge equals the execution latency (et) of the consumer task. Given a buffer size between the producer actor and consumer actor, we can derive a set of scheduling constraints among the producer and consumer actor firings. Consumer actors should fire in time to consume the data tokens so that the data tokens in the communication channel will not increase in a cumulative manner and exceed the capacity of the buffer. We adopt a conservative model as in [18] where the buffer space to produce output data token is assumed to be available at the beginning of the actor firing.

Given produce actor n_0 and consumer actor n_1, we add an edge from n_1^j (jth firing of n_1) to n_0^i (ith firing of n_0), if the following equation holds:

$$j = \min\{k|(i+1)*p - (k+1)*c \le buf\}, \qquad (3)$$

where p is the producer rate and c is the consumer rate. buf is the given buffer size. $(i+1)*p$ is the number of produced data tokens, and $(k+1)*c$ is the consumed data tokens. (It is not $i*p$ since in our model label i starts from 0.) The intuition is that enough data tokens should have been consumed before the ith firing of the producer n_0. Fig. 7 shows an example. If the buffer size is only 1, then actor n_0^1 cannot start firing until n_1^0 finishes, which consumes the data in the FIFO. If the buffer size is 2, then actor n_0^1 can always start firing regardless of actor n_1^0. The detailed ILP formulation for buffer-constrained edges is omitted here due to page limitation.

4.3   Problem Statement

The design space exploration problem for streaming applications requires selecting implementations from the library for each actor under throughput constraint while minimizing the total area cost. To meet the throughput target, the selected hardware implementations from the libraries can be replicated.

Given a scheduling graph $G(V, E)$ and $n_{i1}^j, n_{i2}^k \in V, e(n_{i1}^j \to n_{i2}^k) \in E$ denotes an edge between the jth firing of actor n_{i1} and kth firing of actor n_{i2}. Based on our discussion in Sec. 4.2, weight $w(e)$ of the edge $e(n_{i1}^j \to n_{i2}^k)$ can be derived as

$$w(e) = \begin{cases} et(P_{n_{i1}}^{sel}), & \text{if } e \text{ is data dependency edge} \\ \delta(P_{n_{i1}}^{sel}), & \text{if } e \text{ is module pipeline edge} \\ et(P_{n_{i1}}^{sel}), & \text{if } e \text{ is buffer} - constrained\ edge \end{cases} \qquad (4)$$

where $P_{n_{i1}}^{sel}$ is the selected implementation from the actor n_{i1}'s library. Although the formulation of the data dependency edge and the buffer-constrained edge look similar, the difference is that a buffer-constrained edge is an edge from a consumer node to the producer node, while a data dependence edge is an edge from a producer node to a consumer node. Our design space exploration problem can be described as the following:

Input: (1) Scheduling graph $G(V, E)$ of the streaming applications, (2) throughput target Thr_{tar}, and (3) the implementation libraries.

Output: (1) Selected implementation P_n^{sel} from the library for each actor n, (2) number of replicas rep_n^{sel}, (3) buffer size for each communication channel, and (4) start firing time t_i^j for each actor firing n_i^j.

The selected implementations should satisfy the following constraints:

Constraints:

$$\forall e(n_{i1}^j \to n_{i2}^k) \in E,\ t_{i2}^k - t_{i1}^j \ge w(e), \qquad (5)$$

$$\forall n_i^j \in V,\ t_i'^j - t_i^j = c, \qquad (6)$$

$$c = \frac{1}{Thr_{tar}}. \qquad (7)$$

Optimization goal:

$$minimize : \frac{BufSize}{TotalBufSize} + \frac{Logic}{TotalLogic} \qquad (8)$$

Constraint (5) ensures the precedence of actor firings. Constraints (6) and (7) guarantee that the schedule is periodic and should meet the system throughput. Variable denotations are listed in Table 1 for references. Buffers can be implemented as on-chip block RAM, and hardware modules are implemented using slices. The area metric we used here is the sum of occupied percentages of buffer and logic. The optimization goal can be extended to other area metrics as well. Note that we do not consider the BRAM utilization of the modules. In fact, we assume that modules can always use distributed RAM instead of BRAM whenever possible. This is easy to achieve in many high-level synthesis tools where resource types are explicitly defined by users.

Previous work [16] tries to solve a subset of the above problem with an integer linear program (ILP) formulation where module selection/replication is performed concurrently with scheduling. However, buffer size is not considered in that formulation. Moreover, ILP has an exponential worst-case complexity which may have scalability problems in complex designs. In Sec. 5, we present an efficient iterative exploration algorithm to solve the overall problem.

5.   PROPOSED APPROACH: ST-SYN

In this section we present our algorithm called ST-Syn (streaming synthesis), as summarized in Algorithm 1. It is an iterative exploration algorithm that contains schedulability checking and efficient implementation improvement techniques. The algorithm starts from an implementation that utilizes the minimum logic and buffer size. For each computation kernel, the implementation with the smallest area is selected. Number of replicas is set as 1. The buffer size is set to the larger value between the producer rate and the consumer rate, which is the least buffer size required by both the producer actor and the consumer actor to fire. Given such configurations, we try to schedule all the actor firings under the performance requirement. If the schedulability check fails, we try to improve the implementation by either selecting a faster implementation or increasing the buffer size. We repeat the schedulability checking and implementation improvement process until the system performance can be satisfied.

More specifically, the schedulability checking is formulated as a *system of difference constraints* (SDC) problem. Implementation improvement is formulated as a minimum cut problem in a weighted penalty graph. Both of these problems can be solved in polynomial time using LP relaxation with integer solution guaranteed.

5.1   Schedulability Checking

In this section we show that schedulability checking can be formulated as a system of difference constraints, and thus can be done in polynomial time. As discussed in Section 4.2, given selected hardware modules and buffer size, we can add the data dependency edges, module pipeline edges and buffer-constrained edges in the scheduling graph, thus finalizing the graph structure as well as the edge weights. The only unknown variables are the scheduling variables t_i^j.

Algorithm 1: ST-Syn Overall Algorithm

1 Step 1: Update the scheduling graph with newly selected hardware modules or newly allocated buffer size (*e.g.,* update the edge weight).

2 Step 2: Schedulability checking process. Check if there is a feasible schedule that can satisfy the system throughput given the current setting of modules and buffer size. If not, go to Step 3. Otherwise terminate.

3 Step 3: Module/Buffer size improvement. Go to Step 1.

The edges in the scheduling graph represent the scheduling constraints. We can mathematically model the scheduling constraints as a set of *difference constraints*. Using the definition in [28], *difference constraints* is defined as follows:

DEFINITION 3. *An integer difference constraint is a formula in the form of $x - y \leq w$ for integer variables x and y, and constant w.*

The schedulability check problem is to determine whether there is a solution satisfying the constraints (5), (6) and (7). Note that in constraints (5), $w(e)$ is now a known value since we already decided the module implementations and buffer size.

LEMMA 1. *SDC-based schedulability checking can be solved in polynomial time.*

Proof is based on the results in [28]. Although t_i^j and t'^j_i are integer variables, schedulability check can be solved in polynomial time using linear programming relaxation. This is because the underlying matrix for SDC is a *totally unimodular* matrix [28]. Thus, if there is a feasible solution under linear programming relaxation, it is also a feasible integer solution.

5.2 Iterative Improvement

Algorithm 2: Iterative Improvement

1 Step 1: Identify ϵ-critical paths in the scheduling graph.

2 Step 2: Associate an area penalty with each edge.

3 Step 3: Perform a min-cut on the graph.

Algorithm. 2 shows our iterative improvement algorithm. When the current settings of hardware modules and buffer size cannot meet the system throughput target, we need to either find a "better" module (a faster module or a larger number of replicas) which can contribute to system performance, or increase the buffer size of the communication channels. We do so by first identifying the bottlenecks in the system. The current system is delineated as a weighted directed scheduling graph, and scheduling bottlenecks can be viewed as critical paths in the graph.

DEFINITION 4. *The **critical path** of the scheduling graph $G(V,E)$ as the longest path among all the paths between node n_i^j and node n'^j_i, $\forall i, j, n_i^j \in V, n'^j_i \in V$.*

The general idea here is that the newly selected modules or buffer size should be able to contribute to the system performance in the sense that the length of the critical path is decreased. For the efficiency of the algorithm, instead of identifying a single critical path, we adopt the network flow theorem to find all the ϵ-critical paths ([29]) in the system.

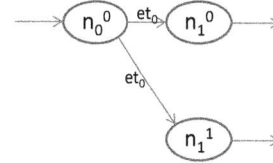

Figure 8: An example of part of an ϵ-critical path. An improved hardware module of n_0 will contribute to both paths in the graph.

DEFINITION 5. *Denote the length of the critical path of the scheduling graph is L. The ϵ-**critical paths** of the scheduling graph $G(V,E)$ are the set of paths between node n_i^j and node n'^j_i whose length is $L(1-\epsilon), \forall i, j, n_i^j \in V, n'^j_i \in V$.*

Then for each edge on the ϵ-critical paths, we calculate the area penalty needed to improve this edge. (a) If the edge is a data dependency edge, then we can select a module with a smaller execution latency from the implementation library. (b) If the edge is a module pipeline edge, then we can select a module with a smaller initiation interval or we can increase the number of replicas. (c) If the edge is a buffer-constrained edge, then we can increase the buffer size by $gcd\{p, q\}$ (the greatest common divider between the producer rate and consumer rate). It is shown in [18] that buffer size should be a multiple of $gcd\{p, q\}$ to be used usefully. Area penalty is calculated as the increased percentages of logic or buffer utilization. To assign a fair penalty to each edge, in both case (a) and (b), we require that the newly selected module be able to reduce the critical path by at least Δ. And Δ can be used to adjust the convergence speed of the algorithm.

The ϵ-critical paths and the associated weight (area penalty) on the edges form a weighted directed graph. Denote such a graph as $H(V,E)$. We perform a minimum cut on the graph so that all the critical paths can be improved and the total area penalty is minimum.

The **minimum cut** problem is formulated as follows. Associate each node in the graph $H(V,E)$ with a variable p_i. p_s and p_t denote the variables for the source and sink node. Associate each edge $(i, j) \in E$ with a binary variable d_{ij} to indicate whether this edge is cut or not. Let c_{ij} denote the edge weight. Thus the problem constraints are:

$$\begin{aligned}
d_{ij} - p_i + p_j &\geq 0, \quad (i,j) \in E \\
p_s &= 1 \\
p_t &= 0 \\
p_i &\geq 0, \quad i \in V \\
d_{ij} &\geq 0, \quad (i,j) \in E \quad (9)
\end{aligned}$$

Note that d_{ij} is not explicitly specified as a binary variable in the constraints. Nevertheless, we will show later that such relaxation can still guarantee that d_{ij} is binary.

The tricky part is how to formulate the optimization goal. It is not simply a summation of $d_{ij} * c_{ij}$. This is because improvement of one hardware module/buffer will have an effect on multiple edges in the ϵ-critical paths. For example, in Fig. 8, assume both edges from n_0^0 to n_1^0 and n_1^1 are on the ϵ-critical path; to decrease the edge weight, a faster module of n_0 will be selected. The area penalty would be the same on both edges. Let us denote it as ap_0. Thus, if a min-cut cuts through both these two edges, then the total area penalty should be ap_0, rather than $2 * ap_0$, since only one module is improved. In this case, the optimization goal can be formulated as $max\{d_0 * ap_0, d_1 * ap_0\}$, where d_0 and d_1

are the binary variables to denote whether these two edges are cut or not in the min-cut.

Generally, we can divide the edges in $H(V, E)$ into several sets ϕ_k. The edges that require improvement of the same module/buffer are grouped into the same set ϕ_k. Thus, the optimization goal of the min-cut problem is:

$$\sum_k \max_{(i,j) \in \phi_k} d_{ij} * c_{ij}. \tag{10}$$

The above optimization goal is convex and the underlying matrix is *totally unimodular*. Thus the problem can be solved by LP relaxation with integer solution guaranteed.

LEMMA 2. *The minimum cut problem (constraints in (9) and objective in (10)) can be solved in polynomial time.*

5.3 Update Scheduling Graph

When a new implementation or number of replicas is selected, or a new buffer size is allocated, we need to update the scheduling graph: (1) Module pipeline edges are deleted and new edges are added as the number of replicas changes. For example, assume that originally the number of replicas is two, then there is a module pipeline edge between every two actor firings. When the number of replicas changes to 3, there should be such an edge between every three actor firings. (2) Module pipeline edge weights are changed to initiation intervals of the newly selected modules. (3) Data dependency edge weights are changed to the execution time of the newly selected modules of the producer actor. (4) Buffer-constrained edges are updated as buffer size changes. The edge weight is changed to the execution time of the newly selected modules of the consumer actor.

Note that we will add buffer-constrained edges into the scheduling graph after we add all the data dependency and module pipeline edges. The reason is that adding buffer-constrained edges may result in cycles in the scheduling graph. If a cycle is detected, then no feasible schedule exists. In this case, we continue to increase the buffer size. Intuitively, if the buffer size is large enough, no buffer-constrained edges will need to be added into the scheduling graph.

5.4 Complexity of ST-Syn

In each iteration we perform a scheduling graph update, schedulability checking, and module improvement. For each kind of edge (data dependency, module pipeline and buffer-constrained), the maximum number of edges is $O(V^2)$, where V is the number of nodes (actor firings in the scheduling graph). Thus, complexity of the scheduling graph update is polynomial to the number of edges in the system. Together with theorem 1 and theorem 2, we can obtain the following theorem:

THEOREM 1. *Each iteration of ST-Syn takes polynomial time.*

To avoid oscillation during the iterative improvement, we adopt a simple heuristic where a selected hardware candidate will be excluded from the implementation library. A hardware candidate refers to both the selected hardware module and the number of replicas. It means that in the current iteration, if implementation P_n^i is selected with the number of its replicas equal to r, then in any following iterations, P_n^i can no longer be selected with the number of replicas equal to r. However, we still allow P_n^i to be selected if the number of replicas is not equal to r. Thus, the algorithm is guaranteed to converge since there are only limited design points to explore.

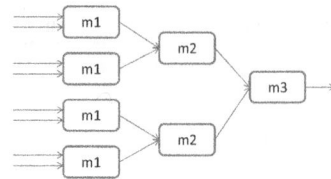

Figure 9: An example of merge sort to sort 8 values. $m1$ takes one value from each of its two input channels, reorders the two values and then sends them out to $m2$. $m2$ takes two values from each of its two input channels, merges them into one sorted stream that contains 4 values. $m3$ works in a similar fashion and outputs a sorted stream that contains 8 values.

6. EXPERIMENTS

In this section we discuss two case studies for evaluating our algorithms. The first case is a FIFO-based merge-sort. FIFO-based merge sort is shown to be a high-performance sorting architecture on FPGAs for large sorting problems [30]. The design is bounded by communication resources. Thus it is a BRAM dominate design. The second case is MPEG-4 where the logic and BRAM utilizations are comparable under different system performance requirements.

We implement three methods: (1) ILP_Separate, the ILP formulation in [16] which solves the module selection/replication problems without considering buffer size, and then the required buffer size is minimized according to the system scheduling result of the computation optimization. (2) ILP_Buf, an integrated ILP formulation that combines module selection, replication and buffer size optimizations. (3) Our proposed ST-Syn algorithm.

6.1 Settings

The high-level synthesis tool *Vivado_HLS* from Xilinx (version 2013.2) is used to perform the estimation of performance and resource usage. We argue that detailed logic synthesis in physical design, although providing us with accurate performance and resource usage information for the hardware design, is too time-consuming, and thus not suitable for use in the early stage of hardware design. To generate different hardware modules for each actor, we adopt several design techniques, such as (1) loop unrolling, (2) loop pipelining, (3) array partitioning, and (4) software pipelining. Each implementation has three attributes: initiation interval, execution time, and area cost. Initiation interval and execution time can be retrieved from the *Vivado_HLS* synthesis report. The area metric we use is a combination of the on-chip resources (*i.e.*, FF and LUT for computation, and block RAM for data communication). The logic utilization is estimated as the maximal value between FF utilization and LUT utilization. The area metric used in the ILP objective function is the sum of logic utilization and BRAM utilization. Thus the area cost is reduced whenever BRAM or logic consumption reduces. The target platform in hardware design is Zynq XC7Z020, and the target FPGA clock cycle is set at 100M Hz.

The ILP solver we use is GLPK [31]. If the ILP solver fails to achieve the optimal results within two hours, we use the suboptimal result returned from the solver, which is the best solution that it can get in two hours.

6.2 FIFO-based Merge Sort

FIFO-based merge sort [30] contains a cascaded chain of merge kernels. Each merge kernel merges two sorted streams of data into a single sorted stream. Fig. 9 shows an exam-

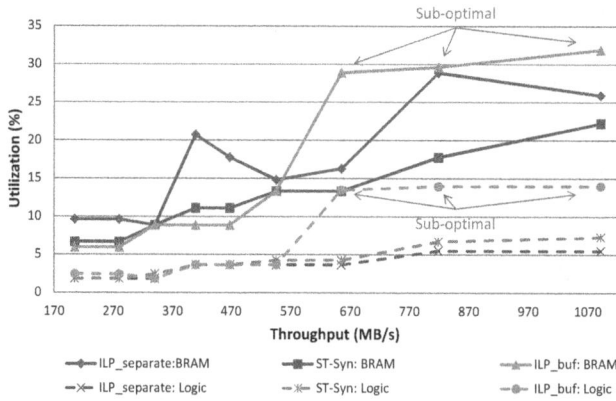

Figure 10: FIFO-based merge sort: area utilization (logic & BRAM) under different throughput settings. 16384 values are merged. Runtime of ILP_buf is limited to up to 2 hours, and thus ILP_buf only generates sub-optimal results.

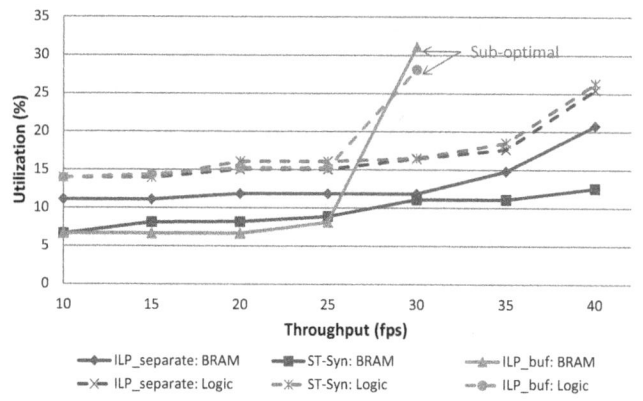

Figure 11: MPEG4: area utilization under different throughput settings. Runtime of ILP_buf is limited up to 2 hours. ILP_buf does not return a feasible integer solution at 2 hours when throughput is 35 fps and 40 fps.

ple. All the data produced are first streamed into FIFOs before the consumer starts to process it. Thus the FIFO size increases as the size of sorting problems increases.

Fig. 10 shows the area utilization under different throughput settings. Results from ILP_separate, ILP_buf and ST-Syn are all shown in the figure. The following are some resource usage numbers from this set of experiments:

(1) The BRAM utilization (resource for communication channels) is much larger than the logic utilization. Variation of logic utilization (range: 2% to 8%) under different throughput is much smaller compare to the variation of BRAM utilization (range: 5% to 30%). Therefore, it is important to consider buffer size optimizations together with module selection and replication in system synthesis. Moreover, we can see from the gap between ILP_buf:BRAM and ILP_separate:BRAM curves that the BRAM usage overhead of ILP_Separate is 62% compared to ILP_buf. (BRAM overhead is calculated as: (BRAM utilization of ILP_separate - BRAM utilization of ILP_buf)/(BRAM utilization of ILP_buf). Logic overhead is calculated in the same fashion.)

(2) The proposed ST-Syn can achieve near-optimal quality of results. BRAM usage overhead of ST-Syn is only 12% on average. Runtime of ST-Syn is less than 1 second in all cases.

(3) In terms of total area cost (logic + BRAM), the overhead of ILP_separate and ST-Syn are 41.3% and 7.9% compared to ILP_buf respectively.

Moreover, there are several observations that match our expectations:

(4) Logic utilization does not strictly correlate with the system performance requirement. For example, comparing the second point and third point on the ILP_buf curve, we can see that logic utilization actually drops when system throughput increases. This is not surprising since we are optimizing the sum of logic and BRAM utilization, and in this case, the BRAM utilization has significantly increased from the second point to the third point.

(5) BRAM utilization does not strictly correlate with the system performance requirement. The size of BRAM reflects the data balance between the producer and consumer kernels. Intuitively, if the producer produces data too early while the consumer consumes data too late, a large FIFO size is needed. Thus, BRAM size highly depends on the selected implementations, number of replicas and scheduling.

And it may not increase as system throughput requirement increases.

6.3 MPEG4

We show the area utilization of MPEG4 under different throughput settings in Fig. 11. In our experiment, throughput varies from 10 fps (frames/second) to 40 fps. In the case of MPEG4, logic utilization is higher than the BRAM utilization. Compared with ILP_buf (suboptimal results are excluded from the comparison), logic overhead is -8.2% and BRAM overhead is 61.5% in the case of ILP_separate. In the case of ST-Syn, logic overhead is -0.02% and BRAM overhead is only 12.4%. Runtime of ST-Syn is less than 10 seconds in all cases, while ILP_buf takes minutes to hours.

6.4 Overall Speedup and Area Overhead

Fig. 12 shows runtime of FIFO-based merge sort and MPEG4, as well as JPEG. We try to cover different designs by varying the problem size and the throughput requirement. In the case of merge sort, two different problem sizes are considered — 4096 and 8192 values are sorted. The number of variables (including intermediate variables) in ILP formulation is also listed. Note that given the same problem size, when throughput changes, the runtime of the ILP solver also varies. When throughput is set high, ST-syn usually runs for more iterations and thus takes a longer time. We compare our ST-Syn with ILP_buf in terms of speedup as well as logic and BRAM overhead. The average logic overhead is 3.1%, and the average BRAM overhead is 8.5%. However, our ST-Syn is 1174x faster than ILP_buf on average.

7. CONCLUSIONS

Communication and computation optimizations are two central aspects in system-level synthesis. System-level synthesis should consider both aspects in a unified framework rather than decouple them into two processes. In this paper we investigate an efficient system-level synthesis algorithm for a combined communication and computation optimization problem. More specifically, we provide a complete formulation and solution to deal with the throughput-driven module selection/replication and buffer size optimization problem. We first derive a scheduling graph and then perform an iterative exploration algorithm by formulating the schedulability checking as a system of difference constraints problem and the module improvement as a min-cut

	problem size	through-put	# of variables	Runtime (s)			Logic Utilization (%)			BRAM Utilization (%)		
				ILP_buf	ST-Syn	speedup	ILP_buf	ST-Syn	overhead (%)	ILP_buf	ST-Syn	overhead (%)
sort	4096	250MB/s	154	0.05	0.01	5	1.80	1.80	0.0	4.40	4.40	0.0
	4096	500 MB/s	154	1.05	0.03	35	3.60	3.60	0.0	5.20	5.60	7.7
	8192	500 MB/s	462	177	0.05	3540	3.60	3.60	0.0	6.70	6.70	0.0
	8192	1 GB/s	462	422	0.08	5275	6.02	7.20	19.6	9.26	9.30	0.4
MPEG4		10 fps	3058	3	0.02	150	14.00	14.00	0.0	6.70	6.70	0.0
		15 fps	3058	72	0.1	720	14.40	14.00	-2.8	6.70	8.15	21.6
		20 fps	3058	46	4.1	11	15.20	16.10	5.9	6.70	8.20	22.4
		25 fps	3058	3297	9	366	15.20	16.00	5.3	8.20	8.90	8.5
JPEG		1 fps	878	23	0.05	460	12.64	12.64	0.0	7.41	8.60	16.1
average						1174			3.1			8.5

Figure 12: Overall speedup and area overhead

problem. The proposed algorithm runs in polynomial time with little area overhead.

Currently, the complexity of the algorithm mainly comes from the large scheduling graph. In the future, we would like to devise design space exploration algorithms where we can use SDFG directly. Also, our current algorithm relies on the numbers in the high-level synthesis reports. The reported number (latency, initiation interval and area usage) is a conservative estimation. For example, worst-case latency of the program is used in the synthesis report. However, at the run-time, latency of the modules can be data-dependent. Thus, we would also like to investigate algorithms that can handle such a data-dependent variance.

8. ACKNOWLEDGEMENTS

This work is partially supported by Center for Domain-Specific Computing. The authors would like to thank anonymous reviewers for their time and valuable comments.

References

[1] E. Lee and D. Messerschmitt, "Synchronous data flow," *Proceedings of the IEEE*, vol. 75, no. 9, pp. 1235 – 1245, 1987.

[2] M. I. Gordon, W. Thies, and S. Amarasinghe, "Exploiting coarse-grained task, data, and pipeline parallelism in stream programs," *SIGOPS*, vol. 40, pp. 151–162, 2006.

[3] M. I. Gordon et al., "A stream compiler for communication-exposed architectures," *SIGARCH*, 2002.

[4] M. Kudlur and S. Mahlke, "Orchestrating the execution of stream programs on multicore platforms," *SIGPLAN*, vol. 43, pp. 114–124, 2008.

[5] A. Hormati et al., "Flextream: Adaptive compilation of streaming applications for heterogeneous architectures," in *PACT*, 2009, pp. 214–223.

[6] S. Liao et al., "Data and computation transformations for Brook streaming applications on multiprocessors," in *CGO*, 2006.

[7] A. Udupa, R. Govindarajan, and M. J. Thazhuthaveetil, "Synergistic execution of stream programs on multicores with accelerators," *SIGPLAN*, 2009.

[8] J. Zhai, M. Bamakhrama, and T. Stefanov, "Exploiting just-enough parallelism when mapping streaming applications in hard real-time systems," in *DAC'13*, 2013, pp. 1–8.

[9] A. Hagiescu et al., "A computing origami: Folding streams in FPGAs," in *DAC*, 2009, pp. 282 –287.

[10] M. Ishikawa and G. De Micheli, "A module selection algorithm for high-level synthesis," in *ISCAS*, 1991.

[11] I. Ahmad, M. Dhodhi, and C. Chen, "Integrated scheduling, allocation and module selection for design-space exploration in high-level synthesis," *CDT*, 1995.

[12] K. Ito, L. Lucke, and K. Parhi, "ILP-based cost-optimal DSP synthesis with module selection and data format conversion," *VLSI*, 1998.

[13] W. Sun, M. J. Wirthlin, and S. Neuendorffer, "FPGA pipeline synthesis design exploration using module selection and resource sharing," *TCAD*, 2007.

[14] D. Chen, J. Cong, and J. Xu, "Optimal module and voltage assignment for low-power," in *ASP-DAC*, 2005.

[15] H. Javaid et al., "Optimal synthesis of latency and throughput constrained pipelined mpsocs targeting streaming applications," in *CODES+ISSS'10*, 2010, pp. 75–84.

[16] J. Cong et al., "Combining module selection and replication for throughput-driven streaming programs," in *DATE*, 2012.

[17] S. Bhattacharyya, P. Murthy, and E. Lee, "Software synthesis from dataflow graphs," in *Kluwer*, 1996.

[18] S. Stuijk, M. Geilen, and T. Basten, "Exploring trade-offs in buffer requirements and throughput constraints for synchronous dataflow graphs," in *DAC*, 2006.

[19] R. Govindarajan, G. R. Gao, and P. Desai, "Minimizing buffer requirements under rate-optimal schedule in regular dataflow networks," *Journal of VLSI Signal Processing*, 1994.

[20] Q. Ning and G. R. Gao, "A novel framework of register allocation for software pipelining," in *Proceedings of the 20th ACM SIGPLAN-SIGACT symposium on Principles of programming languages*, ser. POPL. ACM, 1993.

[21] M. Geilen, T. Basten, and S. Stuijk, "Minimising buffer requirements of synchronous dataflow graphs with model checking," in *DAC*, 2005.

[22] W. Liu et al., "An efficient technique for analysis of minimal buffer requirements of synchronous dataflow graphs with model checking," in *CODES+ISSS'09*, 2009, pp. 61–70.

[23] Y. Chen and H. Zhou, "Buffer minimization in pipelined SDF scheduling on multi-core platforms," in *ASP-DAC*, 2012.

[24] B. Kienhuis, E. Deprettere, K. Vissers, and P. van der Wolf, "An approach for quantitative analysis of application-specific dataflow architectures," 1997.

[25] Q. Liu, G. Constantinides, K. Masselos, and P. Cheung, "Combining data reuse with data-level parallelization for fpga-targeted hardware compilation: A geometric programming framework," *Computer-Aided Design of Integrated Circuits and Systems, IEEE Transactions on*, 2009.

[26] E. A. Lee and D. G. Messerschmitt, "Static scheduling of synchronous data flow programs for digital signal processing," *Computers, IEEE Transactions on*, 1987.

[27] S. Sriram and S. Bhattacharyya, "Embedded multiprocessors scheduling and synchronoization," in *Marcel Dekker, Inc., New York*, 2000.

[28] J. Cong and Z. Zhang, "An efficient and versatile scheduling algorithm based on sdc formulation," in *DAC'06*.

[29] K. Singh et al., "Timing optimization of combinational logic," in *ICCAD'88*, nov 1988, pp. 282 –285.

[30] D. Koch and J. Torresen, "FPGASort: a high performance sorting architecture exploiting run-time reconfiguration on FPGAs for large problem sorting," in *FPGA'11*.

[31] "GNU Linear Programming Kit," http://www.gnu.org/software/glpk.

Quantifying the Cost and Benefit of Latency Insensitive Communication on FPGAs

Kevin E. Murray
Dept. of Electrical and Computer Engineering
University of Toronto, Ontario, Canada
kmurray@eecg.utoronto.ca

Vaughn Betz
Dept. of Electrical and Computer Engineering
University of Toronto, Ontario, Canada
vaughn@eecg.utoronto.ca

ABSTRACT

Latency insensitive communication offers many potential benefits for FPGA designs, including easier timing closure by enabling automatic pipelining, and easier interfacing with embedded NoCs. However, it is important to understand the costs and trade-offs associated with any new design style. This paper presents optimized implementations of latency insensitive communication building blocks, quantifies their overheads in terms of area and frequency, and provides guidance to designers on how to generate high-speed and area-efficient latency insensitive systems.

Categories and Subject Descriptors

B.4.3 [**Input/Output and Data Communications**]: Interconnections (Subsystems); B.5.1 [**Register-Transfer-Level Implementation**]: Design—*Styles*

General Terms

Design, Performance

Keywords

FPGA; Latency Insensitive; Pipelining

1. INTRODUCTION

Modern process technology scaling has introduced many challenges related to the design and implementation of FPGA systems. In particular, the different scaling characteristics of devices, local interconnect, and global interconnect [10] are making it more difficult to achieve timing closure in a predictable and timely manner.

The difference in scaling between local and global interconnect[1] is illustrated for FPGA devices in Figure 1. This shows that the speed of local communication within a relatively small amount of logic (i.e. 40K LEs) has more than

---

[1]This is particularly important for FPGAs where interconnect already contributes significantly to overall delay.

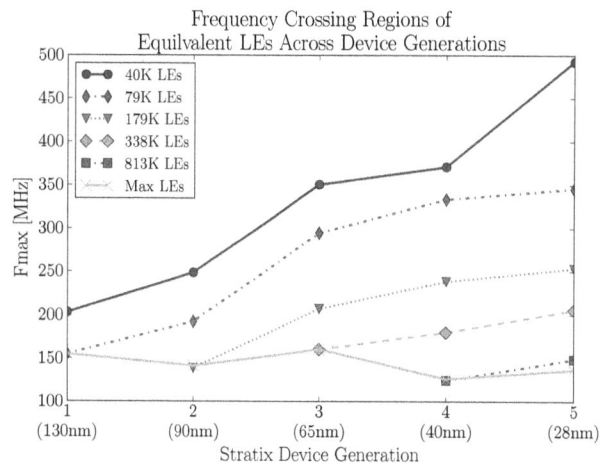

Figure 1: Achievable register to register operating frequency across regions containing an equivalent number of Logic Elements (LEs) for Stratix devices; measured with Altera's Quartus II. Max LEs corresponds to the largest device available each generation.

doubled over five generations. In contrast, the speed of global communication across the full device (i.e. Max LEs) has not improved. This growing mismatch between local and global communication speed makes it difficult to close timing on large designs.

One solution to the interconnect scaling problem is to insert pipeline registers on communication links that traverse large portions of the chip. This breaks the link into shorter segments which can operate at higher speed, and allows multiple clock cycles for the signal to propagate.

The problem with this solution is that it modifies the latency of the communication link. This changes the RTL behaviour of the system, requiring the re-design and re-verification of the system's control logic. Furthermore, the impact of these RTL changes are not known until after the time consuming physical design flow (which may take multiple days [16]) has been completed, making this a slow and iterative process.

Latency Insensitive Design (LID) [4] has been proposed as a design methodology to avoid these issues by making design components insensitive to the latency of the communication between them. This enables the pipelining of communication links while ensuring that the correctness of the design does not change. As a result the insertion of pipeline registers could potentially be pushed to later stages in the design flow, since they no longer require the designer to manually change the system's RTL description. This further abstracts the design from the implementation details of the FPGA, potentially enhancing the timing portability of designs when re-targeting larger or newer FPGAs. Additionally, this also makes the process of inserting pipeline registers much more amenable to design automation. Potential CAD optimizations could include automatic pipeline register insertion during early floorplanning, or pipeline register insertion during routing. These capabilities could be beneficial for architectures featuring pipeline registers embedded in the routing fabric [18, 7].

However, the extra flexibility and abstraction provided by LID will come at some cost. This has not been well characterized, particularly for FPGAs. This paper aims to quantify the costs of latency insensitive communication on FPGAs and present design recommendations to help minimize overhead. Our contributions include:

- Quantification of the area and frequency overhead of LID on FPGAs

- Identification of potential frequency limitations in LI systems and optimizations to improve operating frequency

- A comparison of the efficiency of LI and non-LI pipelining

- Design guidelines for determining the LI communication granularity appropriate to produce area-efficient systems

2. LATENCY INSENSITIVE MOTIVATION

Several different design methodologies have been proposed to address the design issues outlined in the introduction. This section compares these and further explains why this paper focuses on latency insensitive design.

2.1 Limitations of Synchronous Design

Synchronous design is the dominant paradigm for digital design. This is largely due to its amenability to design automation, simple conceptual model and flexibility. However, synchronous design is also restrictive, enforcing the *synchronous assumption* – that all communication must occur within a single clock cycle. On modern devices where it may take multiple clock cycles to traverse the chip this can be too restrictive.

The work-around, adding pipeline registers, is time consuming and error prone. After compiling their system and identifying timing issues, designers must manually insert pipeline registers, modify their system's control logic and re-verify the overall system. They must then re-compile their system (which could take days) before being able to evaluate the impact of their changes. However, after this process, the problem may not be solved. Timing paths may have moved or new critical paths could have appeared, requiring the whole process to be repeated with no guarantee of convergence.

2.2 Why Not Wave-Pipelining?

In a conventional synchronous system each data bit transmitted along a wire must be latched by a clocked storage element before the following bit is launched. With wave-pipelining, multiple data bits are allowed to be in flight along the same wire. This allows the interconnect to behave as if pipelined – with the wire itself storing the multiple data bits in flight rather than registers. This saves the area, power and timing overhead of using registers. It was shown in [20] that wave-pipelined interconnect could be used in an FPGA.

Wire-pipelining however, does not avoid the problem of re-designing a system's control logic to account for the additional communication latency, and also introduces further design issues. Since no stable storage element is used to separate the multiple bits transmitted along a wire, wave-pipelining systems must be meticulously designed to ensure correct operation and avoid interference between subsequent bits. One challenge for these systems is that they can not be run at lower speeds, which makes debugging difficult. This undesirable behaviour is caused by tying the latency of a wave-pipelined link to the (constant) delay of a wire, rather than to the number of registers. As a result, the effective latency of a wave-pipelined link changes with clock frequency. Additionally, wave-pipelining systems must operate robustly in the presence of die-to-die and on-chip variation, as well as in the presence of crosstalk and power supply noise [20]. These non-idealities are expected to become more significant in future process technologies, and the flexibility of FPGAs would make verifying such systems difficult.

Wave-pipelining does not resolve the problem of re-designing control logic, introduces additional limitations to system behaviour, and increases design complexity. As a result, wave-pipelining fails to be a practical solution.

2.3 Why Not Asynchronous Design?

Asynchronous design has long been touted as an alternative to synchronous design. Under this design methodology no clock is used to enforce globally synchronized communication. Instead components of the design detect when their inputs are valid and only then compute their results.

However, despite decades of research, asynchronous design methodologies have seen limited adoption. The reasons for this include a lack of CAD flows and tools to implement and verify designs, the difficulty designers have reasoning about the correctness of their systems, and the challenges of testing asynchronous devices [9].

2.4 Why Not GALS?

Another alternative design methodology is Globally Asynchronous Locally Synchronous (GALS). In this methodology small sub-modules are designed synchronously, but global communication between modules occurs asynchronously, typically through a wrapper module. This allows timing paths to be isolated within each sub-module easing timing closure. Furthermore, since smaller more localized clocks with lower skew are used, this may help to improve performance and power.

One of the key challenges in any GALS design methodology is avoiding metastability when transferring data between sub-modules, since their clocks are no longer synchronous. Several different GALS design styles have been proposed to address this issue [19, 12]. One approach is based on pausable clocks, where each sub-module has a locally generated clock which is paused before data arrives to ensure that metastability is avoided. Alternately, GALS can be implemented using asynchronous FIFOs to handle communication between sub-modules. Additionally in some cases, where the relationships between sub-module clocks are known, conventional flip-flop based synchronizers can be used.

On current FPGAs, it is not possible to locally generate clocks for sub-modules as would be done on an ASIC. As a result these clocks would have to be centrally generated (with a PLL/DLL) and distributed to the local sub-modules. FPGAs typically contain a relatively small number of fixed clock networks, consisting primarily of global, and large regional/quadrant clock networks. Since these clock networks are pre-fabricated, there is not much to gain (in terms of skew and power) by using them to distribute small clocks. This is different from an ASIC where custom smaller clock trees can be designed. While FPGAs do also support some smaller fixed clock networks, these are typically quite small (limiting the size of sub-modules), restrict placement flexibility, and may be difficult to reach from clock generators. While it is possible to distribute clocks with the regular inter-block routing, it is undesirable. The inter-block routing network is not designed for clock distribution, lacking shielding (increasing jitter), and having unbalanced rise-fall times which may distort the clock waveform. Such a clock network would also consume more power and typically have more skew than an equivalent fixed clock network.

GALS also faces problems similar to fully asynchronous design for the asynchronous portions of the system, including difficulty implementing, verifying and testing such systems. While CAD flows for GALS design are perhaps better developed than for fully asynchronous design, they still require substantial design knowledge and manual intervention [23]. These challenges make adopting a GALS design methodology for FPGAs quite disruptive.

2.5 Latency Insensitive Design

LID can be viewed as a middle ground between the synchronous and asynchronous design methodologies. It breaks the synchronous assumption, but does not go so far as to totally remove global synchronization. Instead, LID allows the latency of communication links to vary. This means that while communication is still synchronized to a clock at the physical level, it may take multiple clock cycles for communication to occur in the designer's RTL description.

This yields additional flexibility during the design implementation process compared to synchronous design, but is more tractable than asynchronous design. Keeping communication synchronous at the physical level means conventional synchronous CAD flows and tools can be used to implement designs, and designers can still reason about the correctness of their systems from the perspective of timing constraints. Additionally, emerging FPGA communication styles such as embedded NoCs [6, 1] result in variable latency communication, essentially requiring designs to be latency insensitive. LID also does not require modification of existing FPGA architectures, as would be required to fully support wave-pipelining [20], asynchronous, or GALS [17] design styles.

Furthermore, the formal theory of latency insensitive design [4] shows that any conventional synchronous system, typically called a *pearl*, can be transformed into a latency insensitive system, provided it is stall-able[2]. This is ac-

complished by placing it in a special (but still synchronous) wrapper module, typically called a *shell*. The theory further shows that such wrapped modules can be composed together, and the latency of communication links between them varied, by inserting relay-stations (analogous to registers), without affecting the correctness of the overall system.

An example system is shown in Figure 2. The logical system, as described by an RTL designer, is shown in Figure 2a. After implementation with a latency insensitive CAD flow the design implementation may appear as in Figure 2b.

The scheme described above (and in additional detail in Section 3) implements dynamically scheduled LID, where the validity of a module's inputs are determined dynamically at run time by the shell logic. Statically scheduled LID schemes have also been proposed [5], which determine when inputs are valid at design time before implementation. As a result, statically scheduled LID severely limits the flexibility of the system implementation and significantly restricts any potential CAD optimizations, such as automated pipelining. It also precludes operation with variable latency interconnect such as an NoC. Accordingly, we evaluate only dynamically scheduled LID in this work.

An interesting question is what level of granularity is appropriate for latency insensitive communication. While it is possible to use latency insensitive communication at a very fine level, this is not necessarily required. As shown in Figure 1 local communication can still occur at high speed, the problem is with long distance (global) communication. As a result it may make sense to implement latency insensitive communication at a coarser level that captures primarily global communication.

Some previous work has looked at latency insensitive communication in FPGA-like contexts. In [8], explicit latency insensitive communication was used to improve the design and implementation of multi-FPGA prototyping systems. The authors of [11] proposed an elastic CGRA architecture exploiting latency insensitive communication to avoid static scheduling, and to allow simpler translation of high level languages (i.e. C) into circuits. For their system, which implements latency insensitive communication for each ALU element, they identify the area and delay overhead of their elastic CGRA (compared to an inelastic CGRA) as 26% and 8% respectively. The work presented in [3] describes an FPGA overlay architecture that uses latency insensitive communication. The authors report area overheads (compared to a baseline system) of 3.4× and 10.6× for a floating point and integer based overlay respectively. The high overheads can be attributed to the additional routing flexibility required for the overlay and the use of fine-grained latency insensitive communication.

This work differentiates itself from the above by focusing on the overheads of using latency insensitive communication for RTL design targeting conventional FPGAs, rather than as part of an overlay layer or hardened into a device architecture.

3. LATENCY INSENSITIVE DESIGN IMPLEMENTATION

In order to quantify the costs of a LI design methodology we have created a set of LI wrappers and relay stations based on those presented in [14] and implemented them on Stratix IV FPGAs. Example wrappers are shown in Figure 3.

---

[2]Informally, capable of maintaining its state independent of its current inputs (i.e. no outputs combinationally connected to inputs). See [4] for a formal definition.

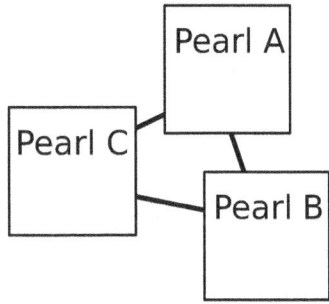

(a) Logical system connectivity.

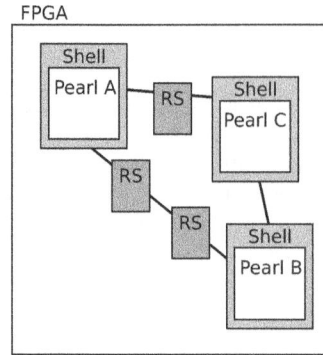

(b) Latency insensitive system implementation, showing shells and inserted relay stations (RS).

Figure 2: Latency insensitive system example.

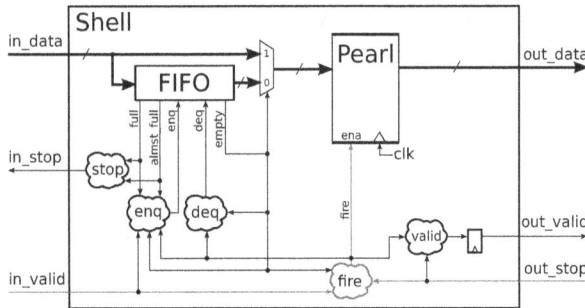

(a) Baseline latency insensitive wrapper (one input, one output). Critical paths highlighted in red.

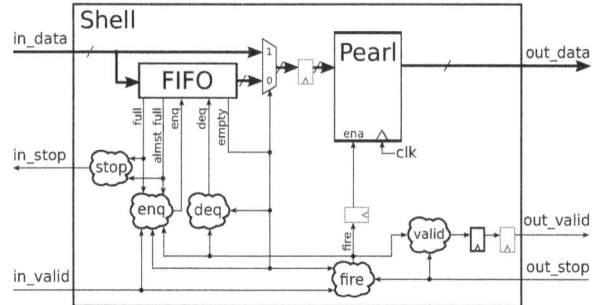

(b) Optimized latency insensitive wrapper (one input, one output). Additional registers added in the optimized version shown in dashed-blue.

Figure 3: Latency insensitive wrapper implementations.

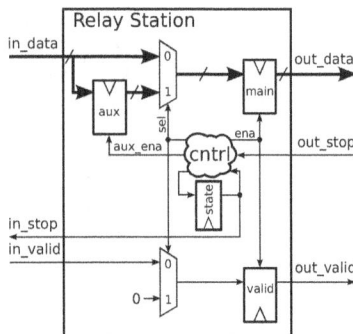

Figure 4: Latency insensitive relay station

One of the key differences between a LI and a traditional synchronous system is the addition of *stop* and *valid* signals on communication channels, forming a 'bundled data' protocol. The *valid* signal allows for data to be marked as invalid and ignored by downstream modules. The wrapper is responsible for stalling the pearl (typically by clock gating) if all of its inputs are not valid. To ensure that no information is lost if valid inputs arrive at a stalled module, they are queued in FIFOs. The *stop* signal provides back-pressure to ensure the FIFOs do not overflow.

Relay stations (Figure 4) are used in place of conventional registers to perform pipelining. Relay stations include addi-

tional logic to handle the *valid* and *stop* signals and must be capable of storing two data words to account for the latency of back-pressure communication.

3.1 Baseline Wrapper

The LI wrapper shown in Figure 3a consists of several components. The *pearl* is the original synchronously designed module which is to be made latency insensitive. This is surrounded by a wrapper *shell* which stalls the pearl if one or more inputs are not available, and queues incoming valid data in FIFOs. In [14] stalling was performed by gating the pearl's clock. However, the granularity of clock gating available on FPGAs is very coarse. On some FPGAs the clock is only gate-able at the root of the clock tree [2], requiring a separate clock networks to be used for each gated clock. On other FPGAs clock gating is enabled at lower levels of the clock tree [22]. However, there are still a relatively small number of gating points, and their fixed locations may overconstrain the physical design tools. As a result clock gating was not considered. Instead, the clock gating circuitry was inferred as a clock enable signal sent to all flip-flops in the pearl.

One of the limitations observed with the baseline wrapper was that it reduced the achievable operating frequency of the pearl module (see Section 4.1). Since the motivation behind latency insensitive design is to enable high speed long distance communication, this was undesirable. The cause was identified as long combinational paths leading from the upstream module's valid signal and from the downstream module's stop signal (highlighted in Figure 3a). As a result the 'fire' logic, responsible for generating the pearl's clock enable signal, was subject to two competing timing paths. This was further exacerbated by the high fan-out clock enable signal. For the relatively small modules presented in Section 4.1, the clock enable fanned-out to nearly 1400 registers. This forced the CAD tool to produce a compromise solution which decreased operating frequency.

One of the largest components of LI wrappers are the FIFOs. To avoid unnecessary stalls these FIFOs require single cycle read/write capability, single cycle updates to full and empty signals and 'new data' behaviour (i.e. the read receives the new data being written) when a write and read occur at the same address. The 'new data' behaviour required additional logic to be inferred around the RAM elements since this mode of operation is not natively supported by the Stratix IV RAM blocks. While it was possible to infer the FIFOs into the MLAB/LUTRAM structures on Stratix IV FPGAs, the choice was left to the CAD tool, which usually implemented them as M9K RAM blocks. Adding native support for 'new data' behaviour in future FPGA RAM blocks would help reduce the overhead associated with these FIFOs.

3.2 Optimized Wrapper

To improve the frequency limitations of the baseline wrapper, an improved wrapper was created by inserting an additional register after the fire logic as shown in Figure 3b. This broke the combinational paths before they became high fanout and greatly improved achievable frequency. However this required several changes to the wrapper architecture. To ensure that all components remained correctly synchronized with the clock enable signal, additional registers also had to be inserted after the FIFO bypass mux and valid signal generation logic. Overall, this introduces one extra cycle of round-trip communication latency between modules. To handle the additional cycle of latency, the FIFO must reserve an additional word to handle the possibility of an additional data word in flight.

While further pipelining of the LI wrapper was attempted, it resulted in only marginal improvement.

4. RESULTS

To evaluate the cost and overhead of LID, we created a program to automatically generate LI wrappers based on a Verilog module description[3]. This program was used to generate wrappers for a design consisting of cascaded FIR filters, and also to more generally investigate the scalability of LI wrappers.

All area and frequency results were determined by implementing the design with Altera's Quartus II CAD tool (version 12.1) targeting the fastest speed grade of Stratix IV devices. To compare area between implementations that make use of hardened blocks (e.g. DSPs and RAM blocks), we calculated 'equivalent Logic Array Blocks (LABs)' based on the normalized block sizes from [21]. Since Quartus II may purposefully spread out the design soft logic and reg-

isters for timing purposes (inflating the number of LABs used), we calculated the required number of LABs by dividing the number of required LUT+FF pairs by the number of pairs per LAB.

4.1 FIR Design Overhead

FIR systems are simple to pipeline manually, because of their limited control logic and strictly feed-forward communication. As a result they do not require LID to enable easy pipelining. An FIR system is used here as a high speed[4] design example, which allows us to quantify the impact of LID while varying the level of pipelining in both the LI and Non-LI implementations. A more general investigation of LID overhead is presented in Sections 4.3 and 4.4.

The FIR filter design consists of 49 cascaded FIR filters as shown in Figure 5. Each of the instances is a 51 tap symmetric folded FIR filter with 16-bit data and coefficients, that is deeply pipelined internally (11 stages) to achieve high operating frequency. The structure of each FIR filter is shown in Figure 6. Its characteristics are listed in Table 1.

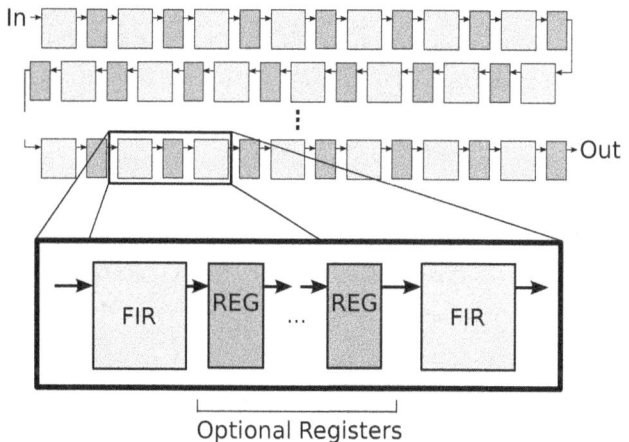

Figure 5: System of 49 cascaded FIR filters with optional registers inserted between instances.

Table 1: Cascaded FIR Design Characteristics

Resource	Number	EP4SGX230 Util.
ALUTs	23,084	13%
Registers	65,256	36%
LABs	4661	51%
M9K Blocks	1	<1%
M144K Blocks	0	0%
DSP Blocks	160	99%

Comparisons of the area and achieved frequency for the LI and non-LI designs are shown in Table 2. In these results each instance of the FIR is made latency insensitive by wrapping it (automatically) using one of the shells from Figures 3a or 3b.

---

[3]The program, along with the LI wrappers and relay stations are available from: `http://www.eecg.utoronto.ca/~vaughn/software.html`

[4]This is important as it allows us to investigate whether the LI wrappers and relay stations would limit such high speed systems.

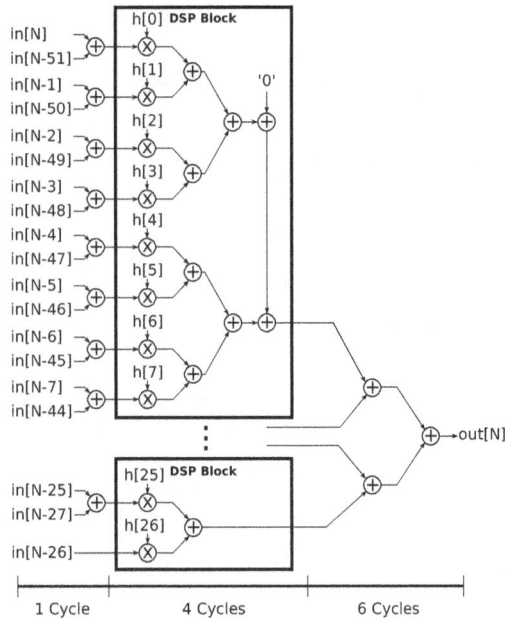

Figure 6: FIR filter architecture. Number of clock cycles required by each portion of the design are annotated.

Table 2: Post fit resource usage and operating frequency for the cascaded FIR design using different communication styles. Values normalized to non-LI system are shown in parenthesis.

Resource	Non-LI	Base LI		Opt. LI	
LUT+FF Pairs	54,940	60,086	$(1.09\times)$	60,299	$(1.10\times)$
DSP Blocks	160	160	$(1.00\times)$	160	$(1.00\times)$
M9K	1	49	$(49.00\times)$	49	$(49.00\times)$
M144K	0	0		0	
Equiv. LABs	4,654	5,049	$(1.08\times)$	5,060	$(1.09\times)$
Fmax [MHz]	377	253	$(0.67\times)$	348	$(0.92\times)$

It is interesting that despite implementing a fine grain latency insensitivity system[5], the area overhead is only 8% or 9%. This could be easily decreased further by implementing latency insensitivity at a coarser level. When viewed from the device level (since many FPGA designs do not fully utilize the device resources) the area overhead amounts to less than 3% of the device resources.

The 33% decrease in frequency, from 377 MHz to 253 MHz, observed when implementing the baseline wrapper (Section 3.1) was both surprising and concerning. This motivated the development of the optimized wrapper (Section 3.2) which improved frequency to 348 MHZ, only 8% below the latency-sensitive system. While this is still a notable impact compared to the non-LI system, it is significantly lower than the baseline wrapper, and comes at only a marginal increase in area overhead.

It was also informative to compare what level of pipelining was required between filter instances when using the LI wrappers to achieve an operating frequency comparable to the non-LI system. As shown in Figure 5 additional pipeline registers (or relay stations) are inserted between FIR filter

[5]Each FIR module is approximately 95 equivalent LABs in area or 0.6% of the EP4SGX230 device.

instances. A summary of these results is shown in Figure 7 for various sizes of the cascaded FIR filter design.

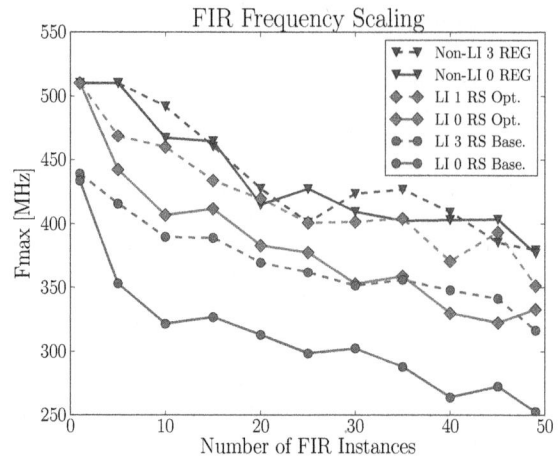

Figure 7: Measured operating frequency versus design size for various communication implementations. The number of registers (REG) or relay stations (RS) inserted between FIR instances are shown in the legend.

The first thing to note is the downward trend in operating frequency associated with increasing design size. This is an artifact of the imperfect nature of the CAD tools used to implement the design. The design is highly pipelined, with no combinational paths between instances. Despite finding a high speed (510 MHz) implementation with one instance in the non-LI system (Non-LI 0 REG) the quality decreases as the design size increases, resulting in a 26% drop in operating frequency when scaling from one to 49 instances. The magnitude of this effect also varies between implementations. For the baseline LI wrapper (LI 0 RS Base.) the frequency dropped 42% across the same range. This disparity is likely a result of the different difficulties these implementations present to the CAD tool, with the baseline LI wrapper containing difficult to optimize timing paths (Section 3.1).

Studying the relative achieved frequency of the different communication implementations, further insights can be drawn. While the baseline wrapper operates at the lowest frequency (LI 0 RS Base.), adding relay stations between filter instances does improve performance (LI 3 RS Base.). However, inserting more than 3 relay stations failed to improve operating frequency. As a result the baseline wrapper fails to match the operating frequency of the non-LI system. The optimized wrapper (LI 0 RS Opt.) performs better than the baseline wrapper, and by inserting only one relay station (LI 1 RS Opt.) performs comparably to the non-LI system. Additional pipelining between filter instances in the non-LI system (Non-LI 3 REG) did not significantly improve operating frequency over the un-pipelined version (Non-LI 0 REG).

4.2 Pipelining Efficiency

One of the interesting questions when comparing different forms of pipelining, whether different latency insensitive implementations or non-LI and LI pipelining, is how much delay overhead is associated with inserting pipeline registers. In the ideal case, on a wire delay dominated path, inserting a pipeline stage would effectively double the operating frequency. However this is not the reality. The setup and clock-to-q times of registers and, in FPGAs, the cost of entering and exiting a logic block to access registers, all reduce the frequency improvement. In latency insensitive systems there is additional overhead in the form of control logic used to determine data validity and handle back pressure.

To evaluate this, a wire delay limited critical path was created between two instances of the FIR filter from Section 4.1 by constraining the two filters to diagonally opposite corners of the largest Stratix IV device (EP4SE820). The impact of pipelining this long communication link is shown in Figure 8.

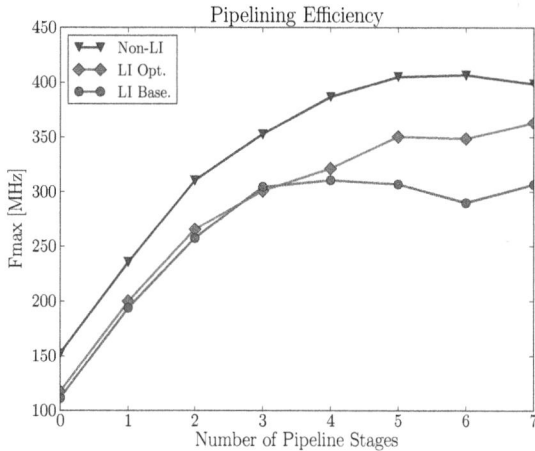

Figure 8: Operating frequency for various numbers of inserted pipeline stages. Results are the average over five placement seeds.

As expected, for an equivalent pipeline depth the non-LI system operates at a higher frequency than the LI systems. The non-LI system ultimately saturates after 5 stages of pipelining. In contrast the baseline LI system saturates after only 3 stages of pipelining and does so at 25% lower frequency. This early saturation is caused by the movement of the critical path from the communication link to the high fan-out clock enable signal internal to the wrappers. The optimized wrapper was not affected by this. While the gap between the optimized LI and non-LI systems grows in absolute terms, the percentage frequency overhead stays fairly constant, ranging from 14-17% for 1 to 5 pipeline stages.

4.3 Generalized Latency Insensitive Wrapper Scaling

While the previous results on the FIR filter design show the potential overheads are manageable, they represent only a limited part of the design space. It is therefore interesting to more generally explore the design space and investigate how LI wrappers scale for different sets of design parameters.

The key design parameters for the LI wrapper are: the number of input ports, the number of output ports, the port widths, and the FIFO depths. While ideally we would investigate all of the interactions between these parameters, this represents a large design space. To decrease the size of this design space, but still gain useful insight into the scal-

ing characteristics of the LI wrappers these parameters were swept individually over a wide range of values.

For the baseline parameters, two input and two output ports were chosen to ensure reasonable control logic was generated, a low port width of 16 was selected to emphasize the scaling impact of ports, and a FIFO depth of 4 (deeper than the typical depth of 1 or 2 words) was used to ensure at least 2 words were available to both the baseline and optimized LI wrappers. While the area results presented do not include the area associated with the pearl used, it is not possible to isolate the pearl's frequency impact. For this reason we chose a very small pearl designed to minimize any impact on the system's critical path. The results are shown in Figure 9. Several useful conclusions can be drawn from the scaling results.

First, as seen in Figure 9a, FIFO depth can be increased with minimal area overhead. This cost is low since the FIFOs are implemented in block RAMs. The large size of these block RAMs means that at shallow depths, the block RAMs are underutilized. As a result, the FIFO depth can be increased at little to no additional cost. This is distinctly different from an ASIC implementation (which would size the FIFO exactly) and highlights the different trade-offs facing FPGA designers. The low incremental cost of increasing FIFO depth may be beneficial for some latency insensitive optimization schemes, which increase FIFO depth to improve system throughput [15]. The frequency overhead of increasing FIFO depth is moderate, staying above 300 MHz until a depth of 16K words.

Second, increasing the width of ports (Figure 9b) or increasing the number of input ports (Figure 9c) are fairly expensive, in terms of both area and frequency overhead. However it is interesting to contrast the relative costs of both. Increasing port width results in a lower area overhead than increasing the number of input ports for the same number of overall module input bits. This is perhaps not surprising, since increasing the port width improves the amortization of the FIFO logic, and does not introduce additional control logic (while adding input ports does). The results are similar from a frequency perspective, with scaling input ports more expensive than scaling port widths. The wrappers have no problem operating above 300 MHz (using only two ports) for port widths up to 2048 bits. In contrast, this speed is only possible if fewer than 32 ports are used.

Finally, increasing the number of output ports (Figure 9d) is less costly, since it adds only a small amount of control logic to handle back-pressure and valid signals. It is however, important to note from a system perspective that each output port has an associated FIFO at the downstream input port. Similarly to the area overhead, the frequency overhead of increasing output ports is low, with 300 MHz operation possible with up to 256 output ports.

4.4 Latency Insensitive Design Overhead

One of the challenges when designing a LI system is determining the level of granularity at which to implement latency insensitive communication. To get the most flexibility, a fine level of granularity may be desired, but this could come at an unacceptably large area overhead.

To provide some guidance, a coarse estimate of the area overhead associated with latency insensitive communication for various module sizes was developed by combining the

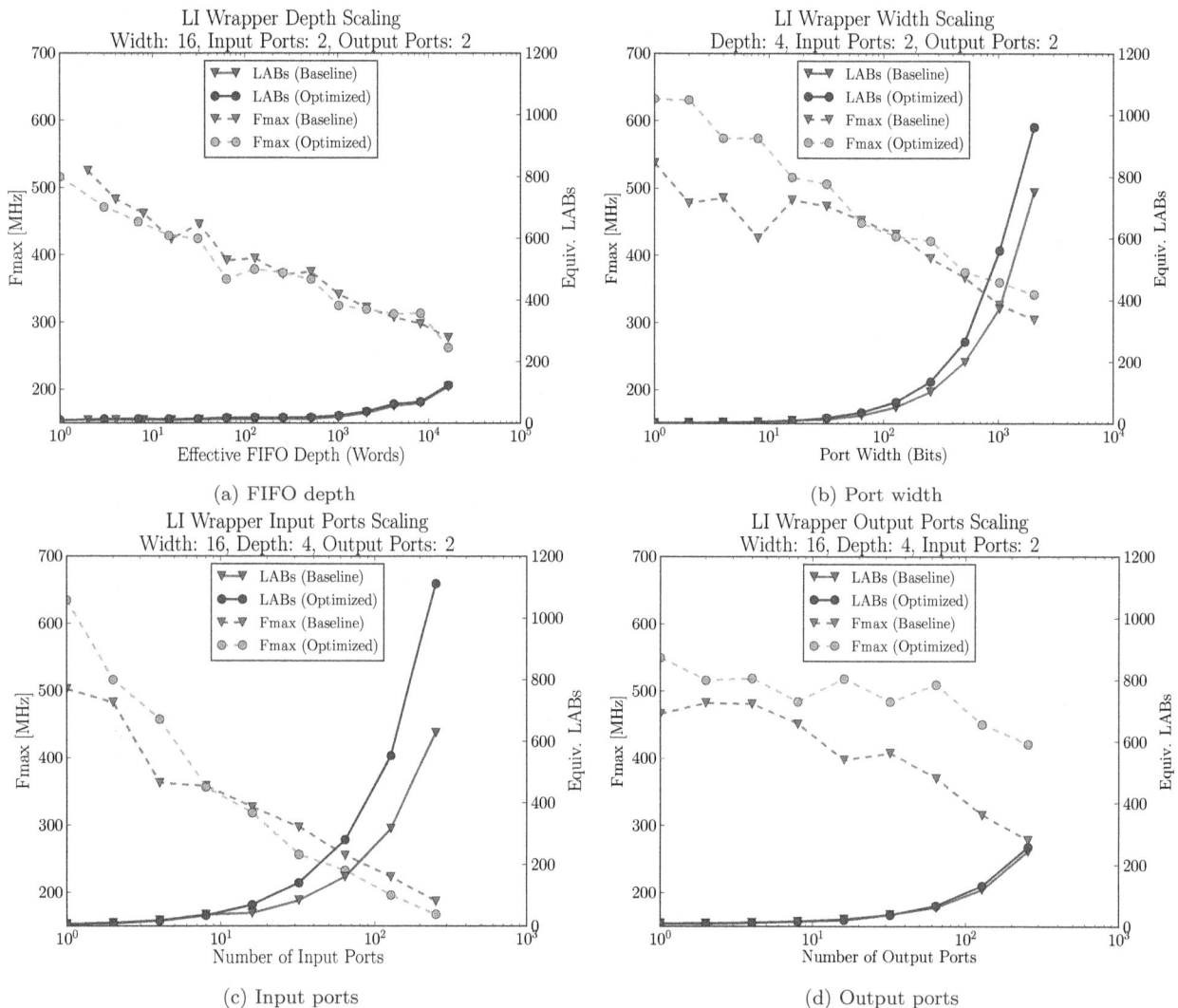

(a) FIFO depth

(b) Port width

(c) Input ports

(d) Output ports

Figure 9: Latency insensitive wrapper scaling results.

results of Section 4.3 with Rent's rule, which relates I/O requirements to module size.

Rent's rule [13], stated as:

$$P = KN^R \qquad (1)$$

is an empirically observed relation between the average number of blocks in a module (N) and its average number of externally connecting pins (P), where K is the average number of pins per block and R is the design dependant Rent parameter. The Rent parameter captures the complexity of the interconnections between modules. A Rent parameter of 0.0 corresponds to a linear chain of modules, such as the FIR design presented in Section 4.1. A Rent parameter of 1.0 corresponds to a clique where all modules communicate with each other. Typical circuits have Rent parameters ranging from 0.57 to 0.75 [13].

It was found for a modern FPGA benchmark set [16] that K was 32.2 for Stratix IV LABs. Assuming the number of pins predicted by Rent's rule split evenly between inputs and outputs, that each port is 64 bits wide, and FIFO depths of 4 are used, it is possible to estimate the area overhead of

a module's latency insensitive wrapper based on the data from Section 4.3.

The area overhead of LI communication compared to module size is shown in Figure 10 for various Rent parameter values. It is clear that modules with low to moderate Rent parameters are amenable to the creation of area-efficient latency insensitive systems. Circuits with good communication locality ($0.5 \leq R \leq 0.6$) can achieve low area overhead ($< 10\%$) when wrapping modules ranging in size from 50K to 300K LEs. Circuits with moderate communication locality ($0.6 < R \leq 0.7$) can achieve moderate area overhead ($< 20\%$) when wrapping modules from 160K to 700K LEs in size. Circuits with poor communication locality ($R > 0.7$) are problematic, and will likely result in latency insensitive systems with high area overhead.

5. CONCLUSIONS

In conclusion, a quantitative analysis of the impact of latency insensitive design methodologies on FPGAs has been presented. We have shown that system level interconnect speeds are not scaling, while local interconnect speeds con-

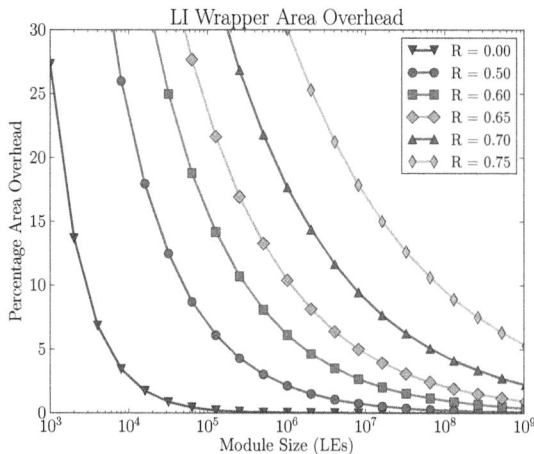

Figure 10: Estimated latency insensitive module area overhead for various rent parameters, assuming equal numbers of input/output pins, 64-bit wide ports and FIFO depths of 4 words.

tinue to improve. This mismatch, along with increasing design sizes, make LI techniques attractive to simplify timing closure, since they allow pipelining decisions to be made late in the design cycle; possibly even by new physical CAD tools. An improved LI wrapper that addresses some of the frequency limitations of conventional LI wrappers was presented, and was used to evaluate the area and frequency overheads of LID. On an example system the area and frequency overheads were found to be only 9% and 8% respectively, with the frequency overhead reducible with further pipelining. The pipelining efficiency of LID was also compared to conventional non-LI pipelining and found to have an overhead of 14-17%. Finally, a more general exploration of the scalability of LI wrappers was conducted, and used to provide guidelines to designers regarding the level of granularity at which latency insensitive communication should be implemented to maintain reasonable area overheads.

While this work shows that the frequency and area overhead of LI systems can be manageable, it remains untenable for some classes of designs, such as those with poorly localized communication ($R > 0.7$) and those unwilling to accept a 14-17% reduction in pipelining efficiency. Previous work on statically scheduled LI systems [5] helps address this, but does so by removing much of the flexibility at late stages of the CAD flow that LID promises. Future work to develop higher performing and lower area overhead LI systems would be beneficial. One potential method to do so would be to improve support for low cost FIFOs requiring 'new data' behaviour in future FPGA architectures.

It would also be useful to extend the overhead quantification to include a power analysis of LID, particularly since unlike ASICs, stalled modules on FPGAs do not have their clocks gated. Similarly further work on evaluating the holistic costs and benefits of LID on real world systems, and with larger more complex benchmarks, would be of value.

While LID will have a cost in area and frequency compared to a perfectly pipelined non-LI system, as design sizes continue to grow and CAD run time for each design iteration increases, the design costs of such systems become large

enough to make LID attractive at the system level to interconnect large modules. However, to fully exploit the promise and benefits of LID it must be integrated into CAD flows and exploited by CAD tools to improve designer productivity and design quality.

6. ACKNOWLEDGEMENTS

This work was supported by Altera, Texas Instruments, the Semiconductor Research Corporation, and a QEII-GSST scholarship. We would also like to thank the anonymous reviewers for their helpful comments.

7. REFERENCES

[1] M. S. Abdelfattah and V. Betz. Design Tradeoffs for Hard and Soft FPGA-based Networks-on-Chip. In *FPT*, pages 95–103, Dec. 2012.

[2] Altera Corporation. *Stratix IV Device Handbook*, September 2012.

[3] D. Capalija and T. Abdelrahman. A High-Performance Overlay Architecture for Pipelined Execution of Data Flow Graphs. In *FPL*, 2013.

[4] L. P. Carloni, K. L. McMillan, and A. Sangiovanni-Vincentelli. Theory of Latency-Insensitive Design. *IEEE Transactions on Computer-Aided Design of Integrated Circuits and Systems*, 20(9):1059–1076, 2001.

[5] M. R. Casu and L. Macchiarulo. A New Approach to Latency Insensitive Design. In *DAC*, pages 576–581, June 2004.

[6] E. S. Chung, J. C. Hoe, and K. Mai. CoRAM: An In-Fabric Memory Architecture for FPGA-based Computing. In *FPGA*, pages 97–106, Feb. 2011.

[7] K. Eguro and S. Hauck. Armada: Timing-Driven Pipeline-Aware Routing for FPGAs. In *FPGA*, pages 169–178, Feb. 2006.

[8] K. E. Fleming, M. Adler, M. Pellauer, A. Parashar, A. Mithal, and J. Emer. Leveraging Latency-Insensitivity to Ease Multiple FPGA Design. In *FPGA*, pages 175–184, Feb. 2012.

[9] S. Hauck. Asynchronous Design Methodologies: An Overview. *Proceedings of the IEEE*, 83(1):69–93, 1995.

[10] R. Ho, K. W. Mai, and M. A. Horowitz. The Future of Wires. *Proceedings of the IEEE*, 89(4):490–504, 2001.

[11] Y. Huang, P. Ienne, O. Temam, Y. Chen, and C. Wu. Elastic CGRAs. In *FPGA*, pages 171–180, Feb. 2013.

[12] M. Krstic, E. Grass, F. K. Gürkaynak, and P. Vivet. Globally Asynchronous, Locally Synchronous Circuits: Overview and Outlook. *IEEE Design & Test of Computers*, 24(5):430–441, Sept. 2007.

[13] B. Landman and R. Russo. On a Pin Versus Block Relationship For Partitions of Logic Graphs. *IEEE Transactions on Computers*, C-20(12):1469–1479, Dec. 1971.

[14] C.-H. Li, R. Collins, S. Sonalkar, and L. P. Carloni. Design, Implementation, and Validation of a New Class of Interface Circuits for Latency-Insensitive Design. In *International Conference on Formal Methods and Models for Codesign*, pages 13–22, 2007.

[15] R. Lu and C. Koh. Performance Optimization of Latency Insensitive Systems Through Buffer Queue Sizing of Communication Channels. In *International*

Conference on Computer Aided Design, pages 227–231, 2003.

[16] K. E. Murray, S. Whitty, S. Liu, J. Luu, and V. Betz. Titan: Enabling Large and Complex Benchmarks in Academic CAD. In *FPL*, 2013.

[17] A. Royal and P. Y. K. Cheung. Globally asynchronous locally synchronous FPGA architectures. In *FPL*, pages 355–364, 2003.

[18] D. P. Singh and S. D. Brown. The Case for Registered Routing Switches in Field Programmable Gate Arrays. In *FPGA*, pages 161–169, Feb. 2001.

[19] P. Teehan, M. Greenstreet, and G. Lemieux. A Survey and Taxonomy of GALS Design Styles. *IEEE Design & Test of Computers*, 24(5):418–428, Sept. 2007.

[20] P. Teehan, G. G. Lemieux, and M. R. Greenstreet. Towards reliable 5Gbps wave-pipelined and 3Gbps surfing interconnect in 65nm FPGAs. In *FPGA*, pages 43–52, Feb. 2009.

[21] H. Wong, V. Betz, and J. Rose. Comparing FPGA vs. Custom CMOS and the Impact on Processor Microarchitecture. In *FPGA*, pages 5–14, 2011.

[22] Xilinx Inc. *7 Series FPGAs Clocking Resources*, March 2011.

[23] A. Yakovlev, P. Vivet, and M. Renaudin. Advances in Asynchronous logic: from Principles to GALS & NoC, Recent Industry Applications, and Commercial CAD tools. In *Design, Automation and Test in Europe*, pages 1715–1724, Mar. 2013.

MPack: Global Memory Optimization for Stream Applications in High-Level Synthesis

Jasmina Vasiljevic and Paul Chow
Edward S. Rogers Sr. Department of Electrical and Computer Engineering, University of Toronto
10 King's College Road, Toronto, ON, M5S 3G4, Canada
{vasiljev, pc@eecg.toronto.edu}

ABSTRACT

One of the challenges in designing high-performance FPGA applications is fine-tuning the use of limited on-chip memory storage among many buffers in an application. To achieve desired performance the designer faces the burden of packaging such buffers into on-chip memories and manually optimizing the utilization of each memory and the throughput of each buffer. In addition, the application memories may not match the word width or depth of the physical on-chip memories available on the FPGA. This process is time consuming and non-trivial, particularly with a large number of buffers of various depths and bit widths. We propose a tool, MPack, which globally optimizes on-chip memory use across all buffers for stream applications. The goal is to speed up development time by providing rapid design space exploration and relieving the designer of lengthy low-level iterations. We introduce new *high-level* pragmas allowing the user to specify global memory requirements, such as an application's on-chip memory budget and data throughput. We allow the user to quickly generate a large number of memory solutions and explore the trade-off between memory usage and achievable throughput. To demonstrate the effectiveness of our tool, we apply the new high-level pragmas to an image processing benchmark. MPack effectively explores the design space and is able to produce a large number of memory solutions ranging from 10 to 100% in throughput, and from 12 to 100% in on-chip memory usage.

Keywords

FPGA, on-chip memory, stream computing, buffer packing

1. INTRODUCTION

Difficulties in the FPGA programming environment have motivated the development of high-level synthesis tools and high-level programming models. One such programming model is the separation of memory and computation. Here the programmer focuses on designing computation kernels and relies on an automated optimization of memory.

In this work, we present a tool, called *MPack* that performs push-button on-chip memory optimization for streaming applications.

MPack is built on top of VivadoHLS [4], a high-level synthesis tool by Xilinx. MPack automatically generates memory solutions utilizing the memory related pragmas available in VivadoHLS. We introduce new *high-level* pragmas that enable global memory optimization goals, such as application throughput and total available on-chip memory budget.

A trade-off between data throughput and on-chip memory use can be explored by altering the mapping of buffers onto physical memories, or Block RAMs (BRAMs). Often, buffer dimensions (bit-width and depth) do not match those of physical memories, resulting in low memory utilization. *Buffer packing* can increase memory utilization and in turn reduce BRAMs. MPack automatically generates the optimal buffer packing approach, creating a memory solution with the highest data throughput at the minimum BRAM budget.

This paper is organized as follows. Section 2 describes the motivation behind our work, and Section 3 introduces VivadoHLS on top of which we built our tool. Section 4 presents the MPack tool, including the high-level pragmas and the buffer packing algorithm. Section 5 describes our stream benchmark. Section 7 presents results, and Section 8 concludes.

2. MOTIVATION

The extensive list of design space options often results in an order of magnitude performance difference between naive and optimized FPGA implementations. A large number of design iterations is common in FPGA development, however, it is tedious and time consuming. Iterations explore many design aspects of the application, such as: parallelization, workload balancing among the accelerator logic, latency and throughput. Modifying these parameters can be achieved through the use of various VivadoHLS pragmas, such as UNROLL and PIPELINE [4].

Each design iteration of the computation logic imposes a different set of requirements onto the memory (buffers of the application). A *buffer* is any application storage component, such as an array or FIFO. The buffer dimensions (depth and bit-width) and throughput, as well as global design requirements (BRAMs budget and throughput), can all change with design iterations.

In general, the design goal is to achieve the best system performance using the available resources. In terms of memory, for stream applications, this translates to achieving the highest data throughput at the lowest BRAM cost. This is a very time consuming and difficult iterative optimization, which motivates the search for programming models and tools that separate the development of computation and memory.

We extend the VivadoHLS programming model to allow the user to express *global* memory design requirements such as the maximum memory resource usage and data throughput. In terms of

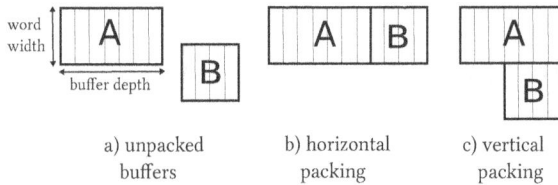

a) unpacked buffers   b) horizontal packing   c) vertical packing

Figure 1: Buffer packing approaches

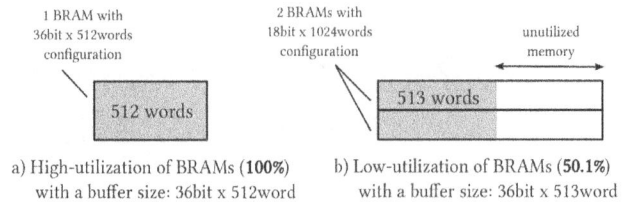

a) High-utilization of BRAMs (**100%**) with a buffer size: 36bit x 512word

b) Low-utilization of BRAMs (**50.1%**) with a buffer size: 36bit x 513word

Figure 2: BRAM concatenation

memory, VivadoHLS provides a variety of *low-level* pragmas that can optimize memory implementation when applied to each buffer (i.e., buffer packing). In contrast, MPack's *high-level* pragmas can be applied to entire functions or sections of code, resulting in an automated, behind the scene, memory optimization across many buffers. The high-level MPack pragmas expose a single knob, through which the user can scale the entire design up or down, allowing for global control of the application's throughput or BRAM use.

3. VIVADOHLS

MPack solutions are expressed in terms of VivadoHLS buffer packing memory pragmas: horizontal and vertical. In this section, we describe the properties of each packing approach and their impact on throughput. Second, we describe how BRAM usage is determined based on buffer dimensions. In particular, we present the technique used by VivadoHLS to concatenate BRAMs to create buffers with large bit-widths and depths.

3.1 VivadoHLS Memory Pragmas

As mentioned, two buffer packing approaches, horizontal and vertical, are explored. Multiple buffers packed together create a *buffer group*, where all buffers within the group share the two read-/write ports (using True-Dual port BRAMs). VivadoHLS allows only homogeneous packing, i.e., all buffers in a group have to be packed either vertically or horizontally. This means that in a group of three buffers, we cannot have two packed horizontally and one vertically. However, a memory solution may contain many buffer groups, each with a different packing approach.

Horizontal packing allows buffers to share BRAM depth, shown in Figure 1b). For example, two horizontally packed 100 word buffers can share the BRAM depth of 512 words. Memory port limitations determine the achievable throughput. Unpacked buffers each have two ports. When packed, a buffer group has a total of two ports - an equivalent of one port per buffer, and can therefore support only half of the original throughput.

Vertical packing allows buffers to share a BRAM's bit-width, or a word at a particular memory address, shown in Figure 1c). For example, two 9-bit buffers, can be vertically stacked and placed into a single 36-bit BRAM. However, writing to one of the buffers would cause data at the same memory address belonging to the other buffer to be overwritten. To prevent unwanted data corruption, every write must be preceded by a read at the same address, to record the un-altered portion of the memory word. Now, each write to a buffer requires two as opposed to one clock cycle. As a result, two vertically packed buffers will have one third of their original throughput, due to the reduced number of available memory ports, and due to the slower write operation.

```
1.  #pragma MPACK system_thr=50% "function_A"
2.  void function_A() {
3.      unsigned8 buffer_A1[1200];
4.      unsigned8 buffer_A2[1600];
5.      unsigned8 buffer_A3[1800];
6.      .. }
7.  #pragma MPACK bram_resources=40 "function_B"
8.  void function_B() {
9.      unsigned16 buffer_B1[8200];
10.     unsigned16 buffer_B2[6200];
11.     unsigned16 buffer_B3[4200];
12.     .. }
```

Figure 3: Sample application C-code with MPack pragmas

3.2 BRAM Concatenation

Understanding how BRAMs are concatenated to produce buffer memories is important in evaluating BRAM utilization, which affects buffer packing. Often, the bit-widths and depths of application buffers do not match those of BRAMs. Small buffers fit into a single BRAM, however, large buffers require many concatenated BRAMs to form a memory with the required buffer dimensions. VivadoHLS automatically performs this concatenation using a simple technique described next.

An 18K BRAM can be used in any of the following configurations, i.e., buffer bit-width and depth combinations: $36\text{bits}\times512\text{words}$, $18\text{bits}\times1024\text{words}$, $9\text{bits}\times2048\text{words}$, $4\text{bits}\times4096\text{words}$, $2\text{bits}\times8192$ words and $1\text{bit}\times16384\text{words}$ [5]. VivadoHLS chooses a BRAM configuration such that the BRAM's depth is at least as large as the buffer depth. Next, the BRAMs are vertically concatenated until the buffer's bit-width is satisfied. Buffers are always created using only one type of BRAM configuration, instead of a heterogeneous mix.

Figure 2a) shows a $36\text{bit}\times512$ word buffer that perfectly fits into a single 18K BRAM. Because the BRAM is 100% utilized, the buffer has no potential for reducing BRAM usage through buffer packing. However, for a buffer larger than 512 words, the next larger BRAM depth configuration is required: the $18\text{bit}\times1024\text{word}$. As shown in Figure 2b), two of these BRAMs are concatenated to create the required bit width. As a result, only 50.1% of the BRAMs is used to store the buffer contents and 49.9% is left unutilized. Buffer sizes just larger than BRAM configuration depths provide an opportunity to increase BRAM utilization through packing.

4. MPACK

MPack automatically generates a memory solution, with the goal to maximize throughput at the given BRAM budget. Using MPack allows the user to focus on optimizing computation, without concern for low-level memory optimization. Once an application is written and tested, the user would apply a variety of VivadoHLS loop and function pragmas to parallelize and pipeline the application code. For every parallelization approach the user can change the MPack high-level pragmas, and quickly generate a memory solution to match the optimized computation. Automating memory design implementation speeds up the design space exploration of the entire system, allowing the user to reach their high-performance goals sooner. MPack defines its new high-level pragmas and has a tool flow that sits on top of VivadoHLS. In this section, we present the high-level pragmas, the buffer packing algorithm and MPack tool flow.

4.1 High-Level Pragmas

C-code can be annotated with MPack pragmas allowing the designer to specify memory optimization goals. We introduce two types of high-level pragmas: 1) system throughput and 2) BRAM resources. High-level pragmas are used to specify global system design requirements. They expose a single knob through which the user can modify the entire on-chip memory solution space.

System throughput is the user-specified data throughput for a function (*system_thr*). This pragma is used to scale up or down all buffer throughputs within that function. For example, a system throughput of 50%, allows for buffers in that function to be packed until their throughputs are halved. In a video application, reducing the system throughput from 100% to 50% would result in a reduction in processing from 30 to 15 frames per second. Because all of the buffer throughputs are reduced by the same factor, the likelihood of creating throughput bottlenecks is minimized. The use of the *system_thr* pragma is shown in line 1 of Figure 3.

The **BRAM resources** pragma, when applied to a function, generates a memory solution such that the sum of all BRAMs used by all of the function's buffers is less than or equal to the number of BRAMs specified by the pragma (*bram_resources*). As the BRAMs from each buffer are reduced, the relative buffer throughput values are preserved to avoid creating throughput bottlenecks. If a solution within the BRAM budget is not feasible, MPack will generate the smallest possible solution and report a warning. The use of the *bram_resources* pragma is shown in line 7 of Figure 3.

4.2 The Algorithm

The MPack algorithm manipulates the mapping of buffers onto BRAMs, by choosing a combination of VivadoHLS packing pragmas to create a memory solution that meets user specified data throughput and BRAM budget. In stream applications throughput is the most important performance measurement metric. Also, buffers and memories in these applications are typically streamed, i.e., accessed with steady and predictable data flow rates (in contrast to random data fetches). In addition, stream buffers are active during the entire run-time of the application. As a result, decreasing the throughput even of a single buffer would create a throughput bottleneck, and decrease the performance of the entire system.

We designed an algorithm to generate memory solutions with minimized throughput bottlenecks. As the number of buffers packed into a group increases, the available throughput of each buffer decreases. The algorithm minimizes throughput bottlenecks by ensuring that the reduced throughputs are approximately the same across all buffers in the application. For example, the MPack pragma *system_thr=30%* indicates that throughput can be reduced to a third of the maximum available. As a result, some buffers will be horizontally packed into groups of three and some buffers will be vertically packed into groups of two.

The algorithm performs a full brute force search of the buffer packing design space. It evaluates all possible packing combinations of all buffers in the design, thus an optimal solution is guaranteed. The algorithm returns one of two possible results. First, if the user specified a desired *system_thr*, the algorithm returns the minimum number of BRAMs required to achieve that throughput.

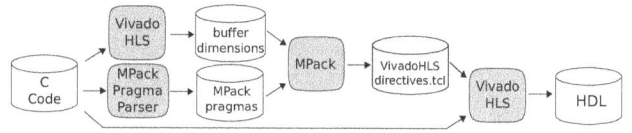

Figure 4: Tool flow

Second, if a BRAM budget was provided (*bram_resources*), we return the maximum throughput achievable at that budget.

A brute force algorithm was chosen as a first step in evaluating the potential buffer packing has to reduce BRAM usage. Future work will include an implementation of a packing algorithm based on heuristics, replacing the brute force search and reducing the algorithm run-time.

4.3 Tool Flow

As shown in Figure 4, MPack requires two types of data as input: 1) buffer dimensions and 2) MPack pragmas. All buffer dimensions are parsed from the synthesis report generated by VivadoHLS.

The application C-code is parsed and the MPack pragmas translated into input parameters for memory optimization.

The generated memory solution is expressed in terms of VivadoHLS memory related pragmas. They are written into the *directives.tcl* file, which may contain other user-specified pragmas and directives (e.g. parallelizing computation or optimizing I/O). Finally, the C-code and *directives.tcl* file are sent to VivadoHLS for synthesis.

5. BENCHMARK

The Gaussian pyramid [1] is an image processing technique used in algorithms such as the Laplacian filter to enhance local contrast. This benchmark creates a stack of successively smaller images (i.e., a pyramid of images) from a single input image, where each pixel is a local average corresponding to a pixel neighbourhood on a lower level of the pyramid. The benchmark performs multiple stages of 5×5 Finite Impulse Response (FIR) filtering and $2 \times$ down-sampling. On-chip storage is used to buffer only the pixels required for FIR filters of all stages of the down-sampling (instead of storing full images). For example, for an input image width w, buffers with three different depths are used: five buffers with depth w, five with depth $w/2$ and five with depth $w/4$.

The benchmark was written in C and synthesized in VivadoHLS 2013.1, targeting the Virtex-6 XC6VLX240T FPGA. To maximize data throughput we applied VivadoHLS pipeline pragmas, which are especially effective when implementing loops, present in our benchmark. Pipelining allows for instructions to be scheduled concurrently, instead of waiting for all instructions in the loop body to complete before starting the next loop iteration [4].

6. RESULTS

To demonstrate the effectiveness of MPack, we perform packing on a large range of buffer dimensions. To generate a range of buffers, we synthesize many versions of the Gaussian pyramid benchmark, each with a different input image width (*w*). As explained in Section 5, the input image width determines the depth of the internal buffers.

Each *line* in Figure 5 represents a version of the benchmark with a different input image width *w*. Benchmark versions are labelled in the format *w<input_image_width>*; e.g., *w800* represents a benchmark with a buffer depths of 800, 400 and 200. (all buffers are 32-bits wide). Each *point* on the line represents

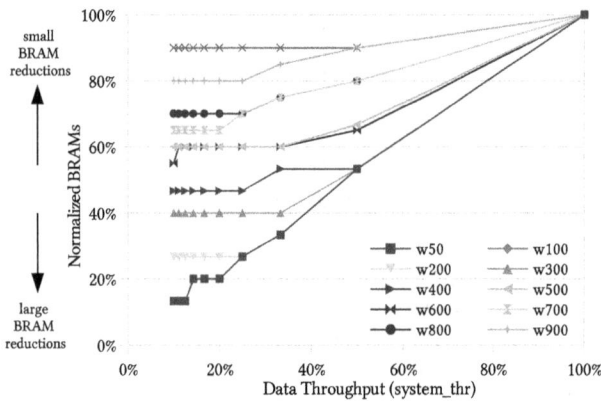

Figure 5: MPack buffer packing results for various system throughputs.

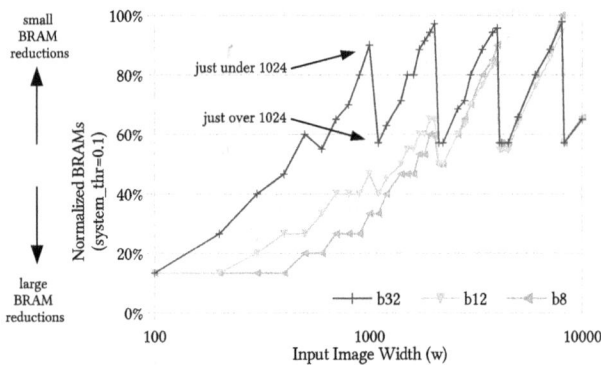

Figure 6: Maximum achievable BRAM reduction: buffer packing results for various buffer depths and bit widths.

a benchmark version synthesized with a different MPack pragma *system_thr* value, shown on the x-axis. A *system_thr=100%* represents the maximum achievable data throughput of the application i.e., the throughput with no buffer packing. We observe that, through the use of the MPack pragmas, the designer can reduce the throughput to a percentage of the maximum available. A reduction in throughput allows for the opportunity to save BRAMs through buffer packing. The y-axis shows the reduced BRAM usage normalized to the number of BRAMs used at the maximum throughput (*system_thr=100%*).

Figure 5 shows that MPack can trade throughput performance for BRAM usage, and allow the user easy and fast access to a large design space of BRAM budgets. We observe that benchmarks with small input image widths ($w = 50, 100, 200$), having small buffers, can be efficiently packed to achieve large BRAM reductions. For example, *w50* can be reduced to use 12% of its original BRAMs. However, as the input image width increases and buffer depths approach the BRAM block's depth of 1024 words (Xilinx 18Kb BRAM), the potential for achieving memory reduction lowers. For example, *w900* can only be reduced to 90% of its original use.

Next, we examine how effective MPack is over a much larger range of buffer depths. Figure 6 shows the maximum BRAM reductions achievable across an input image width ranging from 100 to 10000 pixels (x-axis). The y-axis shows the BRAM usage synthesized using the MPack pragma set at *system_thr=10%*. We synthesized all benchmark versions with a low throughput setting to measure the *maximum* achievable BRAM reduction possible.

Each *line* in Figure 6 represents a version of the benchmark with a different buffer bit-width, and each *point* a different buffer depth. For example, in the benchmark version *b8*, all buffers are 8 bits wide. As shown in the figure, both buffer depth and bit-width impact the BRAM usage, however, there exists a zig-zag trend, explained next.

We observe that memory usage can be reduced by buffer packing if there is a low utilization of BRAMs. For example, due to a large bit-width, in *b32* the MPack algorithm chose mostly horizontal buffer packing, thus making the BRAM utilization vary with buffer depth. Benchmarks with buffer depths just larger than the BRAM configuration depths (e.g., 1100, 2200, 4200 etc.) have low BRAM utilization. In these cases, MPack can achieve large BRAM reductions through buffer packing. However, buffer depths just under BRAM configuration depths (e.g., 1000, 2000, 4000 etc.) have lower potential for packing. These buffer sizes already have high BRAM utilization, therefore buffer packing is only able to slightly decrease memory use.

The presented results show that, through automated buffer packing, MPack can sweep a large design space and allow the user to rapidly explore trade-offs between on-chip memory use and data throughput.

7. RELATED WORK

Our approach of evaluating buffer packing solutions is similar to MemPacker [2], however their implementation is limited only to horizontal packing. In [3] the authors implement horizontal and vertical packing but do not target FPGAs. Their problem space is different, as they optimize for memory cost and data path routing, as well as generate different computation schedules. In contrast, our development approach fully relies on the user to specify a computational schedule (i.e., the amount of parallelism and pipelining); in addition, we define high-level pragmas for fast global optimization.

8. CONCLUSION

In this work we explored an approach to automating the design of on-chip memory solutions. The MPack tool allows for fast exploration of the memory resources vs. data throughput design space. To demonstrate the effectiveness of packing, we implemented and tested a packing algorithm on a stream application benchmark. MPack generated a large number of memory solutions ranging from 10 to 100% in throughput, and from 12 to 100% in on-chip memory usage. These results show that, through automated buffer packing, MPack can sweep a large design space and allow the user to rapidly explore trade-offs between low on-chip memory use and high data throughput.

9. REFERENCES

[1] E. H. Adelson et al. Pyramid methods in image processing. *RCA engineer*, 29(6):33–41, 1984.

[2] D. Karchmer and J. Rose. Definition and solution of the memory packing problem for field-programmable systems. *ICCAD*, 1994.

[3] H. Schmit and D. Thomas. Synthesis of application-specific memory designs. *IEEE Trans. on VLSI Systems*, 5(1):101–111, 1997.

[4] Xilinx Inc. *User Guide High-Level Synthesis*, 2012.

[5] Xilinx Inc. *7 Series FPGAs Memory Resources*, 2013.

A Soft Error Vulnerability Analysis Framework for Xilinx FPGAs

Aitzan Sari
Department of Informatics
University of Piraeus, Greece
aitsar@unipi.gr

Dimitris Agiakatsikas
Department of Informatics
University of Piraeus, Greece
agiakatsikas@gmail.com

Mihalis Psarakis
Department of Informatics
University of Piraeus, Greece
mpsarak@unipi.gr

ABSTRACT

Today's SRAM-based FPGAs provide a reach set of computing resources which makes them attractive in demanding and critical application domains, such as avionics and space. Unfortunately, their high reliance on SRAM configuration memory arise reliability issues due to the single-event upsets (SEUs). Considering the criticality of these applications, the vulnerability analysis of FPGA designs to SEUs becomes essential part of the design flow. In this context, we present an open-source framework for the soft error vulnerability analysis of Xilinx FPGA devices. The proposed framework will allow researchers to evaluate their reliability-aware CAD algorithms and estimate the soft error susceptibility of the designs at early stages of the implementation flow for the latest Xilinx architectures.

Categories and Subject Descriptors

B.8.1 [**Performance and Reliability**] Reliability, Testing, and Fault-Tolerance.

Keywords

Soft errors; Single-Events Upsets (SEUs); FPGAs; SEU mitigation; Sensitive configuration bits; Placement algorithms

1. INTRODUCTION

FPGA companies have followed closely the rapid advances in silicon nanometer technologies gaining significant benefits into device capacity and performance due to the increasing circuit scaling [4]. However, the aggressive shrinking of circuit dimensions to nanometer regime along with the high-reliance of modern FPGAs on SRAM configuration memory has revealed the susceptibility of the FPGA devices to various failure mechanisms raising several reliability issues [10]. Among these failure mechanisms, the radiation-induced single-event upsets (SEUs) are a major cause of failure in-the-field in contemporary FPGAs [7]. An SEU caused by high energy particles, such as heavy ions and protons, striking a memory cell may flip its value producing a *soft error*. Several fault tolerant approaches have been proposed in the past that cope with soft errors in FPGAs [3], [6]. However, given that the feature sizes of the future beyond nanometer technologies will continue to shrink, the implications caused by soft errors are expected to deteriorate [10] drawing the attention of researchers from both domains of fault-tolerant computing and design automation. For the assessment of SEU mitigation methodologies,

the research community needs analysis tools able to measure the soft error vulnerability of the designs and provide useful insights.

Several approaches have analyzed in the past the vulnerability of SRAM-based FPGAs into soft errors. These approaches are based either on fault injection experiments (using accelerated radiation testing [7], [14] or fault insertion software tools [12], [13]) or analytical methods [3] to measure the sensitive configuration bits. The analytical methods classify the configuration bits as *sensitive* or *non-sensitive* depending on their impact in the design operation. A sensitive configuration bit may affect the circuit operation if it is flipped by an SEU. However, some sensitive bits may be not critical for the application because their soft errors are masked and not propagated to the outputs. The fault injection approaches provide a more accurate estimation of critical configuration bits. The drawback of the experimental approaches is that they cannot be applied during the FPGA design flow in order to provide early sensitivity estimation. On the other hand, most previous analytical approaches have been implemented in proprietary software tools targeting specific FPGA architectures, and consequently, they cannot be easily reproduced for other FPGA families. Due to the absence of a soft error vulnerability analysis tool for industrial FPGA devices, all previous approaches that propose SEU-aware placement and routing algorithms [1], [15] have been demonstrated on the academic VPR tool targeting virtual FPGA architectures.

The research community has intensively addressed the last years the problem of bridging the academic CAD tools with commercial CAD tools [8], [9], [11]. Motivated by the above approaches and the need for FPGA reliability analysis tools, we have developed an open–source soft error vulnerability analysis framework based on RapidSmith [9] that is able to target Xilinx FPGAs. The framework supports vulnerability analysis at any phase of the FPGA design flow (e.g. post-mapping, post-placement and post-routing analysis) based on the XDL description of the circuit and can interact with any other XDL-enabled FPGA design flow. To demonstrate the proposed framework, we analyze the soft error vulnerability of various benchmarks mapped in a Virtex-5 device and compare different mapping/packing/placement algorithms in terms of soft-error awareness. We also evaluate our method correlating its sensitivity analysis results with the Xilinx sensitivity report. The framework is available at eslab.cs.unipi.gr.

2. SOFT ERROR VULNERABILITY ANALYSIS FRAMEWORK

Figure 1 depicts the main functions supported by the proposed framework. The user is free to run the entire flow and calculate the soft error vulnerability of the final FPGA design or run individual tools at the intermediate stages of the flow for an early sensitivity estimation of the design. The functions supported by our framework are the following:

- *Post–mapping analysis of the block configuration bits*: It extracts the FPGA resource utilization data from the XDL

FPGA'14, February 26–28, 2014, Monterey, CA, USA.
Copyright 2014 ACM 978-1-4503-2671-1/14/02...$15.00.
http://dx.doi.org/10.1145/2554688.2554767

netlist produced by the packing/mapping step and analyses the sensitivity of the block configurations bits based on a precompiled resource usage profile of the target architecture.

- *Post–placement analysis of the interconnection configuration bits*: It takes into consideration the actual sites of the resources obtained by the placement process and analyses the possibility of a net connecting two or more components to become open or short due to a soft error in a programmable interconnection point (PIP).
- *Post–routing analysis of the interconnection configuration bits*: It provides a more accurate analysis since it relies on the final routed circuit. It considers all possible defects that can be caused by a soft error in a PIP, i.e. open faults, bridging faults and antenna faults. The results are written in a text file (.rsba stands for routing sensitive bit analysis) for further processing.
- *Analysis of the Xilinx report for essential configuration bits*: It parses the Xilinx sensitivity report (essential bitmap file, .ebd) and the bitstream file using RapidSmith packages and classifies the essential bits into block, interface and interconnection bits and allocates them to configuration frames. This step generates the xsba file used in the visualization of the ebd sensitive bits on the FPGA layout.
- *Visualization of soft-error vulnerable areas:* A Graphic tool built as an extension of the Rapidsmith Device.Explorer class reads the results from the two previous analysis steps and illustrates the vulnerable areas of the FPGA layout.

Given that RapidSmith can manipulate the XDL description of any FPGA device, our framework can analyze all Xilinx FPGA families with XDL support. Currently, the tools have been tested for Virtex-5 and Virtex-6 families supporting all the available devices. The .xml file provided to the post–mapping analysis includes the results of the usage profiling of the programmable resources for a specific FPGA architecture. According to this profile, each primitive resource has been mapped with its theoretical configuration bits based on its possible usage mode. We have performed the profiling of Virtex-5 and Virtex-6 architectures and we plan to integrate the profiles of more Xilinx architectures in the future. Furthermore, for demonstration purposes, we have implemented the simulated annealing placer [5] (SA placer) in the RapidSmith in order to compare the Xilinx placer and the SA placer in terms of soft error awareness.

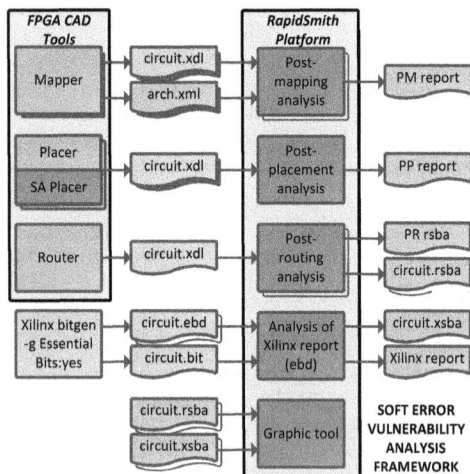

Figure 1. Soft error vulnerability analysis framework.

3. ESTIMATION OF SENSITIVE CONFIGURATION BITS

The analysis distinguishes the sensitive bits to interconnection and block configuration bits, while the interconnection bits are being further classified to open, short and antenna sensitive bits.

3.1 Sensitive Block Configuration Bits

The estimation of sensitive block configuration bits can be applied as early as the mapping process on the FPGA design flow. The block configuration bits are classified into CLB, IOB, BRAM and DSP configuration bits, while two estimation methods are proposed: a black-box method and a structural analysis method. The former method depends only on the post-mapping resource utilization data and a fixed number of sensitive bits per block while the latter uses a structural sensitivity analysis of the programmable resources to improve the accuracy.

3.1.1 Black-Box Estimation Method

The black-box estimation approach assumes that all configuration bits of a used programmable resource are sensitive. According to this pessimistic assumption, the number of sensitive bits per programmable resource is fixed and can be extracted from the documented structure of the configuration bitstream. The sensitive bits of programmable R-type blocks are calculated by dividing the total configuration bits of an R-column ($ColumnBits_R$) to the number of blocks in the column ($ColumnBlocks_R$) and multiplying with the number of R-type blocks (N_R) in the design. For example, a single slice generates 352 sensitive configuration bits ((11 frames*1280 bits/frame)/40 slices/CLB column) in a Virtex-5 FPGA.

$$Sensitive\ bits\ (R) = \frac{ColumnBits_R}{ColumnBlocks_R} * N_R \qquad (1)$$

3.1.2 Structural Analysis Method

A more accurate estimation can be performed by analyzing the structure of each programmable resource block. In this paper, we have explored the CLB/slice as well as the IOB programmable resources of the Virtex-5 and Virtex-6 family.

3.1.2.1 Sensitive Slice Configuration Bits

In order to improve the estimation of the slice configuration bits, we analyze the LUTs utilization and the slice control bits. Regarding the LUT, we consider as sensitive only the portion of the LUT that actually participates in the implementation of the function, e.g. for a j-input function 2^j entries of the LUT are considered as sensitive. For the analysis of the slice control bits we have applied a *resource-usage profile*, where each primitive resource has been mapped with its theoretical configuration bits based on its possible usage mode. The different resource-usage profiles of a single slice for Virtex-5 are listed in Table 1. The theoretical analysis has been also verified experimentally at a large extend; we implemented a simple circuit which occupies a single slice and we measured the sensitive configuration bits of the slice (from the Xilinx sensitivity report) after several slight modifications in order to see how each modification affects the sensitive bits. An example of a slice resource is the storage element which can be configured as FF or Latch. The usage of a single storage element introduces 16 sensitive bits (7 bits for properties configuration and 9 bits for global configuration).

Table 1. Resource usage profile for Virtex-5 slice.

Resource usage	Sensitive configuration bits
LUT for slice L/M/Global	2/9/4
Storage element/Global	7/9
OUTMUX/CARRY/CLKINV	3/11/2

For a given FPGA design the estimation of sensitive bits for the slice resources *Sensitive bits(slice)* can be derived using Equation 2, where N_{slice} is the number of used slices, LUT_j is the number of inputs for the 4 LUTs of the slice and c_{slice} denotes the control bits of the slice.

$$Sensitive\ bits(slice) = \sum_{i=1}^{N_{slice}}\left(\sum_{j=1}^{4} 2^{LUT_j}\right) + c_{slice} \qquad (2)$$

3.1.2.2 Sensitive IOB Configuration Bits
Depending on its direction mode, an IOB could be bounded with an input (ILOGIC) or an output (OLOGIC) logic which in addition can be combined with a programmable delay element (IODELAY). Moreover, a single IOB can use the ILOGIC and OLOGIC resources for the implementation of dedicated circuits such as ISERDES (Input Serial-to-Parallel Logic) or OSERDES (Output Parallel-to-Serial Logic) which in conjunction with the large number of programmable primitive resources makes the IOBs difficult to analyze. In order to come through this difficulty we use the structural approach applied to slices but instead of analyzing theoretically the configuration bits of the IOB resources we rely our analysis on the functional mode of the IOB and observations made by the analysis of Xilinx sensitivity report. More specifically, we configured a single IOB in different functional modes and measured the sensitive bits of every configuration analyzing the .ebd file. Table 2 summarizes the sensitive bits measurements for the different functional modes of an IOB (PAD: Pad bits, I: ILOGIC, O: OLOGIC, IOD: IODELAY). For example, the sensitive bits for an IOB configured as input are 72 bits in total (53 bits for the PAD and 19 bits for the IOLOGIC). The estimation of the sensitive IOB configuration bits can be derived by Equation 3.

$$Sensitive\ bits(IOB) = \sum_{i=1}^{N_{IOB}}(c_{PADi} + c_{Ii} + c_{Oi} + c_{IODi}) \qquad (3)$$

Table 2. Sensitive configuration bits for Virtex-5 IOB.

IOB functional mode	PAD	I	O	IOD	Total
Input/Output	53/54	19/0	0/31	0/0	72/85
Input-single register	53	70	0	0	123
Output-single/two registers	54/54	0/0	48/54	0/0	102/108
IODELAY-input/output	53/54	0/0	0/0	67/80	120/134
ISERDES/OSERDES	53/54	96/0	0/85	0/0	149/139

3.2 Sensitive Routing Configuration Bits
The fault modeling and the vulnerability analysis of the FPGA routing resources have been studied extensively in the past [1], [12], [13]. Here, we adopt the fault modeling of routing resources proposed by several previous approaches, according to which the routing faults due to soft errors in the PIPs can be open, short or antenna. So, an interconnection configuration bit is termed as open-sensitive when a soft error causes an open wire, as short-sensitive when it causes the bridging of two distinct nets, and finally as antenna-sensitive when it results to a hanging wire connected to a net. Our estimation method is based on the simple interconnection block model which consists of a switch-matrix and an interface block. The interface block is used to connect the terminals (inputs/outputs) of a resource block (CLBs, IOBs, etc.) to the switch matrix which in turn provides access to the global interconnection network. The information required by the above analysis (e.g. which PIPs are in use, which wires can be connected through PIPs, etc.) is extracted from the XDL model of the circuit.

3.2.1 Post-placement analysis
We adopt the method introduced in [1] to calculate the open-sensitive and short-sensitive bits of an FPGA design. The open-sensitive bits for a single net are calculated using the Manhattan distance applied on its Bounding Box (BB) assuming $X_{min}Y_{min}$ and $X_{max}Y_{max}$ being the coordinates of the BB. Equation 4 is used to calculate the number of open-sensitive bits. We adopt the q factor used also in the simulated annealing placement algorithm to characterize the pin-count of the particular net.

$$Sens.\ bits\ (open) = (|X_{max}-X_{min}| + |Y_{max}-Y_{min}| + 1) * q \qquad (4)$$

The method for the estimation of short-sensitive bits is based on the usage probability of switch matrices within the BB of a net. To find the short-sensitive bits between two nets N1 and N2 the method just uses the product of their usage probabilities over the overlap area (Equation 5).

$$Sens.\ bits\ (short) = \sum_{\forall(i,j)\ in_{overlap\ area}} p^{N1}(i,j) * p^{N2}(i,j) \qquad (5)$$

where $p^{N}(i,j)$ is the probability of net N to be routed through switch matrix (i,j).

3.2.2 Post-routing analysis
Although post-placement analysis provides a useful tool to estimate sensitive bits at an early phase of the design flow it lacks accuracy, overestimating the susceptibility of routing resources to soft errors. A more accurate calculation can be done analyzing the final routed circuit through its XDL netlist. The calculation of the open-sensitive bits is almost a straightforward process since it requires a simple exploration of the nets and an aggregation of the used PIPs. In order to calculate the short sensitive bits, we first check the wires used in the design and for each wire we identify its possible connections. The possible connections for a given wire (i.e. connections supported by the switch matrix) are extracted using the appropriate APIs of the RapidSmith framework. The last factor of the post-routing analysis is the antenna sensitive bits. The antenna sensitive bits are calculated by finding the alternative connections of the used wires in the switch matrix which do not produce a short circuit.

The total sensitive configuration bits for an FPGA design can be calculated summing-up the block configuration bits (Section 3.1) and the interconnection configuration bits using either the post-placement analysis (Section 3.2.1) or the post-routing analysis (Section 3.2.2).

4. EXPERIMENTAL RESULTS
We carried out a set of experiments to demonstrate the functions of our vulnerability analysis framework. The first experimental set has been used to evaluate the *post-placement* and *post-routing* analysis methods. We use the QUIP benchmarks [2] shown in Table 3 which have been adapted to the design flow of Xilinx ISE and synthesized on a Virtex-5 device FPGA (XC5VLX30FF67). For the above benchmarks we have run both *post-placement* and *post-routing* analysis methods. Figure 2 presents the results of the two steps in terms of sensitive interconnection bits (open-sensitive, short-sensitive and total) considering the SA placer and Xilinx ISE placer. The two placers present the same behavior in terms of SEU awareness. Precisely, SA placer produces slightly less *open-sensitive* bits than the Xilinx placer by a percentage of 6.9% but generates more *short-sensitive* by a factor of 7.4%. Figure 2 can be also used to evaluate the accuracy of the *post-placement* estimation of interconnection sensitive bits compared to the *post-routing* estimation. The *post-placement* estimation introduces a small overestimation of 7.8% in the case of *open-sensitive* and a high overestimation of 64.4% in the case of *short-sensitive* bits.

Table 3. QUIP benchmarks

	benchmark	SLIC	IOB	DSP	BRA	LUT
1	oc_des_des3pe	2279	298	0	0	5652
2	mux_128bit	327	140	0	0	256
3	fip_risc8	90	113	0	0	225
4	oc_mem_ctrl	699	267	0	0	1494
5	oc_vid_cm_jpe	1672	46	32	0	5485

The second experimental set has been performed to evaluate our vulnerability analysis method compared to the sensitivity report of Xilinx (.ebd file). All benchmarks have been implemented using the SA placer and the Xilinx router. Figure 3 compares the sensitive block configuration bits and the interconnection configuration bits for the two methods. The results obtained from the tools are similar for the block configuration analysis, except circuit b5 where Xilinx reports 42.37% more sensitive block configuration bits. Regarding the sensitive interconnection bits, where we adopt the results of our post-routing analysis, the two methods present significant differences. The Xilinx sensitivity analysis results to a significantly larger number of sensitive interconnection bits for all categories.

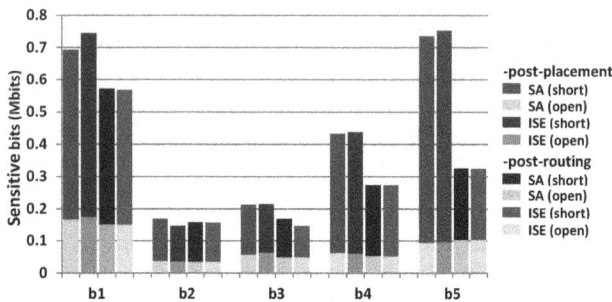

Figure 2. SA placer vs. ISE placer: Post-placement & post-routing analysis (interconnection configuration bits).

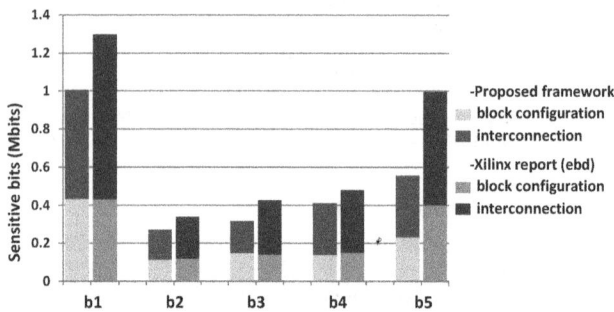

Figure 3. Proposed framework vs. Xilinx report (interconnection and block configuration bits).

5. CONCLUSION AND FUTURE WORK

In this paper we present an open-source, soft error vulnerability analysis framework for Xilinx FPGA devices. The proposed framework, which is based on RapidSmith tools and APIs, will allow researchers to evaluate new soft error aware CAD (packing, placement, routing) algorithms, estimate the soft error susceptibility of FPGA designs at various stages of the implementation flow, and analyze the soft error vulnerability on latest commercial FPGA architectures. The framework tools are available at eslab.cs.unipi.gr. In the future, we intend to extend the list of supported devices and perform fault injection experiments in order to evaluate our analysis results and calculate the actual sensitivity of the FPGA designs.

6. ACKNOWLEDGMENTS

This research has been co-financed by the European Union and Greek national funds through the project "Hardware and Software Techniques for Multi/Manycore Processor Architectures Reliability Enhancement (Thalis/HOLISTIC)".

7. REFERENCES

[1] Abdul-Aziz, M.A. and Tahoori, M.B., 2010. Soft error reliability aware placement and routing for FPGAs. In *Test Conference (ITC), 2010 IEEE International*, 1-9.

[2] Altera, 2010. Benchmark Designs For The Quartus University Interface Program (QUIP) Version 1.1, https://www.altera.com/support/software/download/altera_design/quip/quip-download.jsp.

[3] Asadi, G. and Tahoori, M.B., 2005. Soft error rate estimation and mitigation for SRAM-based FPGAs. *ACM/SIGDA 13th international symposium on Field-programmable gate arrays*, ACM, 1046212, 149-160.

[4] Betz, V., 2009. FPGA challenges and opportunities at 40nm and beyond. In *Field Programmable Logic and Applications, 2009. International Conference on*, 4-4.

[5] Betz, V. and Rose, J., 1997. VPR: a new packing, placement and routing tool for FPGA research, 213-222.

[6] Bolchini, C., Miele, A., and Sandionigi, C., 2011. A Novel Design Methodology for Implementing Reliability-Aware Systems on SRAM-Based FPGAs. *Computers, IEEE Transactions on 60*, 12, 1744-1758.

[7] Hiemstra, D.M. and Kirischian, V., 2012. Single Event Upset Characterization of the Virtex-6 Field Programmable Gate Array Using Proton Irradiation. In *Radiation Effects Data Workshop (REDW), 2012 IEEE*, 1-4.

[8] Hung, E., Eslami, F., and Wilton, S.J.E., 2013. Escaping the Academic Sandbox: Realizing VPR Circuits on Xilinx Devices. In *Field-Programmable Custom Computing Machines (FCCM), 21st Annual Intern. Sympos. on*, 45-52.

[9] Lavin, C., Padilla, M., Lamprecht, J., Lundrigan, P., Nelson, B., and Hutchings, B., 2011. RapidSmith: Do-It-Yourself CAD Tools for Xilinx FPGAs. In *Field Programmable Logic and Applications*, 349-355.

[10] Srinivasan, S., Krishnan, R., Mangalagiri, P., Yuan, X., Narayanan, V., Irwin, M.J., and Sarpatwari, K., 2008. Toward Increasing FPGA Lifetime. *Dependable and Secure Computing, IEEE Transactions on 5*, 2, 115-127.

[11] Steiner, N., Wood, A., Shojaei, H., Couch, J., Athanas, P., and French, M., 2011. Torc: towards an open-source tool flow. *19th ACM/SIGDA international symposium on Field programmable gate arrays*, ACM, 1950425, 41-44.

[12] Sterpone, L. and Violante, M., 2007. A New Partial Reconfiguration-Based Fault-Injection System to Evaluate SEU Effects in SRAM-Based FPGAs. *Nuclear Science, IEEE Transactions on 54*, 4, 965-970.

[13] Violante, M., Sterpone, L., Ceschia, M., Bortolato, D., Bernardi, P., Reorda, M.S., and Paccagnella, A., 2004. Simulation-based analysis of SEU effects in SRAM-based FPGAs. *Nuclear Science, IEEE Trans. on 51*, 6, 3354-3359.

[14] Wirthlin, M., Johnson, E., Rollins, N., Caffrey, M., and Graham, P., 2003. The reliability of FPGA circuit designs in the presence of radiation induced configuration upsets. In *Field-Programmable Custom Computing Machines, 2003. FCCM 2003. 11th Annual IEEE Symposium on*, 133-142.

[15] Zarandi, H.R., Miremadi, S.G., Pradhan, D.K., and Mathew, J., 2007. SEU-Mitigation Placement and Routing Algorithms and Their Impact in SRAM-Based FPGAs. In *Quality Electronic Design, 2007. ISQED '07*, 380-385.

Poster Session 1

FPGA LUT Design for Wide-band Dynamic Voltage and Frequency Scaled Operation

Monther Abusultan, Sunil P. Khatri
Texas A&M University

Field programmable gate arrays (FPGAs) are the implementation platform of choice when it comes to design flexibility. However, the high power consumption of FPGAs (which arises due to their flexible structure), make them less appealing for extreme low power applications. In this paper, we present a design of an FPGA look-up table (LUT), with the goal of seamless operation over a wide band of supply voltages. The same LUT design has the ability to operate at sub-threshold voltage when low power is required, and at higher voltages whenever faster performance is required. The results show that operating the LUT in sub-threshold mode yields a (~80x) lower power and (~4x) lower energy than full supply voltage operation, for a 6-input LUT implemented in a 22nm predictive technology. The key drawback of sub-threshold operation is its susceptibility to process, temperature, and supply voltage (PVT) variations. This paper also presents the design and experimental results for a closed-loop adaptive body biasing mechanism to dynamically cancel these PVT variations. For the same 22nm technology, we demonstrate that the closed-loop adaptive body biasing circuits can allow the FPGA to operate over an operating frequency range that spans an order of magnitude (40 MHz to 1300 MHz). We also show that the closed-loop adaptive body biasing circuits can cancel delay variations due to supply voltage changes, and reduce the effect of process variations on setup and hold times by 1.8x and 2.9x respectively.

ACM Categories & Descriptors: B.7.1 VLSI

Keywords: FPGA; LUT; Subthreshold; Dynamic Body Bias; DVFS; Low Power; VLSI; PVT Control

A Configurable MapReduce Accelerator for Multi-core FPGAs

Christoforos Kachris, Ch. Sirakoulis
Democritus University of Thrace
Dimitrios Soudris
National Technical University of Athens

MapReduce is a widely used programming framework for the implementation of cloud computing application in data centers. This work presents a novel configurable hardware accelerator that is used to speed up the processing of multi-core and cloud computing applications based on the MapReduce programming framework. The proposed MapReduce configurable accelerator is augmented to multi-core processors and it performs a fast

indexing and accumulation of the key/value pairs based on an efficient memory architecture using Cuckoo hashing. The MapReduce accelerator consists of the memory buffers that store the key/value pairs, and the processing units that are used to accumulate the key's value sent from the processors. In essence, this accelerator is used to alleviate the processors from executing the Reduce tasks, and thus executing only the Map tasks and emitting the intermediate key/value pairs to the hardware acceleration unit that performs the Reduce operation. The number and the size of the keys that can be stored on the accelerator are configurable and can be configured based on the application requirements. The MapReduce accelerator has been implemented and mapped to a multi-core FPGA with embedded ARM processors (Xilinx Zynq FPGA) and has been integrated with the MapReduce programming framework under Linux. The performance evaluation shows that the proposed accelerator can achieve up to 1.8x system speedup of the MapReduce applications and hence reduce significantly the execution time of multi-core and cloud computing applications. (Action: "Supporting Postdoctoral Researchers", "Education and Lifelong Learning" Program (GSRT) and co-financed by the ESF and the Greek State.)

ACM Categories & Descriptors: C.1.2 Multiple Data Stream Architectures (Multiprocessors); D.1.3 Concurrent Programming

Keywords: Mapreduce; Cloud computing; Hardware accelerator; multi-core programming; FPGA; Reconfigurable computing

A New Basic Logic Structure for Data-Path Computation

Pierre-Emmanuel Gaillardon, Luca Amarù,
Giovanni De Micheli, *EPFL*

Nowadays, *Field Programmable Gate Arrays* (FPGA) implement arithmetic functions using specific circuits at the logic block level, such as the carry paths, or at the structure level adopting *Digital Signal Processing* (DSP) blocks. Nevertheless, all these approaches, introduced to ease the realization of specific functions, are lacking of generality. In this paper, we introduce a new logic block that natively realizes arithmetic functions while preserving the versatility to implement general logic functions. It consists of a partially interconnected matrix of signal routers driven by comparators. We demonstrate that this structure can realize (i) any 2-output 2-input logic function or (ii) any single-output 3-input logic function or (iii) specific logic, such as arithmetic functions, with up to 4-output and 8-inputs. As compared to a standard 6-input *Look Up Table* (LUT), the proposed block requires roughly the same area but is 35.3% faster. Even though the proposed block has not the same exhaustive configurability of a 6-input LUT, there are arithmetic functions realizable in a single block that do not fit in one, or even more, 6-input LUT. For example, a single block inherently implements an entire 3-bit adder that requires 3× more resources with LUTs plus also custom circuitry. From a system level perspective, we show that a 256-bit adder is implemented with a gain on area×delay product of 31% as compared to its traditional LUT-based counterpart.

ACM Categories & Descriptors: B.7 Types and Design Style

Keywords: FPGA; Arithmetic functions; BBDD; Logic Element

A Methodology for Identifying and Placing Heterogeneous Cluster Groups Based on Placement Proximity Data

Farnaz Gharibian, *Simon Fraser University*
Lesley Shannon, *Simon Fraser University*
Peter Jamieson, *Miami University*

Due to the rapid growth in the size of designs and Field Programmable Gate Arrays (FPGAs), CAD run-time has increased dramatically. Reducing FPGA design compilation times without degrading circuit performance is crucial. In this work, we describe a novel approach for incremental design flows that both identifies tightly grouped FPGA logic blocks and then uses this information during circuit placement. Our approach reduces placement run-time on average by more than 17% while typically maintaining the design's critical path delay and marginally increasing its minimum channel width and wire length on average. Instead of following the traditional approach of evaluating a circuit's pre-placement netlist, this new algorithm analyzes designs post-placement to detect proximity data. It uses this information to non-aggressively extract heterogeneous cluster groupings from the design, which we call "gems," that consist of two to seventeen clusters. We modified VPR's simulated annealing placement algorithm to use our Singularity Placer, which first crushes each cluster grouping into a "singularity," to be treated as a single cluster. We then run the annealer over this condensed circuit, followed by an expansion of the singularities, and a second annealing phase for the entire expanded circuit.

ACM Categories & Descriptors: B.7.2 Design Aids; H.3.3 Information Search and Retrieval

Keywords: FPGA; Placement; CAD; Clustering

A Scalable Routability-driven Analytical Placer with Global Router Integration for FPGAs

Ka Chun Lam, *The Chinese University of Hong Kong*
Wai-Chung Tang, *Queen Mary University of London*
Evangeline F.Y. Young, *The Chinese University of Hong Kong*

As the sizes of modern circuits become bigger and bigger, implementing those large circuits into FPGA becomes arduous. The state-of-the-art academic FPGA place-and-route tool, VPR, has good quality but needs around a whole day to complete a placement when the input circuit contains millions of lookup tables, excluding the runtime for routing. To expedite the placement process, we propose a routability-driven placement algorithm for FPGA that adopts techniques used in ASIC global placer. Our placer follows the lower-bound-and-upper-bound iterative optimization process in ASIC placers like *Ripple*. In the lower-bound computation, the total HPWL, modeled using the Bound2Bound net model, is minimized using the conjugate gradient method. In the upper-bound computation, an almost-legalized result is produced by spreading cells linearly in the placement area. Those positions are then served as fixed-point anchors and fed into the next lower-bound computation. Furthermore, global routing will be performed in the upper-bound computation to estimate the routing segment usage, as a mean to consider congestion in placement. We tested our approach using 20 MCNC benchmarks and 4 large benchmarks for performance and scalability. Experimental results show that based on the island-style architecture which VPR is most optimized for, our approach can obtain a placement result 8× faster than VPR with 2% more in channel width, or 3× faster with 1% more in channel width when congestion is being considered. Our approach is even 14× faster than VPR in placing large benchmarks with over 10,000 lookup tables, with only 7% more in channel width.

ACM Categories & Descriptors: B.7.2 Design Aids

Keywords: FPGA; Placement; Routability-driven

Towards High Performance GHASH for Pipelined AES-GCM Using FPGAs

Karim M. Abdellatif, Roselyne Chotin-Avot
University of Paris VI
Zied Marrakchi, *FlexRas Technologies*
Habib Mehrez, Qingshan Tang
University of Paris VI

AES-GCM has been utilized in various security applications. It consists of two components: an Advanced Encryption Standard (AES) engine and a Galois Hash (GHASH) core. The performance of the system is determined by the GHASH architecture because of the inherent computation feedback. This paper introduces a modification for the pipelined Karat-suba Ofman Algorithm (KOA)-based GHASH. In particular, the computation feedback is removed by analyzing the complexity of the computation process. The proposed GHASH core is evaluated with three different implementations of AES (BRAMs-based SubBytes, composite _eld-based Sub-Bytes, and LUT-based SubBytes). The presented AES-GCM architectures are implemented using Xilinx Virtex5 FPGAs. Our comparison to previous work reveals that our architectures are more performance-efficient (Thr. /Slices).

Keywords
AES-GCM, GHASH, Karatsuba Ofman Algorithm (KOA), FPGAs

Hierarchical Library-Based Power Estimator for Versatile FPGAs

Hao Liang, *HK University of Science & Technology*
Yi-Chung Chen, *University of Pittsburgh*
Wei Zhang, *HK University of Science & technology*
Hai Li, *University of Pittsburgh*

FPGAs are becoming promising hardware accelerators for high performance computing systems, such as cloud computing, big-data processing, etc., where power is a key factor due to thermal and energy saving considerations. Current CAD tools for FPGA power estimation either support specific hardware provided by vendors or contain power models for mainly conventional FPGA architectures. However, with technology advancement, versatile novel FPGA architectures are being proposed to further augment current FPGA architecture at various aspects, such as emerging FPGA based on non-volatile memory, improved logic and DSP design, etc. In order to evaluate the power consumption of versatile FPGA designs, the power estimator has to be made more flexible and extendable to support new devices and architectures.

In this work, we proposed such a tool that the power estimation can be performed based on a hierarchical library which contains power models at different levels, such as circuit components or devices. The tool can collect resource utilization of FPGA for the implemented circuit, and then perform power estimation at coarse-grain or fine-grain levels based on the hierarchical library to achieve the desired complexity-accuracy trade-off. The flexibility is provided that users can customize the hierarchical library for new circuit components or devices with power number of their own study.

In this work, benchmarks evaluation results are verified against commercial power estimation tool to show the accuracy of the proposed tool. Case study on RRAM FPGA is also presented to demonstrate the tool's flexibility to support emerging technology and novel design.

ACM Categories & Descriptors: J.6 Comuter-aided design (CAD)

Keywords: FPGA; Power Estimation; Library-based Power Model

FPGA'14, February 26–28, 2014, Monterey, California, USA.
ACM 978-1-4503-2671-1/14/02.

Poster Session 2

Transformations for Throughput Optimization in High-Level Synthesis

Peng Li, *Peking University*
Louis-Noel Pouchet, *UCLA*
Deming Chen, *UIUC*
Jason Cong, *UCLA*

Programming productivity of FPGA devices remains a significant challenge, despite the emergence of robust high level synthesis tools to automatically transform codes written in high-level languages into RTL implementations. Focusing on a class of programs with regular loop bounds and array accesses (so-called affine programs), the polyhedral compilation framework provides a convenient environment to automate many of the manual program transformation tasks that are still needed to improve the QoR of the HLS tool.

In this work, we demonstrate that tiling-driven affine loop transformations, while mandatory to ensure good data reuse and reduce off-chip communication volumes, are not always enough to achieve the best throughput, determined by the Initiation Interval (II) for loop pipelining. We develop additional techniques to optimize the computation part to be executed on the FPGA, using Index-Set Splitting (ISS) to split loops into sub-loops with different properties (sequential/parallel, different memory port conflicts features). This is motivated by the presence of non-uniform data dependences in some affine benchmarks, which are not effectively handled by the affine transformation system for tiling implemented in the PolyOpt/HLS software. We develop a customized affine+ISS optimization algorithm that aims at reducing the II of pipelined inner loops to reduce the program latency. We report experimental results on numerous affine computations.

Categories and Subject Descriptors
B.5.2 [Hardware]: Design Aids — optimization;
D 3.4 [Program-ming languages]: Processor — Compilers; Optimization

Keywords
Program Optimization; High-Level Synthesis; Pipelining

On Hybrid Memory Allocation for FPGA Behavioral Synthesis

Qian Zhang, Chenfei Ma, Qiang Xu
The Chinese University of Hong Kong

FPGA behavioral synthesis has gained significant momentum recently with the growing interests in accelerating high-performance computing applications. While the latest generation of high-level synthesis (HLS) tools has made significant progress, they still lack the support for certain high-level language features such as dynamic memory allocation, despite the fact that efficiently utilization of the on-chip memory resources in FPGAs is critical to achieve the performance and power consumption target for many designs.

To tackle the above problem, in this paper, we propose a novel hybrid memory allocation scheme to map *malloc/free* in C programing language onto FPGA platforms. By estimating the memory usage and available FPGA memory resources, the scheme judiciously allocates static memory blocks and/or instantiate hardware allocators for memory requests. And the partition between these two parts is based on estimated access counts and solving an ILP to minimize overhead from dynamic memory allocation.

Experimental results on benchmark circuits demonstrate the efficacy of the proposed technique.

ACM Categories & Descriptors: B.5.2 [Hardware]: [Design Aids] – Automatic synthesis

Keywords: High-Level Synthesis; FPGA; Dynamic Memory Allocation

Pushing the Performance Boundary of Linear Projection Designs Through Device Specific Optimisations

Rui Policarpo Duarte, Christos-Savvas Bouganis
Imperial College London

The continuous scaling of the fabrication process combined with the ever increasing need of high performance designs, means that the era of treating all devices the same is about to come to an end. The presented work considers device oriented optimisations in order to further boost the performance of a Linear Projection design by focusing on the over-clocking of arithmetic operators. A methodology is proposed for the acceleration of Linear Projection designs on an FPGA, that introduces information about the performance of the hardware under over-clocking conditions to the application level. The novelty of this method is a pre-characterisation of the most prone to error arithmetic operators and the utilisation of this information in the high-level optimization process of the design. This results in a set of circuit designs that achieve higher throughput with minimum error. FPGA devices are suitable for such optimisations due to their reconfigurability feature that allows performance characterisation of the underlying fabric prior to the design of the final system. The reported results show that significant gains in the performance of the system can be achieved, i.e. up to 1.85 times speed up in the throughput compared to existing methodologies, when such device specific optimisation is considered.

ACM Categories & Descriptors: B.8.1 Reliability, Testing, and Fault-Tolerance; C.4 PERFORMANCE OF SYSTEMS

Keywords: Linear Projection; FPGA; Over-Clocking; Device Characterisation

Accelerating Massive Short Reads Mapping for Next Generation Sequencing

Chunming Zhang, Wen Tang, Guangming Tan
Chinese Academy of Sciences.

Due to the explosion of gene sequencing data with over one billion reads per run, the data-intensive computations of Next Generation Sequencing (NGS) applications pose great challenges to current computing capability. In this paper we investigate both algorithmic and architectural accelerating strategies to a typical NGS analysis algorithm -- short reads mapping -- on a commodity multicore and customizable FPGA coprocessor architecture, respectively. First, we propose a hash buckets reorder algorithm that increases *shared cache parallelism* during the course of searching hash index. The algorithmic strategy achieves 122Gbp/day throughput by exploiting shared-cache parallelism, that leads to performance improvement of 2 times on an 8-core Intel Xeon processor. Second, we develop a FPGA coprocessor that leverages both *bit-level and word-level parallelism* with scatter-gather memory mechanism to speedup inherent irregular memory access operations by increasing effective memory bandwidth. Our customized FPGA coprocessor achieves 947Gbp per day throughput, that is 189 times higher than current mapping tools on single CPU core, and above 2 times higher than a 64-core multi-processor system. The coprocessor's power efficiency is 29 times higher than a conventional 64-core multi-processor. The results indicate that the customized FPGA coprocessor architecture, that is configured with scatter-gather memory's word-level access, appeals to data intensive applications.

ACM Categories & Descriptors: C.1.3 Heterogeneous (hybrid) systems; C.3 Special-purpose and application-based systems

Keywords: Next generation sequencing; Shared cache parallelism; bit-level parallelism; Word-level parallelism; Hash; Data intensive

Application Specific Processor with High Level Synthesized Instructions

Pavel Benáček, Viktor Puš, *CESNET*

The paper deals with the design of application-specific processor which uses high level synthesized instruction engines. This approach is demonstrated on the instance of high speed network flow measurement processor for FPGA. Our newly proposed concept called Software Defined Monitoring (SDM) relies on advanced monitoring tasks implemented in the software supported by a configurable hardware accelerator. The monitoring tasks reside in the software and can easily control the level of detail retained by the hardware for each flow. This way, the measurement of bulk/uninteresting traffic is offloaded to the hardware, while the interesting traffic is processed in the software. SDM enables creation of flexible monitoring systems capable of deep packet inspection at high throughput. We introduce the processor

architecture and a workflow that allows to create hardware accelerated measurement modules (instructions) from the description in C/C++ language. The processor offloads various aggregations and statistics from the main system CPU. The basic type of offload is the NetFlow statistics aggregation. We create and evaluate three more aggregation instructions to demonstrate the flexibility of our system. Compared to the hand-written instructions, the high level synthesized instructions are slightly worse in terms of both FPGA resources consumption and frequency. However, the time needed for development is approximately half.

ACM Categories & Descriptors: C.3 Microprocessor/microcomputer applications; B.6.3 Design Aids

Keywords: High-Level Synthesis; FPGA; Processor; Network Measurement

Optimally Mitigating BTI-Induced FPGA Device Aging with Discriminative Voltage Scaling

Yu Bai, Mohammed Alawad, and Mingjie Lin
University of Central Florida

With the CMOS technology aggressively scaling towards the 22nm node, modern FPGA devices face tremendous aging-induced reliability challenges due to Bias Temperature Instability (BTI) and Hot Carrier Injection (HCI). This paper presents a novel antiaging technique at logic level that is both scalable and applicable for VLSI digital circuits implemented with FPGA devices. The key idea is to prolong the lifetime of FPGA-mapped designs by strategically elevating the VDD values of some LUTs based on their modular criticality values. Although the idea of scaling VDD in order to improve either energy efficiency or circuit reliability has been explored extensively, our study distinguishes itself by approaching this challenge through analytical procedure, therefore able to maximize the overall reliability of target FPGA design by rigorously modelling the BTI-induce device reliability and optimally solving the VDD assignment problem.

Specifically, we first develop a systematic framework to analytically model the reliability of an FPGA LUT (look-up table), which consists of both SRAM memory bits and associated switching circuit. We also, for the first time, establish the relationship between signal transition density and a LUT's reliability in an analytical way. This key observation further motivates us to define the modular criticality as the product of signal transition density and the logic observability of each LUT. Finally, we analytically prove, for the first time, that the optimal way to improve the overall reliability of a whole FPGA device is to fortify individual LUTs according to their modular criticality. To the best of our knowledge, this work is the first to draw such a conclusion.

Keywords: Criticality Analysis, VLSI, Logic Circuit, Discriminative,Voltage Scaling.

Design, Implementation and Security Analysis of Hardware Trojan Threats in FPGA

Devu Manikantan Shila, Vivek Venugopal,
United Technologies Research Center

Hardware Trojan Threats (HTTs) are stealthy components embedded inside integrated circuits (ICs) with an intention to attack and cripple the IC similar to viruses infecting the human body. HTTs are easily introduced into the IC using untrusted tools and unauthenticated intellectual property (IP). Previous efforts have focused essentially on systems being compromised using HTTs and the effectiveness of physical parameters including power consumption, timing variation and utilization for detecting HTTs. Less attention has been devoted to the monitoring of the system to analyze the HTT infection using a combination of affected physical parameters. We propose a novel metric for hardware Trojan detection, termed as HTT detectability metric (HDM) that leverages a weighted combination of normalized physical parameters. As opposed to existing studies, this work investigates a system model from a designer perspective in increasing the security of the device and an adversary model from an attacker perspective exposing and exploiting the vulnerabilities in the device. Based on the models, seven malicious HTTs were designed and implemented on a FPGA testbed to perform a variety of threats ranging from sensitive information leak, denial of service to beat the Root of Trust (RoT). Security analysis on the implemented Trojans clearly showed that existing detection techniques based on physical characteristics such as power consumption, timing variation or utilization does not necessarily capture the existence of HTTs as HTTs can be optimally designed and placed into the hardware that masks within these parameters. Our results showed that using HDM, 86% of the implemented Trojans were detected as opposed to using power, timing and utilization alone.

ACM Categories & Descriptors: K.6.5 [Security and Protection]: Invasive software; Authentication; Unauthorized access

Keywords: Design; Resiliency; Security; Hardware Trojan Threats; Trojan Detection; Root of Trust

A Power-Efficient Adaptive Heapsort for FPGA-based Image Coding Application

Yuhui Bai, Lab ETIS, *Université Cergy-Pontoise, ENSEA,* Lab LIP6, *Sorbonne Universités, UPMC*
Syed Zahid Ahmed, Bertrand Granado, Lab LIP6, *Sorbonne Universités, UPMC*

This paper presents an adaptive heap sort architecture for an image coding implementation on FPGA, which specifically addresses the issue of sorting different amount of data located in each subband during the coding. The proposed sorting architecture is easily scalable. Performance of the sorter only depends on the amount of data sorted. The efficient usage of dual

port memories yields high throughput up to 50 Msamples/s and their adaptive trigger/shutdown provide the average dynamic power reduction up to 20.9%. We designed this architecture and incorporated it in our Adaptive Scanning of Wavelet Data (ASWD) module which reorganizes the wavelet coefficients into locally stationary sequences for a wavelet-based image encoder. We validated the hardware on an Altera's Stratix IV FPGA as an IP accelerator in a Nios II processor based System on Chip. The architectural innovations can also be exploited in other applications that require high throughput and scalable sorting. Our experiments show that compared to an embedded ARM CortexA9 processor running at 666 MHz, our architecture at 100 MHz can provide around 13X speedup while consuming 242 mW average core dynamic power.

ACM Categories & Descriptors: C.3 Real-time and embedded systems; I.4.2 Compression.

Keywords: FPGA; Embedded System; Image Compression; Heap Sort; Power efficiency

Big Data Genome Sequencing on Zynq based Clusters

Chao Wang, Xi Li, Xuehai Zhou
University of Science and Technology of China
Yunji Chen, *ICT, Chinese Academy of Sciences*
Ray C.C. Cheung, *City University of Hong Kong*

Next-generation sequencing (NGS) problems have attracted many attentions of researchers in biological and medical computing domains. The current state-of-the-art NGS computing machines are dramatically lowering the cost and increasing the throughput of DNA sequencing. In this paper, we propose a practical study that uses Xilinx Zynq board to summarize acceleration engines using FPGA accelerators and ARM processors for the state-of-the-art short read mapping approaches. The heterogeneous processors and accelerators are coupled with each other using a general Hadoop distributed processing framework. First the reads are collected by the central server, and then distributed to multiple accelerators on the Zynq for hardware acceleration. Therefore, the combination of hardware acceleration and Map-Reduce execution flow could greatly accelerate the task of aligning short length reads to a known reference genome. Our approach is based on preprocessing the reference genomes and iterative jobs for aligning the continuous incoming reads. The hardware acceleration is based on the creditable read-mapping algorithm RMAP software approach. Furthermore, the speedup analysis on a Hadoop cluster, which concludes 8 development boards, is evaluated. Experimental results demonstrate that our proposed architecture and methods has the speedup of more than 112X, and is scalable with the number of accelerators. Finally, the Zynq based cluster has efficient potential to accelerate even general large scale big data applications.

This work was supported by the NSFC grants No. 61379040, No. 61272131 and No. 61202053.

ACM Categories & Descriptors: C.1.3 Other Architecture Styles

Keywords: Bioinformatics; Genome Sequencing; RMAP; FPGA; Hardware Acceleration.

BMP: A Fast B*-Tree based Modular Placer for FPGAs

Fubing Mao, *Nanyang Technological University*
Yi-Chung Chen, *University of Pittsburgh*
Wei Zhang, *Hong Kong University of Science and Technology*
Hai Li, *University of Pittsburgh*

With the wide application of FPGAs in adaptive computing systems, there is an increasing need to support design automation for PR FPGAs. However, there is a missing link between CAD tools for PR FPGA and existing widely used CAD tools, such as VPR. Hence, in this work we propose a modular placer for FPGAs because each PR region needs to be identified during partial reconfiguration and treated as an entity during placement and routing, which is not well supported by the current CAD tools. Our proposed tool is built on top of VPR. It takes the pre-synthesized module information from library, such as area, delay, etc, and performs modular placement to minimize total area and delay of the application. Modular information is represented in B*-Tree structure to allow fast placement. We amend the operations of B*-Tree to fit hardware characteristic of FPGAs. Different width-height ratios of the modules are exploited to achieve area-delay product optimization. Experimental results show comparisons of area, delay and execution time with original VPR. Though it may have disadvantage in area because of blank area among modules, it improves the delay of most of benchmarks comparing to results from VPR. At the end, we show PR-aware routing based on the modular placement.

ACM Categories & Descriptors: C.3 Special-purpose and Application-based systems; J.6 Computer-aided Engineering;

Keywords: FPGA; Partial Reconfiguration; CAD; B*-Tree

Redefining the Role of FPGAs in the Next Generation Avionic Systems

Venkatasubramanian Viswanathan
Nolam Embedded Systems
Rabie Ben Atitallah, *University of Valenciennes*
Jean-Luc Dekeyser, *University of Lille1*
Benjamin Nakache, Maurice Nakache
Nolam Embedded Systems

Embedded reconfigurable computing is becoming a new paradigm for system designers in avionic applications. In fact, FPGAs can be used for more than just computational purpose in order to improve the system performance. The introduction of FPGA Mezzanine Card (FMC) I/O standard has given a new purpose for FPGAs to be used as a communication platform. Taking into account the features offered by FPGAs and FMCs, such as runtime reconfiguration and modularity, we have redefined the role of these devices to be used

as a generic communication and computation-centric platform. A new modular, runtime reconfigurable, Intellectual Property (IP)-based communication-centric platform for avionic applications has been designed. This means that, when the communication requirement of an avionic system changes, the necessary communication protocol is installed and executed on demand, without disturbing the normal operation of a time-critical avionic system. The efficiency and the performances of our platform are illustrated through a real industrial use-case designed using a computationally intensive application and several avionic I/O bus standards. The reconfiguration latency can be hidden totally in many cases. While in certain others, the overhead of reconfiguration can be justified by the reduction in the resource utilization.

Keywords: Dynamic Partial Reconfiguration, Avionic IP cores; Modular and Reconfigurable I/Os; FPGA Mezzanine Module; Intensive Signal Processing Applications;

Co-processing with Dynamic Reconfiguration on Heterogeneous MPSoC: Practices and Design Tradeoffs

Chao Wang, Xi Li, Xuehai Zhou
University of Science and Technology of China
Yunji Chen, *ICT, Chinese Academy of Sciences*
Koen Bertels, *TU Delft, Netherlands*

Reconfiguration technique has been considered as one of the most promising electronic design automation (EDA) technologies in MPSoC design paradigms. However, due to the unavoidable latency in the reconfiguration procedure, it still poses a significant challenge to efficiently analyze the trade-offs for the software/hardware execution, static reconfiguration and dynamic reconfiguration. In this paper we first present a heterogeneous MPSoC middleware to support state-of-the-art dynamic partial reconfigurable technologies. Furthermore, we evaluate the reconfiguration latency and analyze the trade-off for the dynamic partial reconfiguration technologies.

As a practical study, a heterogeneous MPSoC prototype with JPEG application has been developed on Xilinx Zynq FPGA with state-of-the-art static/dynamic partial reconfigurable technologies. Experimental results on the JPEG case studies demonstrated the leverage among the software execution, hardware execution, and static/dynamic reconfiguration. For the quantitative approach, we have demonstrated the execution time for the different configuration of the hardware steps in JPEG, and the quantitative impact of the dynamic reconfiguration execution. The dynamic reconfiguration could gain the performance benefits for large scale (larger than a certain threshold) computational tasks. Furthermore, overheads and HWICAP hardware utilization have been measured discussed.

This work was supported by the NSFC grants No. 61379040, No. 61272131 and No. 61202053.

ACM Categories & Descriptors: C.1.3 Other Architecture Styles

Keywords: EDA; FPGA; Dynamic Partial Reconfiguration; Heterogeneous MPSoC; Trade-offs

Control Signal Aware Slice-Level Window Based Legalization Method for FPGA Placement

Yu Wang, Donghoon Yeo, Sohail Muhammad,
Hyunchul Shin, *Hanyang University*

The control signal sharing while packing flip-flops and other instances in slices is a necessary constraint in the placement of instances in FPGAs. Global placement usually does not consider signal sharing. In this paper, we propose a control signal aware slice-level packing algorithm within the framework of window based legalization method to obtain an optimized legal layout, satisfying all constraints, after global placement. We select a target window with the highest number of overlaps. Then, we check the capacity of the target window and adjust its size to secure enough space required for legalization. Lastly, window based legalization takes three constraints into account: 1) Control Signal Sharing: Two Flip-Flops in a slice must share a single control signal in FPGA architecture. 2) CLB Architecture Matching: Instances should be placed within a half slice to minimize the routing requirement. 3) Slice Level Packing: Instances are packed into slices for effective utilization of available empty space within a window. The experimental results show that our algorithm performs better with 45% less block displacement and 10% less runtime with the same wirelength when compared to a previous well-known mixed size block greedy legalization method [1].

ACM Categories & Descriptors: B.7.2 Integrated Circuits

Keywords: Analytical placement; Legalization; FPGA; CLB; Signal Sharing

Acknowledgement: This work was supported by the Technology Innovation Program (KI002168, Development of Configurable Device & SW Environment) funded by MOTIE, Korea and by Samsung Electronics Co.

[1] A. Agnihotri, et al. Mixed block placement via fractional cut recursive bisection. IEEE Trans. on CAD of IC&S, 24(5):748-761, 2005.

FPGA'14, February 26–28, 2014, Monterey, California, USA.
ACM 978-1-4503-2671-1/14/02.

Poster Session 3

Future Inter-FPGA Communication Architecture for Multi-FPGA Based Prototyping

Qingshan Tang, *Université Pierre et Marie CURIE,*
Matthieu Tuna, *Flexras Technologies,*
Habib Mehrez, *Université Pierre et Marie CURIE*

Multi-FPGA boards are widely used for rapid system prototyping. Even though the prototyping is trying to reach the maximum performance, the performance is limited by the inter-FPGA communication. As the capacity per I/O for each FPGA generation is increasing, FPGA I/Os are becoming a scarce resource. The design is divided into several parts, each part's capacity fits in a single FPGA. Signals crossing design's parts located in different FPGAs are called cut nets. In order to resolve pin limitation problem, cut nets are sent between FPGAs in pipelined way using the Time-Division-Multiplexing technique. The maximum number of cut nets passing through one FPGA I/O is called the TDM ratio. There are two multiplexing architectures used for multi-FPGA based prototyping: Logic Multiplexing and ISERDES/OSERDES. In this paper, a new multiplexing architecture Multi-Gigabit Transceiver (MGT) is proposed. Experiments are done in a multi-FPGA board with the testbench LFSR to validate the achieved performance. Assume that all the FPGA I/Os used for inter-FPGA communication are MGT capable in the future. Analyses show that the proposed multiplexing architecture can achieve higher performance when the TDM ratio exceeds 67. The gain in performance of the proposed architecture over the existing architecture augments as the TDM ratio increases.

ACM Categories & Descriptors: B.7.2 Design Aids

Keywords: Multi-FPGA Based Prototyping; Inter-FPGA Communication; Logic Multiplexing; ISERDES/OSERDES; Multi-Gigabit Transceiver

1K Manycore FPGA Shared Memory Architecture for SOC

Yosi Ben Asher, *CS. University of Haifa, Israel*
Jacob Gendel, *IBM HRL,*
Gadi Haber, *Intel Development Center, Haifa Israel*
Oren Segal, *EE. UMass Lowell, USA*
Yousef Shajrawi, *IBM HRL*

Manycore shared memory architectures hold a significant premise to speed up and simplify SOCs. Using many homogeneous small-cores will allow replacing the hardware accelerators of SOCs by parallel algorithms communicating through shared memory. Currently shared memory is realized by maintaining cache-consistency across the cores, caching all the connected cores to one main memory module. This approach, though used today, is not likely to be scalable enough to support the high number of cores needed for highly parallel SOCs. Therefore we consider a theoretical scheme for shared memory wherein: the shared address space is divided between a set of memory modules; and a communication network allows each core to access every such module in parallel. Load-balancing between the memory modules is obtained by rehashing the memory address-space.

We have designed a simple generic shared memory architecture, synthesized it to 2,4,8,...1024-cores for FPGA virtex-7 and evaluated it on several parallel programs. The synthesis results and the execution measurements show that, for the FPGA, all problematic aspects of this construction can be resolved. For example, unlike ASICs, the growing complexity of the communication network is absorbed by the FPGA's routing grid and by its routing mechanism. This makes this type of architectures particularly suitable for FPGAs. We used 32-bits modified PACOBLAZE cores and tested different parameters of this architecture verifying its ability to achieve high speedups. The results suggest that re-hashing is not essential and one hash-function suffice (compared to the family of universal hash functions that is needed by the theoretical construction).

ACM Categories & Descriptors: C.1.4 Parallel Architectures

Keywords: Manycore, Shared-Memory, DMM, SoC, FPGA

Non-Adaptive Sparse Recovery and Fault Evasion using Disjunct Design Configurations

Ahmad Alzahrani, Ronald F. DeMara
University of Central Florida

A run-time fault diagnosis and evasion scheme for reconfigurable devices is developed based on an explicit Non-adaptive Group Testing (NGT). NGT involves grouping disjunct subsets of reconfigurable resources into test pools, or samples. Each test pool realizes a Diagnostic Configuration (DC) performing functional testing during diagnosis procedure. The collective test outcomes after testing each diagnostic pool can be efficiently decoded to identify up to d defective logic resources. An algorithm for constructing NGT sampling procedure and resource placement during design time with optimal minimal number of test groups is derived through the well-known in statistical literature *d-disjunctness property*. The combinatorial properties of resultant DCs also guarantee that any possible set of defective resources less than or equal to d are not utilized by at least one DC, allowing a low-overhead fault resolution. It also provides the ability to assess the resources state of failure. The proposed testing scheme thus avoids time-intensive run-time diagnosis imposed by previously proposed adaptive group testing for reconfigurable hardware without compromising diagnostic coverage. In addition, proposed NGT scheme can be combined with other fault tolerance approaches to ameliorate their fault recovery strategies. Experimental results for a set of MCNC benchmarks using Xilinx ISE Design Suite on a Virtex-5 FPGA have demonstrated d-diagnosability at slice level with average accuracy of 99.15% and 97.76% for d=1 and d=2, respectively.

ACM Categories & Descriptors: B.8.1 Reliability, Testing, and Fault-Tolerance; G.2.3 Applications

Keywords: Reconfigurable Hardware; Non-Adaptive Group Testing; Reliability; Fault Tolerance; Fault Diagnosis; Fault Evasion; Sparse Recovery; d-Disjunct Matrix

Novel FPGA Clock Network with Low Latency and Skew

Lei Li, Jian Wang, Jinmei Lai, *Fudan University*

Clock network is a dedicated network for distributing multiple clock signals to every logic modules in a system. Be significantly different from ASIC where the clock tree is custom built by users, clock network in FPGA is usually fixed after chip fabrication and cannot be changed for different user circuits. This paper is committed to design and implement FPGA clock network with low latency and skew. We first propose a novel clock network for FPGA□which is a backbone-branches topology and can be easily integrated to the tiled FPGA with reasonable area. There are one clock backbone and several primary clock branches in the network. When the chip scales up, this clock network can be extended easily. Afterwards, series of strategies such as hybrid multiplexer, bypassing, looping back and Programmable Delay Adjustment Unit (DAU) are employed to optimize latency and skew. Moreover, the prominent couple capacitance and crosstalk effect of clock routing in nanometer are also given consideration in physical implementation. This clock network is applied to own-designed FPGA with 65nm technology. Post-layout simulation results indicate that our clock network with normal loads can uphold 600MHz clock with the maximum clock latency and skew being typically 2.22ns and 40ps respectively, 1.79ns and 39ps in the fast case, achieving up to 78.2% improvement for skew as well as 47.5% for latency, compared to a commercial 65nm FPGA device.

This project is supported by the National High Technology Research and Development (863) Thematic Program of China, No. 2012AA012001.

ACM Categories & Descriptors: B.7.1 Types and Design Styles;

Keywords: Clock network; FPGA; Latency; Skew; DAU

Asynchronous Physical Unclonable Function Using FPGA-based Self-Timed Ring Oscillator

Roshan Silwal, Mohammed Niamat
The University of Toledo

Recently, electronic industries have been facing an increased amount of hardware counterfeits. These counterfeit components, when assembled into a product or a system, can not only jeopardize performance and reliability but also create safety issues. Physical Unclonable Function (PUF) provides means to enhance physical security of Integrated Circuits (IC) against piracy and unauthorized access. The proposed design illustrates the feasibility of using self-timed ring oscillators as a novel approach towards PUF implementation for FPGA authentication. The proposed Self-Timed Ring Oscillator PUF (STRO-PUF) consists of two groups of identically laid-out self-timed ring oscillators. Inputs to the PUF are given through a challenge generator, which selects two self-timed ring oscillators from each group. Outputs of oscillators are fed to multiplexers of corresponding groups. Self-timed ring oscillators exploit the inherent features of random process variations by producing varying frequencies. These unpredictable variations in frequencies are captured using frequency comparator, which generates a output bit. A unique set of output bits , or response is generated for each set of input bits, or challenge. This unique Challenge Response Pair (CRP) is used in identifying a particular device. Frequencies generated from these oscillators are read through a logic analyzer. The varying frequencies observed from all the oscillators mapped across different regions of FPGAs range from 16.234 MHz to 125 MHz with the average frequency of 101.446 MHz. Experimental result shows the uniqueness for the PUF response is 49.92% which is very close to the desired 50% factor.

ACM Categories & Descriptors: K.6.5 [Management of Computing and Information Systems]: Security and Protection--- Physical security, Authentication

Keywords: Physical Unclonable Function (PUF), FPGA authentication, Asynchronous Design, Self-Timed Ring Oscillator, STRO-PUF

APMC: Advanced Pattern based Memory Controller

Tassadaq Hussain, Oscar Palomar, Osman S. Ünsal, Adrian Cristal, Eduard Ayguadé, Mateo Valero and Santhosh Kumar Rethinagiri
Universitat Politecnica de Catalunya

In this paper, we present APMC, the Advanced Pattern based Memory Controller, that uses descriptors to support both regular and irregular memory access patterns without using a master core. It keeps pattern descriptors in memory and prefetches the complex 1D/2D/3D data structure into its special scratchpad memory. Support for irregular Memory accesses are arranged in the pattern descriptors at program-time and APMC manages multiple patterns at run-time to reduce access latency. The proposed APMC system reduces the limitations faced by processors/accelerators due to irregular memory access patterns and low memory bandwidth. It gathers multiple memory read/write requests and maximizes the reuse of opened SDRAM banks to decrease the overhead of opening and closing rows. APMC manages data movement between main memory and the specialized scratchpad memory; data present in the specialized scratchpad is reused and/or updated when accessed by several patterns. The system is implemented and tested on a Xilinx ML505 FPGA board. The performance of the system is compared with a processor with a high performance memory controller. The results show that the APMC system transfers regular and irregular datasets up to 20.4x and 3.4x faster respectively than the baseline system. When compared to the baseline system, APMC consumes 17% less hardware resources, 32% less on-chip power and achieves between 3.5x to 52x and 1.4x to 2.9x of speedup for regular and irregular applications respectively. The APMC core consumes 50% less hardware resources than the baseline system's memory controller.

ACM Categories & Descriptors: D.1.3 Concurrent Programming; D.3.2 Language Classifications

Keywords: FPGA; HPC; Memory Controller; Access Patterns;

On Energy Efficiency and Amdahl's Law in FPGA Based Chip Heterogeneous Multiprocessor Systems

Sen Ma, David Andrews, *University of Arkansas*

This poster presents our preliminary findings on the relationship between speedup and energy efficiency on FPGA based Chip Heterogeneous Multiprocessor Systems (CHMPs). While researchers have investigated how to tailor combinations of heterogeneous compute engines within a CHMP system to best meet the performance needs of specific applications, exploring how these optimized architectures also effect energy efficiency is not as well studied. We show that a simple relationship exists between the speedup these systems gain and their associated energy efficiency. We show that the simple relationship between Amdahl's law and energy efficiency. All the experiments result achieved through actual run time measurements on homogeneous and heterogeneous multiprocessor systems implemented within a Xilinx Virtex6 FPGA. We further show how a systems with 6 MicroBlaze soft processors' dynamic power and hence the overall energy efficiency of the system can be effected through transparent operating system control of the compute resources. We also present how to use clock gating to control the dynamic power consumption for each processor and with this careful power-aware management unit, the system's dynamic power consumption can follow the requirements of each application.

ACM Categories & Descriptors: C.1.4 - Parallel Architectures; D.4.9 - Systems Programs and Utilities

Keywords: Dynamic power; power-optimization algorithm; reconfigurable computing

Producing High-Quality Real-Time HDR Video System with FPGA

Tao Ai, Mir Adnan Ali, Gregory Steffan,
Kalin Ovtcharov, Sarmad Zulfiqar, Steve Mann,
University of Toronto

Video cameras can only take photographs with limited dynamic range. One method to overcome this is to combine differently exposed images of the same subject matter (i.e. a Wyckoff Set), producing a High Dynamic Range (HDR) result. HDR digital photography started almost 20 years ago. Now, it is possible to produce HDR video in real-time, on both high-power CPU/GPU systems, as well as low-power FPGA boards. However, other FPGA implementations have relied upon methods that are less accurate than current CPU and GPU-based methods. Namely, the earlier FPGA approaches used weighted sum for image compositing.

In this paper we provide a novel method for real-time HDR compositing. As an essential part of an upgraded HDR video production system, the resulting system combines differently exposed video stream (of the same subject matter) in Full HD (1080p at 60fps) on a Kintex-7 FPGA. The proposed work flow, implemented with software written in C, estimates the camera response function according to its quadtree representation and generates the compositing circuit in Verilog HDL from a Wyckoff Set. This circuit consists of parts that perform addressing using multiplexer networks and estimation with bilinear interpolation. It is parameterizable by user-specified error constraints, allowing us to explore the trade-offs in resource usage and precision of the implementation.

Here is an MD5 hash function sum generated for the rest of the paper: 07897e61027d15dc3600fadbccfbd67d, citation date: December 18, 2013.

ACM Categories & Descriptors: B.5.1 [Register-Transfer-Level Implementation]: Design; I.4.1 [Image Processing and Computer Vision]: Digitization and Image Capture

Keywords: High Dynamic Range Video; Quadtree; FPGAs; Real-time HDR; Comparametric Camera Response Function; CCRF Compression

xDEFENSE: An Extended DEFENSE for Mitigating Next Generation Intrusions

James Lamberti, Devu Manikantan Shila,
Vivek Venugopal, *United Technologies Research Center*

In this work, we propose a modified DEFENSE architecture termed as xDEFENSE that can detect and react to hardware attacks in real-time. In the past, several Root of Trust architectures such as DEFENSE and RETC have been proposed to foil attempts by hardware Trojans to leak sensitive information. In a typical Root of Trust architecture scenario, hardware is allowed to access the memory only by responding properly to a challenge requested by the memory guard. However in a recent effort, we observed that these architectures can in fact be susceptible to a variety of threats ranging from denial of service attacks, privilege escalation to information leakage, by injecting a Trojan into the Root of Trust modules such as memory guards and authorized hardware. In our work, we propose a security monitor that monitors all transactions between the authorized hardware, memory guard and memory. It also authenticates these components through the use of Hashed Message Authentication Codes (HMAC) to detect any invalid memory access or denial of service attack by disrupting the challenge-response pairs. The proposed xDEFENSE architecture was implemented on a Xilinx SPARTAN 3 FPGA evaluation board and our results indicate that xDEFENSE requires 143 additional slices as compared to DEFENSE and incurs a monitoring latency of 22ns.

ACM Categories & Descriptors: K.6.5 [Security and Protection]: Invasive software; Authentication; Unauthorized access

Keywords: Security Monitor; Architecture; Denial of Service Attacks; Root of Trust; Information Leakage; Hardware Trojan Threats; Trojan Detection

Coordinating Routing Resources for Hex PIPs Test in Island-style FPGAs

Zhang Fan, Chen Lei, *Beijing Microelectronics Technology Institute*
Xu Wenyao*, University at Buffalo, The State University of New York*
Zhao Yuanfu, Wen Zhiping, *Beijing Microelectronics Technology* Institute

The significance of FPGA test and the challenge of its increasing cost can never be ignored. In island-style FPGA architectures, hex lines are the principal interconnect resources. Testing hex lines and hex Programmable Interconnect Points (PIPs) have remained as the major technical difficulty in FPGAs test due to complex interconnect rules. Particularly, test in oblique direction of hex PIPs has rarely been addressed in previous studies. Towards this challenge, this paper for the first time proposes a coordinate system and formulates the interconnect rules of hex lines as mathematical equations. For hex PIPs in horizontal and vertical direction, an efficient circle test structure is formed by coordinate equations. For hex PIPs in oblique direction, the coordinate method is used to generate the partial-cascade pattern. The corresponding test vector is also generated, which ensures the ergodicity of hex PIPs in oblique direction. In addition to hex PIPs, hex lines are also covered without extra effort. Compared to previous researches, the configuration number for hex lines is decreased significantly. We evaluate this method on Xilinx XC2V1000, and experimental results show that our proposed method achieves 100% fault coverage for hex PIPs and can be generally applied to all mainstream island-style FPGAs with a similar interconnect structure currently.

ACM Categories & Descriptors: B.7.3 testability.

Keywords: Hex PIPs; Coordinate; Mathematical Equations; Horizontal and Vertical Direction; Oblique Direction; Partial-cascade

Pipelining FPPGA-based Defect Detction in FPDs

Lin Meng, Keisuke Matsuyama, Naoto Nojiri, Tomonori Izumi and Katsuhiro Yamazaki
Ritsumeikan University

The real-time detection of defects in Flat-Panel Displays (FPDs) is very important during the production stages. This paper describes the manner in which defects induced by bubbles are detected as fast as possible by using 4-stage image processing pipelines with 3-line buffers on a Field-Programmable Gate Array (FPGA). The image processing consists of reading a Time Delay Integration (TDI) image, Laplacian filtering, binarization, and labeling. TDI is applied to the initial image of the FPD to reduce noises induced when taking the FPD images. Laplacian filtering and binarization are used to detect the edges in the image, and labeling is used to number the objects in the image for defect detection. In the 4-stage pipelining, the first stage reads the TDI image from the Block Random Access Memory (BRAM), the second stage implements Laplacian filtering and binarization, the third stage implements labeling, and the final stage revises the labels and writes them into the BRAM. The target pixel and its eight surrounding neighbors are required during Laplacian filtering, and four neighbors are necessary during labeling. Thus, three line registers (3-line buffer) are used as a general pipeline register between two neighboring stages in our system. The pipelining system accesses these 3-line buffers and runs four image processing steps in parallel. Therefore, the system uses four different addresses to access the BRAM and the 3-line buffers. Further, to facilitate performance comparison, we implemented sequential image processing systems with 3-line buffers on FPGA and CPU software. The experiments reveal that Laplacian filtering, binarization, and labeling for FPD defect detection can be executed in less than 1 ms by using four-stage pipelining on an FPGA, which is 3.62 times faster than the sequential system and 158.7 times faster than the CPU software. The pipelining system is 28% larger as compared to the sequential system in terms of the size of the LUTs.

ACM Categories & Descriptors: B.2.1 Design Styles; B.2.4 High-Speed Arithmetic

Keywords: FPD Defect Detection; Pipelining; Line Buffer; FPGA

FPGA'14, February 26–28, 2014, Monterey, California, USA.
ACM 978-1-4503-2671-1/14/02.

Poster Session 4

EPEE: An Efficient PCIe Communication Library with Easy-host-integration Property for FPGA Accelerators

Jian Gong, Jiahua Chen, Haoyang Wu, Fan Ye
Peking University
Songwu Lu, Jason Cong
University of California, Los Angeles
Tao Wang, *Peking University*

The rapid growth in the resources and processing power of FPGA has made it more and more attractive as accelerator platforms. Due to its high performance, the PCIe bus is the preferred interconnection between the host computer and loosely-coupled FPGA accelerators. To fully utilize the high performance of PCIe, developers have to write significant amount of PCIe related code. In this paper, we present the design of EPEE, an efficient PCIe communication library that can integrate with hosts easily to alleviate developers from such burden. It is not trivial to make a PCIe communication library highly efficient and easy-host-integration simultaneously. We have identified several challenges in the work: 1) the conflict between efficiency and functionality; 2) the support for multi-clock domain interface; 3) the solution to DMA data out-of-order transfer; 4) the portability. Few existing systems have addressed all the challenges. EEPE has a highly efficient core library that is extensible. We provide a set of APIs abstracted at high levels to ease the learning curve of developers, and divide the hardware library into device dependent and independent layers for portability. We have implemented EEPE in various generations of Xilinx FPGAs with up to 12.7 Gbps half-duplex and 20.8 Gbps full-duplex data rates in PCIe Gen2X4 mode (79.4% and 64.0% of the theoretical maximum data rates respectively). EEPE has already been used in four different FPGA applications, and it can be integrated with high-level synthesis tools, in particular Vivado-HLS.

ACM Categories & Descriptors: B.4.3 Interfaces

Keywords: FPGA; PCIe; DMA; Efficient; Easy-host-integration; Extensible

Implementing FPGA-based Energy-efficient Dense Optical Flow Computation with High Portability in C

Zhibin Wang, Wenmin Yang, Jin Yu, Zhilei Chai
Jiangnan University

Optical flow computation is widely used in many video/image based applications such as motion detection, video compression etc. Dense optical flow field that provides more details of information is more useful in lots of applications. However, high-quality

FPGA'14, February 26–28, 2014, Monterey, California, USA.
ACM 978-1-4503-2671-1/14/02.

algorithms for dense optical flow computation are computationally expensive. For instance, on the ARM Cortex-A9 processor within ZYNQ, the popular linear variational method Combine-Brightness-Gradient (CBG), spends 26.68s per frame to compute optical flow when the image size is 640×480. It is difficult to be sped up especially when embedded systems with power constraints are considered. Poor portability is another factor to limit current implementations of optical flow computation to be used in more applications. In this paper, a high-performance, low-power FPGA-accelerated implementation of dense optical flow computation is presented. One high-quality dense optical flow method, the Combine-Brightness-Gradient model, is implemented. C code instead of VHDL/Verilog HDL is used to improve the productivity. Portability of the system is designed carefully for deploying it on different platforms conveniently. Experimental results show 12 fps and 0.38J per frame are achieved by this optical flow computing system when 640×480 image is used and optical flow for all pixels are computed. Furthermore, portability is demonstrated by implementing the optical flow algorithm on different heterogeneous platforms such as the ZYNQ-7000 SoC and the PC-FPGA platform with a Kintex-7 FPGA respectively.

ACM Categories & Descriptors: C.3 Special-Purpose and Application-based Systems; B.2.4 Arithmetic and Logic Structures

Keywords: Optical Flow Computation; Energy Efficient; High-Level-Synthesis; FPGAs; Portability

Methodology to Generate Multi-Dimensional Systolic Arrays for FPGAs using OpenCL

Nick Ni, *Altera Corporation*

Systolic arrays (SA) in a FPGA provide a significant speed up on many scientific calculations through massive parallelism exploitation. The low-level hardware design of such complex SA is becoming more time-consuming and non-scalable with more transistors being available on a single chip. In this paper we present a novel methodology to generate multi-dimensional SA for FPGAs using a well-accepted high-level language, OpenCL. Kernels written in OpenCL can then be compiled directly into hardware using an OpenCL high-level synthesis tool. A complex case study using our methodology is presented. We were able to design, generate, verify and optimize the entire FPGA based hardware accelerator using the Smith-Waterman, in only three man weeks. The accelerator's top performance was 32.6 GCUPS (Giga-Cell-Updates-Per-Second) on a DNA similarity search with 1.3 GCUPS/watt efficiency. The result is superior to most state-of-the-art CPU/GPU implementations and competitive against a hand-crafted hardware design which took many months to develop.

ACM Categories & Descriptors: C.0 [Computer Systems Organization]: General – System architectures and Systems specification methodology.

Keywords: Systolic Arrays, Smith-Waterman, Bioinformatics, Algorithm, Generation, FPGA, Productivity, High-level Synthesis, OpenCL

Improving the Security and the Scalability of the AES Algorithm

Alessandro A. Nacci, Vincenzo Rana,
Marco D. Santambrogio, Donatella Sciuto
Politecnico di Milano

Although the reliability and robustness of the AES protocol have been deeply proved through the years, recent research results and technology advancements are rising serious concerns about its solidity in the (quite near) future. In fact, smarter brute force attacks and new computing systems are expected to drastically decrease the security of the AES protocol in the coming years (e.g., quantum computing will enable the development of search algorithms able to perform a brute force attack of a 2n-bit key in the same time required by a conventional algorithm for a n-bit key). In this context, we are proposing an extension of the AES algorithm in order to support longer encryption keys (thus increasing the security of the algorithm itself). In addition to this, we are proposing a set of parametric implementations of this novel extended protocols. These architectures can be optimized either to minimize the area usage or to maximize their performance. Experimental results show that, while the proposed implementations achieve a throughput higher than most of the state-of-the-art approaches and the highest value of the *Performance/Area* metric when working with 128-bit encryption keys, they can achieve a 84× throughput speedup when compared to the approaches that can be found in literature working with 512-bit encryption keys.

ACM Categories & Descriptors: E.3 Data Encryption;

Keywords: cryptography; AES; Advanced Ecryption Standard; security; FPGA

Power Estimation Tool for System on Programmable Chip based Platforms

Santhosh Kumar Rethinagiri, Oscar Palomar,
Adrian Cristal and Osman Unsal
BSC-Microsoft Research Center, Barcelona, Spain

The ever increasing complexity of the applications result in the development of power hungry processors. There is a scarcity of standalone tools that have a good trade off between estimation speed and accuracy to estimate power/energy at an earlier phase of design flow. There are very few tools that addresses the design space exploration issue based on power and energy. In this paper, we propose a virtual platform based standalone power and energy estimation tool for System-on-Programmable Chip (SoPC) embedded platforms, which is independent of in-house tools. There are two steps involved in this tool development. The first step is power model generation. For the power model development, we used functional parameters to set up generic power models for the different parts of the system. This is a one-time activity. In the second step, a simulation based virtual platform framework is developed to evaluate accurately the activities used in the related power models developed in the first step. The combination of the two steps lead to a hybrid power estimation, which gives a better

trade-off between accuracy and speed. The proposed tool has several benefits: it considers the power consumption of the embedded system in its entirety and leads to accurate estimates without a costly and complex material. The proposed tool is also scalable for exploring complex embedded multi-core architectures.

The effectiveness of our proposed tool is validated through dual-core RISC processor designed around the FPGA board and extended to accommodate futuristic multi-core processors for a reliable energy based design space exploration. The accuracy of our proposed tool is evaluated by using a variety of industrial benchmarks such as Multimedia, EEMBC and SPEC2006. Estimated power values are compared to real board measurements and also to McPAT. Our obtained power/energy estimation results provide less than 9% of error for heterogeneous MPSoC based system and are 200% faster compared to other state-of-the-art power estimation tools.

ACM Categories & Descriptors: I.1.6 Simulation and Modeling

Keywords: ASIC; Accuracy; Design space exploration; FPGA; Functional power models; Heterogeneous architecture; Multi-core; Power/Energy Estimation; Speedup; SystemC; TLM; Virtual Platform

Using DSP Blocks to Compute CRC Hash in FPGA

Lukáš Kekely, Viktor Puš, Tomáš Závodník, *CESNET*

Hash table and its variations are common ways to implement lookup operations in FPGA. The process of adding to, deleting from, and searching in the hash table uses one or more hash functions to compute the address to the table. A suitable hash function must meet statistical properties such as uniform distribution, use of all input bits, large change of output based on small change of input. Other desirable parameters are high throughput and low FPGA resources usage. We propose a novel approach to the CRC hash computation in FPGA. The method is suitable for applications such as hash tables, which use parallel inputs of fixed size and require high throughput. We employ DSP blocks present in modern FPGAs to perform all the necessary XOR operations, therefore our solution does not use any LUTs. We propose a Monte Carlo based heuristic to reduce the number of DSP blocks required. Our experimental results show that one DSP block capable of 48 XOR operations can replace around eleven 6-input LUTs. Our results further show that our solution performs less XOR operations than the solution with LUTs optimized by the synthesizer.

ACM Categories & Descriptors: B.2.4 High-Speed Arithmetic; B.7.1 Gate Arrays

Keywords: FPGA; CRC; DSP; Hash

An Automatic Netlist and Floorplanning Approach to Improve the MTTR of Scrubbing Techniques

Bernhard Schmidt, Daniel Ziener, Jürgen Teich
University of Erlangen-Nuremberg

We introduce a new SEU mitigation approach which minimizes the scrubbing effort by a) using an automatic classification of the criticality of netlist instances and their resulting configuration bits, and by b) minimizing the number of frames which must be scrubbed by using intelligent floorplanning. The criticality of configuration bits is defined by the actions needed to correct a radiation-induced SEU at this bit. Indeed, circuits that involve feedback loops might still and infinitely cause a malfunction even if scrubbing is applied to involved configuration frames. Here, only supplementary state-restoring might be a viable solution. By analyzing an FPGA design already at the logic level and partition configuration bits of the resulting FPGA mapping into so-called essential bits and critical bits, we are able to significantly reduce the number of time consuming state-restoring actions. Moreover, by using placement and routing constraints, it is shown how to minimize the number of frames which have to be reconfigured or checked when using scrubbing. By applying both methods, we will show a reduction of the Mean-Time-To-Repair (MTTR) for sequential benchmark circuits by up to 48.5% compared to a state-of-the-art approach.

ACM Categories & Descriptors: B.5.3 Reliability and Testing

Keywords: SEU Mitigation; MTTR; Scrubbing; Netlist Analysis; Floorplanning; Checkpointing

Exploring Duty Cycle Distortions along Signal Paths in FPGAs

Matthias Hinkfoth, Ralf Joost, Ralf Salomon
University of Rostock

Non-trivial hardware architectures consist of a significant number of fine-grained modules that communication with each other via dedicated signal lines. In field-programmable gate arrays (FPGAs), these communication lines are provided in forms of global vertical and horizontal routing channels, and are subject to the routing process. Since the effects of physical properties on the signal skew along these lines is well understood, this paper investigates the observable effects on a signal's duty cycle. Practical experiments show that the distortion on the duty cycle progressively increases along such wires (connections) and that in the extreme case, a signal may entirely vanish.

ACM Categories & Descriptors: B.7.1 Types and Design Styles: Gate Arrays

Keywords: FPGA; Routing; Signal Path; Duty Cycle

FPGA'14, February 26–28, 2014, Monterey, California, USA.
ACM 978-1-4503-2671-1/14/02.

Author Index

www.ingramcontent.com/pod-product-compliance
Lightning Source LLC
Chambersburg PA
CBHW061356210326
41598CB00035B/5996